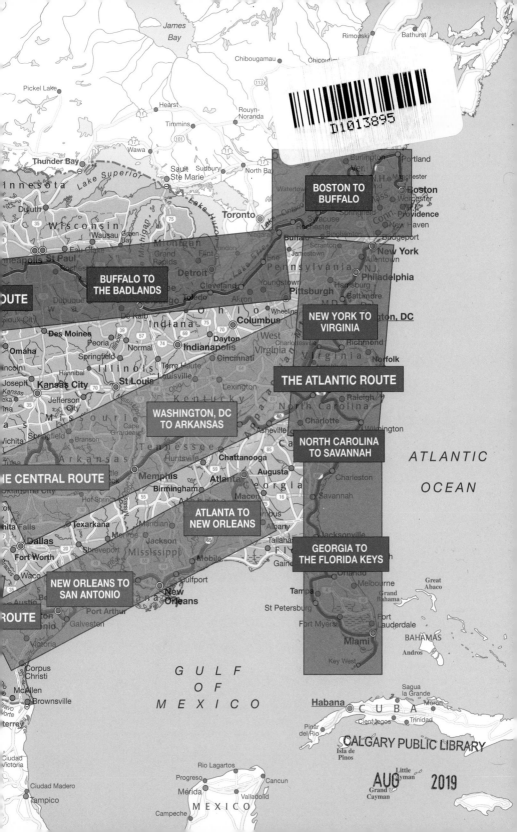

BOSTON TO BUFFALO

BUFFALO TO THE BADLANDS

NEW YORK TO VIRGINIA

THE ATLANTIC ROUTE

WASHINGTON, DC TO ARKANSAS

NORTH CAROLINA TO SAVANNAH

THE CENTRAL ROUTE

ATLANTA TO NEW ORLEANS

GEORGIA TO THE FLORIDA KEYS

NEW ORLEANS TO SAN ANTONIO

ROUTE

OUTE

ROUTE

INSIGHT ⊙ GUIDES

USA ON THE ROAD

◉ Walking Eye App

YOUR FREE DESTINATION CONTENT AND EBOOK AVAILABLE THROUGH THE WALKING EYE APP

Your guide now includes a free eBook and destination content for your chosen destination, all for the same great price as before. Simply download the Walking Eye App from the App Store or Google Play to access your free eBook and destination content.

HOW THE WALKING EYE APP WORKS

Through the Walking Eye App, you can purchase a range of eBooks and destination content. However, when you buy this book, you can download the corresponding eBook and destination content for free. Just see below in the grey panels where to find your free content and then scan the QR code at the bottom of this page.

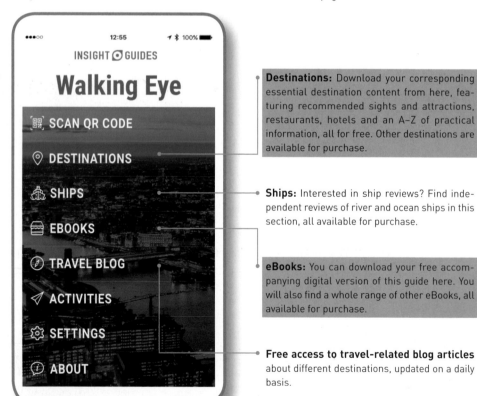

Destinations: Download your corresponding essential destination content from here, featuring recommended sights and attractions, restaurants, hotels and an A–Z of practical information, all for free. Other destinations are available for purchase.

Ships: Interested in ship reviews? Find independent reviews of river and ocean ships in this section, all available for purchase.

eBooks: You can download your free accompanying digital version of this guide here. You will also find a whole range of other eBooks, all available for purchase.

Free access to travel-related blog articles about different destinations, updated on a daily basis.

HOW THE DESTINATION CONTENT WORKS

Each destination includes a short introduction, an A–Z of practical information and recommended points of interest, split into 4 different categories:

- Highlights
- Accommodation
- Eating out
- What to do

You can view the location of every point of interest and save it by adding it to your Favourites. In the 'Around Me' section you can view all the points of interest within 5km.

HOW THE EBOOKS WORK

The eBooks are provided in EPUB file format. Please note that you will need an eBook reader installed on your device to open the file. Many devices come with this as standard, but you may still need to install one manually from Google Play.

The eBook content is identical to the content in the printed guide.

HOW TO DOWNLOAD THE WALKING EYE APP

1. Download the Walking Eye App from the App Store or Google Play.
2. Open the app and select the scanning function from the main menu.
3. Scan the QR code on this page – you will then be asked a security question to verify ownership of the book.
4. Once this has been verified, you will see your eBook and destination content in the purchased ebook and destination sections, where you will be able to download them.

Other destination apps and eBooks are available for purchase separately or are free with the purchase of the Insight Guide book.

CONTENTS

Travel tips

TRANSPORTATION

A – Z

FURTHER READING

Maps

Inside front cover Routes across america
Inside back cover Mileage chart across
   America and road signs of America

LEGEND

⦿ Insight on
◎ Photo story

THE BEST OF THE UNITED STATES: TOP ATTRACTIONS

△ **The Grand Canyon.** The Colorado River carved out the colorful bluffs, mesas, and rock formations, creating one of the great natural wonders of the world. See page 224.

◁ **Saguaro cactus.** This symbol of the American Southwest is a stunning sight against the backdrop of an Arizona sunset. These prickly giants grow only in the Sonoran Desert. See page 299.

△ **Savannah.** Dripping with Spanish moss and Southern charm, this town is the jewel of the Old South. Take a carriage round its cobbled squares and visit its gracious antebellum mansions. See page 78.

▽ **San Francisco**. Fisherman's Wharf, Golden Gate Park, hill-climbing historic cable cars, and an incomparable peninsular setting make this city the jewel of America's Pacific coast. See page 344.

△ **The Everglades.** This unique environment forms the largest subtropical wilderness in the country. It protects rare and endangered plant and animal species, some found nowhere else in the world. See page 90.

▷ **Big Sur.** California's rugged cliffs and pounding surf fringe one of the most dramatic stretches of the Pacific coast, a road trip you'll never forget. See page 338.

▷ **Yellowstone National Park.** Spewing geysers, bubbling mudpots, sizzling hot springs, and other geothermal features are scattered amid the spectacular beauty of the Rocky Mountains. See page 157.

◁ **New York City.** This is the nation's capital of art, commerce, fashion, and culture, with world-class museums, restaurants, and shopping. From its skyscraper skyline to the lights of Times Square, it never fails to impress. See page 52.

▽ **Olympic Peninsula.** Walk among towering ancient trees, lush ferns, and dripping mosses, which form one of the largest areas of temperate rainforest in the country. See page 168.

△ **Niagara Falls.** The thundering cascades mark the border between the United States and Canada. The boat ride into the mist at the base of the falls is an unforgettable thrill. See page 120.

THE BEST OF THE UNITED STATES: EDITOR'S CHOICE

Monument Valley.

BEST FOR FAMILIES

Orlando. Nonstop entertainment at Walt Disney World's four theme parks, Universal Studios, the Kennedy Space Center, and a host of family attractions. See page 86.

San Diego. From SeaWorld and the San Diego Zoo to whale-watching cruises and trolley tours, there's plenty to delight all ages. See page 316.

Williamsburg. Step back in time and see how people lived in the American Colonial era. See page 62.

Monterey Bay Aquarium. One of the best in the world, with mesmerizing exhibits and touch tanks that allow an up-close look at the undersea world. See page 342.

Tombstone. The Wild West lives on in this historic town of boardwalks, Boot Hill, and shoot-outs at the OK Corral. See page 297.

Arizona-Sonora Desert Museum. Watch raptors in flight and observe javelinas, coyote, mountain lions, and other desert creatures in their natural setting. See page 300.

BEST SCENIC DRIVES

The Pacific Coast Highway. Highways 1 and 101 take you from California's rugged shores to Oregon's idyllic beaches. See pages 333 and 347.

Blue Ridge Mountains. Enjoy the stunning vistas of this romantic mountain chain along Skyline Drive and the Blue Ridge Parkway. See page 185.

Going-to-the-Sun Road. Traversing Glacier National Park, this is one of the most dramatic drives in the Rocky Mountains. See page 163.

Atchafalaya Swamp Freeway. Watch out for alligators as you drive across the largest swamp in the country. See page 263.

Monument Valley. These awesome buttes and mesas rising from the desert floor have been used as the backdrop for many Hollywood Westerns. See page 221.

Outer Banks. Pristine dunes, beaches, islands, and lighthouses along the Atlantic coast are preserved in two national seashores. See page 70.

The Badlands. A starkly beautiful landscape of rolling grasslands and twisted rocky canyons stretches right across the windswept plains of South Dakota. See page 139.

BEST MUSEUMS AND GALLERIES

Getty Villa at Malibu. The re-created 1st-century Roman villa is an impressive home for this collection of Greek and Roman antiquities. See page 333.

Smithsonian Institution. A group of museums highlighting the nation's best achievements in art, history, and science line the Mall in Washington, DC. See page 178.

National Civil Rights Museum. The moving story of the Civil Rights movement, set around the Memphis motel where Martin Luther King, Jr was assassinated. See page 194.

Heard Museum. This beautiful collection of Native American arts and crafts in Phoenix, Arizona is among the finest in the country. See page 310.

New Mexico Museum of Space History. Fly a space shuttle simulator and follow the story of early pioneers in the space race. See page 288.

BEST HISTORICAL SITES

Independence National Historical Park. The United States was founded in these Philadelphia buildings. See page 58.

Charleston. The first shots of the Civil War were fired in the harbor of this city of elegant 18th-century houses. See page 75.

Freedom Trail. A walking trail through Boston links the hallowed sites of the American Revolution's birthplace. See page 100.

Washington, DC. The heart of the US capital includes the White House, Capitol, and memorials to Washington, Lincoln, FDR, King, WWII, and the Vietnam War. See page 179.

St Augustine, Florida. The oldest city in the US preserves its Spanish Colonial past in a stone fortress and old-world downtown. See page 84.

Little Bighorn Battlefield. The tragic clash of cultures that defined the Old West came to a head at "Custer's Last Stand" on the high prairie. See page 153.

The Chrysler Building.

BEST ARCHITECTURE AND BUILDINGS

Miami's Art Deco District. Pastel-painted hotels and shops with striking nautical motifs line Miami's South Beach. See page 94.

Hearst Castle. Filled with exquisite art and furnishings, this opulent hilltop residence was a playground for Hollywood's elite. See page 337.

Midtown Manhattan. New York's skyward climb reached its pinnacle in the Empire State Building, Rockefeller Center, and the Art Deco exuberance of the Chrysler Building. See page 52.

Las Vegas. Kitsch is king in Sin City's neon-lit casino resorts, which re-create in miniature such landmarks as the Egyptian pyramids and the Eiffel Tower. See page 228.

Golden Gate Bridge. Graceful and romantic, this San Francisco landmark is said to be the most photographed bridge in the world. See page 344.

French Quarter. Beautiful wrought-iron galleries line the historic buildings in the heart of old New Orleans. See page 258.

Find Greek and Roman sculpture at the Getty Villa.

The open road in
Monument Valley.

Skyscrapers and Highway I-280
as seen from Potrero Hill,
San Francisco.

An armed guard accompanies a stagecoach in John Marchand's depiction of an Old West journey, *The Narrow Pass*.

WE'RE ON THE ROAD TO SOMEWHERE

Americans are always on the move. A French observer in the 1800s identified this unique trait and called it "restlessness amidst prosperity."

The most basic images of American life – the heavy wagon train rumbling across the prairie, a railroad car speeding through the night, the arrival of immigrants at Ellis Island – are powerful symbols of the United States' timeless obsession with movement. In fact, in a nation where change is the only constant, movement and travel have established the ever-quickening tempo of American history, from Lewis and Clark's exploration of the territories west of the Mississippi River to Neil Armstrong's historic walk on the moon.

Highway 101 sign

If the exploration and colonization of America is an example of travel, is there any real connection with the day trip into the countryside? Is it possible seriously to suggest that the 17th-century Puritan seeking refuge in Boston has anything in common with the 22-year-old computer whiz who moves from Lexington, Massachusetts to Seattle, Washington, in search of a higher-paying job? Do Lewis and Clark have any common bond with vacationers of the 1950s rolling down Route 66?

Every one of these travelers believed that movement might bring prosperity, discovery, and renewal. The difference lies in the purpose of the journey. Travel in premodern America was a very serious affair: an essential part of discovering and populating the continent. While a few wealthy Americans embarked on European wander-jahrs, and some even traveled for pleasure to Newport and Saratoga Springs, we do not associate such ease and comfort with the days of old. Rather, we recall Dan-

Oil painting The Immigrants, by Ellen Bernard Thompson, 1899.

iel Boone leading pioneers through the Cumberland Gap; young men heeding Horace Greeley's advice and going West to grow up with the country; the Mormons' perilous flight across the Great Plains; or the stagecoach company that warned its riders not to "point out where murders have been committed, especially if there are women passengers." Given the harsh landscape, we think of travel in early America as a dangerous and epic adventure.

In the early 21st century, when we take a trip there is little heroic about it. Yet, Americans still migrate for economic reasons, particularly to the Sunbelt states in the South or the Pacific Northwest. But this isolated movement of people lacks the drama of the pioneers or the great "Dust Bowl" migration of the 1930s, immortalized in the ballads of Woody Guthrie and in John Steinbeck's novel The Grapes of Wrath. Still, it is very likely that future historians will judge this movement to be as significant a force as it was in past times.

The number of automobiles in America today suggests that the experience of travel is now available to almost everyone. Travel has been democratized and plays no small role in contributing to the American tendency to view cars, boats, and planes as symbols of equality. For better or worse, to be an American is to believe that personal liberty and the freedom to travel are inseparable.

Rush-hour congestion on a Los Angeles freeway.

Is there any truth in this belief? Is there a vital link between the uniquely democratic culture of the United States and the transportation revolution of the past two centuries? Michael Chevalier thought so. Chevalier, a French aristocrat sent to the United States in the 1830s to study its public works, believed that improved means of travel would hasten the collapse of the old order and play an important role in the emergence of "modern society." During his tour, he was amazed by the readiness with which Americans embraced new means of travel: first (after initial disinterest), roads had been constructed with passionate intensity, then canal building had become a national mania. And Chevalier bore witness to the birth of the age of the railroad, for which he rightly forecast a glorious future.

As avenues of economic exchange opened to increasing numbers of people, both ideas and populations were transmitted hither and yon along with pelts, peppers, and teas. Travel became, in Chevalier's words, a catalyst "to equality and liberty."

RESTLESS SPIRITS

Chevalier was writing at the beginning of the Industrial Revolution in America and believed deeply in the 19th-century maxim of progress through science. Today, faced with global warming, oil shortages, and soaring gas prices, people look to the promise of hybrid cars and alternative sources of energy to keep them on the road. The pursuit of freedom and adventure at the end of the road is now costlier, but the allure of crossing America has nevertheless lost little of its appeal to restless spirits.

As Alexis de Tocqueville – author of the quote about "restlessness amidst prosperity" – observed two centuries ago: "An American will build a house in which to pass his old age and sell it before the roof is on; he will plant a garden and rent it just as the trees are coming into bearing; he will clear a field and leave others to reap the harvest; he will take up a profession and leave it, settle in one place and soon go off elsewhere with his changing desires. If his private business allows him a moment's relaxation, he will plunge at once into the whirlpool of politics. Then, if at the end of a year crammed with work he has a little spare leisure, his restless curiosity goes with him traveling up and down the vast territories of the United States. Thus he will travel 500 miles in a few days as a distraction from his happiness."

The barren landscape of Death Valley

DECISIVE DATES

1492
Explorer Christopher Columbus reaches America, landing at San Salvador.

1607
Jamestown, Virginia settled by the British.

1620
Sixty-six Puritans found Plymouth Colony, Cape Cod Bay.

1773
In the Boston Tea Party, men dump tea crates into the harbor to fight against taxes.

1775
Paul Revere rides from Boston warning of the arrival of British troops. The American Revolution begins.

1776
On July 4, the Continental Congress adopts the Declaration of Independence, penned by Thomas Jefferson.

1789
George Washington takes the first presidential oath at New York's Federal Hall.

1804
Lewis and Clark set out on their 8,000-mile (13,000km) expedition to the Pacific Coast.

Henry Ford, American automobile manufacturer.

1848
Gold is discovered at Sutter's Fort, California, bringing over 200,000 prospectors within the next three years.

1860
South Carolina secedes from the Union, and the Confederate states are born.

1861
Confederates open fire on Fort Sumter, in the first shots of the Civil War.

1863
Abraham Lincoln frees slaves in rebelling states by issuing the Emancipation Proclamation.

1864
The transcontinental telegraph connects Seattle, Washington, with the rest of the US.

1865
The Civil War ends. President Abraham Lincoln is assassinated in Washington, DC. The 13th Amendment to the Constitution ends slavery throughout the US.

1869
The Central Pacific and Union Pacific railroads meet in Ogden, Utah, completing the first transcontinental railroad.

1876
Lieutenant Colonel George A. Custer and his men are wiped out by Sioux and Cheyenne warriors at Little Bighorn Creek.

1890
A US Army regiment attacks a camp near Wounded Knee Creek

in South Dakota's Pine Ridge Reservation, killing 300 Indians.

1906
A massive earthquake measuring 8.2 on the Richter Scale, followed by a devastating fire, flattens San Francisco.

1908
Henry Ford begins mass production of the Model T car.

1920
Nineteenth Amendment to the Constitution guarantees women's right to vote. Thirteen-year experiment with prohibition of alcohol begins; law widely flouted.

1929
Wall Street crashes, heralding the Great Depression. US unemployment reaches 25 percent.

1930s
The Dust Bowl forces thousands from farmlands around Oklahoma on a migrant trek west to California in search of work.

1932
Franklin D. Roosevelt elected president in a landslide; commences New Deal programs in response to Depression; FDR re-elected a record three times.

1941
Japan attacks Pearl Harbor, and the United States enter World War II.

1945
First atomic bomb detonates in New Mexico; bombs dropped

on Hiroshima and Nagasaki. United Nations charter drafted in San Francisco.

1955
Rev. Martin Luther King, Jr. leads the Montgomery (Alabama) Bus Boycott.

1963
President John F. Kennedy is assassinated while touring Dallas, Texas.

1968
Martin Luther King, Jr. and Senator Robert Kennedy are assassinated.

1969
Apollo 11 lands on the moon.

1974
Richard M. Nixon, 37th President, resigns after facing impeachment over Watergate.

1981
The Space Shuttle *Columbia* is launched for the first time.

1989
The Loma Prieta earthquake in San Francisco devastates the city.

1995
Domestic terrorists blow up a federal building in Oklahoma City, claiming 168 lives.

1998
President Bill Clinton is mired in a sex scandal with intern Monica Lewinsky. American politics grinds to a halt as the President's personal life is debated in Congress, where he is eventually impeached.

2001
Passenger jets hijacked by suicide bombers destroy New

Resident in Houston being saved after Hurricane Harvey.

York City's World Trade Center. The US invades Afghanistan to pursue al Qaeda.

2003
President George W. Bush orders the invasion of Iraq to overthrow Saddam Hussein.

2005
Hurricane Katrina causes major flooding and destruction in New Orleans and along the Gulf Coast, killing more than 1,000 residents.

2008
The collapse of the housing bubble and the failure of several large banking establishments triggers an economic recession.

2009
Barack Obama is sworn in as the 44th President of the United States, becoming the first African-American to hold the nation's highest office.

2010
Congress passes President Obama's controversial health care reform. Deeply conservative Tea Party movement pushes Republican Party to the right as Democrats lose control of House of Representatives.

2011
American combat forces leave Iraq.

2012
Barack Obama is re-elected for a second term as President.

2014
Riots in Ferguson, Missouri, after shooting of a black teenager by a white policeman.

2015
Supreme Court ruling legalizes same-sex marriage in all states. USA restores diplomatic relations with Cuba ending over half a century of hostility.

2016
Republican businessman Donald Trump is elected President of the United States after winning the Electoral College; however, his opponent, former First Lady Hillary Clinton, senator from New York, wins the popular vote.

2017
An extremely active hurricane season causes devastation in short order across the Caribbean, Florida, and Gulf states. Hurricane Harvey stalls over the Houston metropolitan area for four days, causing flooding, displacing 30,000 people. Category 5 Hurricane Irma, the most powerful hurricane on record in the open Atlantic region, slams into the Florida Keys and the Naples area causing massive damage.

2018
A mass shooting at Marjory Stoneman Douglas High School in Parkland, Florida, results in 17 deaths. Student survivors organize the huge March for Our Lives across the states to lobby for gun control.

Lewis and Clark sculpture and the Gateway Arch in St Louis.

THE TRANSPORTATION REVOLUTION

From wagon trains to the iron horse to today's superhighways,
travel is at the heart of America's history.

During the 17th and 18th centuries, white settlers in early America followed the network of paths that Native Americans had carved out for themselves, and travel conditions were notoriously wretched. During the time of colonization from Great Britain, it cost less to transport goods across the Atlantic Ocean from London to Philadelphia than to carry those same goods 100 miles (160km) to Lancaster, Pennsylvania. In 1776, news of the Declaration of Independence took 29 days to reach the people of Charleston, South Carolina. No wonder New England delegates at the Constitutional Convention in 1787 had more things in common with their brethren in Britain than with their fellow countrymen down South in the Carolinas and Georgia.

Fifty years later, when Alexis de Tocqueville, Michael Chevalier, and a host of European travelers examined the American experiment of self-government, conditions on dry land were little improved. Whereas the Roman Empire made the construction of great roads an important function of its central government, in 19th-century America laissez-faire attitudes predominated, leaving the construction of highways as a state and local responsibility. Often, farmers and laborers who were unable to meet their tax obligations ended up doing the little roadwork that was done.

Bygone mode of transportation recalled in song.

TOLERANCE OF MUD

As a direct consequence of the American belief in "the less government the better," roads suffered from neglect and disrepair. Pioneers such as Abraham Lincoln's father, Thomas, for example, had to possess courage, physical strength, and an incredible tolerance of mud. William Herndon, Lincoln's law partner and biographer, described the Lincoln family's move from Indiana to Illinois in March of 1830 as one which

"suited the roving and migratory spirit of Thomas Lincoln." With the "obscure and penniless" 21-year-old Abe commanding a wagon drawn by two oxen, "the journey was a long and tedious one." Basing his literary account of the trip on Lincoln's recollections, Herndon memorably evokes the experience of thousands of similar travelers. "The rude, heavy wagon," he wrote, "with its primitive wheels, creaked and groaned as it crawled through the woods and now and then stalled in the mud. Many were the delays."

In antebellum America, geography created a formidable barrier to migration. Even as late as the 1830s, approximately 80 percent of the American population still lived east of the Allegheny Mountains.

Thomas Jefferson's decision to send Captain Meriwether Lewis and Lieutenant William Clark to explore the territories west of the Mississippi River charted the way for settlement of the vast region. The president dispatched Lewis and Clark shortly after the Louisiana Purchase in 1803. His motives for asking for a $2,500 appropriation from Congress to finance the expedition were mixed. Even at this late date, it appears Jefferson had not abandoned all hope that a passage to Asia might be found. He was also confident that the explorers would discover trade routes to benefit fur traders.

displayed in the face of physical deprivation, and eloquence is inspiring. Lewis and Clark prepared the way for the invasion of the West that is still in progress today.

In the 1840s, the journalist John O'Sullivan popularized the phrase "manifest destiny" to describe a widespread expansionist ideology.

Western politicians such as Stephen Douglas based their political fortunes on promoting the future greatness of the West as the ultimate destination and demanded the construction of a transcontinental railroad in order to link the nation's

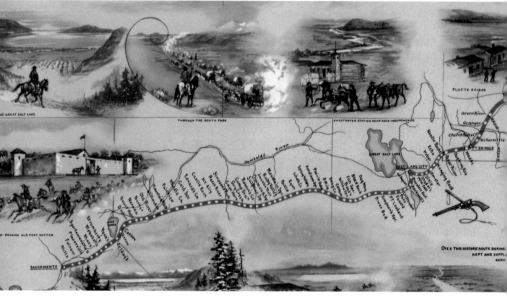

Map depicting the Pony Express Trail.

Thomas Jefferson thought it would take close to a thousand years to settle the lands west of the Mississippi River; he was off by more than 900 years.

Jefferson wanted to expand his "Empire of Liberty" – but as a child of the Enlightenment, he was equally interested in the advancement of knowledge of the physical world. Lewis and Clark did not disappoint Jefferson. Their voluminous journals provided detailed descriptions of Native American tribes, flora and fauna, and topography along their route. Their wide range of learning, courage

rapidly expanding economy. But even before the tracks were laid, settlers were heading west along wagon routes such as the fabled Oregon Trail.

AGE OF THE IRON HORSE

Before the Union could be linked by rail, the United States was plunged into the Civil War. It took four weeks for the news of the opening volley at Fort Sumter to reach San Francisco, but by the end of the war, the nation was forging the bonds of union. The age of the turnpike, steamboat, and canal had been overtaken by the iron horse; it is widely conceded that the North's superior transportation system played a crucial role in crushing the Southern rebels. In 1863, the North was able to transport 25,000 troops by rail from Washington, DC, to Chattanooga, Tennessee, to turn the tide in a major battle.

Mark Twain and Charles Dudley Warner dubbed the final third of the 19th century "the Gilded Age," an era of conspicuous consumption and corruption. Perhaps it might better be thought of as the age of the railroad. The railroad barons – the Goulds, Huntingtons, and Vanderbilts – all understood that the railroad was the lubricant of both a booming economy and sleazy politics.

The railroads, with their new sleeping and dining accommodations, also made long-distance travel for pleasure a realistic possibility for middle-class Americans. Although a period of rest and relaxation did not sit well with those devoted to work, publicists for the new leisure ethic stressed that Americans were growing unhealthy – both physically and spiritually – as a result of their obsession with success. Regeneration through contact with the great outdoors and the vigorous life was a stock promise from popularizers of the West.

In 1893, the year of the Chicago World's Fair, two bicycle mechanics, Charles and J. Frank Duryea,

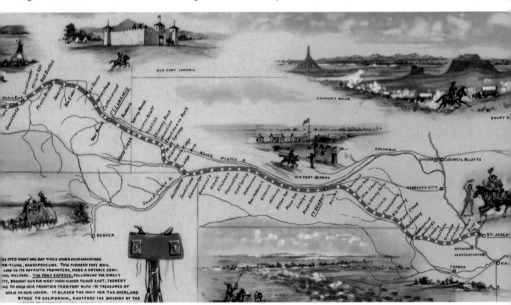

⊙ THE PONY EXPRESS

One of the 19th century's most romantic enterprises, the Pony Express galloped across the western landscape and into the history books in just over 18 months. From April 1860 through October 1861, Pony Express riders formed a record-setting, trans-Mississippi relay team that won over the hearts of Americans, if not the pocketbooks of the US Congress. The daring young mail carriers braved rain, snow, sleet, dead of night, and Indian attacks between St Joseph, Missouri, and Sacramento, California, to deliver over 35,000 letters, telegrams, and newspapers. The riders tallied up 650,000 miles (1 million km) on the 1,966-mile (3,164km) -long Pony Express Trail. And they lost only one mailbag.

Newspaper ads for Express riders did not mince words: "WANTED – Young, skinny, wiry fellows not over 18. Must be expert riders willing to risk death daily. Orphans preferred." Eighty riders, almost all weighing less than 125lbs (57kg), were hired initially, including a fatherless 15-year-old named William F. Cody, later known as Buffalo Bill. The pay was attractive – at least $50 a month, plus free lodging and food. Each rider took an oath, agreeing not to use profane language, not to get drunk, and not to fight with other employees. Each horseman also received a copy of the Bible, plus two Colt revolvers, a knife, and a carbine. The journey took 10 days each way.

successfully tested what became the first commercially successful American automobile on the streets of Springfield, Massachusetts, and a new age began.

CAR CRAZY

Public roads were among the initial benefits of the age of the automobile. The movement to upgrade the quality of highways had begun during the 1880s, when bicycling organizations led the call for improved roads. When automobiles began to appear in the streets in greater numbers after 1900, the drive for surfaced roads

Gridlock on a New Jersey highway – with paved roads and cheaper cars came traffic jams.

attracted increasing support. In 1916, President Woodrow Wilson signed a Federal Aid Road Act, marking the first of a series of occasions when Federal intrusion into the nation's transportation system met with widespread public approval.

The constituency for such governmental action grew larger with each passing decade. The person who probably deserves the greatest share of credit for democratizing the automobile and travel is Henry Ford, who introduced the assembly line, which revolutionized the production and sale of cars; by 1922, he was selling an astonishing 1.3 million Model Ts. The Tin Lizzie had made the automobile a badge of social distinction as well as a necessity.

The impact of the widespread ownership of cars upon travel cannot be overstated. It was probably the single most important factor in the opening of American life not only to travelers seeking remote scenes but also to 20th-century movers and migrants.

What would the 1930s have been like, after all, if John Steinbeck's literary Tom Joad and his fellow wandering poor could not have climbed into a car and headed for California where, as a Jimmie Rodgers song promised, the "water tastes like cherry wine"? The increased mobility the automobile offered underscores the judgment of George F. Pierson, who in his book *The Moving American* describes this freedom as "the great American permit to be both more free and more equal than our contemporaries could manage to become in the more static societies of Europe."

But the early years of the new millennium brought a challenge to this American dream. Concern over air pollution had already led to government-imposed emission standards; now, the realities of global warming forced people to look harder at the environmental cost of their cherished mobility. As gas prices hit a record high in 2008, Americans realized that they could no longer take for granted the cheap transportation that they had enjoyed from birth. At the same time, a world economic recession, triggered by severe problems in the financial sector, imposed further pressures on mobility as the nation faced unemployment, plunging house values, and the near collapse of its automotive industry.

As in the past, Americans are rising to the challenge with the production of ethanol blends that mix grain fuels with gasoline and the exchange of gas-guzzling SUVs for a new breed of hybrid cars that can run partly on electricity. Some 12 car manufactures offer over 25 models of highway-capable electric cars. The American company Tesla's fully electric sedan Model S, introduced in 2010, is one of the top selling plug-in vehicles, and its recent Model 3 is quickly catching up. With 769,252 electric cars sold between 2008 and year end 2017, and sales continuing to soar in 2018, the country boasts the largest fleet of highway-capable plug-in vehicles in the world. Conventional engines have also reduced in size: new cars purchased in the US are now mostly powered by four-cylinder motors. A new transportation revolution is underway – in hearts and minds, as well as on the road.

Marlon Brando as *The Wild One,* one of the first anti-heroes of the silver screen.

AMERICAN ARTISTS AND THE ROAD

America's creative spirit is forever energized by the allure of the open road. Novelists, poets, songwriters, filmmakers – all are seduced by the romance of going places.

American artists are perpetually on the run. Their work epitomizes the wanderlust of the American people: the belief in movement for movement's sake. "The sound of a jet," John Steinbeck wrote in 1961, "an engine warming up, even the clopping of shod hooves on pavement brings an ancient shudder, the dry mouth and vacant eye, the hot palms and the churn of stomach high up under the rib cage."

A century before Steinbeck, Herman Melville depicted travel as a balm to a depressed soul. "Whenever I find myself growing grim about the mouth," he mused in the famous first paragraph of *Moby Dick*, "whenever it is a damp, drizzly November in my soul; ...whenever my hypos get such an upper hand of me, that it requires a strong moral principle to prevent me from deliberately stepping into the street, and methodically knocking people's hats off – then, I account it high time to get to sea as soon as I can." In the classic American fiction of Melville, Edgar Allan Poe, James Fenimore Cooper, and Mark Twain, we encounter characters fleeing the inertia of polite society for a jaunt into the wild.

Tom Hanks as Forrest Gump, who runs across America and participates in much of its recent history.

A STAY AGAINST CONFUSION

The great writers of 19th-century America celebrated the movement away from complex modern life. They viewed travel as a "stay against confusion" in a society committed to material gain. Melville, Nathaniel Hawthorne, and Cooper felt alienated from the climate of the times and sought refuge in foreign travel.

Their despair with the democratic masses stands in marked contrast to one of the greatest American poets of the open road, Walt Whitman. A journey along the open highway suited his desire to comprehend the whole of life: the casual meeting, the encounter between the eye of the seer and the landscape, and the timelessness of nature. Whitman saw the open road as the passage to wisdom and fraternity.

The very act of traveling is a democratic gesture to the poet, a source of inspiration, and a symbol of his personal liberty. Not only were the "American people the greatest poem," but the American environment itself was an incubator of freedom and unity. As he wrote in his acclaimed "Song of the Open Road:"

I think all heroic deeds were all conceiv'd
in the open air, and all free poems also,
I think I could stop here myself and do miracles,
I think whatever I shall meet

on the road I shall like, and
whoever beholds me shall like me.
I think whoever I see must be happy.

Mark Twain used the voyage as a metaphor for change. In his novel *The Adventures of Huckleberry Finn*, he made it clear that the voyage was a learning experience and a rebellion against conventional morality. Some of the book's most moving passages are Huck's accounts of life on the river. Each time Huck and the escaped slave Jim encounter people on shore, trouble, trickery, and cruelty pre-

but his celebration of finding spiritual truths while racing across the continent makes the work transcend conventional literary canons.

I wish for a change of place, The hour is come at last, that I must fly from my home and abandon my farm!
J. Hector St John de Crevecoeur, Letters from an American Farmer.

Jack Kerouac.

Woody Guthrie.

dominate. The book ends with Huck's famous vow to flee civilization and its hypocrisy. But, of course, the old-fashioned frontier was disappearing when Twain was writing in the 1880s, so Huck's dream of flight belonged to a vanishing world. Still, Huck's words at the close of *Huckleberry Finn* bring to mind another characteristic of American literature: loneliness, and the traveler as a solitary figure.

Since World War II, the accelerated pace of travel has produced a literature equally frenetic. The most famous road book has been Jack Kerouac's *On the Road*, the definitive statement of his "Beat Generation" and an incalculable influence on the counterculture of the 1960s and 1970s. Kerouac's prose may impress less now,

Kerouac's work continued the tradition of writer as pathfinder and spiritual voyager, as did Native American writer William Least Heat Moon's *Blue Highways*. Heat Moon traversed the nation in his van "ghost dancing." His report is both a rumination on travel literature and a revealing study of the state of the nation. Richard Grant, a British journalist, fell in love with the American nomadic lifestyle. His *Ghost Riders* tells the story of nomads present (in their own words from boxcar slang to cowboy drawl) and past.

Whereas Kerouac filtered experience through a historical frame of mind, Heat-Moon and Grant, by letting people speak for themselves, capture the diversity of the landscape that often overwhelms the trans-American traveler.

Travel continues to be a method by which writers question where we have come and where we are going, whether collectively as a society, as in Dave Gorman's *American Unchained*, or personally, as in Dan Jackson's *Old Bug: The Spiritual Quest of a Skeptical Guy on a Road Trip Across America with a Long Lost Friend in a Beat-Up Beetle*. Both are comic and touching odysseys of self-discovery.

Today, television, which has replaced literature as the medium for the masses, has picked up the tradition and writers have adapted to a visual role. In *Stephen Fry in America*, the writer and

stampeding, often reworked old Irish and English ballads about murder and betrayal. Much of the music produced under such circumstances was grim and filled with resignation. In the 1940s and 1950s, cowboy singers such as Roy Rogers and Gene Autry evoked the nostalgia of the open range for a populace increasingly constrained by urban and suburban conventions.

Not all country music is downbeat, however. A whole genre of music has arisen devoted to the lives of the modern riders of the open range: truck drivers. These contemporary folk figures

John Steinbeck.

Walt Whitman.

comedian traveled across all 50 states to find the heart and psyche of the nation, while historian Simon Schama took to the road to understand the contemporary political situation in *The American Future*. BBC environmental journalist Justin Rowlatt spent six weeks traveling 6,500 miles (10,400km) across the US on public transportation while reporting on climate change.

MUSIC TO THEIR EARS

It is not just literary artists who have sung of the loneliness and vagaries of the open road. Country music in particular often focuses on that "lonesome guy" Hank Williams sang about on "the lost highway." Cowboys, singing at night to fight off despair and keep cattle from

*I'm going down that long, lonesome road
And I ain't gonna be treated this a-way.*
Bill Monroe, "Lonesome Road Blues"

form a loyal audience for country music, and songs like the admired and much-recorded "Six Days on the Road" are pure Walt Whitmanesque whoops of triumph over the law, the cops, and anything that might get in the way.

The theme of the open road extends to rock music and blues as well. Is it any wonder that one of the rock anthems of the 1970s was Bruce Springsteen's "Born to Run"? Ace bluesman Robert Johnson evoked the road as a haunting meeting place. In his highly influential song "Crossroad Blues," the narrator's fear and anguish are clear as he prays at the crossroad for mercy for (so the legend goes) having sold his soul to the devil in exchange for mastery of the guitar.

Surely Woody Guthrie is the "bard of the open road." Even a simple listing of some of his songs – "Dust Bowl Refugees," "I Ain't Got No Home," "Walkin' Down the Railroad Line" – suggests the

figures in an uncomfortable relationship with polite society. Ready to right wrong wherever he finds it, the cowboy must move along in the last reel.

George Stevens' 1953 classic *Shane* set the pattern for all the films about righteous, wandering loners to follow. Clint Eastwood's *Pale Rider* attempted to revive this formula in the 1980s, but, since the 1960s, motor-driven outlaws have replaced the cowboy as the stars of road films. From Marlon Brando in the *The Wild One* to Mel Gibson in *The Road Warrior*, films set on the road have focused on wandering antisocial anti-heroes.

Dennis Hopper and Peter Fonda hit the open road in Easy Rider.

prominence he assigned to "walkin' down the line." Like Whitman, he attempted to capture the whole of America in the verses of "This Land is Your Land." Guthrie lived the life he wrote about after his family was wrecked by tragedy and disease. His best work is timeless – many of his tunes borrow heavily from hymns and ballads – and will live as long as there are roads to walk and people to sing.

SAGAS OF THE SILVER SCREEN

The great road films of Hollywood are the best visual sagas of the open plains. People all over the world think of the United States as a land of wide-open spaces, thanks to the images they receive from the films of directors such as John Ford and other Western moviemakers. Again we encounter solitary

Bonnie and Clyde (Arthur Penn, 1967) is an example of the perfect tragi-comic road picture. Viewed through the countercultural lens of the 1960s, the story of Clyde Barrow and Bonnie Parker seems like a folk tale of the Depression-era 1930s. Bonnie and Clyde rob banks that rob the poor of their dreams and make their getaway to the sound of rebellious country music.

Few films of the recent past inspired more real-life voyages than *Easy Rider* (Dennis Hopper, 1969). Those who see the film as a period piece and high camp have no idea how its original viewers saw it. *Rider* was probably the most powerful advertisement for the counterculture to appear in movie houses throughout the heartland of the nation. To this day, there are middle-aged workers who dream of throwing away their cellphones, mounting a Harley motorcycle, and setting off for Mardi Gras in New Orleans.

Thelma and Louise (Ridley Scott, 1991) updated this story, using cars and women to illustrate the hi-jinks and low life of on-the-road escapism. The final scene, where the women end it all, is in the tradition of the best Westerns of the 1950s.

But the public also has an appetite for softer films that portray the road as an antidote to modern angst. Witness the hit sleeper *Little Miss Sunshine*, which has a dysfunctional family hobbling across the miles in a broken-down VW bus to help a little girl pursue her dream of entering a beauty pageant. Or a man shaking off a midlife crisis in California's wine country in *Sideways*.

The swoop of history follows us down every highway, and the traveler has many teachers to choose from before embarking on an adventure. For William Least Heat Moon, Walt Whitman served as the model. For Ridley Scott, John Ford was the inspiration. As you head out on the highway, listen to these voices, but be aware that there is no experience like an original one.

Pursuing a family dream in Little Miss Sunshine.

⊘ ON THE ROAD MOVIES

About Schmidt (Alexander Payne, 2002)
Badlands (Terrence Malick, 1973)
Bonnie and Clyde (Arthur Penn, 1967)
Due Date (Todd Phillips, 2010)
Duel (Steven Spielberg, 1971)
Easy Rider (Dennis Hopper, 1969)
The Grapes of Wrath (John Ford, 1939)
Joy Ride (John Dahl, 2001)
Little Miss Sunshine (J. Dayton and V. Faris, 2006)
Natural Born Killers (Oliver Stone, 1994)
The Outlaw Josey Wales (Clint Eastwood, 1976)
O Brother, Where Art Thou? (Joel Coen, 2000)
On the Road (Walter Salles, 2012)

Paris, Texas (Wim Wenders, 1984)
Planes, Trains, and Automobiles (John Hughes, 1987)
Rain Man (Barry Levinson, 1988)
Sideways (Alexander Payne, 2004)
The Sugarland Express (Steven Spielberg, 1974)
Stranger Than Paradise (Jim Jarmusch, 1984)
The Searchers (John Ford, 1956)
The Wild One (Laslo Benedek, 1953)
Thelma and Louise (Ridley Scott, 1991)
Transamerica (Duncan Tucker, 2005)
Two Lane Blacktop (Monte Hellman, 1971)
Vanishing Point (Richard C. Sarafian, 1971)
Wild at Heart (David Lynch, 1990)

ROUTE 66: AMERICA'S MAIN STREET

Quirky motels, mom 'n' pop diners, drive-in movie theaters: in its heyday, many thought this was the most magical road in the world.

In 1926, a road with its eastern terminus at the corner of Michigan Avenue and Jackson Boulevard in Chicago, Illinois received its official designation as Route 66. With its catchy double-six road markers, this ribbon of asphalt and concrete stretched westward for 2,448 miles (3,940km) through three time zones and across eight states – Illinois, Missouri, Kansas, Oklahoma, Texas, New Mexico, Arizona, and California – to the shores of the Pacific Ocean at Santa Monica. Route 66 was one of the country's first continuous spans of paved highway, linking the eastern part of America with the vast spaces and burgeoning new cities of the West.

NO OTHER ROAD LIKE IT

US Highway 66 reigns as the most storied highway in the annals of American travel. A recurring theme in American literature, Route 66 has been the star of more stories, books, songs, movies, and television shows than any other road. From the mid-1920s to the mid-1970s, it was more heavily traveled than scenic Highway 101 on the Pacific Coast, better known than the Pennsylvania Turnpike or the Alcan Highway, and surely better loved than busy US 1 between Maine and Key West, with its maddening traffic snarls around metropolitan New York. And before the advent of the interstate systems, US 66 came closer than any other highway to becoming the National Road. Route 66 was soon known as "the most magical road in all the world." A legend was in the making.

And what a legend it would be. Nobody could possibly know how many Americans – from Oklahoma's Dust Bowl refugees, to starry-eyed aspirants to Hollywood fame, to 1960s counterculture types "splitting for the Coast" – followed Route 66 on their way from their old lives to new ones in the California sun.

Happy Lou Phillips made headlines by roller-skating from Washington, DC to San Francisco.

The nation first became aware of US Highway 66 when the 1928 International Transcontinental Foot Marathon (affectionately known as the Bunion Derby) tramped along the road from Los Angeles to Chicago, then on to Madison Square Garden in New York, a distance of 3,448 miles (5,548km). The winner was handed $25,000. Andy Payne, a part-Cherokee Indian from Oklahoma, won the purse.

Three decades later, for a fee of $1,500, Peter McDonald walked on stilts from New York City to Los Angeles, a distance of 3,200 miles (5,150km). From Chicago to Los Angeles, his way out west was Route 66. Pete was neither the first nor the last to place the road in the public eye – wild, weird, and wondrous celebrants were

*If you ever plan to motor west;
travel my way, take the highway that's the best.
Get your kicks on Route Sixty-six!*

to follow. Two such celebrities were Happy Lou Phillips and his friend Lucky Jimmy Parker. The pair of intrepid travelers strapped on skates and rolled their way along America's Main Street, as it was called, during their cross-country journey

The Mother Road has also seen its share of high school baton twirlers, who have marched along Old 66 setting dubious records.

Route 66 was a highway of flat tires, overheated radiators, motor courts, cars with no air-conditioning, tourist traps, treacherous curves, narrow lanes, and detour signs.

In the Roaring Twenties, desperadoes and bootleggers – the likes of John Dillinger, Al Capone, Bugs Moran, Bonnie and Clyde, and Ma Barker and her god-fearing boys – lurched down Old 66, using it as an escape route. Occasionally, the Associ-

Whimsical establishments like the Iceberg Café in Albuquerque, New Mexico, have been demolished.

from Washington, DC, to San Francisco. Through the state of Arizona, a newspaper reported, "They walked a great deal, since at that time (1929) Route 66 was only paved through towns."

Another student of perambulating the old highway was "Shopping Cart" Dougherty, who, sporting a white beard and turban, traveled 9 to 16 miles (14 to 26km) a day on Route 66 with all his worldly possessions in a shopping cart. History doesn't tell us the final destination of Dougherty.

JOGGERS AND BATON TWIRLERS

In 1972, John Ball, a 45-year-old South African, jogged from California to Chicago on Route 66, and then became a hero on the East Coast. The journey took 54 days.

ated Press warned travelers of the dangers of "the criminally few who mix with the tourist throng."

Route 66 was Burma Shave signs, neon signs, full-service gas stations, mom 'n' pop diners, blue-plate specials, homemade pies, and waitresses who called everybody "honey," winked at the kids, and yelled at the cook. Hitchhiking was safe, and billboards along the highway were legal. People guzzled Grape Nehi, and summer lasted longer because of drive-in movies, miniature golf, and slow-pitch softball under the lights. Motels didn't take reservations. And doctors didn't mind making house calls.

Through good times and hard times, the highway became a symbol of faith for the future. Novelist John Steinbeck set the tone of the highway in his

Pulitzer Prize-winning book *The Grapes of Wrath*, when he found a nurturing quality in Route 66 and called her "the mother road." It was the "Road of Second Chance." To some, like the immigrants of the Dust Bowl, it was the "Glory Road." To archi-

It winds from Chicago to L.A.
More than two thousand miles all the way.
Get your kicks on Route Sixty-six!

to the next. In Vega, Texas, a story – probably sprinkled with a little local folklore – is told of the town's baseball team. They wanted to play the team in a nearby community, but there was no connecting road. So the ambitious folks in this small Texas town built one. Today, that former deep-rutted path is said to be part of Route 66.

Route 66 was all-night radio out of Del Rio, Texas; Continental Trailways and Greyhound buses; lemonade stands; family reunions; 25-cent haircuts and a 5-cent cup of coffee. Kids

DJ Wolfman Jack was the voice on the radio accompanying most long-distance drives.

tect Frank Lloyd Wright, it was the chute of a tilting continent, on which everything loose seemed to be sliding into Southern California. And to travel agencies it was the chosen thoroughfare of the growing numbers of discriminating American tourists.

Route 66 was to carry a sundry of names at different locations throughout her history – names like the Pontiac Trail, Osage Indian Trail, Wire Road, Postal Highway, Grand Canyon Route, National Old Trails Highway, Ozark Trail, Will Rogers Highway, and, because it went through the center of so many towns, the Main Street of America.

ALL-NIGHT RADIO

Route 66 was hundreds of locally improved and maintained lanes going from one town

counted telephone poles on the road, waved at engineers on trains, slept in a wigwam in Holbrook, Arizona, and signs in New Mexico promised (and still do) "Tucumcari Tonight."

"Route 66," Bobby Troup's hit song of 1946, became a highway national anthem. Originally crooned by Nat King Cole, the simple tune went on to be immortalized by Bing Crosby, Chuck Berry, The Rolling Stones, and a host of other recording artists – at last count over 100 of them. Nothing captured America's love affair with the road more than this song.

It celebrated the end of World War II and the end of gas and food rationing. The lyrics invited Americans to get their kicks on Route 66, and millions of motoring adventurers, addicted to

BURMA SHAVE

Exploiting the potential of a captive audience, the verses along the Mother Road entertained the road-weary and accelerated sales.

The Burma Shave company was founded by an imaginative insurance salesman to provide a speedy, brushless shave for the businessman on the go. Clinton Odell, father of the company's former CEO, collaborated with pharmacist Carl Noren to produce an item that became one of the most famous in America by virtue of being seen along every highway.

Burma Shave signs were once a familiar sight along US highways.

"By the start of the year we were getting the first repeat orders in the history of the company – all from druggists serving people who traveled these roads," Odell told Frank Rowsome, Jr, who wrote the history of the company.

Does Your Husband/Misbehave/Grunt and Grumble/ Rant and Rave/Shoot the Brute Some/Burma Shave was one of the earliest signs, its lines spaced 100 paces apart – like most of the thousands that followed. In his book, *The Verse by the Side of the Road*, Rowsome explained that, traveling at 35mph, the sequence took 18 seconds to read – "far more time and attention than a newspaper or magazine advertiser could reasonably

expect from the casual viewer." Alexander Woollcott maintained that it was as difficult to read a single sign as it was to eat one salted peanut.

In those early days, rival advertisers soon became jealous. Many of them had been spending thousands on marketing their product, only to see a perky upstart impress its name on the consumer in a way that was remembered long after the signs ceased to exist. Sensing their annoyance, the signs cheekily responded by rubbing it in: *Let's Give the/ Clerk a Hand/Who Never/Palms Off/Another Brand.* Burma Shave also knew how to needle the latest electric competition: *A Silky Cheek/Shaved Smooth/ And Clean/Is Not Obtained/With a Mowing Machine.*

There were once 35,000 Burma Shave signs, but by 1963 they had been removed. They were now costing the company almost a quarter of a million dollars a year and were clearly having a diminishing effect on sales.

"The commercial fortunes of the Burma-Vita Company can be read like tea leaves in the jingles themselves," wrote Rowsome. There were many reasons for the downturn in sales: people were driving too fast, superhighway rights of way frequently banned commercial signs, and possibly people were becoming too sophisticated to regard them as anything more than corny relics.

Most people were sad to see the Burma Shave signs disappear, as their growing insignificance proved to be just one more nail in the coffin of the vibrant Mother Road. As early as 1930, the company had been spending $65,000 a year (prompting $3 million in annual sales), but it was not only passing drivers that enjoyed them: friendly relations had been established with hundreds of farmers on whose land the red-and-white signs appeared. Although rentals rarely topped $25 per year, many farmers were so proud of the signs that they made their own repairs when necessary.

There was never a chance that Burma Shave would run out of slogans. An annual contest offering $100 for each jingle used drew more than 50,000 entries. These would be whittled down to the best 1,000 stanzas. Of course, there were thousands of entries that were not considered "appropriate" and hence never used: *Listen, Birds/These Signs Cost Money/So Roost a While/ But Don't Get Funny.*

the smell of gasoline and the drone of rubber on the pavement, took Bobby's suggestion to heart.

ITCHY FEET

Americans with itchy feet were ready to hit the road. They removed the musty canvas that had covered and protected the Plymouth ragtop and the Oldsmobile Woody since the outbreak of the war. And although the cars had been stored on blocks, folks replaced the prewar tires with a set of six-ply Allstate clinchers at a total cost of $43.80. Vacationers polished their new post-

The 1950s saw Route 66 reach genuine celebrity status. Families could leave their homes in the East and Midwest and drive to the Painted Desert or the Grand Canyon. They

"Hobo" Dick Zimmerman routinely walked Route 66 from California to Michigan pushing a wheelbarrow in order to visit his 101-year-old mother. Dick was 78.

Route 66, the 1960s weekly TV series, sold more Corvette sports cars than any TV commercial.

war sedans and thumbed through state maps and plotted a course on the road to adventure – Route 66.

Mom wrote "Wish you were here" messages on picture postcards of roadside attractions. The kids bought rich, gooey Pecan *Log Rolls* at Stuckey's *Candy Shoppe* while Dad filled the gas tank at 17 cents a gallon and bought the entire family sticky, orange-flavored popsicles out of the freezer.

The toll charge at the Chain of Rocks Bridge over the mighty Mississippi River was 35 cents per automobile, and brightly colored signs on the outskirts of St Louis, Missouri advertised "the Greatest Show under the Earth" at the nearby Merimac Caverns.

could drive all the way to the Pacific Ocean on a highway that passed through towns where the young outlaw Jesse James robbed banks and Abraham Lincoln practiced law and cross the great river Mark Twain wrote about. Tourists could see snake pits and caged wild critters, mysterious caverns and real-life cowboys and Indians, and visit Mickey's Magic Kingdom in Disneyland, California.

Route 66 reached even greater popularity when a nomadic potboiler of a book by the same name as the highway became a hit TV show from 1960 to 1964. *route 66* (yes, the "r" was not capitalized in the show title) was the story of two young adventurers, Buz (George Maharis) and Tod (Martin Milner), getting their kicks on Route

66 in a Corvette. Of its 116 episodes, few were actually filmed on Route 66. Sponsored in part by Chevrolet, the show itself inspired more Cor-

> Because Route 66 is no longer marked on most road maps, many sections are often hard to find. But the website www.historic66.com gives a turn-by-turn route description of old Route 66 through every state.

Vintage Wurlitzer jukeboxes keep the romance of the open road alive in diners along the Mother Road.

vette sales than any TV commercial and established the Vette as an American icon.

When the Federal Highway Act of 1956 called for the construction of interstate systems throughout the United States, it looked as if the bright lights of fame and fortune that had shone on Route 66 for so many years were beginning to dim.

Little by little, here and there, pieces of Route 66 were replaced by the interstate. Bypassing of the towns that the fabled highway served was a task that took five different superhighways to achieve – Interstate 55 from Chicago to St Louis, Interstate 44 from St Louis to Oklahoma City, Interstate 40 from Oklahoma

City to Barstow, Interstate 15 from Barstow to San Bernardino, and Interstate 10 from San Bernardino to Santa Monica.

The last stretch of Route 66 was bypassed in 1984 at Williams, Arizona, when the old highway was replaced by Interstate 40. There was a ceremony, almost a wake. Bobby Troup, now deceased, was there to give a speech. As tears streamed from his eyes, he called the occasion "a very sad day."

WURLITZER JUKEBOXES

In 1985, US Highway 66 was decertified, giving way to superhighways of diesel fumes and fast-food chains. Because the road is no longer classified as a federal highway, some folks will tell you the road is no longer there. For a while, the route that symbolized America's love affair with the open road seemed destined to live on only in memories and museums.

But progress does not necessarily conquer all. Beyond the endless blandness of the interstates, there is a powerful rhythm in an old two-lane highway that still rises and twists and turns across rolling hills, mountains, and deserts. Slowing through quiet towns, then rushing on and up again to the next ridge, you'll find the road waiting to be discovered in each of the eight Route 66 states.

In rural areas you may come across abandoned and decaying remnants that pay an evocative tribute to the heyday of Route 66. Elsewhere, cafés and roadside attractions have been revived, restored, and reopened. Vintage Wurlitzer jukeboxes blare out old road songs. Folks in classic cars cruise into a drive-in for a hamburger and shake. Service station attendants offer to check under the hood and wash the windshield. Family-owned restaurants serve homemade pie, and a waitress in a starched pink uniform still calls you "Hon!" and yells at the cook. The old road still beckons pilgrims not only from across the US but from nearly every compass point of the world.

With the car open to the wind and an AM radio station riddled with static from a thunderstorm on the horizon, memories flicker in the sweetness of the moment. The miles themselves dissolve every question except the one that matters: What lies waiting, there, just over the next rise of Route 66?

ORIGINA

OLD ROUTE

66

CLUB CAFE
SINCE 1935

A-1 AUTO UPHOLSTERY

A-1 SERVICE & BODY SHOP   472-3887

ICE

Pit stop for a Corvette by the now demolished Club Café in Santa Rosa, New Mexico.

TT·6T6
New Mexico USA · Land of Enchantment

Route 66 passing through
Amboy, California.

Downtown Ybor City
neighborhood in Tampa,
on the Atlantic route.

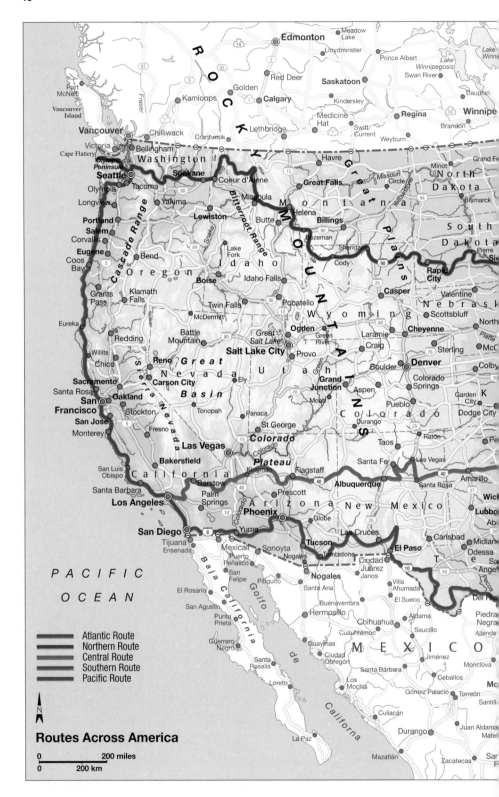

Routes Across America

Atlantic Route
Northern Route
Central Route
Southern Route
Pacific Route

PACIFIC

OCEAN

N

0   200 miles
0   200 km

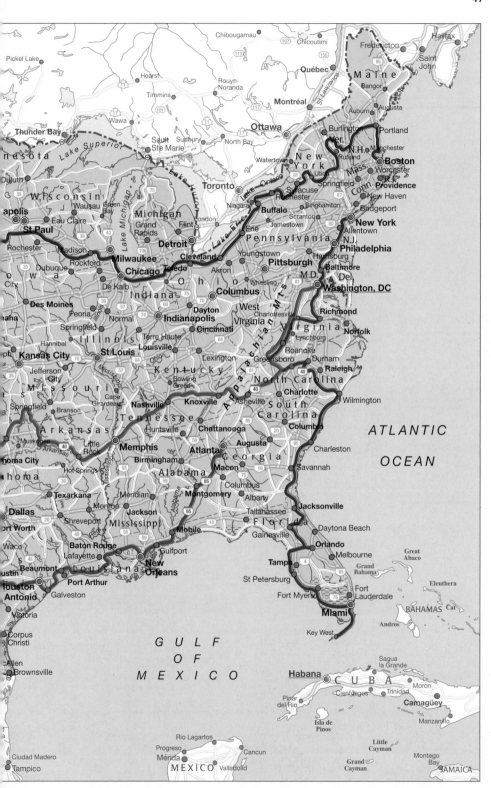

The Blue Ridge Parkway, Virginia.

THE ATLANTIC ROUTE

A detailed guide to the attractions of the Eastern seaboard, with principal sights cross-referenced by number to the maps.

Right at the start of US 1 in Key West, Florida.

Britain's colonization of America's East Coast was accomplished only after settlers had learned to use its waterways: the Atlantic coastline's bays, the long rivers running out of the Appalachian Mountains, and the languid tidal inlets so vital to inland transport in the flat but densely foliated Southern states. It was at the mouths of rivers and ports that virtually every important Eastern city sprang up.

It is appropriate, then, that our route south will rarely stray far from water. Beginning in New York City, undisputed king of America's cities, we will pass through a close succession of two more important cities, each with its own distinct personality: Philadelphia, cradle of American independence, and Baltimore, originally a fishing town and one still largely dependent on port activities.

From there, we will move inland to travel two exceptionally scenic drives in Virginia, passing at last into North Carolina and examining one of the South's most pleasantly diverse states. We will cut east through tobacco fields to the coastline and ride along water once again through South Carolina and Georgia, each time stopping to linger over a beautiful old city or a small, half-forgotten town.

Once in Florida, the weather – and the temperature of the water – will turn steadily warmer as we zigzag south from the nation's oldest settlement, St Augustine on the Atlantic Ocean, to Orlando's lakes, Tampa's mild Gulf of Mexico waters, and past the edge of South

Row houses in Baltimore.

Florida to the vast (and moist) natural area known as the Everglades. At long last, we will emerge at the Atlantic coast once more, skimming past Miami and its attached beaches (returning later) – continuing on to the Florida Keys, a place where water may be more influential and obvious than it is anywhere else in North America.

📷 A SHORT STAY IN NEW YORK CITY

New York is the city that never sleeps. It has energy and confusion, culture, and great charm. Here's a list of the not-to-be-missed attractions.

Central Park, stretching from 59th to 110th streets, hosts ice skating in winter and outdoor concerts in summer. You can also hire a boat on the lake.

9/11 Memorial. Passes are required to tour the site. They are best obtained online (www.911memorial.org).

The Ellis Island Immigration Museum provides a visual history of the port that 40 percent of all Americans can trace their roots to, and documents the migration from the world to the United States.

New York's Museum of Modern Art (MoMA) houses over 200,000 individual pieces of art. Founded in 1929, the world-class institution, which almost doubled in size between 2002 and 2004, is undergoing a $400 million renovation due to be completed in 2019.

Famous for the Rockettes, **Radio City Music Hall** hosts spectacular music and theater shows. Tours are available during the day.

Lincoln Center, on the Upper West Side, is home to the **New York City Philharmonic**, the **New York City Ballet**, the **Vivian Beaumont Theater**, and the **Metropolitan Opera**.

The hub of much of New York City's nightlife, **Greenwich Village** is still a center for musicians, artists, shoppers, and the eccentric.

SoHo and **Tribeca**, with their art galleries and restaurants, are perfect for Saturday strolling. **Chinatown** is close by if you're hungry.

Although its financiers are no longer lords of the universe, **Wall Street** in historic downtown New York is lined with some notable architecture.

USEFUL INFORMATION

Population: 8.55 million
Dialing codes: 212, 347, 929, 718, 917
Website: www.nycgo.com
Tourist information: 810 Seventh Avenue, 3rd floor, NY 10019; tel: 212-484-1200

The famous skyline viewed from Brooklyn Bridge.

Times Square. The bright lights of the renovated square, gateway to Broadway, have made it a tourist magnet once again.

Chinatown is one of the city's most vibrant areas.

The Big Apple

There is a mix of fantasy and foreignness in New York that is unsurpassed anywhere. You want to have a cocktail on a level with the clouds? Go dancing when the moon is high and the mood overtakes you? Want to go in-line skating, ice skating, or take in that Broadway show? You've come to the right town. New York's skyline is instantly recognizable; its attractions the best in the world. Its cultural life is matched only by its culinary awareness; there are over 24,000 eating places. If there are more ways of making it here, there are also more ways of spending it, so bring a fat wallet and lots of stamina.

...om up to the 102nd-floor observation deck of the ...mpire State Building for a different perspective. The ...0° views over Manhattan and beyond are stunning.

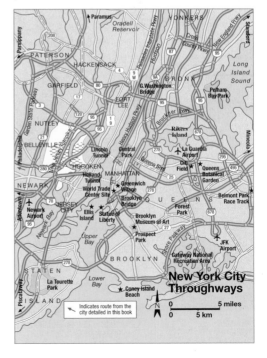

Mabry Mill near the Blue Ridge
Parkway, Virginia.

NEW YORK TO VIRGINIA

Just beyond the frenzy of New York City lie national historic sites and cities of colonial and Civil War importance, as well as the green, green hills of Virginia.

This first leg of the Atlantic route takes in some of the most historic sites in the United States – places where the Revolutionary and Civil wars were fought, and where the brash, new nation was conceived. But in order to take this cruise through history, a bit of contemporary, behind-the-wheel negotiation is required first. There are three ways to leave **New York City ❶** (see page 52) and cross the Hudson River into the neighboring state of New Jersey. From downtown Manhattan, your escape routes are the **Holland** or **Lincoln tunnels**, both of which are in the southern end of Manhattan. Your ultimate objective is I-280W toward the **Oranges**. From the Holland Tunnel, take US 1/9 to I-95N to I-280. From the Lincoln Tunnel, take I-495 to I-95S to I-280. Your other option is the **George Washington Bridge** at the north end of Manhattan. From the bridge, take I-95S to I-280. The drive is more hair-raising than a thrill ride at a theme park; New Jersey and New York drivers have a reputation for almost pathologically aggressive driving.

EDISON'S LAB AND HOME

Sometimes described as "the cradle of American industry," **Edison National Historical Park** (tel: 973-736-0550 ext. 11; www.nps.gov/edis; Wed–Sun) offers

a fascinating look at the complex that was the Silicon Valley and Research Triangle of its time. To reach the site, take I-280W to Exit 10 (West Orange) and follow the brown signs. Most of the buildings are as they were the day the company closed in 1931, with the original lathes, tool shop, drafting tables, and equipment waiting patiently for the inventive workers, chemists, and engineers to return. Edison's desk is covered with papers and notepads; his office is part of a fabulous library that workers used daily, lined with

⊘ **Main attractions**
New York City
Independence National
  Historical Park
Baltimore
Brandywine Valley
Fredericksburg
Williamsburg
Richmond
Monticello
Blue Ridge Parkway

Map on page 56

George Washington Bridge spans the Hudson River.

New York to South Carolina

New York City **1**
Edison National Historical Park
Morristown

Princeton **2**
Lambertville
New Hope
3 Trenton ● Washington Crossing State Park

New Jersey
Pennsylvania

Philadelphia **4**

Pennsylvania
Maryland

Brandywine Valley

5 Baltimore

US Naval Academy
Washington, DC
Maryland
Annapolis **6**

Virginia

Exit 7

Exit 57A

Fredericksburg
7 Exit 130A

8 Richmond

Williamsburg

Exit 121
Charlottesville **9**
Monticello
Exit 124

Natural Bridge
State Park

George
Washington
National Forest

Roanoke **10**

Virginia
North Carolina

Mount Airy **11**

Bethania

Winston-Salem **12**

Greensboro

Durham **13**

Outer Banks

Sanford **14**
Lillington
Fayetteville **15**
Exit 58
Exit 46

Wilmington **16**
USS North Carolina Battleship Memorial

North Carolina
South Carolina
Myrtle Beach

thousands of leather-bound volumes. Ranger-led tours of the Laboratory begin at the visitor center, which offers information, exhibits, and a film about Edison's work. Also shown is *The Great Train Robbery*, the 1903 film made by Edison's film company at the Black Maria – the first onsite film studio in the nation.

A few minutes away is **Glenmont** (tel: 973-736-0550; Aug Wed–Sun, May–July Fri–Sun tours only; tickets available at the Laboratory), Edison's grand estate, which he purchased for his second wife, Mina. (His first wife, Mary, died at the age of 29). Mina was well aware of her husband's reputation and legacy and protected both the house and the factory for posterity.

MORRISTOWN

There are two ways to reach **Morristown**: you can return to I-280, and traverse it and I-80 for about 15 miles (24km) before joining the I-287, or you can follow Route 508 and then 510. The benefit of the country road is that it goes through some pleasant, tree-lined areas and toney neighborhoods rather than less-than-scenic highways.

A lovely village that dates back to Colonial times, Morristown is home to several Revolutionary War sites, protected as Morristown National Historical Park (tel 973-539-2016; www.nps.gov/morr). Six universities and colleges are nearby, and it is also home to the **Seeing Eye** (tel: 973-539-4425; www.seeingeye.org; telephone for tour information), an organization that trains guide dogs for the blind. You will see dogs in training all over town.

Ford Mansion (230 Morris Street; tours Wed–Sun, summer daily; telephone for times) was the elegant home used by George Washington as his headquarters during the bitter winters of 1777 and 1780. Behind it, the WPA-era **Washington's Headquarters Museum** (tel: 973-539-2016 ext. 210; www.nps.gov/morr; Wed–Sun, summer daily) displays original documents, china, maps, and period weapons. **Morris Museum** (tel: 973-971-3700; www.morrismuseum.org; Tue–Sun) features a delightful collection of working mechanical instruments and toys, while the **Museum of Early Trades and Crafts** (tel: 973-377-2982; www.metc. org; Tue–Sun) is housed in a building that is itself an attraction, with stained glass windows, stenciled walls, and mosaics. In nearby **Parsippany**, the **Stickely Museum at Craftsman Farms** (tel: 973-540-0311; www.stickleymuseum. org; Thu–Sun tours only) is a national historic landmark preserving the 1911 home of Gustav Stickely, one of the patriarchs of the American Arts and Crafts Movement.

Head south on US 202 and find yourself surrounded by deep forests and more small towns. **Jockey Hollow**, a Revolutionary War encampment that is part of the national park, is 6 miles (10km) from Morristown; stop at the visitor center for information. A driving or walking tour goes past re-created cabins where reenactors sometimes demonstrate life in the Continental Army.

PRINCETON

At Bridgewater, take the sharp left onto US 206 and you will soon arrive at **Princeton ❷**, home to **Princeton University**. The epitome of the Ivy League campus, Princeton exudes an air of intellectual aspiration, youthful idealism, and more than a touch of privilege. Two American presidents, James Madison and Woodrow Wilson, graduated from Princeton, as did former First Lady Michelle Obama.

Nassau Hall, the oldest building on campus, hosted the Continental Congress in 1783, when mutinous soldiers forced Congress to leave Philadelphia. Note: tours of the campus are available through local tour operators; student-led tours of the campus are available but they are aimed at incoming students (www.princeton.edu/main/visiting/tours).

Backtrack north up US 206 to State 518, then head west for a detour through the lovely **Delaware River**

A Princeton University graduate.

Fall foliage mirrored in a lake in Morristown, New Jersey.

Signpost marking an intersection named after two great cities on the Atlantic Route.

Philadelphia's South Street attracts big crowds on weekend nights.

Valley. Look sharp for the right-hand turn to Lambertville on Broad Street in the village of Hopewell, itself worth a stop. At the river, quiet **Lambertville** has old inns, antique shops, and a narrow bridge connecting it to **New Hope**, Pennsylvania. The Pennsylvania side has several riverside dining establishments. Follow the river on the New Jersey side along Route 29. There are excellent displays at **Washington Crossing State Park** (tel: 609-737-0623; daily), where General George Washington landed on Christmas Eve, 1776, and at the **Old Barracks Museum** (tel: 609-396-1776; www.barracks.org; Mon–Sat) in **Trenton ❸**, where Washington's army captured Hessian soldiers in battle that night. The **New Jersey State Museum** (tel: 609-292-6300; www.state.nj.us/state/museum; Tue–Sun) in Trenton is a one-stop exploration of the archeology, fine arts, culture, and natural history of The Garden State. The **State House** is the second-oldest in the country (Maryland's is number one); across the street is the **New Jersey World War II Memorial.**

From Trenton, take US 1 to I-95 into Philadelphia.

PHILADELPHIA

At the time of the American Revolution, **Philadelphia ❹** was the economic and political center of the fledgling United States. During the early years of the Republic, however, the nation's economic heart was transplanted north to New York City while governmental power traveled south to the new city of Washington, DC. This left the city with a bit of an identity crisis. An interesting ethnic mix has sustained the place ever since, however, making it today one of America's most vibrant large cities.

The nation's fifth most populous city, Philadelphia is right up there with Boston as an American city *par excellence.* Situated at the conjunction of the Schuylkill (pronounced "skoo-kill") and Delaware rivers, the city was founded in 1682 by the English Quaker William Penn. Penn envisioned a colony in which the right to freedom of religious expression would not be quashed. That open-minded attitude pervaded the colony and the city, so it's not surprising that when representatives of the 13 colonies convened to debate independence, they did so here. The result was, of course, the signing of the Declaration of Independence on July 4, 1776, which gave birth to the United States of America.

REVOLUTIONARY SITES

The best place to start a tour is in **Independence National Historical Park** (tel: 215-965-2305; www.nps.gov/inde; daily), where its **Independence Visitor Center** (Sixth and Market streets; tel: 800-537-7676; www.phlvisitorcenter.com; daily) has free films about the city's history, computer kiosks with tourist information, costumed interpreters, and a reservation service for many tours and attractions.

It also issues the free tickets necessary between March and December for entry to **Independence Hall**

at Chestnut Street between Fifth and Sixth streets (tel: 877-444-6777 or www.recreation.gov for ticket reservations; daily), where the Declaration of Independence and the Constitution were signed. Tickets are issued for timed entry; the earlier the tour, the better your chances of getting tickets. The Assembly Room contains the inkstand used by the signers of the Declaration as well as the chair on which George Washington sat during the drafting of the Constitution. To the west of Independence Hall is **Congress Hall**, where the US Congress convened between 1790 and 1800, when Philadelphia was briefly the nation's capital. On Sixth Street, between Market and Chestnut streets, stands the **Liberty Bell Center**, with exhibits about its origins and role as an international icon of freedom. Reservations are not necessary, but expect lines at peak times.

On Independence Mall, between Race and Arch streets, is the **National Constitution Center** (tel: 215-409-6600; www.constitutioncenter.org; daily). Using interactive exhibits and live actors, the museum tells the story of the constitution – its creation in early America, its application in history, and its continuing impact on the lives of Americans today.

On Market Street, toward the Delaware River, is **Franklin Court**, site of Ben Franklin's residence. His home no longer exists but is commemorated by an evocative outline of painted white steel beams. Benjamin Franklin Museum opened in 2013 (tel: 215-965-2305; www.nps.gov/inde/planyourvisit/benjaminfranklinmuseum.htm; daily) and contains artifacts, computer animations, and interactive exhibits. **Christ Church**, at Second Street just above Market Street, was built in 1695 and was the preferred house of worship for the men of the Continental Congress. Plaques mark pews once occupied by George Washington, Ben Franklin, and Betsy Ross. Tours are given daily. **Betsy Ross House** at 239 Arch Street

(tel: 215-686-1252; www.historicphiladelphia.org/betsy-ross-house; Mar–Nov daily, Dec–Feb Tue–Sun) was the place where Ross stitched the new nation's first flag.

READING TERMINAL MARKET

After the Liberty Bell and Independence Hall, Philadelphia's most popular tourist attraction is **Reading Terminal Market** at 12th and Arch streets (tel: 215-922-2317; www.readingterminalmarket.org; daily). First opened in 1893, the market is a gastronomic bazaar of 80 stalls tended by farmers, bakers, butchers, and greengrocers. With numerous restaurants under one roof, it's a good place to pick up lunch. Try a Philly cheese steak, the regional favorite, and look for Tasty Cakes – butterscotch krimpets are sweet decadence.

HISTORIC AND LIVELY NEIGHBORHOODS

From Independence Hall, wend your way toward South Street via the cobblestone streets and garden paths of **Society Hill**, Philly's

⊙ Tip

Parking is available in central Philadelphia in an underground lot beneath Independence Mall. Entrances are at Fifth and Sixth streets between Market and Arch. Parking is also available at the National Constitution Center at Fifth and Arch streets.

Philadelphia's Independence Hall.

BALTIMORE: CHARM CITY

Baltimore is a big city with a small-town feel – the home of good food, great baseball, and "The Star Spangled Banner".

Start with an overview of the city from the **Top of the World** Observation Deck (tel: 410-837-VIEW (8439); www.viewbaltimore.org; daily), located on the 27th floor of the pentagonal World Trade Center. The Inner Harbor is the focus of the city's attractions and the Water Taxi (www.baltimorewatertaxi.com) is a good way to visit the sights. Here, waterfront pavilions house restaurants and specialty shops and an outdoor amphitheater hosts street performers and planned performances. On the water, you can tour the historic **USS *Constellation*** (tel: 410-539-1797; www.historicships.org; daily) a 22-gun, three-masted sloop-of-war that launched in 1854.

A short stroll along the brick waterfront boulevard leads to the fine **National Aquarium** (tel:

Washington Monument in Mount Vernon Place.

410-576-3800; www.aqua.org; daily), one of the nation's best, with a simulated Australian outback, Amazon rainforest, coral reef display, and 220,000-gallon (830,000-liter) open ocean tank. Across the harbor on Light Street, the Maryland Science Center (tel: 410-685-5225; www.mdsci.org; Tue–Sun) has hands-on exhibits on topics such as dinosaurs and space travel. Nearby, the Visionary Art Museum (tel: 410-244-1900; www.avam.org; Tue–Sun) features fantastic visions of self-taught and experimental artists. Take a picnic to **Federal Hill** and enjoy a wonderful view of the harbor. Baseball fans will relish the memorabilia-filled **Babe Ruth Museum** (tel: 410-727-1539; www.baberuthmuseum.org; daily) at 216 Emory Street. Babe Ruth, often hailed as the game's greatest ever player, was born in this modest house in 1895. **Oriole Park at Camden Yards** started the trend of ballparks reflecting the classic era of baseball, and its behind-the-scenes tour is fascinating (tel: 410-547-6234; www.mlb.com/orioles/ballpark; daily). **Geppi's Entertainment Museum** (tel: 410-625-7060; www.geppismuseum.com; Tue–Sun) next to the stadium celebrates comics and pop culture from the 1940s onward.

Fell's Point, Baltimore's first ship-building and maritime center, still has the charm of an old port town. Among the cobbled streets stand more than 350 original Colonial townhouses. Interspersed are old pubs, antique shops, and great places to eat. Further east, the renovated, formerly working-class neighborhood of Canton boasts upscale shopping and dining venues along a yacht-filled marina.

The waterfront's best-known attraction is **Fort McHenry** National Monument and Historic Shrine (tel: 410-962-4290; www.nps.gov/fomc; daily). During the War of 1812, this fort withstood a 25-hour bombardment from the British fleet, prompting Francis Scott Key in 1814 to pen the lyrics that in 1931 became America's national anthem, "The Star Spangled Banner."

Head up Charles Street to visit The Walters Art Museum (tel: 410-547-9000; www.thewalters.org; Wed–Sun) with its renowned collection of Oriental art, and the **Baltimore Museum of Art** (tel: 443-573-1700; www.artbma.org; Wed–Sun), which contains works by Picasso and Matisse, art from Africa, and a beautiful modern sculpture garden.

original residential district and a place of elegant 300-year-old Federal-style homes. Its boundaries are roughly Walnut, Lombard, Front, and Eighth streets.

During the late 1970s, Philadelphia's waterfront underwent considerable rehabilitation. **Penn's Landing**, between Market and Lombard streets along the Delaware River, is where William Penn came ashore in 1682. Today, the area features the **Independence Seaport Museum** (tel: 215-413-8655; www.phillyseaport.org; daily) – several historic ships moored in the harbor – and views of **Camden**, New Jersey (home to the American poet Walt Whitman), across the river. One block below Lombard at **South Street**, you will find a stimulating array of punk haberdashers as well as chic boutiques. It's easily the most interesting shopping district.

City Hall, at Broad and Market streets, is the largest municipal building in the US. It was patterned after the Louvre. The 37ft (11-meter) -high rooftop statue of William Penn is the tallest atop any building in the world. Until recently, the Philadelphia skyline was capped by an ordinance declaring no structure could exceed the height of Penn's hat.

The **Benjamin Franklin Parkway**, built in the 1920s, was modeled after the Champs-Elysées in Paris. This broad road cuts diagonally through Philly's square grid from City Hall to Fairmount Park. On the parkway at 20th Street, visit the **Franklin Institute** (tel: 215-448-1200; www.fi.edu; daily), a science museum that is also a memorial to Franklin and contains many of his personal possessions. Four floors of science exhibits and a planetarium amuse and educate all ages.

ART IN THE CITY

Two blocks away is the popular **Rodin Museum** (tel: 215-763-8100; www.rodin museum.org; Wed–Mon), the only dedicated Rodin museum outside France. It has nearly 150 bronzes, marbles, and plasters by the great French sculptor, among them *The Thinker*, one of the world's most beloved sculptures, and The Kiss.

The Rodin Museum is administered by the **Philadelphia Museum of Art** (tel: 215-763-8100; www.philamuseum.org; Tue–Sun), located at the other end of the parkway. One of the great American art museums, among the works in its collection are Breughel's *Village Wedding* and Picasso's *Three Musicians*, as well as an extraordinary collection of art and artifacts from the Middle Ages.

After hours spent walking the streets of Philly's historic districts and visiting its museums, the greenery of **Fairmount Park** rejuvenates even the most exhausted traveler. The country's largest municipal park, historically it was a system of 63 parks and green spaces throughout the city but is now separate. In addition to grassy meadows and acres of woodland, it features a horticultural center, zoo, Japanese house, tea garden, and several historic homes along the banks of the Schuylkill. Once you have rested, take to the highway again

Rodin Museum.

> ⊘ Tip

In Baltimore, the Old City Art Association sponsors First Friday. On the first Friday evening of every month, galleries host open houses (www. oldcityarts.org). The event is followed by First Saturday, when galleries and museums offer workshops, lectures, and other informal get-togethers.

toward **Baltimore** ❺ (see page 60). From Philadelphia, it's about two hours down I-95. Far lovelier is the ride down US 1 through the **Brandywine Valley**. Between **Chadd's Ford** and **Kennett Square**, you'll pass the **Brandywine Battlefield**, (tel: 610-459-3342; www. brandywinebattlefield.org) site of an early Revolutionary battle the Colonials lost; **Brandywine River Museum** (tel: 610-388-2700; www.brandywinemuseum.org; daily), which displays the works of the famed painting dynasty of Andrew, N.C., and Jamie Wyeth; **Longwood Gardens** (tel: 610-388-1000; www.longwoodgardens. org; daily) with a 4-acre (1.6-hectare) indoor conservatory and 1000 acres (405 hectares) of outdoor gardens; and **Winterthur Museum, Garden, and Library** (tel: 302-888-4600; www.winter thur.org; Tue–Sun), Henry DuPont's one-time home and the premier museum of American Decorative Arts. From here, you'll traverse the northern Maryland landscape, the Conowingo Dam over the Susquehanna River, and Baltimore suburbs before connecting with I-695, the Baltimore Beltway and I-95.

Shoemaker in Colonial Williamsburg.

ON TOWARD VIRGINIA

Leaving Baltimore, take I-695 (the Baltimore Beltway) to I-97, the direct road to Annapolis. Connect with US 50 East and take the Rowe Boulevard exit to reach downtown **Annapolis** ❻. The city sparkles in a way particular to towns built on and sustained by the sea – at dusk its elegant Georgian houses and winding narrow streets shimmer in the dying light of day. Walking is an easy way to see the town, starting at the top where the **Maryland State House** (daily) sits. It was here that the Continental Congress ratified the Treaty of Paris, which officially ended the War of Independence, and Washington resigned his commission.

Wind your way toward the beautifully preserved 18th-century waterfront to the **US Naval Academy** and its US Naval Academy Museum in Preble Hall (tel 410-293-2108; www.usna.edu; daily), with exhibits on maritime life and the history of this venerable institution. There are hourly walking tours of the Academy which leave from Armel-Leftwich Visitor Center. You'll be feeling suitably red white, and blue by the time you climb

⊘ DETOUR TO WILLIAMSBURG

A 54-mile (87km) drive from Richmond along SR 60 ends at Colonial Williamsburg, which recreates the everyday life of the nation's infancy. Established in 1633, Williamsburg grew into a center of culture, fashion, and festive living. After the state government moved to Richmond in 1780, the city languished until 1926, when Dr William R. Goodwin approached John D. Rockefeller, Jr for funds to save those historic buildings still standing and to rebuild others. Using original blueprints and materials, Goodwin resurrected the entire town, from the Congress – where George Mason's Declaration of Rights to the House of Burgesses laid the foundation for the Constitution – to the Raleigh Tavern, where George Washington plotted military strategy in the revolt against Great Britain. Nearly 2,000 "residents" recreate the original Williamsburg community. The blacksmith pounds away at glowing iron; a maid in a bonnet weaves linen; horse-drawn carriages trundle through the streets; militiamen drill on the town green. The baker, the printer, and the glassblower are represented, too. For the full Early American heritage experience, the Jamestown settlement (both the original site with archeological digs and an authentic recreation) and Yorktown, where the British surrendered to the Americans, are less than an hour's drive away. For information, tel: 888-965-7254; www.colonialwilliamsburg.com.

back into your car and drive the short 30 miles (48km) west along US 50 toward America's capital, **Washington, DC** (see page 178). For our purposes on this route, we'll bypass the city using the I-495 loop; take Exit 57A to I-95. While Maryland is below the Mason-Dixon Line, which traditionally separates the "North" and "South," it's not until you enter Virginia that the accent softens and the true South begins.

CONFEDERATE SOUTH

Located halfway between Washington, DC, and Richmond, the capital of the Confederacy, it is not surprising that **Fredericksburg ❼** was a major battleground during the Civil War. In fact, with 110,000 casualties occurring during the four major battles fought in the vicinity of the city, it has been said that it is the "bloodiest ground" on the North American continent.

Fredericksburg and Spotsylvania National Military Park (tel: 540-693-3200; www.nps.gov/frsp; daily), is the second-largest military park in the world. It incorporates the battlefields

of Fredericksburg, Chancellorsville, the Wilderness, and Spotsylvania Court House. Both the Fredericksburg battlefield, near the town's historic district, and the Chancellorsville battlefield, west of town on State Route 3, have visitor centers. They are open daily and offer brochures, knowledgeable staff, and information on touring options.

On a bluff above the Rappahannock River overlooking Fredericksburg, just north of Route 3, imposing brick **Chatham Manor** (tel: 540-373-6122; www.nps.gov/frsp; daily), built in 1771, welcomed Washington and Jefferson in Colonial times. It served as Union headquarters and hospital during the battle of Fredericksburg. American Red Cross founder Clara Barton and poet Walt Whitman joined the efforts to treat hundreds of wounded soldiers there.

Fredericksburg was also the childhood home of George Washington. **Ferry Farm** (tel: 540-370-0732; www.kenmore.org; daily), where he grew up, is also on Route 3 (look sharp for the small sign by a gravel driveway). Archeologists recently found the site of

Sign depicting the past action on Spotsylvania, a Civil War battlefield.

Civil War cannon at Chatham Manor.

the original house, which burned when Washington was still a child; visitors can observe, and sometimes participate in, the on going excavations.

The nation's fifth president, James Monroe, also hailed from here; the **James Monroe Museum and Memorial Library** (tel: 540-654-1043; http://james monroemuseum.umw.edu; daily) on Charles Street contains a collection of the personal possessions, furnishings, and papers of Monroe and his wife, Elizabeth.

Today's Fredericksburg still retains its historic ambiance. The 40-block downtown is a national historic district with antiques shops and restaurants sharing space with museums like the **Hugh Mercer Apothecary Shop** (tel: 540-373-3362; www.washingtonheritagemuseums.org; daily) – where visitors can hear about how to treat a lady's hysteria – and the **Rising Sun Tavern** (tel: 540-371-1494; www.washingtonheritagemuseums.org; daily), which provides an interpretation of 18th-century tavern life.

George Washington's sister Betty and her husband, Fielding Lewis, built elegant **Kenmore Plantation and Gardens** (tel: 540-373-3381; www.kenmore.org; Mar–Dec daily). Including it in a visit gives a rounded idea of life in that era.

RICHMOND

Head back down for the 55-mile (88km) trip to **Richmond** ❽. Exit 92 leads to Scotchtown, home of Patrick Henry. The day after he buried his young wife on its grounds, Henry rode to Richmond to deliver his "Give Me Liberty, or Give Me Death" speech.

Take Exit 75 to the Richmond Visitor Center (www.visitrichmondva.com). You'll find free off-street parking right in front of the building, and inside, brochures, maps, and a staff well versed in the region's attractions and history who can also make hotel reservations and suggest restaurants and shopping. The gift shop features Virginia-made products. Important in both Revolutionary and Civil War history, the city is worth your time. At pretty **St John's Church** on Broad Street, the Second Virginia Convention met in 1775. The debate that culminated in Patrick Henry's cry is reenacted every Sunday in the summer,

The Rotunda, University of Virginia.

with visitors sitting alongside the delegates. Laid out on the fall line of the James River, its location made Richmond a natural center for commerce. By 1779, the city had replaced Williamsburg as the capital of Virginia.

Thomas Jefferson designed the striking neoclassical **State Capitol** (www.virginiacapitol.gov; daily), which is home to Jean-Antoine Houdon's full-size statue of George Washington, one of America's most valuable pieces of sculpture. During the Civil War, Richmond was the capital of the Confederacy. Much of it was destroyed when Union troops set fire to the city. Perhaps the best museum about the Civil War anywhere is The **American Civil War Museum** (tel: 804-649-1861; https://acwm.org; daily), which comprises three distinct locations. Historic Tredegar, west of the State Capitol at 500 Tredegar Street, offers an interactive film and exhibits that require visitors to examine the political, ethical, military, moral, and practical aspects of the war from the point of view of the Union, the Confederates, African-Americans, and themselves. (Note: a new museum is currently under construction at this site and will open in 2019.) At 12th and Clay streets, the Museum and White House of the Confederacy has the largest collection of Confederate memorabilia in the world. The Confederate White House, adjacent to the museum, has been restored as a shrine to the Lost Cause. The American Civil War Museum – Appomattox, at the intersection of US 460 and Route 24, commemorates Confederate surrender and national reunification.

Confederate President Jefferson Davis and 18,000 Confederate dead are buried at the **Hollywood Cemetery** (www.hollywoodcemetery.org; daily) on Cherry Street. The expansive, park-like grounds are also the final resting place of US presidents James Monroe and John Tyler. Downtown Richmond is a pleasant business and government center. Modern office buildings are designed around plazas and fountains; historic buildings are restored as shops and restaurants; the 1.25-mile (2km) Canal Walk opens the James River waterfront for recreation. The city is renowned for its symphony, opera, and ballet, as well as for

Linn Cove Viaduct on the Blue Ridge Parkway.

Every aspect of Thomas Jefferson's home, Monticello, was designed by the inventive US President.

Virginia's limestone Natural Bridge.

the **Virginia Museum of Fine Arts** (tel: 804-340-1400; http://vmfa.museum; daily) on Grove Avenue.

JEFFERSON AND MONTICELLO

From Richmond, take I-64W for 74 miles (119km) toward Charlottesville, site of the University of Virginia and the home of Thomas Jefferson. For a more scenic route, take Exit 167 to US 250 West. The two-lane road rolls through the hills and past the horse farms, rolls of baled hay, ponds, and old-timers sitting in their front yards. The curvy roads were the ones Jefferson knew. As you near the town, signs on Route 729 direct you to Monticello; if you took I-64, take Exit 121.

Americans arriving at **Monticello** (tel: 434-984-9800; www.monticello.org; daily), the "little mountain" estate of Thomas Jefferson, will be familiar with its shape; its image adorns the tail side of the US nickel. This elegant, dome shape is particularly Jeffersonian, for not only does it appear on the Rotunda at the University of Virginia but also as the roof of the Jefferson Memorial building in Washington, DC. Jefferson designed every aspect of Monticello, and the imprint of his active mind is everywhere apparent.

Try to arrive early, as the wait for the mandatory tour is known to extend up to two hours at midday. The tour takes you through the ground floor of the residence, with guides pointing out Jefferson's inventions and innovations, such as a double-writing machine and dumbwaiter system. Equal attention is spent on the family's personal lives. The self-guided exploration of the work areas underneath the mansion is fascinating, as it shows how slaves, servants, and hired hands kept the estate operating. Shuttle buses from the visitor center to the mansion stop at the family plot where Jefferson and about 200 of his family are buried.

Jefferson's good friend James Monroe, fifth president of the United States, lived about 3 miles (4.8km) away, at **Highland** (tel: 434-293-8000; www.highland.org; daily). Turn left out of Monticello on Route 53, then right on Route 795. The unpretentious retreat of Highland reflects Monroe's introverted, thoughtful nature, with its lane lined with ash trees and post-and-rail fencing leading to a simple country home. As in life, Monroe's home offers a peaceful contrast with Jefferson's frenetic energy.

As you backtrack past Monticello toward I-64 to continue to Charlottesville, you pass by **Michie Tavern**, (tel: 434-977-1234; www.michietavern.com; lunch and tours daily), a pre-Revolutionary watering hole that is now both museum and restaurant. Its museum is filled with Colonial furniture and artifacts, while the dining room offers a period-inspired lunch menu.

CHARLOTTESVILLE

It is barely 6 miles (9km) from Monticello to **Charlottesville** ❾ and the **University of Virginia** (www.virginia.edu). Continue on Route 53; turn right onto Route 20 and then take I-64W to the Fifth Street exit, which leads directly into the heart of the town and the

university area. Jefferson designed the original buildings and campus in the 1820s and claimed that it was of this achievement he was most proud. His architecture is based on European classical style, adapted to local red brick and painted wood. Looking out from the elevated walkway of the **Rotunda**, you see the splendid swath of grass known as "**The Lawn**," bordered by columned pavilions. Originally, these were the residences of all the students and professors of Jefferson's "academic villages"; now they are inhabited by school officials and top students. **West Range** on McCormack Road is where poet Edgar Allan Poe (1809–49) lived during his unsuccessful tenure here. His former room is open to visitors.

Continue down University Avenue to "**The Corner**," a collection of restaurants and shops catering to students, tourists, and local residents.

THE BLUE RIDGE PARKWAY

Take I-64W to Rockfish Gap, where the breathtaking 459-mile (739km) **Blue Ridge Parkway** (www.blueridgeparkway.org) begins. Cutting through **George Washington National Forest** (www.fs.usda.gov/gwj), the Parkway – like its nearby counterpart, the Skyline Drive – rides atop the Blue Ridge Mountains. However, as this is not a national park, you will note one big difference: this drive is filled not only with forest and flowers but also with working farms. Trees carpet the surrounding mountains, which seem bluer and bluer as they recede into the distance. This is caused by chemicals emitted by the trees, a prosaic explanation that in no way diminishes the beautiful result. If you're traveling alone, don't allow the superb views to lure your eyes too far from the road or you will end up driving into a tree.

At Mile Marker 61, State Route 130 West leads to **Natural Bridge** State Park (tel: 540-291-1326; www.dcr.virginia.gov/state-parks/natural-bridge; daily), which preserves a 215ft (66-meter)

-high natural rock formation that was cherished as "The Bridge to God" by the Monocan tribe. You can hike and picnic here, making it a good place to take a break from the road.

ROANOKE

Back on the Parkway, continue south. Route 220 leads to the pretty town of **Roanoke** ⑩ (see page 185). Mabry Mill at Milepost 176 is a restored 1900-era gristmill, smithy, and moonshine still. The gem of this trip is at Milepost 210. The Blue Ridge Music Center (tel: 276-236-5309; www.blueridgemusiccenter.org; daily) chronicles the distinctive mountain music played on fiddle, mandolin, guitar, and banjo via excellent displays and videos. Musicians jam in the covered courtyard every afternoon.

Depart the Parkway at Route 89 and head southeast into North Carolina where the pace of life is as relaxed as a sigh and the conversation is laced with the slow Southern drawl that's sometimes difficult for outsiders to understand. You have now entered the Deep South.

Star-gazing in Roanoke.

Entrance to Bethesda, the
former orphanage near
Savannah.

NORTH CAROLINA TO SAVANNAH

This diverse region offers university towns and sandy beaches, antebellum plantations and Civil Rights landmarks, pastoral farmland and history-filled cities, plus the unique culture and cuisine of the Lowcountry.

All that remains of the first-known settlement in present-day North Carolina is one word. That word – Croatan – has kept etymologists and philologists busy for centuries, ever since it was found scraped into a tree in the vanished colony of Fort Raleigh on Roanoke Island. Nothing else was left of the "lost colony," which was founded in 1587.

Today, the state is experiencing rapid transformation from a country backwater to a manufacturing and educational power. Jobs and suburbs are sprouting up all along the I-85 corridor, particularly in light industrial trades. Charlotte has become the banking power of the South. And the Raleigh-Durham area contains a very high concentration of quality universities. It's a measure of this success that you can now watch ice hockey in a state where it rarely snows, and professional football, too; both have recently arrived along with the new jobs. Strains of folk and bluegrass music are still the anthem heard in the mountainous Appalachian west.

MORAVIAN HISTORY

US 52 takes you over the border from Virginia's Blue Ridge Parkway through trim **Mount Airy** ⓫ – birthplace of the late actor and producer Andy Griffith, a Carolina hero, and the model town for his wildly popular classic TV program *Mayberry RFD* – then on down to Winston-Salem.

US 52 leads to **Winston-Salem** ⓬ (see page 186), home of the R.J. Reynolds Tobacco Company. Despite the negative image of the product, tobacco remains the second-largest industry in North Carolina (textiles are first).

The Salem half of Winston-Salem was founded by Moravians in 1766. The name is derived from the Hebrew word "shalom," meaning peace. In 1913, it was incorporated with its neighbor Winston, and when its old buildings

Main attractions
Greensboro
Durham
Chapel Hill
Fayetteville
Outer Banks
Wilmington
Georgetown
Charleston

Maps on pages
56, 82

Vintage diner table jukebox and 1932 Ford Model B in Winston-Salem.

Winston-Salem man in Moravian costume working with tobacco.

fell into disrepair, a restoration project during the 1930s saved them. The success of this effort can be seen in **Salem Old Town**, which is entered from the Old Salem Road near the center of town. Particularly interesting are the **Winkler Bakery**, a restored Moravian bakery that produces lovely bread and unique wafer-thin cookies, and the **Salem Tavern** (http://thetaverninoldsalem.ws). **God's Acre**, a Moravian graveyard nearby, holds 4,000 graves, many graced with flat marble markers symbolizing the equality of the deceased.

Busy four-lane US 421 leads to **Greensboro**, site of a pivotal moment in the Civil Rights movement: the first peaceful sit-in by black activists demanding an end to segregation in 1960. The Woolworth store where the sit-in occurred is now preserved as the **International Civil Rights Center & Museum** (tel: 336-274-9199; www.sitinmovement.org; Mon–Sat), a top North Carolina attraction. The hour-long guided tour takes visitors on an uneasy journey through the historical and moral elements of America's

Bodie Island lighthouse, Cape Hatteras National Seashore, Outer Banks.

legacy of slavery and segregation and the struggle for civil and human rights. The lunch counter where the four college students – Joseph McNeil, Jibreel Khazan (formerly Ezell Blair Jr.), David Richmond, and Franklin McCain – sat has remained untouched since the event. Other exhibits revisit "Jim Crow" laws, the role of churches in the non-violent movement, and a Wall of Remembrance of those who died during the Civil Rights struggle.

DURHAM

Continue along either US 70 or I-40E to **Durham** ⑱. On the way, look for the **Piedmont Triad Farmers' Market** at Exit 208 off I-40. This is a massive covered green market occupying three buildings where area farmers sell produce, meats, cheese, and flowers. (tel: 336-606-9157; daily).

Durham is home to **Duke University** (https://duke.edu). Along with **Chapel Hill** and **Raleigh**, it is part of the Research Triangle, a liberal oasis in the middle of North Carolina with some of the highest numbers of PhDs per capita in the

⊘ DETOUR TO OUTER BANKS

A leisurely 193-mile (311km) drive along SR 64 from Raleigh leads to the Outer Banks, which emerge like the head of a whale breaching into the Atlantic. Two national seashores, Cape Hatteras and Cape Lookout, preserve 120 miles (190km) of these beaches on Bodie, Hatteras, and Ocracoke islands, and Core and Shackleford banks. While most coastal islands lie within 10 miles (16km) of shore, the Outer Banks belong to the realm of the sea; in places, 30 miles (48km) of water separate Hatteras Island from the mainland. The national seashores of the Outer Banks have personalities unique to the rest of North Carolina. The islands have wide, water-thrashed beaches, while scattered patches of sea oats and beach grasses bind low dunes behind them. Clumps of shrubby marsh elder and bayberry dot the swales. The mainland side of each island hosts extensive tidal marshes of swaying cordgrass. Distinctly patterned lighthouses mark the shores for passing ships, in particular the spiral-painted Cape Hatteras lighthouse. Beach erosion threatened to topple the lighthouse into the sea, so in 1999 the 4,400-ton lighthouse was carefully rolled along steel tracks to a new location 1,600ft (487 meters) inland. For more information, contact the Official Tourism Authority for Dare County's Outer Banks (tel: 877-629-4386; www.outerbanks.org).

nation. This is also the place to come for top-tier college basketball. North Carolina is a hoops-crazy state, and the Duke Blue Devils, North Carolina Tar Heels, and North Carolina State Wolfpack – all playing in the Triangle – do the state proud. Duke's campus is among the most beautiful in the South, with Gothic and Georgian buildings filling neat quadrangles. Sarah P. **Duke Gardens** (tel: 919-684-3698; http://gardens.duke.edu; daily) is 55 acres (22 hectares) of formal gardens, fountains, picnic areas, and ponds. Find a legal place to park, then head for the Duke University Chapel to see the **Benjamin N. Duke Memorial Flentrop Organ**, a 5,000-pipe extravaganza. Walking tours of the university are coordinated through the Admissions Office.

DURHAM'S CULTURE

The city is a lively mixture of abandoned tobacco warehouses and factories transformed into businesses, artists' galleries, and chic restaurants. Working-class mill hands and college professors, old Southerners and new Yankee upstarts share their love of the city to create an involved community. **Ninth Street** is the place to go, with plenty of good vintage record shops, bookstores, coffee shops, and eateries.

Make a point of finding the Durham Bulls' minor-league ballpark, one of the nation's finest and the perfect spot to spend a warm summer evening. (Don't miss the outfield bull, which snorts steam when a home run is hit!) The Bulls' former ballpark, El Toro Field, was even more authentic – one side consisted of tobacco warehouses. The steam-snorting bull made its debut here during the filming of the popular baseball film *Bull Durham*. It is easily walkable from downtown.

Durham is also a magnet for culinary excellence. Several chefs with national reputations cook here, including Ashley Christensen of Alpaca. There are over 300 locally owned restaurants, a high number for a relatively small city. **Durham Performing Arts Center** (www.dpacnc.com) is one of the busiest in the country.

Just southwest of Durham, smaller **Chapel Hill** is the home of the pleasant

Downtown Winston-Salem.

A rural mailbox in North Carolina.

1950s stock car, South Carolina.

University of North Carolina campus. UNC was the first state university chartered in the US. Fans of astronomy will enjoy the **Morehead Planetarium and Science Center** at 250 East Franklin Street (tel: 919-918-1155; www.moreheadplanetarium.org; Tue–Sun). Visitors to the campus can park in the lot adjacent to the Planetarium. Franklin Street is the center for shopping, eating, and socializing with students. The 80 acres (32 hectares) of the **North Carolina Botanical Garden** (tel: 919-962-0522; http://ncbg.unc.edu; daily) display the indigenous plants of the state's different regions in natural settings. The James & Delight Allen Education Center is housed in a LEED (Leadership in Energy and Environmental Design) Platinum-certified green building and worth a visit in its own right.

TOWARD THE COAST

From Durham, take US 15-501 (also known as the Jefferson Davis Highway) south toward **Sanford ⑭**, where pottery has become a popular cottage industry. You can visit several potteries

and an annual pottery festival is held here, the largest in the state. At Sanford, change onto US 421. Roadside fields are again densely covered with tobacco plants and the occasional weeping willow or algae-covered pond does little to dispel summer's oppressive heat.

This road runs through farm country, through corn and tobacco fields extending for acres back from the highway. There are innumerable small churches along the road, the majority of which are Baptist with billboards exhorting passersby to reconsider their sin-filled lives. At **Lillington**, turn south on US 401 toward **Fayetteville ⑮**, home to the US Army's Fort Bragg military installation, a highly respected and honored facility. The **Airborne & Special Operations Museum** (tel: 910-643-2778; www.asomf.org; Tue–Sun) tracks the development of paratroopers from World War II through their missions today. Life-sized, walk-through dioramas give a unique sense of being part of the action, be it a French village in 1944 or an Afghan camp in 2012. A separate exhibit of the ordeal of POWs in Vietnam is chilling.

Adjacent, the moving **North Carolina Veterans Park** (tel: 910-433-1457; https://fcpr.us/parks-trails/parks/north-carolina-veterans-park; Tue–Sun) honors those Tar Heels who have served since Revolutionary times. Casts of hands from veterans, raised as though being sworn in, cover the surface of 100 obelisks – one for each county in the state. Inside, rows of dog tags of each North Carolinian who died in the wars line one wall. One empty row is labelled "Future."

Cape Fear Botanical Garden (tel: 910-486-0221; www.capefearbg.org; daily) at 536 North Eastern Boulevard is a tonic after contemplating the impact of war. However, it is a little disconcerting to discover that the police firing range sits nearby; the sound of cicadas and bird songs are sometimes drowned out by

the popping of small arms fire. The garden encompasses 77 acres (31 hectares) of pine and hardwood forest. Cultivated garden areas showcase more than 2,000 varieties of ornamental plants, and include beautiful daylily, camellia, and hosta gardens. There are plenty of viewing areas, including rope hammock-style stools overlooking a pond.

WILMINGTON

If you have an audio book, the two-hour drive from Fayetteville to Wilmington along State Route 87 is the time to listen to it. The road is flat, the scenery is unexciting, and the "towns" little more than gas stations.

Your reward is the coastal town of **Wilmington ⑯**, on the Cape Fear River near the Atlantic Ocean; it's been a deep water port since Colonial times. After the long, hot drive, treat yourself to one of the many sightseeing cruises along the river, or sign on for a kayak or nature trip to the surrounding coastal islands. The breeze almost always blows along the 2-mile (3km) -long boardwalk stretching past former warehouses and chandlers' stores which now house shops, restaurants, and hotels, all with water views. Many fine old houses line the cobblestone streets near the waterfront, including the **Zebulon Latimer House** (126 South Third Street; tel: 910-762-0492; www.lcfhs.org/latimer-house; tours daily) and the 1770 **Burgwin-Wright House & Gardens** (Third and Market streets; tel: 910-762-0570; www.burgwinwrighthouse.com; tours daily), the only Colonial-era house in Wilmington. A triple-ticket promotion allows you to visit both houses as well as Bellamy Mansion Museum for one low price, valid for one week. Walking tours of historic downtown Wilmington leave from Zebulon Latimer House every other Saturday morning.

On the other side of the river, visit the **USS North Carolina Battleship Memorial** (tel: 910-399-9100; www.battleshipnc.com; daily). Commissioned in 1941, she was considered the greatest fighting vessel in the United States of her time. The self-guided tour allows visitors to envision the daily life and fierce combat her crew experienced in the Pacific.

SOUTH CAROLINA

Of all the southern states, South Carolina was the most outspoken in defending slavery and its right to leave the Union. On December 20, 1860, it became the first state to secede from the Union. Six other states quickly followed suit. When Confederate forces opened fire on Union troops stationed at Fort Sumter in Charleston Harbor in April 1861, it plunged the nation into a war with itself.

Holding South Carolina responsible for the war, General William Tecumseh Sherman was particularly harsh in the region during his march to the sea, devastating its agricultural base and torching its ports, and South Carolina's economic base was destroyed. It wasn't until after World War II, when the state's economy began to switch

⊙ Tip

Southerners are great storytellers. In Wilmington, North Carolina, ask about the unsolved murder of 1760, which involved a man, a snake ring, and a riderless horse on a rainy night.

Myrtle Beach State Park Pier.

Pineapple-shaped fountain in Waterfront Park, Charleston.

Mature trees and elegant porches provide welcome shade in Charleston.

from agriculture to textiles, furniture, and chemical industries that the state's fortunes began to improve. (Agriculture remains a mainstay today – South Carolina is one of America's top peach producers and virtually its only producer of tea (which is usually drunk iced and sweet in the South.) Tourism is another economic mainstay along the Carolina coast, which is lined with beach resorts and historic cities.

As you leave the *USS North Carolina*, turn left onto US 17 and head south into South Carolina. You enter the 55-mile (88km) stretch of beach resort known as the **Grand Strand**. Several towns dot the sandy shore, each one with its own personality. Atlantic Beach retains much of its fishing village atmosphere. Pawley's Island is an enclave of summer cottages. Surfside attracts families, and Muretta Inlet attracts surfers. The largest and busiest town is **Myrtle Beach ⓱**, the third most popular tourist resort on the East Coast, after Disney World and Atlantic City. The extraordinary commercialization of the area can feel overwhelming,

as the grandly named King's Highway (US 17) consists of mile after mile of miniature golf courses, shopping centers, theaters, and shops dispensing the accessories that go with beach culture. But the town's hotels and resorts are removed from the highway and share a broad, clean, sandy beach that rarely feels crowded, even at the height of the summer tourist season. South of Myrtle Beach on US 17, on the Sampit River, lies the quieter and more genteel **Georgetown ⓲**. A thriving port during the lumber era, it is still the state's second busiest seaport, although you wouldn't know it from the slow pace of life and its lovely downtown with grand old houses and a boardwalk along the river. The **Rice Museum** (tel: 843-546-7423; www.ricemuseum.org; daily) gives a look at the crop that sustained this area for much of its early history. Just a few steps away, the **South Carolina Maritime Museum** (tel: 843-520-0111; www.scmaritimemuseum.org; Mon–Sat) chronicles 300 years of maritime commerce. **Kaminski House** (1769) and **Parker House** (1740) are side by side

on Front Street; the tours are friendly and informal (tel: 843-546-7706; www.kaminskimuseum.org; Mon–Sat).

HISTORIC CHARLESTON

South again along US 17, you'll notice small frame structures on the side of the road from Awendaw to Mount Pleasant. This is the **Sweetgrass Basketweavers Highway**, the heart of the Gullah region. Gullah culture developed among the slaves from West Africa who worked the vast rice plantations along the coast. They adapted their traditional lifestyle, crafts, language, and cuisine to create a unique folkway. About 300,000 people who claim Gullah roots live along the coast from South Carolina to northern Florida. The women in the roadside stands practice the craft of weaving that was brought from Africa by their enslaved ancestors and passed down through the generations as part of the Gullah culture. Pull off the road to watch, browse, and buy.

In 1670, English colonists founded Charles Towne, named after Charles II, on the Ashley River, 5 miles (8km) from the present location of **Charleston** ⑲. This was the first permanent settlement in the Carolinas. After 10 years of battling malaria, heat, flooding, and the Kiawah tribe, they packed up and headed to the peninsula where modern Charleston was built. The prosperity of the city's early days is reflected in elegant 18th-century homes that fill the residential area south of Broad Street. In fact, this is one of America's top walking cities.

MUSEUM MILE

Charleston Visitor Center at Meeting and Anne streets is at the north end of **Museum Mile** (www.charlestoncvb.com). From there to Charleston Harbor, Meeting Street and the adjacent side streets have over 30 museums, historic houses, churches, and other notable sites. These include

the **Charleston Museum** (tel: 843-722-2996; www.charlestonmuseum.org; daily) across the street from the visitor center. The first museum in America (1773), it showcases artifacts of the natural and cultural history of the Lowcountry – South Carolina's coastal region, including its sea islands. The area is so called because the land is at or near sea level. At one time, agriculture – particularly rice plantations – was the main Lowcountry activity. Now, tourism – focused on seaside resorts, historic sites, cuisine, and culture – drives the economy. Under the aegis of the museum are **Joseph Manigault House** (350 Meeting Street) and **Nathaniel Russell House** (51 Meeting Street), two examples of the luxury the upper classes enjoyed. Meanwhile, newly renovated **Gibbes Museum of Art** (tel: 843-722-2706; www.gibbesmuseum.org; daily) tells Charleston's story through art. The enclosed and outdoor **City Market** (www.thecharlestoncitymarket.com) occupying two blocks of the appropriately named Market Street houses more than 300 market

Interior of a slave cabin.

The wedding cake steeple of St Michael's Episcopal Church, Charleston.

Luxurious houses on the waterfront in Charleston.

entrepreneurs. This is the district for galleries, boutiques, specialty shops, and restaurants.

Meeting Street ends at palmetto-lined **Battery** and **White Point Gardens**. Across the water, the nondescript island at the entrance to the harbor is **Fort Sumter National Monument** (tel: 843-883-3123; www.nps.gov/fosu; daily), where Confederate bombardment of Union fortifications on April 12, 1861, set off the Civil War. Fort Sumter Visitor Education Center at Liberty Square on Concord Street has information and exhibits. Admission to the fort itself is free but you must take a ferry across or use a private boat. Fort Sumter Tours (www.fortsumtertours.com), the official tour boat concessionaire, offers a 2.25-hour cruise and tour leaving from either Liberty Square or Patriots Point. It's best to buy tickets the day before.

At the **Old Slave Mart Museum** (tel: 843-958-6467; www.oldslavemartmuseum.com; Mon–Sat) on Chalmers Street, the first African-American Museum, you can see, among other items, facsimiles of bills of sale used in the slave trade. "A prime gang of 25 negroes accustomed to the culture of Sea Island Cotton and Rice," reads one placard advertising the upcoming sale of 25 human beings into bondage. It is a startling and sobering museum, especially so when one realizes this heinous practice was still in full swing just a century and a half ago. The opulence south of Broad suddenly appears quite different after a thoughtful visit to the slave market.

Charleston is chock-full of historic churches, as well as all its other cultural and social attractions. Two of the more interesting are the **Huguenot Church**, a Gothic structure built by French Protestants, and **St Michael's Episcopal Church** with its 186ft (57-meter) -high steeple. The **Emanuel African Methodist Episcopal Church**, a well-known historic black church, hit international news in July 2015, when a young white supremacist gunman killed nine members of the congregation there, including the minister, while seated among them.

PLANTATIONS AND TEA

Three plantations in the vicinity of Charleston are worth a visit. **Magnolia Plantation & Gardens** (tel: 843-571-1266; www.magnoliaplantation.com; daily), at 3550 Ashley River Road (State Route 61), has a 19th-century plantation house, as well as beautiful gardens planted in 1870, a nature center, and a boat tour of the old rice fields (look for alligators). Five restored slave cabins from the 1850s form the nucleus of the plantation's award-winning From Slavery to Freedom: Magnolia Cabin Project Tour, which allows visitors a hands-on exploration of the area's African-American history and culture.

Middleton Place (tel: 843-556-6020; www.middletonplace.org; daily) has the oldest landscaped gardens in the country, spread over 65 acres (26 hectares). You'll also see a restored stableyard with livestock from the antebellum period and interpreters demonstrating the skills slaves used to keep the place running. **Boone Hall Plantation** (tel: 843-884-4371; www.boonehallplantation.com; daily) has the achingly beautiful avenue of live oak trees featured in *Gone With the Wind*. The mansion is most people's idea of the perfect antebellum residence; in fact, the house was rebuilt in 1935. Boone Hall is the only Low-country plantation to offer a presentation about the unique Gullah culture adapted by African slaves.

Were tea plants faster-growing, the history of the US may have been a little different. The climate of the Lowcountry is perfect for tea propagation, but it takes about four years before tea leaves can be harvested, so the colonists concentrated on faster-growing rice and cotton. **Charleston Tea Plantation** (tel: 843-559-0383; www.charlestonteaplantation.com; daily), on Wadmalaw Island about 30 minutes south of Charleston, is the only remaining tea plantation in America. Using tea plants originally imported from China and grown by Dr. Charles Shepard on Pinehurst Tea Plantation, the operation is now owned by Bigelow Tea Company and cultivates 127 acres (51 hectares) of American tea.

After Charleston, follow US 17 south through the Lowcountry toward the Georgia border. Turning east onto US 21 from US 17, you'll come to **Beaufort** (pronounced "bew-ford"), the second-oldest town in South Carolina. Beaufort is still quite compact and attractive, and Hollywood movie producers use the gorgeous antebellum waterfront homes as set pieces. Indigo and rice cultivation brought wealth during the 18th century, when the majority of these houses (some are inns) were constructed. The best way to experience the town is to wander around, enjoying the friendly locals and dining in one of the seafood restaurants before traveling into Georgia. Take Route 170 south across the Broad River, pick up US 17 again, and cross the bridge to that beautiful "Southern belle" of a city, **Savannah ㉚** (see page 78).

○ **Fact**

The slave cabins at Boone Hall were built of bricks made on the premises; among several other industries, the plantation had a working brick and tile yard.

Azaleas and moss-draped live oaks in Magnolia Plantation and Gardens, Charleston.

SAVANNAH: FIRST CITY OF GEORGIA

The port of Savannah is an enticing, seductive place – equal parts history, gentility, revelry, and eccentricity.

Best known for its gorgeous, moss-draped live oaks, cobblestone streets, and light, pastel-colored buildings, an air of mystique still hovers over Savannah, Georgia's original settlement.

The saucy, best-selling book *Midnight in the Garden of Good and Evil* made this city a household name, with a corresponding increase in the city's tourism. Today, a visit is likely to consist of a horse-drawn carriage ride through stately squares, lunch in an outdoor café, and an evening seeking ghosts in the shadowy passageways. In 1733, James Edward Oglethorpe received a royal

The grand Forsyth Park fountain.

charter to establish "the colony of Georgia in America" and protect the coast from Spanish Florida while producing wine and silk for the Crown. Oglethorpe laid out a grid of broad thoroughfares, punctuated at regular intervals with two dozen spacious public squares. The 20 that remain have been refurbished, forming the nucleus of **Savannah's Historic District,** one of the largest urban national historic landmark districts in the United States, and probably the most beautiful. The district is bounded by the Savannah River to the north and Forsyth Park to the south, covering a 2.5-mile (4km) radius.

Running the length of the district, north to south, Bull Street links some of the most beautiful squares. These squares offer fine examples of some of Savannah's characteristic details: fancy ironwork and atmospheric Spanish moss. They are also enlivened with daily activity, from art vendors and hot dog stands to street performers. Summer brings free jazz concerts to John Square near the river, but early spring is the best time to visit, when the city's azaleas are in full blossom.

TROLLEY AND WALKING TOURS

Walking is the best way to see the city, unless the heat is oppressive, in which case a horse-drawn carriage ride or a trolley tour are better options. **Old Town Trolley Tours** (www.trolleytours.com/savannah) offers on-off tours. You'll see horse carriages near several squares.

One of the most entertaining ways to tour the historic squares is with **Savannah Dan** (tel: 912-398-3777; www.savannahdan.com). Dressed in a seersucker suit, broad-brimmed hat, and bow tie and exuding Southern charm, Savannah Dan is a native with an encyclopedic knowledge of the town and a gift for tale telling. The two-hour walking tours leave you feeling that you know the town like an insider.

Most of the houses surrounding the squares are steeped in history, and several are open for tours. If you only have time to visit one, make it **Owens-Thomas House and Slave Quarters** (124 Abercorn Street; tel: 912-790-8800; www.telfair.org; daily), part of the Telfair Museums. Built with obsessive attention to symmetry, some doors open to blank walls in order to maintain the gracious balance and design. The Marquis de Lafayette stayed there during his visit to the US in 1825. The **Cathedral of St John the Baptist**, near Lafayette Square, is another worthwhile stop. **Juliette Gordon Low's birthplace** (tel: 912-233-4501; www.juliettegordonlowbirthplace.org; Mon-Sat) at 10 East Oglethorpe Avenue is the handsome childhood home of the founder of the Girl Scouts of America and a top Savannah tourist attraction.

Lucas Theatre for the Arts (tel: 912-525-5040; www.lucastheatre.com) at 32 Abercorn Street first opened in 1921, with what was then the largest screen in Savannah. Eventually, TV and suburbia stole its customers, and it closed in 1976. Slated for demolition, local citizens rescued and restored it as a popular opera, theater, film, and concert venue. Around the corner, Broughton Street is the main shopping thoroughfare with a mix of locally owned stores and a few major retailers. **Leopold's Ice Cream** (tel: 912-234-4442; www.leopoldsicecream.com; daily) has been making its own premium ice cream for nearly a century and also serves light meals.

Horticulturists should seek out **Trustees' Garden** (tel: 912-443-3277; www.trusteesgarden. com; daily) on East Broad Street. Planted in the 1700s as Georgia's first experimental garden, it is filled with exotic plants from around the world.

RIVER STREET

In Colonial and antebellum times, cobblestoned River Street, a strip at the foot of a steep hill along Savannah's harborside, was the hub of the city's shipping; now it is the hub of the tourist trade. The old brick warehouses, cotton exchange, and shipping offices are now inns, pubs, restaurants, and gift shops. Parking is a challenge; the lots along the river fill quickly. Better to use the public lots along Bay Street and reach River Street via steep stairways. **Savannah History Museum** (tel: 912-651-6840; www.chsgeorgia.org/SHM; daily) at 303 Martin Luther King Jr. Blvd. is a one-stop blitz of the city's fascinating past, with lots of artifacts, from Forrest Gump's bench to Revolutionary War weapons. It is in the same building as Savannah **Visitor Center** (www.visit-historic-savannah.com/savannah-visitor-center). A block away, at 601 Turner Boulevard, **SCAD**

Museum of Art (tel: 800-869-7223; www.scadmoa.org; Tue–Sun) features ever-changing exhibits by contemporary and avant-garde artists. All the guides are students at the Savannah College of Art and Design. Farther up MLK Blvd, the **Ships of the Sea Maritime Museum** (tel: 912-232-1511; www.shipsofthesea.org; Tue–Sun) is an often-overlooked gem. It is filled with intricately detailed scale models of dozens of ships. Many of them are cutaways with the cargo and crew, fittings, and machinery all looking as though ready to sail to Lilliput.

Leave downtown by heading east on Victory Drive in the direction of the coastal islands to visit **Bonaventure Cemetery** (tel: 912-651-6843; www.bonaventurehistorical.org; daily), a luxurious final resting place for Savannah's most distinguished citizens. A former plantation, Bonaventure is wistfully beautiful, dripping with moss and overflowing with azaleas, jasmine, magnolias, and live oak trees. The images on several of the gravestones have become synonymous with both the *Midnight* book and the city itself.

Colorfully painted clapboard houses.

GEORGIA TO THE FLORIDA KEYS

Small-town ambiance, a tropical paradise, alligators in the Everglades, and the southernmost point in the US highlight the end of the Atlantic Route.

The Georgia coast is one of the Southeast's most interesting natural regions, a string of marshes, largely undeveloped islands, and good beaches rarely sought out by the traveler focused solely on getting through the state via I-95 as quickly as possible. No wonder this region is known locally as the Golden Isles. The inattentive traveler's loss, however, has been others' gain: a number of unusual birds live secreted along this coast, and there are also vestiges of African culture from the dark days when slaves were shipped across the Atlantic to work the plantations of the South.

From Savannah, take Victory Drive (US 17) west out of town, where it shortly becomes Ogeechee Road – and also becomes more rural in character. About 25 miles (40km) along, stop in **Midway ㉑** for a look at the small, whitewashed village church, built in 1792 to replace the 1752 original, erected by displaced New Englanders and destroyed during the Revolutionary War. Note the section that was designated specifically for slaves and a gracefully kept cemetery outside. The church and grounds are managed by the adjacent small **Midway Museum** (tel: 912-884-5837; www.themidwaymuseum.org; Tue–Sat), which houses a collection of period items.

HARRIS NECK NWR TO BRUNSWICK

Past Riceboro, home to an agricultural research station, the highway passes beneath I-95 again and crosses a bridge over a tidal inlet into McIntosh County. To learn more about the politics, poverty, and small-town intrigue of the county, look for the biting nonfiction book *Praying for Sheetrock*, which won awards for its clear-eyed portrait of local life.

If you make a left just after the bridge onto unnumbered Harris Neck Road,

Main attractions
Midway
Cumberland Island
St Augustine
Castillo de San Marcos
Orlando
Clearwater Beach
Alligator Alley
The Everglades
Key West

Map on page 82

Ripe Georgia peaches at a roadside stand.

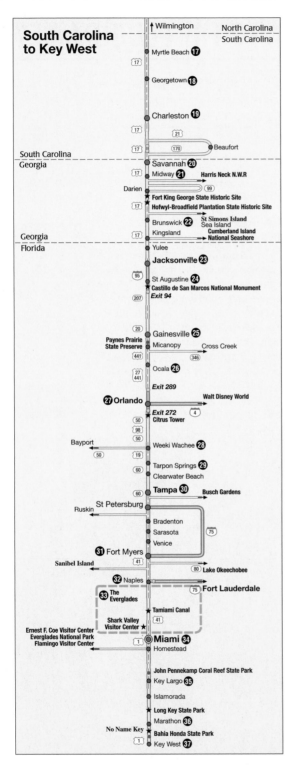

South Carolina to Key West

Wilmington

North Carolina
South Carolina

Myrtle Beach **17**
17

Georgetown **18**

Charleston **19**
17
21
South Carolina
17
170
Beaufort

South Carolina
Georgia
Savannah **20**
17
Midway **21**
Harris Neck N.W.R
Darien
99

Fort King George State Historic Site
17
Hofwyl-Broadfield Plantation State Historic Site

Brunswick **22**
St Simons Island
Sea Island
Kingsland
Cumberland Island
National Seashore

Georgia
Florida
17
Yulee

Jacksonville **23**
95
St Augustine **24**
Castillo de San Marcos National Monument
207
Exit 94

20
Gainesville **25**
Paynes Prairie
State Preserve
Micanopy
Cross Creek
441
346
27
441
Ocala **26**
Exit 289

Walt Disney World
27 Orlando
Exit 272
4
50
Citrus Tower
98
50
Bayport
Weeki Wachee **28**
50
19
60
Tarpon Springs **29**
Clearwater Beach
60
Tampa **30**
Busch Gardens
St Petersburg
Ruskin
Bradenton
Sarasota
75
Venice
31 Fort Myers
Sanibel Island
41
80
Lake Okeechobee
32 Naples
The
33 Everglades
75
Fort Lauderdale
Tamiami Canal
Shark Valley
Visitor Center
41
Ernest F. Coe Visitor Center
Everglades National Park
Flamingo Visitor Center
1
Miami **34**
Homestead

John Pennekamp Coral Reef State Park
Key Largo **35**
Islamorada
Long Key State Park
Marathon **36**
No Name Key
Bahia Honda State Park
1
Key West **37**

you can find **Harris Neck National Wildlife Refuge** (www.fws.gov/refuge/harris_neck), a pocket of wilderness that was saved from development because a former military airstrip occupied the land. Fishing is the most popular activity here, but you can also drive a one-way dirt loop road for a look at the waterfowl in their natural environs. Just offshore sits St Catherines Island, an off-limits island used by the Bronx Zoo as a breeding ground for rare birds and animals.

South again on US 17, make a brief detour onto Georgia 99, which reveals some truly old-fashioned towns and dwellings – shacks, mostly, many of them occupied by the modern-day descendants of freed slaves. These small communities – Crescent, Valona, Meridian, Carnigan, and Ridgeville – are fishing and shellfishing communities now.

At **Darien**, rustic Georgia 99 rejoins US 17 again. **Fort King George State Historic Site** (tel: 800-864-7275; www.gastateparks.org/FortKingGeorge; Tue-Sun) re-creates a Colonial-era blockhouse; this is where the British first settled Georgia and for a brief period administered the area.

Five miles (8km) south, at the mouth of the Altamaha River, sits **Hofwyl-Broadfield Plantation State Historic Site** (tel: 912-264-7333; www.gastateparks.org/HofwylBroadfield; Wed-Sun), prettifying the story of slavery somewhat, as it demonstrates how the know-how of slaves imported from Africa was crucial to the successful cultivation of rice on these islands.

Hold your nose as you enter industrial **Brunswick 22**, a major center for paper and chemical production. Despite its industrial character, Brunswick's downtown is surprisingly slow paced and Old South, with an attractive grid of streets, homes, and moss-draped live oak trees. One such oak tree, the so-called Lover's Oak, is believed to have stood for hundreds – possibly even close to one thousand – years.

The city is also set on a wide, beautiful (if not exactly pure) marsh immortalized by poet Sidney Lanier as the "Marshes of Glynn" (for Glynn County). A turnout facing the marshes has information explaining their formation, which provides an opportunity to stretch your legs, take some snapshots, and pick up lots of tourist information.

LUSH ISLANDS

From the marshes, turn east and cross the toll bridge for a look at lush, though somewhat exclusive, **St Simons Island** (www.explorestsimonsis land.com). Palm fronds, live oak trees, and flowers cover both sides of the road in perpetual green as you drive through the road to the single attractive harborfront, and you might consider staying the night in these restful environs. A museum in the former lighthouse tells the history of coastal Georgia, and there's a good beach out beyond the main settlement. **Sea Island** (www.seaisland.com), an exclusive resort reached via another series of roads on the island, possesses beautiful beaches and a world-class golf course.

South again on US 17, you cross more bridges and then pivot inland through tiny towns. At Kingsland, make a turnoff to catch the ferry for pristine **Cumberland Island National Seashore** (www.nps.gov/cuis), one of the most attractive islands in the Georgia chain, of which 9,800 acres is designated wilderness. Cumberland Island was once the exclusive domain of wealthy families, but federal protection has ensured its delicate environment is undisturbed, particularly by hordes of tourists. Rustic campsites are by advance reservation only (www.recreation.gov); don't expect to waltz in and secure one at the last moment.

FLORIDA

Crossing the St Marys River, a broad watershed that reaches the Okefenokee, you're greeted by a double row of palm trees and, possibly, the presence of police cars: you have arrived in Florida. The first town you reach is **Yulee**, named for legislator and entrepreneur David Yulee. Mr Yulee built a railroad from coast to Florida coast, and it thrived for a short time, but politics and the Civil War soon did it in and the town is of little consequence today. It isn't very long afterward that the rural roads give way to sprawl, announcing the outskirts of **Jacksonville ㉓**.

Jacksonville is trying hard to remake itself as a new urban destination, and corporate headquarters are relocating here to take advantage of the excellent weather and pristine beaches. There are cultural attractions, too – the town is justly proud of its north and south bank **Riverwalks** and the associated **Museum of Science and History** (tel: 904-396-6674; www.themosh. org; daily).**Cummer Museum of Art and Gardens** (tel: 904-356-6857; www.

Taking it easy on a Georgia beach.

Salt marshes edging St Simons Island.

cummermuseum.org; Tue–Sun except holidays) stands on the banks of the St Johns River. The art collection includes 5,000 works of art, from prehistoric to contemporary, but the lush gardens were virtually destroyed by Hurricane Irma in September 2017 and are currently closed for renovation.

Head south on I-95 to the indisputable jewel of northern Florida: **St Augustine ㉔**. Founded by Spanish explorers in 1565 and later occupied by the British, it is America's oldest continuously occupied city. The oldest buildings in the historic district in the heart of St. Augustine date to the 1700s, and the pleasantly Mediterranean atmosphere has been preserved with narrow alleys, flowers, shops, and Spanish architecture. Elegant Casa Monica Resort and Spa, in the heart of downtown, opened in 1888 and was owned by railroad baron Henry Flagler, a name you'll hear a lot in these parts. Other notable buildings constructed by the oil and railroad magnate include the **Memorial Presbyterian Church**, which he built in memory of his daughter. A number of museums and attractions compete for the traveler's attention – some boasting rather dubious "oldest this" or "oldest that" claims – and there are several excellent beaches and state parks just across the Lions Bridge, accessed from the city center.

The city's major attraction is the star-shaped 17th-century **Castillo de San Marcos National Monument** (tel: 904-829-6506; www.nps.gov/casa; daily), a Spanish masonry fort right on the water – the oldest in America – that defended the town from invaders. Nearby, **The Colonial Quarter** (tel: 904-342-2857; http://colonialquarter.com; daily) interprets 16th-, 17th-, and 18th-century Spanish life with blacksmiths, woodworkers, and the like, while the St. Augustine **Pirate and Treasure Museum** (tel: 877-467-5863; http://thepiratemuseum.com; daily) re-creates Jamaican Port Royal in the golden era of piracy. Finally, note the huge round **zero milestone** across the road from the visitor center: this stone marks the endpoint in a string of Spanish missions that once stretched all the way to San Diego. Old Town Trolley Tours (tel: 844-388-6452; www.trolleytours.com/st-augustine) offers a fine tour of the city via trolley or horsedrawn carriage.

GAINESVILLE

From St Augustine, head southwest out of town on Florida 207, passing beneath the interstate and then through fields of sweet potatoes, cabbages, and greens – you are back in Deep South farm country. Across the broad St Johns River, the highway becomes Florida 20, and the route passes Newnans Lake, a beautiful spot for a picnic. It leads directly to **Gainesville ㉕**, home to the University of Florida, where highlights include the spectacular Florida Museum of Natural History's Butterfly Rainforest (tel. 352-846-2000; www.floridamuseum.ufl.edu; daily), a must for young

Castillo de San Marcos, St Augustine, Florida.

and old, and an enjoyable Wednesday afternoon downtown farmers market selling local organic produce, healthy meats, raw dairy, homemade bread, and other fare, where you can pick up treats for the road.

US 441 exits the city south, shortly cutting right through the middle of **Paynes Prairie State Preserve** (tel: 352-466-3397; www.floridastateparks. org/park/Paynes-Prairie; daily), a huge expanse of marsh and grassland bridged by the four-lane highway. Though located here in Florida, it aims to preserve some of the Great Plains species that once thrived in the untamed Wild West. Home to rare bison and horses, alligators and cranes, among other creatures, the park offers glimpses of this lost world either through the viewing tower or from regular park-sponsored tours. Just south is tiny **Micanopy**, a town of dirt roads and simple buildings – an anomaly, something like how the old Florida must have looked.

For an even closer look at the state's recent past, take State Route 346 a few miles east, then follow signs south along Route 325 to **Cross Creek** – a tiny town, not even a town, really, but rather a place strongly identified with Florida author Marjorie Kinnan Rawlings. You can tour her former home, now part of Marjorie Kinnan Rawlings Historic State Park (tel: 352-466-3672; www.floridastateparks.org/park/Marjorie-Kinnan-Rawlings; tours Oct–July Thu–Sun; grounds open daily), where she penned her most famous work, *The Yearling*, and endured a tough life of farming and ranching. Highway 441 continues south through horse country to **Ocala** ㉖, a small Southern market town with surrounding horse ranches, a pretty square, and several old-fashioned eateries. From Ocala, US 441 gets busy and inches through quiet lake towns, lush citrus groves, and sharp-smelling juice-processing plants. Soon enough, you enter the extensive suburbs announcing the most improbable Florida success story of all, **Orlando** ㉗ (see page 86).

SOUTH FLORIDA

ALONG THE GULF OF MEXICO

The vast majority of those travelers heading out of Orlando use the interstates and toll roads, but for more of the real Florida take the state highways a bit longer. Get off the beaten path (in this case the paved four-lane highway) and you'll see small-town life that hasn't changed much for decades. Florida 50 (also called West Colonial Drive) leaves Orlando's city center and cuts due west, shedding the suburbs. In about 15 miles (24km), you come to Clermont, singular for its **Citrus Tower** (tel: 352-394-4061; www.citrustower.com; Mon–Sat), where you can pay to ride an elevator 22 stories to the top for a view of the surrounding lakes and hills. Though eclipsed now by more famous theme parks, the tower, built in 1956, was one of Florida's first tourist attractions.

Marmalade from local oranges makes a great gift.

Shady porch on a rural Georgia log house.

ORLANDO: THE WORLD'S BEST PLAYGROUND

Not long ago, Orlando was just another agricultural town. Now it's Florida's best success story, a transformation made possible by a cartoon mouse.

Orlando's best known, best loved, and best reviled attraction is just southwest of the city. Walt Disney World (tel: 407-939-5277; www.disneyworld.disney. go.com; daily), with its four enormous complexes of entertainments, is thronged year-round by American and international tourists, and similar parks have sprung up around the globe.

The **Magic Kingdom** is Mickey Mouse's domain, and the original facility. It still remains the most popular with visitors of all ages and is divided into four distinctive theme areas – Tomorrowland, Adventureland, Fantasyland, and Frontierland.

Introduced by a glittering "geospherical" dome, the Future World exhibits at **Epcot Center** (the second part of the Disney complex) provide an invigorating look at science past, present, and future. The other half of Epcot is its World Showcase, where you can "travel the world" in less than a day through a variety of cultural (and culinary) attractions.

Cinderella Castle in Fantasyland at the Magic Kingdom.

Rides and tours in the **Disney-MGM Studios** portion of the Disney World experience give a closer look at "show business," with perspectives as seen from both sides of the cameras. Disney's **Animal Kingdom** is the largest of the parks, with over 1,700 animals representing 250 species. The park invites visitors to explore the world of animals on a safari, in a prehistoric world, and at special stage shows held throughout the day.

Not far from Disney World – but a completely separate entity – is **Universal Orlando Resort** (tel: 407-363-8000; www.universalorlando.com; daily). Opened the same year as Disney-MGM's facility, the resort offers a similar experience in its two theme parks, Universal's Islands of Adventure and Universal Studios Florida, where you will have the chance to learn more about live television and film production, with a number of exciting movie-themed rides thrown in as well. The most recent addition to both parks is the immensely popular Wizarding World of Harry Potter, which includes a recreation of Hogwarts, Diagon Alley, and the Hogwarts Express. Look for the spotlights just west of I-4.

There are dozens of similar amusements scattered about the greater Orlando area. Water slides, weird museums, and amusement park rides are especially prevalent, and kids will go crazy with joy as parents just go crazy.

The most intriguing non-Disney non-movie-related non-theme-park attraction nearby isn't within the city limits at all, but is worth traveling the few extra miles to see. Approximately 40 miles (64km) to the east, on a sandy stretch known as Cape Canaveral, the **Kennedy Space Center** (tel: 866-737-5235; www.kennedyspacecenter.com; daily) provides a fascinating up-close look at the workings of America's space program, and the Astronauts' Hall of Fame. You can try the rocket simulators and explore a life-size replica of a space shuttle. The center's popular "Lunch with an Astronaut" allows members of the public to spend an hour with one of NASA's Astronaut Corps, while the flagship centerpiece is the Space Shuttle Atlantis attraction. More recently, launch of Space X Falcon 9 rockets developed by Elon Musk and carrying satellites and other commercial payloads have drawn admiring crowds to Cape Canaveral.

Florida 50 then passes through the limestone spine of central Florida – a land of scrubby pines and prickly plants, sand dunes, citrus groves heavy with fruit in mid-winter, golf courses, even cowboys working cattle herds. Backroad stands sell everything from bovine medicine to boiled peanuts, and you'll also see plenty of churches in all the various denominations.

The route continues west, brushing the edge of Withlacoochee State Forest (tel: 352-797-4140; www.fresh fromflorida.com; daily, visitor center Mon–Fri except holidays) before arriving at whimsically named **Weeki Wachee** ㉘, famous with generations of tourists for its natural warm-water springs and "mermaid" shows. Today, the tradition lives on at Weeki Wachee Springs State Park (tel: 352-592-5656; www.weekiwachee.com; daily), where visitors can catch a water show, take a riverboat cruise, swim, boat, and see live animal shows.

If you're in a hurry to get a glimpse of the **Gulf of Mexico**, press west a few additional miles to tiny **Bayport** with its picnic area overlooking the water. Otherwise, turn south down US 19 and prepare for a spell of thick four-lane traffic and plenty of stoplights. Bring your baseball cap – during early spring, the area from Dunedin to Fort Myers is home to the training grounds for a number of major league baseball teams.

It's 30 miles (48km) down US 19 to the junction with Alt-19. Take Alt 19 to **Tarpon Springs** ㉙, a harbor community that is fascinating not for its physical appearance but its population: the town is largely Greek. Greeks originally settled this area to dive for the sponges that live abundantly in the warm surrounding seas, and today local shops and restaurants continue to reflect this heritage.

Past pretty Dunedin (another good spot to stop for the weekend farmers' market), take Florida 60 west across the causeway to **Clearwater Beach**, a touristy town west of Tampa with an array of seafood restaurants, motels, hotels, and resorts, and beach homes. It's a fine place to swim in warm water and lie on the beautiful – and public – famed white sand beaches.

Turn south down the beach road (which eventually becomes Florida 699). You will pass through more waterfront towns, most with excellent sand but some too overdeveloped for their own good. The finest beach on the entire string is probably the southern-most one, **Passe-a-Grille Beach**, in St. Pete Beach, some 20 miles (32km) of slow driving onward from Clearwater, and adjoining St. Petersburg. Gawk at the huge pink **Loews Don CeSar Hotel,** an Art Deco masterpiece right beside the blue Gulf waters, then pass through the low-key village and hit the sand. For yet another magical beach experience, head over the toll bridge on Route 682 and turn right onto Route 679 to Fort De Soto Park (tel: 727-582-2267; daily); this 1,136-acre (459-hectare) swath of beach, wetlands, and

◉ Tip

Florida Gulf Coast's network of shallow coves and lagoons is great for sport fishing. Yet this is also a prime area for manatees, so boaters should be ever-vigilant and observe the signs and warnings to avoid collisions.

Disney World's Epcot Center.

forest on Tampa Bay is a paradise for both nature and sun lovers (and there's even a historic fort to explore).

TAMPA

St Petersburg is predominantly a retirement community, but on Third Street you'll find the **Salvador Dalí Museum** (tel: 727-823-3767; www.thedali.org; daily), which displays the country's largest collection of the artist's works. It is without question the central cultural attraction of the city (unless you are interested in learning how to play shuffleboard, a popular pastime here). East across Tampa Bay via either I-275 or US 92, and set right on the water facing St Pete across the bay, is **Tampa 30**. This city's historic Cuban influence is nowhere clearer than in **Ybor City**, with its concentration of Cuban restaurants and atmospheric cigar manufacturers. Ybor City was built on empty scrub by a local cigar maker in the late 1800s and retains its authentic Cuban influence; today, though, it also sports posh pubs and hot nightlife, and often hosts movie festivals and other cultural events.

Be mindful here if you are out after dark, but that doesn't mean you shouldn't venture out for a taste of what this city has to offer. Other city attractions include a full February slate of events, kicked off by a wild Mardi Gras–style parade, and Tampa Bay itself – best viewed during a stroll along the sidewalk arcing around upscale Bayshore Boulevard, from the fabulous Florida Aquarium on the water, or by zipping over the stunning Sunshine Skyway, a long, narrow suspension bridge that swoops across this beautiful body of water.

SOUTH FROM TAMPA

Most visitors to Tampa also make a visit to **Busch Gardens** (tel: 888-800-5447; http://seaworldparks.com/en/buschgardens-tampa; daily), the area's "other" famous theme park. This appealing park has an authentic wildlife conservation mission and is home to some 12,000 wild animals of 300 species, including giraffes, zebras, and other animals visible in its African safari park and other animal exhibits—all of it cheek by jowl with heart-dropping roller coasters, water slides, and simulated rapids, not to mention world-famous performances of water ballet, waterskiing skills, and the like.

Take US 41 south out of Tampa, stopping a moment outside **Ruskin** where the Little Manatee River empties into the bay. As you'd expect from the name, you can sometimes find manatees lolling around happily at this inlet in winter, when they swim here to enjoy the warm water. In winter it's not uncommon to see dozens of them clustering around the outflow.

US 41 plunges due south through strings of heavily built-up towns and cities, many catering to retirees. A much faster route would take the parallel I-75.

Locally caught sponges for sale, Tarpon Springs.

Bradenton and Sarasota are next, twin cities on the Gulf of Mexico offering very favorable weather, spring baseball, and more good sandy beaches with warm ocean water. Circus master John Ringling built his glorious Italianate mansion, Ca' d'Zan, on the Sarasota shore, sparing no expense. Now a state museum, the truly wonderful Ringling Museum of Art (tel: 941-359-5700; www.ringling. org; daily) is home to some spectacular European masterpieces collected by Ringling as well as a contemporary installation by light artist James Turrell. Visitors can tour the estate, which encompasses his mansion, art collection, and a circus exhibit.

The beaches continue through lovely Siesta Key and Casey Key to Venice and beyond. The highway circles around Charlotte Harbor and crosses the Caloosahatchee River into Fort Myers ❸❶. The mild climate has long made this a popular winter resort town for Northerners. Indeed, Thomas Edison and Henry Ford were neighbors on the riverfront, for example. You can tour both the Edison & Ford Winter Estates (tel: 239-334-7419; www.edisonfordwinterestates.org; daily) on one combined ticket. Highlights include the magnificently landscaped grounds on the water, Edison's Botanic Research Lab, and the joint Estates Museum.

If you enjoy collecting seashells, follow signs over the toll bridge to resort-rich Sanibel Island, which offers the finest "shelling" in America, as evidenced by scores of people wandering the white sand beaches hunched over in the "Sanibel stoop." The charming Bailey-Matthews National Seashell Museum (tel: 239-395-2233; www.shellmuseum.org; daily) in Sanibel is a perfect destination for shell seekers. Also popular with outdoors lovers is Sanibel's J.N. Ding Darling NWR (tel: 239-472-1100; www. fws.gov/refuge/N_Ding_Darling; daily), a haven for bird watchers in winter when migratory birds are attracted to the largest undeveloped mangrove ecosystem in the world.

Continue south to elegant Naples ❸❷, a good base for visiting southwest

Seminole children operating an airboat in the Everglades.

⊘ DETOUR TO LAKE OKEECHOBEE

A 58-mile (93km) drive along Florida 80 from Fort Myers brings you to Lake Okeechobee and its 750 sq miles (1,940 sq km) of crystal waters. Florida's largest lake is as beautiful as it is sad; the lake reflects the damage being done to the sensitive Everglades' environment by the inexorably burgeoning population of Florida.

The water from Lake Okeechobee once fed the wide shallow river of the Everglades, but dikes, pumping stations, and canals were constructed to tame this dramatic lake and its flooding waters. While this has made the surrounding area an agricultural paradise (the area produces enough sugar to supply the sweet tooth of 15 million Americans for an entire year), the projects have brought ecological hardships to the surrounding environment, and, to some degree, to the residents as well. Both the Everglades and South Florida's cities have been threatened with drought by the dwindling water level of the lake. Excessive pumping of the Everglades' mother waters for the booming population along the Gold Coast is also sucking it dry. Still a popular destination for anglers, fish camps punctuate the lake's perimeter. Okeechobee, the largest town on the north shore of the lake, is the best base if you want to explore the area. Boat trips can be easily arranged. For more information visit www.visitflorida.com.

Tip

Boardwalk trails offer glimpses, but the best way to explore the Everglades is to rent a canoe, take an air boat ride, or hire a licensed outfitters to guide you. Seeing this exotic place only from land does not do justice to its mystery.

SheiKra dive rollercoaster at Busch Gardens, Tampa.

Florida. It's tempting to sit on the beautiful white sand beach, stroll the 1888 pier, or take in downtown's swanky shops and restaurants, boutique hotels, and relax. But make time to visit Naples Zoo at Caribbean Gardens (tel: 239-262-5409; www.napleszoo.org; daily), a historic botanical gardens and zoo renowned for a century of plant and animal conservation work. The zoo was begun in the 1960s by Jungle Larry and Safari Jane Tetzlaff, who introduced wild African animals to the botanical gardens and entertained and educated thousands of visitors. The zoo today still houses lions and other animals from Africa, as well as Madagascar lemurs and endangered Florida species such as panthers, an increasing important focus of the zoo's work. Animals can be viewed close up in well-designed exhibits and fun educational presentations. Note: Naples and nearby Marco Island took the brunt of Hurricane Irma in September 2017 and were badly damaged by flooding, but are recovering well after a lot of clearing up.

INTO THE EVERGLADES

South of Naples is the Gulf section of Everglades National Park, a watery paradise for kayakers dotted with islands. The main drive east through the Everglades can be made via either **Alligator Alley** (on toll route I-75) or farther south, historic US 41 (the Tamiami Trail), which parallels the **Tamiami Canal,** connecting the Atlantic Ocean with the Gulf of Mexico. For close-ups of North America's largest reptile, take the former route – the animals sun themselves in large numbers all along the swampy canal. Pictures are easy to take, but watch for traffic on the busy road, and don't get too close to the water – alligators can move surprisingly fast, and you do not want your last picture to be the one of you getting eaten.

US 41 is the preferable route to take you into the quiet, unspoiled heart of South Florida. There are no towns because you are slowly cutting across the vast wetlands of the **Everglades** ⓭, the largest subtropical wilderness in America, a waterworld made up of coastal mangrove forests, sawgrass marshes, and pine flatwoods semi-protected by law and largely inaccessible to humans.

This magical landscape is home to endangered American crocodiles, manatees, and Florida panthers, venomous snakes, ancient-looking anhingas and other birds, sinuous blackwater creeks overhung by lush vegetation, and a few desperado-like characters; it also supplies the bulk of the drinking water to greater Miami. Authors, including Marjory Stoneman Douglas (a journalist who fought to get the Everglades protected) and Peter Matthiessen, have written about the unique people and creatures here in books like *River of Grass* and *Killer Mister Watson*, but it remains inscrutable. Journalist Susan Orlean's best-seller *The Orchid Thief*, set partially in the entrancing Big

Cypress National Preserve, off US 41, captures the unique landscape and its colorful characters in wonderful detail. You will see "Panther Crossing" road signs, and – if you are really lucky – perhaps even an elusive panther. Boardwalk trails head off into the Everglades for hiking, boating, and truly memorable birdwatching and photo opportunities. At certain times of year, the entire plain floods, sometimes by inches, sometimes by feet. It then gradually drains off into the Gulf of Mexico.

Miccosukee Indian Village/Resort (tel: 305-480-1924; www.miccosukee. com) offers supplies, lodging, food, gambling (legal on the reservation), alligator wrestling, and airboat rides. The tribe's cultural center has art and exhibits but less about the tribe's heroic history, when Seminole warriors like Osceola outfoxed Federal troops in these endless swamps for more than a year rather than surrender. Just east is the first entrance to the main park, at Shark Valley; the other is south of Homestead. Shark

Valley Visitor Center (tel: 305-242-7700; www.nps.gov/ever; daily) offers a boardwalk, bike rentals, and a tram through the 15-mile park loop, as well as an observation tower overlooking miles of wetlands.

FLORIDA KEYS

This string of tiny islands is home to unique plant and animal life, and has long lured celebrities, many of whom put down roots,, most famously writer Ernest Hemingway. In recent decades, the Conch Republic has become popular with LGBTQ travelers, perhaps attracted to its laid-back, party attitude (often referred to as "Keys Disease"). True "Conchs," though, are a tough, resilient, independent lot, riding out the severe storms that have historically made the Keys a paradise for shipwreck treasure. A case in point: many conchs refused to evacuate as Hurricane Irma bore down on the Keys on September 10, 2017, flattening and inundating everything in its path of destruction. Within days, though, all the bridges were open and the

A hawksbill turtle just off the Florida Keys.

clean-up was underway; 10 months later most businesses and attractions are open again.

Laid back is the operative word here. Find a beach chair and a spot in the sun, get a beverage of choice, and leave your worries at the doorstep – or better yet, leave your worries back home. Even the light is different here, a mysterious, turquoise shade of blue that reflects off everything it touches. It is a wonder, really, that these disparate islands are connected to each other or the mainland at all. Yet a series of 42 highway bridges does indeed bridge the many gaps between land and water.

From **Miami** ❸ (see page 94) US 1 proceeds south through the quiet community of **Homestead**. A branch road here, Florida 9336, leads through **Everglades National Park** to Ernest F. Coe Visitor Center and Flamingo Visitor Center at the southernmost point (tel: 305-242-7700; www.nps.gov/ever; daily). The scenic drive and boardwalk trails offer glimpses of cypress swamp, grassland, mangroves, and more, as well as delightfully photogenic anhingas spreading their wings close up on the Anhinga Trail at Royal Palm. Resist the temptation to put pedal to the metal – rangers are polite but zealous about tickets. And be sure to sample Key Lime ice cream at roadside stands.

KEY LARGO

Allow plenty of time to reach Key West. Much of the drive will be at or around 30mph (48kph). US 1 enters the Keys as the Overseas Highway at **Key Largo** ❸, immortalized in the Humphrey Bogart/Lauren Bacall film of the same name (which wasn't actually filmed here), and right away you get an opportunity to view the sea up-close. At **John Pennekamp Coral Reef State Park** (tel: 305-451-6300; www.pennekamppark.com; daily), located at mile-marker 102.5 and one of the most popular parks in Florida, you can gaze through glass-bottomed boats at incredible coral reef formations under the water. Equally compelling are the fish and shellfish living in this delicate ecosystem. Snorkeling and diving are a must, and there are canoe and kayak rentals.

If this reef is the best place to see the nature of the Keys, the next park, **Long Key State Park** (tel: 305-664-4815; www.floridastateparks.org/park/Long-Key; daily), some 30 miles (48km) farther along US 1, is your best bet for a swim or reclining in the sun before proceeding west. There is also a canoe and kayak rental.

For a lesson on what made the Keys into such a unique place, journey 20 more miles (32km) beyond Long Key to the best museum in the region, **Crane Point Museum and Nature Center** (tel: 305-743-3900; www.cranepoint.net; daily) in the resort town of **Marathon** ❸. Be sure to visit the museum's wild bird center. Marathon itself is more like a big town than an island paradise, and is best

Ernest Hemingway Home and Museum, Key West.

used for stocking up on supplies. As you leave Marathon, watch on the left for Pigeon Key Visitor Center (tel: 305-743-5999; http://pigeonkey.net; daily) on Knight Key. Motorboats ferry visitors out to the Key for tours of the museum and quarters housing more than 400 workers on Henry Flagler's historic railroad. Following Hurricane Irma, ferries now depart from Hyatt Place's marina at the Faro Blanco Lighthouse. The mangrove forests thicken beyond here as nature begins reclaiming the westernmost islands. You will get plenty of water views on both sides of the car now as you cross **Seven Mile Bridge**, landing briefly on beautiful **No Name Key** and its **Bahia Honda State Park** (tel: 305-872-2353; www.floridastateparks.org/park/bahia-honda; daily) – yet another wonderful state park, which offers snorkeling tours, kayaking, and an excellent beach. Key deer are an endangered species well worth stopping for and relatively easy to see, especially on No Name Key.

KEY WEST

You cross more bridges still, landing on **Big Pine Key**, **Sugarloaf Key**, and **Looe Key**, each with its own personality and laid-back eateries. Eventually, the highway comes to rest upon balmy **Key West** ㉛, last island in the chain – and also the name of the town that has been drawing interesting characters for a very long time. Today, it's a mixture of fishermen, retirees, Cubans, and tourists, and a large LGBTQ population.

The writer Ernest Hemingway lived here, and purveying "Papa's" image has become one of the town's hottest cottage industries. To get a taste of how he lived, visit the **Ernest Hemingway Home and Museum** (tel: 305-294-1136; www.hemingwayhome.com; daily), where the colorful writer lived for a decade. It's notable for the gardens he personally tended and the unusual 40-50 polydactyl (six-toed) cats that overrun the place. Most are descended from the writer's own cats; others were strays who happened to know a good thing when they saw it. Duval Street – the hub of the town – is lined with tacky tourist shops, restaurants, and extremely noisy bars (several which were patronized by Hemingway himself). The writer's look-alike contest held every year is a highlight of the social season.

The two most popular sights in town, however, are both free. The first is **Mallory Square Dock**, where residents and tourists alike turn out for a nightly arts festival featuring arts and crafts, street performers, food carts, and even psychics and the main event: to cheer the beautiful sunset sinking into the Gulf of Mexico (www.sunsetcelebration.org). The other is the brightly colored buoy that marks the **southernmost point** in the continental 48 states. Locals claim that on a very clear night you can even faintly make out the lights of Cuba, lying less than 100 miles (160km) away.

The Overseas Highway, Florida Keys.

📷 A SHORT STAY IN MIAMI

Spicy and seductive, Miami lures those who enjoy Cuban culture, Art Deco and Spanish architecture, sunny days on the beach, and steamy nights on the town. Here's a list of the not-to-be-missed attractions.

Coral Gables is an enchanting Mediterranean-style neighborhood, home to the glorious **Biltmore Hotel** (1926) and the **Venetian Pool**, sometimes called "the most beautiful swimming hole in the world."

The **Kampong** on Biscayne Bay is the former home of botanical explorer David Fairchild and displays thousands of plants in a lush, tropical garden and Indonesian-inspired architecture and pools.

Coconut Grove is a vibrant, eclectic neighborhood of funky houses, dense natural greenery, and shopping at **Coco Walk**.

Architect I.M. Pei designed futuristic **Miami Tower**, a 47-story building in downtown Miami that changes color at the flick of a switch.

The **Wolfsonian** features an eclectic collection of art and miscellany that businessman Mitchell Wolfson, Jr collected during his lifetime.

Lummus Park preserves the oldest structures in Miami (the **William English Slave Plantation House** and the **William Wagner House**) next to a white-sand beach stretching along the coastline.

Vizcaya Museum and Gardens, the Italian Renaissance-style villa built in 1916 by industrialist James Deering, is one of Miami's top tourist destinations.

Key Biscayne, an island paradise connected by bridge, offers many water-related recreations.

Bill Baggs Cape Florida State Park, on the tip of **Key Biscayne** and with a view of **Cape Florida Lighthouse**, has few facilities – just peace and solitude.

IMPORTANT INFORMATION

Population: 463,347
Dialing codes: 305, 786
Website: www.miamiandbeaches.com
Tourist information: Greater Miami Convention & Visitors Bureau, 701 Brickell Avenue, Suite 2700, FL 33131; tel: 305-539-3000

Art Deco District. Pastel-colored fantasies line Ocean Drive in South Beach.

Lifeguard hut on Miami Beach.

Mile after mile of golden sand, upscale communities, and the eye-catching architecture of Miami Modernism, known locally as MiMo, make up the Miami Beach scene.

City of fantasy

Miami is everything other cities are not. Pastel colors, swaying palms, and Art Deco balconies are not only easy on the eye but also kind to the disposition – it's impossible to fret when there's a cocktail on the table, a pink plastic flamingo on the counter, and a three-piece band playing loud and sassy salsa in your eardrums. If you're staying in trendy South Beach, leave your car behind and stretch those weary legs before getting them tanned on the sandy beach across the street. Or get in a workout surfing some of this area's best waves. Lively Miami is worth discovering. Just don't forget the sunscreen.

...ch volleyball on South Beach, where the buff, bronzed,
and beautiful come to play.

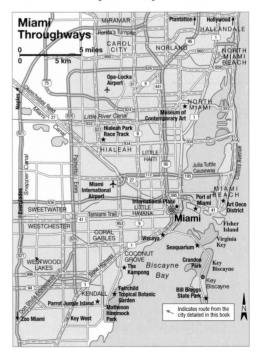

The majesty of Wyoming's Grand Teton National Park.

THE NORTHERN ROUTE

A detailed guide from east to west, with principal sights clearly cross-referenced by number to the maps.

A Montana cowboy.

On our northern route between Boston, Massachusetts, and Washington State's Olympic Peninsula, you will encounter a collage of farmlands, ranches, wilderness, port towns, declining industrial cities, reborn urban centers, and constant reminders of the nation's history.

The first half of the journey is largely marked and guided by water. From Boston, you follow the Atlantic coast through New England up to Maine; later, from the Albany area, your route will swing west alongside the once-busy, now-dormant Erie Canal.

The Great Lakes dominate the next portion of the trip, including Chicago, the great Midwestern crossroads at the southern tip of Lake Michigan. From here to the thriving twin cities of Minneapolis and St Paul, the tour is never far from water, significantly when it runs right beside the mighty Mississippi. Once you reach western Minnesota, however, the character of the land begins to change. As you cut across South Dakota, the geography overwhelms the senses: rising out of the prairie are the otherworldly Badlands, the Black Hills, and Wounded Knee, a reminder of the nation's brutal treatment of Native Americans. Along a legendary stagecoach route come towns of the notorious Wild West. The sky here is huge, and the land seems vast, characterized by small buttes and sagebrush. The route through Wyoming and Montana passes Little Bighorn Battlefield, site of Lieutenant Colonel Custer's last stand against Plains Indian forces.

Brass sidewalk marker on the Freedom Trail.

From here, the tour passes into the northern Rocky Mountains with its gorgeous national parks. Crossing the Continental Divide on paths previously traveled by mountain tribes, gold prospectors, and homesteaders, the route cuts through the forests, lakes, and buffalo reserves of Montana, the Idaho panhandle, and into the state of Washington, where the land modulates between deserts, canyons, and irrigated farmland.

The final portion of the route travels westward toward the Pacific Ocean through Seattle and the Olympic Peninsula. Suddenly, water is abundant again as you enter one of America's largest temperate rainforests. This wildly beautiful spot is an ideal place to reflect upon your just-completed trans-American journey.

📷 A SHORT STAY IN BOSTON

The many colleges in this historic and attractive city ensure it retains a youthful, vibrant outlook. Here's a list of Boston's not-to-be-missed attractions.

Full-scale replicas of three 18th-century ships – *Beaver II*, *Dartmouth*, and *Eleanor* – sit in the harbor at the **Boston Tea Party Ships and Museum**. They commemorate the 1773 dunking of taxed tea from Britain, an incident that fanned the flames of the American Revolution.

Built in 1676, **Paul Revere House** is the oldest residence in downtown Boston; Revere lived here from 1770 to 1800. Exhibits include the saddlebags the patriot used on his famous 1775 midnight ride to warn of a British attack.

The oldest botanical garden in America, **Boston Public Garden** is the city's prettiest green space, with a lagoon surrounded by willow trees and crossed by a mock suspension bridge as its focal point.

Trinity Church, H. H. Richardson's 1877 masterpiece in **Copley Square**, is one of America's finest ecclesiastical buildings. Its wealth of murals, mosaics, carvings, and stained glass makes it Boston's most sumptuous interior space.

Opened in 1895, the **Boston Public Library** is a Renaissance Revival masterpiece by Charles McKim, with a 1972 addition by Philip Johnson. The interior includes murals by John Singer Sargent and Puvis de Chavannes; the courtyard is reminiscent of 16th-century Italy.

The 1903 **Isabella Stewart Gardner Museum** has many architectural elements, from Venetian window frames to Roman mosaic floor tiles. The galleries hold paintings by Titian, Raphael, Degas, and Rembrandt.

IMPORTANT INFORMATION

Population: 685,094 est.
Dialing codes: 617, 857
Website: www.bostonusa.com
Tourist information: Greater Boston C&VB, 2 Copley Place, Suite 105, MA 02116; tel: 888-SEE-BOSTON

Massachusetts State House. On July 4, 1795, Massachusetts Governor Samuel Adams and Paul Revere laid the cornerstone for the "new" State House. The building overlooks Boston Common and can be explored on a free guided tour.

Nichols House Museum. Housed in a splendid 1804 Federal-style townhouse attributed to Bulfinch, Nichols House is a true Beacon Hill period piece.

USS Constitution. Known as "Old Ironsides," the 1797 frigate won all 40 of the battles she fought. Still seaworthy, she is berthed in Charlestown.

The Back Bay City

"I have learned never to argue with a Bostonian," said poet Rudyard Kipling in the early 1900s, and that is still true. By American standards Boston is old, with its cobbled streets lit by gas lamps, national historic landmarks, and individual buildings of great stature and charm. Fifty years ago, Boston was in danger of becoming a museum of living history, forever trapped in its 1700s and 1800s heyday. Then a change took place: the basin was cleaned, the buildings washed and, due to the high-tech industries of nearby Cambridge, businesses began to flock back. Boston is now modern-minded, so go check it out. And no arguing.

wntown. To walk the streets of downtown Boston day is to walk with the ghosts of Colonial settlers on ound now shadowed by modern skyscrapers. Street mes have changed, but the design is much the same it was in the 1600s.

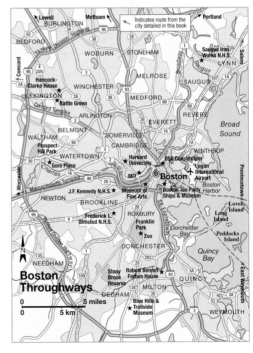

John Hancock building and
Trinity church on Boston's
Copley Square.

BOSTON TO BUFFALO

Take a drive through the prettiest parts of New England before beginning a coast-to-coast trek to the West, starting with the old route of the Erie Canal.

Beginning in downtown **Boston ❶** (see page 100), the Northern route across the United States begins locally, by visiting Greater Boston. Cross the Charles River into busy **Cambridge ❷**, where the combination of old-fashioned leafy streets, active squares, and buzzing student life makes it one of Greater Boston's most interesting areas. The activity focuses on triangular **Harvard Square** and more rough-and-tumble but no less vibrant **Central Square**. While here, explore the brick buildings and carefully manicured greens of **Harvard University**, the second-oldest educational institution in the land; it was chartered back in 1636 and remains one of the finest universities in America, with museums such as Peabody Museum of Archaeology and Ethnology (tel: 617-496-1027; www.peabody.harvard.edu; daily) and Harvard Museum of Natural History (tel: 617-495-3045; www.hmnh.harvard.edu; daily).

The city's beautifully kept **Mount Auburn Cemetery** (tel: 617-547-7105; http://mountauburn.org) is worth seeing as well – its peaceful grounds are the last resting place of the remains of such artistic luminaries as Henry Longfellow, Oliver Wendell Holmes, and Winslow Homer.

Keep following signs for scenic State Route 2A, which continues from Massachusetts Avenue into quieter towns. You soon come to **Arlington**, now suburban and high-tech but once a textile community where retreating British soldiers skirmished with local residents known as "Minutemen" (they were said to have been ready at a minute's notice to fight) in April 1775, as the British backtracked along this road.

PAUL REVERE'S RIDE

At **Lexington**, about 10 miles (16km) outside Boston proper, turn off State Route 2A into the downtown area for a look at the town green, the main stage of the Battle of Lexington on that fateful

Main attractions

Boston
Salem
York
Nubble Light
Appalachian Trail
Norman Rockwell Exhibit
National Baseball Hall of Fame
National Women's Hall of Fame
Niagara Falls

Map on page 104

Paul Revere statue, Boston.

Boston to Buffalo

Massachusetts

- Boston ❶
- Cambridge ❷
- 2A Concord
- Salem ❸
- 225 Lexington
- 127 Gloucester

New Hampshire

- ★ Rye Beach
- Portsmouth ❹

Maine

- 1 York ❺
- Wells
- Kennebunk 99 Kennebunkport
- Portland ❻
- 25 Gorham
- Cornish ❼

Maine / New Hampshire

- Mount 16 Washington
- Center Harbor
- 25 Meredith
- 3 ★ Lake Winnipesaukee ❽
- 104 Potter Place
- 11 New London ❾
- Corbin Covered Bridge
- 114 ★ Lake Sunapee
- 11 Newport ❿
- 10 103 Claremont

New Hampshire / Vermont

- Fairlee Ascutney
- Orford, NH 5
- 5 Windsor ⓫
- Norwich 120 Hanover, NH
- 4 Quechee State Park
- 100A Woodstock ⓬
- Stockbridge 100 ★ President Calvin Coolidge State Historic Site
- ★ Appalachian Trail ⓭
- 125 Bread Loaf 100 Waterbury
- 7 Ripton
- 30 Middlebury
- Pawlet
- 30 Dorset ⓮
- Manchester
- 7A ★ Hildene
- 313 Arlington ⓯

Vermont / New York

- 372 Cambridge
- Saratoga National Historical Park
- 29 Saratoga Springs ⓰
- 50 Schenectady ★ Old Stone Fort ⓱
- 20 Esperance Schoharie
- 30 National Baseball Hall of Fame
- Cherry Valley 80 Cooperstown ⓲
- Richfield Springs
- 167 Little Falls
- Herkimer
- 5S ★ Fort Herkimer Church
- Mohawk ⓳
- Ilion
- 5S Utica ⓴
- 69 Rome ㉑
- 46 Oneida
- 5 Chittenango
- Syracuse ㉒
- Camillus
- Auburn
- ★ Seneca Falls ㉓
- Waterloo
- 20 Geneva ㉔
- Canandaigua
- 21 ★ Granger Homestead & Carriage Museum ㉕
- ★ Sonnenberg Gardens
- ★ Mormon historic sites
- Palmyra
- 31
- Rochester ㉖
- Medina ㉗
- 31
- Lockport
- Niagara Falls ㉘
- Buffalo ㉙

River Rd

---

morning of April 19, 1775. A number of statues and monuments commemorate this spirited American defense of their town, considered the opening battle of the American Revolution (silversmith Paul Revere had ridden his horse here from Boston under cover of night to warn the residents of a British attack). There are also several old taverns in the area, one of which – Munroe Tavern – served as the makeshift British hospital and command center during the battle.

Continue west along State Route 2A, where the sequence of American Revolution events is further interpreted in now-peaceful **Minute Man National Historical Park** (tel: 978-369-6993; www.nps.gov/mima; daily), which occupies both sides of the highway in a green patch just northwest of the village green.

Concord, the next town, was the scene of the second battle on that April morning. The site of the skirmish, at a bridge (now reconstructed) across the Concord River, is preserved as part of the historical park. Concord was a center of literature and philosophy during the 19th century, as evidenced by such prominent residents as Ralph Waldo Emerson, Henry David Thoreau, and Louisa May Alcott, among others. The latter's imposing former home, Louisa May Alcott's **Orchard House** (tel: 978-369-4118; www.louisamayalcott.org; daily), where she wrote *Little Women*, can be seen first, on the right as you approach town. The equally imposing Ralph Waldo **Emerson House** (tel: 978-369-2236; www.ralphwaldoemerson.org; mid-Apr–Oct Thur–Sun) is less than half a mile away, displaying items from the life and work of the influential Transcendentalist thinker.

From the center of town, take Walden Street south a short distance to visit **Walden Pond State Reservation** (tel: 978-369-3254; www.mass.gov/locations/walden-pond-state-reservation), a testament to fellow Transcendentalist Henry Thoreau's life, work, and unique viewpoint. Thoreau built a simple cabin beside this pond in 1845 and lived there for two years, observing wildlife and the seasons. He wrote *Walden* about the experience. "I went to the woods because I wished to live deliberately," he proclaimed, emerging with a view of nature as teacher – rather than slave – of man. Although the book sold poorly in Thoreau's time, it has since become a classic of American literature and the environmental movement. The drive to save Walden Pond was spearheaded by musician Don Henley's Walden Woods Project in 1990. The pond was never as remote or peaceful as Thoreau wrote about, with the commuter train to Boston passing loudly nearby. Nor was Walden as cut off as one imagines – Thoreau frequently visited his mother in town for meals and to have her do his laundry – but the wooded setting still offers a sense of what Thoreau must have felt.

HEART OF NEW ENGLAND

Before leaving behind Boston for the Wild West, consider making a short detour north through the splendid backroads of New England, where America began and where a delightful small-town neighborliness can still be felt today.

Head north from downtown Boston on State Route 1A (North Street from Downtown) toward **Salem ③**. This sea town was one of the earliest capitals of the Massachusetts Bay Colony and is filled with period captains' homes, several of which can be visited, including Peabody Essex Museum (tel: 866-745-1876; www.pem.org; Tue–Sun). It's more famous, though, for the **Salem Witch Trials**, which began in 1692 as an attempt to root out suspected witchcraft among local women and children. Nearly two dozen women were killed during the height of the frenzy – a symbol, ever after, for misplaced persecution. (The term "witch hunt," broadly applied to political activities, remains in the American lexicon today.) **Salem Witch Museum** (tel: 978-744-1692; www.

salemwitchmuseum.com; daily), beside the city's large central green, offers an explanation of the trials. Writer Nathaniel Hawthorne was born in a modest house, now part of the national historical landmark known collectively as **The House of the Seven Gables** (tel: 978-744-0991; www.7gables.org; daily), on the city waterfront nearby. The Georgian-style seven-gabled house, made famous by the novel and officially the Turner-Ingersoll Mansion, is the highlight of a visit but there are also gardens and educational presentations.

State Route 1A continues north from Salem on a scenic route that passes through salt marshes, small drawbridges, farmland, and little fishing and commuter towns such as Ipswich, Rowley, and Newbury. Along the way, you may wish to detour east to **Gloucester**, the entrance to lovely Cape Ann and home port to large numbers of fishing and whale-watching boats.

NEW HAMPSHIRE AND MAINE

After entering **New Hampshire**, State Route 1A frees itself from ticky-tacky

The uniform of a Civil War sergeant of the 13th Massachusetts Volunteers.

Salem Witch Museum.

beach development to reveal the Atlantic itself at **Rye Beach** – your first true glimpse of the open ocean on this tour. Continue a few miles to **Portsmouth** , New Hampshire's most attractive city and one with a salty taste.

Originally known as Strawberry Banke for the wild fruits covering the ground, Portsmouth, founded in 1631, sits at the mouth of the Piscataqua River, where it meets the sea, and has been a fishing and shipping center ever since. Fine old seamen's homes still cluster in the downtown area, and while designer coffee shops and microbreweries are rapidly crowding out the old salts (this is only an hour's commute from Boston, remember), you can still find good clam chowder in the local diners.

Take the bridge north across the river to **Maine**, the "Pine Tree State." Pull off busy US 1 after 6 miles (10km) to visit **York** , Maine's first settlement, where you'll find an old jail and other historic buildings on the waterfront, all connected by Cliff Walk Trail, a rugged 1-mile (1.6km) roundtrip hike from York Harbor Beach along

Portland Head Light, built on Cape Elizabeth in 1794.

the cliffs. Most visitors come for the stretch of attractive beach known as **Long Sands**, framed at one end by a much-photographed lighthouse: the Cape Neddick Light Station, known locally as **Nubble Light**.

Wells is a fairly forgettable beach town, but worth a stop to visit **Wells Reserve at Laudholm** (tel: 207-646-1555; www.wellsreserve.org; daily), a 2,250-acre (911-hectare) coastal reserve comprising Wells National Estuarine Reserve, which is headquartered in a restored 19th-century saltwater farm called Laudholm. Also in Wells, Maine is 9,125-acre (3,693-hectare) Rachel Carson National Wildlife Refuge (tel: 207-646-9226; www.fws.gov/refuge/Rachel_Carson/about.html; daily), honoring famed research scientist Rachel Carson, whose books about the ocean, songbirds, and ecology, particularly Silent Spring in 1962, changed the way Americans thought about the natural world.

PORTLAND AND CORNISH

Farther north, you hit the Kennebunks, two towns physically joined at the hip by a bridge but quite different in character. **Kennebunk** is more workaday, with an exclusive beach several miles east, while **Kennebunkport** is a slice of quaint, upper-crust New England – all gift shops, designer beers, and fish houses, and a bit rich for the blood. Former president George Bush Sr's family compound stands among dramatic shore rocks and crashing waves east of the downtown.

It's 20 more slow miles (32km) north along US 1 (or you can pay to take I-95) to **Portland** , the state's largest city and cultural center. **Eastern Promenade Park** makes a good first stop, with its panoramic view of islands in the bay and part of the city's working waterfront. The **Old Port** district, once a maze of rough streets frequented by sailors, has been tidied up over the past few decades and is now a lively quarter of boutiques and restaurants. The highlight of the **Arts**

District is elegant **Victoria Mansion** (also known as the Morse-Libby House; tel: 207-772-4841; www.victoriamansion. org; May–Oct) on Danforth Street. Built by a luxury hotelier, it is one of the best examples of Victorian Italian villa style in the nation, with 90 percent of the interiors, including paintings, still intact. **Portland Museum of Art** (tel: 207-775-6148; www.portlandmuseum.org; May–Oct Mon–Sun) is known for its permanent collection of Winslow Homer's work. You can also take a ferry across to Peaks Island and enjoy a sea voyage. Make sure to ply parking meters, or risk getting a ticket here.

From Portland, quieter State Route 25 cuts swiftly west through suburbs and rolling farmland (**Gorham**, the rural main campus of the University of Southern Maine, is little more than a crossroads). At East Limington, the bridge crosses the Saco River, a superb canoeing river that winds from deep in western Maine to the sea. A park on the left-hand side of the road provides a scenic picnic spot, rocks make for good sunning, and a path leads to a small swimming beach, out of the sometimes-swift current.

Farther west, the route passes through more countryside to **Cornish** ❼, one of western Maine's handsome towns. The activity here is focused on a small triangular green space lined with small shops and a hardware store, most in typical whitewashed New England fashion. Each September, an annual apple festival showcasing local pies, cider, and other apple products is held here. A highlight is the apple pie contest, which takes place on the porch of the venerable Cornish Inn, next to the village green. The best part comes after the judging, when all pies – winners and losers – are auctioned off to lingering spectators.

LAKE COUNTRY

Keep to Route 25 as it jogs west into New Hampshire, the "Granite State," then briefly north; if you were to keep going north on Route 16, you would soon pass **Mount Washington**, at 6,288ft (1,917 meters) the tallest peak east of the Mississippi, which has the highest recorded winds on the planet.

At West Ossipee, however, make a turn inland again, and follow Route 25 through the communities of Moultonborough; **Center Harbor**, whose little general store features New Hampshire's Squamscot soda; and finally **Meredith**, a resort town with the Annalee Doll Museum, set on pretty **Lake Winnipesaukee** ❽, New Hampshire's largest body of water.

Head south a short way on US 3, which hugs the lake, then, going uphill as you leave town, bear right to take State Route 104, which continues through typical New Hampshire small towns. At Danbury, cut south on US 4 a short distance to Route 11, then turn west again just after **Potter Place**.

It's only 10 miles (16km) more to the prim town of **New London** ❾ (turn right onto State Route 114 just past Elkins), which has good views of the surrounding hills and mountains. This is known locally as a college town, with attractive

Lobster boats in Maine.

Colby-Sawyer College located right next to its very fine village green. This former women's college was long one of America's few remaining single-sex institutions of higher education, and became co-educational only in 1990. Connecting with State Route 11 from State Route 114, the road passes through the hamlets of Georges Mills (little more than a general store and coves on either side of the road) and the lake town of Sunapee, with a pretty harbor on **Lake Sunapee** – reputedly one of the cleanest lakes in America, and one circled by hills of hardwoods.

Six more miles (10km) east on State Route 11 brings you to **Newport** ⓾ spreading out in the Sugar River Valley. It's a small textile and arms manufacturing town, with an old opera house, a covered bridge, and the handsome rectangular "town common" so typical of older New England towns. These green pastures once served as common grazing spaces for local livestock, but today serve mostly as settings for soccer matches, carnivals, and farmers' markets.

Newport is perhaps best known for Sarah Josepha Buell Hale (1788–1879), one of America's earliest feminists and female editors. Despite early tragedies including the loss of her mother, sister, and husband, Hale rose to prominence in Boston and Philadelphia, advocating education and equal opportunity for women. She convinced President Abraham Lincoln to create Thanksgiving Day and penned the popular children's nursery rhyme "Mary Had a Little Lamb." Her birth home is on State Route 11, a few miles before you enter town, across the street from a once-famous woolen mill.

CONNECTICUT VALLEY TOWNS

For a look at the **Corbin Covered Bridge** drive through Newport's main street and continue north on State Route 10 for a mile or so, then turn left, passing the town airport and driving through a corridor of pine trees. The bridge at the edge was constructed as a copy to replace the original jewel, which was burned by a thoughtless arsonist in 1993. Such bridges are sprinkled throughout New England, their distinctive roofed design a way to delay the wood rotting in the absence of creosote protection. They were also, some say, a method of keeping horses drawing carriages from being spooked by rushing rivers below.

The craftsman who built this particular bridge was such a perfectionist he copied the original design and then hauled the bridge to its Sugar River home with an oxen team – both to transport it undamaged and to preserve a sense of history.

From central Newport, State Route 103 proceeds west through **Claremont**, previously a fading mill city that is redeveloping its old decaying riverside mill buildings. The historic Opera House located on Opera House Square, has year-round performances, from opera and theater to comedy and music. Just west of the city, the highway crosses the broad and picturesque Connecticut

A typical New England covered bridge, Vermont.

River dividing New Hampshire from its similar-sized (but very different-thinking) cousin, Vermont.

At **Ascutney**, on the far side of the river, the antenna-topped peak of Mount Ascutney fills the eye; Vermont 5 keeps it to one side and the broad Connecticut River to the other as it heads due north. Shortly thereafter, the road arrives in **Windsor ⓫**, a town that rightly claims to be the "Birthplace of Vermont." In Elijah West's tavern on Main Street, now known as **Old Constitution House** (tel: 802-672-3773; www.historicsites.vermont. gov/directory/old_constitution; late May–mid-Oct Sat–Sun), Vermont's Constitution was drafted and signed in 1777, making it for a time an independent republic that was neither British nor American. This independent streak still marks Vermonters today. In the 1990s, they elected and reelected a socialist and Independent, Bernie Sanders, to sit in the US House of Representatives. In 2005, Sanders became the first socialist senator, and in the 2016 election, he ran strongly against Senator Hillary Clinton in the race for the Democratic presidential nomination.

The **Simon Pearce** glassblowing shop (www.simonpearce.com), also in Windsor, may be one of the nation's finest such shops. The establishment also operates a restaurant and bar, The Mill at Simon Pearce, on Main Street in **Quechee**, where meals are served on glassware from the shop.

Still heading north on Vermont 5, you dip and curve riverside and soon enough come to **Norwich** (pronounced Nor-witch), a tiny, typical Vermont town with its classic general store, the first of many you'll see on this drive. **The Baker's Store** (www.kingarthurflour.com), run by King Arthur Flour, sells the famous company's superior stone-milled flour, top-grade cooking supplies and cookbooks, and delectable treats in its cafe/bakery at a light, bright and spacious wood-paneled store right off Vermont 5. Outside town, **Montshire Museum of Science** (tel: 802-649-2200; www. montshire.org; daily) provides children with a terrific hands-on look at ecology and nature amid riverside fields.

IVY-CLAD DARTMOUTH

Cross the Connecticut River into New Hampshire once more on State Route 120 to **Hanover**, an attractive town, largely thanks to the elegant, ivy-clad presence of **Dartmouth College**. Dartmouth was founded in 1769 by the Reverend Eleazer Wheelock to educate (and, of course, convert) local Native American children. Now, it is one of America's finest Ivy League colleges, with especially strong programs in the sciences, humanities, and Native American studies. The pleasing Dartmouth Green is a center of town life, surrounded on all sides by college buildings, including the **Hopkins Center for the Arts** (https://hop. dartmouth.edu), designed by Wallace K. Harrison, lead architect of New York's Lincoln Center and UN Headquarters.

The downtown district also features the excellent Dartmouth Bookstore,

Famous Dartmouth College alumni include Daniel Webster, Robert Frost, Theodore "Dr" Seuss, and Nelson Rockefeller.

Kids (and grownups) will love the tour of Ben & Jerry's ice-cream factory in Waterbury, Vermont.

It is estimated that hiking the entire length of the Appalachian Trail requires five million steps.

Killington Resort has reliably good snowfall and a long season.

as well as one of New England's most beloved natural food cooperatives. It is not unusual to see haggard, unshaven hikers lugging huge backpacks tramping through town, either, as the bridge from Norwich and downtown Hanover forms one of the most civilized stretches of the popular Appalachian Trail.

For a little more New England character before moving west, continue north on Vermont 5, which snuggles between the interstate and the river, mostly passing through dairy pastures and cornfields. Several of the small towns have interesting gathering spots, such as the Fairlee Diner in **Fairlee**, Vermont. Across a small bridge from Fairlee, in **Orford**, New Hampshire, beautiful white wooden and red brick homes from the early 1800s – not to mention the Orford Social Library and a general store full of local characters – line the town's main street. It was from here that local car salesman Mel Thomson rose to become a multi-term governor of the state, never straying from his extremely Republican view of things. **Mount Cube Sugar Farm** (daily),

in the hills east of Orford, down State Route 25A, has 9,000 taps and has been making organic maple syrup since 1952. It's a delicious taste of the region that should not be missed if you are in the area (and be sure to buy a jug to go, too – it's unrefined, filled with B vitamins, and a healthy sugar in moderation). Locals swear by it.

From Hanover, cross back to Vermont, and proceed a short distance south before turning west on US 4 at White River Junction. Nondescript little Quechee is primarily known for **Quechee Gorge**, "Vermont's Little Grand Canyon,"** a 165ft (50-meter) cut in the rock made by the Ottauquechee River. A bridge goes over the gorge, which is accessible from several viewpoints. Hiking and camping are available nearby in **Quechee State Park** (tel: 802-295-2990; www.vtstateparks.com/quechee; daily).

WOODSTOCK

Ten miles (16km) farther, and you come to compact **Woodstock** , which sits prettily among trees, ridges, and river. On an autumn afternoon, the town is jammed tightly with leaf-peepers touring the area to view the fall foliage, but early October is the time to come – an annual chili cook-off and apple festival, and other autumn events compete with the stunning foliage. From downtown, it is just a few paces to the handsome **Middle Bridge** covered bridge, which is located beside a row of exceptionally fine homes surrounding the village green.

Woodstock Historical Society leads tours of some of these homes. **Billings Farm & Museum** (tel: 802-457-2355; www.billingsfarm.org; May–Oct daily, Nov–Feb Sat–Sun) preserves and interprets a 19th-century dairy farm and **Vermont Institute of Natural Science** (tel: 802-359-5000; www.vinsweb.org; daily) is known for nursing birds of prey back to health. Don't miss **Marsh-Billings-Rockefeller National Historical Park** (tel: 802-457-3368; www.nps.gov/mabi;

grounds: daily, tours: June–Oct), a 500-acre (202-hectare) park that preserves the former home of famed botanist George Perkins Marsh, forester Frederick Billings, and philanthropist Laurance Rockefeller, who left the property to the National Park System. Just 2 miles (3km) west of town via US 4, the community of **West Woodstock** has a slightly less manicured feel. The seasonal White Cottage Snack Bar serves up fried clams, ice cream, and similar summertime snacks, while Woodstock Farmer's Market sells fresh local produce next door. Drive several more miles to **Bridgewater Corners**, home of Long Trail Brewing Company and its locally popular Long Trail Ale.

Turn left onto State Route 100A for a beautiful detour through some of the state's loveliest scenery – hay bales and maple syrup signs, red barns, spotted cows, and grazing horses: pure Vermont. The stretch is particularly beautiful when leaves are changing color. About 6 miles (10km) along, take a right onto the dirt drive for a look at **President Calvin Coolidge State Historic Site**

(tel: 802-672-3773; www.nps.gov/nr/travel/presidents/calvin_coolidge_homestead; late May–mid-Oct daily), the farm homestead where "silent Cal" was raised and to which he periodically returned.

When President Warren G. Harding died in office in 1923, Coolidge was sworn into office here by his father, a notary public. He remains to this day a hero to Vermonters, symbol of a kind of taciturn, humanistic work ethic that still drives Vermont farmers and politicians alike.

GREEN MOUNTAINS AND SOUTHERN VERMONT

Continue on State Route 100A until it ends at State Route 100, making a right and driving north. You pass numerous bed-and-breakfasts in the agreeable small towns; if you're in a hurry to get west, turn left where State Routes 100 and 4 split, at **Killington,** and cut through the scenic mountains to Rutland. Near this junction is where two of America's famous hiking trails – the **Appalachian Trail** ⓭ (see page 111) and Vermont's **Long Trail** – diverge. If

(see page 111)

> **⊙ Fact**
>
> Although Vermont had almost all of its timber removed in the late 19th century, more than 75 percent of the state's area is now forested.

Bright fall foliage heralds the "leaf-peeper" season.

⊙ APPALACHIAN TRAIL

A pleasant 19-mile (31km) drive along State Route 100A, then State Route 100, from the town of Bridgewater Corners, Vermont, leads to one of the longest marked trails in the world, winding a total of 2,178 miles (3,505km) from Maine to Georgia. Benton MacKaye, who proposed the trail in 1921, wrote about his great project: "The ultimate purpose? There are three things: 1) to walk; 2) to see; 3) to see what you see. Some people like to record how speedily they can traverse the length of the trail, but I would give a prize for the ones who took the longest time." His idea was for a super-trail running the length of the industrialized East Coast. This would be a trail that was wild, yet within reach of major urban centers and the throngs of workers who were alienated from outdoor life. He felt the trail would grace all who spent time on it with the healing tonic of wilderness.

Winding from north to south, it traverses the many distinct ranges that make up the Appalachian chain, touching the tops of many of the states it enters. Though it was not the first of its kind, the Appalachian Trail remains a favorite with outdoors people, enjoying celebrity status among the great hikes of the world. For more information, contact the Appalachian Trail Conservancy (tel: 304-535-6331 or visit www.appalachiantrail.org).

you continue north on State Route 100 for a short distance, you can park and take a short stroll on the trail to the left (through Gifford Woods State Park) or the right, around the shore of Kent Pond.

Heading north on State Route 100, continue through little **Stockbridge** until State Route 100 connects with State Route 125, then make a choice: food or nature? If you have a sweet tooth, continue north up State Route 100 to **Waterbury**, and take a tour of the Ben & Jerry's ice-cream factory. A more scenic route, however, is to turn left onto State Route 125 to begin 13 gorgeous miles (21km) of national forest land. You will discover why it's been designated a state scenic route as you wind through **Green Mountain National Forest** (www.fs.usda.gov/greenmountain). Partway along, just before **Ripton**, pull over for a peek at several Robert Frost—related sites.

Frost, one of America's best-loved poets, moved to this area and wrote his finest poetry in a farmhouse here. **Bread Loaf**, the complex of yellow buildings on the right, is a campus of Middlebury College that becomes an internationally

famous school of writing each summer; the yellow Bread Loaf Inn offers lodging on-site. The **Robert Frost Interpretive Trail**, on the left, combines passages from his writing with the typical elements – stone walls, maple trees – that inspired it. There are also a number of impressive hikes off the main road, clearly signposted, although to reach them requires driving some rough gravel and dirt roads. The twisty final miles of State Route 125 snake down the western slope of the Green Mountains beside the Middlebury River and must be driven carefully, but you are rewarded with a stunning view of the misty stacks of the Adirondacks as the route coasts down into the village of East Middlebury. At US 7, turn right and enter **Middlebury**, a college town with its own handsome buildings and microbrewery.

State Route 30 angles almost due south, and provides delightful driving through classic Vermont scenes of grazing spotted cows, rivers, red barns, and the like. You pass several quiet lakes with pleasant campgrounds, then **Pawlet**, where you'll find one of Vermont's best country stores, now called Mach's: among the wooden iceboxes of beer and stacks of rakes and rubber boots, you can actually see the brook running beneath the store through a grate. It was once a hotel, and there's a sepia 1900s photograph of dapper men with mustaches who once stayed at the place.

Next comes East Rupert, and then **Dorset ⓮**, an attractive town with a golf course and summer theater and classic New England homes, many of which are now bed-and-breakfasts.

SHOPPING, HISTORY, AND ART

Crowds begin appearing again in **Manchester**, a tourist-filled town nestled on the **Battenkill River**, one of the world's finest fly-fishing rivers. You can learn more at the **American Museum of Fly Fishing** (tel: 802-362-3300; www.amff.com; Tue–Sun), which displays the rods and gear of famous fishermen like

Race meet at Saratoga Race Course.

Hemingway and Eisenhower, among others. Not surprisingly, this is also home to the outdoor equipment and clothing manufacturer Orvis and numerous designer outlet stores.

Breeze through town and continue south down State Route 7A, here known as "Historic 7A," as it passes **Hildene** (tel: 802-362-1788; www.hildene.org; daily), the former home of Abraham Lincoln's son, Robert Todd Lincoln. This beautiful Georgian Revival mansion features a huge pipe organ. The road then takes in the pleasing ridge of **Mount Equinox**, especially stunning in fall. A toll road ascends to the summit, if you wish to drive it. Apple orchards, meadows, and cows continue to be the prevailing themes along State Route 7A.

At **Arlington** ⑮, you can have a look at the famed **Norman Rockwell Exhibit** at Sugar Shack (tel: 802-375-6747; www.sugarshackvt.com/norman-rockwell-exhibit; Feb–Dec daily), a collection of the artist's work. The artist lived in two homes in this area, and locals often served as models for his all-American portraits.

Turn west onto State Route 313, and as you leave Vermont, there's one final treat. Just before the New York state border, you pass the covered **West Arlington Bridge**, a small bridge over the Battenkill River with a typically plain New England church behind it, a composition Rockwell himself was said to have especially loved. These are a local specialty, and as this is the last one you'll see on this cross-country trip, linger awhile, contemplating the river and the lush beauty of New England.

NEW YORK STATE

As you greet the sign welcoming you to the state of **New York**, you have not only crossed a line on a map separating one state from another, you have also crossed an imaginary but no less real boundary, where yard sales at once become "tag sales," tonic water becomes "soda," and an Empire State mindset takes over from the "think small" Vermont mentality.

Entering the Hudson Valley, you'll also discover a history forged by Dutch settlers rather than New England Yankees.

Entering on State Route 313, you arrive shortly at a pleasant picnic spot beside the Battenkill River. Then you pass through **Cambridge**, a small town with antiques and an attractive little general store, more form than function these days. You'll also pass the Cambridge Hotel, built in 1885, self-proclaimed home of "pie à la mode." Change to State Route 372, join State Route 29, and continue driving west. Ten or 12 miles (16 to 19km) on, the road crosses the **Hudson River** at Schuylerville, unimpressive here since it's split into so many parts; in fact, the great river seems tame indeed – there is no hint yet of the power and beauty that will soon fill a great valley and inspire countless artists.

It was only a few miles downstream from these banks that the two Battles of Saratoga were fought in 1777, resulting in a crushing defeat of British troops – a crucial momentum swing in the Revolution. A turnoff leads to **Saratoga National Historical Park** (tel:

⊙ Fact

The illustrator Norman Rockwell (1894–1978) was known for his realistic and humorous scenes of small-town life. His best work appeared as covers for the magazine *The Saturday Evening Post*.

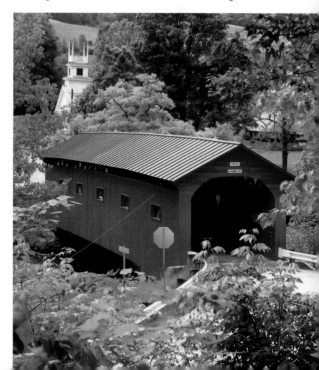

West Arlington covered bridge.

Fresh spring water from Saratoga Springs.

The impressive 16-sided Nott Memorial Building on Schenectady's Union College campus integrates symbols from major world religions.

518-670-2985; www.nps.gov/sara; battle-field: daily, tour road: Apr–Nov daily), commemorating the battles, where you can drive or be guided through the fields.

Continue to **Saratoga Springs** N, long a resort town due to the mineral springs that bubble up beneath it and more recently a popular weekend town. It is also home to Skidmore College students and faculty, and thus a fair number of coffeehouses, ice-cream shops, and bookstores speckle the downtown district. Saratoga Perform-ing Arts Center, within a green park on the southern edge of town, frequently hosts big-name concerts. Summertime also brings crowds to the harness track here, where horse racing is king – wit-ness the presence here of the **National Museum of Racing and Hall of Fame** (tel: 800-JOCKEY4; www.racingmuseum.org; racing season daily, Sept–Dec and Mar–July Wed–Sun). Finally, don't miss **Caffé Lena** (www.caffelena.org), an upstairs joint on a central street, which is said to have been the first American coffeehouse to host regular folk music performances in 1960. It still does.

ERIE CANAL

State Route 50 brings you south through Ballston Spa, home of the eccentric **National Bottle Museum** (tel: 518-885-7589; http://nationalbottlemuseum.org; June–Sept Fri-Tue, Oct–Dec and Mar–May Tue–Sat), to the Mohawk River and the Erie Canal. Tracing this great inland water route west to Buf-falo is not the shortest way to get from here to there, but it is a route that runs rich with American history.

The idea of a canal connecting the port cities of Albany (on the Hudson River) and Buffalo (on Lake Erie) was greeted with skepticism and derision at first. Detrac-tors called it "Clinton's Ditch" after New York Governor DeWitt Clinton, champion of the project. Completed in 1825, and eventually bypassed in the early 20th century, the Erie Canal was responsible for the settling of the Midwest and the rise of the state of New York. The old canal towns, once the sites of boister-ous activity, are quiet now, many down on their luck.

Begin tracing the route in **Schenec-tady** O. A plaque in this town sums up its early history: "Settled by Van Curler 1661. Burned by French and Indians Feb 8, 1690."

Because it was the farthest west of all Dutch settlements in the New World, the town's settlers built a stockade around the land, which was bounded by the Mohawk River and a branch called the Binne Kill. The stockade is now gone, dismantled during the American Revolution, but the area it protected is still known as the **Stockade** and is now a historic district containing an eclectic array of buildings that spans over three centuries of American life.

Schenectady's strategic riverfront location has historically made it an important center for commerce and transportation. The city supplied Revo-lutionary troops battling in the Mohawk Valley, and in the 19th century it was a major port. In 1931, it became the ter-minus of the nation's first passenger steam train, the "DeWitt Clinton," an innovation stimulated by the protracted process of traversing the 23 locks between Albany and Schenectady.

Schenectady has not been exempt from the exodus of industry out of the Northeast. In the 19th century, it progressed from being a center for the manufacture of brooms to "the city that lights and hauls the world." The Schenectady Locomotive Works (later the American Locomotive Company) opened in 1851, followed by Edison and his Machine Works, which later became General Electric. The Locomotive Company pulled out of town in 1969, but the lights are still switched on at GE.

LEATHERSTOCKING TRAILS

New York's heartland is generally considered to begin west of the industrial triangle of Albany, Troy, and Schenectady. This essentially rural area north of the Catskill Mountains and south of the Adirondacks is also known as the **Leatherstocking District**, after the protective garb once worn by trailblazers. Native son James Fenimore Cooper immortalized the region in his *Leatherstocking Tales* and other works. And the numerous Revolutionary War battles that took place throughout the Mohawk River Valley are the subject of Walter D. Edmonds' historical novel *Drums along the Mohawk*.

Schenectady's Broadway leaves town in a southwesterly direction (State Route 7). It passes through Rotterdam and Duanesburg, where State Route 7, US 20, and I-88 converge. From there, US 20 travels to **Esperance** on Schoharie Creek. This pleasant town features old houses, antique shops, and the obligatory country store. About 8 miles (13km) south of here, along State Route 30, which follows the creek, is the town of **Schoharie**, the third-oldest village in upstate New York. The **Old Stone Fort Museum Complex** (tel: 518-295-7192; www.theoldstonefort.org; May–Oct daily) started as a church in 1772, became a fort during the Revolution, and has served as museum and library specializing in early Americana since 1889.

An interesting chapter out of Schoharie's past includes the Middleburgh and Schoharie Railroad, built in the late 1860s. This 5.7-mile (9.2km) train run down the Schoharie Creek Valley transported hops and other local products. The railroad's president was fond of pointing out that although it wasn't as long as other railroads, it was just as wide. In its last days, the line's single locomotive faltered physically and financially, and operation was finally stopped in 1936.

A SHRINE TO BASEBALL

US 20 west of Sharon and Sharon Springs is one of the loveliest stretches of road in central New York, providing a panoramic view of **Cherry Valley**, the site of an infamous massacre in 1778, now crimson only in autumn.

It would be a mistake not to detour 10 miles (16km) south at Springfield Center down State Route 80 to visit **Cooperstown ⑱**, a charming town with several important attractions. Fenimore Art

Actors by the encampment tents at a Revolutionary War re-enactment in Mohawk Valley.

Museum (tel: 607-547-1400; www.fenimor eartmuseum.org; Apr–mid-May, Oct–Dec Tue–Sun, mid-May–early Oct daily) and Farmers Museum (tel: 607-547-1450; www.farmersmuseum.org; mid-May–mid-Oct daily, Apr–mid-May and mid-Oct–end Oct Tue–Sat) are worthwhile, but the main draw is the **National Baseball Hall of Fame** (tel: 888-HALL-OF-FAME, 607-547-7200; www.baseballhall.org; daily), a tremendous experience, which highlights the history of the sport, one that has inspired countless novels, films, and even poems. Make time for a visit to the monuments, biographies, and collections here.

Past **Richfield Springs**, known for its sulfur springs and fossil-hunting grounds, State Route 167 travels north toward **Little Falls**. Not far up this road stands the **Russian Orthodox Holy Trinity Monastery** (tel: 315-858-0940; www.jordanville.org; overnight visits to the guesthouse by arrangement), startling to the eye in a land of Colonial history, 19th-century buildings, and rustic farmhouses. Little Falls' **Herkimer Home**, former residence

Patriotic Paul Revere mural in Rome, New York state.

of Revolutionary War hero Brigadier General Nicholas Herkimer, provides a glimpse of Colonial life, with maple syrup tapping, sheep shearing, and other exhibitions. This canal town once had the world's highest lock, at 41ft (12.5 meters).

West along State Route 5 is Herkimer, named after Nicholas Herkimer, the Revolutionary War general whose statue still commands attention. **Herkimer County Courthouse** was the site of the Gillette murder trial, which inspired Theodore Dreiser to write *An American Tragedy*, depicting the dark side of the American dream. George Stevens' film version, *A Place in the Sun*, featured Montgomery Clift, Shelley Winters, and Elizabeth Taylor. Between Herkimer and **Mohawk** along State Route 5S, stands the **Fort Herkimer Church**, built in 1730.

Ilion, a small industrial pocket, is located just beyond Mohawk. The interesting **Remington Arms Museum** (tel: 315-895-3200; Mon–Fri) here is devoted to the great guns made by Remington Arms Company, past and present. Continuing west, the road terminates in **Utica** ⑳, the only city of any size you will have seen since Schenectady.

Utica, once named Fort Schuyler, is rich in Colonial and Revolutionary history. But the biggest attraction here is the **Munson-Williams-Proctor Arts Institute** (tel: 315-797-0000; www.mwpai. org; Tue–Sun), reputed to have one of the finest collections of 18th- through 20th-century American and European art in the northeast, housed in a building designed by Philip Johnson. On a much less cultural note, Utica's **Saranac Brewery** (tel: 315-624-2490; www.saranac.com tours: June–Aug Mon–Sat, Sept–May Fri–Sat) serves its microbrewed beer in a Victorian tavern built in 1888. It's all part of a brewery tour that culminates in a trolley ride to the tavern.

ERIE CANAL VILLAGE

Route 69 leaves Utica for **Rome** ㉑, best known for its crucial role in the building of the Erie Canal. Beyond this point, there were no continuous natural water routes westward. This is where excavation began. The canal brought industry to Rome, some of which remains. Rome has always been serious about America: this, after all, is where native son Francis Bellamy wrote the famous "Pledge of Allegiance" that every American school child learns by heart.

Route 46 takes you from Rome to **Oneida**, home to the Oneida Indian Nation. The Oneida Community – associated with this town, but actually just southeast in Sherrill – was established in the mid-19th century by John Humphrey Noyes and his followers. Calling themselves perfectionists, they adhered to a strict sexual code as part of a community-determined system of selective breeding. In their spare time, they produced high-quality silver-plated flatware. The community was dissolved in 1881, but the silver-plate business continues to thrive.

From Oneida, **Chittenango** is a short drive along State Route 5. Don't be surprised, in town, to see a yellow brick sidewalk, for this is "**Oztown, USA**." The sidewalk is a tribute to L. Frank Baum, author of the beloved *Wizard of Oz*. Route 5 will lead right into Syracuse, the biggest city for miles around.

FINGER LAKES

Busy **Syracuse** ㉒ is the urban gateway to the Finger Lakes. State Route 5 becomes Erie Boulevard as it cuts through the heart of the city along a path carved by the Erie Canal. The **Weighlock Building**, built in 1849 in the Greek Revival style, once weighed canal boats for the purpose of toll collection. At the turn of the 20th century, it was converted into an office building. In its most recent reincarnation, it serves as the **Erie Canal Museum** (tel: 315-471-0593; www.eriecanalmuseum.org; daily).

Thanks to the canal, this was once a center for the salt trade, and some still refer to it as "Salt City." The town boomed during the 19th and early 20th centuries on the back of salt and other industries, and its well-preserved architecture testifies to former prosperity. The **Landmark Theatre** (tel: 315-475-7979; www.landmarktheatre.org), an ornate "fantasy palace" built in the 1920s, now functions as an entertainment center. But the main draw here is **Syracuse University**, on a hill above the city, which brings crowds of students, sports fans, and other audiences to its huge **Carrier Dome** (www.carrierdome. com). Basketball games are especially well attended, though football games and rock concerts follow a close second. For more cerebral pursuits, visit the on-campus **SUArt Galleries** (tel: 315-443-4097; http://suart.syr.edu; mid-Aug–June) in Shaffer Hall, which offers enjoyable exhibits such as 2018's Rodin: The Human Experience. Or check out **The Everson Museum of Art** (tel: 315-474-6064; www.everson.org; Wed–Sun), designed by renowned architect I.M. Pei and dedicated to all American art. State Route 5 leaves Syracuse on its way to **Camillus**, where you can canoe

⊙ **Eat**

Try a *pustie* (short for *pasticciotti*, an Italian custard-filled tart), one of Utica, New York's signature dishes.

The village of Cooperstown.

⊙ Tip

"I would make a home for them in the North, and the Lord helping me, I would bring them all here."

Harriet Tubman

and kayak to your heart's content along 7 miles (11km) of navigable canal in **Camillus-Erie Canal Park**. Farther along, State Route 5 merges with US 20, a route that strings together the northern tips of the largest **Finger Lakes**.

The Finger Lakes consist of 11 long, thin glacial lakes carved during the Ice Age. Famed for its vineyards, the Finger Lake region is particularly photogenic when the vines turn copper in late summer and can best be appreciated from a hot-air balloon. Other pleasures include water sports and many gracious inns. **Auburn**, on US 20/State Route 5, is home to **Harriet Tubman National Historical Park** (tel: 315-882-8060; www.nps.gov/hart; daily), designated in 2017 to preserve the former home of Harriet Tubman, the escaped slave who founded the Underground Railroad, a freedom network that spirited slaves out of the South. She was an uncommon woman, and it's quite inspiring to spend time here.

SENECA LAKE

After Auburn, US 20/State Route 5 passes Cayuga Lake and follows the Seneca River to **Seneca Falls ㉓**, where the first Women's Rights Convention was convened and is now a designated **Women's Rights National Historical Park** (tel: 315-568-0024; www.nps.gov/wori; daily) protecting a number of important historic sites, including the Elizabeth Cady Stanton Home, the Wesleyan Chapel, the Waterfall at Declaration Park, and the McClintock House. To plan your visit with rangers, stop at the visitor center on Fall Street. Don't miss the **National Women's Hall of Fame** (tel: 315-568-8060; www.womenofthehall.org; June–Aug daily, Sept–May Wed–Sat), which highlights women's accomplishments and makes a good complement to the other sites here. **Waterloo**, between the Finger Lakes, prides itself on being the birthplace of Memorial Day. The road passes by the old Scythe Tree, upon which local farm boys planted their scythes on their way to wars past.

The jewel of **Seneca Lake** is the town of **Geneva ㉔**, known for its elegant inns and mansions and for its Seneca Lake Wine Trail (tel: 607-535-8080; www.senecalakewine.com), which visits 35 vineyards, including four specializing in sparkling wine and mead (honey wine). It is pretty in fall, when the grape and maple leaves are changing color. Seneca Lake may seem small and thin, but it's actually one of the deepest freshwater lakes in the world, reaching a depth of more than 600ft (180 meters). The US Navy used the lake to test depth charges during World War II.

Approximately 20 miles (32km) west of Geneva, on US 20/Route 20, is **Canandaigua**, at the northern tip of Canandaigua Lake. Of interest here is the Federal-style **Granger Homestead and Carriage Museum ㉕** (tel: 585-394-1472; www.grangerhomestead.org; late May–late Oct Tue–Sun), built in 1816, with its collection of nearly 70 horse-drawn vehicles. North of town – take State Route 21 – is **Sonnenberg Gardens & Mansion State Historic Park** (tel: 585-394-4922; www.

International Museum of Photography and Film.

sonnenberg.org; May–Oct daily), which offers nine formal gardens, a Queen Anne–style mansion, and Finger Lakes Wine Center in historic Bay House, showcasing gourmet foods and wines from 40 local purveyors and a tasting bar in the cellar.

State Route 21 passes through Shortsville on the way to **Palmyra**. Members of the Church of Latter Day Saints, or Mormons, make pilgrimages to this town because it is the site of the Smith Family Farm (tel: 315-597-1671; daily), the boyhood home of first Mormon prophet Joseph Smith who, according to Mormon belief, received and translated ancient records in the Book of Mormon, buried the tablets in nearby woods known as the Sacred Grove, and founded the LDS Church in the 1820s. For more information, stop at **Hill Cumorah Visitor Center** (tel: 315-597-5851; daily), which is run by the LDS for information on other LDS sites here including the 1850 Martin Harris Farm a cobblestone house typical of gentleman farmers' homes that sprang up along the Erie Canal.

It is approximately 20 miles (32km) from Palmyra to Rochester along State Route 31. The names of the towns along the way are perhaps more exotic than the towns: after Palmyra comes Macedon and then Egypt, where the New York State Barge Canal stands in for the Nile.

ROCHESTER

Like other upstate cities, **Rochester** ㉖ thrived during the canal era and suffered economically with the advent of alternative modes of transportation. But it has adjusted to change better than its siblings and is on the upswing as a center for high-tech industries, while continuing to preserve much of its 19th-century architectural ambiance. Eastman Kodak, struggling since the advent of digital photography, is still a presence here, as is Xerox Corporation.

The former mansion of George Eastman, who founded Kodak, now houses the **George Eastman Museum** (tel: 585-327-4800; www.eastman.org; Tue–Sun), the world's oldest photography museum, devoted to the history of this art and science. The **Eastman School of Music** (tel: 585-274-1000; www.esm. rochester.edu) sponsors musical events, from jazz to rock to folk to symphonic works, while the **Eastman Theatre** is the home of the Rochester Philharmonic (www.rpo.org). For those in touch with their inner child, the **Strong National Museum of Play** (tel: 585-263-2700; www.museumofplay.org; daily) has one of the most extensive collections of dolls and toys in the world, in addition to a butterfly garden and coral reef aquarium. Winters are severe in Rochester, thanks to its northern location on Lake Ontario, the easternmost Great Lake. But in spring, when **Highland Park** is in bloom, Rochester is as colorful as one of Kodak's Kodachrome slides. During May, the park (which bills itself as the "Lilac Capital of the World") is the setting for the Lilac Festival featuring the world's largest display of these blossoms.

Clinton Square in Syracuse, New York state.

ON TO THE FALLS

State Route 31 continues along the path of the Erie Canal from Rochester to Niagara Falls. The names of the towns along this route, including Spencerport, Brockport, Middleport, and Gasport, continue to remind the traveler of the canal's former importance. But there are other reminders as well. **Medina ㉗** has its cobblestone buildings and Culvert Road, which passes beneath the canal. **Lockport** also has its share of cobblestone houses, though it is best known for its magnificent flight of five locks.

From Lockport, Route 31 (here called Saunders Settlement Road) travels directly to **Niagara Falls ㉘**. Once known as America's "Honeymoon Capital," the town is fond of referring to itself as an international tourist destination. And, indeed, it remains one of the top tourist draws in all the US, despite its endless tackiness. Quite simply, the 700,000 gallons (3 million liters) of water plummeting from top to bottom each second here are a wondrous assault on the senses, something that must be experienced while in America. The magnetic draw of these falls has even inspired some visitors to attempt crossing them on a tightrope or riding them in a barrel, with sometimes-tragic results; both activities are now illegal, though daredevils still occasionally try.

The natural beauty of the site might have been irreparably compromised had it not been for the efforts of landscape architect Frederick Law Olmsted, landscape painter Frederic Church, and others. Their "Free Niagara" (from commercialism) campaign resulted in the establishment of the Niagara Reservation in 1885. One of the best ways to experience the falls today is by donning the provided foul-weather gear and taking a boat ride on the *Maid of the Mist*. Make sure you have your passport with you in the border region (a good idea for US citizens as well as overseas visitors in this era of frequent Border Control checks within 100 miles of the borders now), you might drive across the river to Canada and enjoy what many consider to be a superior view.

River Road hugs the eastern branch of the Niagara River, past the falls, and through an industrial landscape to **Buffalo ㉙**. As with other industrial giants past their prime, New York's second-largest city has acquired a somewhat bad reputation. As the 19th-century terminus of the Erie Canal, Buffalo once served as a funnel through which raw materials, cash, pioneers, and immigrant labor flowed into the Midwest. Today, it is a bit ragged. Nevertheless, there are reasons to stop for a visit. Landmarks include the 398-ft art deco City Hall, the Frank Lloyd Wright–designed Darwin D. Martin House, and the Albright-Knox Art Gallery, a Greek Revival museum with works by Picasso and Warhol. You can also eat well and cheaply here. A local specialty is spicy chicken wings, which anywhere else are called "Buffalo wings," but here are "wings." The owner of the Anchor Bar is said to have invented the dish.

Seneca Lake.

Niagara Falls and the famous
Maid of the Mist boat tour.

Beach volleyball on Chicago's lakefront.

BUFFALO TO THE BADLANDS

Follow the shores of Lake Erie into New York, Pennsylvania, and Ohio, then continue through the Midwest and the Great Lakes to the starkly beautiful hills of the Badlands.

Buffalo was an important point of departure for 19th-century settlers heading for the Midwest. From Buffalo, they traveled to major ports of the Great Lakes in order to start their new life. Today, the road from Buffalo to the Midwestern states follows the shore of Lake Erie through New York, Pennsylvania, and Ohio. Although known primarily as an industrial area, there are still some unspoiled stretches of coastline that are remarkable for their beauty. At Toledo, the highway diverges from the shoreline on its way to big, busy, beautiful Chicago.

South of Buffalo, along US 62, is the town of **Hamburg**, where the hamburger – perhaps America's greatest contribution to world cuisine – was purportedly invented in 1885. In celebration of the centennial of this event, J. Wellington Wimpy came to town and was honored as the undefeated hamburger-eating champion of the world. Essentially a rural town, Hamburg has been host to America's largest county fair since 1868. It's only about 5 miles (8km) from here to Lake Erie, where you can pick up State Route 5, a lakeside road that takes you to Ohio.

ANTIQUE TRAIL

Lake Erie has suffered more than its sister Great Lakes at the hands of industry, yet miles of its beautiful, sandy, ocean-like shoreline are still unspoiled. The stretch from Silver Creek, New York, to the Pennsylvania border is designated New York Antique Trail (www.antiquetrail.com) for its abundance of antique shops.

State Route 5 takes you past terrain blanketed with grapevines and other fruit trees. In **Silver Creek**, go straight to the site of the **Skew Arch Railroad Bridge** on Jackson Street. Built on an angle in 1869, it is one of only two such bridges in the world.

Dunkirk and Fredonia follow, in the heart of the Lake Erie Concord Grape

⊙ Main attractions
Lake Erie State Park
Chain O'Lakes State Park
Chicago
Taliesin
Walker Art Center
Minnesota State Fair
Corn Palace
Badlands National Park

Map on page 124

Chicago Cubs fans.

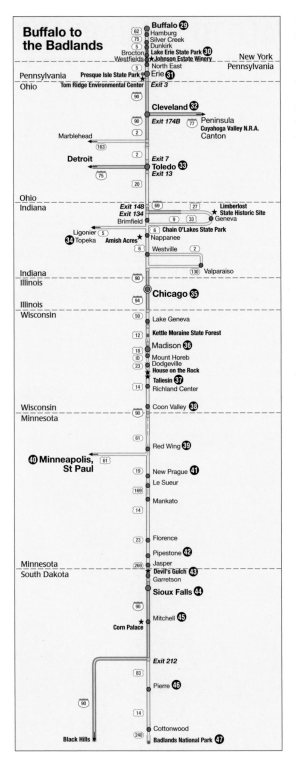

Buffalo to the Badlands

Buffalo **29**
62
75 Hamburg
Silver Creek
5 Dunkirk
Brocton Lake Erie State Park **30**
Westfields ★ Johnson Estate Winery New York
5 North East Pennsylvania
Presque Isle State Park ★ Erie **31**
Pennsylvania
Ohio Tom Ridge Environmental Center *Exit 3*
90

Cleveland **32**
90 *Exit 174B* 77 Peninsula
Marblehead 2 Cuyahoga Valley N.R.A.
163 Canton
2
Detroit 2 *Exit 7*
75 Toledo **33**
20 *Exit 13*

Ohio
Indiana
Exit 148 69 27 Limberlost
Exit 134 ★ State Historic Site
Brimfield 9 33 Geneva
Ligonier 5 6 Chain O'Lakes State Park
34 Topeka Amish Acres★ Nappanee
6 Westville 2

Indiana
Illinois
90 130 Valparaiso

Illinois
Wisconsin
94 Chicago **35**
50 Lake Geneva
12 Kettle Moraine State Forest
18 Madison **36**
10 Mount Horeb
23 Dodgeville
House on the Rock
14 Taliesin **37**
Richland Center

Wisconsin
Minnesota
90 Coon Valley **38**

61
Red Wing **39**
40 Minneapolis, 61
St Paul 19 New Prague **41**
Le Sueur
169
Mankato
14

23 Florence
Pipestone **42**
Minnesota 269 Jasper
South Dakota Devil's Gulch **43**
Garretson
Sioux Falls **44**
90
Mitchell **45**
★
Corn Palace

Exit 212
83
Pierre **46**
90
14
Cottonwood
Black Hills 240 Badlands National Park **47**

Belt (the world's largest; www.grape discoverycenter.com), which extends into Pennsylvania. **Dunkirk**, with its natural harbor, is a center for boating as well as winemaking. **Fredonia**, to the south, is home to the Fredonia campus of the State University of New York, which was co-designed and modernized in the late 1960s by renowned architects I.M. Pei and Henry N. Cobb.

Continuing along the lake, the road passes pretty **Lake Erie State Park 30** (tel: 716-792-9214; http://parks.NY.gov/ parks/129; campground reservations www.reserveamerica.com; May–Oct; daily) in **Brocton**, which has beautiful lakeside campsites and cabins by reservation May through October. **Westfield** follows, calling itself "The Grape Juice Capital of the World" and dominated by the various production facilities of a popular grape jelly and grape juice. Combined with peanut butter and two pieces of bread, the peanut butter and jelly sandwich vies with Hamburg's hamburgers as *the* American food.

There is no obvious transition between New York and its westerly neighbor, Pennsylvania. The landscape remains the same – a sparkling lake on one side and lush vineyards on the other. In season, roadside stands sell the local grapes in every imaginable form. Only 63 miles (101km) of Lake Erie shoreline prevent Pennsylvania from being a landlocked state (an economic decision to do with lake access), and it knows just what to do with it. Past the state line is the town of **North East**, center of the state's tiny wine industry (www.lakeeriewinecountry.org). Twenty boutique wineries now operate here and all offer tours and tastings. New York's oldest winery, Johnson Estate Winery (http://johnsonwinery.com) in Westfield, is a good bet.

About 15 miles (24km) west of Lake Erie Wine Country, on State Route 5 sits the city of **Erie 31**. It was off these shores that Commander Oliver Hazard Perry's fleet defeated the British in the Battle of Lake Erie during the War of

1812. Despite his motto – "Don't give up the ship!" – flagship *Niagara* was left to sink in what later became known as **Misery Bay**. That bay is now a quiet fishing cove off Presque Isle, and the ship was rescued a century later. A reconstructed *Niagara* is now docked behind **Erie Maritime Museum** (tel: 814-452-2744; www.flagshipniagara.org; Apr–Sept daily, Oct Mon–Sat, Nov–Mar Thu–Sat). When the flagship is docked here, guided tours are included with museum admission, but note: its sailing schedule is active in summer.

On the other side is Erie's finest physical feature, **Presque Isle** (www. goerie.com/presque-isle), a claw of land – an island, really – reaching out into the lake. You can drive its length, pass Presque Isle Lighthouse, and do a loop around the southern end passing Misery Bay. You'll find lovely sand beaches, wooded trails, fishing holes, and lazy lagoons. While in Presque Isle, visit Tom Ridge Environmental Center (tel: 814-833-7424; www.trecpi.org; daily), which offers interactive exhibits on the natural history of the region as well as a big

screen theater screening documentaries on environmental issues. Due south of Erie is Pittsburgh, the quintessential American city, so eloquently recalled in Pulitzer Prize–winning writer Annie Dillard's memoir *An American Childhood*.

CLEVELAND

Before you can say "knee high by the Fourth of July," you're in Ohio. I-90 cuts through the gently rolling farmland of this part of the state, past Ashtabula, Geneva, and Euclid before reaching the **Cleveland ㉜** area. Cleveland has its share of high culture – the Cleveland Orchestra and its home, Severance Hall, as well as the **Cleveland Museum of Art** (tel: 216-421-7350; www.clevelandart.org; Tue–Sun) – and pop culture – the **Rock and Roll Hall of Fame** (tel: 216-781-ROCK; www.rockhall.com; daily). The latter covers everyone from Louis Jordan to John Lennon, with exhibits including report cards and Jim Morrison's Cub Scout uniform. And let's not forget the **Museum of Contemporary Art** (tel: 216-421-8671; www. mocacleveland.org; Tue–Sat) located in a modern mirrored structure at University

Cleveland skyscrapers catch the setting sun.

Circle and designed by renowned London architect Farshid Moussavi. Popular American chef Michael Symon hails from Cleveland and has three award-winning restaurants here.

It's well worth a short detour south from Cleveland to explore the green **Cuyahoga Valley National Park** (www.nps.gov/cuva). The valley's ridges were settled during the late 18th century by the New Englanders who first surveyed its boundaries, and their influence remains today.

PRO FOOTBALL HALL OF FAME

Sport fans will want to make a brief detour south down I-77, through Akron – tire and rubber capital of America – to the city of **Canton**. Here, the **Pro Football Hall of Fame** (tel: 330-456-8207; www.profootballhof.com; daily) offers a look at the heroes of American football. Things peak in August, when an annual game is played here to kick off each season and to celebrate the new class of inductees.

State Route 2 leaves Cleveland on its way west, diverging from I-90 and running closer to Lake Erie. At Ceylon it comes right to the lake, loops around Sandusky, then bridges Sandusky Bay to arrive on the Marblehead Peninsula. State Route 163 takes you out to land's end and reveals the peninsula as a slightly rundown but refreshingly unpretentious place, full of lively harbors, the African adventure–themed Kalahari Waterpark Resort, orchards, and fruit stands. At its rocky tip is **Marblehead Lighthouse** (www.marbleheadlighthouseohio.org), which has been in continuous use since 1822, longer than any other beacon on the Great Lakes. The quaint Kelleys Island is a 20-minute ferry ride from Marblehead and offers boating, swimming, wineries, and even the South Shore Historic District, which was placed on the National Register of Historic Places in 1975. Looking back south across the bay, you'll see the roller coasters of **Cedar Point** (tel: 419-627-2350; www.cedarpoint.com; mid-May–Aug daily, Sept–Oct Sat–Sun), a popular 364-acre (147-hectare) amusement park in Sandusky. Off the Marblehead Peninsula, State Route 2 proceeds toward Toledo. This region was once part of the **Great Black Swamp**, a glacially fed wetland refuge for wildlife, from Sandusky to Detroit. Small remnants have managed to survive along this route.

TOLEDO

The road emerges from the swamp and continues straight as an arrow to the town of **Toledo** ㉝, past bait shops, drive-through liquor stores and drive-in movie theaters. The "Toledo Strip" was once the subject of a border dispute between Ohio and Michigan. When Ohio got the Strip, Michigan got its Upper Peninsula from Wisconsin Territory as compensation.

Toledo seems like an industrial wasteland, but it has its moments. Internationally renowned **Toledo Museum of Art** (www.toledomuseum.org; Tues–Sun) has a terrific collection of modern and Renaissance art, while

An Indiana farm.

's Glass Pavilion showcases Toledo's fame as a glass production center (Owens Corning Glass Company is headquartered here) and exhibits thousands of glass works. Signs of redevelopment can be found in the downtown riverfront area along the Maumee River. On the east side is the Hungarian neighborhood of Birmingham when you'll find Tony Packo's Café – made famous by Corporal Max Klinger in the long-running TV series *M*A*S*H* – which is known for authentic Hungarian food and a quirky collection of hot dog buns autographed by celebrities.

Leaving Toledo and Lake Erie behind, US 20 heads west, straight through Ohio farm country to the Indiana border, a distance of about 60 miles (100km). The road parallels the Michigan border, just a few miles to the north.

INDIANA

They call **Indiana** the Hoosier state, and native Indianans Hoosiers. Some say the name comes from a common inquiry from the pioneer days, "Who's

yer?" Others say the nickname comes from a canal-builder named Samuel Hoosier, who liked to hire Indiana men over other workers; the workers became known as Hoosiers, and the name stuck. (There was even a film called *Hoosiers* – widely considered one of the best sports films ever made – which told the story of an Indiana high school basketball team that wins the state championship.) Whatever the origin of the name, this state has produced such high-profile celebrity residents as basketball star Larry Bird, singer John Mellencamp, and television talk show host David Letterman.

HISTORIC STATE PARKS

Ten miles (16km) inside the state, at Angola, leave US 20 for I-69S fifteen miles (24km) later, cut over to US 6, which will carry you westward through northern Indiana to Illinois. Fields of golden grain (mostly corn) and silos announce it: you are solidly in the Midwest now. Driving I-69 south toward Fort Wayne, hop on State Route 27 south to **Limberlost State Historic Site** (tel:

Marblehead Lighthouse on Lake Erie.

Michigan Avenue's brick road in Detroit.

⊘ DETOUR TO DETROIT

A 45-mile (72km) drive beside Lake Erie on I-75 leads from Toledo to Detroit, Michigan, better known as Motor City. Henry Ford was the single most influential American in motoring history, forming the Ford Motor Company in 1903. Six years later, he had 10,000 orders for his newest car, the Model T, and, by 1919, was selling close to a million cars. His innovations bolstered Detroit's economy, increased the automobile's popularity, and gave people jobs. Ford was shaken by the global financial crisis and business remains volatile. The 260-acre (105-hectare) Henry Ford Museum of American Innovation (www.thehenryford.org) and Greenfield Village complex in nearby Dearborn is the world's largest indoor/outdoor museum and highlights Ford's contribution to the city. The Museum exhibits Ford's collection of early automobiles and airplanes, while Greenfield Village houses recreations of famous businesses and residences, including Thomas Edison's Menlo Park laboratory. Detroit is also famously home to Motown records, created by former Ford assembly line worker Berry Gordy, Jr, in 1958, which produced stars of the Detroit Sound, such as Smokey Robinson and Diana Ross. Motown Museum (www.motownmuseum.org) in "Hitsville USA," former Motown HQ, charts the label's rise, from the 1960s to present. For information, contact Detroit Metro Convention and Visitors Bureau (tel: 800-338-7648; www.visitdetroit.com).

⊙ Fact

The Amish splintered off from Swiss Anabaptists in 1693 and settled in Pennsylvania. Now nearly half the states in the US have communities, and the number of followers is growing.

260-368-7428; www.indianamuseum.org/limberlost-state-historic-site; mid-Apr–mid-Dec Tue–Sun, mid-Dec–mid-Apr Tue–Sat), a log cabin in Limberlost Swamp in Geneva, where Gene Stratton-Porter lived and wrote her well-loved books and essays about northern Indiana's natural history. It's a peaceful spot among trees on a lake, perfect for a picnic.

Head back north to Fort Wayne, where you can catch State Route 33 north to State Route 9 north, which takes you to **Chain O' Lakes State Park**, a string of refreshing oases in the middle of Noble County.

INDIANA'S AMISH COUNTRY

Back on US 6, tiny towns punctuate a landscape known for its productivity considerable Amish population, which has been in this area for more than a century. These inventive, industrious, and deeply religious people go about their business while shunning worldly things such as buttons, zippers, electricity, and motor vehicles. Cut north up State Route 5 for a look at their farms, homes, and horse-drawn buggies. Be respectful: most Amish do not like to have their photo taken as they believe it is an act of pride. It's also a good idea to drive slowly while in Amish country as you never know when a horse-drawn buggy might round the corner.

Ligonier is a quaint small town known for its Jewish heritage. It has an attractive Main Street and a number of handsome Victorian mansions. The town clock was erected by John Cavin, son of pioneer Isaac Cavin, who laid out the town in 1835. **Ligonier Historical Museum** (tel: 260-894-9000; May–Oct Tue–Sat) is in a former one-room Jewish temple, one of the few surviving 19th-century synagogues in the US. Exhibits include items from now-shuttered Wilkinson Quilt Factory and the original Kidd's Marshmallow Company (Ligonier's Marshmallow Festival is held every Labor Day) and a dozen antique radios on loan from Indiana Historical Radio Society.

Continue north on State Route 5 and then turn right at a gas station to reach **Topeka** ③④, a tiny town whose slogan is "Life in the Past Lane." It's the kind of place where Amish buggies line up in parking lots and hardware and feed stores outnumber banks three to one. The Amish ride bicycles around town, work the counter at restaurants, and generally blend into life in this farming community. For a more intimate experience, check out Amish Country lodging (www.amishcountrybb.org), a network that offers 30 Amish bed-and-breakfasts from log homes and farmhouses to lakeside residences and historic mansions. As you drive county roads in this area, white farmhouses with full clotheslines and empty driveways are usually Amish but don't intrude on a private home without checking first with tourism offices.

Now, retrace your steps to US 6 and continue west. **Amish Acres** in **Nappanee** (tel: 800-800-4942; www.amishacres.com; variable days Mar–Dec), a historic farm homestead that interprets the Amish lifestyle for visitors, is fur

Amish buggy on a country road.

hough a bit over-commercialized. he round red barn hosts theater erformances.

Beyond that, it's more lovely country riving through fields of corn and occaional stands of maple trees. Drifting long US 6 like the "Windiana winds" hrough the last of rural Indiana before hicago's industrial fringe, the route akes you over the Kankakee River (a ood fishing stream) and on to **Westille**, home of an annual Pumpkin Fesval that brings a carnival – and piles f orange pumpkins, of course – to wn in late September.

RVILLE REDENBACHER'S OMETOWN

you're hungry, make a quick swing own to US 30, on State Route 2, and he town of **Valparaiso**, where Schoop's amburgers serves up old-fashioned tmosphere in the form of "Green iver" sodas. The town was also the ome of famed American bow-tied opcorn magnate Orville Redenbacher, nd you'll still find occasional popcorn tands in this part of northern Indiana.

In fact, this region of America sometimes appears permanently frozen in 1950 – you are likely to encounter classic cars, crew cuts, and friendly folk. Make the most of it before you reach the sensory assault – and very different pace – of **Chicago** ③⑤ (see page 140).

WISCONSIN

Leaving Chicago, take Lake Shore Drive north out of the city, and follow either US 41 or hop onto I-94 for a spell. Soon enough, you're in **Wisconsin**, the unofficial Cheese Capital of America, a friendly place settled by blond Scandinavians who are still very much in evidence today.

A few miles inside the state, turn west on State Route 50 for a lovely country drive past orchards, fruit stands, and small lake towns – one of which is called **Lake Geneva**, attractive if not exactly a match for its counterpart in Switzerland. Turn north on US 12, passing plenty of maple trees, small cafés, burger joints, and rustic roads (so marked by state road signs). You'll also pass through **Kettle Moraine State**

The Amish shun worldliness for small-scale values, with emphasis on the community.

Downtown Valparaiso, Indiana.

Wisconsin's rural road sign is in the shape of the state.

A Wisconsin dairy farm.

Forest, so named for its major feature: Kettle Moraine, ridges of rock and silt and circular ponds, left behind when this area of Wisconsin was carved by glaciers during the last ice age. Rent a bicycle from LaGrange General Store to explore at your leisure.

At Whitewater, a small university town, you'll note a preponderance of custard stands serving burgers and the Wisconsin specialty dessert of frozen custard, a concoction invented in nearby Milwaukee (it's not just beer that made Milwaukee famous). By law, custard must contain a certain percentage of cream and a certain number of eggs. It's like ice cream but richer; a spoon is barely adequate to pry it from the cup.

MADISON

US 12 leads to **Madison ㊱**, Wisconsin's capital and one of the Midwest's most agreeable cities. Madison boasts a splendid downtown with a handsome central capitol modeled on the US Capitol. Its excellent university contains the archive of the father of US conservation, Aldo Leopold, author of Sand County Almanac. The lakefront campus attracts joggers, cyclists, boaters, skiers, and skaters, depending on the season (it gets frigid here in winter; bring your arctic gear and stay warm). Visit a proper pub for microbrew beer and "brats" (short for German-style bratwurst sausage) and don't miss one of the nation's top farmers' markets, wrapped around the capitol on summer Saturdays, offering everything from organic produce to goat, bison, and emu meat. The spirit of Aldo Leopold is still strong at on-campus Lakeshore Nature Preserve, a lovely place to walk, and at Olbrich Botanical Gardens (www.olbrich.org), a total delight with 16 acres (6.47 hectares) of hardy Wisconsin plants and the tropical Bolz Conservatory, resplendent with hothouse orchids, a waterfall, and free-flying birds and butterflies in summer.

From Madison, take US 18 west through green pastures and roadcuts revealing the limestone underlying the countryside. This area is an anomaly in the normally flat Midwest, with numerous ridges popping up between you and the horizon; farms top distant hilltops like ships on sea swells. At the little town of **Mount Horeb**, exit onto County Road ID – in Wisconsin, unusually, minor roads are lettered instead of numbered – for a look at two attractions. **Cave of the Mounds National Natural Landmark** (tel: 608-437-3038; www.caveofthemounds.com; daily) is a natural limestone cave near Blue Mounds that offers tours of stunning subterranean crystalline formations.

Returning to US 18 and County Road BB, a short detour south leads to **Folklore Village** (tel: 608-924-4000; www.folklorevillage.org; Tue–Sun with exceptions), a small complex of period buildings set amid tallgrass prairie. It offers folk art workshops ranging from cooking to dancing and spinning wool. Call about the culture and recreation programs when in the area or visit the website to check upcoming events. The highlight

s a one-room 1882 church, very simple but nicely restored; it was jacked up and moved from a nearby town.

Dodgeville, home to outdoor clothing company Land's End, is just a few miles on. Take Wisconsin 23 north past the headquarters. On the way out of town, you will pass the **Don Q Inn** (www. donqinn.net), an eccentric motel built in the sixties by pilot Donald Quinn. Twenty-five themed rooms include an igloo built for two, a hot-air balloon gondola, a cave, and more. Quinn's Boeing C-97 airplane is parked next door. Tours are offered on weekends.

Donald Quin was inspired to build his inn by nearby **House on the Rock** (tel: 608-935-3639; www.thehouseontherock. com; May–mid-Oct daily, Mar–May, mid-Oct–mid-Nov Thu–Mon), Wisconsin's quirkiest roadside attraction. This unique complex of buildings on top of an odd rock formation was built up over a period of decades by inveterate collector Alex Jordan, Jr. Its many attractions include rooms and rooms of art, antiques, and oddities; an "Infinity Point" glass bridge with views down a gorge; a huge assemblage of dolls' houses; a collection of rare books and vintage cars; and the world's largest carousel. It's well worth the expensive admission price, if only for a look at the fruits of a single man's manic obsession – you could easily spend the better part of a day roaming this kitschy complex. If you don't have time for a long visit, there's an attractive spot just north of the entrance where you can park, walk a spell and get a distant glimpse of the house.

FRANK LLOYD WRIGHT'S WISCONSIN

State Route 23 soon arrives at the sandy banks of the Wisconsin River, where you suddenly come upon famed organic architect Frank Lloyd Wright's **Taliesin** ㉗ (tel: 608-588-7900; www. taliesinpreservation.org; May–Oct daily, Nov, Apr Fri–Sun), which means "shining brow" in Welsh. This 800-acre

(324-hectare) private estate includes Lloyd Wright buildings from the 1890s to the 1950s, including the Taliesin residence, Hillside Home School, Midway Barns, and Tan-y-Deri, the house that Wright designed for his sister and brother-in-law, Jane and Andrew Porter. Access is by tour only, which vary in destinations covered and length. They sell out fast, so book ahead and plan your time. There is a cafe on campus; the setting is peaceful and lovely.

The route continues to the pretty little town of Spring Green, turns west onto US 14 and abruptly flattens before passing through **Richland Center**, where you can view the A.D. German warehouse designed by Wright in 1915. Known today as "The Warehouse," this red-brick structure topped by a band of concrete frieze illustrates a distinctive Mayan influence. Then the road begins climbing and wrinkling again, indicating the approach of the Mississippi River. At **Coon Valley** ㉘, neatly tucked into a surprisingly deep valley, you'll marvel at the surroundings and the town's solid Lutheran church. **Norskedalen Nature**

Wisconsin State Capitol, Madison.

Canoeing on a Minnesota lake in the morning calm.

St Paul's Cathedral.

and Heritage Center (tel: 608-452-3424; www.norskedalen.org; May–Oct daily, Nov–Dec, Apr Sun–Fri, Jan–Mar Mon–Fri) outside town provides a pleasant look at Norwegian heritage in a quiet natural setting. Speed right through industrial La Crosse, hop onto I-90, and take the big bridge across the Mississippi; get off again on the other side at signs for State Highway 61, the road Bob Dylan called attention to in his namesake album and song. You have entered **Minnesota** and are now following the **Great River Road** toward the river's source. The route north clings to the bluffs of the Mississippi River, revealing spectacular colors in fall and outstanding river views at any time of the year. Patrons once rode steamboats all the way upriver from St Louis to gaze upon these high, beautiful bluffs.

Highway 61 is mostly grand views and ordinary towns from here to the Twin Cities, but there are a few worthy stops along the way. **Pepin**, back across the great river on the Wisconsin side, is renowned for being the birthplace of Laura Ingalls Wilder, author of Little House on the Prairie. There's a copy of the cabin "Little House Wayside" just north of town, and a small museum (mid-May–mid-Oct daily) as well.

North again, **Red Wing** , with an especially good vista of the valley, makes a good place for a picnic and a photograph. The Prairie Island Indian Community of the Mdewakanton Sioux Indian Tribe lies mostly within the boundaries of the city, and the tribe has developed a casino here. You may like to have a look round before plunging into the suburban ring of towns and highways that have replaced what were once cornfields but now serve as the suburban bases for legions of commuters into Minneapolis and St Paul.

THE TWIN CITIES

Because of their proximity, **Minneapolis** and **St Paul** , on opposite sides of the Mississippi, will eternally be known as Minnesota's "Twin Cities." Fraternal rather than identical, they are like sides of the same coin: different, yet inseparable. St Paul, the more conservative, ethnic, and parochial of the two, presents an earthier and more weatherbeaten appearance. There's a more neighborly feel, too, and malt shops, health-food stores, and homes are more common here than the apartments, condos, and skyscrapers across the river.

Minneapolis, more competitive and cosmopolitan, dresses for success while living and breathing the concept of quality time. Author and local radio humorist Garrison Keillor, who created the News from Lake Wobegon segment (and later popular books) about a fictitious iconic Minnesota community for his weekly show A Prairie Home Companion, put it this way: "The difference between St Paul and Minneapolis is the difference between pumpernickel and Wonder Bread."

Yet together they are responsible for an urban success story, the envy of every overcrowded and crime-ridden

metropolis. Minnesota pioneers were forced by circumstances to cooperate with one another, and a genuine spirit of friendliness toward strangers prevails to this day.

People here put a lot of stock in politics and have developed a rather civic, populist bent: this state nourished the careers of Hubert Humphrey and Walter Mondale, the late Senator Paul Wellstone, and, outrageously, former Governor Jesse "The Body" Ventura, once a professional wrestler, who continued this populist tradition, if in very different ways. Minneapolis is also famously the home of the late musician Prince, whose Paisley Park recording studio and home was located here, and may become a museum one day.

MINNESOTA: LAND OF 10,000 LAKES

It always comes back to the lakes. Without its waters, Minnesota wouldn't even be Minnesota; the name itself comes from the Sioux, meaning "sky-blue water." The shore of **Lake Superior** marks the border of its northeast corner and the **Mississippi River** courses down its eastern flank. State license plates affirm "Land of 10,000 Lakes," but there are even more than that in the state.

During the 18th century, French explorers stumbled onto this region and named it *L'Etoile du Nord* (the Star of the North). Over the following 150 years, the Sioux and Ojibwa who originally occupied the territory were frequently set upon by hundreds of white settlers, and violent clashes between encroaching whites and Indian groups inevitably escalated.

In order to protect the early settlers and establish a secure trading station, **Fort Snelling** was built in 1819, high on river bluffs at the site of what is now Minneapolis. As Indian warriors crossed the Plains in an effort to hold onto their lands, white farmers fled to the fort for refuge, andthus the city was born. Today, Fort Snelling has been

reconstructed and staffed with actors who give visitors a first-hand glimpse of frontier life, *c.*1825.

An increase in commerce along the river gave birth to the towns of St Paul and Minneapolis. The former sprang up as a local center of navigation and was originally known as Pig's Eye, after "Pig's Eye" Parrent, proprietor of a riverfront saloon. Seeking a better image, its residents renamed it St Paul.

Ever-industrious Minneapolis, "the city of water," evolved upstream around **St Anthony Falls** (www.mnhs.org/places/safhb), source of power for sawmills and gristmills. Both towns were flooded with a wave of immigrants, mostly northern Europeans, on their way to harvest the bounty of the Great North Woods: lumber and iron ore. In the wake of the Homestead Act, more settlers then poured in to help cultivate a sea of wheat.

The Twin Cities' status in the world of agriculture, in fact, is never far from the minds of Minnesotans. Reports from the Minneapolis Grain Exchange, the nation's largest cash market, monopolize the local airwaves;

Minneapolis.

⊙ **Fact**

Based at the University of Minnesota's Northrup auditorium, the Northrop Dance Season hosts the greats from national and international ballet and contemporary dance companies.

General Mills and Pillsbury are headquartered here (as is the Target Corporation, the second largest retailer in the United States.) Magnificent grain elevators, standing tall above the Mississippi, vie for attention with the likes of Minneapolis's **Investors Diversified Services** (IDS) building, the tallest in the state; **St Paul's Cathedral;** and the handsome **State Capitol**.

METRODOME AND WALKER ART CENTER

Characterized by stable neighborhoods and superbly planned public places and open spaces, the Twin Cities run smoothly even in cold weather. They've given a lot of thought to the weather here, after all, and over the years have refined methods of dealing with a winter that is typically cruel and unrelenting. Glass-enclosed skywalks radiate from the Crystal Court of the IDS building, as they do in downtown St Paul, and the enclosed **Hubert H. Humphrey Metrodome** hosts sports events and concerts year-round – and was the setting for two World Series titles for

baseball's Minnesota Twins and success for the football team, the Vikings.

Yet people here are also perversely proud of their ability to withstand record-cold temperatures, and they celebrate the ice and snow at the St Paul's Winter Carnival, an annual event since 1886.

Culture is well endowed and thriving, particularly in Minneapolis. The **Walker Art Center** (tel: 612-375-7600; www.walkerart.org; Tue–Sun), along with its sculpture garden, is a forum for contemporary visual and performing arts that The New York Times called "one of the best contemporary art exhibition facilities in the world." The **Guthrie Theatre** (www.guthrietheater.org), sited next to the Mississippi River with great views of St Anthony Falls, is indisputably one of the premier repertory theaters. The **Northrop Dance Season** (http://northrop.umn.edu/events/ dance) puts together one of the most impressive dance series. The **American Swedish Institute** archives and the European collections of the **Minneapolis Institute of Arts** (tel: 888-642-2787; http://new. artsmia.org; Tue–Sun) are within a short distance of each other; both are terrific.

And there's still more to be found – avant-garde films, classical music, art galleries, jazz. The **Dakota Jazz Club** features the best local and international musicians nightly in downtown Minneapolis.

MINNESOTA STATE FAIR

The annual **Minnesota State Fair** (www. mnstatefair.org) the nation's second-largest (behind Texas's), should not be missed if you're coming through in late summer. Held at the State Fairgrounds over a week and a half, it is a stream of fishing and farming demonstrations, folk and country music performances, horse shows, special exhibitions for children, and carnival rides – accompanied by every sort of meat or cheese one can imagine, placed onto a stick and fried. The fair has been running

University of Minnesota marching band at the state fair.

or over a century – it's a huge dose of Midwestern popular culture, a little overwhelming but absolutely authentic.

THE MISSISSIPPI TO THE BADLANDS

The region extending from the Mississippi River in Minnesota to the Missouri River in South Dakota marks the transition from the midwestern to the western states – geographically, culturally, and spiritually.

The transition can be subtle. If you listen to the car radio, up-to-the-minute reports from the floor of the Minneapolis Grain Exchange will be heard less frequently. Western idioms begin to turn up in small farm towns. The changes in geography are more abrupt, as the Missouri River serves as a sharp boundary between the Grain Belt and the true West.

MINNESOTA FARM COUNTRY

The region of Minnesota southwest of "The Cities" is unmistakably farm country. This land was settled by European and Scandinavian immigrants during the latter half of the 19th century. Some called them "sodbusters," as they indiscriminately cleared land and penetrated virgin sod, exposing the rich soil of the midwestern prairie. Many of their grandchildren and great-grandchildren still farm the land here, an occupation known these days as "agribusiness."

The founders of **New Prague** ㊶, a town dominated by **St Wenceslaus Church**, clearly had no desire to conceal their Eastern European heritage. West of the town, along State Route 19, are peculiarly medieval-looking buildings with domed roofs, looking incongruous in the midst of all-American corn country.

Those who believe the Valley of the Jolly Green Giant to be a mythical place created by television advertising executives are mistaken. At **Le Sueur**, renowned for its peas, US 169 intersects the Minnesota River and passes through this lush, green valley, marked by the Green Giant himself sprouting from the top of a billboard.

Branching southwest toward **Mankato**, the road enters Blue Earth

Harvested hay bales in a Minnesota field.

Gondola Ferris Wheel, one of the many rides at the Minnesota State Fair.

country across the **Blue Earth River**. This is some of the most productive farmland in the state, a green expanse interrupted only by lakes. Modern farming is still a family business here, and it isn't unusual to see an entire family out in the fields working various pieces of machinery.

From Mankato, take US 14 west as far as tiny Florence, passing many more farms along the way, and then turn south onto State Route 23 for a more scenic stretch. **Pipestone** 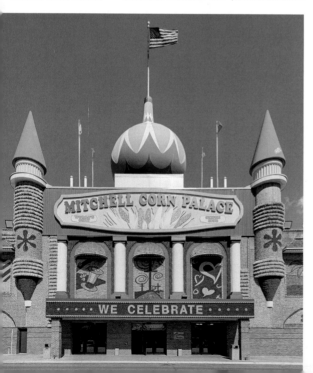, near the South Dakota border, is better known for the pinkish local Sioux quartzite found in its buildings than for agriculture, which can be viewed on historic Main and Hiawatha streets.

The buildings are significant not only because they are lovely to look at but because they are among the last of their kind – the use of Sioux quartzite is no longer considered cost-effective. But in the last two decades of the 19th century, Pipestone went to town with it, literally: the **County Courthouse**, the **Public Library**, the **National Bank Building**, the **Calumet Historic Inn** (www.calumetinn.

com), and, most impressively, **Moore Block** (1896) are all made of this material. L.H. Moore, a local businessman who owned a Sioux quartzite quarry, embellished the block bearing his name with fanciful images of the sun, angels, gargoyles, a jester, and the devil.

Underlying and veining Sioux quartzite is catlinite, a metamorphosed mudstone, or argillite, that was used by the Sioux and other tribes to make pipes, hence its popular name of pipestone and that of the nearby town. Longfellow's *The Song of Hiawatha* tells of "the great Red Pipestone Quarry," and the quarries in Pipestone and the land that surrounds them are still sacred to the Sioux and other tribes today. To learn more, visit **Pipestone National Monument** (tel: 507-825-5464, ext. 214; www.nps.gov/pipe; daily), where the **Circle Trail**, a 1-mile (1.6km) scenic loop through the prairie surrounding the quarries, takes in **Hiawatha Lake**, **Winnewissa Falls**, quartzite cliffs, and wind-carved formations known as **Old Stone Face** and the **Oracle**. Watch for a stone inscription that records the passage of the Nicollet expedition through here in 1838, while exploring the isolated Upper Mississippi region.

Continue south from Pipestone along State Route 23, passing through **Jasper** (which, as you might guess from its rocky name, also has its share of quartzite buildings). Angle onto State Route 269, and in a few miles, you'll cross another state line and be exactly halfway between the Atlantic and Pacific oceans.

THE PINK ROAD TO SOUTH DAKOTA

The South Dakota Department of Highways chose to make use of the locally plentiful quartzite, and so a pink road unfolds at the border of their state. It takes you to **Garretson**, known for its **Devil's Gulch** 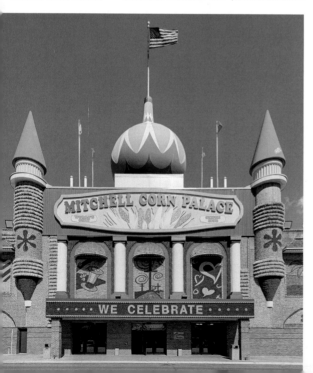. The gulch is a sliver in the quartzite cliffs that loom above **Split Rock Creek**. According to Indian legend, the rocks were split by the

The Corn Palace, Mitchell, South Dakota.

Great Spirit's tomahawk. According to Wild West legend, outlaw Jesse James jumped across the gap while being pursued by a posse. Fortunately for modern travelers, they can now cross the gap over a short bridge. Devil's Gulch lends Garretson an Old West image, but it is primarily a small farming community.

The prairies of eastern South Dakota and the pioneers who settled this land have been immortalized both on canvas and in popular literature. The paintings of Harvey Dunn, son of homesteaders and sodbusters, depict the reality and the dignity of these people. These same themes are mirrored in the work of Laura Ingalls Wilder, author of the beloved *Little House on the Prairie* and other books concerning life in the pioneer era before it was changed by modern times. (The books have now become an enormous industry, with over 50 million volumes having been sold. With the aid of some of Ingalls' descendants, ghostwriters have been employed to continue the series.)

To save time through this stretch of the Great Plains, get onto I-90, which cuts through eastern South Dakota in a nearly straight line through terrain that becomes a bit hillier and less green as rainfall becomes scarcer and the cultivation of hay and wheat mingles with that of corn.

These crops will eventually be taken to industrious **Sioux Falls ㊹**, the state's commercial center. While agriculture and meat packing have always featured strongly here, Sioux Falls became the most prosperous city in the state almost overnight when Citibank moved its headquarters here in 1981. It now provides over 16,000 jobs to a growing population of over 250,000, and with more than $3 trillion in commercial and savings bank assets, is ahead of every other state. Apart from the waterfalls themselves in Falls Park, though, visitors will find little to keep them here.

Farther west, in **Mitchell ㊺**, they have created a monument to – and with – all the amber-colored grains: the **Corn Palace** (tel: 866-273-2676; www.cornpalace.org; daily). It's one good reason to stop in Mitchell – the other being to take a much-needed break from the interstate. The Corn Palace is most certainly the world's only Byzantine structure decorated with murals of corn and other grains; each year, the patterns change according to local whim. It is a slice of quintessential Americana.

As I-90 approaches the Missouri River, which divides South Dakota into "East River" and "West River," a very different type of terrain lies ahead.

DEADWOOD TRAIL AND COTTONWOOD

Western South Dakota is unquestionably where the West begins. Visually, the Badlands and the Black Hills rise out of the prairie and hit you with a one-two punch; they are equally unexpected and stunning. But there is more to these regions than just their bleak beauty. They have been witnesses to some pretty tumultuous history.

Prairie sunset.

> **Tip**

After crossing the Missouri River at Pierre, South Dakota, set your watch back by one hour; Central Time gives way to Mountain Time here.

If you're hurrying, stay on I-90 through to these twin wonders, but if you've got the time and inclination to explore rural South Dakota, then meander west instead along US 14, which you can pick up at the rather ordinary state capital of **Pierre** 46, reached on US 83 North from Vivian. After crossing the banks of the Missouri River, set your watch back an hour to Mountain Time, and prepare to traverse mound after mound of prairie grass. This route also coincides with a section of the old **Deadwood Trail**, a legendary wagon train and stagecoach route.

The wagon trains and stagecoaches were destined for the expanding frontier; nevertheless, they had certain rules. "If you must drink, share the bottle," was one. Chewing tobacco was permitted, though it was requested the chewer spit "with the wind, not against it." And specified topics of conversation were forbidden: stagecoach robberies and Indian uprisings, to name but two.

US 14 cuts due south and then west again toward **Cottonwood**, for grove after grove of cottonwood trees, a fast growing, tall, shady, riparian tree in the poplar family whose shallow roots need adequate water to thrive in the arid West. This deciduous tree was the single most useful tool prairie settlers had: they could build a fence with it, sit under its shade, even cut into its bark to drink a bit of watery pulp in an emergency. Whenever you see the cottonwood's toothed leaves forming a bright green swath across a valley, you know there is water nearby, whether it be in the form of river, stream, or some other hidden source.

Continuing west, motorists are besieged by a growing number of signs imploring them to stop at Wall Drug, located in Wall on the northern edge of the Badlands. Depending on your degree of thirst, hunger, illness or defiance, you can continue west and arrive at Wall in no time at all, or turn south at Cottonwood directly into the Badlands.

This area is also known as the Dakota by the Sioux Indians, which roughly translates as "land bad." French trappers in the early part of the 19th century described it as "a bad land to cross." Many contemporary travelers bypass the Badlands (rarely visible from the interstate) while rushing to the Black Hills and the stone faces of Mount Rushmore, but it is a unique landscape and one that is certainly worth seeing – even if it can be a brutally hot place in summer.

BADLANDS NATIONAL PARK

This constantly eroding landscape has often served as a metaphor of youthful malaise and rootlessness: Terence Malick used it as a title for an acclaimed film (*Badlands*, 1973), and Bruce Springsteen later sang about "Badlands" on his 1978 album "Darkness at the Edge of Town." Despite all the discouraging words, there is a rare and striking beauty to be found here; it is well worth a detour off the interstate

Prairie dog in Badlands National Park.

and the $20 per vehicle charge it costs to enter the national park.

The Badlands have been described as "Hell with the fires burned out," but, fire has played no part in it; it has been shaped chiefly by wind and water. Spires, turrets, and ridges form a silent skyline, which changes with each gust of wind and torrential (although infrequent) downpour. **Badlands National Park** ⑰ (tel: 605-433-5361; www.nps.gov/badl; daily) is not a single piece of land, but rather several chunks of territory loosely strung together and carved out of **Buffalo Gap National Grassland** and the **Pine Ridge Indian Reservation**.

It is possible to be driving through rolling grasslands and suddenly be confronted without warning with Badlands terrain: huge sand castles and canyon walls. A 40-mile (64km) loop road traverses the park and provides access to points of geological and paleontological interest, including a number of hikes through the strange terrain.

This was once the stomping ground of ancient camels, three-toed horses, and saber-toothed tigers, whose fossilized remains continue to be uncovered by the elements. Many of these fossils, dating back to the Oligocene epoch, 24 to 34 million years ago, have been preserved by the **South Dakota School of Mines and Technology** and are exhibited at their **Museum of Geology** (tel: 605-394-2467; http://museum.sdsmt.edu; last Mon of May–first Mon of Sept daily, rest of the year Mon–Sat) in Rapid City. The largest of the Oligocene mammals was the titanothere, known in Sioux mythology as the Thunderhorse. It was believed by the Sioux that this creature descended from the heavens during thunderstorms and killed bison.

Enthusiasts were well on their way toward cleaning out the Badlands of its fossil treasures before the government and Federal protection intervened,

and the abundant wildlife that once roamed here was also largely gone by the 1890s – depleted by the throng of humanity en route to the Black Hills in search of "the devil's metal" – gold.

WILDLIFE SANCTUARY

Thanks to reintroduction and protection, however, the park is today a sanctuary for pronghorn antelope and bison. Prairie dogs also thrive here in their own metropolis. These peculiar rodents employ an elaborate system of tunnels, entry holes, and sentries; a shrill "barking" rings throughout the prairie if anyone ventures too closely.

Ranchers neither particularly like these creatures – as cattle can be severely injured by stepping into their holes – nor the weather, which here is as severe as it is unpredictable. Old-timers still talk about the blizzard of May 1905, when the weather progressed from balmy to icy. Thousands of head of cattle and horses drifted south with the wind and eventually fell to their death by pitching over the north wall of the Badlands.

◔ Fact

The part of the Badlands National Park lying within the Oglala Sioux Nation contains several sites sacred to the tribe. This land, south of Highway 44, has limited road access.

Badlands National Park – a landscape etched by wind and water.

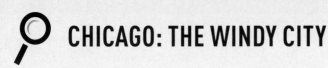
Broad-shouldered and big-hearted, Chicago has a long list of aliases: Chi-Town and Second City are just two.

Although a few people might well dispute the authenticity of some of Chicago's various nicknames, one in particular will remain forever true: Crossroads of the Midwest. Chicago's railroad yards are the largest in the world. O'Hare claims to be the world's busiest airport (by aircraft movement). Even the famed Art Institute of Chicago straddles train tracks. Visitors get around the city by a light railway known as the El, for "elevated," because it usually is.

The site, at the confluence of the midwestern prairie, the Chicago River, and Lake Michigan, was an obvious place for a town to spring up. With the building of a canal in the 1840s – essentially linking the Great Lakes with the Mississippi River drainage system – followed by the advent of railroading, Chicago spread like the proverbial wildfire as commerce and masses of immigrants descended upon it.

Live music venue The Back Room.

Then, in 1871, wildfire became a reality. As the story goes, a certain Mrs O'Leary's cow knocked over a certain lantern, starting a disastrous blaze known as the "Great Chicago Fire." After the fire, the city became the workshop of architects like William LeBaron Jenny (the father of the skyscraper), Louis H. Sullivan, Frank Lloyd Wright, and later Ludwig Mies van der Rohe.

From the **Chicago Water Tower and Pumping Station**, the only public building to survive the Great Fire (which is now home to the Lookingglass Theatre Company), to the **Willis Tower** (formally Sears Tower), the tallest building in America, the city's skyline is built to impress.

A few remnants of the 19th century have managed to survive, particularly in the **Prairie Avenue Historic District**. Once known as the "Avenue of Avenues," the area experienced a mass exodus during the early part of the 20th century. However, the buildings that remain are now being restored and lovingly protected. The city's oldest building is Clarke House (www.clarkehousemuseum.org).

Chicago has made the most of its magnificent lakeshore. A huge front yard encompasses 29 miles (47km) of beaches, wonderful parks with distinct personalities, and some of the nation's finest cultural institutions including the **Museum of Science and Industry** (tel: 773-684-1414; www.msichicago.org; daily) on the South Side; the **Field Museum** (tel: 312-922-9410; www.fieldmuseum.org; daily), the excellent **Shedd Aquarium** (tel: 312-939-2438; www.sheddaquarium.org; daily), and the **Art Institute of Chicago** (tel: 312-443-3600; www.artic.edu/visit; daily), all in **Grant Park**. The Art Institute, with its superb Modern Wing designed by celebrated architect Renzo Piano, is known for its collection of works by the French Impressionists, and is also the home of that famous stoic couple staring out of Grant Wood's 1930 painting *American Gothic*.

Chicago is crazy about outdoor sculpture. All the big names are represented – including Oldenburg, Calder, Picasso, Miro, and Dubuffet. The most recent addition is Anish Kapoor's glistening *Cloud Gate* in the Millennium Park. Chicago is the ultimate *film noir* set piece. Never has a place been so closely associated with gangsters and political corruption, the latter almost an institution. Eternally proud of those things that set it apart, the city has made little attempt to dispel these images even if they are quite unrealistic today. The real life of Chicago is a bit different. Politics are one face of it: black activist Jesse Jackson started his political career here and former mayor Richard J. Daley – gone but never forgotten – pulled the town's strings for so long that time is now measured in years AD ("After Daley"). And of course, no one can forget former Governor of Illinois Rod Blagojevich who was impeached by the Illinois Senate in 2009 for attempting to sell President Barack Obama's former Senate seat then later appeared on Donald Trump's reality TV show, *The Celebrity Apprentice*.

This is also a writer's town, as articulate as it is brash. A steady stream of writers has interpreted their hometown for the rest of the world, everyone from James T. Farrell and Richard Wright to Saul Bellow, Studs Terkel, David Mamet, and the columnist Mike Royko. The Second City, an edgy improv comedy group that originated in Chicago, is an incubator for comedians who then go on to star on the nationally broadcast *Saturday Night Live* late-night show based in New York City.

Dark, smoky blues clubs have long been part of the Chicago scene, ever since players and singers from fields in the rural South relocated and invented "electric blues" here. You can hear all about it at **B.L.U.E.S.** (www.chicagobluesbar.com) on North Halsted.

There's a new brightness to the hip North Side of Chicago; after an impassioned debate, Wrigley Field, the home of the Chicago Cubs, was the last Major League baseball park to get lights, thereby facilitating night games.

The communities flanking Chicago have become part of the silver screen in a number of films poking fun at suburbia. **Glencoe**, to the north, is familiar to many as the home of Joel, the fictional teenager played by Tom Cruise in the movie *Risky Business* who submerges his father's Porsche in Lake Michigan. **Aurora** was the setting for the wacky comedy *Wayne's World*. And Joliet's penitentiary briefly housed John Belushi in *The Blues Brothers*.

Landlocked **Oak Park** is west of Chicago's Loop, via I-290, on the other side of the city limits. Ernest Hemingway grew up here, and architect Frank Lloyd Wright lived and worked here during the early part of his career before moving to Wisconsin. He left behind 25 buildings, making this the world's largest repository of his work. Wright's home and studio, built in 1889, is most revealing of his personality and genius: every touch, from the distinctive and renowned streamlined Prairie Style to the Scottish proverb that's carved over a fireplace, bears his characteristic imprint.

Thanksgiving Day parade on State Street.

THE BADLANDS TO YELLOWSTONE

Drive through the land of Buffalo Bill, Wild Bill Hickok, Calamity Jane, and the Sundance Kid to see Mount Rushmore and the tragic sites of the Indian Wars.

Leaving the Badlands behind and heading west through South Dakota on State Route 44, you will come upon tiny Scenic, a ramshackle place named by someone with a wry sense of humor; in exactly the same spirit, a sign along the main road ("Business District") signals your arrival. There's a tiny church here, a few abandoned shacks, several vintage mobile homes, a hole-in-the-wall US Post Office, a heap of junked cars, and, on the edge of town, the place people come here to see: the Longhorn Saloon.

The Longhorn was established in 1906, and the ankle-deep sawdust on the floor has been collecting ever since, as have the bullet holes and cattle brands on the ceiling. In its heyday, it was always the site of a recent shootout, and even now discomfort pervades the atmosphere. Tractor seats mounted on metal barrels serve as bar stools. Its facade features longhorn skulls and a weather-beaten sign that originally read "No Indians Allowed." ("No" has been removed – staff is often Oglala Sioux from the nearby Pine Ridge Reservation.) From here, State Route 44 will take you on to Rapid City.

WOUNDED KNEE

The Pine Ridge Reservation surrounds the southern tier of Badlands National Park. On this bleak land, Wounded Knee Creek bleeds off from the White River to the site of the infamous massacre of December 29, 1890 – when 250 Sioux, mostly unarmed, were slaughtered by the army. Chief Sitting Bull was a casualty of this skirmish – the last tragic episode of the Indian Wars – and the name "Wounded Knee" has become an enduring symbol of unfathomable loss.

Wall Drug (tel: 605-279-2175; www.walldrug.com), in the town of Wall (located on I-90, after completing a loop of the park), is a unique roadside

Main attractions
Black Hills
Mount Rushmore National Memorial
Devils Tower
Denver
Sheridan
Little Bighorn Battlefield National Monument
Big Horn County Historical Museum
Buffalo Bill Historical Center

Map on page 144

Rock tunnel on Iron Mountain Road in the Black Hills.

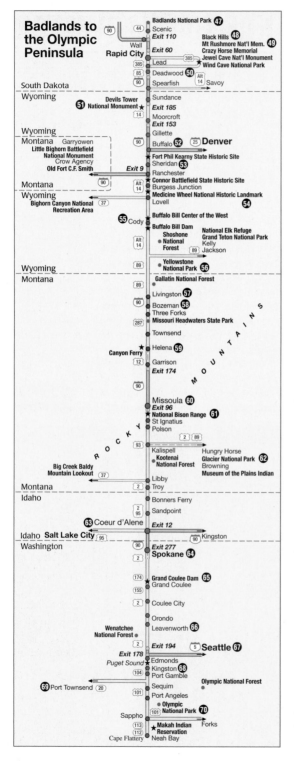

Badlands to the Olympic Peninsula

attraction – though it can't possibly live up to the miles of repeated advertising painted onto abandoned trucks and wooden signs as you drive west. Never has there been a more elaborate drug store: located on the northern wall of the Badlands, next to the interstate, it is difficult to pass through this part of South Dakota without dropping in.

Apothecary Ted Hustead began posting the ubiquitous signs along the highway in the early 1930s, inspired by the old Burma Shave (see page 38) signs. By the time drivers hit the Missouri River, even the most stoic of travelers craves a glass (or maybe even a jug) of Wall Drug's famous ice water, which has been offered free of charge for decades. Hence, what began as the only drugstore in a small, dusty town became famous as the "Ice Water Store" and now takes up most of Main Street.

Wall Drug has, among other things, a chapel for those in need of solace, a clothing and boot shop for those in need of Western duds; a bookstore, jewelry made from Black Hills gold, and a Western art gallery. There is also a staggering assortment of Western "attractions," from a replica of Mount Rushmore (for those tired of driving) to a mythical 6ft (2-meter) "jackalope" (a rabbit with antlers for the uninitiated), a mounted buffalo, and life-sized carvings of Butch Cassidy and the Sundance Kid. Donuts and coffee are free year-round for honeymooners and veterans and during the season for skiers and hunters. Approximately 20,000 folks stop by Wall Drug on a good day. It's the archetypal American success story, but Ted Hustead defines the lesson of his success thus: "There's absolutely no place on God's earth that's godforsaken."

The ride from Wall to **Rapid City** along I-90 is approximately 50 miles (80km) of rolling, treeless prairie and wheat fields. You'll note black cattle dotting the grasslands, rolling hills slowly increasing in elevation, and occasional patches of sunflowers. Rapid City, settled by prospectors in 1876 and slowly becoming a sophisticated place, is the gateway to the Black Hills.

THE BLACK HILLS

". . . as long as rivers run and grass grows and trees bear leaves, Paha Sapa, the Black Hills of South Dakota, will forever be the sacred land of the Sioux Indians." ~ Excerpt, 1868 Treaty between US Government and Sioux Nation
"There's gold in them thar hills." ~ Attributed to US Army scouts, 1874.
Taken together, these words summarize the course of late 19th-century history in the **Black Hills**, ⁴⁸ and indeed throughout the West; an era characterized by greed, deception, and bloodshed. The Sioux were "granted" eternal rights to this land that held little interest for the white man until the discovery of gold. After that, of course, it was a different story.

George Armstrong Custer led an army reconnaissance expedition through here in 1874. The presence of gold was barely confirmed before a deluge of humanity swept through the hills, leaving the treaty of 1868 shredded in its wake. Years of bloodshed followed, and the Sioux would never regain exclusive rights to their sacred *Paha Sapa.* In 2012, a UN Special Rapporteur on indigenous rights conducted a 12-day fact-finding mission in the region and concluded that the Black Hills should be given back to the Sioux, who refuse to take the $1 billion in settlement funds awarded them by the US Supreme Court in 1980. The dispute has yet to be settled. Meanwhile, a stream of travelers flow through the Black Hills every day – mostly past Mount Rushmore, the "shrine of democracy" that was never completed.

Past Rapid City and the rampant commercialism of US 16, you encounter a road of another color, a 17-mile (27km) corkscrew known as the **Iron Mountain Road**. It is one of the spectacular, specially engineered Black Hills highways built in the 1930s and intended for pleasure driving. The inspiration of Highway Commissioner Peter Norbeck, the roads are characterized

You are now in rattlesnake country.

Mount Rushmore National Memorial.

by hairpin turns, switchbacks, granite tunnels (placed to provide remarkable vistas), and pigtail bridges using native pine columns in place of steel.

MOUNT RUSHMORE NATIONAL MEMORIAL

Rather than sashaying around the mountain, Iron Mountain Road heads straight for the top. It passes by **Mount Rushmore National Memorial** ㊾ (tel: 605-574-2523; www.nps.gov/moru; daily), which first appears framed at the end of a tunnel. This sight is akin to watching Hitchcock's *North by Northwest* (1959) on television from across the room. You may find yourself squinting to see if those specks up there are actually Cary Grant and Eva Marie Saint escaping across the six-story granite faces.

Rushmore, the (uncarved) mountain, was purportedly named for Charles E. Rushmore, a New York attorney who visited here in 1885. When he asked a local about the name of the (then-nameless) peak, the fellow is said to have obligingly replied, "It is called Mount Rushmore." In the 1920s, Doane Robinson, the official historian of South Dakota, was considering various projects aimed at attracting visitors to the Black Hills. He decided on the concept of a colossal mountain carving, envisioning statues of legendary mountain men such as Jim Bridger, John Colter, and Kit Carson. But the more universally admired presidential subjects (George Washington, Thomas Jefferson, Abraham Lincoln, and, later, Theodore Roosevelt) were finally chosen.

In 1927, sculptor Gutzon Borglum (then 60 years old) was commissioned to do the work. The enormous endeavor took him the remainder of his life, and work on the mountain came to a permanent halt following Borglum's death and the Japanese attack on Pearl Harbor in 1941. It's interesting to note that Borglum had intended the figures to be carved to the waist, and had he begun from the bottom rather than the top, the US would have been left with a rather peculiar shrine to democracy.

The project was always plagued by controversy and lack of funding

The head of Crazy Horse Memorial.

argely as a result of the Depression nd Borglum's artistic temperament nd egotism. Some say he pushed for he inclusion of Roosevelt because he onsidered the president's spectacles ɔ be a particular challenge to his kills, for instance. Also controversial s the fact that the monument sits on site considered sacred by the Sioux. he granite promontory is part of the nited Nations inquiry and it has been uggested by the UN that the site be iven back to the Sioux.

CRAZY HORSE

Mount Rushmore is not the only mountain carving in the Black Hills. The Crazy Horse Memorial (tel: 605-673-4681; ttps://crazyhorsememorial.org; daily) is work-in-progress begun by the late orczak Ziolkowski. Whereas Mount ushmore remains incomplete, Crazy Horse, even more ambitious in scale, is till in its infancy. Ziolkowski left detailed lans and instructions behind, and the rounds – the town of Crazy Horse now – re literally abuzz with workers.

Ziolkowski was engaged to carve this epiction of the great Oglala Lakota varrior by Chief Henry Standing Bear o that the white man might know that the red man had great heroes, too." lthough some 8 million tons of rock ave been blasted off the mountain ince 1949, it is still difficult to visual-ze a figure on horseback without the id of a 1/34th scale plaster model. till, the figure is gradually taking hape. Come for a look at the mountain and also to visit the ever-expand-ng **Indian Museum of North America**, he Native American Educational and ultural Center, and Ziolkowski's stu-io. Learning about the sculptor, his fe. and his ambitions for this place is me well spent. Ziolkowski was a fas-inating giant of man, as a father, art-st, and humanitarian. He liked to think f himself as a "storyteller in stone," nd these are words he personally nscribed on the door of his tomb.

South of Mount Rushmore and Crazy Horse is **Wind Cave** (tel: 605-745-4600; www.nps.gov/wica; daily), the first cave to be named a national park in 1903. Wind Cave and **Jewel Cave** (its sister to the west) are the fourth- and second-longest caves in the world, respectively. They are characterized by calcite crystals and honeycomb formations known as "boxwork," found more extensively here than anywhere else in the world. The National Park Service offers scheduled Candlelight Cave Tours of Wind Cave during the summer months, a mystical experience for most visitors.

DRIVING NEEDLES HIGHWAY

North of Wind Cave, in the direction of Lead, is Needles Highway, another Black Hills driving experience. The road was built to show off the Needles, spires made from granite that reach for the sky. The highway meanders and climbs several miles up into the firmament, at times through tiny granite tunnels. You must sound your horn before proceeding, and don't let your attention stray too far.

A drive through Spearfish Canyon, South Dakota.

Cathedral Spires – Needles Highway was built to show them off.

Dancing and singing at a South Dakota tribal gathering.

Past Needles Highway, continuing north toward **Lead** on US 385, the aroma of pine pervades the air as the road passes through thick, dark stands of ponderosa pine. The appearance of these trees from afar gave the Black Hills its name. Lead (pronounced *"leed"*), named for a lode or vein of ore, is the site of **Homestake Gold Mine**, which produced more gold than any other gold mine in the Western Hemisphere during its 125 years of operation. It's still a company town of pickup truck-driving roughnecks, though tourists now mix curiously with them on the patchwork Main Street. The town's main tourist attraction is the old **Open Cut**, a gash in the side of the mountain where gold was originally discovered in 1876. For more information visit **Sanford Lab Homestake Visitor Center** (tel: 605-584-3110; www.sanfordlabhome-stake.com; June–Sept daily).

Deadwood ⑩, 3 miles (5km) northeast of Lead, on US 85, is the other Black Hills town built by gold. In fact, this was the original center of local gold mining activity – called to mind in the Eric Taylor/Nanci Griffith song "Deadwood, South Dakota" – before Lead overtook it. During the 1870s, Deadwood gained a reputation as the quintessential Wild West town, thanks to local characters like "Wild Bill" Hickok, Calamity Jane, and others. Wild Bill and Calamity are buried beside each other in **Mount Moriah Cemetery**, high above Deadwood, in accordance with Jane's last wishes, but today the place is rather tame and overdeveloped, its every nook devoted either to perpetuating a faux "Wild West" image or to milking tourists at one of the numerous casinos. *Deadwood* was even the name of a popular, award-winning television series that aired on HBO from 2004 to 2006 and is due to return as a full-length HBO movie in 2019. It depicted the town in its infancy and used newspaper accounts and diaries from the 19th century in the formation of the story and plot lines.

If you must, visit **Saloon No. 10**, where Wild Bill was fatally shot by Jack McCall. You'll have to find it first, as several bars claim the location

– the real one is billed as "Home of the Deadman's Hand" and "The Only Museum in the World with a Bar." The most interesting attractions lie farther west. Descend from the hills via spectacular **Spearfish Canyon** (www. visitspearfish.com), reached by driving north from Deadwood on US 85 for a few miles, then west on I-90, then US Alt-14 south. You can turn off onto a still rougher Forest Service road at the town of **Savoy** to glimpse the landscape where part of the 1990 movie *Dances with Wolves* was filmed.

SPEARFISH RIVER COUNTRY

Along US Alt-14, the canyon is threaded by the highway, which descends in winding fashion alongside the cool, shaded Spearfish River. You'll have plenty of motorcycles and recreational vehicles for company, but there are a number of pull-offs where you can park and hike up or down the canyon and find solitude, noting the striking high cliffs of sandy-colored rock topped with aspen and pine trees. As this is the last green oasis before some very long stretches of lonesome western landscape, you'd be well advised to do so.

WYOMING AND SOUTHERN MONTANA

Quite simply, the West is not like the rest of the country. The professional sport of choice here is not football, nor baseball, but rodeo. The sky seems larger than anywhere else, and indeed, you'll see frequent references to Big Sky Country. This is a land of last stands, last chances, lost dreams; it is also a region of sparsely populated open spaces characterized by a wild natural beauty. The 2005 Academy Award–winning film *Brokeback Mountain*, which was based on author Annie Proulx's novella, directed by Ang Lee, and starred the late Heath Ledger and Jake Gyllenhaal as sheepherders in love in the 1960s, is set in Wyoming and beautifully depicts the state's stark wilderness.

Wyoming and Montana are both quintessential western states. They lead all others in statistical extremity – the most bars, drive-ins, gas stations, cars, and mobile homes per capita. The myths of the West live on here in the hearts and lives of the people who call this vast country home; theirs is not an easy life, they will tell you, but they would not trade it for anything.

Descending from the Black Hills of South Dakota by way of Spearfish Canyon brings you right to I-90, less than 10 miles (16km) from the **Wyoming** border. The "Cowboy State," known locally as simply "Wyo," greets you with a sign proving you are in the West: while neighboring South Dakota has chosen somber presidential faces for its license plates, Wyoming has opted for a silhouette of a cowboy riding a bucking bronco. You'll notice this icon everywhere you go in the state.

Wyoming has a small piece of the **Black Hills National Forest** (www. fs.usda.gov/blackhills), located not far from the border, outside **Sundance,** the town "Where the Kid Got His Name."

"Wild Bill" Hickok's grave in Mount Moriah Cemetery.

Devils Tower is well known to fans of the movie Close Encounters of the Third Kind.

Indeed, Harry Alonzo Longabaugh, better known as the "Sundance Kid," was said to have shot a deputy sheriff near here and subsequently headed for his infamous "**Hole-in-the-Wall**" hideout about 150 miles (240km) southwest, in the Big Horn Mountains. Once little known outside the West, his name has become a household word, thanks to Robert Redford and Paul Newman, stars of the ever-popular 1969 movie *Butch Cassidy and the Sundance Kid*.

Past Sundance, US 14 loops up toward the Black Hills and **Devils Tower** (www. nps.gov/deto) ⑤, the object of obsession in a very different but equally popular film, Steven Spielberg's mesmerizing 1977 movie *Close Encounters of the Third Kind*. Visible from almost 100 miles (160km) away, this 867ft (264-meter) laccolithic butte made of fluted igneous rock exposed by erosion is the tallest of its kind in America. It stands on the other side of the Belle Fourche River, where the Black Hills meet the gullies and grasslands of the Plains.

The first white men to explore this region, supposedly misinterpreting a benign name ascribed to it by Native Americans, called it Devils Tower. It held a prominent place in the folklore and legends of the Sioux, and it later served as a landmark for those traveling west, just as it does today.

You can hike around the base of the tower, but beware of rattlesnakes. The majority of visitors simply stare at its almost supernatural shape and size – particularly luminous at sunrise or by the light of the moon. The sight of it so impressed Teddy Roosevelt that he designated it the nation's first national monument in 1906.

South of the monument, the road loops back onto I-90 at **Moorcroft**, an old cow town. The old Texas Trail made its way through here in the 19th century, trampled by cowboys driving cattle all the way to Montana. Farther west, through and beyond drab **Gillette**, the Plains are vast and beautiful, interrupted only by cattle and the occasional river bottom of aspen and cottonwood trees. Even before crossing the Powder River and its tributary, Crazy Woman Creek, you can see the

Denver State Capitol.

☉ DETOUR TO DENVER

The drive on I-25 from Buffalo, Wyoming, leads after 388 miles (624km) to Denver, the Mile-High City. Celebrating the Gold Rush that built it is the grand Denver State Capitol, covered in 250 oz (7kg) of 28-carat goldleaf. In the mid-1800s, unlucky prospectors flocked to Denver for guns, booze, and women; the gambling halls never closed. Throughout the 1880s, money from silver camps bolstered the economy, and the population increased nearly threefold. The Black American West Museum and Heritage Center (tel: 720-242-7428; www.bawmhc.org; Fri–Sat), features exhibits about Bill Pickett, an early Black cowboy, while Buffalo Bill Museum and Grave (tel: 303-526-0744; www.buffalobill.org; May–Oct daily, Nov–Apr Tue–Sun), atop Lookout Mountain in Golden, celebrates the western legend. Nearby is Coors Brewery, which offers popular tours with free samples. Denver Art Museum (tel: 720-865-5000; www.denverartmuseum.org; Tue–Sun) is one of the largest art museums between the West Coast and Chicago, with over 70,000 exhibits. Specializing in Asian, pre-Columbian, and American Indian art, its spectacular titanium-and-glass Hamilton Building was designed by Daniel Libeskind to feature sails that echo the mountains. In 2018, it began a major renovation of its seven-story North Building designed by renowned Italian architect Gio Ponti as one of the first high-rise museum buildings.

improbable pile of the Crazy Mountains looming, and the snow-streaked peaks of the **Bighorn Mountains** in the distance: a tremendous relief for the traveler weary of the endless expanse of the Great Plains.

BUFFALO, WYOMING

If you're taking US 14, you'll go through towns with colorful names such as Spotted Horse and Ucross. Take I-90, though, and you must drive a sparse (if beautiful) 70-mile (113km) stretch without so much as a town or gas pump to interrupt you, only miles of empty ranch lands. The lone break in this stretch is a forlorn rest area among trees at the crossing of the Powder River.

Traveling westward, the Bighorns gradually become closer. They were named for bighorn sheep, once prevalent here but now infrequently seen. As abrupt as they are majestic, the Bighorns foretell the Rocky Mountains just beyond. These eastern foothills are today traversed by I-90 just as they once were by the Bozeman Trail,

a bloody shortcut in the 19th-century push westward through Sioux, Crow, and Cheyenne hunting grounds.

Buffalo ⑤, where the interstate highway bends north for Montana, was actually named after the town in New York and not for the formidable animals that once thundered across the Plains. It was one of the earliest settlements in this corner of Wyoming, and its Main Street was formerly an old trail that negotiated Clear Creek. The road from Buffalo to Sheridan passes near the remains – now a state historic site – of Fort Phil Kearny (tel: 307-684-7629; www.fortphilkearny.com; daily). This was the most hated army outpost along the Bozeman Trail, and when it was finally abandoned in 1868, it was immediately burned to the ground by Cheyenne Indians.

HISTORIC SHERIDAN

About 20 miles (32km) south of the Montana border lies the small historic city of **Sheridan** ⑤ (www.sheridanwyoming.org), where I-90 and US 14 meet, and county seat in a region once inhabited by Crow Indians but

A bison calf frolicking in the grasslands.

Bison in Yellowstone National Park. A mature bull can weight around 2,000lbs and run up to 40mph.

now a major cattle-producing area. The railroad came to town in 1890 and played a major role in the development of the city. There are a number of historic homes, but the real pleasure comes from strolling Main Street and mingling with real-life cowboys in the saloons. Have a drink at the Mint Bar (www.mintbarwyo.com), the oldest bar in Wyoming, whose walls are lined with cedar roof shingles carved with hundreds of brands – each one different – of the cowboys who drank here. Across the street, through the back of King's Saddlery, is **Don King's Museum** (tel: 800-443-8919, 307-672-2702; www.kingssaddlery.com; Mon–Sat). You could spend hours perusing this fascinating private collection of western items, which includes Indian artifacts, cowboy memorabilia, historic photos, leatherwork, and around 600 saddles, many with intricately carved decoration.

Across the street from the old railroad station is the **Sheridan Inn** (https://sheridaninn.com), a gracious structure with a long, inviting front porch. It was built in 1893 by the Burlington Railroad

and Sheridan Land Company. William F. "Buffalo Bill" Cody once owned part of this inn and made it his second home; it was customary for Cody to sit on the wraparound porch and audition acts for his Wild West Show.

Modeled after a Scottish inn, most of the materials used in its construction were shipped from back East by rail. In its day, it was considered to be the finest hotel between Chicago and San Francisco; presidents and such celebrities as Ernest Hemingway, General Pershing, and Will Rogers all stayed the night here, and this was the first building in the area to feature bathtubs and electric lights. The lights were powered by an abandoned threshing machine and illuminated from dusk until midnight, when a whistle was blown to warn of impending darkness. It was the first inn in the country to install a telephone. But the inn's pride and joy was its bar, constructed in England from oak and mahogany and hauled from Gillette by ox team. Still in use today, it's known as the "Buffalo Bill Bar." The historic inn changed hands in 2013, and following restoration work it now offers 22 rooms for overnight stays.

Along I-90 north of Sheridan, as you approach the Montana border, sit two of the most infamous sites of the 1860s "Indian Wars." **Ranchester** is the location of **Connor Battlefield** (www.wyohistory.org/encyclopedia/connor-battlefield), where General Patrick E. Connor led a division of more than 300 soldiers in an ambush of an Arapaho encampment. The Arapaho lost 64 of their people, and their camp was virtually destroyed. Women and children were brutally massacred here, and as a result Connor lost his command.

Just north of Ranchester is the **Montana** line, where I-90 enters the massive **Crow Indian Reservation**, homeland of the Crow Nation, and passes through the heart of desolate-looking but neatly kept ranchlands, home to 11,000 enrolled members of the tribe.

Graves at Little Bighorn Battlefield National Monument, Montana.

BATTLE OF LITTLE BIGHORN

The town of Garryowen, named after an Irish drinking song, leads to legendary **Little Bighorn Battlefield National Monument** (tel: 406-638-2621; www.nps.gov/libi; daily). The Battle of Little Bighorn, popularly known as "Custer's Last Stand," took about as long as it takes for a white man to eat his dinner, according to one observer. But the Sioux and Cheyenne who won the battle that day eventually lost the war. Two hundred and sixty white marble stones, along with the words of Oglala Chief Black Elk, in Lakota and English ("Know the Power that is Peace") now sanctify the field where Custer's men died.

Beyond the battle site is **Crow Agency**, headquarters of this 2.5 million-acre (1 million-hectare) reservation – far less than the lands outlined in the original treaty, which designated 38 million acres (15 million hectares) as Crow land. This area, bisected by the Bighorn River and characterized by rolling hills, was described by Crow Chief Rotten Belly in the 1830s as being "exactly in the right place. Everything good is to be found there. There is no country like the Crow Country." To get a glimpse of modern Indian life, stop at a gas station or grocery store and mingle. You won't find any "museum Indians" here but people who move effortlessly between two worlds, a sovereign nation within the larger US.

Back on the highway, you'll begin to notice the first of many signs indicating "Chain Up" areas – turnouts where truckers wrap heavy chains around their tires in foul weather to obtain better traction through the treacherous mountain passes farther inside Montana.

Make time at the northern edge of the Crow Reservation, just south of Hardin, for a stop at the **Big Horn County Historical Museum** (tel: 406-665-1671; www.bighorncountymuseum.org; May–Sept daily, Oct–Apr Mon–Fri). This collection of architectural structures from around the huge, spare county – which leads in agricultural production for the state – includes a train station, German church, and the original farmhouse and barn that occupied the site. The museum also serves as your first pickup point for Montana information, and its helpful staff can direct you to area attractions such as the superb fishing in **Bighorn Canyon**. Crow guides will take you up the canyon for a price, and if you'd like to stay on the reservation, lodges and motels abound in **Fort Smith**.

From Crow Agency to Billings, I-90 skirts the northern boundary of the reservation through towns with names like Big Timber. It doesn't get interesting again until you reach Livingston and Bozeman. If you wish to see Yellowstone, you can also reach those towns via a scenic – if roundabout – method, by backtracking south a bit to Ranchester, Wyoming.

TOWARD YELLOWSTONE

Approaching the Bighorn Mountains via I-90 in clear weather, you can sometimes discern a road switch-backing up the snowy slopes. Traveling west

Bighorn Canyon.

Buffalo Bill rose to fame through a series of dime novels based on his character. His Wild West show hit the road in 1883, and by the 1890s was performing in Europe in front of royalty.

Winding highway near Buffalo Bill State Park, Cody.

from Ranchester to Lovell allows you to experience it firsthand. US 14 out of Ranchester climbs into Bighorn National Forest past bullet-ridden signposts to Burgess Junction. The road is treacherous beyond this point: several runaway truck ramps and brake-cooling turnouts help drivers negotiate the steep grades and sharp turns.

About 20 miles (32km) beyond Burgess Junction is a 3-mile (5km) bumpy gravel road, US 14A, leading to the largest ancient **Medicine Wheel** site in North America. Although well paved, the road is extremely narrow and winding, at one point crossing a narrow ridge. But the views from these highest reaches of the Bighorns are stupendous, and the immediate countryside is sprinkled with wildflowers. Near its end, the road forks and presents you with a clear choice: the 20th-century radar facility to the left or the medicine wheel to the right. Go right. This medicine wheel is the most elaborate of a series of stone circles found east of the Rocky Mountains, its 28 spokes forming an almost perfect circle 74ft (23 meters)

in diameter. It is thought to be about 600 years old, but its creators and its purpose still remain a mystery. According to Crow legend, the wheel was here when they arrived in the 1770s, and today, it serves a ceremonial function for tribes. Looking at the radar station, you may well wonder how *that* structure will be interpreted centuries from now.

Past the Medicine Wheel, US 14A, also known as Big Horn Scenic Byway, plunges down the mountain into the **Big Horn Basin**. Protected by the mountains, this region enjoys a milder climate than the rest of Wyoming. It is a prime cattle-producing area that saw one of the last great range wars between cattlemen and sheepherders in the early 20th century.

Stay on US 14A to travel from Lovell to Cody through Shoshone River Valley. **Lovell**, a well-groomed town, was founded by ranchers in the 1870s and remains identified with cattle, though it is also known as the "Rose Town of Wyoming." Past Garland, the Rocky Mountains come into view for the first time, with square-topped **Heart Mountain** in the foreground. A short drive from here is Cody, a town named after William F. "Buffalo Bill" Cody.

CODY

You can't pass through **Cody** without encountering all things Buffalo Bill, the one-time Pony Express rider, soldier, buffalo hunter, army chief scout, rancher, frontiersman, actor and showman. He has accurately been called a "kaleidoscope of the white man's western experience." Through his Wild West Show, his own screen roles, and other films that dealt with his character (played by everyone from Roy Rogers to Charlton Heston and Paul Newman), he has, more than any single person, influenced the world view of the West, for better or worse. And he certainly left his mark on Cody.

The place is unquestionably tourist-crazy. When Yellowstone attained

national park status, this town jumped in with both feet, billing itself as gateway to the park. Today, there are so many tour buses and tourist attractions in the town, you may be inclined to step on the gas and get the hell out of Dodge. If you can look beyond souvenir shops and the phony facade, however, you will discover the Old West here.

To do that, head over to the exceptional **Buffalo Bill Center of the West** (tel: 307-587-4771; http://centerofthewest.org; Mar–Nov daily, Dec–Feb, Thu–Sun), which is actually five outstanding museums and a research library in one. **Buffalo Bill Museum** is devoted to the man's vast collection of memorabilia. He was known for his flamboyance and excess, and the collection is all the better for it. **Whitney Western Art Museum** spans the period from the 1800s to the present. All the greats are represented – Catlin, Bierstadt, Moran, Remington, Russell; Remington's studio has been re-created here, as well. **Plains Indian Museum** displays perhaps the world's finest collections of Sioux, Cheyenne, Shoshone, Crow, Arapaho, and Blackfoot artifacts. Of interest is a series of pictographs made by Chief Sitting Bull while imprisoned at Fort Randall in 1882. Drawn on Fort Randall stationery, they depict what he considered to be the important events in his life.

RODEO CAPITAL OF THE WORLD

Cody is known for its Night Rodeo, which, along with the annual Fourth of July Cody Stampede, has led the town to claim to be the "Rodeo Capital of the World." Old Trail Town (tel: 307-587-5302; www.oldtrailtown.org; mid-May–Sept daily), which includes the Museum of the Old West, is located west at the original town site. The beloved obsession of Bob and Terry Edgar, this is an impressive collection of authentic frontier buildings, horse-drawn vehicles, and other artifacts from Wyoming's past. The "Hole-in-the-Wall Cabin" used by Butch Cassidy and the Sundance Kid is also here, marked by a rock with the oldest inscribed date in northern Wyoming (1811).

A number of legendary frontiersmen have been reburied here at the cemetery, among them John "Jeremiah Liver-eating" Johnson, portrayed by Robert Redford in the film *Jeremiah Johnson*. Johnson died in an old soldiers' home far from the mountains where he lived, and his reburial was marked by a moving ceremony attended by Robert Redford and the Utah Mountain Men, who served as pallbearers. The plaque on his grave simply reads "No More Trails."

US 14 West out of Cody follows the Shoshone River, winding through the formations of **Shoshone Canyon** past **Buffalo Bill Dam**, the world's first concrete arch dam (www.bbdvc.com; visitor center May–Sept daily). It tunnels through **Rattlesnake Mountain** and continues on through **Shoshone National Forest** (the nation's first) and soon thereafter, the entrance to Yellowstone National Park.

William F. Cody's buffalo hide coat (c.1871) in the Buffalo Bill Museum.

Geothermal landscape of
Yellowstone National Park.

YELLOWSTONE TO THE OLYMPIC PENINSULA

The Northern Route concludes its coast-to-coast journey by traveling through several of the country's most glorious national parks to the farthest northwestern corner of the US.

The national parks of the northern Rockies – Yellowstone, Grand Teton, and Glacier – are regions of breathtaking natural beauty, vignettes from a more primitive North America. These mountain parks all share an abundance of wildlife, but each possesses a distinct personality. Yellowstone has its geysers; Grand Teton encompasses the incomparable Teton Range, rising above cattle country; and Glacier has its spectacular mountain passes (and a diminishing number of glaciers).

The route between Yellowstone and Glacier passes through the westernmost **Great Plains**, the traditional hunting grounds of the Plains Indians. First described by Lewis and Clark in the early part of the 19th century, and later depicted by Western artist Charles Russell, the landscape is now dominated by cattle ranches and wide-open fields of wheat.

OLDEST NATIONAL PARK

Yellowstone National Park 56 (tel: 307-344-7381; www.nps.gov/yell; July, Aug only months all facilities open, but Albright Visitor Center and Mammoth Hot Springs roads and facilities are open year round; othewise, roads close in winter, and times vary for different facilities) is both symbol and sanctuary. Located in the northwest corner of Wyoming, it was the world's

first national park – and for many people is still the most magnificent. This primitive landscape, forged by fire and water, has been called the "greatest concentration of wonders on the face of the earth," its shapes and colors "beyond the reach of human art." It is a hotbed of geothermal activity, with more than 10,000 thermal features, as well as being one of the last remaining habitats of the grizzly bear in the United States outside of Alaska. All this and enough canyons, cliffs, and cataracts to please the most jaded eye.

Main attractions

Yellowstone National Park
Grand Teton National Park
Museum of the Rockies
Montana Historical Society
National Bison Range
Glacier National Park
Museum of the Plains Indian
Lake Pend d'Oreille
Seattle
Olympic National Park

Map on page 144

Pike Place Market, Seattle.

Though Native Americans hunted here for centuries, credit for the region's discovery goes to John Colter, the first white man to set foot in what is now Wyoming. Later in the 19th century, trappers and prospectors passed through, among them Jim Bridger, a celebrated mountain man and teller of tall tales. Impressed by the petrified trees of **Specimen Ridge**, he embellished his description a bit, raving of "petrified trees full of petrified birds singing petrified songs." In 1870, Henry Washburn, Surveyor General of Montana Territory, headed up a more illustrious expedition endeavoring to set the record straight. They returned awestruck and committed to the creation of a "nation's park" – a dream realized in 1872.

Yellowstone encompasses an area of more than 2 million acres (800,000 hectares). Those who prefer being at one with nature can rest assured that 95 percent of this area is backcountry. For the less intrepid, there are nearly 300 miles (480km) of roads. The **Grand Loop Road** provides access to most of the major attractions, from **Yellowstone** Lake and the **Grand Canyon of Yellowstone** to **Mammoth Hot Springs** and **Old Faithful**. They are simply magnificent.

Many visitors view Old Faithful's performance with a sense of obligation. Although not as faithful as it once was, the geyser pleases the crowd regularly – 21 to 23 times daily. This is also a prime location for people-watching; a chance to glimpse a real slice of American life frozen in anticipation.

YELLOWSTONE WILDLIFE

Many visitors come to Yellowstone primarily to view wildlife, and few depart disappointed. Stopped cars along the road generally indicate that some large mammal is grazing nearby. Unfortunately for both man and beast, visitors tend to forget their natural fear of and respect for these truly wild creatures. A park ranger relates that people who would ordinarily be reluctant to pet a neighbor's dog have no qualms about posing for a snapshot with a wild animal twice their size. Bison are best left alone – visitors getting too close are not infrequently gored, and the result can be fatal. Of ever-greater concern to park officials are bears – both black bears and grizzlies; the latter are more dangerous and are protected as an endangered species. To avoid bears, visit the park in winter, when they are hibernating, a season that arrives early in Yellowstone.

GRAND TETON NATIONAL PARK

With the arrival of winter, the Yellowstone elk population leaves the high country and heads for the National Elk Refuge outside Jackson, Wyoming. Though not exactly following in their hoofprints, US 89 South nevertheless takes you from the southern boundary of Yellowstone National Park through majestic **Grand Teton National Park** (tel: 307-739-3300; www.nps.gov/grte; daily) and Jackson Hole alongside the refuge, to Jackson, the perennial boomtown.

If the Rockies are the crown, then the **Teton Range** is its jewel. Exquisite

Cowboy country around Yellowstone is also bison, elk, and black bear country.

eautiful, amethyst-tinged, jagged, nowcapped, and hypnotic, they loom bove the horizon west of the highway. he **Snake River**, true to its name, hreads in between. The Teton and **Gros Ventre** ranges, which in turn ncircle the **Jackson Hole** valley. Trappers worked this territory in the early 9th century, and it was named for David E. Jackson, a prominent member f the trade. Settlers came in the 1880s s outlaws, homesteaders, and ranchrs. This is a gorgeous landscape, ever more visually stunning than in he classic 1953 western movie *Shane*, lmed on location here.

It is still cattle country, but tourism has become the economic maintay now. People flock from all over he country to ski here, especially the vell-to-do. Nearby is **Rendezvous Mountain**, whose claim to fame is its ertical drop, the greatest of any US ki resort. The sheer ascent of nearly mile (1.6km) can be appreciated even n summer by riding the aerial tram el: 307-733-2292; www.jacksonhole. om; usually late May–early Oct). The view from the summit is stupendous – across Grand Teton and far beyond.

JACKSON

The Old West and the New West have converged in **Jackson**, land of condos and cowboys. This is a big-name resort with its share of local color; you just have to look for it. Look beyond the boutiques, the ski chalets, the nightly "shootouts," and the stagecoach rides. Bars are generally the best place for this sort of quest, so pull up a saddle (mounted on a bar stool) at the **Million Dollar Cowboy Bar** (www.milliondollarcowboybar.com) and hoist a few beers with the locals.

North of Jackson is the **National Elk Refuge** (tel: 307-733-9212; www.fws.gov/refuge/national_elk_refuge; daily), established in 1912 and now the winter habitat of a herd some 11,000 strong. Once victims of starvation and disease, these elk are now protected by law. Regularly scheduled sleigh rides transport visitors briefly into the company of these graceful creatures. In spring, the elk shed their antlers, which are expeditiously retrieved by area Boy Scouts

> ### ⊙ Tip
> The best way to explore the Yellowstone and Tetons backcountry in winter is on Nordic skis or snowshoes. Snowmobiles and snowcoaches only provide limited access as roads are closed to most vehicles. The thermal areas are good places to spot wildlife warming their hooves and paws.

The stunning Grand Tetons.

> **Tip**

Finger pickers should check out Bozeman, Montana. Highly desirable Gibson guitars are made at a factory just outside town. For information, call 406-556-2100 or visit www.gibson.com.

and later auctioned off at a considerable profit.

MONTANA

Gardiner, Montana, sits along US 89 just north of Yellowstone on the southern fringe of **Gallatin National Forest** (www.fs.usda.gov/gallatin). Out of Yellowstone, the road passes through barren plains, irrigated farms, and a land of many hot springs – mineral bath resorts are thick on the ground here – before reaching the forest, rich in minerals. The road plays hide-and-seek with the Yellowstone River a while longer before intersecting with US 191 at Livingston.

Livingston (www.livingstonmontana.org) ⑤⑦ was put on the map by both the Northern Pacific Railroad and its proximity to Yellowstone, just 56 miles (90km) to the south. Retaining some of its authentic Old West character, it has also been the popular haunt of Western authors and painters such as Russell Chatham and Jim Harrison – not to mention modern movie stars and media types such as Andie MacDowell and Ted Turner, among others. The town consists of a small grid

of streets with bars and cafés; its proximity to Bozeman has also brought an increasing number of university students and professors.

A little west along I-90 sits **Bozeman** (tel: 406-586-5421; www.bozemancvb.com) ⑤⑧, nestled in the Gallatin Valley beneath 9,000ft (2,700-meter) peaks that seem close enough to touch in the clear air. This was known as the "Valley of Flowers" by the Blackfeet, Crow, Cheyenne, and Snake tribes who hunted here. William Clark passed through the area with the blessing of the tribes in 1806, on the return trip of he and Meriwether Lewis's path-finding expedition. John Bozeman and Jim Bridger later guided wagon trains through in direct violation of the Indian treaty, a considerable risk. The trail became Bonanza Trail, the Bridger Cut-Off, and the Bloody Bozeman – a treacherous shortcut for impatient pioneers.

Like many other cities out West, Bozeman has a historic Main Street, though several of its century-old buildings were rebuilt from scratch after a gas explosion in 2009. It is also a popular and growing university town, and has many stores selling outdoor gear and health foods and a thriving food scene. On campus, you'll find the **Museum of the Rockies** (tel: 406-994-2251; www.museumoftherockies.org; daily), devoted to the physical and cultural heritage of the northern Rockies. Gibson Guitar (www.gibson.com) manufactures quality guitars at a plant just outside town, while the **American Computer and Robotics Museum** (tel: 406-582-1288; www.compustory.com; June–Aug daily, Sept–May Tue–Sun) traces the history of changing computer technology. Bozeman's own "Boot Hill" is **Sunset Hills Cemetery**, final resting place of journalist Chet Huntley, pioneer John Bozeman, and Nevada miner Henry T.P. Comstock.

LEWIS AND CLARK

Northwest of Bozeman, along Montana 2, sits Manhattan – which doesn't hav

Around 5,000 elk spend the winter near Jackson, Wyoming.

much of a skyline at all – followed by the town of **Three Forks**, across the Madison River. This town was named for the Missouri Headwaters – the Gallatin, Madison, and Jefferson rivers – all named by Lewis and Clark. Meriwether Lewis and William Clark led their historic expedition through here in July 1805, having accepted the challenge of exploring the recently acquired Louisiana Purchase by tracing the Missouri River and its tributaries to (they hoped) the Northwest Passage. By the time they reached the Three Forks area, however, they realized that the Missouri drainage system did not in fact lead to the Pacific. Nevertheless, the success of their expedition remains undisputed. They opened up the West for a generation and for all time; a deluge of exploration – and exploitation – soon followed.

Gone today is the abundant wildlife Lewis and Clark found at the headwaters, but **Missouri Headwaters State Park** (tel: 406-285-3610; www.stateparks.mt.gov/missouri-headwaters; campground reservations at www.reserveamerica.com; daily) now protects and interprets the area's historical significance. Here, you can camp or picnic at the very spot where the expedition stopped for breakfast on July 27, 1805, then climb up to **Lewis Rock**, where Lewis sketched a map.

At the park entrance are the remains of a ghost town, **Second Gallatin City**. The town moved here from across the headwaters for the main stagecoach route, after being abandoned by the steamboat. Sadly, it was short lived, as it was again bypassed by the next wave of transportation – the "iron horse": the mighty railroad.

A few miles west of Three Forks, on I-90, the color suddenly changes to wheat gold, and the route heads north on US 287 toward Helena. Past **Townsend, Canyon Ferry Lake** appears to the east of the road like an oasis on the prairie. Behind it stand the **Big Belt Mountains**. US 287 continues north and merges with I-15, skirting **Helena** ⑤, Montana's seat of government.

ACROSS THE DIVIDE TO GLACIER

Helena, the state capital, was founded on the site of an 1864 gold-mining camp, Last Chance Gulch. Tours of Helena Historic District take you through Last Chance Gulch, where you will find many historic buildings, including one that houses Lewis & Clark Brewing Company (www.lewisandclarkbrewing.com), which makes handcrafted ale (albeit sold in cans). **Montana Historical Society Museum** ("Montana's Museum") (tel: 406-444-2694; http://mhs.mt.gov; Mon–Sat), has galleries displaying the work of Western artist Charlie Russell and an exhibit on Lewis and Clark, and offers tours of the **Original Governor's Mansion**. You may also visit the **State Capitol** for a self-guided tour.

From Helena, US 12 runs up and over 6,300ft (1,920-meter) MacDonald Pass (don't try this if winter is approaching) and the **Continental Divide**. Watersheds from this point flow into the Pacific

Sunrise over the Bitterroot Mountains, near Bozeman, Montana.

⊘ **Fact**

Cowboy-artist Charles Russell's enormous mural, *Lewis and Clark Meeting the Flathead Indians at Ross' Hole*, graces the chambers of the House of Representatives in Helena, Montana.

Montana State Capitol in downtown Helena.

instead of the Atlantic. West of the Divide, at Garrison, get back onto I-90 for another stretch of rugged mountains; you are solidly within the Rockies now, with minor ranges such as the Garnet Range to either side of the road. A rest area on the interstate provides a good chance for you (and your vehicle) to take a break from all the mountain climbing while gazing at the surrounding peaks.

Five valleys converge at **Missoula ⑥**, the Garden City, the state's most liberal-leaning town, thanks to the influence of the 1895 University of Montana, whose presence is marked by a giant "M" carved in the hills (the trail leading to the "M" is a popular hike). Of interest here is the historical museum and restored buildings of 1877 Fort Missoula and the city's role as the largest base for US Forest Service firefighting smoke jumpers in the country. Downtown Missoula has attractive Victorian buildings, a great farmers' market, health-food shops, bookstores (writer Rick Bass lives here), and live music – the perfect place to spend the night and enjoy cultural activities.

From Missoula, take US 93 due north, which climbs again as you enter the **Flathead Indian Reservation**, home to the Bitterroot Salish, Kootenai, and Upper Pend d'Oreille tribes. Roadside stands and restaurants sell delicious bison burgers and huckleberry shakes. The 1855 Hellgate Treaty established the Flathead Reservation, but over half a million acres (202,343 hectares) passed out of tribal ownership due to land allotment in 1906. Today, Indian and non-Indian residents coexist harmoniously amid lovely, wild scenery.

At the junction of Montana 200, turn west a short way to tour the **National Bison Range ⑥** (tel: 406-644-2211; www.fws.gov/refuge/national_bison_range; daily, weather permitting), established in 1908 by President Theodore Roosevelt. Today, 350–500 bison and many other species roam more than 19,000 acres (7,700 hectares) of beautiful grassland and park-like patches of timber. Note: for your safety and that of the bison, you are not permitted to get out of your car while traveling through the range.

A few miles north again on US 93, **St Ignatius** beckons as a turn-off beneath the splendid Mission Mountain range. The town's chief draw today is its impressive mission church (tel: 406-745-2768; daily), built in 1854 and containing interesting fresco work. The surrounding mountains belong to the Confederated Salish and Kootenai Tribes of the Flathead Reservation (tel: 406-675-2700; www.csktribes.org), and you must obtain a tribal permit to fish, hunt, or visit. It's beautiful and rugged country, and bears and mountain lions are frequently seen.

To the North, US 93 is ramrod-straight. It's one of the most accident-prone stretches of highway in the land, so look sharp. It continues along the mountains to the folksy town of **Polson**, where huge **Flathead Lake** drains through a gorge, then the road bends to circle the lake's western shore. Tribally owned KwaTaqNuk Resort and Casino

ntrudes somewhat on what was once ristine scenery here, but offers food, odging, and entertainment. The lake is marvelous to contemplate as you climb round it to **Kalispell**, population center of the area and a base for excursions nto Glacier National Park. Fittingly, its name means "prairie above the lake."

US 2 turns east to pass through Columbia Falls and then **Hungry Horse**. The highway crosses the middle fork of the Flathead and meanders through the pristine, cathedral-like wilderness of **Flathead National Forest** (www.fs.usda. gov/flathead) before finally reaching the natural wonders of the park.

GLACIER NATIONAL PARK

Glacier National Park ⊕ (tel: 406-888-7800; www.nps.gov/glac; daily) is more remote and less crowded than Rocky Mountain or Yellowstone national parks but traffic can still be heavy, so it's best to visit at quieter times – sunrise or sunset, early summer and fall. Roads are usually plowed and open between mid-June and mid-October, but check the website for alerts and current road status.

Near the park's western edge is **McDonald Creek**, a final resting place for kokanee salmon, which spawn here in late fall after traveling from Flathead Lake. The annual salmon migration attracts hundreds of bald eagles, a bonanza for birdwatchers.

The Continental Divide forms Glacier's backbone, crossed by spectacular **Going-to-the-Sun Road** at Logan Pass. Opened in 1933, this is the only road that crosses the park, neatly bisecting it. It has been called "the most beautiful stretch of road in the world," its twisting 50 miles (80km) of two-lane pavement climbing from the settlement of West Glacier to the shore of Lake McDonald, to Garden Wall, and finally crossing Logan Pass and descending to St Mary. The entire road is usually open mid-June to mid-September, weather permitting.

Pull over for spectacular vistas of the **Hanging Garden Trail**, which leads to vast alpine meadows. Columbian ground squirrels greet hikers at the trailhead, which proceeds past wind-deformed trees known as *Krummholz* (the German word for "elfin timber" or "crooked wood") and across the meadow, which explodes with a changing repertoire of glacier lily, Indian paintbrush, red monkeyflower, and mountain heath throughout the short growing season. Mountain goats can sometimes be sighted from here, as well as grizzly bears, which feed on the meadow's plentiful bulbs and roots. **The Highline Trail**, across the road from the Hanging Garden, is a more challenging and potentially dangerous trail – not recommended for the faint-hearted. Opportunities for backcountry hiking abound inside the park. Its remaining 25 glaciers, 200 lakes, alpine meadows, and forests are a haven for fishermen, hikers, and wildlife alike. And two rustic stone chalets (**Granite Park** and **Sperry**; www.graniteparkcha let.com, www.sperrychalet.com), reached

Glacier National Park.

only by foot or horseback, offer overnight accommodations; both were built around 1914 by the Great Northern Railroad. The 150 glaciers that were here when this magnificent park was set aside are rapidly dwindling due to global warming, and the only way to see many of them is on foot.

At the eastern edge of the park sits the small, friendly town of **St Mary**, which separates Lower St Mary Lake from St Mary Lake proper. Even the drive out of the park, along US 89, is dramatically beautiful, descending rapidly from St Mary to Kiowa and winding sharply, then turning due east out of the mountains. From there, the road continues to **Browning**, headquarters of the 17,321-member **Blackfeet Nation** (www.blackfeetnation. com), one of the largest tribes in the nation. Its fascinating **Museum of the Plains Indian** (tel: 406-338-2230; www.doi. gov/iacb/museum-plains-indian; June–Sept Tue–Sat, Oct–May Mon–Fri) houses the most comprehensive collection of Blackfeet artifacts in existence, including the work of Blackfeet sculptor John Clarke and murals by Blackfeet artist Victor

Horseback ride in Washington State.

Pepion. Of particular note are the Assiniboine drums, some of which have been painted with wonderful visionary designs suggesting hallucinatory images; it is thought the hallucinations were caused by prolonged fasting.

BEYOND THE GREAT DIVIDE

As waters flow west of the **Continental Divide** toward the Pacific, so too do paths of civilization. The Nez Percé the Kootenai, the Pend d'Oreille, the Bitterroot Salish, and other mountain tribes once lived and hunted here in peace. Later, the Blackfeet came from the plains across the Divide on horse-stealing raids, a journey many have since followed for different reasons.

The first white people to arrive were trappers and traders in the early part of the 19th century, followed by prospectors in search of gold and silver. Homesteaders heading west conquered the Rockies and moved on, some settling in eastern Washington. With the coming of the railroad, the lumber industry found a permanent home in the forests west of the Divide.

⊘ DETOUR TO SALT LAKE CITY

A major detour of 793 miles (1,276km) on US 95 from Coeur d'Alene, Idaho, goes through five national forests to reach the pilgrimage city for Mormons worldwide: Salt Lake City, Utah. It was founded in 1847 by Brigham Young, the Church leader who led persecuted Mormons out of the Midwest on a long, exhausting journey on foot to find Deseret, the Promised Land. Proclaiming this mountain basin "the right place," Young "called" converts worldwide, particularly those with practical skills from the British Isles, to help settle first Salt Lake City then other parts of Utah. Today, 70 percent of the current population belongs to the Church, although the number is diminishing. Downtown's 10-acre Temple Square is headquarters for the Church, where activities center on the beautiful white Temple. Only LDS members in good standing may enter, but the immaculate grounds and visitor center offer exhibits and films about the Church. Mormons live by a strict code, shunning alcohol, tobacco, and even hot drinks, and tithing 10 percent of their income to the Church. Other historic sites include the Mormon Tabernacle; Beehive House, home of Brigham Young; mirage-like Great Salt Lake; and hiking trails and four popular ski resorts in the towering Wasatch Mountains, which form a spectacular backdrop to this unique and prosperous city. Salt Lake Convention and Visitors Bureau can be reached via www.visitsaltlake.com.

VAST TIMBERLANDS

From Browning, take US 2 west over **Marias Pass** and skirt the southern edge of Glacier National Park, passing through Hungry Horse and Kalispell once more. West of Kalispell, **Kootenai National Forest** takes over where the Flathead leaves off. Along the highway toward **Libby**, the lumber industry's presence in this area becomes progressively more apparent. Lumber has been big business here since 1892, when the Great Northern Railroad arrived. As with all national forests, Kootenai National Forest supports many uses, but within its boundaries (an area nearly three times the size of Rhode Island) lie many acres of wilderness, home to elk, moose, deer, and Rocky Mountain bighorn sheep.

A network of fire lookout towers, manned around the clock, was once the primary method of forest fire surveillance. As fire detection methods became more sophisticated, these structures were gradually retired (although many famous writers found them good places to work, including environmental writer Ed Abbey and Beat writer Jack Kerouac). **Canoe Gulch Ranger Station** (tel: 406-293-7773; lookout reservations www.recreation.gov/camping/big-creek-baldy-lookout-rental/r/campground; June–Sept, weather permitting; office Mon–Fri) opens **Big Creek Baldy Mountain Lookout** to overnight visitors by reservation. You will be given the combination to the lock and directions and will have to pack in supplies on foot. To get there, follow State Route 37 out of Libby and take 5-mile (8km) Forest Road 309, which winds up to the lookout. The last mile or so is rough and steeply graded, and a four-wheel-drive is recommended. It's a real high to make it to the top and take in the breathtaking panoramic views, which only get better after you climb the steps and enter the 41ft (12-meter) tower.

The 225-sq-ft (21-sq-meter) space inside has unobstructed windows and an observation deck on all sides. It contains items essential to survival and comfort and nothing more – save a fire-sighting device smack in the middle of the floor. Below, the tranquil

Hidden Lake, Glacier National Park.

beauty of the forest stretches for many miles in all directions; the wind becomes much more than a whistle, no longer muffled by the trees. This is a solitary, spiritual, romantic place to spend the night.

From Libby, where the **Cabinet Mountains** can be seen from downtown, it is a short drive west along US 2 to the Idaho border along the Kootenai River, passing near lovely and dramatic **Kootenai Falls** and through **Troy**. You are leaving a land of cowboy hats and rejoining a land of loggers and miners.

INTO IDAHO

The road enters Boundary County – aptly named, as it borders not just Montana but also British Columbia in Canada and Washington – joining US 95 just north of **Bonners Ferry**. Backed by the Selkirk Mountain Range, **Sandpoint** lies on the shores of huge **Lake Pend d'Oreille**.

Here, US 2 splits off to the west, while US 95 crosses the lake on the two-mile Long Bridge on its way southwest toward Coeur d'Alene. From 1890

to 1910, three transcontinental railroad lines forged their way through this part of Idaho, creating a string of towns that dot the highway.

Before reaching **Coeur d'Alene** ⑬ US 95 greets the interstate. It is worth back-tracking east along I-90 a little here, not only because the road hugs the banks of **Coeur d'Alene Lake** for some 11 miles (18km), but primarily because it leads to two vestiges of 19th-century Idaho, both unique in their way.

The **1848 Mission of the Sacred Heart**, or Cataldo Mission, in Old Mission State Park (tel: 208-682-3814; daily) stands atop a hill overlooking the interstate. It is the oldest standing building in Idaho, constructed of timber, mud, and wooden pegs in 1853 by Father Anthony Ravalli and members of the Coeur d'Alene tribe.

The Jesuits came to this part of Idaho as missionaries knowing that they would be welcomed by the Coeur d'Alene people, who had been told by neighboring tribes of the great powers of the "Black Robes." Truly a Renaissance man, Ravalli designed the Indian mission in European style, perhaps best described as Native American-Italianate. The spacious, cathedral-like interior is decorated with chandeliers made from tin cans, whitewashed newspaper painted with floral motifs, carved pine crosses, a wooden altar painted to resemble marble, and many other precious artifacts.

In 1877, the Coeur d'Alene were forced to abandon their beloved mission for a reservation to the south, but they still consider it their mission today, and return each August 15 to celebrate the Feast of the Assumption. Due to its location, the mission also became a rendezvous point for mountain men, fur traders, and "all sorts of riff-raff," in the words of the cavalrymen who were often called in to maintain peace and order. The annual Historic Skills Fair in July recalls those days with traditional crafts, music, and food.

The Washington State Ferry system, the largest in the US, runs ferries to the Olympic Peninsula from Seattle, via Bainbridge Island.

The Old Mission had no confessional until the late 1800s when one was established, presumably to serve white settlers, some of whom may have sinned at an establishment formerly called the **Enaville Resort**, which has now returned its early days' name of **Snake Pit** (tel: 208-682-3453; www.snakepitidaho.com; daily), located in **Kingston**, east of the mission along I-90 and then north on Coeur d'Alene River Road. It was built in 1880 as an overnight stop en route to gold and silver country, gaining several nicknames over the years – and one that has stuck is the Snake Pit. Located across from a lumberyard, a rail crossroads, and a fork of the Coeur d'Alene River, it has served in its time as boomtown bar, hotel, and house of ill repute.

Today, the Snake Pit is merely a relaxing place to stop for a drink and a bite to eat. Furnishings have piled up over the years and include many pieces hand-wrought by a mysterious man from Finland known only as Mr Egil. His materials were pine burls, antlers, horns, and animal hides; his only recompense was a room, board, and free beer.

WASHINGTON STATE

A short drive west on I-90 takes you out of Idaho and into eastern **Washington**, a land of deserts, canyons, coulees, wheat fields, and irrigated farmland – a sharp contrast to the densely forested terrain of northern Idaho. Historically, this region was home to numerous tribes, most of whom lived along the banks of the Columbia River. Their descendants, members of the Colville Confederated Tribes, live today on a reservation bordered on two sides by the Columbia River. This was uninviting territory for early white explorers. The Grand Coulee itself presented a major obstacle, with few openings through which to pass. In the 1880s, the first white settlers in the region faced enormous hardships. Their numbers remained relatively few until the completion of the Grand Coulee Dam. Built during the height of the Great Depression, the dam and the Columbia Basin irrigation and electrification project changed the face of this region for all time.

Outside **Spokane** ➏, US 2 travels through golden wheat fields toward the dam. Road signs become a little confusing as the road approaches not only the Grand Coulee Dam but the towns of Electric City, Grand Coulee, Grand Coulee Dam, and Coulee City. At Wilbur, State Route 174 goes north to the town of Grand Coulee, where State Route 155 continues on to the dam. As they say, "You can't miss it." The impact of the **Grand Coulee Dam** ➏ (tel: 509-633-3865; www.usbr.gov/pn/grandcoulee; daily) cannot be overestimated – economically or visually. Its aims, achievements, and sheer size are all on a grand scale, and the design of the dam is of such stylistic integrity that it still looks modern today.

The drive along State Route 155, from the dam to **Coulee City** and US 2, is surprisingly scenic. The road skirts the lake on one side and the algae-clad

Sol Duc Falls, Olympic Peninsula.

⊙ Tip

The community of Forks' status as "logging capital" has been overshadowed by its fame as "vampire capital," since it became the setting for the teen novels and films of Stephanie Meyer's *Twilight* series. Fans can pick up a *Twilight* tour packet at the tourist office.

coulee walls on the other. West of Coulee City, along US 2, gently sloping fields of wheat, dotted with the occasional farmhouse, give the appearance of a vast desert. Layers of blue mountains appear in the distance like a mirage – the first of the coastal chains.

At **Orondo**, the highway meets, follows, and crosses the **Columbia River** and then branches off, tracing its tributary, the Wenatchee, into foothills of the **Cascade Range**. This is orchard country: green patches of fertile land jut into the river and contrast with the golden hills; some of the local stands put out ripe apricots for sale.

Now US 2 climbs and enters a realm of tall timber, passing through the town of **Leavenworth** ⑥⑥ – an attractive Bavarian-style ski resort and gateway to the **Wenatchee National Forest** (www.fs.usda.gov/okawen). Over the rushing south fork of the Skykomish River, and through the **Snoqualmie National Forest** (www.fs.usda.gov/mbs), past several small towns with no-nonsense names like Gold Bar and Startup, US 2 continues west, bringing you just to the

Hiking in the verdant Olympic National Forest.

northeast of **Seattle** ⑥⑦ (see page 172) where you catch the expressway and (hopefully) breeze into one of America's most interesting and attractive cities.

THE OLYMPIC PENINSULA

Before digging into Seattle, however, another nearby destination beckons. Washington's **Olympic Peninsula** is the northwesternmost corner of the contiguous 48 states – a remote, exotic and wildly beautiful region within easy reach of both Seattle and Victoria, British Columbia, Canada. It is set apart from these places not merely by Puget (pronounced "*pyew*-jet") Sound and the Strait of Juan de Fuca but by its climate, its geology, the mystery of its peaks and forests, and by the natural rhythms that guide the pace of life.

From **Edmonds**, due north of Seattle, a ferry crosses the short, scenic distance across the sound to **Kingston** ⑥⑧ on the neighboring Kitsap Peninsula. From here, it is a lovely drive west to the Olympic Peninsula, where US 101 heads north in circular fashion around the Olympic Peninsula, which sustains the rain forests of the Hoh, Quinault, and Queets river valleys; the glacial peaks of the Olympic Mountains; the rugged Pacific coastline; lumber towns; fishing villages; and nine small Indian reservations.

At the heart of the peninsula are the majestic **Olympic Mountains**, snow-streaked even in summer. Long a subject of myth, these mountains remained unexplored until the 1890s, when an expedition from Seattle set off in search of man-eating savages. Even the peninsula's various tribes avoided venturing into the interior, fearing the wrath of mighty Thunderbird, who was believed to reside atop Mount Olympus.

Today, the mountains are protected as part of Olympic National Park, which comprises 923,000 acres (374,000 hectares) of the peninsula. Most of the park lies inland but includes a 50-mile (80km) strip of Pacific Ocean coastline that includes wilderness beaches on the ortheastern edge and the Hoh Rain Forest a bit farther south, keeping mountain, forest, and coastal ecosystems largely intact. Only a few roads penetrate the park, which is primarily backpacking and mountaineering terrain for those who are well prepared. The park is surrounded by **Olympic National Forest** (www.fs.usda. gov/olympic) and is largely under federal ownership. There has been a long history of conflict between conservationists and the longtime logging industry, particularly as regards protection for the endangered northern spotted owl.

Heading west from the Kitsap Peninsula, charming **Port Gamble**, the first town along the route, is an authentic lumber town reflecting a bygone era. Just beyond it, scenic Hood Canal Bridge crosses the Hood Canal – the work of glaciers rather than men. At the town of **Discovery Bay**, State Route 20 veers off and up to Port Townsend.

VICTORIAN TOWN

Port Townsend ⑥, first settled in 1851, is the peninsula's oldest town. Sea captains and storekeepers from back East made their homes here, and it was quick to become a boomtown, built in anticipation of being linked with the Union Pacific Railroad and consequently becoming the major seaport of the Northwest. All this came to pass – for Seattle, not Port Townsend. After the bust, settlers tore up the train tracks, closed down the banks, and departed for more prosperous parts.

Left behind is the best example of a Victorian seacoast town north of San Francisco. Declared a national historic district, Port Townsend has become a haven for artists and writers (poetry publisher Copper Canyon Press is based here), while nearby, in Port Hadlock, is the headquarters of the **Northwest School of Wooden Boatbuilding** (tel: 360-385-4948; www.nwswb.edu; Mon–Fri), where a dying art has been revived and is showcased during the Wooden Boat Festival every September.

Also worth visiting is the Kelly Art Deco Light Museum (tel: 360-379-9030; www. kellymuseum.org; Mon–Sat), where you can see magnificent vintage chandeliers or wall sconces.

US 101 loops around the peninsula like a misshapen horseshoe, open at the bottom. In the north, it passes through Olympic National Forest and on to the lumber towns of the "West End." The region between Discovery Bay and Port Angeles has been called the "banana belt," sitting as it does in the rain shadow of the Olympics. Farmers here see an average rainfall of only 17 ins (43cm) compared with upwards of 140 ins (356cm) on the other side of the mountains. Irrigated farms are a common sight along this stretch, as are madrona trees, twisted and terracotta in color.

SMALL TOWNS AND A RAINFOREST

The towns along the way are small and distinctive. **Blyn** is gone before you can say "Little Brown Church of Blyn," its one and only landmark. Just north of **Sequim** (pronounced *skwim*), on the

Victorian B&B in Port Townsend.

Strait of Juan de Fuca (explorer De Fuca thought this was the Northwest Passage), is **Dungeness**, which like its British namesake protects a long shingle spit where Dungeness crabs are landed. Camping is really good nearby.

The plants of several major lumber companies are located at **Port Angeles**, and the smell of wood permeates the air; here you can catch big cruise boats to Victoria, British Columbia, on gorgeous Vancouver Island. Port Angeles is the gateway to **Olympic National Park** ⓱ (tel: 360-565-3130; www.nps.gov/olym; daily). Drive up to Hurricane Ridge Visitor Center for Sound of Music views of Mount Olympus and its surrounding glaciers and some lovely alpine hiking. Heading west, US 101 traces Elwha Creek, enters the national forest, and winds down to crystalline Lake Crescent within the park, a nice place to camp. The highway is lined with towering conifers, the roadside carpeted with ferns, as you continue west toward the ocean and the rainfall amounts suddenly begin rising again.

Second Beach, Olympic National Park.

WEST END

Logging is a way of life in the peninsula's "West End," and evidence of this is everywhere: clearcut hillsides denuded of all trees, reforested plantations, and logging trucks barreling down the roads. Most of the large old-growth forest is long since gone, and what remains is usually – though not always – off-limits to these lumber companies.

US 101 passes through the towns of **Sappho** and **Forks**. The village of **La Push**, on the **Quilayute Indian Reservation**, is reached by way of La Push Road (State Route 110) from Forks. Those who live here fish for a living, and those who visit here visit for the fishing. If La Push were not so unpretentious, it would surely proclaim itself driftwood capital of the world: its beach is beautiful at night, a string of warming campfires and sea-stacks visible through the perpetual mist.

The temperate rain forests west of the mountains, some of the finest in North America, may be the most mesmerizing of all the sights in Olympic National Park (and there is a lot of competition in this spectacular park). A jewel-green dripping environment, these rain forests contain some of the tallest timber in the world. The easiest to visit is the **Hoh River Valley**, located south of Forks and inland on Hoh River Road. Here, along the boardwalk trail that leaves from the Hoh Visit Center, you find awe-inspiring ancient evergreens – western red cedar, Sitka spruce, Douglas fir, and western hemlock – shrouded with club moss, filtered by light, surrounded by ferns and the sound of the river. It is an eerie, overgrown, magical place, barely touched by the presence of man – with one exception.

John "The Iron Man of Hoh" Huelsdonk came to the Hoh Valley from Iowa in 1891. Discouraged by all who met him, he nevertheless poled his canoe up the wild river and made his home in is forest. What he could not carry by canoe, such as his cast-iron stove, he strapped to his back. Hence the nickname – and the birth of a legend. The Iron Man died and is buried in the forest he so loved, as is his wife.

US 101 continues south to another glorious, sandy, driftwood-strewn shoreline at **Ruby Beach**; look for rock oysters and starfish clinging to the rocks when the tide is out. On the south side of the park, the **Quinault Rainforest** on national forest land offers accessible hiking trails through the big trees.

LAND'S END

You can't get any farther northwest in the continental United States than isolated **Neah Bay** (www.neahbaywa.com). Forking off the loop of US 101 at Sappho, State Route 113 and then State Route 112 wind their way to the ocean along the strait. Vancouver Island is now visible in the distance. Neah Bay is the ancestral and current home of the **Makah Tribe** (www.makah.com), whose presence here for at least 3,000 years has been confirmed by archeologists from the University of Washington. Once renowned whale and seal hunters who took to the sea in cedar canoes, the Makah still live off the ocean, though the catch today is more likely to be salmon. On entering town, a sign proclaims: "Makah Nation – a Treaty Tribe Since 1855." The Makah do not underestimate the importance of this treaty, which guarantees their territorial and fishing rights, which to them means survival. To learn more, don't miss the fabulous **Makah Museum** (www.makahmuseum.com), which tells their history from a native point of view and displays many of the thousands of artifacts that were recovered by University of Washington archeologists from a buried Makah village at Ozette.

Neah Bay is gateway to one of America's most splendid stretches of wilderness coastline. A network of gravel and dirt roads goes part of the distance, but to reach land's end it is necessary to go on foot. If you want some adventure, drive as far as you dare and then hike the precipitous trail down to pretty **Shi-Shi Beach** (pronounced shy-shy) and simply gaze out to sea. Be aware of time – and tidetables – as the water rushes in quickly around here.

The trail to **Cape Flattery** is shorter and less dangerous. It descends an intricate stairway of tree roots through the forest, a clearing, and a stand of huckleberry bushes before reaching the cliff's edge. Look out over Cape Flattery, knowing you stand as far northwest as possible in the lower 48 states of the US – and that you have reached the end of a journey that began, thousands of miles ago, beside a different ocean in busy Boston Harbor.

Then retrace your steps to Seattle, or follow US 101 around the rest of the peninsula and down to the town of Aberdeen, where you can, if you wish, drive all the way to Mexico on US 101.

Young buck in the Hoh Rainforest.

📷 A SHORT STAY IN SEATTLE

Seattle is youthful and friendly, business-minded, busy, and beautiful: a city of the 21st century. Here's a list of the not-to-be-missed attractions.

Glide into the **Seattle Center**, home of the Space Needle, on the monorail and explore its many attractions, from theaters and a children's museum to the excellent **Pacific Science Center**.

Seattle Aquarium features 200 varieties of fish native to Puget Sound, plus environments simulating rocky reefs, sandy seafloors, eelgrass beds, and tide pools. It's part of the vibrant Waterfront area, which also has ships, piers, stores, and restaurants.

Famed movie martial artist Bruce Lee, Seattle's founding fathers, and other famous folk lie in the cemetery on **Capitol Hill**, an eclectic neighborhood of coffeehouses, funky shops, hip bars, and restaurants.

Housed in an extraordinary Frank Gehry building, **Experience Music Project (EMP)** is a rock music museum conceived by Paul Allen of Microsoft, featuring artifacts like Eric Clapton's guitar, state-of-the-art technology, and interactive exhibits. It stands adjacent to the very cool **Science Fiction Museum**, whose exhibits are out of this world.

From spy planes to supersonic jets and a Space Shuttle trainer, explore more than 85 aircraft at the fascinating **Museum of Flight**. Then head for the **Future of Flight Aviation Center** in **Everett**, with hands-on exhibits, and take the Boeing Tour to watch these famous airplanes being assembled.

"The Mountain" (as Mount Rainier is known to locals) looms southeast of Seattle, in **Mount Rainier National Park**. A scenic loop travels around the base through miles of parkland and timbered canyons.

IMPORTANT INFORMATION

Population: 725,000
Dialing code: 206
Website: www.visitseattle.org
Tourist information: One Convention Place, 701 Pike Street, Suite 800, WA 98101 (no drop in); tel: 866-732-2695

Built for the 1962 World's Fair, Seattle's iconic Space Needle offers 360-degree views of the city and surrounding hills from its observation deck.

Like the Space Needle, the Monorail dates from the 1 World's Fair. Trains run between Seattle Center and downtown's Westlake Center.

The oldest part of the city, Pioneer Square's 19th-century buildings are now home to unique shops and bars.

The Emerald City

Seattle is rated one of the most livable cities in the US. With a diverse, growing population, multi-billion-dollar employers like Boeing, Starbucks, and Microsoft, and one of the most beautiful locations of any city in America, between the Cascade Mountains and Puget Sound, who wouldn't want to live in the Emerald City (if you can afford the sky-high rent)? Named for local Suquamish Chief Sealth, Seattle was once a coastal paradise for salmon-fishing tribes who were displaced in the 1800s by white settlers outfitting prospectors en route to the Alaska gold rush, Scandinavian fishermen, and loggers attracted by old-growth forests. Home to The Mountaineers Club and outdoor retail cooperative REI, Seattle is a hearty place. It attracts residents who work hard and play hard – and appreciate coffee strong enough to beat the ever-present rain.

...gned by Robert Venturi, Seattle Art Museum (SAM) has ...xceptional collection of Northwest Indian art, paintings ...odern artists, and an Australian Aboriginal Gallery.

...fish is a long established, Greek-influenced fish and ...shop at Alki Beach, West Seattle.

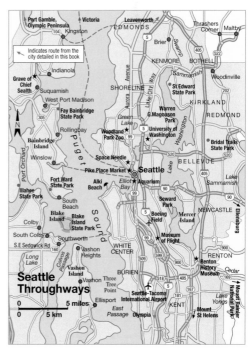

A cattle rancher.

Moonrise over the US Capitol, Washington, DC.

THE CENTRAL ROUTE

A detailed guide to the Central US, with principal sights clearly cross-referenced by number to the maps.

Civil War memorial.

It is perhaps fitting to begin a journey across America from the nation's capital of Washington, DC; the many museums and landmarks that give a glimpse into the country's past do much to set the scene for the rest of your trip west. We've chosen a south-central route that combines enough history and beauty to sate any traveler's appetite.

The history lesson begins as soon as you leave Washington, heading first west and then sharply south along Skyline Drive and the Blue Ridge Parkway through the Appalachian Mountains of Virginia. This was Stonewall Jackson territory, and the route is sprinkled with Civil War sites. Interstate 40, which we'll be following for much of the trip, continues into North Carolina and through the Great Smoky Mountains, taking you past the fine old homes of Knoxville, Tennessee, before reaching Nashville, the capital of Tennessee and of country music.

From there, it's truly into small-town America as you hit Arkansas, stopping in Little Rock, with its impressive state capitol, historic district, and hot springs, then into Oklahoma, where we pick up historic Route 66. Some know Route 66 from legend, others from childhood, when every weathered telegraph pole and zany-shaped motel was a milestone on a journey into a wonderland, whose roadside attractions included snake pits, live buffaloes, and Indian dancers.

Fuel brand inspired by Route 66.

Oklahoma's section of Route 66 passes through many interesting small towns but also Tulsa and Oklahoma City, cities where oil and cattle are king. After crossing the Texas Panhandle, you'll travel into New Mexico and visit the attractive adobe city of Santa Fe and its 19 surrounding Indian pueblos, home to Native people for a millennium. As you drive through northwest New Mexico into northeastern Arizona on I-40, you cross the immense Navajo Nation, passing Petrified Forest National Park before reaching Flagstaff, in northern Arizona, gateway to the incomparable Grand Canyon. The sweeping pine forests and volcanic mountains of the Colorado Plateau give way to the basin-and-range topography of the torrid Mojave Desert in western Arizona, as you reach Kingman, and enter California on the other side of the Colorado River at Needles. The desert stretches long and hot for hundreds of miles, dotted with iconic Joshua trees and hazy ranges, before touching the Inland Empire cities like Barstow well before metro Los Angeles appears. With some 2,900 miles (4,700km) behind you, the Pacific beaches beckon.

📷 A SHORT STAY IN WASHINGTON, DC

Planned as a city of monuments and memorials, the nation's capital is also one of its most beautiful. Here's a list of the not-to-be-missed attractions.

Tours of the **White House** are restricted, but its visitor center at the Department of Commerce, 15th and E streets NW, provides a good sense of the building's history since 1792.

Whether you wish to retrace the path of Martin Luther King Jr, whose "I Have a Dream" speech came from these steps, or simply take a look at the huge statue of Abraham Lincoln, the **Lincoln Memorial** celebrates the liberty sought by the founding fathers.

The world's largest museum and research complex, the splendid **Smithsonian Institution** exhibits outstanding collections of artifacts and fine arts.

Maya Lin's haunting **Vietnam Veterans Memorial**, at Bacon Drive and Constitution Avenue, lists on polished granite the names of more than 58,000 American soldiers killed in the 1960s conflict.

At first a strategic stronghold in the Civil War, **Arlington National Cemetery** contained 16,000 headstones by the end of the struggle. The eternal flame at the grave of John F. Kennedy honors the fallen President, and the Tomb of the Unknowns commemorates the nameless soldiers felled in battles over the past 100 years.

The striking granite sculpture of the **Martin Luther King, Jr Memorial** at Independence Avenue and West Basin Drive is surrounded by 17 quotes from the Civil Rights leader.

The **World War II Memorial**, on the Mall between the Washington and Lincoln memorials, honors those Americans who fought for their country.

IMPORTANT INFORMATION

Population: 703,608 (metro area: 6.2 million)
Dialing code: 202
Website: www.washington.org
Tourist information: 901 Seventh Street NW, Fourth Floor, Washington, DC, 20001; tel: 800-422-8644 or 202-789-7000.

Basilica of the Immaculate Conception and the dome of the Capitol.

The Smithsonian Institution's Mary Livingston Ripley Garden. It lies between the Arts and Industries Building and the Hirshhorn Museum and Sculpture Garden.

The White House in winter.

The nation's capital city

A visit to Washington, DC, is nothing less than a lesson in history, literally a living history, since the President of the US lives here. The city also has a unique beauty, the credit for which should go to George Washington. The new President insisted on creating a new city as the nation's capital, a place as grand as Paris or London. With this in mind, he hired French architect Pierre Charles L'Enfant to create a "city of magnificent distances." L'Enfant's plan was only partially realized, but Washington *is* magnificent. The distances between monuments are deceptively large; bring a pair of good walking shoes.

n-air fish market on Maine Avenue, where dozens of
dors along the Washington Channel hawk fresh seafood.

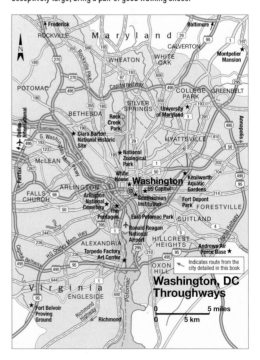

Washington, DC
Throughways

Re-enacting a Civil War battle.

WASHINGTON, DC TO ARKANSAS

This route traces the essence of Americana: Civil War battlefields, American Indian reservations in pine-scented mountains, blues and country music in Memphis and Nashville, and pioneer history in Arkansas.

Our route begins in **Washington, DC ❶** (see page 178), the first leg of which explores Northern Virginia and the Appalachian Mountains to Winston-Salem, North Carolina. Some of the route requires driving I-66 and I-81, but the secondary roads parallel the interstates and are generally more scenic, less busy, and without 18-wheelers.

Leaving Washington on I-66, look for the **Virginia Welcome Center** (www. virginia.org) west of Fairfax, where you will find information about every possible site, lodging, or activity in the "Old Dominion."

MANASSAS

Take Exit 47B to visit **Manassas National Battlefield Park ❷** (tel: 703-361-1339; www.nps.gov/mana; daily), site of two great Confederate victories during the Civil War – the First and Second Battles of Manassas (or locally, Bull Run). Ten hours of deadly fighting on July 21, 1861, resulted in a Union defeat, but the cost was horrific: 3,000 Union casualties and 2,000 Confederate. Spectators arriving in carriages from Washington planned to picnic while watching what they expected to be an afternoon of colorful heroics. They were overwhelmed by the carnage,

as were the troops who anticipated a day of almost schoolboy playground fighting.

It was here that General Thomas J. Jackson earned the nickname "Stonewall," for sitting on his horse in the face of enemy fire "like a stone wall." The second Confederate victory one year later convinced Union Army General Robert E. Lee to cross into Maryland in an unsuccessful attempt to invade Pennsylvania. The visitor center has information about self-guided and ranger-led tours.

⊙ Main attractions

Washington, DC
Manassas National
  Battlefield
Shenandoah National Park
Old Salem
Great Smoky Mountains
  National Park
Nashville
Memphis
Little Rock Central High
  School National Historic
  Site

Map on page 182

On stage at the Grand Ole Opry, Nashville, Tennessee.

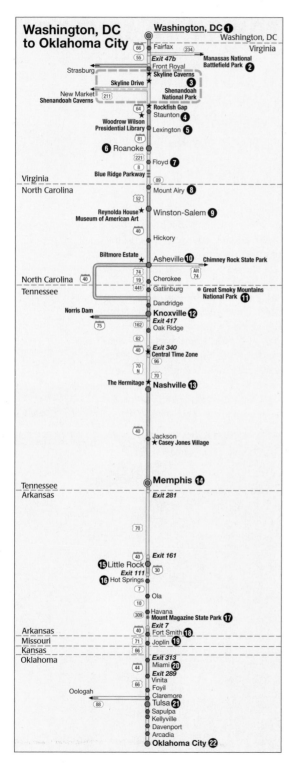

Washington, DC to Oklahoma City

Washington, DC **1**
Washington, DC
Virginia
66
Fairfax
234
55
Exit 47b
Front Royal
Strasburg
Skyline Drive
Skyline Caverns
Manassas National Battlefield Park **2**
Shenandoah National Park **3**
New Market
Shenandoah Caverns
211
64
Rockfish Gap
Staunton **4**
Woodrow Wilson Presidential Library
81
Lexington **5**
6 Roanoke
221
8
Blue Ridge Parkway
Floyd **7**
Virginia
North Carolina
89
52
Mount Airy **8**
Reynolda House Museum of American Art
Winston-Salem **9**
40
Hickory
Biltmore Estate
Asheville **10**
Chimney Rock State Park
North Carolina
40
74
Alt 74
Tennessee
19
Cherokee
441
Gatlinburg
Great Smoky Mountains National Park **11**
Dandridge
Norris Dam
Knoxville **12**
Exit 417
Oak Ridge
75
162
62
40
Exit 340
Central Time Zone
96
70 N
70
The Hermitage
Nashville **13**
40
Jackson
Casey Jones Village
Tennessee
Arkansas
Memphis **14**
Exit 281
70
40
Exit 161
15 Little Rock
30
Exit 111
16 Hot Springs
7
Ola
10
309
Havana
Mount Magazine State Park **17**
Exit 7
Arkansas
40
Fort Smith **18**
Missouri
71
Joplin **19**
Kansas
66
Oklahoma
Exit 313
Miami **20**
44
Exit 289
Vinita
66
Foyil
Oologah
Claremore
Tulsa **21**
88
Sapulpa
Kellyville
Davenport
Arcadia
Oklahoma City **22**

TOWARD VIRGINIA'S MOUNTAINS

The Civil War looms large in these parts, as Virginia was the site for more than half of its major battles. Almost every exit off the interstate leads to the site of a skirmish, raid, or other event.

Even if this page of history does not appeal to you, it's a good idea to abandon the interstate and enjoy the more scenic and leisurely alternate route. Try taking Exit 23, turning left, and then right onto State Route 55. Cattle graze near faded red barns, and roadside stands sell fresh produce. In the fall, orchards sell apples by the bushel, along with desserts made from apples (look for apple-cinnamon donuts). This is also a center of Virginia's wine industry, and signs direct you to vineyards along the way. You can pick up a brochure for the Blue Ridge Whiskey and Wine Loop at most of them.

Around 70 miles (112km) west of Washington, DC, at the junction of I-66 and State Route 55, on the eastern edge of the Shenandoah Valley, is **Front Royal**. Like most of the small towns dotting the valley, it was once a bustling center for farmers and mountain folk, Improvements in transportation and communication, however, sapped much of the vitality from their economies. Located at the northern end of the Skyline Drive, a few miles north of the entrance to Shenandoah National Park, Front Royal fares better than most of the valley towns, providing food and services for tourists. Front Royal **Town Tourism Office** at 414 East Main Street (tel: 540-635-5788 or 800-338-2576; www.frontroyalva.com; daily) has an enthusiastic staff and useful information about the area.

SHENANDOAH NATIONAL PARK

Settlers from Europe turned the fertile Shenandoah Valley into a successful agricultural area. During the Civil War, its meat, grain, leather, and wool supplied the rebels, and Union forces evastated the valley. After the war, the ecline continued as logging, poor farm-ng techniques, and a chestnut blight led) soil exhaustion and erosion.

In 1926, Congress created **Shenan-oah National Park** ❸ (tel: 540-999-500; www.nps.gov/shen; daily). At the edication in 1936, President Franklin oosevelt announced an experiment in and reclamation, restoring the nearly ne-third of the park's land that had een deforested by decades of logging nd intense cultivation to its natural tate. Between natural regrowth and vigorous restoration program, crop-and and pastures were replaced with ak, pine, mountain laurel, and berry ushes. Wildflowers and azaleas now righten the landscape, and wildlife has eturned: the park now has the largest lack bear population in the eastern Jnited States. White-tailed deer stroll onchalantly along the roads. Bobcats nd coyote are sometimes sighted, and atbirds and juncos fly overhead.

Br eathtaking 105-mile (169km) kyline Drive National Scenic Byway vas completed in 1939 and runs the ength of Shenandoah National Park. side from the entrance to the park ear Front Royal, there are three other ccess points, about an hour's drive part. The per-car park entrance fee s good for a week. The speed limit is leisurely 35mph (56kph) along the vinding, two-lane road. Don't hurry; ou will want to pull off at the 82 over-ooks and picnic locations for views of he **Shenandoah Valley** and **Shenan-loah River** to the west and the **Pied-nont Plateau** to the east.

At **Dickey Ridge Visitor Center** (Apr–lov; daily), you can purchase guides for niking and identifying flora and fauna. larry F. Byrd Senior Visitor Center daily in season, winter Sat–Sun if Sky-ine Drive is open) at Mile Marker 51 las exhibits on the creation of the park nd the people who once lived there.

Don't leave without getting out of our car and experiencing the forest

close up. At Mile Marker 50.7, a 1.4-mile (2.25km) round-trip hike leads to **Dark Hollow Falls**. It's a bit steep in places, but the wide, well-maintained trail leads to a 70ft (21-meter) water-fall, which is especially impressive during spring run-off.

You can finish the drive in one day, but if you want to linger, Skyland and Big Meadow Lodges and Big Meadow Campground are well equipped and comfortable.

UNDERGROUND SCENERY

The limestone rock under the Blue Ridge was eroded over eons by under-ground streams, leaving dozens of caverns nestled in the foothills near Front Royal. **Skyline Caverns** (tel: 540-635-4545; www.skylinecaverns.com; daily), **Luray Caverns** (tel: 540-743-6551; www.luraycaverns.com; daily), **End-less Caverns** (tel: 540-896-2283; www.endlesscaverns.com; daily), and **Shenan-doah Caverns** (tel: 540-477-3115; www.shenandoahcaverns.com; daily; elevator service for guests with mobility issues) are all near **New Market**. From Skyline

Magnificent view from a summit above Shenandoah Valley.

Drive, take State Route 211 West to reach both Luray and New Market.

In New Market, the **Virginia Museum of the Civil War** (tel: 866-515-1864; www.vmi.edu/vmcw; daily) chronicles the conflict as it impacted the state. The Battle of New Market is most remembered for the 257 teenaged cadets from the Virginia Military Academy who fought there. Ten of the boys were killed, another 47 wounded.

Skyline Drive ends at **Rockfish Gap.** You can take I-64 to **Staunton** or opt for the more relaxed State Route 250.

STAUNTON AND LEXINGTON

Staunton **4**, (pronounced "Stanton") tucked into the steep hillsides of the Appalachians, is a pleasant former mining town with buildings dating to the 19th century. **Woodrow Wilson Presidential Library & Museum** (tel: 540-885-0897; www.woodrowwilson.com; daily) portrays the 28th president's political career and two-term (1913–21) White House stint.

Don't miss a performance at **Blackfriars Playhouse** (tel: 540-851-1733 or 877-MUCHADO; www.americanshakespeare center.com). The home of the American Shakespeare Center is an exact replica of the stage the Bard knew, and performances return to that time. The audience sits on the stage, lighting is from chandeliers, sets are minimal, and the actors play to the lively spirit of Elizabethan times. There are daily backstage tours. Also worth visiting is the **Frontier Culture Museum** (tel: 540-332-7850; www. frontiermuseum.org; daily), which compares transplanted farmsteads from Europe and West Africa with American frontier farms from 1750 to 1840 to demonstrate the merging of different traditions.

From Staunton take the I-81, or the more scenic US 11, to another town with deep connections to the Civil War. Attractive **Lexington **5**, is where ol' Stonewall was teaching cadets at the Virginia Military Institute (VMI) shortly after its founding in 1831. The VMI Museum (tel: 540-464-7334; www.vmi. edu/VMI_Museum; daily) includes the coat Jackson was wearing when he was accidentally shot by his own men. It also has the mounted hide of his horse, Little Sorrel (which ranks very high on the tasteless and creepy scale), an extensive collection of 19th-century firearms, and seven Medals of Honor bestowed on VMI graduates.

In town, you can tour the **Stonewall Jackson House** (tel: 540-464-7704; www.vmi.edu/museums-and-archives/ stonewall-jackson-house; daily), the only residence Jackson ever owned.

Jackson's commander, **General Robert E. Lee**, became president of **Washington College** after the Civil War. In contrast with the discipline at VMI, his only "rule" was that "every student must be a gentleman." Lee and his family are interred in the crypt beneath the school's chapel. An excellent museum about the close ties between Virginia "aristocracy" and Lee's life after the war can be found in the chapel's basement. The remains of Traveler, Lee's beloved horse, are respectfully interred outside

A young spotted fawn taking its first steps in Shenandoah National Park.

Savoring the Blue Ridge Parkway scenery from Raven's Roost.

the chapel. The school was renamed **Washington and Lee College** after the general's death.

LIVELY ROANOKE

Continue south on State Route 11, which rolls through Virginia's alluring landscape to **Roanoke ❻**, a pleasantly relaxed and sophisticated city close to the Blue Ridge Parkway. Mill Mountain, topped by the huge, illuminated **Roanoke Star**, overlooks the city. The outstanding outdoor **City Market**, with about 50 stalls selling produce, plants, baked goods, and meats – all from local sources – operates daily in the heart of the city's historic district. The **Center in the Square** (tel: 540-342-5700; www.centerinthesquare.org) has museums focusing on science, regional history, and African-American culture, rooftop gardens, and the largest living coral reef in the East. The ultramodern **Taubman Museum of Art** (tel: 540-342-5760; www.taubmanmuseum.org; Wed–Sun) owes some of its design to Australia's Sydney Opera House. Inside, the comprehensive collection runs the gamut of artistic inspirations: folk and visionary art, American masters, and contemporary regional artists. Adjacent to **Virginia's Blue Ridge Visitor Information Center** (tel: 800-635-5535; www.visitroanokeva.com; daily) is the **O. Wilson Link Museum** (tel: 540-982-5465, www.linkmuseum.org; daily), an evocative collection of photographic vignettes that record the last years of steam railroads.

BLUE RIDGE MOUNTAINS AND MUSIC

Leaving Roanoke, take US 221 south. It coils up Bent Mountain, past Baptist churches preaching redemption and houses flying the Confederate flag. Motorcyclists will be in heaven; RVers will need to stay in second gear. The trek ends in **Floyd ❼**, where Bluegrass music is in the air. Floyd is one of the venues for The Crooked Road, Virginia's Heritage Music Trail, a driving route through southwest Virginia. At the **Floyd Country Store** (tel: 540-745-4563; www.floydcountrystore.com; daily), home of the Friday Night Jamboree, you can buy penny candy, a field guide to cows, bib overalls, eco-friendly cleaning supplies, and a map of the Crooked Road. Musicians gather Tuesday and Friday evenings, and Sunday afternoons to jam. The town is a magnet for craft artisans; there are galleries and almost weekly art and music fests.

Take State Route 8 south for 6 miles (9.6km) to Tuggle's Gap and the **Blue Ridge Parkway** (www.blueridgeparkway.org). The national scenic byway connects Shenandoah and Great Smoky Mountains national parks, passing through forests and past farms and crossroad hamlets. There are several scenic overlooks, but not as many as along Skyline Drive. Pick up a free guide at **Rocky Knob Visitor Center** at Milepost 169.

Mabry Mill at Milepost 176 has a picture-worthy restored 1900-era gristmill and moonshine still. At Milepost 210, **Blue Ridge Music Center** (tel: 276-236-5309; www.blueridgemusiccenter.

Long-established barbecue joint in Eureka Springs, Arkansas.

View of Roanoke from Mill Mountain.

Tip

Leave yourself plenty of time to enjoy the walking and hiking excursions offered along the way; even a tiny walk to a beautiful waterfall can relieve the tedium of driving.

org; June–Oct daily, Nov–May days may vary) recounts the story of the distinctive folk music of these mountains: bluegrass, ballads, gospel, and traditional songs played on fiddle, mandolin, guitar, and banjo. Musicians jam in the covered courtyard every afternoon.

Leave the Parkway at State Route 89 and follow it southeast into North Carolina to **Mount Airy** ❽. The birthplace of the late Andy Griffith and setting for *Mayberry RFD* has a museum of Griffith's career and a recreation of the gas station, city hall, and sheriff's office.

WINSTON-SALEM

Continue south on US 52 to **Winston-Salem** ❾. The city's history is split between the Moravian settlers who arrived in the 1750s and the R.J. Reynolds Tobacco Company, which began packaging tobacco in 1875. The **Winston Cup Museum & Special Event Center** (tel: 336-724-4557; www.winston cupmuseum.com; Thu–Sat) commemorates the Winston Cup era of NASCAR stock car racing (1971-1993) and 33 years of company sponsorship.

The Moravians were here first at **Old Salem** (tel: 336-721-7300; www.olds lem.org; Tue–Sun). Slightly removed from the modern city, the "Salem" part of Winston-Salem is one of the most authentic and inviting living history districts in the US. A covered bridge transports you from the visitor center to the village. At its foot, the **Museum of Early Southern Decorative Arts** in the Frank L. Horton Museum Center (tel: 336-721-7360; www.mesda.org Tue–Sun) has an Antiques Road Show feel to its collection. Each piece has a family history tale of where it was made, when, by whom, and why.

Most of the Old Salem buildings are privately owned, and there are modern concessions. Air-conditioners hum behind houses, and cars park on the streets, but costumed guides roam the village, and buildings operating as examples of the historic period feature hands-on demonstrations of daily life. Its old tavern is an upscale restaurant. The printing shop of John Christian Blum, founding publisher in 1828 of *The Farmers' and Planters' Almanac*, is one of the exhibit buildings. Be sure to stop at the **Winkler Bakery** for impossibly thin Moravian ginger cookies. And what of the giant-size metal coffeepot standing on the village green? Built by the sons of Salem's founders Samuel and Julius Mickey, it was used to advertise their tinsmith's shop.

Living history interpreters roam another restored Moravian village, **Historic Bethabara Park** (tel: 336-924-8191; www.cityofws.org/departments/recreation-parks/historic-bethabara; exhibit buildings Apr–mid-Dec Tue–Sun; grounds and gardens all year daily) in a pleasant green setting off University Parkway. The open-air museum has a 1788 church, archeological ruins, and 20 miles (32km) of nature trails.

Reynolda House Museum of American Art (tel: 888-663-1149; www.reynoldahouse.org; Tue–Sun) is the former home of Katharine Smith and

Cycling along the Blue Ridge Parkway.

Richard Joshua Reynolds (founder of R.J. Reynolds Tobacco). The home, its gardens, and adjoining Reynolda Village, in which the old buildings have been converted into shops, offices, and restaurants, are open to visitors. **Southeast Center for Contemporary Arts (SECCA)** (tel: 336-725-1904; www.secca.org; Tue–Sun) is connected to the Reynolda Museum via an enclosed passageway. It is as contemporary as the Reynolda is traditional.

From Winston-Salem, I-40 heads west. About 73 miles (117km) along the route is the town of **Hickory**, the center of the state's furniture industry.

ASHEVILLE

With the Blue Ridge Mountains as a backdrop, **Asheville** ⑩ enjoys great natural beauty. It also enjoys a gallery of elegant buildings commissioned by paternalistic businessmen in the early 1900s. They successfully promoted Asheville to investors. In the early years of the 20th century, the city was booming. When the Depression hit, it became the most indebted city in the nation. Rather than default, the Asheville community swore it would repay all loans; it signed the final check in the 1970s.

That economic disaster prevented Asheville from participating in the Urban Renewal projects of the 1960s, which saw many downtowns replacing classic buildings with "Nouveau Gulag" architecture. So the block-square Grove Arcade – the original indoor shopping mall – remains as it was when it was completed in 1923, and the surrounding streets retain their period charm. Only Miami has more Art Deco buildings. You will find no national retailers downtown; by community consensus, all businesses are locally owned. The River District along the French Broad River houses the studios of nearly 200 artists (www.ashvillerad.com/www.riverartsdistrict.com).

At Grovewood Village adjacent to the **Omni Grove Park Inn**, you can view arts and crafts exhibits in Grovewood Gallery (www.grovewood.com; daily) and the Antique Car Museum. **Thomas Wolfe Memorial State Historic Site** (tel: 828-253-8304; www.wolfememorial.com; Tue–Sat) preserves the boardinghouse where author Thomas Wolfe grew up and which he used in his novel *Look Homeward, Angel*. The unflattering novel about Asheville so angered residents (many of whom recognized their fictional selves) it was banned in the city.

A winery, sporting activities, shops, and restaurants are all part of the immense landscaped property of the 250-room **Biltmore Estate** (tel: 800-411-3812; www.biltmore.com; daily). It is America's largest privately owned home. George Vanderbilt's vision took root in 1887, when he visited Asheville on vacation and became enchanted by the mountain scenery. Vanderbilt set out to create a mansion modeled after the French Loire Valley chateaux. The self-guided tour includes three floors and the basement. Inside you'll find 16th-century tapestries, many priceless antiques, and a banquet hall with

⊙ Tip

Winston Salem Visitor Center at 200 Brookstown Avenue (tel: 336-728-4200; http://visitwinstonsalem.com; Mon–Fri, Mar–Nov also Sat) distributes free maps and other information about the city and surrounding area.

Hiking in Shenandoah National Park.

Nicknamed The Batman Building for its resemblance to the superhero's mask, the 32-story AT&T Building in Nashville is the tallest in the state of Tennessee.

Knoxville's springtime celebration, the Dogwood Arts Festival.

a 70-foot (21-meter) ceiling. The former village for employees is now a shopping district. All new buildings must reflect the original Tudor-style architecture, even the McDonald's, which has faux-marble floors and a fireplace.

Southeast of Asheville, near the intersection of US 64 and US 74A, is **Chimney Rock State Park** (tel: 800-277-9611; www.chimneyrockpark.com; Mar–Dec daily, Jan–Feb Fri–Tue), a 1,000-acre (405-hectare) natural heritage site that includes Chimney Rock itself. An elevator whisks visitors 26 stories to the top of the formation, 1,200ft (366 meters) above sea level. The waterfalls of majestic **Hickory Nut Falls** were the backdrop for the climactic scenes in the movie *The Last of the Mohicans*.

THE GREAT SMOKIES

Great Smoky Mountains National Park ⓫ (tel: 865-436-1200; www.nps.gov/grsm; daily), 16 of whose peaks exceed 6,000ft (1,800 meters), sprawls majestically over the North Carolina and Tennessee borders. Access on the North Carolina

side is via the town of **Cherokee** by taking I-40W Exit 27 (US 74) from Asheville, then Exit 103 (US 19). The arrival in Cherokee is jarring, with the 21-story Harrah's hotel and casino dominating the townscape. The resort is vital to the economy of the Cherokee Nation, whose reservation surrounds the town.

The town of Cherokee is the unofficial capital of the Eastern Band of the Cherokee. About 12,000 members of the tribe live on the Quallah Boundary, the name of the 56,000-acre (23,000-hectare) reservation that is adjacent to the national park.

A string of souvenir shops sells mass-produced moccasins, beadwork, key rings, and other gee-gaws. Many schedule "Indian dances" for entertainment. The 11,000 years of documented Cherokee history is presented with dignity at the **Museum of the Cherokee Indian** (tel: 828-497-3481; www.cherokeemuseum.org; daily). An introductory film describes the Cherokee's use of stories and nature to define their place in the world. Displays explain their non-material social order, the visit to England by their leaders to meet King George III, and their efforts to have their land recognized as an independent nation. Although the US Supreme Court upheld their claim in 1831, Jackson ignored it.

Qualla Arts and Crafts Center (tel: 828-497-3103; www.quallaartsandcrafts. com; daily), next to the museum, is the oldest Native American arts co-operative in the country. Contemporary Cherokee artists display traditional and interpretive takes on pottery, fetishes, and both decorative and ceremonial objects. **Oconaluftee Indian Village** (tel: 828-497-2111; http://visitcherokeenc. com; May–Oct Mon–Sat) recreates life in a Cherokee village in the year 1760.

US 441 climbs out of Cherokee across the Great Smoky Mountains toward **Gatlinburg**. As you start the trek, a sign warns of "35 miles of steep, winding road." You soon reach **Oconaluftee Visitor Center** in Great Smoky Mountains

National Park, a recently built green building that enjoys an impossibly beautiful location in a broad glade surrounded by the blue-grey mountains.

There are many overlooks along the way. It is impossible to capture the views on camera, but you will try anyway. There's a stop light at the end of the forest; drive out of the park proper and you will abruptly find yourself in the commercial center of **Gatlinburg**, confronted with every chain restaurant and souvenir shop known to man. **Sky Lift Gatlinburg** (tel: 865-436-4307; www.gatlinburgskylift.com; Apr–Oct daily, Nov–Mar times vary) lifts riders 1,000ft (459 meters) above the valley for peaceful views of the vast forest. There's free parking at the visitor center and a shuttle service into town.

Pigeon Forge, 4 miles (6.5km) away is home to Dollywood Theme Park (tel: 800-365-5996; www.dollywood.com) – the creation of Dolly Parton, the buxom country singer and actress, who grew up in Pigeon Forge – and more resort attractions. To bypass them turn on State Route 449 and continue to the T-intersection at Dolly Parton Parkway. Turn right to rejoin US 441.

TOWARDS KNOXVILLE

Driving northeast from Gatlinburg, you will pass through pleasant hills and pastures for 23 miles (37km) to **Chestnut Hill**, home of **Bush's Baked Beans** (tel: 865-509-3077; www.bushbeans.com; Mon–Sat). The visitor center is in the original 1897 family general merchandise store on the highway. The brand is best known for a popular US television ad featuring Duke, a talking dog, who schemes to sell the secret family recipe. There is a video virtual tour of the factory and the company's story (the recipe really does come from the family matriarch), a scale telling your weight in beans, and the opportunity to have your photo taken with Duke via backdrops. The café features Southern dishes and the "bean of the day."

From the visitor center, take State Route 92 to **Dandridge**. The views along Lake Douglas will have you ready to buy lakefront property. From here, I-40 is a straight shot to **Knoxville ⑫**, home of the University of Tennessee. Tennessee is proud of its musical heritage, and it starts at Knoxville **Visitor Center** at 301 Gay Street (tel: 865-523-7263; www.visitknoxville.com; daily), the location of *The Blue Plate Special*, a Monday to Saturday, live, free noontime performance of traditional music broadcast over radio station WDVX.

In 1982, Knoxville was the site for the World's Fair, which attracted 11 million visitors from 30 countries and established Knoxville – considered an unlikely location for the event – as a sophisticated urban venue. The most attractive downtown feature is an extensive park with a lake and rock-lined creek, which was created for the World's Fair. None of the buildings erected for the fair remain.

The exhibit "Voices of the Land" at the **East Tennessee Historical Society** (tel: 865-215-8824; www.easttnhistory.

Breathtaking view across Great Smoky Mountains National Park.

org; daily) consists of written and oral excerpts from diaries, letters, and official documents, which give the region's history a personal perspective. "Betsy," Davy Crockett's rifle, is on display, as are relicts from the Civil War (which quickly degenerated into personal vendettas here), and of logging. Main Street in the **Old City** is a pedestrian shopping and business area. A few blocks away, **12th Street** is an up-and-coming residential and entertainment district.

James White's Fort (tel: 865-525-6514; www.jameswhitesfort.org; Apr–Nov Mon–Sat, Dec–Mar Mon–Fri) is the restored farm of Knoxville's founder. As many as 100 people, along with livestock, stayed inside the palisaded compound, which is not much bigger than a lot in a suburban housing development. Across the street, at the **Women's Basketball Hall of Fame** (tel: 865-633-9000; www.wbhof.com; May–Labor Day Mon–Sat, Labor Day–Apr Tue–Sat), you can watch videos of past moments of glory, as well as shoot some hoops. **Volunteer Landing** along the riverfront has a walking trail and the dock for a dinner cruise boat.

North of the city, on US 441, **Norris Dam** was the first to be built by the vast and important New Deal–era Tennessee Valley Authority, which brought electric power to this region in the 1930s. **Norris Lake** (www.norrislake.com), acclaimed as one of the cleanest in North America, has several marinas and supports houseboats and fishing. There are trails and campgrounds in the surrounding woods. On State Route 61, in Clinton, the **Museum of Appalachia** (tel: 865-494-7680; www.museumofappalachia.org; daily) is a "living mountain village" and does a superlative job of interpreting rural Tennessee. The extensive collection of transplanted buildings, demonstrations of basic skills of daily life, personal items, and the stories told by their owners make you deeply aware of how hard it was to survive in the mountains.

THE SECRET CITY OF WORLD WAR II

West of Knoxville at Exit 364 off I-40 is **Oak Ridge**, the "secret city" built in 1942; 75,000 people lived there in total secrecy to work on production of the first atomic bomb. The **American Museum of Science and Energy** (tel: 865-576-3200; www.amse.org; daily) tells the stories about life there, and includes a photo of guards frisking Santa. The rest of the museum is an explanation of nuclear energy and displays about the Y-12 National Security Complex, which is responsible for various aspects of nuclear activity, and dealing with nuclear vulnerabilities. Back on I-40, you enter the **Central Time Zone,** just past Exit 340. Take Exit 268, turn right on to State Route 96 to US 70 North. Turn left. You are now about 50 miles (80km) from Nashville. This rolling ride through the last of the mountains starts as a two-lane road on a thread-thin strip of land with steep ravines on one side. It levels out to pastures and cultivated fields where weathered, silver grey barns with faded red roofs pose for photos.

The Hermitage, Andrew Jackson's Tennessee home.

Just before you reach Nashville, stop to visit President Andrew Jackson's gracious and beautiful mansion, **The Hermitage** (tel: 615-889-2941; www.thehermitage.com; daily), on whose grounds still stands the pre-existing farmhouse in which Jackson lived before becoming America's seventh President. He died there in 1845.

NASHVILLE

In the 1850s **Nashville** ⑬ was considered the most refined and sophisticated city in the South, calling itself "The Athens of the South." In 1897, the city built a full-scale replica of the **Parthenon** for its centennial celebration. It still commands its imposing location on a hill in Centennial Park, complete with a 42ft (12.8-meter) -tall, gilded statue of Athena. The Parthenon also serves as **Nashville's art museum** (tel: 615-862-8431; www.parthenon.org; Tue–Sun) with a permanent collection devoted to 19th- and 20th-century American artists.

Frist Center for Visual Arts (tel: 615-244-3340; www.fristcenter.org; daily), located in the magnificent Art Deco former Post Office on Broadway, has no permanent collection. Instead, it stages three or four rotating visual exhibitions at any time. Often they complement each other; just as often, they demonstrate the great variety of visual expression.

Tennessee State Museum (tel: 615-741-2692; www.tnmuseum.org; Tue–Sun; free) offers a comprehensive exploration of Tennessee history and culture from the days of the mastodon to the early years of the 20th century. The centerpiece of the museum is an illustrated history of the Civil War accenting the role of Tennessee, a Confederate state. Occupying an entire floor are interactive exhibits with sound effects, film, battle flags, and personal effects of soldiers. There are also exhibits about the New South that Tennessee helped create during Reconstruction (the period after the Civil War), Davy

Crockett's powder horn, and a Conestoga wagon in which some long-forgotten family from Virginia migrated to the state in about 1800.

MUSIC CITY

Despite its other attractions, Nashville is known primarily as the epicenter for country music. Musicians, singers, songwriters, and performers have gravitated to the city since 1925, when radio station WSM began broadcasting the WSM Barn Dance show on Saturday nights. Two years later, it was renamed the **Grand Ole Opry** (tel: 615-871-OPRY or 800-SEE-OPRY; www.opry.com), a joking parallel to the program broadcasting classical opera that preceded it. In 1943, the show moved to **Ryman Auditorium** (tel: 615-889-3060; www.ryman.com; daily). With acoustics second only to the Mormon Tabernacle, it was originally built as the Union Gospel Tabernacle, hence the nickname of the auditorium as "The Mother Church of Country Music." But it staged theatrical and music performances of all genres, from Katherine Hepburn to Caruso.

> **Tip**
>
> Take a stroll along Nashville's Walk of Fame, found along the 1-mile stretch connecting downtown with Music Row. Star-and-guitar sidewalk markers commemorate Jimi Hendrix, Roy Orbison, and Emmylou Harris, among others.

All ages welcome at the annual Country Music Association (CMA) Festival in Nashville, Tennessee.

⊘ **Fact**

Interstate 40, the road
that connects Nashville
with Memphis, is known
as "Music Highway."

The Opry moved to expanded, modern facilities in 1974, and the Ryman closed until 1994. It now hosts a schedule of musical performances in the classic theater with its church pews and stained glass windows.

Today, the Grand Ole Opry is housed in a large, custom-built facility north of Nashville. To honor the Opry's history, a large circle of wood from the Ryman's stage is inlaid at the front of the new Opry stage. Performances are Friday and Saturday, with Tuesday shows during the summer. Every country artist dreams of being invited to perform there; to be chosen as a member of the Opry roster is a career highlight.

The Ryman is a cornerstone of a district devoted to country music defined by Second to Fifth avenues and Church to Demonbreun streets. Broadway, between Second and Fourth avenues, is lined with tiny honky-tonk bars that never close and where undiscovered musicians perform at all hours, each hoping that they'll be noticed by a passing talent agent. Stop at **Hatch Show Print** at 316 Broadway (tel: 615-577-7710; http://hatchshowprint.com daily). Since 1875, the company has produced handbills and posters for entertainers using wood block, letterpress techniques little changed from Gutenberg's press. Across the street, **Ernest Tubb Record Shop** (tel: 615-255-7503; www.etrecordshop.com; daily) opened in 1947. Its inventory, both CD and vinyl, is second to none.

The **Country Music Hall of Fame & Museum** (tel: 615-416-2001; www.countrymusichalloffame.org; daily) occupies an entire city block along Demonbreun Street. From above, the building is shaped like a bass clef; the windows mimic piano keys; the soaring northwest corner resembles the fins of cars from the 1950s. Allow at least three hours to even casually explore the exhibits. Starting with the origins of a music that deals with "real people and real lives," it honors singing cowboys and Western swing, Tennessee Ernie Ford, and the television variety show *Hee-Haw* (with the original cornfield set). Songwriters explain their musical inspiration, listening booths play

Country Music Hall of Fame, Nashville, Tennessee.

classic and forgotten recordings. Elvis' gold Cadillac, scores of guitars from famous owners, and Taylor Swift's laptop are on display. In the center of the buildings, the Hall of Fame has bronze tablets honoring members of the creative and business communities who are dedicated to advancing country music. The random placement of the plaques in the circular hall demonstrates the equality of all of the members.

The **Johnny Cash Museum** (tel: 615-256-1777; www.johnnycashmuseum.com; daily) on Third Avenue honors the memory and career of one of country music's iconic performers. The **Musicians Hall of Fame and Museum** (tel: 615-244-3263; www.musicianshalloffame.com; Mon–Sat), located at the Nashville Municipal Auditorium, is dedicated to "studio musicians," those who accompany artists and stars and who are rarely recognized. The **Willie Nelson and Friends General Store** (www.willienelsongeneralstore.com), near the new Opry, shows off Nelson's long career and sells all manner of Nashville and Nelson souvenirs.

MUSIC HIGHWAY

Most of the towns along I-40 claim connection to some musical star. Exit 143 leads to **Loretta Lynn's Ranch** (tel: 931-296-7700; www.lorettalynnranch. net; daily Apr–Oct, limited attractions Nov–Mar) with a replica of the "house in Butcher Holler" where the Coalminer's Daughter was born and tours of the 1837 plantation house she bought when she became a star.

Jackson, at Exit 82, claims Tina Turner, Isaac Hayes, and Carl Perkins. At **Casey Jones Village** (tel: 731-568-1222; www.caseyjones.com; daily), a museum and performance venue shows off all of the genres. Jackson was the home of John Luther Jones, nicknamed Casey, who entered into history when he rode his engine, *The Cannonball Express,* into the rear of a stalled freight train, slowing his train enough that all of his passengers

survived. The house where he lived with his wife and three children is open for tours. The train depot is filled with articles about the Casey Jones legend and the history of Tennessee railroads. Hank Williams, Jr lives in nearby Paris.

West Tennessee Delta Heritage Center at Exit 56 (tel: 731-779-9000; www.westtnheritage.com; daily) is a good place to stop to gather information about attractions throughout the region. If you have time, swing past The Mindfield in **Brownsville** on South Main/Highway 54. Tennessee's largest outdoor sculpture, at first glance it looks like an electrical substation. A closer look shows it to be an ever-expanding, visionary reflection on life by self-taught artist Billy Tripp.

Tennessee's music and cultural heritage rolls right on in to **Memphis** ⑭ (see page 194).

ARKANSAS

At Memphis, the I-40 crosses the **Mississippi River** into Arkansas. With barely 3 million people in an area of 53,000 sq miles (138,000 sq km),

Lunch break at a Civil War re-enactment event.

Wildflowers on a farm in Ozark Mountain Country.

MEMPHIS: MUSIC CITY USA

The gateway to the Mississippi delta, Memphis is home of the blues, Beale Street, and the memory of two kings: Elvis and Martin Luther.

The guest list at Memphis's ornate and venerable **Peabody Hotel** (pronounce it ho-*tel;* www.peabody memphis.com) has included US Presidents as well as General Robert E. Lee, but today's notables are the Peabody ducks. Every day at 11am, they take a ride in the elevator from their rooftop home to the lobby, waddle across a red carpet and, to the strains of John Philip Sousa, hop into

Beale Street music clubs, Memphis, Tennessee.

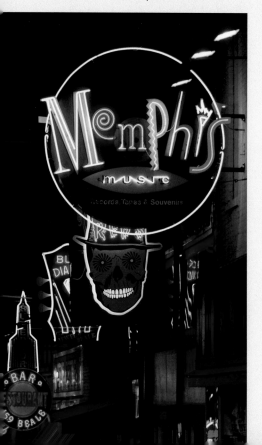

the fountain, where they happily paddle around until 5pm, when the performance is repeated in reverse.

Memphis is best known, of course, for **Graceland** (tel: 800-238-2000; www.graceland.com; Mar–Nov daily, Dec–Feb Wed–Mon), home and final resting place of Elvis Presley. The in-depth, self-guided audio tour covers the bottom floor and basement of the mansion. Other buildings contain his awards, and concert and movie memorabilia. Arrive early: on busy days, the wait for the shuttle to the mansion can be over an hour.

Sun Studio (tel: 800-441-6249; www.sunstudio. com; daily) was where "the King" recorded, but B.B. King, Ike Turner, and many other artists preceded him here. In recent years, Bono, U2, and Paul Simon have been Sun clients. Half-hourly tours are given. The **Stax Museum of American Soul Music** (tel: 901-942-7685; www.staxmuseum. com; Tue–Sun) celebrates musicians like Aretha Franklin and Otis Redding, who lived, worked, or are buried in the Memphis area called Soulsville, while the **Memphis Rock 'n Soul Museum** (tel: 901-205-2533; www.memphisrocknsoul.org; daily) on Beale Street has seven galleries that examine the history of the city's music.

There are plenty of other music venues, among them the **Center for Southern Folklore** (tel: 901-525-3655; www.southernfolklore.com; daily), which puts the music in a larger cultural and social context and runs the annual Music and Heritage Festival. **Beale Street** is where it all began, and the street's bars and nightclubs swell with the strains of the Delta blues created by W.C. Handy (1873–1958).

On Mulberry Street, the **National Civil Rights Museum** (tel: 901-521-9699; www.civilrightsmuseum.org; Wed–Mon) incorporates the Lorraine Motel, where Martin Luther King, Jr was assassinated on April 4, 1968. The sight of the rumpled bed, breakfast tray, and a few objects in Room 306 – the last things Dr King saw before stepping onto the balcony – somehow make the event very personal. Other exhibits chronicle key moments in the American Civil Rights movement and global efforts toward human and civil rights.

much of Arkansas remains undeveloped, which accounts for one of its nicknames, "The Natural State." The state capital, Little Rock, has just over 200,000 people; Fort Smith, the second largest, has just over 88,000.

Instead of taking the interstate, consider traveling US 70 west to Little Rock. Take time to observe some of the best of Arkansas' natural landscapes along this route – rich Delta bottomland, prairie, pine forests, and cypress swamps – before rejoining I-40 at Galloway at Exit 161.

LITTLE ROCK

The Arkansas River carves a gateway between the Ouachita and Ozark mountains to the delta at **Little Rock ⑮**. The city is, therefore, first and foremost, a river city. **Breckling Riverfront Park** is a wonderful outdoor space with great walking along the water, a fountain that's filled with laughing kids and more than a few adults in hot weather, and the "Little Rock" after which the city is named.

Markham Street has hotels and the convention center. Cross Broadway, and the street becomes President Clinton Avenue. This is **River Market District**, the center of activity for tourists and entertainment. At the **Clinton Presidential Library** (tel: 501-374-4242; www.clintonlibrary.gov; daily), the self-guided tour includes the only full-scale replica of the Oval Office, a timeline of President Clinton's career, and many of the gifts collected by the Clintons during their time in the White House. Outside, a refurbished railroad bridge is now a pedestrian walkway crossing the river to North Little Rock, a developing neighborhood.

Behind the library is the headquarters of **Heifer International** (tel: 855-948-6437; www.heifer.org; Mon–Sat). The charity develops self-sufficiency by giving livestock to poor communities in the Third World. The exhibits at Heifer Village in Little Rock explain how this

leads to better living conditions and social progress.

Arkansas Museum of Discovery (tel: 501-396-7050; www.museumofdiscovery.org; Tue–Sun) is fun for kids and adults, so much so that the museum has "adults only" nights. Tornado Alley Theater places you inside a tornado shelter during a storm. Even knowing that it's not real, it is still very frightening.

Surrounded by the modern city, the **Historic Arkansas Museum** (tel: 502-324-9351; www.historicarkansas.org; daily) is a collection of the first buildings in Little Rock. The city's oldest structure, the **Hinderliter Grog Shop**, sadly no longer serves customers. The museum's pride is the printing press used to produce the state's first newspaper.

The modern history of Little Rock is inexorably linked to the ordered desegregation of **Central High School**. In 1957, nine black students entered the school past scores of violent protesters. The city already planned to desegregate the high school that year, but the Governor swore that Arkansas schools

Re-living a Civil War battle in Arkansas.

> **⊙ Tip**
> You may want to roll down your windows when traveling through Arkansas: a highway department program has resulted in the planting of 600 kinds of wildflowers, some of which attract hummingbirds.

would remain segregated. Inside **Central High School Visitor Center** (tel: 501-374-1957; www.nps.gov/chsc; daily), interactive displays re-create the tension-filled weeks and includes recollections of the Central High Nine and others who were involved at the school and in the community.

Arkansas Arts Center (tel: 501-372-4000; www.arkansasartcenter.org; Tue–Sun) is committed to building a collection of outstanding works on paper, from the Renaissance to the present. You can wander past art by Van Gogh, Cézanne, and Jackson Pollack. Contemporary crafts are another focus, with pieces from glass artist Dale Chihuly and Dorothy Gill Barnes.

A submarine is about the last thing you'd expect to find on the Arkansas River, but the **USS *Razorback*** is berthed at the **Inland Maritime Museum** (tel: 501-371-8320; http://aimmuseum.org; Wed–Sun). The sub saw duty in the Pacific, during the Cold War, and in Vietnam before being decommissioned in 2001, after near 65 years of service. Guided tours show off the extremely complicated machinery and tight quarters the crew tolerated.

HOT SPRINGS

The hour-long drive from Little Rock to **Hot Springs** ⑯ is purely functional. Take I-30W to Exit 111 and US 70. The last part of the drive goes through some steep mountain terrain; hikers can explore the trails around the resort town. There are several access points to the trailheads, which are clearly marked. Native Americans called Hot Springs "the Valley of the Vapors" for the steam rising from the thermal waters. By the 1880s it was an elegant resort town, when Bathhouse Row, with its elaborate spa houses, was completed. Today, two of the bathhouses still operate. Buckstaff Bathhouse (tel: 501-623-2308; www.buckstaffbaths.com; Mon–Sat) offers traditional tub baths, while Quapaw Baths and Spa (tel: 501-609-9822; www.quapawbaths.com; Wed–Mon) has a more modern atmosphere and amenities. Impressive **Hot Springs National Park** (tel: 501-620-6715; www.nps.gov/hosp; daily) preserves Bathhouse

Country star Charlie Daniels performing at the Grand Ole Opry, Nashville, Tennessee.

Row and Fordyce Bathhouse. The self-guided tour includes bathing rooms, lounges, and the gym where Babe Ruth worked out.

Before there was Las Vegas, there was Hot Springs. In the 1930s and 1940s, this was the hangout of the famous and notorious. Al Capone and Lucky Luciano vacationed here. Many of the buildings that are shops now were speakeasies then. For an entertaining version of that era, visit the **Gangster Museum of America** (tel: 501-318-1717; www.tgmoa.com; daily). Wearing fedoras and using just enough New York accent, guides tell stories – most of them true – about the decades when Hot Springs was synonymous with vice, corruption, and good times.

A few miles from town, **Garvan Woodland Gardens** (tel: 501-262-9300; www.garvangardens.org; daily) is a welcome break from the hustle of Hot Springs. Operated by the University of Arkansas' Department of Landscape Architecture, the gardens were once a timber clear-cut area. Restoration began about 40 years ago, and the gardens are now a showcase of blooms, bulbs, and perennials, mature trees and shrubs, a koi pond, and flowing streams and waterfalls. There are golf cart tours for those with mobility issues.

MOUNT MAGAZINE

The two-hour drive from Hot Springs to **Mount Magazine State Park** 🕗 (www.arkansasstateparks.com/parks/mount-magazine-state-park) goes through some of the loveliest scenery in Ouachita National Forest. Leave Hot Springs on State Route 7, continue to State Route 10, and turn onto State Route 309 to the park. This is the crown jewel of Arkansas' superior state park system. The "Island in the Sky" is the highest peak in the state, rising 2753ft (839 meters) above the valley where Blue Mountain Lake shimmers. It's a natural destination for nature lovers, with dozens of hiking trails, facilities for rock climbing, backpacking, hang-gliding, and mountain biking. On the east side of the mountain, **Mount Magazine Lodge** has breathtaking views of the valley.

⊘ Tip

Stop by Old State House Museum in Little Rock, the place where Bill Clinton gave his election night victory speeches (tel: 501-324-9685; www.oldstatehouse.com; daily).

The State Capitol, Little Rock, Arkansas, where former US President Bill Clinton served five times as governor.

⊘ MINIATURE MISSISSIPPI

Spend a pleasant, relaxing day at **Mud Island River Park** (tel: 901-576-7241; www.mudisland.com; mid-Apr–Oct Tue–Sun), a scaled down version of the Mississippi River in a lovely riverside setting.

Among activities here, you can walk in miniature the entire 954 miles (1,535km) of the Mississippi, from Cairo, Illinois to the Gulf of Mexico, with accurate, real-time water levels and geographic, geologic, and historic details. Running the length of this island in the middle of the Mississippi, it takes about an hour to complete the journey. The museum focuses on the days of the Mississippi riverboats, including a nearly full-scale replica of a paddle wheeler to explore. There are also small boats and bikes to rent (the park includes cycling trails).

Fact

Fort Smith features in *True Grit*, a novel by Charles Portis that inspired two movie adaptations.

From Hot Springs, take State Route 7 north to Ola, switch to State Route 10, then turn onto State Route 309 in Havana. The 90-minute drive is one of the most scenic in the state.

FORT SMITH

From Mount Magazine, take State Route 309 north to I-40W to **Fort Smith** ⑱. The town revels in its Wild West heritage. The lovely restored Victorian mansion at 2 North B Street that houses **Miss Laura's Visitor Center** (tel: 479-783-8888 or 800-637-1477; www.fortsmith.org/miss-laura's-visitor-center; daily) was once Miss Laura's Social Club, one of the town's more upscale bordellos. It is now on the National Register of Historic Places, and many of the rooms are restored to their "business" appearance, and staff cheerfully give tours.

Fort Smith National Historic Site (tel: 479-783-3961; www.nps.gov/fosm; daily) tells the rest of the lively history. The courtroom of "Hanging" Judge Parker and the jail where many of the defendants in the 13,490 cases he heard were incarcerated have been restored. Excellent displays recount the hard, dangerous, violent, and exciting time when outlaws slipped across the river into "Indian Territory," followed by US marshals.

Fort Smith Museum of History (tel: 479-783-7841; www.fortsmithmuseum.org; Tue–Sat, June–Aug also Sun) pays more attention to the city's "respectable" times and its citizenry, who often maneuvered around the lawless residents. The old-time soda fountain is a good place for refreshment. At Fort Smith Trolley Museum (www.fstm.org), a railcar museum, hop aboard a restored vintage **trolley**, which circulates through the downtown historic district. The scenic railroad ride that chugs through the countryside is especially grand in the fall.

When Elvis Presley joined the army, he reported to Fort Chafee, just south of Fort Smith, to the east of I-540. **Chaffee Barbershop Museum** (tel: 479-434-6774; Mon–Sat) is where he had that famous haircut. Located in the Chaffee Crossing Historic District (http://chaffee-crossing.com), the barbershop is restored with the chair Elvis sat in and videos of the famous buzzcut. Fort Smith has played a major role in other events, including helping Vietnamese refugees and housing evacuees from Hurricane Katrina. The building has exhibits about those more important activities.

FAYETTEVILLE

Although I-40 will carry you all the way through the state of Oklahoma and westward, it you are interested in a more colorful journey, we suggest taking I-49 to **Fayetteville**, about an hour north of Fort Smith. The city is home to the University of Arkansas and the first house owned by Bill and Hillary Clinton when they were both instructors at the university. The **Clinton House Museum** (tel 479-444-0066; www.clintonhousemuseum.org; Thu–Tue) is a modest, Tudor-style house on a side street near the school

Paddle steamer on the Arkansas River, Little Rock.

Pull into the gravel driveway and knock on the front door. Volunteers have great stories about how it took Bill six months to put tiles around the fireplace, a job he told Hillary would take a weekend.

BENTONVILLE: FINE ART AND WAL-MART

Further along I-49, just below the Missouri line, is **Bentonville**, home of Walmart, the largest retailer in the US. One of the storefronts facing the town square is the original five-and-dime store that Sam Walton ran and where his Walmart plans were made. The store is now the **Walmart Museum** (tel: 479-273-1329; www.walmartmuseum.com; daily). After viewing a video tribute to Sam Walton and a promotional cheerleading piece about the corporation, you go through many displays about the growth of Sam's empire and its operations today.

The Waltons are the richest family in America, with a combined wealth of 151.5 billion dollars. So when Alice Walton decided to build a museum dedicated to American art and history, she went on a cultural shopping spree that wowed the art world. (She purchased the Hudson River School landscape *Kindred Spirits* by Asher B. Durand from the New York Public Library for a reported $35 million.) The result is the stunning **Crystal Bridges Museum of American Art** (tel: 479-418-5700; www.crystalbridges.org; Wed–Mon). Every "master" in American art from Colonial to modern times is represented; you will see Charles Wilson Peale's portrait of George Washington and Andy Warhol's tribute to Dolly Parton. The building, designed by Moshe Safdie, is notable: eight linked pavilions bordering two large pools fed by Crystal Springs, which gives the museum its name.

From here, continue north on US 71 into Missouri. At **Joplin** ⑲, you can pick up America's Mother Road, Route 66, which cuts across the southeast corner of Kansas before entering Oklahoma. Parts of Joplin were devastated by a massive tornado that ripped through the southeast corner of the city in May 2011.

Bill and Hillary Clinton's former home in Little Rock, Arkansas.

Tempting rural road in Oklahoma.

OKLAHOMA TO NEW MEXICO

Take "a stroll on wheels" along Route 66 through Oklahoma and the Texas Panhandle, then cruise through Santa Fe and Albuquerque before heading west to Gallup. The highway anthem begins here.

Oklahoma was the site of one of the most dramatic land rushes in the country in 1889. Today, the Sooner State, as it's known, is where we finally get to know 2,448-mile (3,940km) -long Route 66 (see page 35), the Mother Road of John Steinbeck's *Grapes of Wrath*, which has one of its longest drivable stretches in Oklahoma.

Be prepared to get lost. In some cases, the brown "Historic US 66" signs vanish, with little or no indication as to where the road has gone, or whether it has been subsumed by the nearby inter-state. Time, patience, and guesswork are the keys to a successful trip – along with a reliable segment-by-segment map. Expect to take at least eight days to drive the whole route – from the road's origin in Illinois to the final mile in California. A thorough exploration will take longer.

ROUTE 66 INTO OKLAHOMA

Route 66 enters Oklahoma at **Quapaw** in the northeast corner, then traverses 400 miles (644km) of the state, running parallel to (or being replaced by) I-44 as far as Oklahoma City, where you pick up I-40 west through New Mexico, Arizona, and much of California.

Starting in 1817, Oklahoma became Indian Territory, where tribes living on lands east of the Mississippi were force-ably resettled by an expansionist US

government. But after the creation of Oklahoma Territory and the subsequent Land Rush, Indian Territory was halved almost overnight and Oklahoma's tribes were forced to abandon communal ownership in favor of small individual plots. More than 65 Indian tribes are represented in the state, and you will drive across numerous reservations as you follow Route 66 west.

MIAMI TO CLAREMORE

The first major town you'll come to after entering Oklahoma, **Miami** ⑳

⊙ Main attractions
Gilcrease Museum
Philbrook Museum of Art
National Cowboy & Western Heritage Museum
Oklahoma Route 66 Museum
Santa Fe
Albuquerque Old Town
Acoma Sky City
El Morro National Monument

Map on page 202

Open-road relic along the Oklahoma leg of Route 66.

Oklahoma City to Los Angeles

Oklahoma

Oklahoma City 22
Yukon
66 El Reno
Exit 108 ★ Fort Reno 23   Geary
Hydro
281 Weatherford
Clinton
40 Foss
Elk City
Sayre
Erick
Texola

24 Oklahoma Route 66 Museum

Texas

66 Shamrock
★ Pioneer West Museum
McLean 25
Groom
40 Conway 87 217
26 Amarillo Stanley Marsh's   Palo Duro
★ Cadillac Ranch Canyon State Park
66 Vega
Adrian 27

New Mexico

40 Tucumcari 28

Santa Rosa
Exit 256 ★ Route 66 Auto Museum
84 Las Vegas
25 Santa Fe 29   40
285
Cline's Corner Exit 218
Moriarty
40 ★ Albuquerque 30
Pueblo Laguna
Cubero
23 Acoma Sky City
Exit 81 Grants 53 El Morro National Monument
Milan Bandera Volcano & Ice Cave
Zuni
Window Rock 40
264 Gallup 31

Arizona

Painted Desert Petrified Forest
★ National Park 32
33 Holbrook
40 Joseph City
Homolovi Winslow 34   Meteor Crater
State Park Exit 233

Winona Walnut Canyon National Monument
Monument Valley 35 Flagstaff Oak Creek Canyon
89 Parks ★ 89A
Sedona 36
38 Grand Canyon 40 Williams 37 Jerome
64 Ash Fork 89
Exit 139 Seligman 39
Grand Canyon West Grand Canyon National Park
(Grand Canyon Skywalk) 66 Peach Springs
Truxton
Las Vegas 93 Kingman 40
★ Goldroad
Oatman 41
Exit 1 Topock

California

Needles
Goffs
40 Essex **Desert**
Mojave Amboy
Ludlow
Newberry Springs
40 Daggett
Barstow 42
Rainbow Basin Natural Area 66 Helendale
Calico Ghost Town
Early Man Archeological Site Victorville
15 ★ California Route 66 Museum
215 San Bernardino 43
66 Rancho Cucamonga
La Verne
San Dimas
Glendora
210 Azusa
Monrovia
Arcadia
◎ Los Angeles 44

(pronounced "My-am-er"), is named for a local tribe (as is Quapaw). Located in what was once a prominent zinc mining region, Miami is still a commercial center and an early segment of Route 66 passes right through town. Miami's pride and joy is its restored Spanish Revival landmark **Coleman Theatre** (tel: 918-540-2425; www.colemantheatre.org; free tours Tue-Sat), built in 1929, which still has its Wurlitzer organ. Look for **Waylan's Ku-Ku Burger**, a classic 66 drive-in as you leave town.

Southwest of Miami, you can drive one of two stretches of original 9-foot-wide old alignment Route 66 "sidewalk highway" to **Afton**, named for the daughter of a Scottish railroad engineer after a river in Scotland. It's worth a stop to visit **Afton Station Route 66 Museum** (tel: 918-284-3829; www.aftonstationroute66.com; Tues-Sun), a restored vintage DX gas station with a Route 66 museum on First Street.

Vinita was founded in 1871 by Elias Boudinot, son of one of the Cherokees who sold ancestral lands to the US government, resulting in the Cherokee Trail of Tears mass migration in 1838. Boudinot renamed the community after a friend, Miss Vinnie Ream, who, at the age of 18, sculpted the lifesize Lincoln statue in the US capitol. Route 66 is still alive and kicking in Vinita. **Clanton's Cafe** (www.clantonscafe.com), opened in 1927, is the oldest continually owned family restaurant on Route 66 in the state, and you'll find many vintage 66 buildings in town.

Four miles (6km) east of **Foyil** is the world's largest totem pole. At 90ft (27 meters) tall, it is one of several sculpted by Ed Galloway in the 1940s. Foyil's main street sits on Oklahoma's first stretch of original Portland Cement concrete-paved Route 66. It's named after Andy Payne, the local man who won the 84-day "Bunion Derby" in 1928, which required contestants to hike 2,400 miles (3,862km), from ew York to Los Angeles, mostly along oute 66.

In **Claremore**, stop to visit the inter-sting **Will Rogers Memorial Museum** el: 918-341-0719; www.willrogers.com; aily Mar–Nov; Wed–Sun Dec–Feb). ight galleries with interactive exhib-s commemorate the Cherokee-born owboy, vaudeville performer, social ommentator, and renowned wit, one of klahoma's most famous native sons. he section of I-44 between Miami nd Tulsa is known as the Will Rogers urnpike. It's the subject of a folk song elebrating Route 66 by Woody Guthrie, ho was born in Okemah, southeast f Oklahoma City, where the popular oodyfest (www.woodyguthrie.com) is elebrated every July.

Just outside Tulsa is **Catoosa**, home a classic Route 66 roadside attrac-on: a large, smiling papier-mâché **lue Whale** sculpture next to a swim-ing hole and picnic area popular ith Tulsans. Adjoining **Molly's Land-g Restaurant** (http://mollyslanding. om) is a scenic spot for a barbecue inner before heading into Tulsa, here there's plenty more good od ahead in the cultural capital of klahoma.

ULSA: BIRTHPLACE OF OUTE 66

ulsa ㉑ with a population of just over 08,000, on the banks of the winding rkansas River, was once known as he Oil Capital of the World. It paraded s wealth in a number of glorious, ow-restored downtown Art Deco usinesses and hotel buildings, and legant mansion-filled neighborhoods uch as Brookside, south of 11th Street n the post-1933 Route 66 alignment.

Plan on spending a day visiting Tul-a's two most important museums, /hich are housed in the former homes nd extensive gardens of two men who nade their money in oil but whose love f art and beauty created a lasting leg-cy in their hometown.

The **Gilcrease Museum** (tel: 918-596-2700; www.gilcrease.org; Tue–Sun), northwest of downtown, houses one of the largest collections of Western and Native American art in the US, the life's work of Thomas Gilcrease, who deeded his home and collection to Tulsa in 1955. Part of the University of Tulsa School of Art, the museum includes the satellite Henry Zarrow Center for Art & Education (www.utulsa.edu/zarrow-center) in the vibrant Tulsa Arts District downtown (www.thetulsaartsdistrict.org).

Also in the Tulsa Arts District is the **Woody Guthrie Center** (102 East M.B. Brady Street; tel: 918-574-2710; http://woodyguthriecenter.org; Tue–Sun), which houses a major Guthrie archive, including the original lyrics to the sing-er's famous anthem, "This Land is Your Land." The archive was purchased for $3 million by the George Kaiser Fam-ily Foundation in 2012. It represented something of a homecoming for Guthrie, Oklahoma's prodigal son, in the year of the centennial of his birth.

The gorgeous **Philbrook Museum of Art** (tel: 918-749-7941; www.philbrook.

> ## Tip
>
> 1-44 is a turnpike, or toll road, between Miami, Oklahoma and Oklahoma City. Not all tollbooths are manned, and automatic entries may require exact change, so be sure to carry plenty of quarters and dollar bills with you. Ask for and keep your receipt; if you get on and off to visit Route 66 towns, you'll get a refund at those exits.

Tulsa, Oklahoma.

org; Tue–Sun), south of 11th Street, in a leafy neighborhood off Peoria Avenue, is housed in a 1927 Italian villa-style home and gardens built by Waite Phillips. The wide-ranging art collection, which is displayed thoughtfully in its intimate home setting, includes many fine works by Native American and Southwestern artists, a passion of Phillips, whose former home in northeastern New Mexico, Philmonte, is now another fine art museum. No matter your age or inclination, this is truly a romantic and inspiring place to visit. The European-style café overlooking 23 acres (9 hectares) of classical gardens created by Phillips himself, a renowned gardener, is a welcome respite from sticky heat in summer.

Tulsa's disappearance from Route 66 literature is perplexing, all the more so because, as Tulsa historian Michael Wallis, author of the best-selling *Route 66: The Mother Road*, says: Route 66 owes its very existence to the tireless efforts of Tulsa resident Cyrus Avery. Avery was the owner of a gas station and restaurant on Mingo Circle near the 11th Street Bridge (now Cyrus Ave Memorial Bridge) and was a drivin force in getting Route 66 built in 1926.

After decades of neglect, Tulsa finally getting round to promoting i important role in Route 66 histor Funds have been allocated to bui gateway signs at the east and we ends of 11th Street, the main Route drag through Tulsa. Already built is th **Cyrus Avery Centennial Plaza**, next the Cyrus Avery Memorial Bridge. Th plaza has a large bronze statue entitle "East Meets West," depicting the Ave family in a Model T Ford encounter ing a horse-drawn carriage on its wa back to Tulsa from the western Okla homa oilfields. Officials are hopin to break ground on the long-planne state-of-the-art Route 66 Experienc in 2018/2019 at the plaza. Followin news that Congress is finally consid ering recognizing Route 66 as a desig nated National Historic Trail, hopes a high for additional federal funding an that Tulsa will feature on every tou ist's Route 66 itinerary.

DINERS, MOTOR COURTS, AND WINERIES

After crossing the river, Route 66 con tinues through the rough-'n'-tumbl of industrial West Tulsa to nearb **Sapulpa**, which became an impor tant cattle shipping center with th arrival of the railroad (cowboy sta Gene Autry once sang in the local ice cream parlor here). Sapulpa is hom to **Frankoma Pottery** (www.frankomap tery.com), founded in 1933 and locate on an old alignment of Route 66. Th attractive vintage ceramics were popu lar with Route 66 eateries like Norma Diamond Café, which closed when it longtime owner died, and have becom collector's items. The pottery was so to a Texas owner in 2012, and output now reduced to pieces mainly aimed the art market.

The stretch of Route 66 betwee Sapulpa and Edmond is one of th

The "Welcome Sundown" statue at the National Cowboy & Western Heritage Museum.

ongest and most scenic Route 66 segments in Oklahoma and a popular day trip destination. The country is rolling, and its lush greenery contrasts nicely with the bright red Oklahoma soil, fields of corn, and distinctive grain silos, signs that you are still in the fertile confluence of the Midwest and South and have not yet reached the arid West.

The route follows the train tracks through **Kellyville** and **Bristow**. Don't miss the turnoff for **Depew**, a Route 66 near-ghost on the old alignment where the old Main Street has been restored by Route 66 enthusiasts. This is an unexpected and charming photo op.

Stroud is certainly no ghost; in fact, it's roaring to life as the center of what is becoming Oklahoma wine country, with some 47 wineries in the area on a wine trail. You'll find wine tasting rooms as you pass through town, but be careful about drinking and driving around here – Oklahoma's finest are often out in force, particularly on weekends. Best to stop a while and soak up any alcohol with a buffalo burger

at the historic **Rock Café** (www.rock cafert66.com) in a 1939 redrock building in the center of town. The Rock Café is famous in these parts. It burned down in 2008, but its fans helped rebuild it, and it reopened (its owner, Dawn Welch, by the way, was the model for Sally in the movie *Cars*).

It's worth a quick stop at **Davenport** to drive its bumpy 1925 brickway to view the enormous murals depicting scenes from its past painted on the buildings. The Early Bird Diner on the corner is covered in license plates – a classic Route 66 montage.

The winding road through the pretty town of **Chandler** has a classic Route 66 feel. The **Lincoln Motel** with its cabins and garages, is a classic motor court motel, albeit one that has seen better days, but don't miss the innovative **Route 66 Interpretive Center** (tel: 405-258-1300; www.route66interpretivecenter.org; May–Sept Tue–Sun, Oct–Apr Tue–Sat) in the 1937 redrock building that once housed the armory, where the Route 66 experience includes lying on beds and doing a virtual Route 66 trip.

Fancy hood ornament on an antique Ford at a classic car rally.

Clinton, Oklahoma, has one of the best Route 66 museums along the historic road.

There are two major landmarks at the appropriately pastoral **Arcadia**: the large and distinctive restored 19th-century **Old Round Barn** (www.arcadiaroundbarn.com) and **POPS Dine** (www.pops66.com/arcadia-ok-on-route-66; daily), a fun retro gas station and diner in a massive glass cantilevered building in the Deep Fork River Valley. POPS was designed by the same firm that created the Oklahoma Route 66 Museum in Clinton, and driving in here on a busy Saturday night feels just like arriving on the set of *Happy Days*. Another branch has opened in Nichols Hills, Oklahoma City.

Just past **Lake Arcadia** in Edmonds, Route 66 is a fickle customer as you enter the sprawling Oklahoma City suburbs. Plan on taking I-44 south to visit the state capital.

AN EXUBERANT STATE CAPITAL

Oklahoma City ㉒ sprang up overnight on April 22, 1889, when the Oklahoma Land Rush opened up the adjoining territory to settlement, attracting 50,000 hopeful prospectors. Its appeal for visitors today is its attractive **downtown**, filled with renovated Art Deco bank buildings and boutique hotels and the adjoining **Bricktown Historic District**, where restored warehouses house hip restaurants and nightclubs as well as an unexpected treasure, the delightful **American Banjo Museum** (tel: 405-604-2793; www.americanbanjomuseum.com; Tue–Sun) – a must-see for bluegrass fans.

Downtown has benefited from the planning genius of architect I.M. Pei who, in the 1960s and 1970s, helped develop the city's urban renewal plan, creating an elegant mix of lakes, parks, landscaped hills, distinct neighborhoods, and stylish buildings. Highlights are **Myriad Botanical Gardens** (tel: 405-445-7080; www.myriadgardens.org; daily), a 17-acre (7-hectare) oasis with a seventh-floor illuminated Crystal Bridge housing a plant- and tree-filled tropical conservatory and waterfall and **Oklahoma City Museum of Art** (tel: 405-236-3100; www.okcmoa.com; Tue–Sun), which has one of the country's most extensive collections of art glass by master glassblower Dale Chihuly.

Water, plants, light, and art also feature prominently in what, for many visitors, is Oklahoma City's most important destination: the poignant **Oklahoma City National Memorial & Museum** (tel. 405-235-3313; www.oklahomacitynationalmemorial.org; daily), commemorating the April 1995 bombing of the Alfred P. Murrah Federal Building which killed 168 adults and children. At the memorial, which is managed and well interpreted by the National Park Service, the dead are remembered with 168 empty cast-bronze chairs on a grassy slope under a canopy of trees facing a reflecting pool. A surviving building to the north now houses the memorial museum. In front is the Survivor Tree, a large spreading oak that escaped destruction and is now a symbol of hope. Dusk, a reflective time of day, is a good time to visit

The historic first Phillips gas station in McLean, Texas.

You can sit quietly with other pilgrims to Oklahoma's Ground Zero, watching birds swooping overhead and the lights beneath the chairs turn on, so that they appear to float ethereally between heaven and earth – an apt metaphor.

CLASSIC NEON, COWS, AND OIL

Even more than Tulsa, Route 66 seems to hide in plain sight in OKC, but buildings on old alignments along 23rd Street and Beltline 66 are still visible. The 1930 **Milk Bottle Grocery Building**, just north of 23rd Street on an old alignment of Route 66, is the epitome of Route 66 roadside vernacular architecture, with its large milk bottle advertising local Braum's milk atop a 350-sq-ft (33-sq-meter) triangular building. Its last incarnation – as a Vietnamese sandwich shop – ended when the fast food outlet closed its door. Plans to restore the landmark are still in the works.

Oklahoma's State Capitol (right on Route 66, at NE 23rd Street and Lincoln Boulevard) is unique in having a working oil pump on its grounds, a reminder that the city's wealth stemmed from a major gusher 75 years ago; oilfields still operate in the state. Cotton was once king here, but cattle ranching dominates today. This heritage is celebrated at **Stockyards City** (www.stockyardscity.org), a few minutes southwest of downtown, off I-40, where ranchers and real cowboys have been coming since it grew up in the early 1900s as a place for apparel, equipment, supplies, and a good meal.

NATIONAL COWBOY & WESTERN HERITAGE MUSEUM

If you're drawn to the cowboy lifestyle, check out the **National Cowboy & Western Heritage Museum** (tel: 405-478-2250; www.nationalcowboymuseum. org; daily), just northeast of downtown, off I-44 (Exit 129). This sprawling museum feels overscaled and rather "old school," and emphasises contemporary and historic Western art, which

might make it rather boring for kids (although there is a frontier town they can walk through). As always, the Hollywood Cowboy gets good treatment: movie posters of Gene Autry, Tom Mix, and John Wayne decorate one gallery, close to a larger-than-life statue of Ronald Reagan and the museum's famous centerpiece: the huge statue titled *The End of the Trail*, by James Earle Fraser.

Continue west on Route 66 or I-40; either will do, as the two highways become one, anyway, about 40 miles (64km) west of the city. The Chisholm Trail, which was used to trail cattle to market, ran along what is now Ninth Street in tiny **Yukon,** just outside the OKC limits on Route 66, hometown of country music star Garth Brooks. Sid's Diner and Johnnie's Grill in neighboring **El Reno** claim to be the home of that distinctive Oklahoma treat – the Fried Onion Burger. The El Reno Hotel, built in 1892 when rooms cost all of 50 cents a night, is now part of the Canadian County Historical Museum (tel: 405-262-5121).

⊘ Fact

Famous Texans include Larry McMurtry, the Pulitzer Prize-winning author of *Lonesome Dove*, the definitive Western novel based loosely on real-life people and events.

The Big Texan in Amarillo, Texas, offers a free meal of 72-ounce steak and fixings as long as you eat all of it in an hour.

CHISHOLM TRAIL

Fort Reno ❷❸ (tel: 405-262-3987; www.fortreno.org; daily) displays exhibits from the days when it served as a cavalry post during the Indian Wars. El Reno is now the headquarters for the Cheyenne-Arapaho tribe.

If you take Exit 108 off I-40, a short detour north on US 281 leads to **Geary**, bypassed by Route 66 in 1933 despite the locals' work in grading and graveling the road in the hope of enticing the route, and its dollars, through their town. Not far away is **Left Hand Spring Camp**, where Jesse Chisholm, who gave his name to the famous Chisholm Trail, is buried. The trail, which stretched 250 miles (400km) from San Antonio to Abilene, was first laid in 1860, when bison still roamed nearby. Twenty years later, when the trail was more or less abandoned, it had seen the passage of more than 10 million cattle.

STEEP HILLS AND HISTORIC GAS STATIONS

Near where I-40 intersects with US 281 is the 3,944ft (1,202-meter) -long "pony bridge" crossing the South Canadian River, a multiple simple-span bridge typical of the type used in the construction of Route 66. In addition to offering superb vistas of the river, the William H. Murray Bridge starred in a scene in John Ford's 1940 movie version of *The Grapes of Wrath*.

The hill leading to the bridge is so steep that Model T Fords – their engines generating more power in reverse – had to climb it backward (something that was also a problem on New Mexico's infamous La Bajada Hill on the pre-1938 Route 66 alignment between Santa Fe and Albuquerque).

Continuing west on I-40, just north of Exit 88 is Lucille's gas station and store at **Hydro.** Lucille ran the property for 59 years till her death in 2000, and it's still a sentimental stop for Route 66 regulars, some of whom had been buying gas and groceries here since 1941. In 2004, a local resident bought Lucille's and restored the exterior; he later opened Lucille's Roadhouse (http://lucillesroadhouse.com) in nearby **Weatherford**, as a tribute to this 66 landmark and its longtime owner. Other Weatherford landmarks include a building with Greek columns (formerly a bank, now a dress shop) and the century-old Lee Cotter's Blacksmith Shop, where the **General Thomas P. Stafford Air and Space Museum** (tel: 580-772-5871; www.staffordmuseum.com; daily), a Smithsonian Institution affiliate, has fighter jets and moon rocks and commemorates Oklahoma's premier astronaut.

A MOTHER ROAD MUSEUM

You really begin to feel like you're traversing the old road at sleepy **Clinton**, with a population of just 9,500, where the state-sponsored **Oklahoma Route 66 Museum** ❷❹ (tel: 580-323-7866; www.okhistory.org/sites/route66; Feb–Nov daily, Dec–Jan Tue–Sat) is the most comprehensive – and memorable – of many similar places found along the famous highway. In 2012, it underwent a major

The Cadillac Ranch art installation just west of Amarillo, Texas.

enovation to improve its audiovisual
xhibits in each of the rooms dedi-
ated to a single decade in the history
f Route 66. Kids will love the com-
uter game that allows you to stick to a
oute 66-era daily budget while trave-
ng across country. Each room has
crapbooks containing headlines of
ie era and typical family memorabilia.

There are photographs of the road's
onstruction in the 1920s. In the
930s, Oklahoma was still "dry," and
ie rise of the bootlegger prompted a
orresponding increase in the num-
er of law enforcement officers, who
re pictured in their intimidating uni-
orms. A typical garage from the same
ra – with its glass-topped Red Crown
asoline pump – flanks pictures of a
w of the three million Okie migrants
ı their battered trucks bearing "Cali-
ırnia or Bust" signs. The photos
f trucks, crammed with furniture,
edding, pots and pans, and crated
ıickens, typify the Dust Bowl years,
ıen parched farmlands induced the
estward-flight of almost one-fifth of
ıe state's population.

A Greyhound bus and a VW bus evok-
g the hippies-on-the-road era of the
960s are among the vehicles on show,
ıe "bug" illuminated by fluorescent
ghting in a room whose walls display
xties album covers from records by
rank Sinatra and Dina Shore to Hank
'illiams and Chuck Berry.

A poster promoting a one-time rat-
esnake show, a map made by a retired
ostmaster with franking stamps from
very post office along the route, a glass
ase of souvenirs from long-vanished
ft shops, a diner, and a video running
ʋaint family movies on an endless loop
·e also part of the museum tour, which
imaxes with a nostalgic and heart-
ıgging movie celebrating the ongoing
ɔmance of the road and its characters
ıd places, written and narrated by
other Road historian Michael Wallis
ou can also rent an audio tour of the
ıuseum by Wallis).

GRAPES OF WRATH TOWNS

The ghost town of **Foss** and the Old
Town Museum complex of relocated
old buildings at **Elk City** (misleadingly
dubbed the National Route 66 Museum
– it's not) might draw you off the road
after leaving Clinton. When the US
Highway 66 Association held its convention in Elk City's Casa Grande Hotel
in 1931, more than 20,000 enthusiasts
attended. Songwriter Jimmy Webb
("Up, Up, and Away") was born here.

Sayre is also alarmingly empty
these days. Its main claim to fame
is that its somewhat grand county
courthouse featured fleetingly in the
movie The Grapes of Wrath. The small,
fairly ordinary town of **Erick** and the
almost deserted **Texola** have each
– at different times by different surveys – been declared as sitting on the
100th meridian, the longitudinal arcs
running through both the North and
the South poles that are used as geographical definitions.

On the stretch heading through Erick,
Route 66 is renamed Roger Miller Boulevard – a tribute to its songwriting ("King

*Tinkertown is an
eccentric miniature
roadside attraction on
the Turquoise Trail,
north of I-40, a scenic
back route to Santa Fe.*

*Mascot outside the Big
Texan steak ranch.*

⊙ Tip

Remember to set your watch back an hour as you cross the border between Texas and New Mexico and move from the Central to Mountain time zone.

of the Road") native son, who is celebrated in a small downtown museum.

THE TEXAS PANHANDLE

As you make your way west, the high plains of Oklahoma merge into the Texas Panhandle, and the air becomes drier, the prairie grass shorter, and the hills eroded buttes and mesas. There's an overwhelming sense of insignificance in the face of the wide, open space stretching as far as the horizon. As might be expected in Texas, there is also a palpable feeling of having arrived in the real West, reflected in the expansive confidence of its residents.

At **Shamrock**, Texas, don't miss the lime-green-and-sand-colored Art Deco masterpiece, the **U Drop Inn** (now a tourism office; www.shamrocktexas.net), and adjoining gas station with matching tower. Early gas stations had to fight hard for customers in a competitive market, and the filling pump station took many forms. One, on the site of Albuquerque, New Mexico's present-day Lobo Theater, was shaped like a giant chunk of ice.

The Jemez Mountains are northwest of Santa Fe, New Mexico.

Picturesque, sleepy **McLean** (pop. 778), which describes itself as "the heart of old Route 66," feels like the backdrop to *The Last Picture Show*. Here, an old Phillips 66 gas station has been restored by volunteers and is one of a surprisingly small number along the route (there are none at all in Arizona). The Phillips Petroleum Company records some of the many erroneous explanations people have offered for the "66" in the company's name. Historian Michael Wallis claims to have the real story from Phillips himself in his book: Phillips was traveling 66mph (106kph) on Route 66, when the new name came to him.

BARBED WIRE: THE DEVIL'S ROPE

At the **Devil's Rope Museum** (tel: 806-779-2225; www.barbwiremuseum.com; Mon–Sat, in winter call to check if open), the "rope" in question is barbed wire, a large rusty ball of which sits outside. Although the museum has only a small selection, more than 8,000 different types exist. In the mid 1800s, there were hundreds of competing designs, but it was Joseph F. Glidden's patent for fencing material consisting of barbs wrapped around a single strand of wire, that eventually dominated.

The unpaved section of Route 66 between Alanreed and **Groom** has always been a problem for unwary drivers. Jericho Gap, as it was known, "was notorious for bogging down cars and trucks in a black gumbo mud every time it rained," according to Route 66 guidebook authors Bob Moore and Patrick Gauwels. As you get to Groom, be on the lookout for the huge leaning water tower defying gravity beside the road.

PALO DURO CANYON

Just before Amarillo (where local rancher J.F. Glidden invented his barbed wire), turn south on US 87 to visit **Palo Duro Canyon State Park** (tel:

806-488-2227 ext.100; www.paloduro canyon.com), dubbed "Texas's Grand Canyon" and closely associated with legendary cattleman Charles Good-night. Goodnight – inventor of the chuckwagon and once owner of the largest ranch in Texas – was the first rancher to move into the Panhandle in the 1870s. Chuckwagon tours, begin-ning or ending with Cowboy Breakfast or Dinner, are offered on the rim of the canyon, where part of an Indiana Jones movie was filmed.

AMARILLO

Dusty **Amarillo** ㉖, redolent with the smell of feedlots, stages regular rodeos; for more information contact Amarillo Convention and Visitor Coun-cil (tel: 800-692-1338; www.visitamarillo. com). Route 66 fans know it for its big-and-cheesy **Big Texan Steak Ranch** (http://bigtexan.com), a fun roadside attraction offering 72oz (2kg) steaks free to anybody who can eat one (along with the sides) within an hour. The city's one-way traffic system can be confusing, but you'll be back on Route 66 proper if you follow Sixth Street, which leads into "**antique row**," where plenty of Route 66 shops and modern cafés entice visitors with their colorful signage, such as the Golden Light Café (http://goldenlightcafe.com).

Just west of town is **Cadillac Ranch**, the much photographed chorus line of graffiti-covered Cadillacs, an art instal-lation by the Ant Farm and funded by local art patron Stanley Marsh. The Cadillacs, with their rear ends stick-ing out of the earth, are literally in the middle of a field, south of I-40. To get closer, look for a frontage road parallel to the interstate, where you can park for free and walk through a gate to take your snapshots of the cars.

MIDPOINT OF ROUTE 66

Vega is largely a ghost now, but you can still see old buildings roadside, including the restored 1926 Magnolia Gas Station and the Vega Motel, which is now closed. Tiny **Adrian** ㉗ has one big claim to fame: it sits at the exact halfway point of the Mother Road: 1,139 miles (1,833km) to Chicago and 1,139 miles to Los Angeles. A sign announc-ing this fact can be found at the west end of town, right across from a restau-rant that has been operating on Route 66 since its earliest days, the **Midpoint Café** (tel: 806-538-6379; www.facebook. com/MidpointCafe; breakfast, lunch daily), a classic diner famed for its Midpoint Ugly Pie and burgers.

NEW MEXICO

Nothing can prepare you for the pleas-ure of your first encounter with the aesthetic beauty of New Mexico, a high-desert landscape of dun-colored earth, sagebrush, dwarf pinyon and juniper trees, floating mesas, and dis-tant high volcanic peaks. A big yellow sign announcing "Welcome to New Mexico, Land of Enchantment" is an invitation that generations of dreamers along Route 66 have happily accepted: many have never left.

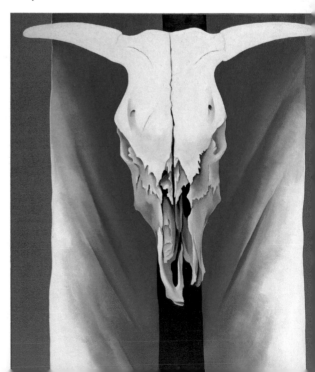

Cow's Skull: Red, White and Blue by Georgia O'Keeffe, who has a museum dedicated to her in Santa Fe, New Mexico.

The country here, the Llano Estacado (Staked Plains) – a high plateau covering 33,000 sq miles (85,430 sq km) – is one of the hottest, flattest areas of the continental US. Spanish explorer Francisco Vasquez de Coronado unsuccessfully combed the region for the fabled Seven Cities of Cibola back in 1540, expecting to uncover unimaginable hoards of gold and silver. Instead, he discovered innumerable Indian pueblos, where the glitter came from micaceous adobe homes and jewelry crafted from local turquoise by native artisans. Nineteen of these pueblos remain today and are open to visitors.

TUCUMCARI CURIOS AND NEON

Route 66 extends more than 300 miles (483km) across the state along I-40. On its eastern end, the road crosses and re-crosses I-40 before running through **Tucumcari** ㉘ ("Two Miles Long and Two Blocks Wide"), where the **Tee Pee Curios Store** (1944) is one of the oldest souvenir shops along the route. Every conceivable type of souvenir item turns up here, and in dozens of independently

run shops in one small town after another along the route: pop-up art of paper buildings, old postcards, caps jackets, scarves, traffic signs, sheriff's badges, playing cards, mugs, glasses, paperweights, ashtrays, earrings, belt buckles, money clips, and even baby bibs bearing the Route 66 logo.

Homely Tucumcari once trumpeted its "Thousands of Motel Rooms" on its famed "Tucumcari Tonite" roadside signs. With the decline in traffic, that is no longer the case, but the town is home to a famous motel veteran of the highway, the historic **Blue Swallow** (http://blueswallowmotel.com), famous for its Southwest Vernacular style, bright neon blue swallow sign, and old-style garages. It was run for decades by Lillian Redman, a kind and charitable innkeeper who was given the motel as an engagement present by her future husband. Under new family ownership since 2011, it has been upgraded sensitively but remains an essential stop for Route 66 buffs.

SANTA ROSA

Santa Rosa, famous for its sparkling freshwater lakes, maintains strong links to Route 66. **Route 66 Auto Museum** on Will Rogers Boulevard (tel: 575-472-1966; daily) displays classic cars, and the town hosts a Route 66 Festival every September. Joseph's Bar and Grill (www.josephsbarandgrill.com) has been serving burgers and New Mexican food to Route 66 travelers since 1956 (look for its historic Fat Man logo, which once graced the 1935 Center Café, a Route 66 landmark).

A DETOUR TO SANTA FE

Just past Santa Rosa, at Exit 256 from I-40, is a major Route 66 detour that you won't want to miss. The old pre-1938 alignment of Route 66 swings north on US 84, crosses the Pecos River, and passes through tiny Hispanic villages toward Las Vegas, New Mexico, before turning sharply west

Painting the Santuario de Nuestro Señor de Esquipulas, in Chimayó, New Mexico.

o reach **Santa Fe** ㉙, the oldest state apital in the US.

Santa Fe was the end of the Santa 'e Trail, which, beginning in 1821, an from here for almost 800 miles 1,290km) to Kansas City, Missouri, nd was the major western trade and mmigration route until the railroad rrived in the 1880s. You can still ollow the old Route 66 alignment o the Santa Fe Plaza on Old Santa 'e Trail (Pecos Trail exit from I-25), long Water Street, out on Cerrillos Road (Highway 14), and south through anto Domingo Pueblo and Algo- ones to Albuquerque; it was decom- nissioned in 1938, when a straighter oute through Albuquerque super- eded it and cut 126 miles (200km) ff the journey.

Today, the traditional adobe build- ngs in Santa Fe's attractive historic lowntown district, with their flat oofs and large portals, are filled with ntriguing museums, superb restau- ants, small inns, lively bars, art gal- eries, and unique boutiques selling outhwest arts and crafts. Santa Fe is nown as the "City Different" because f its unique blend of Ancestral 'ueblo, Colonial Spanish, and early american history and contemporary rtistic culture, which make the city ne of the most popular destinations n the Southwest.

N HISTORIC CULTURAL MECCA

'he heart of Santa Fe is its **Plaza**, vhich dates to the founding of the ity by Spanish settlers from Mexico round 1610. With its bandstand, vrought-iron benches, and seasonal edestrian-only streets, it offers good eople-watching and free outdoor oncerts in summer. Stretching along he north side is the **Palace of the iovernors** (tel: 505-476-5100; www. alaceofthegovernors.org; May–Oct daily, Nov–Apr Tue–Sun), where Pueblo ven- lors sell high-quality jewelry, pottery, nd other crafts beneath its portal.

The seat of regional government for 300 years by successive administra- tors from Spain, Mexico, and the US (as well as, briefly, local Pueblo dur- ing the 1680 Pueblo Revolt), the pal- ace is the oldest public building in the country. It's now part of the **New Mexico History Museum** (tel: 505- 476-5200; www.nmhistorymuseum.org), a fascinating interactive museum that opened in 2009. In the next block is the **New Mexico Museum of Art** (tel: 505-476-5072; www.nmartmuseum. org), with works by Southwest artists. These two museums, as well as the **Museum of Indian Arts and Culture** (www.indianartsandculture.org) and the **Museum of International Folk Art** (www.internationalfolkart.org), both on Museum Hill, are part of the **Museum of New Mexico Foundation** (www.muse- umfoundation.org; all museums May– Oct daily, Nov–Apr Tue–Sun; free Fri 5–8pm and first Fri of Nov–Mar).

Nearby is the **Georgia O'Keeffe Museum** (tel: 505-946-1000; www.oke effemuseum.org; daily). Inspired by the light and landscapes, the artist made

Museum of Indian Arts and Culture, Santa Fe.

northern New Mexico her home. The museum holds the largest collection of her works.

East of the Plaza is the **Museum of Contemporary Native Arts** (tel: 888-922-IAIA; www.iaia.edu/iaia-museum-of-contemporary-native-arts; Wed–Mon) in the Santa Fe–style historic post office building. Run by the Institute of American Indian Arts, it contains the largest collection of contemporary Native American art in the country. Opposite is the **Cathedral Basilica of St Francis**, whose founding archbishop, Jean Baptiste Lamy, is buried below the altar. He was the model for the archbishop in Willa Cather's novel, *Death Comes to the Archbishop*.

Just past the cathedral is **Loretto Chapel** (tel: 505-982-0092; www.loretochapel.com; daily) with its "Miraculous Staircase." South of the river is Santa Fe's oldest section, home to the much-photographed **San Miguel Chapel** (tel: 505-983-3974; http://sanmiguelchapel.org; daily) and the **State Capitol**, or **Roundhouse** (tel: 505-986-4589; Mon–Fri). Even this governmental seat is an art

gallery, with works by New Mexico artists on its circular walls.

ART TOWN

Art is everywhere in Santa Fe. **Canyon Road**, off the Paseo de Peralta loop around downtown, was once a dirt track over the mountains used by locals but is now lined with art galleries housed in historic adobes (Friday night is Art Walk night, when many galleries stage openings; www.visitcanyonroad.com). West of the Plaza, South Guadalupe Street leads to **The Railyard** (www.railyardsantafe.com), the city's newest arts and entertainment district, with native plant gardens and converted warehouses containing a year-round farmers' market and art galleries, and the Rail Runner train depot, linking Santa Fe and Albuquerque.

Off Old Santa Fe Trail is Museum Hill, home to the delightful **Museum of International Folk Art** (tel: 505-476-1200; www.internationalfolkart.org; May–Oct daily) as well as the **Museum of Spanish Colonial Arts** (tel: 505-982-2226; www.spanishcolonialblog.org;

Lunch on the plaza at La Hacienda, Albuquerque.

Tue–Sun, May–Oct daily), **Wheelwright Museum of the American Indian** (tel: 505-982-4636; www.wheelwright.org; daily), and impressive **Museum of Indian Arts and Culture** (tel: 505-476-1250; www.indianartsandculture.org; Tue–Sun, May–Oct daily).

The city makes a good base for visiting other highlights in northern New Mexico, including the Eight Northern Indian Pueblos (www.santafe.org); the Santuario de Chimayó, "the Lourdes of America" (www.holychimayo.us); ancestral cliff dwellings at Santa Clara Pueblo (www.puyecliffs.com) and those protected in nearby Bandelier National Monument (www.nps.gov/band) and artsy Taos, to the north via the Rio Grande Gorge.

TOWARD ALBUQUERQUE

To continue, drive I-25 south, the fast route that parallels the old alignment to Albuquerque, or pick up the new alignment by heading south through Galisteo Basin on US 285 to I-40, a lovely scenic route. At the junction, you can't miss the roadside emporium **Cline's Corners** (www.clinescorners.com), in business since the 1930s, at a spot that founder Roy Cline described as "the coldest, the meanest, the windiest place on Highway 66."

The longest remaining stretch of Route 66 in New Mexico runs through **Moriarty**, a dusty ranch town. Nostalgic reminders here include a Whiting Brothers Gas Station and the huge 1960s "rotosphere" rotating neon Sputnik sign atop the former El Comedor de Anayas restaurant. This is one of only 264 remaining rotospheres created by Warren Milks between 1960 and 1971 and thought to be the only one on Route 66 still in use.

The State Fairgrounds in Albuquerque were the site of the 2001 75th anniversary celebration of Route 66. Post-1938 Route 66 bisects **Albuquerque ㉚**, running past the University of New Mexico at Nob Hill on

what is now Central Avenue. The Civic Center, the tourist office (www.visitalbuquerque.org), and a handful of vintage buildings are across the Atchison, Topeka, and Santa Fe railroad tracks, just past Second Street, in downtown Albuquerque. A multi-million dollar revitalization project has transformed this stretch of the route into a vibrant downtown scene with neon, theaters, nightclubs, hotels, and restaurants. A notable landmark is the **KiMo Theater** (www.kimotickets.com), built in 1927 in a fusion of Pueblo Revival and Art Deco styles.

ALBUQUERQUE'S OLD TOWN

Two miles (3km) farther west, before you reach the Rio Grande and the western edge of the city, **Old Town**, with its attractive shops and restaurants, is one block to the north of Central Avenue, its Plaza dominated by the adobe **San Felipe Church** (1706). Five flags have flown over this plaza: Spanish, Mexican, Confederate, the Stars and Stripes, and that of New Mexico (a red zia cross on a yellow background).

> **⊘ Fact**
>
> The redstone arch for which the Navajo Nation's capital, Window Rock, is named stands in a small park near the Navajo Nation Administration Center.

A 20ft (6-meter) arrow pierces the ground outside a store in Gallup, New Mexico.

In the heart of Old Town are the excellent **Albuquerque Museum** (tel: 505-243-7255; www.cabq.gov/cultural services/albuquerque-museum; Tue–Sun), covering Southwest art and history; the shuddery **American International Rattlesnake Museum** (tel: 505-242-6569; www.rattlesnakes.com; daily); and useful **Turquoise Museum** (tel: 505-247-8650; www.turquoisemuseum.com; Mon–Sat), which will guide you with jewelry purchases. Nearby are the **New Mexico Museum of Natural History and Science** (tel: 505-841-2800; www.nmnatu ralhistory.org; daily) with its planetarium, and **Explora** (tel: 505-224-8300; www. explora.us; daily), a hands-on learning center for kids. West of Old Town is the popular **Albuquerque BioPark** (tel: 505-768-2000; www.cabq.gov/biopark; daily), which offers a zoo, aquarium, and botanical garden at one location.

If you don't have time to visit an Indian pueblo, the next best thing is the excellent **Indian Pueblo Cultural Center** (tel: 866-855-7902; www.indian pueblo.org; daily), which has galleries telling the stories of each of the 19 pueblos. It has a gift shop, restaurant serving Pueblo-inspired cuisine, and free traditional Native American dance performances on weekends. Whatever your politics, the **National Museum of Nuclear Science and History** (tel. 505-245-2137; www.nuclearmuseum.org daily) presents an intriguing look at the Atomic Age and New Mexico's role in developing the atom bomb. Fans of the HBO series *Breaking Bad* may be interested in taking a 3-hour film location tour of Walter White's and Jesse Pinkman's Albuquerque (www.breaking badrvtours.com).

ACOMA SKY CITY

West of the Duke City, Route 66 passes near **Laguna Pueblo** (tel: 505-552-6654; www.lagunapueblo-nsn.gov), with its early 18th-century church, and **Cubero**, where an apocryphal tale claims that Ernest Hemingway wrote *The Old Man and the Sea* in a motor court motel. A side road heads south a few miles to **Acoma Sky City**, which, perched on a mesa 367ft (112 meters) above, claims to be the oldest continuously occupied village in the country (Taos Pueblo also makes that claim). Tribal members lead guided tours from **Sky City Cultural Center** (tel: 800-747-0181; www.acomaskycity.org; daily) up to the Old Pueblo and its historic church, explaining its complex history. The cultural center has an excellent small museum and a cafe serving traditional Acoma and Contemporary American cuisine.

Grants (named after three brothers) feels like a Route 66 town. In the mid-20th century it was a center for uranium mining, a history that can be explored in the **New Mexico Mining Museum** (tel: 505-287-4802; www. grants.org; Mon–Sat). The multiagency **Northwest New Mexico Visitor Center** (tel: 505-876-2783; www.nps.gov/elma/ planyourvisit), just south of I-40, has information about nearby national parks (remote Chaco Culture National Historical Park is to the north and will

The 1950s-style 66 Diner in Albuquerque.

equire at least a day trip) and other regional attractions.

Your best bet is to drive scenic Highway 53 between Grants and Gallup – a small detour south paralleling I-40 – or a taste of this glorious country of sandstone mesas and ancient volcanic lava flows from nearby Mount Taylor. Family-run **Bandera Volcano and Ice Cave** (tel: 888-423-2283; www.icecaves. com; daily) and **El Malpais National Monument** (tel: 505-783-4774 ext.801; www.nps.gov/elma; daily) interpret the volcanic features of the area; the highlight, though, is **El Morro National Monument** (tel: 505-783-4226; www. nps.gov/elmo; daily), a sandstone bluff whose base is covered in carvings (petroglyphs) and paintings (pictographs) made by centuries of travelers stopping for water at the pool below the rock. These included Native Americans, Spanish explorers and dignitaries, and the US Army Camel Corps, pioneers heading west, and railroad surveyors in the mid-1800s. A trail leads to ruined Atsinna Pueblo atop the rock.

Just before you reach Gallup, the highway passes through **Zuni**, the largest pueblo in the state, famous for its Our Lady of Guadalupe Mission dating from 1629 and intricate silver jewelry skilfully inlaid with turquoise and coral.

GALLUP'S MOVIE STAR HANGOUT

Although its redrock setting is glorious, the spit-and-sawdust railroad town of **Gallup** ㉛ isn't pretty to look at. It is, however, a classic Route 66 town, one you should not miss. The highlight, on the east end of town, is **El Rancho Hotel and Motel**, built in 1937 by Raymond E. Griffith, who passed himself off as the brother of movie pioneer D. W. Griffith. From the beginning, the hotel was a favorite with movie stars shooting on location; by the 1960s, at least 15 movies had been shot using the hotel as headquarters, among them *Sundown*, *Streets of Laredo*, and *The Hallelujah Trail*.

Gallup tags itself "Where the Indian Southwest Begins" and is a major trading center for the Navajo, or Diné – 300,000 in number – who live on the 9,817-sq-mile (25,426-sq km) adjoining **Navajo Nation**. The Navajo capital of **Window Rock** is 25 miles (40km) northwest of Gallup, just across the border in Arizona, on State Route 264.

Indian arts and crafts, such as handmade rugs and jewelry, can be bought at longtime trading posts like Richardson's and Ortega's in downtown Gallup, a 12-block area around Hill Avenue and Fourth Street. The **Rex Museum** (tel: 505-863-1363; www. gallupnm.gov/208/Rex-Museum; Mon–Fri) is in the century-old Rex Hotel, while the historic train depot houses a cultural center staging nightly ceremonial Indian dances in summer. In August, check out the world-famous Intertribal Indian Ceremonial (tel: 505-863-3896; https://gallupceremonial. com), an enormous powwow held over 10 days in **Red Rock Park** (tel: 505-722-3839), east of town. This park has nicely developed campsites.

Swapping gas for leg power on a desert road.

Frank Lloyd Wright Spire,
Scottsdale.

ARIZONA TO LOS ANGELES

Wigwam motels, vintage gas stations, soda fountains that work – the cruise along Route 66 continues, taking in ghost towns and the Grand Canyon along the way.

The Mother Road becomes difficult to follow over the border from New Mexico into Arizona, so if cruising the length of Route 66 is not a priority, you can remain on I-40 through Holbrook, Arizona. Approximately 25 miles (40km) inside the state, Exit 311 from I-40 leads to **Petrified Forest National Park** ㉜ (tel: 928-524-6228; www.nps.gov/pefo; daily), whose 220,000 acres (89,000 hectares) preserve giant petrified logs. More than 200 million years ago, the region was a swampy, tropical zone in which mineral-rich soil helped to preserve the fossilized bones of prehistoric animals. In the northern section of the park is **Painted Desert Inn National Historic Landmark**, now a museum and bookstore (no lodging; tel: 928-524-3522).

Dinosaur statues line the road on the way to **Holbrook** ㉝, whose outstanding attraction is the roadside **Wigwam Motel** (www.sleepinawigwam. com), a long-standing favorite (particularly with kids) on Route 66. Each of the 15 cozy rooms is inside its own tall, stone tepee built by owner John Lewis' father in the 1940s from plans by architect Frank Redford. He allowed seven similar motels around the country to be built from his plans, stipulating only that each be equipped with a radio that played 30 minutes for 10 cents.

Parked outside the tepees is the family collection of 1950s Fords and Buicks, while inside the main building a small museum exhibits chunks of petrified trees, Native American artifacts, and rifles and powder horns from the frontier days. A visitor center and historical museum can be found in the **Historic Navajo County Courthouse** (tel: 928-524-6558; http://holbrookazmuseum.org; daily), built in 1898, on Navajo Boulevard (Route 66), which runs through the center of town. Native American dances are performed

◎ Main attractions
Petrified Forest National Park
Meteor Crater
Monument Valley
Grand Canyon
Grand Canyon Skywalk
Kingman Route 66 Museum
Las Vegas
Route 66 Mother Road Museum
California Route 66 Museum

Map on page 202

1920s Route 66 gas station, Cool Springs.

⊙ Tip

If you want a letter to be carried via the Hashknife Posse in the spirit of the old Pony Express, send it, stamped, preferably in the first two weeks of January. Put that envelope in another stamped envelope addressed to the Holbrook Postmaster, Pony Express Ride, Holbrook, AZ, 86025. In the lower left-hand corner write: *Via Pony Express*. For more information, log on to https://nationalponyexpress.org/annual-re-ride/send-a-letter.

nightly on the courthouse lawn in summer. The local trading posts are a good place to buy Apache baskets, silver and turquoise jewelry, and pottery.

PONY EXPRESS

The spirit of the short-lived but legendary Pony Express, whose demise was sealed by the telegraph system some 150 years ago, is kept alive in Holbrook by riders in the Navajo County Hashknife Sheriff's Posse, who carry mail to Old Town Scottsdale (in metro Phoenix) in late January every year.

Under a contract with the US Postal Service, the 40-strong Hashknife Posse continues a tradition begun in 1954, when a similar posse carried an invitation to the state governor to attend a stampede. Some 20,000 letters (sent in from all over the world) are hand-stamped with the official ride logo and franked with a Pony Express postmark before being sent off in mailbags relayed by riders every few miles in the course of the 200-mile (320km) journey. A similar national Pony Express Re-Ride also takes place annually.

The posse's name is derived from The Hash Knife Outfit, a branch of the third-largest cattle company in the country, which began shipping out thousands of cattle after 1881 when the life-changing railroad began to go through here.

Holbrook's preserved **Blevins House** across from the Santa Fe Depot was the scene of a spectacular shootout on September 4, 1887, when the county sheriff went to arrest a horse thief and was wounded while gunning down several members of the thief's family. Nearby are the notorious Bucket of Blood Saloon, the 1910 J&J Trading Post, and the one-time Campbell's Coffee House, which became famous for its "Son of a Bitch stew."

ANCESTRAL PUEBLO RUINS

Five miles (8km) off I-40 near **Joseph City** ("Joseph Small Town" would be more appropriate) is the Jack Rabbit Trading Post, with its original crouching rabbit sign, while 16 miles (26km) farther on, a turn north on State Route 87 – just before you get to Winslow – will take you to the extensive 14th-century Ancestral Pueblo site of **Homolovi State Park** (tel: 928-289-4106; www.azstateparks.com/homolovi; daily). The name Homolovi is the Hopi word for "Place of the Little Hills," and this is a Hopi ancestral site.

Winslow ㉞ achieved fame from its inclusion in the Eagles' hit "Take It Easy," written by Jackson Browne. The song refers to "Standin' on a corner in Winslow, Arizona," and visitors pour into town to do just that at Standin' on the Corner Park (Kinsley and Second streets), where there is a bronze statue of a man with a guitar. The lyric goes *Well, I'm standing on a corner in Winslow, Arizona/Such a fine sight to see/It's a girl, my Lord/In a flatbed Ford/Slowing down to take a look at me.*

Until the 1960s, Winslow – born with the arrival of the railroad in 1880 – was the largest town in northern Arizona.

Homolovi State Park, near Winslow, Arizona.

out business began to fade when it was bypassed by the interstate. Its rebirth began with the reopening of **La Posada** (tel: 928-289-4366; www.laposada.org), the 1930 Fred Harvey railroad hotel designed by Mary Elizabeth Jane Colter and lovingly restored by Allan Affeldt.

South of Winslow, off State Route 99, Ancestral Pueblo petroglyphs can be admired in **Chevelon Canyon**, via tours conducted from Rock Art Canyon Ranch (tel: 928-288-3260; www.facebook.com/rock-art-ranch; Mon–Sat, advance reservations required). Anglers rate the area for its rainbow and (more enticingly) brown trout, which live in the lake and creek here.

About 20 miles (32km) west on I-40, Exit 233 leads to **Meteor Crater** (tel: 800-289-5898; www.meteorcrater.com; daily tours), a 600ft (183-meter) -deep hole almost a mile across created by the impact of a meteorite nearly 50 centuries ago. Astronauts were trained here before the moon visit, and Astronaut Memorial Park has an Apollo Space Capsule. The museum has exhibits documenting the history of meteorites impacting the earth

and a theater recreating those impacts as if you were at ground zero. Back on the interstate heading west, the ghost town of **Two Guns** sits on an abandoned portion of Route 66.

Although **Winona** features in Bobby Troup's "Route 66" song (it rhymes with "Arizona"), it's actually a dead-end, and what Route 66 historian Tom Snyder calls "a one-blink town." Near Winona, 7 miles (11km) before Flagstaff, is **Walnut Canyon National Monument** (tel: 928-526-3367; www.nps.gov/waca; daily), where a short hike down a paved trail reveals Sinagua Indian cliff dwellings that were abandoned hundreds of years ago.

FLAGSTAFF

The main commercial center in Northern Arizona is **Flagstaff** ㉟, a good base for trips to the South Rim of the Grand Canyon, 80 miles (129km) north. The trip up US 89 and then along State Route 64 is longer but more scenic than the shorter route from Williams, a small town to the west that also offers historic

The skeleton of a sickle claw dinosaur at the Museum of Northern Arizona in Flagstaff.

Navajo shepherd by the Ear of the Wind formation in Monument Valley Navajo Tribal Park.

⊙ MONUMENT VALLEY

A 182-mile (293km) journey from Flagstaff, Arizona, leads to one of the most famous sights in the Southwest. Monument Valley is easily recognized from far away thanks to scenes from countless Westerns, especially those by director John Ford, who often used it as the backdrop for his movies. With its serene rock formations dominating this high desert valley, these iconic landmarks were not just attractive to Hollywood but more importantly, formed a sacred cultural landscape for ancestors of modern Pueblo people and for the Navajo, who still live here. Medicine men may have journeyed to Rain God Mesa, site of a sacred burial ground, to pray for rain. The Totem Pole formation appears in Navajo origin stories, while the Yei-Bi-Chei formation resembles holy Navajo figures performing a traditional dance. Like the Grand Canyon or Sedona, the timeless mystery of these rocks is humbling, but geologically, they were shaped by differential erosion of local sandstone and shale into hoodoos, odd-shaped stone landmarks that make the landscape feel alive. You can hire a tour guide at the visitor center (tel: 435-727-5870) to show you around or do a self-guided tour of the famous landmarks on the rugged scenic loop. Stop at the visitor center to pay the entrance fee and pick up a map. For more information, contact Navajo Nation Parks and Recreation in Window Rock (tel: 928-879-6647; www.navajonationparks.org).

railroad day trips to the canyon. Two Flagstaff museum attractions, the **Pioneer Museum** (tel: 928-774-6272; www.arizonahistoricalsociety.org/museums; Mon–Sat) and the **Museum of Northern Arizona** (tel: 928-774-5213; www.musnaz.org; daily), are not far apart on North Fort Valley Road, (US 180) enroute to the canyon. Flagstaff's other attractions are either in or near the Downtown and Southside historic districts, which are separated by the railroad and Route 66 (the tourist office is in the historic railyard depot). A Route 66 Days Charity Car Show takes place each September with live music, a parade of classic cars, and displays of arts and crafts.

Route 66 rolls into Flagstaff from the east, north of the interstate and train tracks, with motels, neon, and history. Check out the **Museum Club** (tel: 928-526-9434; www.themuseum club.com; daily), a 1931 huge log roadhouse that began as a "zoo" filled with stuffed animals during Prohibition. Now listed on the National Register of Historic Places, it has just reopened under new management (no restaurant but food trucks are planned). It remains a popular dance club, where country musicians like Willy Nelson have played. On Mars Hill, just west of downtown, is **Lowell Observatory** (tel: 928-774-3358; www.lowell.edu; daily), filled with astronomy history. South of downtown, off Milton Road, the main route back to I-40, is historic **Riordan Mansion State Park** (tel: 928-779-4395; http://azstateparks.com/Parks/RIMA; daily), built by a pair of brothers and lived in by them and their wives. It adjoins laid-back Northern Arizona University.

Opposite the train station, on Leroux Street, is the historic **Weatherford Hotel**, which opened January 1, 1899. That day, it welcomed among its score of distinguished guests the publisher William Randolph Hearst, President Theodore Roosevelt, and lawman Wyatt Earp. The bar boasts an antique counter that came from Tombstone, and the ballroom is named for Western author Zane Grey, who stayed here while writing *Call of the Canyon*.

On Route 66 near Winslow.

A young reader of Zane Grey's books was one Cecil B. DeMille, who concluded that Flagstaff sounded like a good place to launch his movie career. When he arrived from back East, however, it was snowing, and DeMille decided to continue on the train to Los Angeles, thereby altering the course of movie history forever.

An attractive side trip from Flagstaff travels down winding scenic State Route 89A, off Interstate 17, through spectacular **Oak Creek Canyon** to artsy **Sedona** ❸, 28 miles (45km) south. Its famed red rocks have attracted film directors, hikers, and New Age spiritual seekers drawn to its powerful energy vortexes – visited by Jeep tours. Southwest of Sedona is a less pricy artist's haven, **Jerome**, a former ghost town named after a defunct copper mine, with attractive Old West buildings that house restaurants, cafes, art galleries, and B&Bs.

BACK ON ROUTE 66

Between Flagstaff and Williams, Route 66 is poorly maintained but reaches its highest point on the route, at 7,300ft (2,225 meters) above sea level, just east of **Parks**. Parks in the Pines general store and Union 76 gas station (www.route66historicparksgeneralstore. com) opened in 1910 and also contains a post office. Nearby are the remains of the **Beale Wagon Road Historic Trail**, a sturdy 120ft (37-meter) -wide track constructed in 1857, used by pioneers to travel to the Colorado River.

Back on I-40, the next town, historic **Williams** ❸, as well as its Main Street on Route 66 and the nearby mountain, were named for Bill Williams (1787–1849), an early fur trapper whose statue stands at the west end of town. The excellent *Route 66 Magazine* was once published here, the last town on Route 66 to be bypassed by I-40.

Just north of Williams railroad depot (which also houses an interesting museum run by the US Forest Service) is the Grand Canyon Railway Hotel, a 1995 rebuild of historic Fray Marcos Hotel, one of the original Harvey Houses designed by famed architect Mary Elizabeth Jane Colter and

Monument Valley is an iconic landscape and an epicenter of Navajo culture.

Desert songbird.

Grandview Point, South Rim, Grand Canyon National Park.

located in the railroad depot. The 100-hotel chain was established by legendary restaurant and hotel entrepreneur Fred Harvey, an English immigrant, between 1876 and 1917, partnered with the Santa Fe railroad. Harvey revolutionized hospitality and tourism. One of his rules was that the coffee – served by smiling "Harvey Girls" in black dresses and spotless white aprons and bows who lived on the job and could not marry – was to be made fresh every two hours, even if the urn was full. For 75 cents, customers chose from seven entrees, second helpings included.

A tan-colored 1953 Cadillac and life-size cutouts of James Dean and Marilyn Monroe sit outside family-owned **Twisters Soda Fountain**. A "back-to-the '50s diner," it displays hundreds of snapshots of families taken along Route 66, and an old glass-topped Sky Chief gasoline pump that has been converted into a holder for typical road souvenirs. Sit here and immerse yourself in pure, unadulterated kitsch as you enjoy one of the dozen famous milk shakes, malts, floats, or cherry

phosphates. For dinner, keep with the Route 66 theme at the town's best restaurant, **Rod's Steak House** (www.rods steakhouse.com), which has been serving excellent steak dinners to travelers on the Mother Road since 1946.

THE GRAND CANYON

Williams is the main departure point for the South Rim of **Grand Canyon National Park** ⓸ (tel: 928-638-7888; www.nps.gov/grca; daily). Grand Canyon Railway (tel: 800-843-8724; www.thetrain. com) departs for the canyon every morning and offers a welcome opportunity to ditch driving for the day to ride the train and see one of the essential wonders of the West. The five-hour round-trip – by vintage steam locomotives in summer, diesel locomotives the rest of the year – leaves three hours for sightseeing at the South Rim, but the train journey itself in historic railroad cars is an attraction in itself (particularly for families), with strolling cowboy musicians and a lively "train robbery" on the ride home.

By car from Williams, it's a 40-mile (64km) drive north on US 180 to reach the South Rim. The main Grand Canyon Visitor Center is located opposite Mather Point, the first viewpoint inside the park entrance. The visitor center and park facilities are open 8am to 6pm in summer, but if you arrive after hours, there is a series of excellent large interpretive and trip planning panels in the open air plaza in front that are open 24 hours.

The main tourist hub is just west of here, in Grand Canyon Village. Lines are long, so park your car at the visitor center and hop on one of the free shuttle buses, which operate from March through November, taking you to the village. From there, the West Rim shuttle travels west along the popular 7-mile (11km) Hermits Road. You can hop on and off and walk segments of the pleasant paved Rim Trail to nine of the best canyon overlooks. (Private cars are only allowed on this route in winter.

At **Trailview Point**, you can look back at the village and the **Bright Angel Trail** switchbacking down to the river. In the morning, mule trains plod into the canyon, bearing excited greenhorns who may wish they'd gone on foot when the day is done. Other recommended viewpoints along Hermits Road are the **Hopi**, **Mohave**, and **Pima points**, offering breathtaking vistas of isolated buttes and "temples," many with fanciful names bestowed by early explorers. The road ends at **Hermits Rest**, which has a gift shop, concession stand, and restrooms. Hermit's Trail offers a moderate hike a short way into the canyon that makes a nice canyon day hike. Be sure to wear strong walking shoes, a broad-brim hat, sunglasses, high-factor sunscreen, and bring a liter of water and salty snacks even on short hikes; it is very hot and exposed here and you are at high elevation, so expect to feel some altitude effects, even if you are superfit. Don't push yourself, and try to hike early morning to avoid the heat.

East of Grand Canyon Village, a shuttle travels along **East Rim Drive** for 25 miles (40km), stopping at more breathtaking overlooks, Desert View Watch Tower, an Ancestral Pueblo–style stone tower designed by Mary Colter looking out to the Painted Desert with Hopi murals by Fred Kabotie.

It's worth staying at least a night at the South Rim to appreciate the changing vistas at different times of day, when the rock formations take on different colors and moods. You'll need to plan a stay far in advance. Reservations are taken up to a year ahead for the Grand Canyon lodges run by concessaire Xanterra (tel: 303-297-2757; www.grandcanyonlodges.com). Dinner reservations should be made then too; El Tovar Restaurant in particular books up fast. If unavailable, consider Tusayan, the gateway community outside the park, which has several good lodges and a couple of decent dinner options, though without the killer view.

BEYOND WILLIAMS

From Williams, 19 miles (31km) west along I-40, it's worth getting off the busy road to visit somnolent **Ash Fork**, which

Stomachs and gas tanks fueled here at Delgadillo's Snow Cap Drive-in, Seligman, Arizona.

Delgadillo's Snow Cap Drive-In, Seligman.

Clark Gable and Carole Lombard were married in Kingman, Arizona.

was a stagecoach depot until the arrival of the railroad in 1882. This was also a regular stop along Route 66 until the town was bypassed by the bigger thoroughfare. One of the Harvey Girls lived nearby until her death, and donated several artifacts from the defunct Harvey House chain to a fledgling museum located in a vast, empty warehouse beside the tourist office (tel: 928-637-0204; http://ashforkrt66museum.com). An old Corvette sits on a roof nearby, providing a fun photo opportunity.

SELIGMAN

Return only briefly to the interstate before leaving it again at the Crookton Road exit to drive the longest and most nostalgic section on the entire Historic Route 66. From here, you could stay on Route 66 all the way to the California border, at Topock, a distance of about 180 miles (290km).

Route 66 as it passes through Seligman.

Seligman ③ is a classic Route 66 destination, with the highway running right through town. Main Street is ined with strangely compelling gift shops devoted to the highway's history that carry every conceivable type of souvenir, from Route 66 highway signs, Mother Road license tags, and ol company signs to old Coca-Cola posters and bottles – as well as the now familiar inscribed mugs, glasses, an T-shirts. One of these is the iconi Delgadillo Route 66 Gift Shop (te 928-422-3352; www.route66giftshop.com the former barbershop of Route 6 booster Angel Delgadillo, who helpe revive the bypassed town as a Rout 66 attraction in 1987. It doubles as th town visitor center. Pick up a histori cal walking tour booklet and visit suc iconic Seligman sights as the Rust Bolt Souvenir and Gift Shop (www.rus bolt66.com) with its collection of vintag cars, and Delgadillo's Snow Cap Drive In, which serves classic road fare an kitsch in equal measure. In case yo were wondering: the Road Kill Caf ("You Kill It, We Grill It") does not serv animals squashed on the highway; it just a gimmick to get your attentio The bison burger here is pretty goo though, and don't miss the dollar bill pinned on the walls of the OK Saloon.

Twenty-five miles (40km) west of Seligman is **Grand Canyon Caverns** (tel: 928-422-3223; www.gccaverns.com; daily), into which early visitors paid 25 cents to be lowered 150ft (46 meters) by rope. Today, there's an elevator and illuminated paths on which to walk.

GRAND CANYON SKYWALK

Peach Springs is the tribal headquarters of the Hualapai Nation, whose lands encompass the western end of the Grand Canyon. **Grand Canyon West** (tel: 928-769-2636; www.grandcanyonwest.com; daily) is 242 miles (389km) from the entrance at the South Rim – nearly as long as the canyon itself. Here the Hualapai have built the popular Grand Canyon Skywalk, a U-shaped glass-bottomed walkway that extends from the edge of a clifftop out into the air above the canyon, giving visitors a hawks-eye view of the surroundings and the Colorado River, 4,000ft (1,220 meters) below. It's not for those with vertigo, nor for those on a budget. On top of the pricy Skywalk fee, visitors must purchase a Hualapai tour package to gain access to the site, but it's a fun day of activities and a unique opportunity to walk on air and see the canyon from a new perspective.

Access to Grand Canyon West, 70 miles (112km) north of Kingman, is via minor roads. The last 21 miles (34km) are on unpaved gravel surface, so those with low-clearance vehicles or RVs should use the Park and Ride coach service available at the site.

Kingman ⑩ is where the tubby, gruff-voiced movie star Andy Devine was born. The long boulevard through town is named after him. At the west end of Andy Devine Boulevard, and adjoining Beale Street, opposite the train depot, is Kingman's slowly regenerating historic downtown. Here you'll find a handful of museums, motels, and several eateries in historic buildings, including Beale Street Brews (www.bealestreetbrews.net) for locally roasted coffee before hitting the highway, and across the street, Black Bridge Brewery (www.blackbridgebrewery. com), a lauded place for microbrewed ale at the end of the day.

⊙ Tip

The "almost" ghost town of Chloride, Arizona (10 miles/16km north of Kingman) is a fitting venue for Old Miner's Day held in October each year. Join in the Old West festivities – mock gunfights, pie baking contests, parade, food booths, and more. For further information, call 740-603-4496.

Bright lights of Las Vegas.

Kingman's popular **Route 66 Museum** is located in the Powerhouse Visitor Center (tel: 928-753-9889; http://www.gokingman.com; daily); one of its exhibits is a re-creation of a small-town Main Street, complete with a yellow Fifties Studebaker. **Mojave Museum of History and Arts** (tel: 928-753-3195; www.mohavemuseum.org; Mon–Sat) displays attractive turquoise jewelry and a re-created Hualapai Indian dwelling, among other historical artifacts; Hualapai Indian Reservation is located just east of town.

Heading west, Route 66 takes on a desolate, rocky wilderness appearance – an indicator of what's to come; be sure you have good brakes. Before long, the road is climbing between jagged peaks in a series of seemingly endless switchbacks and scary, blind curves to the 3,500ft (1,067-meter) -high summit at **Sitgreaves Pass** (named, like the Beale Wagon Trail, for a mid-19th-century US Army surveyor), before beginning an equally sinuous route into tiny Oatman, named for a young Illinois girl captured by the Apache.

⊘ DETOUR TO LAS VEGAS

A dusty drive of 101 miles (163km) from Kingman, Arizona, on US 93 leads straight to Sin City. At latest count, over 39 million visitors spend $6 billion annually on gaming alone in this capital of frivolity, greed, and gluttony – not to mention plain old fun. For a long time after gambling was legalized in 1931, Las Vegas remained a sleepy desert town. It took visionary underworld hit man Bugsy Siegel to free this seething neon dragon. In 1946, Siegel opened the Flamingo Hotel, sparing no expense in mob finances for its plush interior, which sported a flashing pink neon facade and set a new standard in sheer swank. From a high-roller's point of view, Las Vegas is divided into two parts. First is the Strip, where modern hoteliers vie with each other to offer the latest in accommodation extravaganzas, replicating Venice, Paris, Rome, ocean liners, and the Egyptian Pyramids. Then there's Downtown – the original Vegas – also known as Glitter Gulch. As for gambling, either way you lose, but Downtown casinos are said to afford better odds. The best advice is to simply enjoy it: win, lose, or draw, there's nothing quite like the Strip at night, ablaze with electric light and self-indulgence. Las Vegas Convention and Visitors Authority is at 702-892-0711; www.lcva.com.

OATMAN AND ITS QUIRKS

On the way down into Oatman, you'll pass **Goldroad**, the site of a mine that produced $2-billion-worth of gold in its early years, but closed down in 1907 when gold prices dropped.

Hundreds of wild burros turned loose by early miners roam the mountains, occasionally straying across the highway and wandering into **Oatman** ④, proving irresistible camera fodder for photographers and inspiring the name of the Classy Ass gift shop (www.classyassgiftsoatman.com), next to the Oatman Hotel, which sells jewelry made from rocks and sand dollars and other one-of-a-kind gifts. Oatman looks exactly the way you'd imagine an Old West town to look, with sagging wooden shacks lining the solitary unpaved street, on which amusing mock gunfights are conducted daily.

Across the street from Fast Fanny's Place (selling clothes, sunglasses, and postcards), a bed on wheels promotes the annual Great Oatman Bed Races, which are held every January. Summer temperatures can reach 118°F (48°C), prompting the annual Sidewalk Egg Fry every Fourth of July (magnifying glasses permitted).

The worn and characterful 1902 **Oatman Hotel** (tel: 928-768-4408), once known as the Durlin Hotel, no longer rents rooms, but will be forever famous as the place where Clark Gable and Carole Lombard spent their honeymoon night in Room 15, after being married in Kingman. The simple room is preserved as a shrine to the glamorous Hollywood couple with pictures of the pair on the walls and a pink nightdress draped over a chair. On the ground floor are an ice-cream shop, a saloon, and restaurant popular with locals.

Twenty miles (32km) of Mojave Desert scrub lie between Oatman and **Topock**, where the bridge over the Colorado River marks the Arizona-California border. Route 66 comes to a dead-end at Moabi Regional Park, with its lake and boat rentals – a refreshing stop after the long drive in the hot sun.

CALIFORNIA

As the car heads ever closer toward the setting sun, spare a thought for those migrants from the early days of Route 66 for whom crossing the border into the Promised Land became an ordeal. Faced with an influx of refugees from the Dust Bowl states, Californians were worried about the impact on property prices and already poorly paid jobs. In some places, guards were posted at the border, and scores of exhausted migrants were turned away. It's a story that is still familiar today, albeit at a different border.

Sadly, once in California, much of the old Route 66, apart from a few parched stretches through the Mojave Desert, has been largely supplanted and is submerged beneath a welter of busy freeways to re-emerge only in occasional short stretches or as the main routes through towns such as Barstow, Victorville, and Rancho Cucamonga.

NEEDLES

Just after crossing into California, you arrive in **Needles**, hellishly hot much of the year, where Route 66 passes through the business section on Broadway. Adjoining the train station is the former 1908 Fred Harvey House, El Garces, a grand Beaux Arts–style building regarded as the crown jewel of the Harvey House chain. Harvey Girls lived in the upper floors. Trained in neatness and courtesy, the girls signed a contract of employment agreeing not to marry for a year. In recent years, El Garces was bought by the city and came close to reopening as a fine hotel in the style of other meticulous Harvey House restorations carried out by Allan Affeldt, owner of La Posada in Winslow, Arizona, and the Plaza and Castaneda hotels in Las Vegas and New Mexico. Sadly, the transfer was disallowed, and the city went ahead and completely renovated the building as a community center with the aid of a large federal grant. The center is worth a look. **Needles Regional Museum** (tel: 760-326-5678; Sept–May Mon–Sat) has a fanciful collection of stuff guaranteed to raise a grin: vintage clothes, old jars and bottles, obsolete currency, pictures curling with sepia, cartridge shells, and Native American artifacts. Fort **Mojave**

Sheep Hole Pass on Amboy Road.

Tribal Center (tel: 760-629-4591; https://fortmojaveindiantribe.com) adjoins Fort Mojave Indian Tribe's (Pipa Aha Macav, the People by the River) resort and casino, PGA championship golf course, RV park, and Colorado River marina. A February Pow Wow celebrates Native American culture.

In World War II, General George Patton established an army training center in the Mojave, to prepare troops for the harsh terrain of the forthcoming Africa campaign. The US Army National Training Center is still headquartered at Barstow, 145 miles (233km) due west of Needles.

The route from Needles to Barstow can be traveled swiftly on I-40, but old Route 66 runs north of the interstate and heads through **Goffs**, before diverting south through the barely existing communities of Essex, Amboy, and Bagdad (famous for its landmark café, inspiration for the 1987 film Bagdad Café and, earlier, another Harvey House). Tiny **Essex** appeared on NBC's *Tonight Show* in 1977, claiming to be the only town in America without television – a Pennsylvania company promptly donated the

necessary equipment. The ghost town of **Amboy** (www.amboyroute66.com) is the property of preservationist Albert Okura, owner of the Juan Pollo chicken chain. It is worth a stop for a photo of the Fifties Googie-style sign outside shuttered Roy's Motel and Café (www.rt66roys.com). It was once a favorite with film makers, and actor Harrison Ford still flies in to visit. The volcanic origins of this landscape, which created its signature basin-and-range appearance, are evident at nearby **Amboy Crater**.

Ludlow, where Route 66 links up once more with the interstate, was once a boomtown served not only by the Santa Fe railroad but also by two other local lines bearing ore from Death Valley, and in fact was named for a Central Pacific repairman. The 1940s Ludlow Cafe building is derelict, as is the abandoned Ludlow Mercantile Building (1908) down by the railroad tracks, but Ludlow Coffee Shop (tel: 760-733-4501), the only eatery for miles, offers standard American diner fare, such as good breakfast pancakes, and of course, coffee to get you to Barstow. Water, always scarce in these parts, was at one time brought in to fill the steam trains by tank cars from **Newberry Springs**, 40 miles (64km) to the west (actual filming site of the cult movie *Bagdad Café*). There really are springs here, and they supplement the water supply from the region's numerous artesian wells.

At the State Agricultural Inspection Station, you will be asked if you are transporting any fruits to California; it's a precaution against pests that might threaten state fruit crops. Eat any fruit before getting there, or they will throw it away. Just before Barstow is **Daggett**, whose landmark **Stone Hotel** (closed for renovation; it will reopen as the Daggett Museum) was popular with Tom Mix and other movie cowboys. On show in the current Daggett Museum (tel: 760-254-2629; www.daggetthistoricalsociety.org; in season Sat) is a scale model of the California Edison Company's Solar One

Calico ghost town near Barstow.

hermal plant (1981–1986) out in the desert. Giant mirrors focused the sun's energy on tanks of nitrate salt intended to convert water into the steam required to power a turbine generator.

BARSTOW

The Mojave Desert was a forbidding yet paradoxically inviting place in the 1870s, when gold, silver, and borax were among the valuable metals and minerals that drew prospectors and miners from all over the country. The arrival of the Santa Fe railroad in 1883 connected – and, in many cases, created – isolated small towns, and the Mediterranean-style Santa Fe Depot at **Barstow** ⑫, and renovated 1911 Casa del Desierto (a former Harvey House and now a route 66 Museum), give some idea of the forgotten splendor of the times. Gift shops and a McDonald's, at which customers eat in converted railroad cars, are among the station's attractions. Among the exhibits in the **Route 66 Mother Road Museum** (tel: 760-255-1890; www.route66museum. org; Fri–Sun) are archival and contemporary prints by photographers who have captured images of the road and its icons. Many are available for purchase.

With the arrival of the pre-World War II National Old Trails Highway, the predecessor to Route 66, Barstow's importance as a transportation center was quite literally cemented. Sitting at the major junction of I-15 and I-40, it has shown little sign of decline. Midway between Los Angeles and Las Vegas, it is a convenient rest stop for drivers on their way to and from Sin City. The older Route 66 motels are to the west end of town. Watch for the El Rancho, built with railroad ties, and whose 100ft (30-meter) -high neon sign has been a landmark since the early days of the highway.

The **Mojave River Valley Museum** (tel: 760-256-5452; www.mojaverivervalleymuseum.org; daily) and the **Desert Discovery Center** (tel: 760-252-6060; www.desertdiscoverycenter.com; Tue–Sat) will together answer all your questions about the desert – past and present.

SIDE TRIPS FROM BARSTOW

There are two worthwhile side trips from Barstow. The first is to **Rainbow Basin Natural Area** (tel: 760-252-6000; www.blm.gov; daily; camping in Owl Canyon Campground), where a 4-mile (6km) loop road circles an area filled with fossilized animal remains and fringed by multicolored cliffs. The second is to **Calico Ghost Town** (tel: 800-8622-2542; www.cms.sbcounty.gov/parks/calicoghosttown; daily; camping by reservation), 11 miles (18km) to the east, whose prosperity between 1881–96 came from mining a $12-million seam of silver, a boom that was supplemented by the discovery of borax nearby.

When both "cash crops" gave out, the town's 22 saloons closed one after another as the population drifted to other areas to seek their fortunes, but many of the old buildings have been rehabilitated, and such tourist attractions as wagon rides, mock gunfights,

Watch out for snakes when hiking in the desert – a rattler taken by surprise may not give you a warning before striking.

Joshua tree in the Mojave Desert.

and gold panning were introduced. A few miles to the east, the **Calico Early Man Site** (tel: 760-252-6000) displays fossils and artifacts such as stone tools from the recent Pleistocene era (2.6 million–11,700 years before present).

VICTORVILLE

It's an uneventful 40-mile (64km) drive on a good road (which parallels I-15) to Victorville, where Route 66 is merely another city street. **Victorville** began as a mining camp in the 19th century and became a magnet during Hollywood's golden age for moviemakers attracted by its Old West feel. For a while, it also attracted the Roy Rogers—Dale Evans Museum, where the galleries glittered with the husband-and-wife cowboy stars' sequined costumes, before the museum moved to the country-music town of Branson, Missouri.

The **California Route 66 Museum** (tel: 760-951-0436; www.califrt66museum.org; Thu–Mon) offers a final fix for westbound travelers who haven't yet had their fill of curios and ephemera from the Mother Road. The modest museum building was

Kitsch mementos of the Mother Road.

once a roadhouse called the Red Rooster Cafe. Its premier exhibit is Hula Ville, an example of the folksy roadside attractions once found all along Route 66. In the mid-1950s, a man named Miles Mahan decided to drive nails into fence posts and hang from them all the bottles left behind by transients. Later, he rescued a huge metal sign of a dancing hula girl and arranged for her to tower over the fences, practically stopping traffic along the route. Locals began to donate other items to Mahan's Cactus Garden and in time Hula Ville became a Route 66 high desert legend.

SAN BERNARDINO

South of Victorville, I-15 heads over 4,300ft (1,310-meter) Cajon Summit. Apart from a brief stretch, I-15 has subsumed much of the old route, but you're on it if you follow Cajon Boulevard into **San Bernardino** ⑬, known to locals as San Berdoo, a Mormon town in the 1850s, and once a major citrus center. It's the gateway to the mountainous **San Bernardino National Forest** (www.fs.usda.gov/sbnf), more than 600,000 acres (243,000 hectares) of wilderness dominated by 11,500ft (3,505-meter) -high Mt San Gorgonio, the highest in Southern California. Deep in the forest are the well-known resorts of **Big Bear** and **Lake Arrowhead**, hideaways for Hollywood stars. State Route 18, romantically known as the Rim of the World Drive, is the lofty 40-mile (64km) highway that leads to these destinations.

RIM OF THE WORLD DRIVE

With panoramic views, switchback turns and lots of overlooks, **Rim of the World Drive** is particularly exhilarating to do on a motorcycle. The best stretch is the 25-mile (40km) run from Redlands up the hill toward **Big Bear Lake**.

Back down on the ground in San Bernardino itself, the classy old (1928) **California Theatre of the Performing Arts** (www.californiatheatre.net), on West Fourth Street, is worth noting. Head out of town on Mt Vernon Avenue past some aged motels and a hard-to-miss Santa Fe railroad smokestack, and eventually you will pass the tepees of another Wigwam Motel (1950) along Foothill Boulevard. This leads into **Rancho Cucamonga** and begins with a series of large and anonymous shopping malls, but at the corner of Vineyard Avenue there is a glimpse of earlier times, with the quaint **Cucamonga Service Station** (tel: 909-271-1024; www.route66ieca.org; Fri–Sun), a vintage Mobil gas station built in 1915, which was restored and reopened as a Route 66 museum in 2015. The historic service station is opposite the historic Thomas Winery building, once a popular stop on Route 66. Today, it is a state landmark, designated as the oldest commercial winery in California and the second-oldest in the country. Sadly, the Thomas vineyards fell victim to development in the 1960s, but the premises are now occupied by a restaurant, a coffee house, and, appropriately, The Wine Tailor, which sells custom wines.

Farther down is the historic **Sycamore Inn** (www.thesycamoreinn.com), a huge, rustic log palace and steak house on the site of an 1848 trailside inn that catered to the Gold Rush adventurers. In 1858, it became a stop along the route of the Butterfield Stage.

Past **Claremont**, where the old route suddenly moves upscale with a grassy median and eucalyptus trees, are a few eating places that old-timers might remember. There's Wilson's restaurant (now La Paloma; http://lapalomamexican restaurant.com) in **La Verne**; the Pinnacle Peak Steak House (www.pinnaclepeaksteak-house.com), in **San Dimas**, where they cut off customers' ties; and the Golden Spur Restaurant (tel: 626-963-9302) in **Glendora**, which began as a hamburger stand over 80 years ago.

There are many old motels and eateries along this part of Route 66, including the 1922 Derby Restaurant (www.thederbyarcadia.com) and Rod's Grill (tel: 626-447-7515) in **Arcadia**. In **Monrovia**, the astonishing renovated one-story Aztec Hotel (tel: 626-358-3231) is a national historic landmark. It was built by architect Robert Stacy-Judd in 1924, in Mayan Revival style to catch the attention of motorists along the route. It is also said to be haunted.

THE END OF THE ROAD

Just before **Los Angeles** ⓮ proper, Route 66 becomes what is now the Pasadena Freeway, but which started life in the closing days of 1940 as the Arroyo Seco Parkway, the first freeway in a bold, new experiment that was eventually to cover the entire state of California with a network of similarly fast highways. Continue driving, and take the Sunset Boulevard exit, then head west along Sunset until it joins Santa Monica Boulevard, which runs all the way to the Pacific Ocean. Here, in Palisades Park overlooking the beach, a modest plaque commemorates the western terminus of this famous American road.

⊙ Tip

If you happen to be in Long Beach, just south of Los Angeles, in August, check out the outdoor waterfront Long Beach Jazz Festival. Greats like Poncho Sanchez and Michael Franks and classic Motown musicians have featured in past years. For details: tel: 562-424-0013; www.longbeachjazzfestival.com.

Santa Monica, Los Angeles.

📷 A SHORT STAY IN LOS ANGELES

The city of fantasy and film, Los Angeles has endless sun, an easy ambiance, and, of course, Hollywood. Here's a list of the not-to-be-missed attractions.

The Hollywood Museum is the place to pay homage to the achievements of the silver screen. Included are displays on history, personalities, and Max Factor movie make-up innovations.

Part amusement park, part working film studio, **Universal Studios Hollywood** is one of the most visited sites in Los Angeles. Go behind the scenes to see sensational stunts and special effects, face dinosaurs and vengeful mummies on heart-pounding thrill rides, or visit Hogwarts School of Witchcraft and Wizardry.

Lined with jewelers, designer studios, upmarket fashion, and accessories boutiques, **Rodeo Drive** in Beverly Hills is one of the most exclusive shopping addresses in the world.

Watch a parade of stars – the celestial kind – at the landmark **Griffith Observatory**. Like the famous Hollywood sign, it stands in Griffith Park, which extends for miles and has far-reaching views over LA and the San Fernando Valley.

Art lovers should not miss the **Los Angeles County Museum of Art**. Its displays of costumes, pottery, silverware, and decorative arts, as well as paintings and sculpture from all eras, are augmented by the new **Broad Contemporary Art Museum** on campus, designed by Renzo Piano. Another Piano landmark, the new home of the **Academy Museum of Motion** Pictures, is under construction nearby. Downtown, a new contemporary art museum, **The Broad** (www.thebroad. org) opened in 2015.

IMPORTANT INFORMATION

Population: Just over 4 million
Dialing codes: 213, 310, 323, 818, 424, 747
Website: www.discoverlosangeles.com
Tourist information: Los Angeles Official Visitor Information Center, 6801 Hollywood Boulevard, Hollywood CA 90028; tel: 467 6412.

Sidney Grauman, who invented the movie premiere, designed Grauman's Chinese Theatre (now TCL Chinese Theatre) in the 1920s. Its main attraction is the forecourt with stars' hand and foot prints.

Made famous by Billy Wilder's magnificent melodrama movie, Sunset Boulevard is an important avenue in Hollywood history.

View over LA from Griffith Observatory, which appeared in Rebel Without a Cause.

City of Angels

In 1781, Father Junípero Serra named a dry, dusty settlement after St Francis of Assisi's first church, St Mary Queen of the Angels. No one could have conceived that this hot, arid place would turn into glittering Los Angeles, the capital of moviedom and a world-famous synonym for glamor and fun. Residents of most big cities pretend to be blasé in the presence of celebrities, but Angelenos really are: movie stars are the stock-in-trade here, as common as scarlet-suited guardsmen in London or yellow cabs in New York. LA is also a city of adventure and innovation: Disneyland, rollerblading, beach culture, West Coast rap music – it all started here.

stars that make up the Walk of Fame on Hollywood *levard.*

fabulous hilltop Getty Center, designed by architect *ard Meier to take advantage of stunning views,* *petes with the treasures inside.*

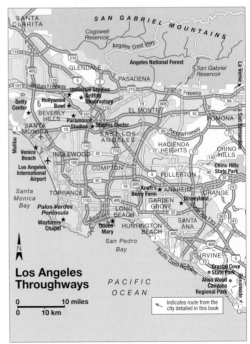

Los Angeles Throughways

Indicates route from the city detailed in this book

Oak Alley Plantation, Louisiana.

Texas rancher.

THE SOUTHERN ROUTE

A guide to the South and the Southwest, with principal sights clearly cross-referenced by number to the maps.

All-American classic.

Sit back and enjoy the ride on the Southern route across the continent. The pace is leisurely, as you meander down a Georgia street lined with trees draped in Spanish moss, relax on a Texas beach, or kick up your cowboy boots in Tombstone.

Our nearly 2,500-mile (3,900km) journey through the South departs from Atlanta, capital of the "New South" and home of slain civil rights leader Martin Luther King. Atlanta is home to well-known global corporations like CNN, but its attractive woodsy setting, foodie leanings, and numerous visitor attractions make it a great jumping-off point. After a detour in charming Macon, the route speeds south along the Civil Rights trail to the architecture-rich state capital of Montgomery, Alabama, and on to oil-rich Mobile on the Gulf of Mexico. From here, you'll be following the Gulf through hurricane-devastated Mississippi and Louisiana, stopping in New Orleans, a sensory explosion of sights and sounds, soulful food, gracious architecture, and resilient citizens defying the odds after Hurricane Katrina.

West of the state capital of Baton Rouge, the highway crosses the country's largest swamp into Cajun Country, one of the cultural highlights of the trip. Ease into Texas by dipping your toes in the Gulf on the resort island of Galveston before driving north into Houston, famed for its space program but also an art destination of note. Superb live music is the draw in the dynamic state capital, Austin. The highway rolls through wildflower-strewn Hill Country before reaching San Antonio, renowned for its historic missions, Alamo, and downtown River Walk.

Louisiana has the highest alligator population in the US.

It's a long haul to El Paso, as the highway follows the Rio Grande, the US border with Mexico, passing through dusty border towns with Wild West links. River trips among beautiful canyons and wildlife viewing draw nature lovers to spectacular Big Bend National Park, just south of Marfa, a rising art and cultural destination in ranch country.

After El Paso and its Mexican sister city of Ciudad Juárez, it's on to New Mexico, with its contrasting scenery, ancient cultures, and modern high-tech weaponry and atomic history. The highway crosses the Continental Divide en route to Arizona, where the Old West survives in places like Tombstone and Bisbee. In Tucson and Phoenix, indulge in some pampering at a spa resort before heading across the Mojave Desert to San Diego, California.

📷 A SHORT STAY IN ATLANTA

Atlanta is bold, brash, and self-confident – a cosmopolitan island surrounded by rural Georgia. Here's a list of the not-to-be-missed attractions.

Atlanta's main attractions are walkable, clustered around the small **1996 Centennial Olympic Park** in **Downtown**. There's plenty for families at the dynamic **Georgia Aquarium**, which has the world's largest fish tank; Imagine It! The **Children's Museum of Atlanta**; and the **New World of Coca-Cola**. Nearby is the recently opened **Center for Civil and Human Rights**, where you can learn the history of the civil rights movement in the US and much more. Fascinating **CNN Studio Tours** offer interesting, behind-the-scenes looks at newscasting at the CNN Center.

Underground Atlanta is filled with shops and watering holes and stretches six blocks above and below ground.

Midtown, centered on 10th and Peachtree streets, is Atlanta's fast-growing arts district. Highlights are the light-filled **High Museum of Art**, designed by Richard Meier, showcasing Rodin sculptures, works by Picasso and Matisse, and big traveling exhibitions, and the 1929 **Fox Theatre**, a Moorish-style former movie palace, best seen on a tour of the Fox Theatre Historic District with the Atlanta Preservation Society.

Gone with the Wind author **Margaret Mitchell** is a hometown literary hero. The modest apartment where the pioneering journalist wrote her one masterpiece is a mecca for fans and is open daily for tours.

Piedmont Park, surrounded by tree-shaded streets and old homes, is a Midtown favorite. Its northside has a botanic garden, while the south side hosts a Saturday Green Market (mid-Mar–Dec) and the April Atlanta Dogwood Festival.

IMPORTANT INFORMATION

Population: City: 464,000; Metro: 5.9 million
Dialing codes: 404, 770, 678
Website: www.atlanta.net
Tourist information: Atlanta CVB, 233 Peachtree St. NE, Suite 1400, GA 30303; tel: 404-521-6600; daily.

Vintage vending machines at the World of Coca-Cola.

Discover more about the Civil Rights leader at Martin Luther King National Historic Site. The four-block Swee Auburn District includes King's birth home (shown), his tomb, and the church in which the King family preache

A studio tour of CNN headquarters shows the professionals at work.

Capital of the New South

Atlanta is a city alert to opportunity. This is not just because it was burned down during the Civil War; it has always been this way. Winning the bid for the 1996 Olympics was just the beginning; now Atlanta is an urban phenomenon, the third fastest-growing metro area in the US, exuding prosperity, self-confidence, self-absorption, and reinvention. Don't be fooled by all the construction, though: Atlanta retains a Southern graciousness and is very welcoming. Its population is diverse – it has one of the largest gay populations in the US – and, once you get used to navigating streets without good signs, you quickly feel at home and want to linger.

Buckhead District is the center of Atlanta's nightlife.

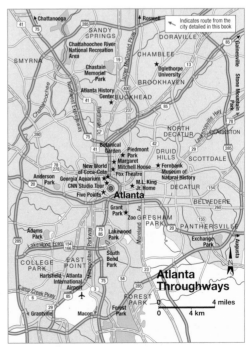

Freight train at a crossing.

ATLANTA TO NEW ORLEANS

The mournful whistle of freight trains, small towns on hot summer nights, and grand, glorious antebellum towns characterize this trip through Georgia and Alabama.

For more than a century after its cataclysmic encounter with historical destiny – as the focus of the Confederacy during the American Civil War (1861–65) – the South set itself apart from its conquerors (the Federal Government, or Union), stubbornly continuing to identify with the antebellum days on the Cotton Belt. Finally – and in part unwillingly, as a result of the changes forced upon it by the civil rights campaigns of the 1950s and 1960s – a New South is emerging. While there is still truth in the popular image of the region as a poor, undeveloped, and uneducated rural backwater, many of its urban communities have recast themselves beyond recognition, as high-tech high-achievers to match any in the nation.

NEW SOUTH MEETS OLD SOUTH IN GEORGIA

Nowhere is this reinvention more true than in the cities of Georgia, particularly its dynamic capital, **Atlanta ❶** (see page 240), on the broad Piedmont Plateau of north-central Georgia. Home to global corporations, from Coca-Cola to CNN, Atlanta justly claims to be the heart of the New South. Nonetheless, it has managed to retain the more appealing aspects of its past, such as the South's traditional mannered gentility and famed flair for hospitality. Macon, too, on the Fall Line that runs from Augusta to Columbus separating northern Georgia from the Coastal Plain, has prospered without losing sight of its heritage, while Savannah, on the Savannah River close to the Atlantic Ocean, surrounds its stunning, antebellum city center with modern industry and shipping activity.

Banking, manufacturing, media, military installations, and tourism may have come to dominate its cities, but much of the rest of Georgia remains

⊘ Main attractions
Hay House
Little White House State
  Park
Carver Museum
Civil Rights Memorial
Bellingrath Gardens
Walter M. Anderson
  Museum of Art
Beauvoir
The French Quarter, New
  Orleans

Map on page 244

Summit Skyride cable car on Stone Mountain, Georgia.

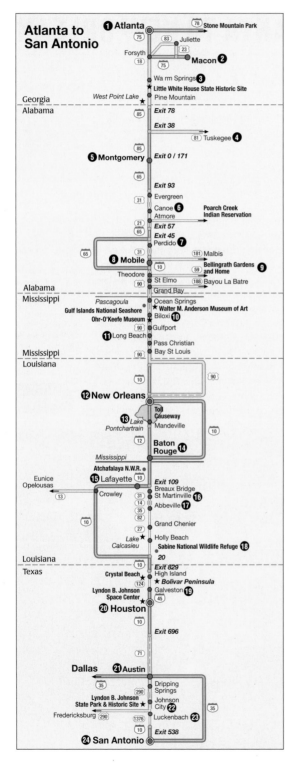

Atlanta to San Antonio

1 **Atlanta**
78 Stone Mountain Park
75
83 Juliette
23
Forsyth
18
75
Macon 2
Wa rm Springs 3
Little White House State Historic Site
Georgia
West Point Lake ★ Pine Mountain
Alabama
85
Exit 78
Exit 38
81 Tuskegee 4
85
5 **Montgomery** *Exit 0 / 171*
65
Exit 93
31 Evergreen
Canoe 6 **Poorch Creek Indian Reservation**
Atmore
21
65 *Exit 57*
Exit 45
Perdido 7
65 31
181 Malbis
8 **Mobile**
10
59 **Bellingrath Gardens and Home** 9
Theodore
90 St Elmo 188 Bayou La Batre
Alabama Grand Bay
Mississippi
Pascagoula
Gulf Islands National Seashore Ocean Springs
Ohr-O'Keefe Museum ★ Walter M. Anderson Museum of Art
90 Biloxi 10
90 Gulfport
11 Long Beach
Pass Christian
Mississippi 90 Bay St Louis
Louisiana
10
90
12 **New Orleans**
Toll Causeway
13 *Lake* Mandeville
Pontchartrain
10
12 **Baton Rouge** 14
Mississippi
Atchafalaya N.W.R.
Eunice
Opelousas 15 **Lafayette** 10
Exit 109
13 Breaux Bridge
Crowley 31 St Martinville 16
14
35 Abbeville 17
82
10 27 Grand Chenier
Lake ★ Holly Beach
Calcasieu **Sabine National Wildlife Refuge** 18
20
Louisiana 10 *Exit 829*
Texas Crystal Beach ★ High Island
124 ★ **Bolivar Peninsula**
Lyndon B. Johnson Space Center ★ Galveston 19
45
20 **Houston**
10
Exit 696
71
Dallas 21 **Austin**
35 Dripping Springs
290 Johnson
Lyndon B. Johnson State Park & Historic Site ★ City 22 35
Fredericksburg 290 1376 Luckenbach 23
10 *Exit 538*
24 **San Antonio**

rural. Agricultural produce, such as the state's trademark peaches, peanuts, and sweet Vidalia onions, and lumber, cattle, and poultry, continue to figure prominently in the economy.

Throughout Georgia, expect hot, humid days and pleasant nights from May through September, temperate comfort in April and October, and cool to cold temperatures November through March, with occasional frigid northerly winds, and even a sprinkling of snow. Georgia blooms most beautifully in the spring, which is the ideal visiting season. Southern Georgia, on the Coastal Plain, is balmiest, often sweltering, in summer.

If finding parking in downtown Atlanta leaves you crying for escape, take a trip 7 miles (11km) east of I-285 on US 78 to **Stone Mountain Park** (tel 800-401-2407; www.stonemountainpark. com; daily), a recreation complex with seasonal attractions, including an ice rink, golf course, campground, hotels, waterslides, boating, fishing, tennis, wildlife trail, scenic railroad ride, and reconstructed plantation. Stone Mountain's plantation showcases buildings from throughout the state.

The park sprawls around its eponymous landmark: **Stone Mountain**. The exposed portion of this granite giant occupies a volume of 7.5 trillion cubic ft (213 million cubic meters) and is thought to be almost 3 million years old. Its gestation period was long, as igneous rock struggled to push through the surface. Stone Mountain's thrust to the sky is a fine metaphor for the concrete explosion of modern Atlanta after its razing by the Union army.

The mountain itself, smooth but for light pocks in the surface, is spectacle enough. Its focus, however, is the **Stone Mountain carving**, over 50 years in production, depicting Confederate leaders Jefferson Davis, Robert E. Lee and "Stonewall" Jackson. The sculpture, which spreads 147ft (45 meters) across and towers 400ft (122 meters above the ground, was completed in 1972. Following the 2015 mass shooting in Charleston, SC, and the 2017 deadly racist attack on a protestor in Charlottesville, VA, (see page 76), there have been calls for the removal of the carving due to its identification with racism and slavery.

MACON

Heading southeast out of Atlanta on I-75, you'll begin to encounter what the Depression-era Federal Writers' Project called "the rolling character of the land [which] makes for undulations in the roadways, the fields, and the pine forests that border them. The clay hills are deeply gullied by erosion and their red color against the dark pines of the wooded regions creates a perpetually vivid landscape." Some 80 miles (130km) after leaving Atlanta, I-75 takes a sharp turn to the south, straight into the heart of **Macon ②** (it rhymes with "bacon"); you can venture into the city from either I-75 or I-16, which continues southeast to Savannah. In recent years, Macon's downtown has experienced something of a cultural resurgence, sparked not only by the largest number of listed historic antebellum mansions and civic buildings in Georgia but also Macon's deserved reputation as a music mecca: it is the hometown of rock-and-roll legends Little Richard, Otis Redding, the Allman Brothers, and REM, among others.

THE OLD SOUTH

Macon's marvelous historic buildings were spared destruction during the Civil War by a simple ruse. In 1864, when General Sherman and his troops fired into the city across the Ocmulgee River, the return fire suggested a substantial resistance. But the troops that diverted Sherman and his all-too-tragic torched earth policy toward Savannah were not Confederate regulars but old men and young children.

The architecture that has been preserved and restored is incredibly diverse, yet thoroughly Southern. As one resident put it: "When people from outside the South come to find the Old

Macon is the epitome of the Old South.

Labor Day crowds prepare to watch the laser show at Stone Mountain. On the side of the mountain is the Confederate Memorial Carving, depicting three heroes from the Civil War: President Jefferson Davis, General Robert E. Lee, and General Thomas J. Jackson.

The Italianate Revival Hay House, Macon.

South, it's not in Atlanta, which is too new, nor is it in Savannah, which by virtue of its settlers and design is closer to a European city. The Old South is right here in Macon."

During the cotton boom of the early 19th century, cotton kings built lavish homes in the early Federal style with classical touches. These were followed by structures in the Greek Temple style adapted to the climate. Over the years, waves of commercial expansion inspired forays into new styles for mansions and civic and commercial buildings. Italianate Revival, Roman Revival, and Academic Revival experiments carried through to the 1920s. Among fine examples open daily to visitors are the huge **Hay House** (tel: 478-742-8155; www.hayhousemacon.org; daily) on Georgia Avenue, and **Cannonball House** (tel: 478-745-5982; www.cannonballhouse.org; Mon–Sat) on Mulberry Street, scarred by a shot from Sherman's artillery and now appropriately housing the **Civil War Museum**.

All can be enjoyed at their best in late March each year, when the Cherry Blossom Festival (www.cherryblossom.com) celebrates the simultaneous flowering of Macon's pride and joy, the incredible 300,000 Japanese cherry trees that have been planted along the downtown streets.

Macon Visitor Information Center (tel: 478-743-1074; www.maconga.org; Mon–Sat) on Martin Luther King Boulevard has a film introducing Macon narrated by Little Richard, interactive exhibits, and offers walking tours of Macon's historic homes and museums. Although sadly, the Georgia Music Hall of Fame in Macon has now closed, the **Georgia Sports Hall of Fame** (tel: 478-752-1585; http://georgiasportshalloffame.com; Tue–Sat), celebrating Georgia athletes such as record home run hitter Henry "Hank" Aaron and golf legend Bobby Jones, remains a popular destination on Cherry Street.

A bridge honoring Macon's best-known hometown musical legend, Otis Redding, leads from downtown across the Ocmulgee River to **Ocmulgee National Monument** (tel: 478-752-8257; www.nps.gov/ocmu; daily). This small, peaceful national park doesn't do much to toot its own horn but is one of Macon's undiscovered treasures. It preserves ceremonial mounds, cornfields, and other remnants of the powerful South Appalachian Mississippian Mound Building culture that thrived here between AD 900 and 1100.

A museum inside the 1930s Art Moderne–style visitor center and trail-side exhibits interpret the lifeways of the Mississippians and 1000 years of Native American culture. Children will enjoy going inside the 42ft (12.8-meter) diameter reconstructed earthlodge. With its thunderbird-shaped altar, fire-pit, and banquette seating, the semi-subterranean structure resembles the great kivas found at Chaco Culture National Historical Park in New Mexico, one of the Mississippians' far-flung trading partners.

WHISTLE STOP CAFE

Taking US 23, which winds north-ward from Macon along the Ocmul-gee River, affords an appealing taste of rural Georgia. Tiny **Juliette**, 20 miles (32km) along, was reinvigor-ated in the early 1990s, when its air of picturesque deep-woods derelic-tion made it the perfect location for the movie *Fried Green Tomatoes at the Whistle Stop Café*, based on Fan-nie Flagg's original novel. The actual **Whistle Stop Cafe** (tel: 478-992-8886; www.thewhistlestopcafe.com; daily), built for the film beside a still-used country railroad station, was almost destroyed by a flood in 1994. It has seen better days, but the food has overall good reviews, and the place still attracts tourists making a pilgrimage to eat the Southern specialty of tempura-style green tomatoes.

From Juliette, pick up State Route 83 east, then State Route 18, which winds all the way to the Georgia-Alabama border. The bucolic town of **Warm Springs ❸**, approximately an hour east of Juliette, is nestled amid the foothills of Pine Mountain. It grew to fame as a therapeutic center for polio sufferers in the 1920s, when then—New York Governor Franklin Roosevelt, who suf-fered from polio himself, began using the warm mineral springs to ease his symptoms. Roosevelt opened a hos-pital with therapeutic pools, now the Roosevelt Warm Springs Institute for Rehabilitation (the pools are not open to the general public).

In 1932, the year before winning the presidency, Roosevelt built a six-room cottage at Warm Springs that served as a regular retreat, where he took the waters, formulated his New Deal policies, and eventually died on April 12, 1945. **Little White House State Historic Site** (tel: 706-655-5870; www. gastateparks.org/LittleWhiteHouse; daily) has a museum on FDR and makes a fascinating stop. This part of Georgia is worth savoring. Using Warm Springs or nearby Franklin D. Roosevelt State Park as a base, you can hike, camp, fish, horse-back ride, and rest up before entering Alabama, a short way to the west on I-85.

⊙ Tip

Jarrell Plantation State Historic Site (http://gastateparks.org/JarrellPlantation) in Georgia preserves an old family homestead and mill and offers bed-and-breakfast in a backwoods setting. It's close to the Whistle Stop Cafe and Piedmont National Wildlife Refuge. To reach it, drive US 23 north of Macon and watch for signs.

The earth lodge at Ocmulgee National Monument.

ATLANTA TO SOUTHWEST ALABAMA

Alabama and much of the land to its west passed through several hands before it was taken over by the United States in the late 18th century. Labyrinthine colonial struggles involving the indigenous "Five Nations" (Cherokee, Seminole, Muscogee, Chickasaw, and Choctaw tribes) mark Alabama's early history, and its coat of arms displays the emblems of the five non-native nations that successively held sovereignty over it: France, Great Britain, the United States, the Confederacy, and again the United States.

The last two of these regimes, of course, have left the clearest stamp on Alabama, named for the Alabama River, itself named after the Alabama tribe. Alabama rose to its economic apex during the cotton boom of the 19th century, and has been markedly reluctant to let go of the memory of its Confederate heyday. Only following bitter campaigns in the 1990s did the state capitol in Montgomery finally cease flying the Confederate

This shack's climbing vine, known as kudzu, was brought from Asia and used by the government to stop soil erosion. It is now virtually unstoppable, smothering thousands of acres of land.

Booker T. Washington statue Lifting the Veil of Ignorance, Tuskegee.

flag. The state has seen better days economically and socially, but its natural resources, hard-working citizenry, and enduring pride refuse to admit decline.

Although in principle the **Chattahoochee River** delineates the boundaries of Georgia and Alabama, in fact, at this point, you cross the Alabama state line a short way west of the river. Even then, you don't join the rest of Alabama on Central Time – one hour earlier – until you're beyond the Lanett Valley here.

TUSKEGEE AND BLACK EDUCATION

After rolling through a forested area along I-85 westbound, you can turn off at Exit 38 to **Tuskegee ❹** via State Route 81 south and State Route 126 west. Tuskegee is the site of Booker T. Washington's **Tuskegee Normal and Industrial Institute**, which is one of the few institutions of higher learning for American blacks that existed during the 19th century.

In the words of the leading black intellectual, W.E.B. DuBois, Booker T. Washington was "the greatest man the South produced since the Civil War." Handsome, politically deft, and enormously inspired, Washington believed in cooperation with the ruling whites and in practical education to serve the needs of the black masses concentrated in the South. Washington's policy of avoiding confrontation made enemies among other educated blacks and liberal whites, but he kept Tuskegee alive from 1881 to 1915.

While the institute remains very much active, much of its historic campus has been preserved with the aid of the National Park Service at **Tuskegee Institute National Historic Site** (tel: 334-727-3200; www.nps.gov/tuin; Mon–Sat). Its centerpiece is the George Washington **Carver Museum** named after the black agricultural chemist George Washington Carver, who worked and taught on campus from 1896 until his retirement to The Oaks in Tuskegee, where he died in 1943.

A former slave, Carver abandoned artistic aspirations in order to forge the pioneer science of industrial agriculture. His discoveries saved the Southern economy from collapse after the boll weevil infestation of 1919 destroyed the cotton industry. Many of his published bulletins are displayed in the museum through such works as *How To Grow The Peanut and 105 Ways of Preparing It for Human Consumption*. A black man saved a region whose elite had oppressed and would continue to oppress his race. The museum also shows two 30-minute films about George Washington Carver and Booker T. Washington, which detail the history of the institution and of their struggles, without shying away from the controversies that surround them.

Among Carver's interests were polio therapies, which brought him to the attention of Franklin Roosevelt. In 1939, Roosevelt visited Tuskegee, and shortly thereafter, Tuskegee became the pilot training base for the first all-African-American 99th Pursuit Squadron.

In 1998, neighboring Moton Field was redesignated **Tuskegee Airmen National Historic Site** (tel: 334-724-0922; www.nps.gov/tuai; Mon–Sat) to celebrate the lives of these unsung heroes of World War II. Hangar No. 1 has an Orientation Room, where you can view a four-minute video on the Tuskegee Airmen, and a museum re-creates some of the sights and sounds of Moton Field during the 1940s, including two World War II aircraft. A visitor center has exhibits and five films on the airmen, as well as views of the airfield. The annual Memorial Day Fly-In held here features vintage aircraft, aeronautical displays, airplane rides, and tours of the museum.

MONTGOMERY

Back on I-85 south, travel 41 miles (66km) from Tuskegee to the boundary of **Montgomery** ❺. Alabama's capital city consists of a small, surprisingly quiet downtown area surrounded by wide outlying neighborhoods whose names smack of agricultural gentility. While the prairie muds are still rich, Montgomery bases its livelihood on government services, construction, and manufacturing. It also benefits from the patronage of the US Air Force, whose elite members are frequently assigned to **Maxwell Air Force Base** on the site of famed aviators Wilbur and Orville Wright's flight school.

The state government complex on Goat Hill has several extraordinary public buildings in the gleaming white antebellum style that simply take your breath away. The marble-columned **State Capitol** (tel: 334-242-3935; www.ahc.alabama.gov; guided tours Mon–Sat) is one of the country's only state capitols designated a national historic landmark: the place where

Civil Rights Memorial, Montgomery.

Confederate president Jefferson Davis took his oath of office.

Two grand structures stand across Washington Street from the Capitol: the **First White House of the Confederacy** (tel: 334-242-1861; www.firstwhitehouse.org; Mon–Sat) and the imposing **Alabama Department of Archives and History** building (tel: 334-242-4435; www.archives.state.al.us; Mon–Sat). The White House, relocated from its original site at Bibb and Catoma streets, was the home of Confederate president Jefferson Davis during Montgomery's stint as first capital of the Confederate States of America. This rebel nation was comprised of the 13 states and territories that seceded from the United States in 1860 and 1861 over the issue of states' rights – among them the right to maintain slavery. Davis has been eclipsed in history by Confederate General Robert E. Lee, but in the South he is still revered as an emblem of distinction and self-determination, as evidenced by the bumper sticker "Don't Blame Me – I Voted for Jefferson Davis."

Quiet spot on a Gulf Coast beach.

The neoclassical Archives Building is a rich storehouse of Native American arts, Confederate history, and state development. It once housed a diverse collection of performing outfits belonging to hometown music legend Hank Williams, Sr. They, and Williams' baby-blue 1952 Cadillac, now take center stage at the enormously popular **Hank Williams Museum** (tel: 334-262-3600, http://thehankwilliamsmuseum.net; daily) on Commerce Street. Literature buffs won't want to miss the delightful **Scott & Zelda Fitzgerald Museum** (tel: 334-264-4222; www.thefitzgeraldmuseum.org; Tue–Sun) where the author of *The Great Gatsby* and his wife lived from 1931 to 1932, after meeting in Montgomery during World War I.

CIVIL RIGHTS SITES

Barely a hundred yards from the Capitol is **Dexter Avenue King Memorial Baptist Church**, whose 26-year-old pastor, Rev. Martin Luther King, Jr, was thrust somewhat unwillingly into the limelight in December 1955, when he was invited to spearhead the civil rights campaign known as the Montgomery Bus Boycott after Montgomery resident Rosa Parks refused to give up her seat to a white man. A mural inside the church, "Montgomery to Memphis, 1955–1968," commemorates the long struggle for dignity and equality. Outside the Southern Poverty Law Center nearby, the powerful **Civil Rights Memorial** (tel: 334-956-8200; www.splcenter.org/civil-rights-memorial; Mon–Sat) designed by Maya Lin (who was also responsible for the celebrated Vietnam Veterans Memorial in Washington, DC), honors King and 40 other martyrs of the movement. A small but well-thought-out visitor center has a stirring audio-visual presentation and an interesting bookstore.

The legacy of slavery and racial inequality in the United States, a longtime project of lawyer Bryan Stevenson's Equal Justice Initiative, is examined in detail at the 11,000-sq-ft (1,022 sq meter) **Legacy Museum: From Enslavement to Mass Incarceration** (tel: 334-269-1803; www.museumandmemorial.eji.org; daily), which opened on Commerce Street in April 2018, in a former slave warehouse. Multimedia presentations, including large-scale photographic interpretive panels, first-person accounts, and haunting sculptures, take visitors on an unflinching journey through slavery to modern-day racial justice. Outside, the haunting 6-acre (2.4 hectare) **National Memorial for Peace and Justice** commemorates the more than 4,400 African men, women, and children lynched by white mobs between 1877 to 1950, using 800 six-foot steel monuments, one for each US county where lynchings took place. It goes without saying that a visit to Montgomery is a powerful and unmissable experience.

BACKROADS ALABAMA

Interstate 85 into Montgomery dovetails into I-65 and continues south into the rural glades of southwestern Alabama. Along the way, the radio bands are striped with black contemporary music, pop, country, gospel, sermons, and jazz. The soil deepens again to red, where it had been sandy and gray in the Black Belt through the midsection of the state.

Deeper exploration of rural Alabama is definitely recommended, and US 31 is a good place to start. A branch off the interstate near the cute town of **Evergreen**, US 31 arcs through Escambia and Baldwin counties, grazing the northwesternmost edge of Florida near Atmore and Perdido. The land surrounding towns such as Castleberry ("Home of the Alabama Strawberry") is dotted with small green ponds and spread with groves of pine and oak. Cattle graze on the muddy soil, and farmhouses call forth images of peaceful backwaters.

Before reaching **Atmore**, you pass through **Canoe** ⑥, where you might see a horse and buggy along one side of the road as a 100-car-long freight train whistles by on the other. Atmore is weary-palmed, open-fielded, and railroad-tied, with churches signposted in all directions off the highway. Eight miles (13km) north of Atmore, you'll find the 2,340-member **Poarch Band of Creek Indians** (www.pci.nsn.gov), the only reservation in Alabama and the only one whose members have never been forcibly moved from their original homeland. You can learn more about the history of these descendants of the Creek Indians at the tribe's large, eye-catching **Wind Creek Casino & Hotel Atmore** (tel: 866-WIND-360; www.windcreekatmore.com) near the interstate (they own another casino/hotel in Montgomery), which has gambling, four restaurants, and a hotel.

ALABAMA WINE

Continue on I-65 along a 13-mile (21km) stretch before the next exit

The Greek Orthodox Malbis Memorial Church.

Pristine Gulf shoreline in Alabama.

(Exit 45) to **Perdido** ❼. Just south of the highway, the fruit of Jim and Marianne Eddins's gumption and perseverance continues to thrive: **Perdido Vineyards** (tel: 251-937-9463; www.perdidovineyards.net; Mon–Sat). Winemaking in Alabama, once a great domestic industry, was effectively killed by Prohibition. Even afterward, Baptist leaders maintained that drinking – let alone manufacturing – alcohol was next to ungodliness. The Eddins family dared the opposition and began their muscadine vineyard in 1971, marketing the grapes to a Florida winemaker. When that arrangement fell through, Perdido Vineyards began producing its own wine in 1979.

The muscadine varieties grown at Perdido – scuppernongs, higgins, nobles, and magnolias – are from a tough vine indigenous to the southeastern United States. Perdido's table wines, which may be sampled at the vineyard, are mostly sweet wines with a few drier varieties, including an extra-dry white that is reminiscent of some California wines. The Perdido venture

met with initial hostility from the community, but its success and the subsequent attention it brought to Baldwin County considerably warmed their reception.

Baldwin County is hot and prone to extremes of humidity. Nature has been hard on American farmers for centuries, but the environment was very attractive to a settlement of Greeks who came to the shores of Mobile Bay before World War II. Under the leadership of a Greek Orthodox priest named Malbis, the community established the lushest plantation in the county. When Malbis died in Nazi hands after he returned to Greece, the community carried out his plan to build an Orthodox Church in what is now the town of **Malbis**, between US 31 and I-10, 4 miles (6km) east of Mobile Bay. The church was constructed from materials imported from Greece and includes stunning tile work and stained glass.

MOBILE TO NEW ORLEANS

The coastline of the Gulf of Mexico, arcing from northwest Florida to southeast Texas, can well lay claim to the title of the American Riviera, though less reverently, it's also known as the Redneck Riviera. Not so much a Côte d'Azur as a Côte de Blanc, the Gulf Coast spreads its white sands beside warm waters stocked with fine shrimp, oysters, and other delicacies. While never quite ranking as an international destination, the superb beaches of Gulf Coast Alabama, Mississippi, and Texas have attracted vacationers from the South and Midwest since the mid-19th century. Tourism, gambling, and fishing are the economic mainstays of the region, but they have been strongly affected by destructive hurricanes and the oil industry, which often drills within sight of sunbathers. Still, whatever the ecological effects of oil retrieval may be, the petrochemical industry has been crucial to the survival of cities like Mobile, Alabama.

Dauphin Street, downtown Mobile, Alabama.

FORMER FRENCH CAPITAL

Interstates 10 and 65 and US 90 (which pick up from US 31) all straddle the mouth of the Mobile River, as they cross westward from Baldwin County into the port of **Mobile** ❽ (pronounced French style as "Mo-beel"). Mobile's location on river and Gulf has made it the most contested area in all of Alabama's twisted power struggles, and to this day it feels resolutely atypical of a state that outsiders regard as the most insular in the South. That sense of rich cosmopolitan diversity is hardly surprising; after all, Mobile began life in 1703 as the capital of the French colony of Louisiana, which covered a far larger, if not precisely defined area than the modern state of the same name.

A pair of illuminated skyscraper spires forms a distinctive skyline, but Mobile's French Colonial past remains evident everywhere. Parallels with Louisiana in general, and New Orleans in particular, range from the intricate iron grillwork that adorns the city's balconies to the

oysters and gumbo sold in its restaurants. Most striking of all is Mobile's Mardi Gras, which pre-dates its more famous counterpart in New Orleans. Arrive the week before Lent, and you'll be dazzled by the parades and costumes, but throughout the year telltale strings of colored Mardi Gras beads festoon the live oaks and telephone wires in downtown.

A stroll along downtown avenues such as lower **Government**, **Church**, and **Dauphin streets** is by far the best way to get a flavor of Mobile. Pick up a historic walking tour brochure at the south end of Royal Street, at Mobile Visitor Center, which is housed in a partial replica of the 1724 **Fort Condé** (tel: 251-208-2000; www.mobile.org; daily), whose cannons now point forlornly across a concrete underpass. Across the street, **Mobile Museum of History** (tel: 251-208-7569; www.historymuseumofmobile.com; Tue–Sun) is housed in an Italianate building and has good exhibits on local history. From there, a short walk will take you through stately historic districts that

Crest of the Historic Development Commission in Mobile, Alabama.

Overlook Lake, Bellingrath Gardens.

⊙ Tip
The popular Blessing of the Fleet (http://fleetblessing.org) takes place in early May in Bayou La Batre, a fishing town near Mobile, Alabama.

flourish with magnolia, azalea, and oak, all of which thrive in the semi-tropical climate. In a familiar pattern, serious commerce has fled to the outlying malls, and the old department stores have closed down. Downtown does, however, have a plethora of hip cafés, clubs, and restaurants, and a restored *grande dame* hotel – the 1852 Beaux Arts—style **Battle House** – established on the site of Andrew Jackson's military headquarters during the War of 1812.

SEMI-TROPICAL JUNGLE

Government Street becomes US 90 as it pulls away from Mobile Bay and widens into the usual mall-motel-and-fast-food sprawl. On reaching the town of **Theodore**, you'll spot a huge billboard directing you south on Bellingrath Road to **Bellingrath Gardens and Home** ❾ (tel: 251-973-2217; www.bellingrath.org; daily). All the hype – "Incomparable," "One of the World's Most Beautiful Year-Round Gardens" – turns out to be true. Originally a semi-tropical jungle serving as

Fat crabs from the warm waters of the Gulf.

a fishing camp along the Fowl River, the land was purchased by Walter Bellingrath, who made his fortune as the first bottler of Coca-Cola in Alabama. Mr and Mrs Bellingrath landscaped 65 acres (26 hectares) of th 905-acre (367-hectare) plot, sculpting an evolving, living work of art to surround their magnificent riverfron home. Azaleas, roses, hibiscus, chenille, chrysanthemums, poinsettias lilies, violets, and dogwood are al part of the "rapturous floral beauty. The Oriental-American Garden, honking geese, flamingos, and teemin bayou will charm even if the gift sho and restaurant depress. This attraction is out of the way. Allow half a da for a visit.

GULF WILDLIFE AND ART IN OCEAN SPRINGS

US 90 is the old highway along the Gul Coast from Florida to Louisiana. You' have to decide for yourself whether th potted roads, frequent traffic lights dreary trailer parks, and gritty fishin ports such as Grand Bay and Bayou L Batre close to Mobile merit taking th slow route the whole way, or whether you want to drive the more efficient an pleasantly grassy freeway some of th way and get off at US 90 communitie that interest you.

If you're taking I-10, **Pascagoul** is your best bet to exit and pick u US 90 as it heads west through Bilox and Gulfport. Just before reachin Biloxi, you'll pass through the delightful beach town of **Ocean Springs**, cultural mecca with the intimate fee of California's Carmel, which seem almost out of place amid the working class towns of the Gulf. The pretty compact downtown – a haven for artists – offers unique boutiques, eateries, cafés, and art galleries, and make a relaxing spot to linger over lunch or cup of coffee.

If you only visit one small-tow art museum on this whole Souther

Route, make it Ocean Springs' mesmerizing **Walter Anderson Museum of Art** (tel: 228-872-3164; www.walterandersonmuseum.org; Mon–Sat). Local boy Anderson (1903–65), a classically trained artist who developed mental health problems, was a passionate recorder of the natural treasures along the Gulf Coast shoreline. His moving artwork combines an inner turmoil reminiscent of Van Gogh with the subtly colored but detailed natural forms found in Georgia O'Keeffe's artwork, all of it expressed in thousands of jewel-like watercolors of his beloved Mississippi Gulf Coast. A huge mural in the adjoining community center, containing numerous spiritual references and natural motifs, was designated a national treasure in 2005. Among the 900 works in the collection are ceramics by Walter's brothers Peter, founder of Shearwater Pottery, and James, a noted painter and ceramist.

At the east end of Ocean Springs, you'll find the Mississippi branch of **Gulf Islands National Seashore** (tel: 228-230-4100; www.nps.gov/guis; daily) – the other branch is in Florida. Its pleasant boardwalk trail offers glimpses of the Gulf and bayous that so entranced Anderson. The visitor center has exhibits and information. This is a good place for nature lovers hoping to view ospreys and other birds and to relax in an unspoiled setting.

BILOXI

Just across the bridge from Ocean Springs is **Biloxi** 🔟 (pronounced locally: "bluxi"), the second base of operations for the French government of the Louisiana Territory, when it moved from Mobile. Founded in 1699 across Biloxi Bay from its present location, the city sits on a peninsula cut by two bays and the Gulf of Mexico, which has created a popular beach. In the 1800s, Biloxi had a reputation as a posh winter resort, but its bayou-front stately homes are mostly gone now, largely due to a succession of severe storms that have made direct hits on Biloxi.

Mailbox with tiny Confederate flag in the Deep South.

Hard Rock and Beau Rivage casinos in Biloxi, Mississippi.

☉ **Tip**

Gulf Islands National Seashore offers a rare unspoiled look at the natural history of the gulf in charming Ocean Springs, an arts town near Biloxi, Mississippi. Ospreys nest near the visitor center and the boardwalk trail through the bayous and gulf shore.

Hurricane Camille wreaked severe damage in 1969; in 1998, Hurricane Georges caused further widespread destruction; then in August 2005, Hurricane Katrina devastated the resort town, killing residents and uprooting homes and businesses.

More heartache for Gulf residents came with the April 2010 Deepwater Horizon explosion and oil spill, which in addition to killing workers on a Gulf oil platform operated by British Petroleum, polluted area beaches, killed birds and other wildlife, impacted tourism, and ruined the livelihoods of numerous Gulf residents. A major cleanup operation and strong advertising campaign promoting the Gulf's clean beaches (including a visit from President Obama) went some way toward allaying tourism fears, but fisheries and small Gulf businesses long counted the costs.

Biloxi's big gambling resorts have survived it all, including Hurricane Nate in November 2017, which made landfall in Biloxi as a Category 1 hurricane but quickly fizzled, the last of a series of destructive hurricanes that hit the US that season. The resilience here demonstrates the corporate incentives at play here, as well as a fierce North-versus-South politics that saw Republican governors like Mississippi's Haley Barbour and Louisiana's Bobby Jindahl emphasizing recovery through private enterprise rather than long-delayed government handouts.

Today, Biloxi is roaring back to life, in part due to gambling resort mainstays like the Hard Rock (www.hardrockbiloxi. com) and Beau Rivage (www.beaurivage. com). State laws only allow for gambling on boats, not on land, so the huge structures you see from the road are in fact just the hotel and restaurant parts of the operation, while the actual gaming takes place on "barges" situated behind. Once inside, however, you can't tell where the buildings end and the barges begin.

The **Ohr-O'Keefe Museum** (tel 228-374-5547; www.georgeohr.org; Tue-Sun), a museum and cultural center designed by celebrated architect

Beauvoir Mansion, Biloxi.

and artist Frank Gehry, is dedicated to Biloxi's "mad potter" George Ohr 1857–1918). The purpose-built, three-story **Maritime and Seafood Industry Museum** (tel: 228-435-6320; www.maritimemuseum.org; daily) on 1st Street boasts life-size replicas of two Biloxi schooners visible through massive glass windows.

GULFPORT AND LONG BEACH

Biloxi still holds one genuine historical attraction – though it, too, suffered enormous damage during Hurricane Katrina and only reopened in 2008. The white-columned 1852 oceanfront mansion of **Beauvoir** (tel: 228-388-4400; www.visitbeauvoir.org; daily), the last home of Confederate President Jefferson Davis, serves as a showcase for his possessions, and also as a wide-ranging Confederate museum. Most of the buildings on the 51-acre (20-hectare) estate were destroyed by Katrina, including the **Jefferson Davis Presidential Library**. Following a huge outpouring of support, the library's reconstruction was completed in 2013 and reopened to the public. The state-of-the-art facilities house many volumes of Confederate literature and artifacts from the Davis family, while on display are Confederate items of interest, including weapons and soldier's clothing.

If it's beach fun you're after, continue along the coast on US 90, where the golden strands of **Gulfport** and **Long Beach** ⑪ are lined with kiosks that rent out jet skis, beach tractors with inflatable wheels, or simply multicolored beach umbrellas. One final community, the intriguingly named **Pass Christian**, once harked back to more gracious days in Mississippi, with the Gulf on one side of US 90 and an avenue of live oaks whose branches intertwined above the highway to create a cool green tunnel. It was a popular retirement community

until Hurricane Katrina destroyed over 2,000 homes, permanently altering the town. Now, more than 13 years after Katrina, while the population is still finding its feet, the town has a new city hall, library, and yacht club, and a busy harbor.

US 90 then curves sharply away from the coast and crosses the Bay of St Louis, where a bridge leads to lovely **Bay St Louis**, "Gateway to the Gulf Coast." With little warning, the road forks: State Route 609 takes the northwestern route toward I-10 and a NASA test site, while US 90 slides southwestward, both bringing you shortly to Louisiana. Eight miles (13km) of bridges form I-10 from shore to shore – from St Tammany Parish (counties are called "parishes" in Louisiana) into Orleans Parish. As the car crosses **Lake Pontchartrain Causeway**, you feel you're dipping and climbing through the water itself. Suddenly, wistful **New Orleans** ⑫ (see page 258) rises from the opposite shore of **Lake Pontchartrain** ⑬, a crescent of skyscrapers amid a green lake of oak.

⊙ **Fact**

Pass Christian was named for a nearby deepwater pass commemorating Nicholas Christian L'Adnier who lived on nearby Cat Island in 1746.

Drawbridge on the Lake Pontchartrain Causeway, gateway to New Orleans.

NEW ORLEANS: THE BIG EASY

Anchor of the Gulf Coast, cradle of jazz, home of exotic food – this is without doubt the most fascinating city in the South.

Curling around a mighty bend in the Mississippi River, New Orleans (Noo-*Orlens*) is known as the "Crescent City" – home of jazz, blues, and complex Creole food, blending French, Latin, and Caribbean influences. Since 1857, it has also been synonymous with Mardi Gras, whose private balls, flamboyant float parades, masks, and glittering costume jewelry capture the towering gothic spirit of this unique American city.

Not even the devastating Category 5 Hurricane Katrina, which narrowly missed hitting New

Bourbon Street, in the heart of the French Quarter.

Orleans in August 2005, stopped Mardi Gras the following year, but it was close. The levees that protect sub–sea level New Orleans from flooding failed in more than 50 places during the subsequent storm surge, flooding 80 percent of the city for weeks. Remarkably, the Vieux Carre, or **French Quarter**, and other historic areas along the river, the high ground on which the French government had wisely built the original walled city in the 1700s, were spared.

In 2015, the city commemorated the 10th anniversary of Katrina, mourning more than 1,800 of its victims. Although New Orleans has been largely rebuilt, people who suffered high levels of trauma have been changed forever. With some 393,000 residents, the area's population is still much lower than before the hurricane, when 500,000 people lived here. To learn more about the events leading up to and following the disaster, visit the **Hurricane Katrina Memorial** at 5056 Canal Street. Plans are underway for the Katrina Memorial Museum and National Memorial Park (see www.knmfno.org to find out how you can support the project).

In the French Quarter, between Canal Street and Esplanade, though, it's business as usual – an eerie contrast with outlying neighborhoods. The heart of the French Quarter is **Jackson Square**, fronted by **St Louis Cathedral** (1794). The sidewalks here are the domain of street musicians, portrait artists, and fortune tellers – not to mention the Lucky Dog hot dog sellers, their carts shaped like garish giant sausages, immortalized in John Kennedy Toole's comic masterpiece *A Confederacy of Dunces*. To either side are the red-brick **Pontalba Buildings** (1849), the oldest apartment buildings in the US. The **Cabildo** and **Presbytere** (tel: 800-568-6968; www.louisianastatemuseum.org; Mon–Tue), two excellent state museums, flank the cathedral itself, housed in cupola-topped Colonial structures. Among their treasures are Napoleon's death mask and the room in which the 1803 Louisiana Purchase was signed.

The main drag (in every sense) is Bourbon Street, a pedestrian circus at all hours. Paralleling Bourbon, one block toward the river but in complete contrast is Royal Street, which hosts elegant art galleries and antique shops as well as formal restaurants such as **Brennan's** – legendary for its breakfasts – and the Court of **Two Sisters**, whose shaded courtyard is a perfect jazz brunch spot.

Along **Decatur Street**, the riverfront thoroughfare, tourist dollars are mined enthusiastically at souvenir shops and restaurants in the legendary **French Market** (www.frenchmarket.org) and former **Jackson Brewery**. It's all accompanied by the deafening blare of tunes played on the whistle of the **steamboat** *Natchez* (www.steamboatnatchez.com), which offers daily sightseeing cruises on the Mississippi. For an appealing half-mile or so, the aptly named "Big Muddy" is lined first by a wooden boardwalk known as the "Moonwalk," then by grassy parks, one of which contains the well-stocked Aquarium of the Americas (tel: 800-774-7394; www.auduboninstitute.org/aquarium; Tue–Sun). A small ferry (http://nolaferries.com) crisscrosses the river to the island of **Algiers**, an interesting vantage point on the city.

Lafitte's Blacksmith Shop (www.lafittesblacksmithshop.com) at 941 Bourbon Street, the tumbledown brick smithy where the pirate Lafitte plotted many a high-seas escapade, is an atmospheric if almost impenetrably gloomy bar that makes an appropriate starting point for nightly walking tours of "Haunted New Orleans," while the stately **Napoleon House** (www.napoleonhouse.com) at 500 Chartres Street, allegedly the focus of a scheme to rescue the exiled emperor from St Helena and bring him to the United States, is another ravishingly Stygian bar with its own courtyard café.

All along Bourbon Street, talented house bands entertain diners at cafés and restaurants. *The* spot for traditional jazz is Preservation Hall (tel: 504-522-2841; www.preservationhall.com), a tiny, dilapidated hall on St Peter Street whose appearance belies the famous musicians who nightly toot their horns here. At legendary clubs like Tipitina's (tel: 504-895-8477 -7095; www.tipitinas.com), featured in Jim Jarmusch's movie *Down by Law*, you'll see local bands like the Radiators tearing up the dance floor.

Best with spicy gumbo, jambalaya, and crawfish étouffée is ice-cold Abita beer, Louisiana's own brew. The definitive local liquor drinks are Sazerac and Ramos Gin Fizz; a rum-based Hurricane at Pat O'Brien's (www.patobriens.com); or

a cooling Pimm's Cup at the Napoleon House. New Orleans is famous for its chicory coffee. It is traditional to enjoy creamy café au lait with beignets – donuts drowned in powdered sugar – at the 24-hour sidewalk **Café du Monde** in the French Market, a great people-watching spot.

West of the Vieux Carré, the **Warehouse District** is New Orleans' up-and-coming arts district. Among its boutique hotels and contemporary restaurants like Cochon, whose Cajun Southern pork dishes celebrate everything but the squeal, you will find art galleries, the **Louisiana Children's Museum** (tel: 504-523-1357; www.lcm.org; May–Sept daily, Oct–Apr Tue–Sun), and the **National WWII Museum** (tel: 504-528-1944; www.ddaymuseum.org; daily). Beyond the Central Business District, the home of the **Mercedes-Benz Superdome** (www.mbsuperdome.com) – a good trip to take by tram – is the lush and wealthy **Garden District**, where antebellum houses stand amid the azalea and dogwood, and baroque oak trees shade marvelous structures built in Greek Revival, Renaissance, and Victorian styles.

St Louis Cathedral.

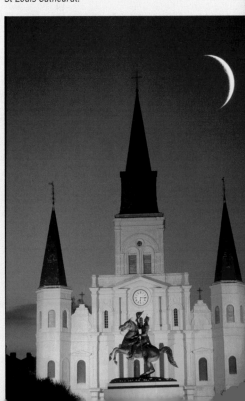

NEW ORLEANS TO SAN ANTONIO

Cruise across what is claimed to be "the longest bridge in the world," take an alligator-enhanced trip through Cajun Country, and end up in Cowboy Country.

This route from New Orleans to the Texas border takes in, first, Cajun Country and then the state's capital. Leaving the city and driving north, Lake Pontchartrain is spanned by **Lake Pontchartrain Causeway** (www.thecauseway. us), "the world's longest bridge." The causeway is a 24-mile (39km) double strip of highway propped above the surface of the lake. For miles, nothing can be seen on the horizon, and the camelback plunge into the void is akin to crossing the barren yet subtle plains of Texas.

On the trip north over the causeway to **Mandeville**, land initially appears as a thin blue sliver on the horizon, an airy gray-blue strip melting off the murky waters into the sky. Gradually, it becomes more distinct, broader, and deeper in color, until it reveals itself as the interface of two great azure bodies: sea and sky.

If you choose to cross the Lake Pontchartrain Causeway, it might be best to do it when leaving the city – a round-trip across the lake can be overwhelming, and concentration may falter on the return stretch. When the Causeway touches land, in Mandeville, it becomes US 190. Four miles (6km) north of the lakeshore, it interchanges with I-12, which runs 61 miles (98km) west to the capital of Louisiana – Baton Rouge.

ACADIAN BAYOUS

Alternatively, follow the efficient but gritty I-10 out of New Orleans, and cut through the boggy, baroque Bayou Country on the southwest bank of Lake Pontchartrain in St Charles and St John the Baptist parishes. The highway is stilted out of grass-fringed still water, where the thin tree trunks that disappear into the mire mirror the poles supporting the parallel powerlines.

Bayous – narrow, sluggish rivers surrounded by wetlands – run in veins throughout southern Louisiana,

Main attractions

Lake Pontchartrain
  Causeway
New Louisiana State Capitol
Atchafalaya Swamp
Breaux Bridge
Jean Lafitte Scenic Byway
St Martinville
Port Bolivar Ferry
Bishop's Palace
Texas State Capitol
Lyndon B. Johnson State
  Park

Map on page 244

Traffic jam on Lake Pontchartrain Causeway.

otherwise known as Acadiana. This expansive region is named after the Acadians, French Catholic refugees driven out of Nova Scotia, Canada, by the British in the mid-18th century. Settling the Louisiana lowlands, mostly Spanish dominions, they were joined by Frenchmen fleeing the American Revolution; together, they created a culture known as "Cajun" (a corruption of "Acadian").

Acadiana, stretching along the Gulf Coast to Texas and west from the Mississippi River up to Avoyelles Parish, has been described as "South of the South," although in many ways it's more conspicuously akin to the societies of the French and Spanish West Indies than to the traditional American South.

BATON ROUGE

Interstate 10 meets the Mississippi River at the city of **Baton Rouge ⓮**, capital of Louisiana and the state's main port. Its French name means "red stick," apparently the "stick" being a tree, red either from the blood of animals hung there by Indians or from the

stripping of its bark. In the latter case the tree may have been used to mark the boundary of Houma and Bayou Goula Indian land. Although Baton Rouge abuts Acadiana, it has little to do with it, except for governing it and shipping its oil. The ambiance is definitely Southern, and you'll notice, in comparison to New Orleans, a deepening of accent and of provincial ways. The rather quiet, laid-back tempo of the streets belies the intense industry and politicking at the city's heart.

The principal sights of Baton Rouge are the old and new trappings of government. **Louisiana's Old State Capitol** (tel: 225-342-0500; www.louisianaoldstatecapitol.org; Tue–Sat) was a Gothic folly constructed beside the Mississippi in 1849 that was derided by all, including writer Mark Twain. It is now home to a museum of political history. In contrast, the 34-story Art Deco **New Capitol** (tel: 225-342-7317; www.brla.gov; Tue–Sun), a national historic landmark, bestrides the north end of town like a scaled-down Empire State Building. The skyscraper was built in

Old State Capitol, Baton Rouge.

1932 by Louisiana's infamous governor Huey Long, the so-called "Kingfish," who reigned supreme throughout the Great Depression. By all accounts a distasteful and corrupt man, Long was nevertheless an enlightened despot who brooked no opposition to his semi-socialistic rule for the "common man." Highways, schools, and hospitals were built; the unemployed put to work; the privileged heavily taxed. He was gunned down in the capitol in 1935 – a plaque on the exact spot admits that he may have been killed by his own bodyguards as they panicked in the face of a supposed assassin who never fired a shot. He is buried in the adjacent garden, alongside a larger-than-life statue.

The twin foundations of the city's wealth appear as you leave. From the huge **Baton Rouge Bridge**, on which I-10 crosses the river, you can see belching petrochemical refineries stretching into the distance. Down below stands Baton Rouge's port, one of the most active in the nation, thanks to being the farthest inland of all deep-water ports serving the Gulf of Mexico. That status was not achieved by chance; one of Long's most brilliant ploys to boost his own state was to build this very bridge too low for ocean-going vessels to continue any farther upstream.

West of the Mississippi, you re-enter Acadiana in West Baton Rouge Parish, and soon pass into Iberville Parish. For the first time on this trip – but not the last, as you head toward the open spaces of the West – you're treated to spectacular scenery without having to leave the interstate. Here, it is the **Atchafalaya Swamp Freeway**, crossing America's largest swamp, which is split into east- and west-headed roadways, supported on precarious-looking concrete stilts and separated by soupy open water dotted with lozenge-shaped islets. It's the most exciting drive on this whole trip.

DROWNED FORESTS IN THE BAYOU

To either side, the landscape is a magical melding of water and drowned forest, punctuated by clumps of trees, telegraph poles, and strangely shaped

'Gator in a glade, Atchafalaya.

◉ Tip

The Cajun language includes many French words: *cher* dear one, *boudin* sausage, *lagniappe* something extra, *beignet* square donut found in New Orleans, *gris-gris* good luck charm or spell, *laissez les bons temps rouler!* let the good times roll!

cypress "knees" *(pneumatophores)* – those parts of the root systems of cypress trees that poke out of the morass. Locals fish sedately, or even race speedboats, just below the highway, and every unidentified piece of flotsam may potentially be an alligator. On the far side of the 20-mile (32km)-wide swamp, you find yourself safely back on terra firma. Louisiana-born residents draw a distinction between the Prairie Cajuns, who farm the soil of south-central Louisiana, and the Bayou Cajuns, the shrimp-fishing river-dwellers of the marshlands closer to the Gulf, jokingly referred to as "half-man, half-gator." In terms of what the rest of the world thinks of as Cajun culture – the accordion- and fiddle-based Cajun music and spicy food – the two are not far apart.

Lafayette ⑮ 50 miles (80km) west of Baton Rouge, is the largest city in Acadiana, and, standing close to the hypothetical line that divides the prairies from the bayous, makes an ideal hub for exploring the region. It's a sprawling city, known for excellent restaurant-cum-music-clubs like **Prejean's** (http://prejeans.com) and **Randol's** (www.randols.com) and living history museums, where costumed interpreters bring local history alive in specially built settings. The best, Vermilionville (tel: 337-233-4077; www.vermilionville.org; Tue–Sun), consists of an idealized village of restored and transplanted 19th-century buildings where experts demonstrate traditional Cajun crafts. Its free weekly Cajun Jam features some of the finest musicians in the area.

LAND OF THE CAJUNS

The Texas border is barely 100 miles (160km) west of Lafayette, but the temptation to explore Cajun Country will prove irresistible, as this is one of the most fascinating and culturally rich areas on the whole route. A short excursion north, for example, leads to the welcoming real-life prairie town of **Eunice**, and to **Opelousas**, home of Cajun music's blacker, bluesier counterpart – zydeco.

If it's a perfect taste of Acadiana you want, leave I-10 at exit 109 before you

An Acadian accordion handcrafted in Eunice.

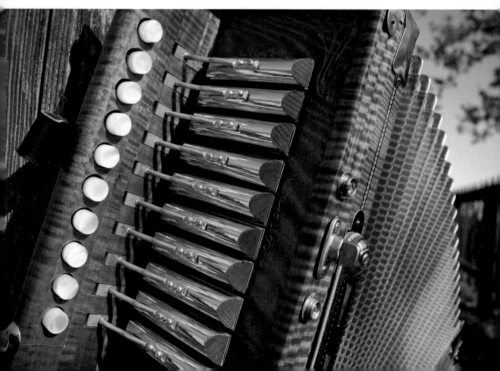

et to Lafayette to visit the delightful own of **Breaux Bridge**, which calls self the Crawfish Capital of the World. he town has an almost English feel o it, with its tiny bridge, main street afés, and antique shops. If you come n a Saturday morning (and do try to o that), don't miss the world-famous ydeco Breakfast with live music and ancing at Buck and Johnny's (www. uckandjohnnys.com) in the historic istrict. The cafe, serving a blend of ydeco and Italian food, has carried on his longtime tradition since historic afe des Amis closed in 2017, and eveyone joins in, locals and travelers, to ake a turn on the dance floor. Cafe des mis reopened in 2018 as Cafe Sydnie lae (www.cafesydniemae.com), a steak nd seafood restaurant, but no longer oes the famous Saturday Cajun runch in its lovely old space.

RIVING THE JEAN LAFITTE CENIC BYWAY

lore ambitious travelers can connue on a long detour south to pick p State Route 82 to parallel the more interesting coast along the **Jean Lafitte Scenic Byway**. From Breaux Bridge, State Route 31 follows Bayou Teche another 11 miles (18km) south to **St Martinville** ⑯, one of the most unspoiled towns you will find in your travels in America. A former indigo plantation and Spanish holding, it was populated by Acadians and Frenchmen in the late 18th and 19th centuries, an era when its culture was so rich that its inhabitants nicknamed it "Petit Paris." After its transformation as a minor port on the bayou, St Martinville settled into its current form of small agrarian center, with visible Cajun and French roots.

Locals are glad to recite half-remembered and half-invented histories in small cafés, which might serve Coca-Cola and catfish *étouffée*. The town is infused with the legend of Evangeline (subject of a well-known Henry Wadsworth Longfellow poem), who allegedly walked from Nova Scotia to St Martinville in search of her lover.

The venerable **Evangeline Oak** next to the **St Martin de Tours** church (1765),

St Martin de Tours Catholic church.

Spanish moss is found draped over live oak trees. It is not really Spanish nor is it really moss; it is an air plant and a member of the pineapple family.

Cruising a bayou in a traditional Louisiana wooden boat.

where she arrived only to receive the news that her faithless sweetheart had married another, is now a riverside beauty spot where Cajun couples hold their wedding services, while the **Longfellow-Evangeline State Historic Site** (tel: 337-394-3754; Wed–Sun) explores the cultural diversity of peoples along the Bayou Teche, including Acadians, Creoles, Indians, Africans, Frenchmen, and Spaniards. The interesting **Acadian House Museum** (tel: 337-394-2258; www.acadianmemorial.org; Tue–Sat) has more on Acadian history.

South of St Martinville, State Route 675 and then State Route 14 will take you west into Vermilion Parish and the attractive parish seat, **Abbeville** ⓱. Home to the Giant Omelette Celebration (www.giantomelette.org) in November, Abbeville consists of three interlocking and very sleepy squares, as well as a couple of oyster restaurants.

Grazing cattle indicate solid ground, but the next field along may be a waterlogged rice paddy through which cranes and herons meticulously pick their long-legged way. Locals fish in the channels that run alongside the roadway, or wade through with shrimping nets.

The farther you go, the fewer signs of human life there are along this bleak and windswept drive, but the birds are a constant source of delight. The trees are bent at ever more acute angles as you approach the Gulf, and in places it feels as though you're having to force yourself through the thick tangles of Spanish moss that hang from overhead. This wispy, gray, romantic shroud is not a parasite but an epiphyte, an air plant, which draws no sustenance from its host, and is therefore equally at home dangling from telephone wires. Turn on the radio for company and you'll find French- and English-language stations in equal measure, together with Spanish baseball commentaries from Houston as you come within earshot of that city.

MARSH TRAIL

Seventy-two miles (116km) from Abbeville, highway signs announce that you're arriving in **Grand Chenier**

ut apart from a few trailer parks and
a Catholic church surrounded by pray-
ng statues, no recognizable town ever
appears. Another 30 miles (48km) on,
beyond a straggle of run-down motels
and rudimentary restaurants cater-
ng to workers in the occasionally
glimpsed oil refineries, the highway is
interrupted by an on-demand platform
erry that shuttles a dozen vehicles at
a time across the outlet of **Lake Calcasieu**. On the far side, the open ocean
lies barely 50 yards (46 meters) off
to your right, and mighty drilling rigs
are visible far out to sea. It is said
that early Spanish explorers would
beach their vessels here to caulk their
hulls with the mysterious black sub-
stance found oozing on the beaches
– a boon for Louisiana, perhaps, but,
especially after the BP Deep Horizon
oil spill in 2010, many lost the incen-
tive for a quick dip at **Holly Beach**. In
any case, it's time to turn your wheel
back inland. The coastal road ahead
has been closed by one Gulf storm too
many, and to reach Texas you'll have
to head 35 miles (56km) north to rejoin
the interstate.

One final highlight remains, however, in the shape of the **Sabine
National Wildlife Refuge ⑱** (tel: 337-
762-3816; www.fws.gov/refuges; daily), 9
miles (15km) up State 27. Exhibits in
the visitor center and along the Wetland Walkway interpret the natural
history of this wetland. The trail starts
beside the **Intracoastal Waterway** – a
mind-boggling canal that spans almost
the entire length of the state. The best
times of year to see alligators sunning
themselves along the Wetland Walkway are spring and fall.

EAST TEXAS TO SAN ANTONIO

Everyone has at least one picture of
Texas. Tumbleweeds and cacti, oilfields, cowboy millionaires, humming
border towns, cattle ranches – popular culture has disseminated a rugged,
romantic vision of the largest of the
Lower 48 states. Such familiar cultural
snapshots, however, both over- and
underestimate the sprawling diversity
and vitality of Texas. This *is* where the
West begins, but it's a West with no
coherent definition. At the risk of over-
simplifying, think of a passage through
Texas as a microcosmic passage from
East to West, with the point of transition coming at San Antonio, the westernmost of the state's major cities.

Texas's vast wealth and power are
centered within the compact urban
triangle of Houston, Dallas–Fort
Worth, and San Antonio. From Galveston through Houston to Austin, the
Southern tour arcs through the heart
of East Texas – its resort, its port, and
the state capital. Wherever you go,
note the change in the triangular yellow signs that elsewhere in the South
exhort motorists to "Drive Safely."
Here, they read: "Drive Friendly." The
name "Texas," after all, is derived
from "Tejas," meaning "friendly" – the
name given by the Spanish to the Native
Americans they encountered.

*The "drowned forests"
of Louisiana's bayous.*

PORT BOLIVAR FERRY

From the moment you enter Texas on I-10 from Louisiana, highway signs start to count down the mileage to New Mexico. Shortly after the state line, Exit 877 branches off to the town of Orange, and the first sign you will see for El Paso shows it as an incomprehensible 857 mile (1,379km) distant. You'll feel ready to leave this nondescript stretch of highway long before the first city of any size – Houston, 110 miles (177km) – and you're well advised to return to the Gulf coast as soon as possible, and head for the historic island resort community of **Galveston ⑲**.

By far the most enjoyable way of reaching Galveston is to take the free 20-minute Port Bolivar ferry across Galveston Bay. As you approach Exit 829, look for the billboard that lets drivers know it's in operation, and if so, take the scenic island route rather than the straight-shot I-45 south from Houston by picking up State Route 124 South to the ocean at Winnie.

As you cross first Spindletop Bayou and then Elm Bayou, little

about this marshy landscape suggests you've left Louisiana. Ric and even crawfish farms stand o either side of the highway, whil oil pump jacks diligently bob awa atop mounds of scrubby gulf vegeta tion. About 20 miles (32km) south, humpback bridge crosses the Intra coastal Waterway at **High Island** High Island's unique salt-dom geography allows trees to grow tha serve as stopovers for thousands o neotropical migratory birds durin spring migrations. In fact, this tin hamlet is a birding hotspot, with n less than four bird sanctuaries run b Texas Audubon.

State Route 87 runs the 27-mil (43km) length of Bolivar Peninsula t dead-end at the ferry terminal for Gal veston. This once was a wild barrie island, a boon for those with a taste fo nature in the rough. Sparsely inhabite on its eastern end and growing rapidl into a high-end resort community o its west end – by 2008, Bolivar Pen insula had a permanent population o 3,800 residents and attracted thou sands of local vacationers.

All that ended abruptly in Septem ber 2008, when Hurricane Ike, a cate gory 2 storm with winds up to 110mp (178kph), made a direct hit on East Gal veston, creating a massive storm surg that inundated the Bolivar Peninsula The destruction on Bolivar was almos total, flattening homes and businesse and blowing debris into Galveston Ba The historic Bolivar lighthouse, whic survived the Great Storm of 1900, wa destroyed. The remaining signs of Ike' wrath are now loosely strewn, but th hurricane has changed Bolivar Pen insula forever. With the little fishin camps gone, the newly constructe houses are big and expensive, whil the owners of new homes, who wer often attracted here by lower lan prices following the disaster, are b and large a different group of peopl than previous residents.

Flock of pelicans over wooden beach houses in Galveston.

ALVESTON'S PIRATES AND EACHES

alveston grew to prominence during e early 1800s as a seaport and head-arters for the pirate Jean Lafitte, of ew Orleans fame. In the local eco-mic boom that followed the Civil ar, it flowered into a fully fledged ty, becoming Texas' leading manu-cturing center and, by 1899, the rgest cotton port in the world. Gal-ston had the first telephone system Texas, the first newspaper, electric hts, golf course, brewery, and Ford alership, while the Strand (named r the street in London), thanks to its ofusion of great commercial houses, as renowned as "The Wall Street of e Southwest."

Houston's port has entirely over-adowed the island's, but Galveston mains an active shipping center d is heavily involved with the cation industry, being a popular nbarkation point for cruises to the aribbean. Of its 32 miles (51km) of ach, the most popular stretch lies the Gulf side of the island, along awall Boulevard. This broad thor-ghfare is lined on its inland side th numerous sprawling motels d fast-food restaurants, while the ach itself is interrupted by a suc-ssion of privately owned piers that t out into the ocean.

There's lots of family-style enter-inment in Galveston. In the historic wntown, you'll find **Texas Seaport useum** (tel: 409-763-1877; www.gal ston.com/texasseaportmuseum; daily), aturing the 1877 tall ship *Elissa*. **:ean Star Offshore Drilling Rig and useum** (tel: 409-766-7827; www. eanstaroec.com; daily) has a unique orking replica of an offshore oil rig. **alveston Railroad Museum** (tel: 9-765-5700; www.galvestonrrmuseum. m; daily), at the foot of the Strand, is cated in a looming early 20th-cen-ry skyscraper, the former home of merican National Insurance Company

founded by wealthy Galvestonian Wil-liam Moody Jr.

Moody's name is associated with several places on the island. On Broad-way, the 1895 **Moody Mansion** (tel: 409-762-7668; www.moodymansion.org; daily), built in a Romanesque style, was the family home for 50 years. While over on the island's quieter northwest side, a family bequest created the sprawling **Moody Gardens** (tel: 800-582-4673; www.moodygardens.com; daily), a 242-acre (98-hectare) educational com-plex used heavily by Texas schools. It has three themed glass pyramids containing a rainforest, an aquarium, and science-oriented exhibits. Other attractions include a museum, a 3D/4D theater, landscaped waterfront gardens, a huge hotel/convention com-plex, and a ropes course and zipline.

EAST END ARCHITECTURE AND FOOD

The historic Strand has undergone a familiar renovation into tourist attrac-tion, arguably losing its soul in the process, but the East End Historical

Dolphin statue on Galveston's seawall.

The tall ship Elissa, built in 1877 by Alexander Hall & Co. in Aberdeen, Scotland, is now part of the Texas Seaport Museum in Galveston.

Shrimp boats in Galveston's dock.

District, bounded roughly by Broadway, Mechanic, 19th and 11th streets, remains unspoiled. Here, Victorian homes stand, intermixed with buildings that betray neoclassical, Renaissance, and Italianate influences. Bungalows rest in the shade cast by oleanders, oaks, maples, and palms, and are slightly raised from the ground out of respect for the Gulf. Post Office and Church streets are particularly lovely. Several of the town's best contemporary eateries are located on 14th Street. On the corner of Broadway and 14th is **Bishop's Palace** (tel: 409-762-2475; www.galvestonhistory.org; daily), a turreted Gothic fantasy rated as one of the top historic buildings in the US by the American Institute of Architects. It was built for the wealthy Gresham family in 1892 by famed Galveston architect Nicholas Clayton.

Galveston is 50 miles (80km) south of Houston, but the buildup to the megalopolis begins as soon as you cross back to the mainland on the I-45 Causeway, to be confronted by massed ranks of smoke-belching oil refineries.

From there on, strip malls and garish billboards line the interstate for the full 27 miles (43km) up to the Sam Houston Tollway, which encircles the city for 20 miles (32km). As you pass beneath its stacked and spiraling freeways and connecting concrete loops, the futuristic downtown skyline of **Houston** ⑳ (see page 272) finally rises on the northern horizon.

WELL-SHELTERED AUSTIN

If you see Texas as a microcosm of the whole country, then it's as you head west of Houston that you leave the South behind and enter the Great Plains. The state capital, **Austin** ㉑, is approximately 150 miles (240km) west, but as I-10 runs directly to San Antonio instead, along a slightly more southerly route, reaching Austin entails at least 40 miles (64km) of driving off the interstate. Whichever route you choose will be much the same, a relaxing cruise through the lush plains and gently rolling hills of the German- and Czech-influenced ranch country that lies within the Houston–Dallas–San

ntonio triangle. Probably the most ucolic option is to leave I-10 at exit 96, near little Columbus, and join tate 71 as it meanders back and forth cross the equally sinuous Colorado iver (not the one that carved the rand Canyon) all the way up to Austin.

Austin itself nestles amid verdant oodland in the middle of an agricul-ural paradise that's unique among e many Texan climates and terrains. heltered from the humid heat that weeps in waves over Houston, this cale is ideal for ranching and recrea-on. Unlike Houston, and despite hav-g experienced similarly phenomenal rowth, Austin is fairly well contained. xit between Martin Luther King, Jr oulevard and 83rd streets from I-35, nd you'll be in the middle of a walk-ble downtown. For most visitors, the xperience of the city is confined to the rea from First Street and the Colorado iver up to 24th Street and the heart of e **University of Texas** (UT) at Austin long Guadalupe Avenue.

IGH TECH AND OUTLAWS

ustin manages the difficult double ct of being not only Texas's political apital but also its true cultural capi-al. Having attained that distinction uring the 1960s, when it was a hip-ie mecca, it went on to spearhead the utlaw country music movement of e 1970s, when country singers like illie Nelson, Waylon Jennings, and erry Jeff Walker first came to promi-ence. Its reputation as a center for ve music and the arts no doubt con-ibuted to the 1980s growth of its very wn Silicon Hills, when more and more igh-tech and financial firms relocated ere. That process, of course, brought ith it an influx of young urban profes-ionals, and one need look no farther an **Sixth Street** to see the impact of ggressive consumerism on the cul-ure. Experiencing the same gentrifica-on as San Francisco's Haight Street, ormerly gay-dominated Sixth Street

is still a good place to bar-hop but not nearly as much of a community as it used to be. Construction, moreover, has become a constant in downtown – so much so that locals joke that Aus-tin's native bird is the "crane."

Despite its changing face, Austin retains much of its laid-back, toler-ant spirit. With 51,000 students and the largest university campus in the state, the counter-cultural element will always have its place. At heart, it's still got long hair and a beard, though it might also have a Mercedes, a top-of-the-line road bike, and a kid. Hardly surprising, then, that Austin is home base for **Whole Foods Market**, the nat-ural foods giant whose luxurious head-quarters in downtown has become a tourist destination in itself.

Austin is the Live Music Capital of the US. Some 200 venues offer every-thing from hard-edged country, new music, ska, classical, and blues to R&B and jazz, and the taping of the televised live music show Austin City Limits (www.austincitylimits.com; free tickets by random lottery a week ahead online)

View of Houston's skyline from a trail in City Park.

Austin by night.

HOUSTON: SPACE-AGE CITY

Once an oil town, Houston now houses a wide range of high-tech industries and quintessentially Texan self-confidence.

Houston, the nation's fourth largest city, boasts that the first word uttered by the first man on the moon was – you guessed it – "Houston." Mission Control Center is the city's prime tourist attraction. **Space Center Houston** (tel: 281-244-2100; www.spacecenter.org; daily), the official visitor center for **Johnson Space Center**, is located on NASA Road 1, off I-45, about 25 miles (40km) south of Houston. A guided tram tour takes visitors through a campus of structures containing moon rocks and astronauts, into the Mission Control Center and full-scale replicas of the

Johnson Space Center on NASA Parkway.

Space Shuttle used for training. Named for the Sea of Tranquility, the base for the 1969 *Apollo* moonshot, Tranquility Park, in downtown Houston at Bagby and Walker streets, is landscaped to look like Tranquility Base, with craters and mounds, fountains, reflecting pools, and copper tubes representing rockets taking off.

More deserving of the name "Tranquility" is the hushed art temple of **Rothko Chapel** (tel: 713-524-9839; www.rothkochapel.org; daily), located on Sul Ross in the Museum District. American abstract expressionist Mark Rothko was commissioned by collectors Dominique and John de Menil to create 14 of his oversized trademark colorwash paintings for this chapel for nondenominational worship and meditation. More of the de Menil couple's extensive art collection can be viewed at the gorgeous **Menil Collection** (tel: 713-525-9400; www.menil.org; Wed–Sun), which houses arts and artifacts of mankind from the earliest days to the present.

The galleries of Houston demonstrate how "black gold" has enriched the state of Texas through the purchase of works of art. The Matisse bronzes that turn their backs to you at the **Museum of Fine Arts Houston** (tel: 713-639-7300; www.mfah.org; Tue–Sun) at Main and Bissonet streets make their case about Houston's attitude toward the norm. The MFAH's collection is particularly strong in American paintings. Across the street is the **Contemporary Arts Museum Houston** (tel: 713-284-8250; www.camh.org; Tue–Sun), dedicated to contemporary works. At Hermann Park is the **Museum of Natural Science** (tel: 713-639-4629; www.hmns.org; daily, free Thu from 2pm), with a walk-through greenhouse aflutter with butterflies, a giant-screen theater, and a planetarium. George Observatory (tel: 281-242-3055), a satellite facility of the Museum of Natural Science is located in Brazos Bend State Park, approximately an hour's drive south of downtown.

The discount booklet CityPass includes entry to five major Houston attractions for $59, a 49 percent saving. For information, log on to www.visit houstontexas.com.

still a popular gig, broadcast from an open-air theater on the UT campus. Downtown is host to the popular South-by-Southwest (SXSW; www.sxsw. com) Music Fest every March. Theater and literary events are numerous, while good bookstores, record stores, cafés, and Tiffany glass restaurants rub shoulders with low-down, funkier spots. Above all, local legends have persisted despite the changes – for example, **Scholz Garten** (tel: 512-474-1958; www.scholzgarten.com; daily). Scholz Garten was founded in 1866, 16 years before construction began on the State Capitol. You can find good food here, along with unpretentious charm and heartfelt music.

LONE STAR CAPITOL

Scholz Garten is a few blocks from the **State Capitol** (tel: 512-305-8400; www. tspb.texas.gov/plan/tours; daily tours) and the lower edges of UT, two major sources of business. The Capitol itself is unmistakable, a local pink-granite version of the US Capitol in Washington, DC. Its white, classical interior focuses on the great rotunda, commemorating the six governments that ruled Texas (Spain, France, Mexico, the Confederate States, the United States, and, most proudly, the Republic of Texas). Above, at the apex of the dome, is the lone star that is the state's emblem: independence, self-determination, and singularity.

Information on touring the Capitol Complex is available at the **Capitol Visitors Center** (tel: 512-305-8400; daily), located in the distinctive castle-like building southeast of the Capitol that housed the General Land Office in the mid-1800s. The enjoyable **Bullock Texas State History Museum** (tel: 512-936-8746; www.thestoryoftexas.com; daily), behind the Capitol, is housed in an attractive modern building constructed from the same pink granite as the Capitol. Its soaring atrium contains three floors of well-presented audio-visual exhibits covering Texas's Native American, Spanish, and American history, as well as an IMAX theater. The **LBJ Presidential Library** (tel: 512-721-0200; www.lbjlibrary.org; daily), located

Eat

Austin's premier barbecue restaurant is the family-run Salt Lick (tel: 512-858-4959; www. saltlickbbq.com; daily), famous for smoked pork ribs, sausage, and brisket from family recipes.

The Texas State Capitol is guarded by a Texas Ranger statue.

Acoustic band playing at the Continental Club in Austin.

Jam session in the saloon of Luckenbach's general store.

on Red River Street, 2 miles (3km) north of the Bullock Museum, contains a diverse collection of objects ranging from Middle Eastern antiquities and fine art to Oval Office furniture.

HILL COUNTRY

Historic San Antonio is barely an hour's drive southwest of Austin on I-35, but there's a diverting half-day's sightseeing to be had if you make your way between the two along the **Texas Hill Country Trail** (http://txhillcountrytrail.com) to the west instead. At first, leaving Austin, the scenic drive along US 290 crosses a somewhat dreary Western landscape of thin grassland. Beyond **Dripping Springs**, the road starts to climb through a rich rolling terrain of open meadows sprinkled with profuse wildflowers, and then starts to undulate through **Johnson City** ㉒, 50 miles (80km) west of Austin, and pastoral countryside.

Johnson City acquired its name long before local boy Lyndon Baines Johnson became the 36th President of the United States, following the assassination of John F. Kennedy in 1963. Even so, LBJ (who shared his initials with wife Lady Bird Johnson) is the big story here. His downtown birthplace and the LBJ Ranch in nearby Stonewall, to which the couple retired after the Vietnam War put an end to his political career, are now part of **Lyndon B. Johnson State Park and Historic Site** (tel: 830-644-2252; www.tpwd.texas.gov/state-parks/lyndon-b-johnson; daily). Incidentally, the glorious **Lady Bird Johnson Wildflower Center** (tel: 512-232-0100; www.wildflower.org; Tue–Sun) in Austin showcases the First Lady's passion for Texas' spectacular wildflowers, easy to understand if you visit the Hill Country in spring.

Everywhere there is evidence of the German settlers who were attracted here in the 1800s. The Main Street of touristy **Fredericksburg**, another 32 miles (51km) west, for example, is called Hauptstrasse and is lined with pseudo-Teutonic beer gardens and bakeries, while farms along the intervening highway, such

as Der Peach Garten, sell German-style wines and liquors.

LUKENBACK TO SAN ANTONIO

Wander through the real Hill Country down to San Antonio by getting off US 290, 4 miles (6km) east of Fredericksburg, and taking State Route 1376 south. The backroad passes within a few feet of the tiny village of **Luckenbach** ㉓ (tel: 830-997-3224; www.luckenbachtexas.com; daily), another 4 miles (6km) on. Unless you know where to look, however, you'll miss it altogether – the unmarked turning comes immediately before South Grape Creek. A much-loved ghost town – more of a joke, really – Luckenbach was bought in its entirety by humorist Hondo Crouch in 1970, and made famous by a No. 1 Country & Western hit, recorded in 1976 by Willie Nelson and Waylon Jennings, that features the refrain "Let's Go To Luckenbach, Texas."

Hundreds of country fans now do just that, to while away an afternoon in the bar inside the diminutive post office

as the postmaster cracks corny jokes and sings songs, and to perhaps buy a souvenir such as a stuffed armadillo drinking a bottle of Luckenbach beer. Willie Nelson hosts a picnic here every Fourth of July, while most summer weekends there's some sort of large-scale concert in the dancehall. From Luckenbach, State Route 1376 continues south toward San Antonio by way of some beautiful hills, where you're liable to startle wild deer grazing beside the highway. Ten miles (16km) northeast of the city limits, it meets I-10/US 87 at Boerne.

San Antonio ㉔ at first seems deceptively pastoral – not far from the interstate, luxurious Italianate villas perch on isolated rocky knobs that look like Tuscan hill towns. Soon enough, however, you're forced to run the gauntlet of the manic freeways required to reach every large American city, and just before it finally spits you out into downtown, the interstate for no reason splits alarmingly into two separate highways, one stacked on top of the other.

General store, post office, and saloon dating from 1849 in Luckenbach, Texas.

Bank of America Plaza and Renaissance Tower, Dallas.

⓪ DETOUR TO DALLAS

A 195-mile (314km) drive along I-35 from Austin leads to Dallas, which, with 1.3 million residents, attracts visitors with its sky-high architecture, quality art collections, and high-end shopping malls. The city grew up around a cabin built by trapper John Neely Bryan beside the Trinity River, which Bryan believed to be navigable for trade all the way to the Gulf of Mexico. It wasn't, but the Houston and Texas Railroad soon brought people and commerce. The pioneer era comes alive at Dallas Heritage Village (tel: 214-421-5141; www.dallasheritagevillage.org; Tue–Sun), which preserves 38 historic structures in a living history museum. Extravagance rules at the flagship Neiman Marcus (www.neimanmarcus.com), whose Christmas catalog once contained a page entitled "How to Spend a Million Dollars." That extravagance has led to wonderful art collections, such as the Meadows Museum on the Southern Methodist University campus (tel: 214-768-2516; www.meadowsmuseumdallas.org; Tue–Sun), home to the largest collection of Spanish art outside Spain. However, its most visited site is the former Texas School Book Depository, where Lee Harvey Oswald shot President John F. Kennedy in 1963. The Sixth Floor Museum at Dealey Plaza (tel: 214-747-6660; www.jfk.org; daily) overlooks the plaza where the President was assassinated. For more information, contact Dallas Convention and Visitors Bureau (tel: 214-571-1000; www.visitdallas.com).

The Rio Grande flows through
Big Bend National Park, Texas.

SAN ANTONIO TO SOUTHERN NEW MEXICO

Davy Crockett and Billy the Kid are just two of the people who left their mark on the lands that border Mexico and the Rio Grande.

Of all the major cities in Texas, El Paso and San Antonio are the oldest. El Paso began as the first Spanish mission in the future state, while it was in San Antonio that American Texas was born and almost lost back to Mexico at the Alamo. Stretching between the two is the vast expanse of **Trans-Pecos Texas**, a largely barren yet subtly beautiful mountainous desert. There is a timeless quality to the landscape that stands in marked contrast to the booming spectacle of the metropolitan east.

In the anchor cities, Hispanic culture consistently revitalizes itself much more effectively than in Galveston, Houston, or Austin. El Paso and adjoining Ciudad Juárez are bound as a Mexican/American metropolis, a popular gateway to the American Southwest.

CRADLE OF TEXAS LIBERTY

San Antonio ㉔, the "Cradle of Texas Liberty," was the Spanish capital of Texas before Mexico won its independence from Spain in 1821. Mexico was essentially an absentee landlord. It began opening the territory of New Spain to settlement by anyone who would develop the land, including immigrants from the fledgling United States. American Stephen F. Austin, whose father Moses had received a land grant from Spain in 1820,

inherited it and, in 1822, led a group dubbed the Old Three Hundred to settle Los Brazos River. Before Austin's pilgrimage, there were 3,500 persons of European descent in San Antonio and La Bahia. By 1836, 30,000 Anglos, 5,000 black slaves, and 4,000 Mexicans populated Texas.

In the late 1860s, when Spaniards first came to the San Antonio River Valley, which cradles modern San Antonio, they found it occupied by the Payaya people, hunters who supplemented their catches with the fruits of the pecan

Main attractions

The Alamo
Big Bend National Park
Chinati Foundation
Chamizal National Memorial
White Sands National Monument
Cloudcroft
Mescalero Apache Indian Reservation
Gila Cliff Dwellings National Monument

Map on page 278

Tribal ceremonial, Gallup.

San Antonio 24
San Antonio Missions National Historical Park

Kerrville
Fort Stockton
Kent — 10

Castroville 25 — 90

Hondo

Knippa

Uvalde

Del Rio 26 — 90
Ciudad Acuña — 277 377

International
Amistad Reservoir
Amistad National Recreation Area

Langtry 27 — 90

Marathon 28

Big Bend
National Park 29 — 385
The Chisos
Basin

Lajitas 30 — 170
Ojinaga

Presidio 67 — 67

Marfa 31 — 67 90

Alpine — 118
Fort Davis 32
Fort Davis N.H.S.
Davis Mountains S.P.
McDonald Observatory
Kent — 10
Van Horn

El Paso 33
Ciudad Juárez

Texas
New Mexico — 54 — 54

Mescalero Apache
Indian Reservation — 244
Lincoln
N.F. — 82
Orogrande
Oliver M. Lee Memorial State Park

Ruidoso — 70
Ski Apache Resort,
Hubbard Museum of
the American West
Cloudcroft
Alamogordo 34 — 70

White Sands
National
Monument 35
Organ Mountains-Desert Peaks NM
Las Cruces

Rio Grande
La Mesilla 36 — 10

Gila Cliff Dwellings
National Monument 38 — 15
Deming 37 — 180

Silver City

Western New Mexico
University Museum — 90

New Mexico — 10
Arizona
Fort Bowie National Historic Site
Lordsburg
Shakespeare Ghost Town

Exit 362 — 186
Chiricahua National Monument 39 — 181
Gleeson — 191
Benson — 80

Saguaro National Park — 90
Tombstone 40
Bisbee
Kartchner Caverns S.P.

Nogales — 19
Mission San Xavier del Bac
Titan Missile Museum
Tumacácori N.H.P. — 10
Tucson 41
Biosphere 2 — 77

Apache
Exittion — 79
88

Picacho Peak State Park — 60
Mesa
Theodore Roosevelt Dam, 42
Tonto National Monument,
Tortilla Flat

Tempe Scottsdale
Heard Museum
Phoenix 43

Exit 112 — 85

Exit 119 — 10
Gila Bend
Dateland 44 — 8

Arizona
Quartzsite — 95
Yuma Territorial Prison State Historic Park
Yuma 45

California
Colorado
Winterhaven

Imperial Sand Dunes NRA 46
El Centro
Ocotillo
Jacumba — 8

Live Oak
Springs 94
El Cajon 47

**San Antonio
to San Diego**

San Diego 48

and mesquite trees and prickly pear cactus. The Payaya cooperated readily with the Europeans, but the Apache who controlled the plains to the north took more convincing, and the nomadic Comanche were always a threat.

Intent on securing their claims in the area, and on taming people they considered godless heathens, the Spanish established a military barracks or *presidio*, and a mission on the west bank of the San Antonio River in 1718. By 1793, Mission San Antonio de Valero had been relocated to the east bank and secularized, and Mexican troops were transferred there to protect the pueblo that had grown up on the riverbanks. Renamed *El Alamo* (*alamo* means "cottonwood"), it became a crucial fortification.

REMEMBER THE ALAMO

The infamy of the converted mission arose much later, during the early American frontier period, and involved an ill-conceived standoff with the forces of Mexican president General Antonio Lopez de Santa Anna, the self-styled "Napoleon of the West," on March 6, 1836. Mexico's 5,000 troops were met by 187 (or 186, depending on who you ask) "Texian" martyrs-to-be. In the words of memorializer Frank J. Davis, "All dead within one sanguinary hour; yet the heroes of the Alamo are deathless."

"Remember the Alamo!" was adopted as the Texan battle cry, and revenge came swiftly. Seven weeks later, Santa Anna was defeated in a mere 18 minutes at the Battle of San Jacinto, and the Texas Revolution culminated with the declaration of the newly independent Republic of Texas.

DAVY CROCKETT

Riddled with as many contradictions as bullet holes, The Alamo (tel: 210-225-1391; www.thealamo.org; daily) is nonetheless an essential destination. The Alamo's defenders during the battle were, after all, recent arrivals from foreign countries – England, Ireland, Scotland, even Denmark – as well as the United States; nevertheless, their 26-year-old commander, William B. Travis from South Carolina, wrote three days before he died that "the citizens of this municipality are all our enemies."

His associates included opportunists such as Jim Bowie, remembered for his namesake knife (though the museum here can only rustle up one of his less-celebrated spoons), and the legendary Davy Crockett, a three-term Congressman from Kentucky who sought his fortune in the West after the evaporation of his presidential ambitions. The independent Texas for which they fought and died survived just nine years before being subsumed by the United States.

A plaque on the front door of the graffiti-etched **Alamo Shrine**, originally the mission's chapel, requests "Be quiet, friend. Here heroes died to blaze a trail for other men." Most visitors focus on taking photos of the famous exterior of the shrine and then repair first to the lovely garden, shaded by everything from myrtles to a mescal bean tree. This is followed by the all-important souvenir shop, which sells such reverent mementos as Alamo mugs, belts, patches, playing cards, pencils, plaques, postcards, dishware, license-plate frames, pins, coasters, caps, tote bags, and erasers.

Note: There are five missions in San Antonio, all of which are designated Unesco World Heritage Sites. The Alamo is managed by the Daughters of the American Revolution, while the other four, also well worth visiting, are preserved as **San Antonio Missions National Historical Park** (tel: 210-932-1001; www.nps.gov/saan; daily) and managed by the National Park Service.

THE RIVER WALK

Though San Antonio is an enormous desert city, you'd never know it as you amble along the lively, pedestrianized **Paseo del Rio**, or River Walk, an inspired tourist attraction that has done wonders for the rough-around-the-edges downtown. An original and elegantly simple concept, River Walk was instigated in 1939 as part of Franklin

The Alamo, symbol of the Republic of Texas.

The hand-operated Los Ebanos Ferry is the last of its kind on the Rio Grande.

San Antonio's River Walk.

Roosevelt's New Deal. The plan called for confining the San Antonio River into a tight and very narrow little channel as it loops through the city center, paving and landscaping both banks, and garnishing them liberally with restaurants, patio cafés, stores, and gardens.

River Walk stands roughly 10ft (3 meters) lower than the busy downtown streets. Flat-bottomed cruise boats ply gently along the river itself, and at night, in particular, when it's all low-lit, the effect is magical. There's even an open-air theater, the ingenious **Arneson River Theatre**, where the stage is arranged on one side of the river while the audience watches from a stucco Spanish-style amphitheater of benches on the opposite bank.

Downtown San Antonio holds several other worthwhile attractions. The beautifully restored **Spanish Governor's Palace** (tel: 210-224-0601; Tue–Sun), a tranquil gem, is located near the original site of Spain's Presidio de Bexar (1722), the **Plaza de Armas**, where a sign notes that in the Republican era (1836–45), the grounds had

already become a busy market teeming with "noisy vendors of vegetables, fresh eggs, chili peppers, and live chickens."

UTSA Institute of Texan Cultures (tel: 210-458-2300; www.texancultures.com daily), a Smithsonian Institution affiliate in Hemisfair Park, takes an entertaining look at the many different peoples, from Comanches to Czechs, who have contributed to the cosmopolitan blend of modern Texas. There's also a glorious evocation of the cowboy past; one early African-American *vaquero* is quoted as saying, "We loved to work cattle so much we'd just be sittin' around cryin' for daylight to come." **Briscoe Western Art Museum** (tel: 210-299-4499; www. briscoemuseum.org; Tue–Sat), on Market Street, right off the Riverwalk, offers classic and contemporary Western art in its collection. Its name honors former Governor Dolph Biscoe, who was born in nearby Uvalde.

MILES, MESAS, AND MOUNTAINS

It's an exhausting 500-mile (800km) -long haul between San Antonio and El Paso, not recommended as a one-day drive. It's quickest to stick to I-10, but to experience the desolate border country you'll need to take US 90 out of San Antonio and head south toward Del Rio, where the legendary Rio Grande forms the US-Mexico border. Plan on taking two or three days and exploring the dusty backcountry, including the arty towns in the Alpine–Marathon–Marfa–Fort Davis quadrangle and nearby Big Bend National Park (www. nps.gov/bibe), one of the country's most remote yet stunning national parks.

As you leave San Antonio, there's a parched quality to roadside grasslands that presages desiccation ahead. At first, however, agriculture maintains a foothold. Historic **Castroville** ㉕, 15 miles (24km) along on US 90, proclaims itself to be "The Little Alsace of Texas," and has several Alsatian restaurants. **Hondo** feels like the Great Plains, with

huge fields of corn and wheat, while **Knippa** ("Go Ahead and Blink, Knippa is Bigger than You Think") is devoted to stone quarrying.

The Great Depression hit South Texas pretty badly, but Uvalde was fortunate to have President Franklin Roosevelt's vice president, John Garner, as a hometown boy. Among Garner's local projects were **Garner State Park**, a riverfront park created in 1941 by the Civilian Conservation Corps (CCC), and the **Aviation Museum at Garner Field**, a World War II training base that displays old bombers and other aircraft.

THE RIO GRANDE

The US Border Patrol is an ever-vigilant presence along the border. Across most of Texas, the desert makes a far more effective barrier against illegal entrants from Mexico than does the Rio Grande. Rather than monitor every inch of the river, therefore, Border Patrol simply erects roadblocks along the few highways that lead away from it.

Note: Be sure to carry a valid passport or other form of official national identification denoting citizenship, such as birth certificate, and proof of residency. As of 2018, this includes US citizens; drivers' licenses are no longer an adequate form of identification in the border zone. Legally, anyone within 100 miles of the US border can be stopped and asked their citizenship/immigration status.

Past Uvalde, US 90 dwindles to a single lane. **Del Rio** ㉖ is home to Laughlin Air Force base and malls catering to day-trippers from the adjacent Mexican town of **Ciudad Acuña**, but apart from a couple of 19th-century buildings, there's not much to divert tourists.

A further 12 miles (19km) northwest, **Amistad National Recreation Area** (tel: 330-775-7491; www.nps.gov/amis; daily), the third-largest international man-made lake in the world, was created by the completion of Amistad Dam, a huge curving wall of concrete jointly dedicated by the presidents of the US and Mexico in 1969. Above this point, the Rio Grande has been designated a Wild and Scenic River, but you won't get any glimpses of it until you reach Langtry and beyond, in Big Bend.

Another 30 miles (48km) northwest, the highest highway bridge in Texas crosses the deep gorge of the Pecos River, just before its confluence with the Rio Grande. It's worth stopping to admire this, the first of the many western canyons to come and to envy the eagles and falcons that soar so majestically above it.

Beyond the Pecos you've reached true desert, and confirmation that you're in the Wild West arrives soon enough in historic **Langtry** ㉗. This semi ghost town was home to Judge Roy Bean, a storekeeper who was appointed justice of the peace here in 1882. Known as the "Law West of the Pecos," Judge Bean exacted swift frontier justice, despite an ignorance of all legal matters. His saloon-cum-courtroom, a hundred yards shy

⊘ Tip

Road blocks and checkpoints by the US Border Patrol are commonplace even far inland from the US-Mexico border. All travelers, whether US or foreign, should carry photo identification denoting citizenship and residency status, such as a passport or green card. US citizens note: driver's licenses are no longer sufficient photo ID in the border zone.

Morning on the border river – the Rio Grande is known as the Rio Bravo in Mexico.

British actress Lily Langtry, for whom it's said the eccentric Judge Roy Bean named the tiny Texas town of Langtry.

of the dry-as-bones canyon of the **Rio Grande**, is now a tiny state-run museum and official Texas travel information center (tel: 432-291-3340; www.txdot.com; daily). A dusty store offers lukewarm coffee and snacks. Take advantage: this is the only available sustenance in the 120 empty miles (193km) between Langtry and Marathon.

Until you come to **Marathon ㉘**, you've added time but no extra mileage to your trip by taking US 90 rather than I-10. This is where you'll have to decide whether to detour down to Big Bend – a decision best contemplated after a night in the luxury of the beautifully restored **Gage Hotel** (www.gagehotel.com), the first appealing lodging and fine dining since San Antonio.

BIG BEND NATIONAL PARK

Spectacular **Big Bend National Park ㉙** (tel: 432-477-2251; www.nps.gov/bibe; daily) is so out of the way that if you do happen to be nearby, you owe it to yourself to go. The 40-mile (64km) drive south to the park entrance on US 385 is best done at sunset or early morning,

Black bears roam the rugged terrain of Big Bend National Park.

when the long shadows play over a landscape as entrancing as Shangri-la. You head straight toward a misty wall of mountains, only to shimmy around them at the last minute and confront another equally alluring range on the horizon.

Once inside the park, watch for the cute but feisty wild desert boar known as javelinas crossing the road: they have very poor eyesight. Thirty more miles (48km) brings you to the main visitor center, an essential information stop and one of only two places in this vast park where you can fill up with gas during business hours. The prime destination, the mountain-ringed **Chisos Basin** lies another 12 miles (19km) beyond. A scenic road – too narrow for large RVs – climbs steeply into the park's central cluster of mountains, through a labyrinth of towering rocks guarded by tall yucca plants flanked by talus slopes speckled with eye-popping pink-blossomed cacti and other desert succulents. A succession of steep hairpin bends then drops into the grassy basin that holds the park visitor center, lodge, campground, and store. Big Bend is bear and mountain lion country, and you should learn what to do if you encounter these shy but majestic wild creatures. That also goes for rattlesnakes, which sometimes curl up on the doorstep of motel rooms. The highest elevation in the park, Chisos Basin is the park's premier hiking area. From the campground, a superb hike takes you on a 4.4-mile (7km) round-trip trail to the **Window**, a gap in the mountains with views across an eerie desert landscape of buttes and mesas. Note: plan ahead – this park is seeing increasing visitation and visitor facilities are few.

RIVER-RAFTING TRIPS

State 170 west of the park, the **River Road**, is one of Texas's most attractive highways – a rare opportunity to drive along the Rio Grande in all its glory. It reaches the river 17 miles (27km) south of the Terlingua/Study Butte turn-off at the small resort of **Lajitas ㉚**, which

ecializes in river-rafting trips through gh-walled Santa Elena Canyon into e park. For 50 miles (80km) from Laji-s, the River Road sticks close to the er, sometimes scrambling over high ndstone outcrops, at other times eandering through well-watered lds. Cattle can often be seen grazing Chihuahua, Mexico, and in several aces the river is shallow enough for em to wade across. There's another ance to cross into Mexico at **Presidio**, ere **Ojinaga** on the far side holds a uple of seafood restaurants plus cut-te opticians and pharmacies.

G BEND COUNTRY

om Presidio, a 61-mile (98km) drive rth on US 67 returns you to US 90 at arfa ③. The ranch town is celebrated the location for the 1956 movie *ant* – James Dean, Elizabeth Taylor, d other stars took over downtown's arming **El Paisano** hotel as head-arters. In the 1970s, Marfa gained a w kind of fame when the late Donald dd, a New York City native, began talling overscaled art projects in toric buildings around town. Judd's jacy is now safeguarded by the **Chi-ti Foundation** (tel: 432-729-4362; w.chinati.org; Wed–Sun), which also ers morning and afternoon tours by servation to installations. The town s become a haven for hip East Coast ban artists, many of whom have sen-ively restored and opened historic ildings as art galleries, eateries, okstores, even a local public radio tion. The wail of locomotives flying rough town is often the only sound this quiet far West Texas backwater. There are more art, restaurants, and dgings in the small college town of pine, 25 miles (42km) east of Marfa. e excellent **Museum of the Big Bend** l: 432-837-8143; www.museumofthe bend.com; Tue–Sun) on the campus Sul Ross State University has exhib-on the natural and cultural history the Big Bend area.

State 17 heads north to **Fort Davis** ③, in the Davis Mountains. **Fort Davis National Historic Site** (tel: 432-426-3224 ext. 220; www.nps.gov/foda; daily), the best-preserved 19th-century fort in the West, adjoins **Davis Mountains State Park**, a pretty valley with lovely oak-shaded campgrounds. From here, it's a beauti-ful mountain drive on State Route 118 to return to I-10 at Kent. En route, you'll pass right by the entrance to **McDonald Observatory** (tel: 877-984-7827 or 432-426-3640; www.mcdonaldobservatory.org; visitor center, daily), one of the largest astronomical observatories in the world.

EL PASO

Once on I-10, it's roughly two and a half hours to El Paso, gaining an hour as you enter Mountain Time. On the way, you will pass through **Van Horn**, an his-toric crossroads of the old Bankhead Highway and the Old Spanish Trail. **El Paso** ③, a gritty, working-class city of 683,000, spread around the base of the Franklin Mountains, lies in the oldest European-settled area of Texas. In the 16th century, Spaniards first crossing

Hikers on a Big Bend trail.

◎ Tip

Day-trippers to Ciudad Juárez will do better to walk across one of the three footbridges to Mexico. Driving across the border requires the purchase of additional Mexican auto insurance.

the Rio Grande to explore their territories in New Mexico headed along El Paso del Norte – the Pass of the North – which sent the river through a break in the mountain ranges. Soon the trading route of El Camino Real (The Royal Road) was extended from south of Chihuahua City, Mexico, to what is now Santa Fe, New Mexico, by conquistador Juan de Oñate.

When the Spanish colonists were driven out of New Mexico by the Pueblo Revolt of 1680, dispirited refugees regrouped here, around an adobe Franciscan mission they called Ysleta del Sur. Its founder, Fray Garcia, is commemorated in downtown's Pioneer Plaza with a 14ft (4-meter) statue by internationally known sculptor David Houser.

It took 12 years for the Spaniards to reconquer New Mexico under De Vargas, during which time the towns of Ysleta and El Paso had sprung up around the mission. El Paso gradually absorbed Ysleta, but was itself split in two after the designation of the Rio Grande as the United States-Mexico border. The US city remained El Paso

Mission of Nuestra Señora de Guadalupe, Ciudad Juárez, Mexico.

and the Mexican city was dubbed Ciudad Juárez. El Paso's strategic location has made it a travelers' stop for centuries. Forty-Niners during the Gold Rush passed through on their way to fortune in California. Refugees, desperados, and tourists have all met here. Today, it is best known as a major gateway to Mexico.

Much of El Paso's history involves gunfights. The notorious Marshall Dallas Stoudenmire and John Wesley Hardin won many a shootout before finally biting the dust (John Wesley Hardin is buried in Concordia Cemetery). There is a lot of dust to bite in El Paso. Its climate is singularly dry, although rain is not unknown. The city is uniformly beige in look and feel. Its shanty dwellings clinging to barren hillsides have more in common with nearby Mexico than the United States.

El Paso is an inexpensive city, but there's little here to justify it as a destination. Tourism is mainly channeled to its environs and up to **Ranger Peak** in the Franklin Mountains. The **Tigua Indian Reservation**, the pueblo

◎ DETOUR TO MEXICO

Ciudad Juárez, across the bridge from El Paso, Texas, is probably the most interesting Mexican border town outside of Tijuana, which lies south of San Diego. But whereas San Diego is sleek and efficient, confirming the US's superior grasp of the modern world, the difference between El Paso and Ciudad Juárez is definitely in Mexico's favor. El Paso is a rather desolate, depressing city, whereas Juárez, the biggest city in the state of Chihuahua, is vibrant and colorful. Bullfights and bright souvenirs make a strong impression right away, as does lush Chamizal Park, a counterpart to El Paso's memorial. Juárez Museum of History, occupying a dazzling historic building, traces the area's development, with special attention paid to the Mexican Revolution and the Mexican hero Pancho Villa. Our Lady of Guadalupe Mission explores the rich religious tapestry of the country. Juárez's food is wonderful and spicy, but don't drink the water, or eat ice cream or ice cubes. It's certainly worth a day trip to experience another country, but make sure you have all valid documents: a passport or proof of citizenship with photo and a green card to reenter the US, if necessary. If you stay in Mexico more than 72 hours, or travel beyond the border zone (La Frontera), you'll need a Tourist Card, available at the border.

community of the oldest identifiable Indian tribe in Texas, is on the eastern edge of the city, while **Ysleta Mission**, one of three historic Spanish missions restored and run by El Paso Mission Trail Foundation (tel: 915-851-9997; daily tours; www.visitelpasomissiontrail. com), is in the Ysleta neighborhood in western El Paso. **Fort Bliss Military Reservation**, in the northeast, is the site of the largest Air Defense School in the "free world."

CROSS-CULTURAL RELATIONS

The Rio Grande is more of a fortified moat than a river in El Paso, but its political role as the natural boundary between Mexico and the US is important. That interesting story is told well at **Chamizal National Memorial** (tel: 915-532-7273; www.nps.gov/cham; daily), a little-known unit of the National Park System overlooking the river.

The memorial was established to commemorate the Chamizal Convention of 1963, a milestone in diplomatic relations between Mexico and the United States, which resulted in the peaceful settlement of a century-long boundary dispute. It wholeheartedly celebrates Mexico, with art and museum exhibits, regular cultural performances such as folkloric dance and mariachi music, and thoughtful ranger talks. For visitors in town for just a few hours, it's a safe way of experiencing a little of Mexico's infectious *Viva La Vida*, especially if you have neither the time nor the inclination to cross into Mexico itself.

El Paso – notorious as one of the weakest links in the "Tortilla Curtain" between the United States and Mexico – has a decidedly uneasy, schizophrenic relationship with its sister city across El Rio. That friction has been exacerbated by gun violence and crime in Ciudad Juárez, primarily between the warring Sinaloa and Juarez drug cartels, prompting the US Consulate in Mexico to issue a Travel Alert to travelers. Tens of thousands of people have died in drug-related violence since 2006, when then President Felipe Calderon declared war on the drug cartels.

Weigh the risks against the many pleasures of a quick visit: the vast majority of Mexican citizens are hard-working, law-abiding, and hospitable people, equally terrorized by violence, whose livelihood from tourism on La Frontera is being seriously undermined by a tiny minority. Expect a high military presence in Juárez: thousands of troops have been sent in by the Mexican government during the most recent major crackdown.

Symbolic of the tension between the US and Mexico is the 580-mile (933km) -long fence along the 1,989-mile (3201km) US-Mexico border – a series of 18ft (5-meter) -high, steel-and-mesh fences secured with a "virtual fence" of sensors and cameras. The fence has been an effective barrier to illegal entry. In 2000, up to 220,000 illegal aliens were caught and repatriated monthly; by 2018, that figure had nosedived to less than 40,000 per month. Despite

Corner café in a Mexican border town.

> **Tip**

The national parks of Carlsbad Caverns and adjoining Guadalupe Mountains are 152 miles (244km) north of El Paso on US 62/180. Texas's highest mountains and New Mexico's most spectacularly decorated caves are worth an extra day for a detour.

this, President Donald Trump, who campaigned on building a new wall to address illegal immigration, committed to a new wall along the border. In 2018, Congress committed $1.6 billion in funds to replace existing fencing, and work began on key segments, including those in the Rio Grande Valley, in early spring.

NEW MEXICO

Exiting El Paso, US 54 east skirts the eastern slopes of the Franklin Mountains. New Mexico arrives, with the minimum of ceremony, 10 miles (16km) out of El Paso, at which point US 54 contracts to a two-lane undivided highway with virtually no services the entire 83-mile (134km) stretch to Alamogordo and the Tularosa Valley.

New Mexico is among the youngest of US states (the 47th admitted to the Union), but it has one of the longest histories. At its eastern edge, near Clovis, archeologists have dug up beautifully carved arrowheads dating back 12,000 years. By the time the first Spanish *conquistadores* reached the valley of the Rio Grande, in 1540, the Rio Grande Valley held some 150 separate villages, or *pueblos,* each home to a distinct clan-based group specializing in certain handicrafts and trade items. The Spaniards named the infant colony New Mexico in the misplaced hope that it might yield similar treasures to the Aztec empire of Mexico.

By the late 16th century, *El Camino Real* (now US 85) extended along the Rio Grande from Mexico to Santa Fe, site of the oldest government building in North America and the oldest US capital. Yet even though New Mexico covered an area far greater than the current state, including all of modern Arizona and much of Nevada, California, and Utah, until the Yankees arrived in 1846 it remained an impoverished provincial backwater, whose farmers had to battle against not only the unforgiving desert environment but also Navajo, Apache, and Comanche raiders.

Under American rule, New Mexico has attended to its somewhat mundane motto: *Crescit Eunde* ("It grows as it goes"). Railroading, ranching, and mining have all thrived on the state's rocky surface, warm valleys, and subterranean waters. A deliberate US policy during World War II of siting defense installations in remote landlocked locations also brought unexpected dividends, as it was in New Mexico that scientists developed and tested the first atomic bomb. Today military facilities are still an integral part of the state economy. New Mexico is sparsely populated, with just over 2 million people, most of them clustered in the major cities of Albuquerque, Santa Fe, and Las Cruces. Notable residents include sworn enemies Pat Garrett and Billy the Kid, "king of the innkeepers" Conrad Hilton, novelist D.H. Lawrence, artist Georgia O'Keeffe, and famed US Forest Service mascot Smokey Bear (a real bear cub who was rescued from a fire near Capitan).

New Mexico's natural beauty and mesmerizing landscape have

The New Mexico Museum of Space History tells the story of the international space race.

aptivated everyone, from the earliest Indian tribes, to generations of Hispanics and Anglo explorers, traders, ranchers, and artists, to modern new-age tourists drawn to cities such as Santa Fe, Albuquerque, and Taos. Even little green men from outer space seem to love it, if you believe the "evidence" on display in Roswell.

ALAMOGORDO

As you drive the gorge between the Organ Mountains to the west and the Hueco Mountains to the east, you nick the edge of **White Sands Missile Range**. Roadside signs warn of unexploded ammunition lying in the desert, and advise you not to leave the highway. Just south of Alamogordo, in the Sacramento Mountain foothills, is **Oliver M. Lee Memorial State Park**, named for a state legislator with a colorful past. The immaculate 50-site campground makes a good base to explore scenic Dog Canyon and Lee's ranch, once the largest in New Mexico.

After all that emptiness, **Alamogordo ❸4** itself feels positively urban. It's actually a small desert town, with just over 31,000 people, which counts among its population international rocket scientists, astronomers, and military brass. Alamogordo is built atop a large 11th-century Indian pueblo that was abandoned in the 1300s when a long drought and Apache raiding made life too difficult. Earlier, the Jornada branch of the Mogollon culture left behind some 21,000 extraordinary petroglyphs, or incised rock art, on basaltic boulders at **Three Rivers Petroglyph Site** (www.blm.gov/nm/threerivers), north of Alamogordo, many of which have, sadly, now been defaced. Mogollon people introduced farming, pottery, and masonry architecture to New Mexico learned from their southern neighbors. By AD 1000, they had been subsumed into the powerful Ancestral Pueblo (formerly Anasazi) trading culture to the north.

Spaniards passed through here, naming the valley for its fat (*gordo*) cottonwood trees (*alamos*). They settled on the Tularosa River and founded a presidio and mission in 1719 at **La Luz**, but Apache raiding soon forced them to move on. The arrival of the US Army at **Fort Stanton** in 1855 was the beginning of the end for Apache warriors. In the 1880s, they were forced to make peace and move to reservations in the nearby Sacramento and White mountains, allowing Anglo settlement in the Tularosa Basin.

In 1898, C.B. and John A. Eddy founded Alamogordo as a stop on their railroad line. Seduced by the forested valley and its commercial potential for lumber, the Eddys sold the railroad and settled down in Alamogordo to make their fortune from indigenous resources. Alamogordo grew as a trade center, but the development of White Sands Proving Ground and nearby Holloman Air Force Base radically recast the contours of the city. In the words of one local historian, "No longer was it a sleepy, peaceful land of *mañana* (tomorrow), but a hustling, bustling, fast-growing city."

Apache crown dancer (or mountain spirit) at an Apache Changing Woman Ceremony to mark an Apache girl reaching puberty.

Oliver Lee Memorial State Park.

Today, Alamogordo is dominated by the high-tech weaponry community. It also pays tribute to the peaceful uses of technology in the exploration of space, in the shape of the **New Mexico Museum of Space History** (tel: 575-437-2840; www.nmspacemuseum.org; daily), standing prominently on the foothills at the edge of the valley. This well-conceived museum chronicles the international race for the stars, featuring an International Space Hall of Fame, from early dreamers to the moon-walking astronauts of NASA's *Apollo* missions. After admiring space shuttle models, a lunar TV camera and samples of foods brought aboard *Apollo* and *Skylab* missions (including canned vanilla ice cream and dehydrated peach ambrosia), you can watch a video presentation of highlights from the *Apollo* 11, 12, and 14 moon landings, or simulate a space shuttle landing.

CLOUDCROFT TO MESCALERO

In summer, the 12,000ft (3,657-meter) Sacramento Mountains, east of

Alamogordo, provide welcome relie from the 100°F (37.7°C) heat of the torrid Chihuahuan Desert, attracting visitors from southeastern New Mexico and West Texas. Scenic US 82 climb abruptly from 4,350ft (1,325 meters) a Alamogordo to almost 9,000ft (2,740 meters) to reach **Cloudcroft** in Lin coln National Forest (www.fs.usda.gov/li coln), just 20 miles (32km) later. Hiking cross-country skiing, and camping are popular in the cool, piney forest.

The quaint alpine village of Cloud croft is known for its rental cabins and hiking trails. Historic **Cloudcroft Lodge** (www.thelodgeresort.com), buil as a vacation resort for rail workers i 1899 in the Bavarian style, is a must see; it even has a resident ghost. Six teen miles (26km) south of Cloudcroft in tiny Sunspot, are two observatories **Apache Point Observatory** (tel: 575 437-682; www.apo.nmsu.edu) and the **National Solar Observatory** (tel: 575 434-7000; www.nso.edu). Take a tour o the latter to find out how astronomer safely view the sun, using telescope like the Dunn Solar Telescope, a rotat ing instrument that ascends 330ft (10 meters) from a subterranean chamber

Just north of Cloudcroft is th **Mescalero Apache Indian Reserva tion**. A 28-mile (45km) drive throug the reservation on State Route 24 passes through bucolic scenery, wit shimmering little lakes and flower filled meadows, and Apache cowboy riding the range. Any notions you ma have of reservations as desolate o depressing places will evaporate. Se if you can catch a rodeo in July.

The Mescalero are prosperou entrepreneurs; while parts of the res ervation are closed to outsiders, th tribe operates successful commer cial enterprises on adjoining lands These include the elegant **Inn o the Mountain Gods & Casino Resor** (http://innofthemountaingods.com), whos lakeside setting offers a clear view o sacred Sierra Blanca Peak. The peak i

Skiing at the Southern New Mexico Ski Apache resort.

part of the tribe's luxury winter-sports venue, **Ski Apache** (www.skiapache.com), set above busy little **Ruidoso**, home to Ruidoso Downs racetrack and the large **Hubbard Museum of the American West** (tel: 575-378-4142; www.hubbardmuseum.org; Thu–Mon), an affiliate of the Smithsonian with extensive exhibits. Leaving Ruidoso, US 70 drops back down to the Tularosa Valley to tribal headquarters at **Mescalero**, best known for its restored 1939 **St Joseph Apache Mission**. From here, Alamogordo is 46 miles (74km).

WHITE SANDS NATIONAL MONUMENT

From the detour described above, you'll enjoy mountain-top views of the most spectacular feature of the region: **White Sands National Monument** ㉟ (tel: 575-479-6124; www.nps.gov/whsa; daily). Located 15 miles (24km) southwest of Alamogordo, this stunning 144,458-acre (58,505-hectare) expanse is made up of gypsum sand blown in between the San Andreas and Sacramento mountain ranges and deposited as shifting dunes on this corner of the otherwise off-limits White Sands Missile Range. The only access road – the main highway between Alamogordo and Las Cruces, US 70 – is regularly closed for up to three hours at a time, so that military personnel can drive their top-secret cargo along it in peace; call the visitor center the day before arrival for alerts if you are on a tight schedule. As you approach White Sands, you may see eerie V-shaped stealth jets silently speeding through brilliant blue skies, as the glowing dunes rise from the base of the San Andreas Mountains.

The historic visitor center has wonderful Pueblo Revival–style historic architecture and is a good place to pick up information before taking the 16-mile (26km) paved scenic drive that loops through the dunes. The deeper it penetrates into the heart of White Sands, the more the road surface is obscured by drifts of gypsum sand. The effect is both disorienting and remarkable. Gypsum is one of the most common compounds found on Earth, but it's rarely seen on the surface because it dissolves readily in water. Surface sand elsewhere is almost always composed of quartz.

At midday, the sands are a blinding white, reflecting so strongly your eyes sting. As you clamber over the dunes, occasionally pocked by the slither marks and pawprints of nocturnal wanderers, periodically remove your sunglasses to appreciate the hallucinatory expanse fully. As the afternoon cedes to evening, the sands refract the light, breaking it down into a rainbow. In summer the park is open until 9pm, a good time to hunker down quietly and hope to see some of the 500 different animals that populate the dunes, from coyotes and roadrunners to owls and skunks. There is also a sparse scattering of beautiful plant life, including the hedgehog cactus with its brilliant red flowers.

Would-be cowboys should visit the Hubbard Museum of the American West in Ruidoso.

White Sands National Monument.

Sierra Blanca is the highest peak in Southern New Mexico at 12,005ft (3,659 meters).

Concealed amid the roadless wastes of White Sands Missile Range, **Trinity Site National Historic Landmark** preserves the site where, in July 1945, scientists from the Manhattan Project in Los Alamos detonated the first US atomic bomb. If you are interested in visiting, Alamogordo Chamber of Commerce (tel: 800-826-0294; www.alamogordo.com) and White Sands Missile Range (tel: 575-678-8824; www.wsmr.army.mil/Trinity/Pages) sponsor tours of Trinity Site on the first Saturdays of April and October every year. Visitors are accompanied by convoys of army vehicles to the detonation site from an inconspicuous gateway north of Alamogordo.

THE WILD WEST

Leaving White Sands, US 70 slowly ascends the rugged Organ Mountains, climbing over 5,720ft (1,740 meters) **San Augustine Pass** before descending to Las Cruces.

Trinity Site National Historic Landmark.

About 10 miles (16km) east of Las Cruces, you come to **Dripping**

Springs Natural Area (tel: 575-522-1219; open daily 8am-5pm) the most accessible section of New Mexico's newest national monument: 496,330-acre (200,858-hectare) **Organ Mountains–Desert Peaks National Monument** (tel: 575-522-1219; www.organmountains.org daily), with a nicely developed visitor center, campground, and trailheads. One trail leads past **La Cueva Rock Shelter**, dating from the Desert Archaic period (5,000 BC) to the historic period, when it was occupied by Apaches and later by an eccentric recluse named Giovanni Maria Agotino, known as "the Hermit." In the mid-1970s, approximately 100,000 artifacts were recovered from here by the University of Texas at El Paso. Another trail leads to the ruins of **Dripping Springs Resort**, built in 1873 by Colonel Eugene Patten and in 1917, converted to a sanitorium.

Las Cruces ("the crosses") was so named after travelers on a wagon train from Taos were ambushed and slaughtered here in 1830, and white crosses were erected to mark their graves. The city is a bit homely but its regenerating downtown, New Mexico State University campus, and burgeoning business environment have made it New Mexico's fastest-growing city. It has two free downtown art museums: **Branigan Cultural Center** (tel: 575-541-2154; www.las-cruces.org/museums; Tue–Sat) and **Las Cruces Museum of Art** (tel: 575-541-2137; www.las-cruces.org/museums; Tue–Sun). **New Mexico Farm & Ranch Museum** (tel: 575-522-4100; www.nmfarmandranchmuseum.org; daily), on the edge of town, highlights 3,000 years of farming and ranching in the area. Spanish churro sheep, burros, longhorn cattle, and other traditional livestock are kept on the grounds. Demonstrations of weaving, candle making, and other pioneer skills are presented regularly.

LA MESILLA

Historic **La Mesilla** ㊱, a short hop from downtown Las Cruces on State Route 28 and State Route 292 (Motel Boulevard), is worth a look. Its restored historic **Plaza**, dominated by an old gazebo, now a state monument, evokes the colors and sounds of Old Mexico. This was where the Gadsden Purchase was sealed in 1854, establishing the current boundaries of Mexico and the United States, while a gift store in one corner was originally the courthouse where the notorious outlaw Billy the Kid was tried and sentenced to hang for murder in 1881. The Kid managed to escape before his hanging, but subsequently met his maker at the hands of Pat Garrett, near Fort Sumner; Garrett was himself murdered near Las Cruces in 1908. Vendors create a Mexican *mercado* (market) atmosphere and will be happy to sell you rugs, pottery, Indian jewelry, ceramics, and other souvenirs. This is a great spot to relax and do a bit of shopping. Stop at the famed **Double Eagle Restaurant** (www.double-eagle-mesilla.com), in a registered historic building on the plaza for a drink in its elegant Imperial Bar.

ACROSS THE GREAT DIVIDE

A short distance out of Las Cruces, on I-10 west, a double ribbon of landscaped orchards lines the narrow Rio Grande, which flows from its source in southern Colorado via Taos and Albuquerque. Beyond the shallow sandy ridge on the far side, the highway levels out to cross the windblown chapparal of Luna County, where increasing numbers of the ostrich-like state plant, the yucca, scrutinize travelers as they make their way westward. From here to the Arizona state line, freeway exits are commonly lined with frontier-style outlets for supposedly characteristic goods. Behind false facades spring a trading post, Wild West town, or tepee, where moccasins, cactus jelly, and plant candy are sold to tourists.

Fifty-six miles (90km) out of Las Cruces, in New Mexico's "bootheel," is the truck-stop town of

La Mesilla town square.

Deming ③⑦, encircled by four short mountain ranges. Deming was of strategic importance to railroad magnate Charles Crocker, who joined his Southern Pacific line to the Santa Fe Railroad. Early settlers included soldiers, professionals, merchants, and a large population of gunmen who dominated local affairs until the town was "cleaned up" in 1883. Housed in a historic 1917 armory building in the nondescript downtown, the **Deming Luna Mimbres Museum** (tel: 575-546-2382; www.lunacountyhistoricalsociety.com; Mon–Sat) displays local history, including artifacts of the prehistoric Mogollon culture, whose Mimbres branch made spectacular black-on-white pottery for trade.

One exhibit re-creates frontier life, which, in the words of a guide, was "as you can see just by looking around, not easy here. This wasn't a luxury place." Today, Deming is a homely desert town of just over 14,000, where retirees drive and walk slowly, shade trees shield against a fierce sun, and the enticing smell of roasting green chili from

nearby Hatch, the country's leading grower of chili, perfumes the air every August (note the spelling of chili in New Mexico is always the Spanish *chile*).

RELICS OF THE MIMBRES

Rather than stay on dreary I-10 for the 60 miles (97km) west to Lordsburg veer northward on US 180 toward the Gila Mountains toward charming Silver City. Between the 10th and 12th centuries, this region was home to the Mimbres branch of the Mogollon culture, the highland people who took ceramics from its earliest expression in the Southwest to an exquisite, and now highly collectable, art form – a precious trade item throughout North and Central America. Early archeologist and Mogollon specialist Jesse W Fewkes claimed that "no Southwestern pottery, ancient or modern, surpasses that of the Mimbres, and its naturalistic figures are unexcelled in any pottery from prehistoric America."

The Mimbres are named for the Mimbres River, which at lower elevations remains a bone-dry sandy *arroyo* (wash) most of the year. US 180 crosses it repeatedly en route to Silver City, 53 miles (85km) north of Deming. Now one of New Mexico's most popular historic art towns, **Silver City** has successively been the base for Native American turquoise miners, Hispanic silver miners, modern copper conglomerates, and now artists and nature lovers. Billy the Kid lived here as a child, but most of the town he knew was wiped out by a cataclysmic flood in 1895.

Western New Mexico University Museum (tel: 575-538-6386; www.wnmu.edu; daily), 12th and Alabama streets, holds the world's finest collection of Mimbres pottery, decorated with black-on-white snakes, parrots and other animal designs as well as abstract patterns. Each pot is thought to have belonged to a single individual, and to have been buried with its owner,

Gila Cliff Dwellings National Monument.

having first had a symbolic "kill hole" punched through its base.

GILA CLIFF DWELLINGS

Allow a whole day to make the lengthy, winding, and very slow 88-mile (142km) round trip into the Gila Mountains on State Route 15 to visit **Gila Cliff Dwellings National Monument** ❸❽ (tel: 575-536-9461; www.nps.gov/gicl; daily), where cliff dwellings built by a late phase of the Mogollon people in the 14th century are built in caves above the Gila River. A moderate 1-mile (1.7km) trail leads to the dwellings, where rangers conduct regular tours. Be sure to bring water and food: there's none at this remote spot.

State Route 90 runs 44 miles (71km) southwest from Silver City to rejoin I-10 at **Lordsburg**. Along the way, it crosses the Continental Divide, then descends slowly and gloriously to the vast alkali flats, or playas (from the Spanish word for "beach"), in which Lordsburg seems to float alone. The largest settlement in Hidalgo County, Lordsburg sprawls languidly beside the interstate and the Southern Pacific railroad tracks at the northern edge of the Pyramid Mountains. The train tracks themselves tell the story of modern Lordsburg, which eventually eclipsed neighboring **Shakespeare**. Shakespeare had been a stop on the great Butterfield Stagecoach Line run by the post office from St Louis, Missouri, to San Francisco, California, at the time Charles Crocker laid his railroad tracks.

Today, Shakespeare is a ghost town, preserved in its current state of decay after being abandoned for more profitable pastures. A short drive south on Main Street from Lordsburg, Shakespeare is the genuine item, although it *is* inhabited by surviving resident and owner Manny Hough, who opens the town for one weekend each month for folksy one-hour-and-a-half tours at 10am and 2pm (tel: 575-542-9034; www.shakespeareghosttown.com; monthly). Several notable characters are known to have graced the dining room of its **Stratford Hotel**, including an escapee from Silver City jail: Billy the Kid.

Abandoned automobiles and gas pump in Mogollon, a ghost town near Silver City.

Vulture Mine road in the Sonoran Desert.

SOUTH ARIZONA TO SAN DIEGO

Celebrated for its ponderosa pine forests, Colorado River canyons, and Native American ruins in the north and in the Sonoran Desert, and for the towns of Tucson and Phoenix in the south, this part of the Southwest is fascinating to explore.

Water is precious in Arizona, but its name has nothing to do with aridity. It is likely derived from the local Pima word for "little spring place." There are, in fact, many "little spring places" secreted among the desert canyons and mountains of Arizona, as well as just about every climatic, topographic, and ecological variant found in the US.

For millennia, Arizona's Indian tribes clustered around precious water sources. In the north, among the mountains and canyons of the Colorado Plateau, the dominant Ancestral Pueblo culture farmed washes and tributaries of the Colorado River, while to the south, in the Sonoran Desert, the ancient Hohokam developed a complex agricultural civilization based on sophisticated irrigation canals in what is now Phoenix.

Heat, lack of water, and Apache raiding deterred Spanish, Mexican, then Anglo settlement. It was only with the development of sophisticated irrigation for farming and later, during World War II, air-conditioning, that Arizona began its spectacular growth. Much of the desert remains undeveloped. Though beautiful, the Sonoran and adjoining Mojave deserts are dangerously hot in summer. Balmy temperatures make winter peak season in southern Arizona, when you can expect to pay premium prices to enjoy its famous spa resorts, dude ranches, and historic hotels. You'll find excellent discounts during torrid summers, though.

SKY ISLANDS AND FORT BOWIE

After leaving Lordsburg, New Mexico, on I-10, the Arizona state line is just 20 miles (32km) away. You're now driving close to the US-Mexico border, through Arizona's distinctive basin-and-range topography of "sky island" mountains interspersed with heat-hazed low desert. To the north are the Peloncillo

Main attractions

Chiricahua National Monument
Tombstone
Amerind Foundation
Saguaro National Park
Arizona-Sonora Desert Museum
Mission San Xavier del Bac
Titan Missile Museum
Heard Museum, Phoenix
Yuma Territorial Prison State Historic Park

Map on page 278

Heard Museum, Phoenix.

Mountains, while to the southwest the towering Chiricahua Mountains march in serried ranks into Mexico and the Sierra Madre.

Until the late 1800s, these ranges offered protection from white settlers for the nomadic Chiricahua Apache, who, along with other Apache groups, had separated culturally and geographically from their Navajo relatives centuries earlier, after arriving from northwest Canada, and made the mountains of southern Arizona and New Mexico their homeland.

The tragic confrontation between the Apache and the US Army during the Indian Wars is commemorated at Fort Bowie and nearby Chiricahua national monuments. Both can be reached by taking Exit 366 from I-10 at Bowie, then heading south on Apache Pass Road. A small parking lot at the monument marks the start of the hiking trail to **Fort Bowie** (tel: 520-847-2500; www.nps.gov/fobo; daily; visitor center: Sat–Sun). Built in 1886, for the next 25 years the fort was the headquarters of a campaign that eventually drove the

Apache from this region altogether. As you walk the 3 miles (5km) up to its evocative ruined adobe walls, you seem at first to be in a dry, bowl-shaped depression entirely ringed by mountains. Eventually, however, you come to tranquil, well-wooded Apache Spring, teeming with wildlife, which made this spot so precious to the Apache, then to the fort, commanding wonderful views across the valley below.

CHIRICAHUA NATIONAL MONUMENT

A further 8 miles (13km) of easy driving on unpaved road brings you to State Route 186. If you're in a hurry to reach Tombstone, by all means head west to I-10, by way of Willcox and Benson. If you do that, though, you'll miss spectacular **Chiricahua National Monument** ❸❾ (tel: 520-824-3560; www.nps.gov/chir; daily), a mere 14 miles (23km) east. Though a little off the beaten track, this national monument is the most magnificent spot on this part of the route for hiking, camping, scenic drives, and authentic border history.

Chiricahua's unique landscape has taken shape over millennia, as hardened deposits of ash from volcanic eruptions at Turkey Caldera 25 million years ago have been eroded by water, wind, and ice into strangely carved hoodoo rocks. To view them, follow the 6-mile (10km) **Bonita Canyon Drive**, which climbs from the visitor center through lush **Bonita Canyon** to **Massai Point**, the start of a short nature trail and day hikes among the rocks. All the way up, alarmingly balanced stacks of rock loom precariously above the road, while the viewpoint at the top surveys a panorama of odd stone towers and columns.

With twice the rainfall of the Chihuahuan Desert below, these "sky islands" attract numerous plants and animals. Rocky Mountain and Sierra Madrean wildlife from both sides of the border use a natural corridor running through

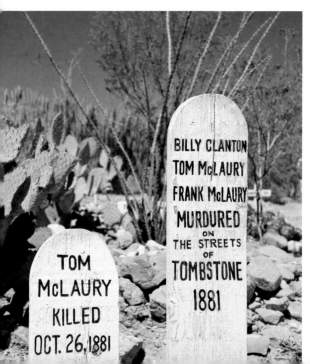

Victims of the OK Corral shootout are buried in Tombstone's Boothill Graveyard.

BILLY CLANTON
TOM McLAURY
FRANK McLAURY
MURDERED
ON
THE STREETS
OF
TOMBSTONE
1881

TOM
McLAURY
KILLED
OCT. 26, 1881

the mountains to Mexico, and Mexican species such as the rare Apache fox squirrel and and Chihuahua and Apache pines live side by side with species more commonly found north of the border. Of note are the birds that summer in Cave Creek, on the east side of the Chiricahua Mountains, at Portal. Top of every birder's list is the elegant trogon, a Mexican native with a long, coppery tail and bright feathers. It returns from the Sierra Madre every May to raise its young at Cave Creek, along with sulphur-bellied flycatchers, tanagers, chickadees, and many hummingbird species.

Heading westward on State Route 181, you pass the lovely **Dragoon Mountains**, a great place to hike and camp and visit **Cochise Stronghold** (http://cochisestronghold.com), a forested hideout used by Cochise. Continuing to Tombstone, you will drive south of Willcox Playa, which floods in winter to form a wetland that attracts up to 10,000 sandhill cranes, Canada and snow geese, and other migratory waterfowl.

Ahead are the dusty mining ghosts of **Gleeson, Courtland**, and **Pearce**. Pearce is now the only site with sizeable ruins (a mercantile store, post office, and jail). Its decrepit state belies the 1894 gold rush that occurred here and is indicative of the boom-and-bust nature of mining in resource-rich Arizona. Today, one mining town is mining a different kind of gold – from tourists – the "Town Too Tough to Die": **Tombstone** ㊵.

TOMBSTONE'S OK CORRAL

Infamous Tombstone was named by founder Edward Schieffelin, as a retort to those who said his mad hunt for silver would end in his own tombstone. But Tombstone sat amid lands rich in silver, and strikes here led to dizzying growth, wealth, and some famous troublemakers. It went into sudden decline in 1886, when its main silver mine flooded, and today is a tacky but endearing tourist trap, cheerfully providing visitors with a sanitized and glamorized taste of the lawless days of the Wild West.

An empty road curving through Saguaro National Park. The tall, slim, armed saguaro cactus flowers in the springtime, with blossoms opening only in the cool desert night air.

Tombstone's history is recalled in the local watering hole Big Nose Kate's Saloon.

Tombstone actors ready for a showdown.

Like Pearce, Tombstone would probably be forgotten now save for the infamous shootout that took place at its **OK Corral** (tel: 520-457-3456; www. ok-corral.com; daily), which pitted Wyatt Earp, his brothers, and the consumptive dentist Doc Holliday against the Clanton and McLaury brothers. The latter were at the forefront of a cowboy gang that allegedly engineered a series of stagecoach robberies, while the Earps – themselves no angels – represented establishment Tombstone. Political and personal clashes culminated in the legendary, bloody "Gunfight at the OK Corral" on October 26, 1881, which left three men dead.

ART, MINES, AND UNDERGROUND CAVERNS

Cowboys rule in Tombstone.

The OK Corral still stands on Allen Street, preserved as it looked on the fateful day, mannequins of the various participants posed in its yard, guns in hand. Staged gunfights take place here every afternoon, with actors re-creating the showdown and keeping the legend alive. Stagecoaches clatter evocatively past landmarks like the **Bird Cage Theatre,** where working girls plied their trade in 14 cages, or "cribs," suspended from the ceiling, and **Tombstone Courthouse State Historic Park** (tel: 520-457-3311; http://azstateparks. com/parks/TOCO; daily), on East Toughnut Street, which has an excellent diorama model of the gunfight. The victims of the shootout rest (or try to) in kitschy **Boothill Cemetery** at the edge of town, on a dusty hillside, where their eternal slumber is disturbed by loudspeakers concealed amid the boulders that play mournful country music.

Things are more authentic, 24 miles (39km) south of Tombstone, in the delightful former mining town of **Bisbee**, an attractive artist's haven, sprawled 3 steep miles (5km) across Mule Pass Gulch and Tombstone Canyon in the 5,000ft (1,500 meter) **Mule Mountains**. Its restored downtown Victorian mansions and buildings house comfortable historic hotels and B&Bs, restaurants, and an intriguing array of unique boutiques, art galleries, and antique stores. The **Queen Mine Tour** (tel: 866-432-2071 or 520-432-2071; www.queenminetour.com; call to book) takes you deep underground to see one of the most productive copper mines of the 20th century.

From Bisbee, take State Route 90 (which initially heads west and then takes a jog north in Sierra Vista) to meet up with I-10 at **Benson**. Don't miss **Kartchner Caverns State Park** (tel: 520-586-4100; http://azstateparks. com/parks/kaca/index.html; daily), just 9 miles (14km) south of I-10 off State Route 90. Arizona's top state park, its focal point is the rare "living" limestone caverns that erosion has carved and decorated in the Whetstone Mountains, which were discovered by cavers on the family ranch in 1974. Tours are given daily, but numbers are limited in order to protect the cave's environment, so you must book ahead (tel: 520-586-2283). Alternatively, stay in

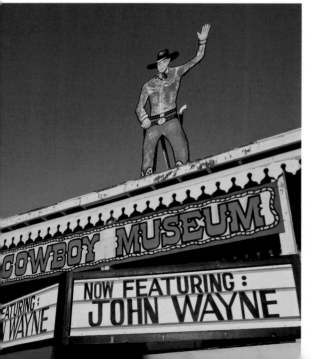

the campground and check at the Discovery Center, in person, first thing to see if tickets are available, and you may get lucky. In addition to the cave, there are 5 miles (8km) of hiking trails, a picnic area, a nicely developed campground, and a hummingbird garden.

Another premier Southwest destination, at a rural location a few miles east of Benson, is the private **Amerind Foundation Museum** (tel: 520-586-3666; www.amerind.org; Tue–Sun), housed in a lovely historic hacienda-style ranch house built by amateur archeologist William Fulton in 1937. An important research center, its museum displays an outstanding collection of Native American art and archeological artifacts, as well as works by Western artists like Frederic Remington and William Leigh.

TUCSON

From Benson, it's a quick 43 miles (69km) via I-10 to **Tucson ㊶** (pronounced "too-sawn"), a sprawling modern desert metropolis of nearly a million, with a well-preserved 18th-century Hispanic downtown, an excellent university, and stunning mountain-and-desert setting. Founded in 1776 as a Spanish settlement on Pima land, Tucson is the same age as the United States, though it only passed into American hands with the Gadsden Purchase of 1854.

Downtown Tucson, or the Old Pueblo as it is known locally, still centers on the area that was originally contained within the adobe walls of the Spanish *presidio*. This delightful spot is now dotted with artisans' shops, cafés, good shade trees, and some extremely interesting architecture, anchored by **St Augustine Cathedral**, built in 1897, and the **Pima County Courthouse** with its mosaic tile dome. Five historic homes stand on the grounds of the **Tucson Museum of Art and Historic Block** (tel: 520-624-2333; www.tucsonmuseumofart.org; Tue–Sun), whose collection features pre-Columbian, Hispanic, Western, and modern art.

SONORAN DESERT WILDLIFE AND MISSIONS

For many visitors, Tucson's greatest appeal lies in the fantastic scenery that

⊙ **Tip**

If you plan to spend some time in southern Arizona, consider buying a Tucson Attractions Passport for $24 from the Tucson Visitor Center (or order the booklet or app online at www.visttucson.org). The booklet contains 2-for-1 offers and discounts on a range of theaters, museums, state parks, and gardens, several of which are mentioned in this guide.

Trail riding at White Stallion ranch, Tucson.

⊙ Fact

The unique Yaqui Easter celebration held in Tucson's Yaqui Indian community blends a lenten all-night fiesta, featuring a Yaqui deer dancer, and Holy Week ceremonies, including matachine dancers and a maypole.

surrounds it. **Saguaro National Park** (tel: 520-733-5153; www.nps.gov/sagu; daily) occupies two separate tracts of land to either side of the city proper. It was established to protect dramatic expanses of multiarmed saguaro (pronounced *sah-WA-row*) cacti. Although it's often considered emblematic of the Wild West, the saguaro – which can live for 200 years and grow to a height of 50ft (15 meters) – is native to the Sonoran Desert, only a small portion of which extends into Arizona from Mexico. The western segment of the park, the **Tucson Mountain District** (tel: 520-733-5158), holds an extraordinary "forest" of younger, towering saguaros, which take on an otherworldly magnificence at sunset.

Nearby, the expansive **Arizona-Sonora Desert Museum** (tel: 520-883-2702; www.desertmuseum.org; daily) is the best place to understand the flora and fauna of the Sonoran Desert. Walk through beautiful gardens of cacti and desert plants to view desert mammals, from prairie dogs to mountain lions, in naturalistic enclosures. One highlight is the walk-through aviaries, alive with darting, iridescent hummingbirds, and the raptor free-flight demonstrations that take place twice a day from late October to mid-April.

The Mexican border at Nogales is 65 miles (105km) south of Tucson via I-19, a good place to enjoy shopping, Sonoran *ranchero*-style food, and lively *norteño* music. But even if you don't visit Mexico, it is worth driving down the lovely Santa Cruz River Valley from Tucson to Nogales. It's known as the **Mission Trail**, for the string of preserved Spanish missions on both sides of the US-Mexico border established by Italian Jesuit missionary Padre Eusebio Kino in the 1600s.

Just 9 miles (14km) from downtown is famed **Mission San Xavier del Bac** (tel: 520-294-2624; www.sanxaviermission.org; daily). The ornate whitewashed mission church, known as the White Dove of the Desert, was begun in 1783 and finished in 1797 and is still in use as a parish church. Both its resplendent facade and intricately painted interior have been restored to their full

Lake Pleasant Regional Park, near Phoenix.

lory. San Xavier Mission was originally established by Father Kino in 1692 to minister to the village of Wa:k (Xavier District) on the Tohono O'odham Reservation. Formerly known as the Pima, the Tohono O'odham people are descendants of the Hohokam culture. Their 2.8-million-acre (1.1-million-hectare) reservation sprawls west of Tucson to the Mexican border and adjoins torrid **Organ Pipe Cactus National Monument** (tel: 520-387-6849; www.nps.gov/orpi; daily), a great place to enjoy the Sonoran Desert backcountry when the weather cools down.

MISSIONS AND MISSILES

Tumacácori National Historical Park (tel: 520-377-5060; www.nps.gov/tuma; daily), 40 miles (64km) south on I-19, preserves the remains of three mission churches built between 1691 and the early 1800s. Its small museum details what mission life was like in the time of the Spanish padres. Nearby is the charming artists' colony of **Tubac**, a former mining town with a rich history and a popular February Festival of the Arts. **Tubac Presidio State Historic Park** (tel: 520-398-2252; http://azstateparks.com/parks/TUPR; daily) preserves part of the presidio erected by the Spanish in 1752.

Titan Missile Museum (tel: 520-625-7736; www.titanmissilemuseum.org; daily underground tours), near Green Valley, 16 miles (26km) south of San Xavier, is an entirely different experience. It preserves the only one of the 27 US Titan Missile II sites not to have been dismantled at the end of the Cold War. Operational July 1963 to November 1982, it held two missiles that were capable of being fired over 5,000 miles (8,000km) in less than 20 minutes.

BIOSPHERE 2

Modern technology also created another Tucson area curiosity: **Biosphere 2** (tel: 520-838-6200; www.biosphere2.org; daily), near **Oracle**, 32 miles (51km) north of the city on State 77. Completed in 1991, Biosphere 2 was a private human experiment that went awry. It was designed as a 3-acre (1-hectare) hermetically sealed replica

The purple prickly pear cactus is native to the Sonoran Desert.

Tumacácori National Historical Park.

of Biosphere 1: planet Earth – albeit cunningly disguised as a giant terrarium – and its grand aim was to pave the way for colonization of Mars. To that end, a group of eight ex-actors and scientists – four men and four women – were locked into it for two full years, to see whether they could survive in a closed and self-sufficient environment. Operated as a department of the University of Arizona's College of Science since 2011, tours are less exciting now that there are no "Biospherians" to be glimpsed, but you do get to go inside the huge and oddly beautiful structure, including its luxurious living quarters, and explore its multiple environments.

THE APACHE TRAIL

The quickest route between Tucson and Phoenix to the north is the long, flat 100-mile (160km) drive on I-10, which takes less than two hours. About 30 miles (48km) north of Tucson, the interstate passes historic **Picacho Peak**, a distinctive, fang-shaped volcanic promontory around which the Battle of Picacho Peak, the westernmost battle in the Civil War took place on April 15, 1862. It's a great place to stop in spring to photograph huge, orange carpets of California poppies and other desert wildflowers.

Alternatively, State Route 79 heads north from Biosphere 2 on a parallel course to Phoenix, east of the interstate. Known as the **Pinal Pioneer Parkway**, it is lush with native vegetation, from the prickly pear and saguaro cactus to the catclaw and mesquite tree, and is worth taking if you have time. It leads to **Apache Junction**, east of Phoenix, the start of the **Apache Trail**. This modern road was constructed in 1905 to provide access to **Theodore Roosevelt Dam** ㊷, the first of the great dams of the West, built to quench the growing thirst of nearby Phoenix. Named the Apache Trail in the hope of encouraging tourism, it was hailed by President Teddy Roosevelt, when he dedicated the dam in 1911, as combining "the grandeur of the Alps, the glory of the Rockies, and the magnificence of the Grand Canyon. Despite the hyperbole, it is indeed a ravishing drive.

The hermetically sealed environment of Biosphere 2.

Shortly after leaving Apache Junction, the Apache Trail passes the touristy ramshackle **Goldfield Ghost Town** (tel: 480-983-0333; http://goldfieldghosttown.com; daily), where you can take horse or jeep rides amid the abandoned mine machinery and false-front stores, or simply buy a snack at the bakery. Beyond that comes your first clear sighting of the **Superstition Mountains**. The Spanish called these peaks the "Mountains of Foam" because of their effusive volcanic ridges, but they're best known for the legends that surround the Dutch prospector Jacob Walz. He seems to have struck a huge lode of gold in the Superstitions in the late 19th century, but no one who followed him on his expeditions was ever seen again, and the Lost Dutchman Mine remains hidden to this day. The Superstition Mountains have taken the life of many an overly curious fortune-seeker.

Apache Trail cuts into **Tonto National Forest** (http://www.fs.usda.gov/tonto), where vistas and foot trails skirt the highway. The fun really begins as it winds its narrow way into the highlands. Drivers beware: you'll have to keep your eyes more on the road than the alpine rises, glorious vistas, and lush canyons. Saguaros and mesquite, dry riverbeds, and wave upon wave of mountain ridges follow a scenic overlook of the **Canyon River**. When you descend into the valley, pull up and strip down, because the blue waters are irresistible.

The trail is well paved for the 18 miles (29km) up to **Tortilla Flat**, a required stop for lovers of desert lore and witty Western character. To experience the essence of Tortilla Flat visit Superstition Saloon, where you can dine on "Killer Chili" in a whimsical setting (www.tortillaflataz.com/restaurant).

INDIAN RUINS, A TEMPLE, AND A UNIVERSITY ENCLAVE

A hotel, post office, café/restaurant, gift shop, riding stable, curio shop, a legend, and a marvelous view – Tortilla Flat is a great place to stop for "the best chili in the West" and a "howdy" from "the friendliest town in America." Admire the hundreds of dollar-bills tacked under business cards on the ceiling and walls of the café before you return to the sun-drenched desert. Roosevelt Dam lies another 30 miles (48km) up the precipitous but passable dirt road beyond Tortilla Flat. Above and behind it spreads **Roosevelt Lake**, the reservoir it created. The best views are from a steep hiking trail in **Tonto National Monument** (tel: 928-467-2241; daily; www.nps.gov/tont; daily), just west of the dam on State 88.

That short but grueling hike culminates in a cliff-dwelling once occupied by the Salado culture, which disappeared from this area before the Apache arrived. Retrace State Route 88 into the valley, where you'll pass through two unique suburbs, as State Route 88 becomes Main Street in Mesa, then Apache Boulevard in Tempe. **Mesa** contains Arizona's largest community of Latter Day Saints (Mormons), and you'll pass by the

Staple ingredients in this region, chilis are made into strings, or ristras, and hung to dry in the sun.

Petroglyph rock art at Signal Hill picnic area, Saguaro National Park.

beautiful **Mesa Arizona Temple**. It is closed to non-Mormons. Its visitor center (tel: 480-964-7164; www.lds.org) is open daily. Note: the temple and visitor center are currently closed for a major two-year renovation. When they reopen in mid-2020, the public will be able to tour the temple before it is consecrated, a rare opportunity to enter an LDS temple.

Tempe is home to Arizona State University, which anchors the south side of Phoenix with its lively Mill Avenue and postmodern buildings along the Salt River. The beautifully designed **Tempe Center for the Arts** (tel: 480-350-2822 box office; www.tempecenterforthearts.com; box office daily, gallery Tue–Sat) is a nice place to relax a while. The community center houses two theaters; an art gallery; a restaurant with a view of Tempe Town Lake, an artificial lake impounded from the Salt River; and an adjoining riverwalk and sculpture garden. Turning left on University, you'll come to I-10, which quickly whisks you into the heart of **Phoenix ④** (see page 310).

Dining at El Charro, Arizona's oldest Mexican restaurant, in Tucson.

PHOENIX TO SAN DIEGO

The 150 miles (240km) between Phoenix and the Colorado River, which marks Arizona's border with California, are interesting for the way the relatively green Sonoran Desert starts to yield to the more monochromatic Mojave Desert, your companion all the way to San Diego. You can stick with I-10 as far as Quartzsite, then change to US 95 south, or drop south much earlier, to meet I-8 at Gila Bend. Either way, your final destination in Arizona will be Yuma, where the words "furnace heat" might have been invented.

Quartzsite is only worth visiting if you're passing through in January or February, when up to a million sun-seeking, northern "snowbirds" (retirees in classic Airstream trailers and RVs) descend on the town for the **Quartzsite Powwow Rock and Mineral Show** (tel: 928-927-6325; www.qiaarizona.org/PowWow), a huge, open-air flea market for seekers and sellers of precious, semi-precious, and not-even slightly-precious stones and gems of various shapes and sizes.

Otherwise, you'd do better to turn off 10, 25 miles (40km) west of Phoenix, and take State Route 85 down to the I-8 truckstop of **Gila Bend**. (In fact, if you're in a hurry to get to the beach from Tucson, I-8 enables you to bypass Phoenix altogether.) Named for its location on a big bend in the Gila River, Gila Bend holds a predictable array of fast-food restaurants and motels, plus one outstanding exception. The **Best Western Space Age Lodge** is a marvelous 1950s-style folly, fitted out with kitsch Sputnik-shaped neon signs. Its **Space Age Restaurant**, which features a dazzling lunar-exploration mural, is well worth a stop for a bite to eat. **Gila Bend Visitor Center and Museum** (tel: 928-683-2255; www.gilabendaz.org/248/Visitor-Center; daily), a mile west, has brochures and small exhibits on the Hohokam culture, the Oatman massacre, and a WWII internment in the area. The most exciting thing to happen in the area recently was Prince Harry's stint in aircraft training in late 2011, while 2013 saw the opening of the 9-11 Memorial Park featuring a Twin Tower's steel beam artifact.

Signs on the interstate near Gila Bend warn that this is a "Blowing Dust Area," while bridges repeatedly cross "rivers" that are little more than dry *arroyos*. Somehow, **Dateland** ⓘ, 50 miles (80km) west of Gila Bend, manages to grow a bumper annual crop of dates. If you're desperate for diversion, stop for a date shake or whatever date-related product may strike your fancy in Dateland's solitary diner.

MEXICO'S DEVIL'S ROAD TO YUMA

There's plenty of notice that you're approaching **Yuma** ⓘ – its avenues are numbered a mile apart, thus you pass an Avenue 51E that's a full 50 miles (80km) east of downtown Yuma. Yuma is growing, but it's not *that* large (about 208,000 people). The road climbs over the pass through the Gila Mountains and descends into the Colorado River valley, before there's any sign of life. That is, apart from the low-flying jets that screech overhead. Southwest Arizona is a proving ground for the US military, and the latest top-secret warplanes are constantly being tested

Space cowboys will want to refuel at the Space Age Restaurant, at the Best Western Space Age Lodge in Gila Bend.

Numerous Hollywood films and television shows were shot at Old Tucson Studios.

Prison gate at the Yuma Territorial Prison State Historic Park.

Cowboy at Rancho de los Caballeros in Wickenburg.

above the barren desert that lies between I-8 and the Mexican border.

When Padre Eusebio Kino, the most tireless of all Spanish missionaries to the American Southwest, opened a trail in 1699 from Sonoita, Mexico, to what is now Yuma, he called the trail *El Camino del Diablo* – the Devil's Road. It seemingly led straight into the inferno. The town subsequently gained a long-standing reputation as one of the worst hellholes in the Wild West. Yuma smolders to this day, but it has been tamed by the air-conditioner into a city fit for human beings. With some 339 days of sunshine and less than 4 inches (10cm) of rainfall annually, it made the *Guinness Book of World Records* as the "Sunniest Place on Earth." All that heat has made Yuma a mecca for sun-seekers, and the gigantic sprawl of RV parks as you approach town in winter just might make you agree with Kino's description.

A HISTORIC FORD ON THE COLORADO RIVER

Set just below the confluence of the Gila and Colorado rivers, Yuma has been known for centuries as the site the only natural ford on the souther trail to the Pacific. As such, it was crucial way-station on the road to Cal fornia, even before the Gold Rush 1849. Originally, local Quechan peopl held a monopoly on the lucrative riv crossing, but as ever-greater number of starry-eyed miners demanded to b ferried into gold country, control wa wrested away in some astonishing bloodthirsty conflicts.

Quechan Indian Museum (tel: 760 572-0661; www.quechantribe.com; dail on the California side preserves 185 Fort Yuma, built to protect traveler prior to the area coming under U control with the 1854 Gadsden Pur chase. Today, the Quechan Tribe use the fort to interpret its culture, a interesting irony.

When gold was also discovered ea of Yuma, in 1858, the city blossome into a port, where ore was transporte by steamboat down the Colorado Riv and into the Gulf of California. Afte the mines dried up and the river wa dammed, Yuma transformed into a

agricultural center, with help from irrigation technology. But it is still a crossroads, where I-8 from San Diego meets US 95. The restored Ocean to Ocean Bridge that spans the Colorado close to the prison was completed in 1915, the only bridge over the Colorado for 1,200 miles (1,931km). It finally spared travelers the ferry ride across the river but was built for Model Ts, not four-wheel-drive vehicles, and only accommodates one lane of traffic at a time.

A TERRITORIAL PRISON AND WETLANDS REFUGE

Thanks to diminished water flow, the Gila and Colorado now meet 5 miles (8km) upstream from downtown Yuma. The bluff that once overlooked their intersection is occupied by the fascinating **Yuma Territorial Prison State Historic Park** (tel: 928-783-4771; http://azstateparks.com/parks/yute; daily, June–Sept Thu–Mon), which preserves the remaining structures of the most infamous prison in Arizona Territory, including its guardhouse, courtyards, cellblock, and notorious Dark Cell for solitary confinement. It housed a total of 3,069 convicts before its closure in 1909, three years before Arizona achieved statehood.

Inside the central building, there's a rogues' gallery of photos of former inmates, including Pearl Hart, the prison's only female inmate, who was jailed for five years for robbery and released two years early when it was learned she was pregnant, presumably by one of her guards. The Hell Hole (no air-conditioning in these cells!) was so dreaded that at least a few desperados surely thought twice before pulling the trigger.

Yuma Crossing Heritage Area (www.yumaheritage.com) is an ambitious multiuse wetlands project that is gradually restoring 1,400 acres (560 hectares) of the riverfront for wildlife and human use, and birds and wildlife are returning, along with native plants and trees. You can walk the Yuma East Wetlands Trail for 3 miles, starting at Gateway Park.

The point from which the ferries once set off, on the fringes of downtown, is now occupied by **Yuma Quartermaster Depot State Historic Park** (tel: 928-329-0471; http://azstateparks.com/parks/YUQU; daily, closed Mon June–Sept), formerly Yuma Crossing State Historic Park, which preserves the original river ford and the quartermaster depot. Living history demonstrations are offered by docents, recalling the bygone era when paddle steamers plied the Colorado. Outdoor interpretive exhibits can be found at Pivot Point Interpretive Plaza (daily) in the restored historic riverfront area, at the location where the first railroad train entered Arizona in 1877. The multiuse pathways provide a pleasant spot for strolling or cycling along the riverbank, linking the West and East Wetlands and other points of interest.

In the downtown core, **Old Yuma** consists of a few blocks of sleepy but atmospheric Victorian-era buildings,

Colorado River at Yuma on the Arizona-California border.

such as quaint Sanguinetti House Museum and Gardens (tel: 928-782-1841). Lutes Casino (www.lutescasino.com), on South Main Street ("Where the Elite Meet"), is a local institution. It resembles a featureless barn on the outside, but the interior of the dive bar/restaurant/casino is filled with memorabila.

CALIFORNIA

Over the Colorado River, down-at-heel **Winterhaven** provides a deceptively low-key introduction to California, the third-largest and most populous state in the nation. Northwest of here, the **Imperial Valley** – thanks to extensive damming and irrigation – is one of the most agriculturally productive regions on Earth. As you follow I-8 to the coast, however, it takes a while before the myth of California is fulfilled. First, there is the desert to deal with.

The Mojave is expansive enough for even the biggest of visions. Exit 164 leads to the **Center of the World** (tel: 760-572-0100; www.felicityusa.com), a unique site built by Jacques-Andre

Istel, French-born author of the children's book *Coe: The Good Dragon at the Center of the World*. The Center of the World is marked on a plaque inside a pyramid in the town of Felicity founded by Istel (also its mayor), who named it for his wife. In addition to the pyramid, there's a giant sundial whose gnomon replicates Michelangelo's Arm of God on the Sistine Chapel, the original staircase from the Eiffel Tower in Paris, and the incredible **Museum of History in Granite** (tel: 760-572-0100; www.historyingranite.org; call to check opening times), an ongoing project that captures the history of mankind on massive etched granite panels. You can spend the night in a little vacation rental apartment here and explore further. To reserve, tel: 928-343-0360.

ALGODONES DUNES AND A DESERT OASIS

The **Algodones Dunes**, immediately west of the Colorado River, were every bit as much of an obstacle to early travelers as the river itself. This strip of deep, shifting sands stretches 40 miles (64km) north to south. It's only around 6 miles (10km) wide at this point, but for the first motorists to attempt to cross, this might as well have been the Sahara Desert. In 1915, the **Old Plank Road**, made from railroad ties, was laid down to enable automobiles to rumble their way over. By 1925, when as many as 30 cars were using the road each day, it had deteriorated alarmingly. A two-lane paved highway, State Route 80, finally opened in August 1926; it has long since been superseded by I-8.

A small segment of the Old Plank Road is still visible by leaving the interstate 20 miles (32km) west of Yuma, on Grays Well Road, to enter **Imperial Sand Dunes National Recreation Area ⑯** (tel: 760-337-4400; www.blm.gov/visit/imperial-sand-dunes) immediately south. Roughly 4 miles (6km) along, parallel to the interstate and to the very long **All American Canal**, the dried-out old planks descend

Migrant worker harvesting lettuce near Yuma.

a short slope. These arid dunes are now a raucous playground for Californian youths, who race their dune buggies and ATVs over the razor-edged inclines, while "snowbirds" tan themselves sleepily beside their RVs.

Islands of irrigated green dotted with palms spell "oasis" at the end of the 58-mile (93km) tumble from Yuma to **El Centro**. Supposedly the largest city below sea level in the western hemisphere, and birthplace of the entertainer Cher, El Centro prospers quietly as a supply center for the Imperial Valley.

Beyond the reach of the canals, the vegetation all but disappears, and you enter the bare **Yuma Desert**. Punctuated by only the occasional 20ft (7-meter) wandlike ocotillo plant, whose tips flame orange in early spring, the desert floor appears to have undergone an unsuccessful hair transplant. The appropriately named **Ocotillo**, 28 miles (45km) west of El Centro, is no more than a flyblown little hamlet.

The mountain ranges that sweep down from the northwest just past Ocotillo are at first obscured by the dust, but soon you find yourself embarking on the very steep climb up their rocky flanks. The east- and westbound lanes of the interstate divide at this point, each plotting its own course across a terrain that consists of no more than piles of rust-colored boulders. Every few hundred yards stand roadside barrels filled with "Radiator Water," as the risk of overheating is so high. Atop a minor eminence at an elevation of 3,000ft (914 meters), 5 miles (8km) out of Ocotillo, the **Desert View Tower** (www.desertviewtower.com) commands a stunning view back across Imperial Valley. Constructed in 1922, using blocks of hewn granite, it contains an enjoyable jumble of exhibits on local history. Entering San Diego County at Mountain Spring, I-8 pulls south to skirt the Mexican border; a minor turn-off leads to the border town of **Jacumba**.

SAN DIEGO REVEALED

Near **Live Oak Springs**, 27 miles (43km) west of Ocotillo, the winds die down and the rises level off. Interstate 8 soon swoops to green valleys and into **Cleveland National Forest** (www.fs.usda.gov/cleveland), winding through Pine Valley and Alpine. As you drop toward Alpine, you should get your first glimpse of the Pacific Ocean, glinting on the horizon ahead. **El Cajon ⑰**, 43 miles (69km) beyond Live Oak Springs, is a nicely landscaped city that marks the first major outpost of the San Diego metropolitan area. **La Mesa** follows, set picturesquely amid the hills that rise on El Cajon's western outskirts.

Past La Mesa, traffic on I-8 becomes increasingly congested; the overpass of I-15 is the portal to San Diego. As the interstate pushes out to the Pacific beaches, its shoulders open onto shopping malls and numerous high-rise hotels. A little farther south, buildings arched by trees glimmer on the slopes. Behind them lies the sunny border city of **San Diego ⑱** (see page 316).

(see page 316).

Performing at a Cinco de Mayo (Fifth of May) celebration.

PHOENIX: VALLEY OF THE SUN

Business is booming in Phoenix, with plenty of industry, tourism, and golf courses. Just be sure to come in winter.

Phoenix may not have had any real ashes to rise from, but its founders were inspired by the knowledge that the merciless heat of the Salt River Valley had been overcome before. Between approximately AD 1100 and 1450, the Hohokam people successfully irrigated this region by means of a network of over 300 miles (480km) of canals. In 1867, Jack Swilling established modern Phoenix by simply redigging the waterways.

During World War II, the military used the desert for aviation training and revolutionized

Central Business District.

Phoenix by introducing air conditioning. Suddenly, life in the torrid Sonoran Desert was a year-round possibility, and the great migration was on. Now, Phoenix, with a metropolitan area population of 4.7 million people, is booming.

The city's setting is impressive. To the east soar the massive Four Peaks and Superstition Mountains, while the Sierra Estrella, sacred to the Maricopa and Gila River Indian Community, rides the southeast horizon. Hemming in the city north and south are lower mountain ranges, framing Camelback Mountain. Day hikes offer visitors an opportunity to witness the beauty (and silence) of the Sonoran Desert, but note: the average high temperature in Phoenix from June through August is 103°F (39°C). Peak tourist season is winter, when daily maximum temperatures hover around 70°F (21°C) and the valley's spa resorts and nearly 200 golf courses fill with tourists.

Once lacking character, downtown Phoenix has transformed in recent years into an enticing venue. Its major cultural attractions and restaurants are located on or near the **Central Avenue downtown** corridor, which now has the appearance of a European boulevard. It is anchored by the popular new 26.3 mile (42km) light rail network connecting downtown with outlying communities and used by 50,000 commuters a year.

Heritage Square, a block east of the Civic Plaza, preserves Victorian buildings in **Heritage and Science Park** (tel: 602-262-5070 visitor center for tickets; http://heritagesquarephx.org; Wed–Sun). The **Rosson House**, a striking red-brick Victorian home built in 1895, stands out from the square's 11 buildings, while two of the city's hottest restaurants – Pizzeria Bianco/Bar Bianco and Nobuo at Teeter House – make the square a popular destination for foodies. Nearby **Arizona Science Center** (tel: 602-716-2000; www.azscience.org; daily), a hands-on funhouse of science housed in a $50 million building designed by famed architect Antoine Predock, has 300 exhibits in five themed galleries on four floors, as well as a planetarium.

If you only visit one Phoenix museum make it the spectacular **Heard Museum** (tel:

602-252-8840; www.heard.org; daily) at 2301 North Central. Founded by Dwight and Mae Bartlett Heard in 1929 to house their collection of American Indian art and artifacts, the recently expanded 12 galleries focus on interpreting Indian arts and crafts, both ancient and modern. The Heard's signature exhibit is Home: Native People in the Southwest, which tells the story of Arizona's Indian tribes, then and now, through multimedia. It includes 250 historic Hopi kachina dolls collected by the late Republican senator Barry Goldwater and donated to the Heard. The classy **Phoenix Art Museum** (tel: 602-666.7104; www.phx-art.org; Wed–Sun), around the corner from the Heard, has also expanded and is now the largest art museum in the Southwest. It displays some 17,000 artworks by American, Mexican, and Asian artists, Southwest painters, as well as Western art by Moran and Remington.

The hugely popular **Musical Instrument Museum** (tel: 480-478-6000; http://mim.org; daily) is located due north of the adjoining city of Scottsdale. Dreamed up by the energetic retired CEO of Target Stores, it tells the story of world music via a dizzying array of exhibits featuring musical instruments and videos of live performances.

The influence of famed architect Frank Lloyd Wright echoes throughout the historic **Arizona Biltmore Resort** (tel: 602-955-6600; www.arizona biltmore.com) at 24th Street and Missouri, north-east of downtown, off Camelback Road, on the Phoenix/**Scottsdale border.** Albert Chase McArthur, a former student of Wright, originally designed the building in 1929, but found himself in trouble and summoned the master for help. Wright probably gave more help than required, for the hotel is a delightful masterpiece from Wright's middle period. Wright stayed in Phoenix to found his architectural school and residence, **Taliesin West** (tel: 480-627-5340; www.franklloydwright.org/taliesin-west; tours daily, June–Aug Thu–Tue), in the Scottsdale foothills. Taliesin still bustles with architecture and design students, offering visitors not only a fascinating look at Wright's organic architecture but glimpses of how his legacy is being continued today.

Luxury spa resorts cluster around Scottsdale's Camelback Mountain. There's good shopping at Scottsdale's Fashion Square and in **Old Town**, where galleries focus on cowboy and Indian art, as does the impressive new Western Spirit: Scottsdale's Museum of the West (tel: 480-686-9539; www.scottsdalemuseumwest.org; daily). Contemporary installations at little Scottsdale Museum of Contemporary Art across the street (tel: 480-874-4766; www.smoca.org; Wed–Sat) make a nice counterpoint.

The entrancing **Desert Botanical Garden** (tel: 480-941-1225; www.dbg.org; daily) is located in **Papago Park** in southern Scottsdale. It displays 139 rare, threatened, and endangered species of plants from around the world as well as the Sonoran Desert, the world's largest collection of desert plants living in a natural environment.

South of the botanical garden is the Salt River, where you will find **Pueblo Grande Museum Archeological Park** (tel: 602-495-0900; http://pueblogrande.com; Tue–Sat), preserving a rare 1,500-year-old Hohokam village ruin built on a mound within sight of the airport. It is an intriguing juxtaposition, one that is common throughout the Valley of the Sun.

The Arizona Biltmore resort.

San Francisco's Golden Gate Bridge enveloped by fog.

Highway 1 on the Big Sur coast.

THE PACIFIC ROUTE

A guide to the Pacific Coast, with principal sights cross-referenced by number to the maps.

On the road in California.

America's historic US 101 – which stretched from San Diego all the way up the coast through Oregon and Washington to the Canadian border, and eventually became, in part, today's California Highway 1 – has a history that is comparable with its more famous companion, Route 66. Until 1909, it had been a narrow, bumpy, dirt-surfaced track on which horse-drawn wagons and primitive autos competed for space. Then a concrete and macadam road began stretching north from the cities of San Diego and Oceanside.

The spiffy new road stimulated the rise of a phenomenon known as "car culture," epitomized in sunny California, which spawned all the enterprises that subsequently came to be associated with travel along the highway, such as gas stations, car dealers, motels, diners, and auto laundries.

The highway led visitors from all parts of the Pacific Coast to San Diego's Balboa Park for the 1915–16 Panama-California Exposition, enticed Hollywood movie stars and others to its pristine beaches, and lured those in search of a good time during Prohibition to Mexico's Tijuana.

In 1925, the road officially became US 101. Increased traffic spelled its doom, however, and by the end of the war a new four-lane highway, eventually to become Interstate 5, bypassed the old route. Today, the Pacific Coast Highway, often abbreviated to "PCH," and also known as El Cabrillo Trail, is a sometimes-scrappy, often sea-scented mixture of the old US 101, California Highway, and roaring Interstate 5. We have fol-

Surfing at Zuma Beach, Malibu.

lowed it here as faithfully as possible, stopping off at breathtaking sites like California's Big Sur and Hearst Castle and sometimes diverting inland and away from its charms to visit vibrant cities like Portland and Seattle. Along the way there are quaint Victorian-era towns, wineries, giant redwoods, romantic windswept beaches, historic sites such as Mission San Juan Capistrano, and countless opportunities to see a fascinating array of wildlife.

The Pacific Coast Highway's villages and towns – as well as much of its old structure – are still here, and for those who have time, and a romantic desire to reclaim an earlier America, following Highway 1 and historic 101 to Seattle can lead to unimaginable pleasures.

📷 A SHORT STAY IN SAN DIEGO

San Diego is a busy, elegant harbor town with a history unsurpassed in the state of California. Here's a list of the not-to-be-missed attractions.

Mission San Diego (1769) offers a peaceful sanctuary with fragrant gardens. A museum and walking tour tell the story of the "Mother of all Missions," and mass is still celebrated in the basilica.

Old Town State Historic Park preserves the site of the original settlement where Spanish soldiers and their families lived until the early 1800s. Its historic structures now house interesting small museums and shops, offering a glimpse of California as it was in the Spanish, Mexican, and early American periods.

Board a **Hornblower yacht** at **Broadway Pier** for a professionally guided whale-watching cruise, where you can expect to see sea lions, harbor seals, dolphins, and, between December and April, large numbers of formerly endangered gray whales during their seasonal migration between Alaska and Mexico, where they give birth over the winter, then return to seasonal Alaskan fishing grounds in spring. Scenic harbor and dinner cruises can be enjoyed all year.

In the heart of San Diego, 1,200-acre (490-hectare) **Balboa Park** is San Diego's major cultural destination, with 17 museums, theaters, beautiful gardens, art galleries, and more. A park pass, available at the visitor center, admits you to 16 of the museums, several in ornate old buildings.

Hire a convertible and cruise the **59-Mile Scenic Drive**, which takes you through **downtown**, **Balboa Park**, the beaches, **La Jolla**, and out to **Cabrillo National Monument** on **Point Loma** for fabulous views of the city and the open ocean.

IMPORTANT INFORMATION

Population: 1.4 million
Dialing codes: 619, 858
Website: www.sandiego.org
Tourist information: San Diego Visitor Information Center, 996-B North Harbor Drive, San Diego, CA 92101; tel: 619-737-2999

Vessels of all sizes line the natural harbor of San Diego Bay, from yachts to the USS Midway aircraft carrier, now a museum.

Hotel del Coronado. Sixteen US presidents have visited this characterful Victorian resort.

Swim, surf, and sunbathe on San Diego's sandy beaches.

The birthplace of California

Although Spaniard Juan Cabrillo was the first European to stake a claim to California in 1542, it wasn't until July 16, 1769, that it became a reality, when Padre Junípero Serra conducted a mass dedicating the newly created Mission San Diego de Alcalá on Presidio Hill (it was moved to its present site in Mission Valley five years later). History and luxury can be found in many parts of this harbor city, which has numerous upscale shops and 90 golf courses. San Diego's harborfront, the Embarcadero, can be touristy, but there are enough historic sites, cultural attractions, fine restaurants, shady walks, harbor cruises, and sandy beaches to appeal to the most discerning of visitors.

ric Gaslamp Quarter of San Diego, the place to head
r entertainment, nightlife, shopping, and dining.

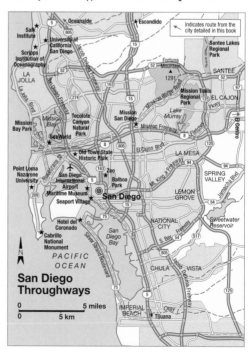

The classic surfer's vehicle –
a VW camper van.

SAN DIEGO TO LOS ANGELES

Beach towns, beach facilities, and beaches themselves – more than 20 of them – line this short stretch of coastline. Is it any wonder the bikini first became famous here?

The journey from seaside **San Diego ❶** (see page 316) to glittering Los Angeles is only around 125 miles (200km), but following the ragged coastal roads can take much longer than that short distance implies. It's also much more rewarding, as the coastal route meanders past Southern California's best beaches, prettiest towns, and most exclusive residential areas. For navigational purposes, the road signs along the way go by a variety of names – Highway 1, US 101, I-5 – but to most Californians, this mix of roads paralleling the ocean is known simply as the Pacific Coast Highway (PCH).

LA JOLLA TO OCEANSIDE

The first stop out of San Diego is **La Jolla ❷** (pronounced "la-hoy-ya"), a seaside community that once boasted "the richest zip code in America." This college community and upscale town can be reached in a few minutes by heading north up I-5, but a more scenic way is to start the drive to Los Angeles as you intend to proceed – using water as your navigator. From SeaWorld, take the road called SeaWorld Drive to West Mission Bay Drive, routes that curl along the bottom of **Mission Bay** itself. The road turns north (changing into Mission Boulevard) to parallel Mission Beach, then the livelier Pacific Beach, before rolling into La Jolla. La Jolla has beautiful homes and a downtown area – which calls itself "the

village" – filled with expensive shops, as well as a branch of San Diego's **Museum of Contemporary Art** (tel: 858-454-3541; www.mcasd.org; Thu–Tue). Described by writer Raymond Chandler as "a nice place for old people and their parents," La Jolla featured in Tom Wolfe's 1960s surfer novel *The Pump House Gang*. On the campus of the University of California is La Jolla Playhouse (www.lajollaplayhouse.org), whose forerunner was founded by the late actor Gregory Peck. The caves carved into its coastal bluffs have long been a paradise for both deep-sea divers

Main attractions

Map on page 320

Sunset over the San Diego coast.

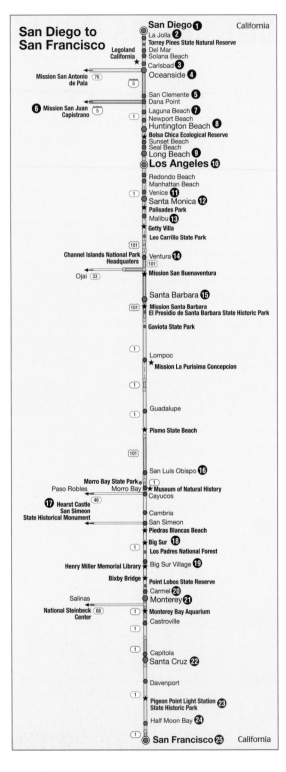

San Diego to San Francisco

San Diego ❶ — California
La Jolla ❷
Torrey Pines State Natural Reserve
Del Mar
Solana Beach
Legoland California ★
Carlsbad ❸
Oceanside ❹

Mission San Antonio de Pala (76) — (5)

❻ Mission San Juan Capistrano — (5) (1)

San Clemente ❺
Dana Point
Laguna Beach ❼
Newport Beach
Huntington Beach ❽
Bolsa Chica Ecological Reserve
Sunset Beach
Seal Beach
Long Beach ❾
Los Angeles ❿
Redondo Beach
Manhattan Beach
(1) Venice ⓫
Santa Monica ⓬
Palisades Park
Malibu ⓭
Getty Villa ★
Leo Carrillo State Park

(101)
Channel Islands National Park Headquaters — Ventura ⓮ (101)
Ojai (33) — ★ Mission San Buenaventura

Santa Barbara ⓯
(101) Mission Santa Barbara
El Presidio de Santa Barbara State Historic Park

Gaviota State Park

(1) Lompoc
★ Mission La Purisima Concepcion

(1)

(1) Guadalupe

(1) ★ Pismo State Beach

(101)
San Luis Obispo ⓰ (1)
Morro Bay State Park ★ Museum of Natural History
Paso Robles — Morro Bay — Cayucos
❿ Hearst Castle (46)
San Simeon State Historical Monument — Cambria
San Simeon
★ Piedras Blancas Beach
(1) Big Sur ⓲
Los Padres National Forest
Henry Miller Memorial Library ★ Big Sur Village ⓳
Bixby Bridge ★ Point Lobos State Reserve
Carmel ⓴
Salinas — Monterey ㉑
National Steinbeck (68) (1) Monterey Bay Aquarium
Center — Castroville

(1)

(1) Capitola
Santa Cruz ㉒

Davenport

(1) Pigeon Point Light Station ㉓
State Historic Park

Half Moon Bay ㉔

(1) San Francisco ㉕ — California

---

and cliff divers, and nearby **Black's Beach** was once legally – now illegally – a nudist beach.

At the north end of town, above Point La Jolla, is the renowned **Scripps Institution of Oceanography**, whose well-stocked **Birch Aquarium** (tel: 858-534-3474; www.aquarium.ucsd.edu; daily) offers whale-watching cruises in season. Among the more than 60 different habitats exhibiting marine life is a two-story sea-filled tank that replicates a kelp bed with all its familiar and unfamiliar creatures. Farther north and also by the sea is the **Salk Institute**, designed by the late Louis I. Kahn, perhaps one of America's most admired contemporary architects. The institute is named after its famous resident scientist, Jonas Salk, who devised the polio vaccine.

TORREY PINES SCENIC DRIVE

La Jolla Shores Drive parallels Torrey Pines Road, which follows a winding hillside out of La Jolla through the affluent suburb of Torrey Pines – both named for the trees of that name, which are environmentally protected. The road accesses **Torrey Pines Scenic Drive**. Look for the windswept hillside that flying enthusiasts have been using to launch gliders over the ocean since the 1930s. **Torrey Pines Gliderport** (tel: 858-452-9858; www.flytorrey.com; daily) offers introductory lessons to paragliding; spectators are welcome. There's also a restaurant and flight sport shop at the site. **Torrey Pines State Natural Reserve** (tel: 858-755-2063; www.torreypine.org; daily) and **Torrey Pines State Beach** are two places perfect for picnics.

DEL MAR AND SOLANA BEACH

A series of small coastal roads, which together make up US 101, parallels I-5 as far as the town of Oceanside, where the mighty interstate takes over until it reaches Dana Point. From then on, PCH becomes Highway 1 more or less until it reaches San Francisco.

Both the coast road and the interstate lead to the community of **Del Mar**, which has an Amtrak station. Its famous racetrack (tel: 858-755-1141; www.dmtc.com) has attracted crowds since the 1930s. It was rescued from collapse by actor Pat O'Brien and singer Bing Crosby, who turned the track into one of America's most popular racing circuit venues. The season begins in July, a week after Del Mar's big fair ends, and runs until mid-September.

The track's sandy-colored main building, in a sort of California-meets-Mediterranean style, can be glimpsed from the interstate, but much of the town itself lies farther down the hill, beside the coast road. Camino del Mar has art galleries, boutiques, and outdoor dining with ocean views.

The road passes **Solana Beach**, with its futuristic-looking railroad station, and the north San Diego communities that make up Encinitas – Old Encinitas, New Encinitas, Leucadia, Cardiff-by-the-Sea, and Olivenhain – which run into each other along this stretch of coast. A profusion of stop signs and red lights can slow progress; otherwise, this is a pleasant stretch to drive, with plenty of roadside trees, the beach and railroad track both near the road, and here and there, a "Historic US 101" sign. Sweet-smelling **San Diego Botanic Gardens** (tel: 760-436-3036; www.sdbgarden.org; daily) in **Encinitas** may be worth a stop to admire the waterfall and extensive collection of exotic plants. The **San Dieguito Heritage Museum** (tel: 760-632-9711; www.sdheritage.org; Thu–Sun) at Heritage Ranch specializes in the history of the area – from the Diegueño tribe of 10,000 years ago to life today – and includes a fine collection of more than 8,000 photographs. The beach is a few blocks away; the railroad parallels the road to the east. At the north end of the community are the golden domes of the Self-Realization Fellowship temple.

CARLSBAD

At **Carlsbad** ❸, the road runs along the beach and through the pretty downtown village, with its antiques stores and historic **Carlsbad Mineral Water Spa** (tel: 760-434-1887; www.carlsbadmineralspa.com), which reflects the heritage of its spa-town namesake in the Czech Republic. The region is known for flowers, particularly flowering bulbs, which are sold nationwide. Almost 50 hillside acres (20 hectares) are resplendent with swathes of brightly colored Giant Tecolote ranunculus at **The Flower Fields at Carlsbad Ranch** (tel: 760-431-0352; www.theflowerfields.com; Mar–May), a big draw every spring. The **Museum of Making Music** (tel: 760-438-5996; www.museumofmakingmusic.org; Tue–Sun) spans a century of music-making in America. Exhibits include vintage instruments, samples of music from each era, and photographs and paintings.

Carlsbad's 128-acre (52-hectare) **Legoland California** (tel: 760-918-5346; www.california.legoland.com; summer daily, closed Tue–Wed during select seasons) was the first Legoland theme park in the

Tip

Birch Aquarium at San Diego's Scripps Institution of Oceanography offers whale-watching cruises through its highly regarded aquarium, December to April. Tel: 858-534-3474 for more information.

These waters form part of the migratory path for gray whales.

US. It used 120 million of its signature toy plastic bricks to depict such scaled-down landmarks as New York City and Washington, DC – as well as Castle Hill with an "enchanted walk" where children can search for hidden treasure. Also on the grounds are a waterpark and Sea Life Aquarium.

OCEANSIDE SURF HISTORY

With almost 4 miles (6km) of white-sand beaches and world-class surf, **Oceanside ❹** is an appropriate place to find the **California Surf Museum** (tel: 760-721-6876; www.surfmuseum. org; daily), which displays the evolution of surfboards from 16-footers weighing 200 pounds (90kg) to fiberglass creations known as "potato-chip boards." There's a huge market among surfer dudes for memorabilia, making much of the museum's collection priceless. Famous surfing veterans like Duke Kahanamoka are honored here.

Also check out **Oceanside Historical Society Museum** (tel: 760-722-4786; www.oceansidehistoricalsociety.org; Thu–Fri, Sat by appointment;); **Oceanside**

Museum of Art (tel: 760-435-3720; www.oma-online.org; Tue–Sun; first Sun of month free); and **Buena Vista Audubon Nature Center** (tel: 760-439-2473; www.bvaudubon.org), beside a lagoon on the highway south of town. Four miles (6km) inland from the beach is the lovely 1795 **Mission San Luis Rey de Francia** (tel: 760-757-3651; www.sanluisrey.org; daily), the largest of the 21 California missions. Nearby is **Heritage Park Village and Museum** (tel: 760-801-0645; Wed–Sun), whose old buildings include the cottage that was once Oceanside's post office.

Watch for the **101 Cafe** (tel: 760-722-5220; www.101cafe.net; daily) as you drive through Oceanside. While the bright mural on its outside wall is a contemporary tribute to Highway 101, the diner itself is the real thing. Built in 1928, it is the town's oldest restaurant and is filled with memorabilia. Oceanside has more cafés and shops located in a pleasant man-made harbor, with a lighthouse that serves as a marina for several hundred boats at the north end. From here, boats run across to **Santa Catalina Island** (for information, contact the Catalina Island Chamber of Commerce and Visitors Bureau, tel: 310-510-1520; www.catalinachamber.com). Oceanside's pier, just north of Mission Avenue, is the longest recreational wooden pier on the West Coast. Hundreds of downtown walkways are marked with the mysterious O.U. MIRACLE, the name of contractor Orville Ullman Miracle, whose construction company submitted the winning bid in the 1920s to improve the community's streets.

OCEANSIDE TO LOS ANGELES

An interesting diversion from Oceanside is to drive inland along State Route 76 for a few miles to **Mission San Antonio de Pala** (tel: 760-742-3317; www.mission sanantonio.org; daily) on the Pala Indian Reservation. This is the only Californian mission still serving local Indian tribes: the Pala Band of Mission Indians and the Rincon, Pauma, and La Jolla bands

Sailboats in Avalon harbor, Santa Catalina Island.

of Luiseño Indians. San Antonio has celebrated its Corpus Christi Festival, with an open-air mass, dances, and games, on the first Sunday of every June since 1816.

The United States Marine Corps occupies the coastal area north of Oceanside, where the coast road is incorporated into I-5 and the sea is half a mile away. Just north of the controversial San Onofre Nuclear Power Plant is **San Clemente ⑤**, where former US president Richard Nixon, an Orange County native, set up a Western White House on his 25-acre (10-hectare) estate. This attractive town, with its Spanish Colonial–style red-tiled roofs and white stucco walls, prompted the *Los Angeles Times* to write in 1927: "If the charms of this place could be shown to the poor, snow-bound, wind-beaten people back East, there would be an exodus so great the hills above San Clemente would be covered like mushrooms."

In 1925, the town's founder, a former mayor of Seattle named Ole Hanson, purchased and designed the community on what was then empty space. He is memorialized at **Casa Romantica Cultural Center and Gardens** (tel: 949-498-2139; www.casaromantica.org; Tue–Sun), his old home near the Parque Del Mar, as well as at the Ole Hanson Beach Club and Ole's Tavern (tel: 949-498-9400; www.olestavern.com).

Writing in the *San Clemente Journal*, Ann Batty claimed that it was San Clemente designers who first popularized the bikini on local beaches, of which there are many (bikinis *and* beaches). San Clemente and Doheny state beaches have campgrounds, and Dana Point and Laguna Beach are protected as state marine conservation areas, where some fishing is permitted (patrolled by state fish and game wardens), but a portion of Laguna Beach is a state marine reserve, where fishing is not allowed.

DANA POINT AND CATALINA ISLAND

Capistrano Beach and Doheny State Beach span San Juan Creek, just before **Dana Point**, where most of the buildings in the harbor complex are a lot younger than they look – although the overall effect is quite attractive. There are dozens of places to shop and eat, and whale-watching excursions depart from here in season (Dec–Mar). Dana Point's annual Festival of Whales (http://festivalofwhales.com) in March is an amusing event, with its imaginative whale costumes, parade of clowns, jugglers, and antique cars, and lively street fair.

The **Ocean Institute** (tel: 949-496-2274; www.ocean-institute.org; daily), at the northern end of the harbor, commemorates Richard Henry Dana, whose seafaring exploits from here resulted in the novel *Two Years Before the Mast*, which became a 1946 movie starring Alan Ladd. **Catalina Island**, 22 miles (35km) off the coast, can be reached from here, too. This makes a fabulous day trip. Hour-long Catalina Express boat trips depart 30 times a day (tel: 800-481-3470; www.catalinaexpress.com) bound for the city of Avalon and town of Two Harbors on Catalina Island.

Laguna Beach.

SAN JUAN CAPISTRANO

Interstate 5 now veers away from the coast and heads inland to the town of San Juan Capistrano. Following it into town, Del Obispo Street leads to Camino Capistrano, on which sits celebrated **Mission San Juan Capistrano** ❻ (tel: 949-234-1330; www.missionsjc.com; daily), seventh in the chain of California missions founded by Spaniards in the late 1700s. There's a statue of Saint Junípero Serra, the controversial Franciscan missionary who founded this and eight other California missions (he was canonized by Pope Francis in 2015, the first Latino saint, causing a backlash among 50 California Indian tribes whose ancestors died in the missions). The Serra chapel behind the church is the oldest building still in use in the state of California. Pick up a free map that identifies and dates the chapel's treasures, including the bells to the left of the church.

San Juan Capistrano is most famous, of course, for its swallows, whose return signals the start of spring. Their scheduled arrival is on St Joseph's Day (Mar 19) and their departure for the warmer climate of Argentina on October 23. By some mysterious alchemy, the swallows have almost always been on time; their arrival here is marked by a week-long festival with mariachi bands leading a parade. Nevertheless, disappointed tourists sometimes arrive to find only pigeons.

HIGHWAY 1

Back on the coast, PCH now officially becomes Highway 1. It's been a while since the long-gone Serpentarium at **Laguna Beach** ❼ advertised *Rattlesnake à la Maryland* on the reptile zoo's menu – today, this upscale beach community is full of art galleries and chic shops. Laguna was always a favorite with Hollywood movie stars, and Mary Pickford, Bette Davis, Judy Garland, and Rudolph Valentino were among the stars who maintained homes here.

The resort has established a worldwide reputation with its annual **Pageant of the Masters** (www.foapom.com) each summer, at which well-rehearsed volunteers take up their roles in living reproductions of famous paintings.

Century-old **Laguna Art Museum** (tel: 949-494-8971; www.lagunaartmuseum.org; Thu–Tue) is a great place to see art; the city and local galleries organize a **First Thursdays Art Walk** (www.firstthursdays artwalk.com), when some 40 galleries stay open from 6 to 9pm and offer music, food, drink, and entertainment; a free trolley is available, or you can walk. Laguna Beach Visitors Center, located at 381 Forest Avenue (tel: 949-497-9229; www.visitlagunabeach.com; daily), has a self-guided Heritage Walking Companion tour booklet of downtown Laguna, which includes the **Murphy-Smith Historical Bungalow** (tel: 949-497-6834; Fri–Sun), one of the few remaining houses in downtown Laguna Beach from the 1920s.

Whale-watching boat trips to view the annual gray whale migrations are popular here, but there are other outdoor activities to enjoy. Lace up your hiking boots, and check out **Laguna Coast**

Balboa Pavilion, Newport Beach.

Wilderness Park (tel: 949-923-2235; www.ocparks.com/lagunacoast), a native plant and wildlife refuge on Laguna Canyon Road; the delightful **Pacific Marine Mammal Center** (tel: 949-494-3050; www.pacificmmc.org; daily), which cares for sick and injured seals; **Laguna Outdoors** (tel: 949-874-6620), which offers guided trail hiking and mountain biking along the coast; and **Glenn E. Vedder Ecological Reserve**, an underwater park at the north end of the main beach, where divers can explore marine life.

BALBOA PENINSULA

Newport Beach's upscale **Balboa Peninsula** features 3 miles (5km) of sandy shoreline on one side and a harbor filled with yachts and a large paddle wheeler moored beside the highway bridge on the other. It's hard to miss **Balboa Pavilion** on Main Street in Newport Beach; it was built in 1905 as a railroad terminal with a distinctive but totally unnecessary steeple. Behind it, if you get here early enough, you'll find fishing boats unloading their daily catch. Almost as old is the ferry that makes the 3-minute trip from the end of Palm Street to **Balboa Island**, with its million-dollar homes and classy shops and cafés. The hour-long walk around the island along the sidewalk hugging the water's edge is enjoyable, particularly at twilight.

On your way back across the narrow channel, someone will surely point out, on nearby islands, the former homes of John Wayne and cowboy hero Roy Rogers. From **Balboa Pier**, you can admire the kite-flyers, frisbee-throwers, and bodysurfers. Check out the restaurant at the end of the pier before finishing up at the Balboa Fun Zone, with its rides and video arcades.

Waves cascade over the breakwater here. It's not a swimming beach; expert bodysurfers are the only people with the right skills to negotiate this water. Kids will enjoy the hands-on experience at **ExplorOcean** (tel: 949-675-8915; www.explorocean.org; Sat–Sun). You can reach

Catalina Island from Newport Beach's Balboa Pavilion by taking the Catalina Flyer (tel: 949-673-5245; www.catalinainfo.com). In **Corona del Mar**, just to the south, the gardens of the **Sherman Library & Gardens** (tel: 949-673-2261; www.slgardens.org) is a pleasant place to pause. The library is an historical research library on the Pacific Southwest while the nicely scaled gardens include a tropical conservatory containing orchids, gingers, among other plants and seasonal displays of Pacific coastal plants. Lunch, crepes, and English afternoon tea are served in Cafe Jardin.

HUNTINGTON BEACH

It's now official – after a long legal trademark dispute with Santa Cruz in northern California, **Huntington Beach** ❽ has earned the right to call itself Surf City, USA. Not that anyone in Huntington Beach was ever in any doubt. In 1994, the city inaugurated a sidewalk **Surfers Walk of Fame** in the presence of its surf-fanatic congressman Dana Rohrabacher. Around the same time it also opened an **International Surfing**

International Surfing Museum at Heritage Beach.

Museum (tel: 714-465-4350; www.surfing-museum.org; Tue–Sun).

The highway heads along the coast past Huntington State Beach and the state's longest municipal pier, rebuilt in concrete after the original was destroyed by a fierce storm. Three blocks up Main Street and directly opposite the pier is **Plaza Almeria**, with an attractive collection of shops, restaurants, and condominiums. Farther uptown, **Bella Terra** is an outdoor entertainment and shopping complex.

Rail tycoon Henry Huntington introduced the railroad here in the late 1800s, and a subsequent oil boom brought prosperity to a city that ironically is now best known for its environmental awareness. Its 350-acre (140-hectare) **Central Park**, 50 percent of which is devoted to wildlife and greenery, is a mere hors d'oeuvre to the main entrée, the 1,300-acre (527 hectare) **Bolsa Chica Ecological Reserve** (tel: 714-846-1114; www.wildlife.ca.gov/Lands/Places-to-Visit/Bolsa-Chica-ER; daily), which preserves the vast coastal salt marsh that serves as a stopover for birds migrating between North and South America.

The best spot for birdwatchers is on the inland side of the highway, between Golden West Street and Warner Avenue, opposite the entrance to the beach. There are walking trails and plenty of parking. **Bolsa Chica Wetlands Interpretive Center**, run by the Bolsa Chica Conservancy, offers bird checklists and is located at Warner Avenue. Not far away, between Warner and Heil avenues, is the **Monarch Butterfly Habitat**, where rare migratory Monarch butterflies gather in the eucalyptus trees between November and March. Passing through the small, waterside community of **Sunset Beach**, you can't miss a huge wooden water tower beside the highway. Now a private residence, it is a local landmark.

SEAL BEACH PIER AND NAPLES GONDOLAS

At the Los Angeles County line, **Seal Beach**, an unspoiled enclave with an 80-year-old inn and a lengthy pier uncluttered with modern diversions, is the last place at which the ocean can be seen from the highway for many miles. To the right of the highway, in the **Belmont Shore** neighborhood of Long Beach, you can detour along Second Street, which skirts the beach of Alamitos Bay. **Gondola Getaway** on East Ocean Beach Boulevard (tel: 562-433-9595; www.gondolagetawayinc.com; daily) operates hour-long tours in real gondolas along canals that pass the elegant homes of neighboring **Naples Island**.

Highway 1 goes inland here, bypassing Long Beach, San Pedro, and the Palo Verdes Peninsula to hit the coast again just south of Redondo Beach.

THE *QUEEN MARY* IN LONG BEACH

Although PCH bypasses **Long Beach ❾**, it's worth passing through town to see some of its attractions, which include one of the world's largest murals, a panorama of marine life

⊘ LA'S PETERSEN AUTOMOTIVE MUSEUM

Lovers of automobiles and travel will want to make a sidetrip into Los Angeles to visit the **Petersen Automotive Museum**, one of the world's largest museums devoted exclusively to the history and cultural impact of the car. For when it comes to vehicles, no city knows them like Los Angeles, and no one can know Los Angeles without a vehicle.

This city, like few others, was designed for the car, and its endless miles of freeway tie it together the way rivers tie together London or Paris. The museum details everything you ever wanted to know about four wheels, and the culture that rides above them. It houses racing and classic cars, hot rods, movie-star cars, and vintage motorcycles. It also hosts events such as auctions and cruise-ins.

But the Petersen is not just about transportation; it's also about style. Although the museum has yet to host an exhibition on why balding old men buy flashy red sports cars, it does have rotating cultural exhibitions covering the Hispanic culture around low-rider cars and the history of that quintessential American icon: the pick-up truck. The museum is at 6060 Wilshire Boulevard, tel: 323-964-6331; www.petersen.org; Tue–Sun.

hat covers the entire surface of the Long Beach Arena on Ocean Boulevard. Other sights include the magnificent **Aquarium of the Pacific** (tel: 562-590-3100; www.aquariumofpacific. org; daily) and the venerable retired British ocean liner **Queen Mary** (tel: 877-342-0738; www.queenmary.com; daily), which made 1,000 transatlantic crossings and was a heroine of World War II before ending her journey here, moored in the harbor. The ship's history is a starry one, having been the carrier of choice for both celebrities and royalty; visitors can pretend to be the same by staying overnight in a cabin, or dine in the elegantly restored Art Deco Sir Winston's restaurant.

Long Beach has positioned itself as a sleek, modern city in recent years, and it certainly has a number of architecturally chic new structures. But it's also anxious to promote its historic downtown buildings from the early part of the 20th century. A walking tour map of more than 40 of these landmarks is available from the Long Beach Convention and Visitors Bureau (tel: 800-452-7829; www.visitlongbeach.com). If you're traveling with kids, note that State Route 22 east from Long Beach hooks up with I-5 and leads to Anaheim, where the attractions include **Disneyland** (www.disneyland.com), Knotts Berry Farm (www.knotts.com), Adventure City (www.adventurecity.com), and Medieval Times (http://medievaltimes.com).

HARBOR TOURS

Headquarters for Southern California's fishing fleet, **San Pedro** once carried the distinction of being a genuine fishing port. The old town is long gone, replaced by an imaginatively designed pseudo-19th-century construction called Ports O'Call Village. Several blocks of saltbox-type weathered-looking shops and numerous restaurants are a pleasure to walk around. Harbor tours and fishing trips leave from here (as well as the

Catalina Express and a beautiful classic sailing ship), and there is plenty of free parking. Green-and-white trolleys run along the waterfront, stopping at the World Cruise center, the maritime museum, Ports O'Call Village, and the Frank Gehry–designed **Cabrillo Marine Aquarium** (tel: 310-548-7562; www.cabrillomarineaquarium. org; Tue–Sun).

San Pedro's **Cabrillo Beach** has earned a reputation as one of the best places to go windsurfing, and beginners especially favor the sheltered waters inside the harbor breakwater. Between March and September – twice a month, like clockwork – milky-white grunion fish ride in on the tide by the thousand to deposit their eggs in the sand.

On the **Ranchos Palos Verdes** peninsula, you'll see multi-million-dollar Italianate villas and French châteaux overlooking the ocean. Abalone Cove Preserve, the beach west of Narcissa Drive, is an ecological reserve at the end of a steep path, perfect for divers and tide-poolers. Just past the

The Queen Mary is a famed Art Deco ocean liner docked in Long Beach. It has a hotel, restaurants, and bars.

Golden Shores mall, next to the Point Vicente Lighthouse, is **Point Vicente Interpretive Center** (tel: 310-544-5375; www.rpvca.gov; daily), a prime whale-watching location. Here, you'll find long-lens telescopes for sighting passing gray whales (Dec–Apr) and earphones to listen in on their mournful songs.

About a mile farther is the wood-and-glass **Wayfarers Chapel** (www.wayfarerschapel.org; daily), designed by Frank Lloyd Wright's son, whose inspiration is said to have been Northern California's majestic redwood trees. The chapel was built in 1951 as a memorial to the 18th-century Swedish theologian Emmanuel Swedenborg. Walking around the peaceful gardens to the sound of songbirds, a fountain, and the gurgling stream is a very tranquil experience. There are services in the chapel at 10am every Sunday.

BEACH TOWNS

By now we are well and truly in **Los Angeles ⑩** (see page 234), although most of this sprawling city's inland tourist attractions lie much farther north. LA's southern beaches are linked by a combination of Highway 1 and minor roads. After its chances of becoming a major port were wrecked by its vulnerability to severe storms **Redondo Beach** turned its attention to tourism. A Pacific Electric Railway developer hired a Hawaiian teenager called George Freeth to demonstrate surfing, and before long visitors were flocking to watch "the man who can walk on water."

In the 1930s, even bigger crowds were lured by the gambling ships moored offshore – the most famous being the *Rex*, which could accommodate 1,500 customers taking the 25 cents ride out to the boat from the town pier. Offshore gaming was outlawed by Congress in 1946, but a pier remains at the center of the town's colorful boardwalk. The current pier is horseshoe-shaped, after several predecessors were destroyed by storms, while Redondo Beach itself is a big draw for bodybuilders.

Gondola tour in Naples.

Follow Catalina Avenue from Redondo Pier to **Hermosa Beach** (www.hermosabch.org). An inland road leads past Kings Harbor Marina, opposite which an enormous ocean mural is painted on the wall of the power plant. Hermosa Avenue continues for quite a way one block from the beach. The beach itself stretches for eight sandy miles (13km) between Kings Harbor and **Marina Del Rey** (www.visitmarinadelrey.com), the longest uninterrupted stretch in Los Angeles County. There are pedestrian-only streets leading from Hermosa Avenue to the beach at every block. At 22nd Street, **Martha's 22nd Street Grill** (tel: 310-376-7786) is a good neighborhood place to sit outside, get a cup of coffee and do some people watching.

Hermosa Beach is known for its nightclubs, particularly the Lighthouse Cafe at the pier, a famed jazz club since 1949. Marina Del Rey is known for its child-friendly beaches. In between the two is **Manhattan Beach**, named by a homesick New Yorker who was living here in 1902, when it was a community of just a dozen families. Its population grew dramatically during World War II, when aircraft plants sprang up along Avalon Boulevard. In recent years, Roy E. Disney, nephew of Walt Disney, built the $90 million Raleigh's Manhattan Beach Studios, a series of 14 enormous sound stages, where series like The O.C. have been filmed. In addition, in the last few years, this part of Orange County has become second only to Hollywood as a venue for moviemakers, with its coastal piers especially attractive to the makers of television commercials. The scene down by the water resembles an old episode of *Baywatch*, with plenty of bronzed and beautiful joggers, rollerbladers, and volleyball players.

VENICE AND ITS CANALS

Just north of Marina Del Rey, the long pedestrian and bicycle path linking **Venice** ⓫ (and **Venice Beach**) with Santa Monica is a hive of activity, especially in Venice itself, where you'll

> **⊘ Fact**
>
> California's Manhattan Beach was named by a homesick New Yorker in 1902. Hermosa Beach stretches for 8 miles (13km) between Kings Harbor and Marina Del Rey, making it the longest in LA County.

Venice canal.

⊙ Tip

If you're passing through LA in September, visit the Greek Festival for a celebration of all things Hellenic, from ouzo and baklava to Greek dancing and raffles. Tel: 323-737-2424; www.lagreekfest.com.

encounter rollerbladers of both sexes, rainbow-haired punks, magicians, fortune tellers, itinerant musicians, and pumped-up bodybuilders flexing their biceps at **Muscle Beach**. You can rent rollerblades on Windward Avenue or a bicycle on Washington Street (opposite the abandoned pier), or just sit at one of the sidewalk cafés and admire the passing parade. The most interesting place to grab a snack in Venice is probably the art- and artist-filled **Rose Café** (www.rosecafvenice.com) on Rose Avenue. If you feel like getting away from the noise and the relentless body-beautiful activities, this is also a good spot from which to begin exploring Venice proper, which is surprisingly different from the image normally associated with the place.

The lesser-visited town of Venice is much more charming than the beach. Take a stroll through the residential area around the inland canals, where a proliferation of bright flowers tumbles over sagging fences and ducks nestle under upturned boats on tiny jetties. Visitors can pick their way along rutted paths, over gentle hump-backed bridges and past lovingly tended gardens, admiring the variegated architecture, numerous birds, and floral displays.

More than 70 years after the death of Abbott Kinney, who acquired and reclaimed what was worthless marshland in anticipation of creating an "Italy in California," some of his vision still remains in what is probably the most pleasant walk in urban Los Angeles.

The original circulation system for the canals – a design that envisaged seawater pulsing through 30-inch (76cm) pipes with every fresh tide – proved unworkable, and the canals themselves became sand-clogged and stagnant. In 1993, a $6 million overhaul dredged and refilled the canals, repaired the adjoining paths, and rebuilt some of the bridges.

SANTA MONICA PIER AND THE MOVIES

Santa Monica ⑫ is a seaside resort where West LA meets the ocean. You have to drive some distance inland on

Dusk falls over Santa Monica Pier.

eeways to reach Tinsel Town's most mous attractions: Hollywood, Bev-ly Hills, Rodeo Drive. But here at e beach, things are much more laid ack, and the "Bay City" of Raymond handler novels is a pleasant place hang out. The boulevards and side reets are attractive places to stroll nd shop. Trendy **Third Street** pedes-ian mall, originally designed in 1980 y Frank Gehry, a Venice resident, and vamped in 2010 as an outdoor mall ned with restaurants, stores, bars, nd movie theaters, is usually filled th street performers by day and ghtlife seekers after dark.

The town's recognizable landmark century-old **Santa Monica Pier** ttp://santamonicapier.org), which has an ssortment of amusement arcades, irground rides, souvenir stands, nack bars, and sedentary fishermen ong its lengthy boardwalk. There's so a wonderful carousel with 44 and-carved horses, which featured in e 1973 film *The Sting*. On either side the wide, sandy beach bordered by a usy bicycle path.

Clifftop **Palisades Park**, a euca-lyptus-fringed grassy stretch along Ocean Avenue, overlooks the beach and offers stunning views of boats and sunsets. The park is popular with the homeless – although their presence should not deter you from visiting. To one side is an information cabin for brochures and useful tips on where to catch local buses. Main Street, with its murals, shops, and numerous excellent restaurants, is also worth exploring. Looming over the corner with Rose Avenue is Jona-than Borofsky's giant sculpture, *Bal-lerina Clown*.

The mansions along the seashore at the northern end of Santa Monica were mostly built by moviedom's former elite. The grandest, at 415 Pacific Coast Highway, was the 118-room compound designed for William Randolph Hearst and his paramour, Marion Davies. The mansion has been demolished, but its restored ornate marble pool is open to the public. The site is now home to Annenberg Community Beach House (http://beachhouse.smgov.net).

San Francisco.

LOS ANGELES TO SAN FRANCISCO

This legendary stretch of Highway 1 takes in California's most famous attractions on the coast: extravagant Hearst Castle and fog-shrouded Big Sur.

The distance from Los Angeles to San Francisco is 380 miles (611km). Taking I-5 all the way means a city-to-city trip can be accomplished in around six hours, but that would be a pity. Highway 1 hugs the coast almost the entire way, presenting heart-stopping curves, breathtaking scenery, pretty inns, scenic sites, and two of California's best attractions – Hearst Castle and Big Sur. With all of this to savor, allowing two days rather than six hours makes far more sense.

LOS ANGELES TO SANTA BARBARA

The Pacific Coast Highway out of Los Angeles cruises through **Malibu** ⑬. Malibu is largely residential – much of the beach is private for the exclusive use of Malibu Colony residents – but you won't want to miss **The Getty Villa** (tel: 310-440-7300; www.getty.edu/visit; Wed–Mon; tickets must be booked in advance). The original home of the Getty Museum replicates an ancient Roman villa and was built by millionaire J. Paul Getty to house his superb collection of Greek, Roman, and Etruscan antiquities. The new Getty Center, an elegant modern travertine structure designed by Richard Meier, sits atop a hillside in the Santa Monica Mountains overlooking the San Diego Freeway (Getty Center Drive exit) and is well worth a visit.

Getty Villa, Malibu.

North of Malibu, get out and walk on some wonderful beaches – **Point Dume**, **Zuma**, and **Leo Carrillo** – before Highway 1 turns inland toward Ventura and merges with US 101 (the "Ventura Freeway" of the old America song). **Ventura** ⑭ has a restored Old Town historic district with the Rubicon Theatre in an old church, art galleries, and interesting shopping. The main attraction is the pretty 1782 **San Buenaventura Mission** (tel: 805-643-4318; www.sanbuenaventuramission.org; daily), Father Serra's last mission.

Main attractions

Malibu
Channel Islands
Santa Barbara
Pismo State Beach
San Luis Obispo
Morro Bay
Paso Robles wine region
Hearst Castle
Piedras Blancas beach
Big Sur
Carmel
Monterey

Map on page 320

You'll find good seafood restaurants at the harbor, connected to the rest of the town by trolley.

CHANNEL ISLANDS NATIONAL PARK

Ventura is important as the main headquarters for **Channel Islands National Park** (tel: 805-658-5730; www.nps.gov/chis; daily), which protects five offshore islands – Santa Barbara, Anacapa, Santa Cruz, Santa Rosa, and San Miguel. Transportation from the mainland is via commercial boat to the islands or chartered flight to Santa Rosa and San Miguel. You can hike and camp on all the islands; one of the most enjoyable is **San Miguel**, a premier spot for viewing six species of seals and sea lions. The National Park Service operates visitor centers in Ventura, Santa Barbara, and on **East Santa Cruz Island**, at the 1866 **Scorpion Ranch Visitor Center**.

Inland along State Route 150, edged by Los Padres National Forest, is **Ojai** (pronounced "o-hi"), a sleepy art colony, near the location for the 1926 movie *Lost Horizon*. The town's Main Street has a graceful tower that offsets a row of unpretentious shops under a portal. Artifacts in Ojai Valley Museum (tel: 805-640-1390; www.ojaivalleymuseum.org; Tue–Sun) include those from prehistoric Chumash Indians through the ranching period to the days when heavyweight boxing champion Jack Dempsey cleared rocks from what became "Pop" Soper's training ranch.

SANTA BARBARA

In **Santa Barbara** ⑮, following a destructive 1925 earthquake, the city fathers ruled that the town should be rebuilt using Spanish Colonial—style architecture – white-washed adobe, red-tiled roofs, and iron grillwork, and today it is one of the most beautiful cities on the California coast. Celebrated as "Santa Teresa" in the late Sue Grafton's popular Kinsey Mulhone private eye stories, Santa Barbara is immediately recognizable. Largely that's due to its unique geography, which juxtaposes the soaring, east—west—trending Santa Ynez Mountains

Zuma Beach, Malibu.

with wildlife-rich beaches beneath steep cliffs, the sparkling waters of the Santa Barbara Channel, and a relaxed, moneyed lifestyle.

The 1782 **Mission Santa Barbara** (tel: 805-682-4713; www.santabarbaramission.org; daily) may have one of the best locations of any California mission: below the lush foothill drive known as the Riviera. Nearby is the tiny **Santa Barbara Museum of Natural History** (tel: 805-682-4711; www.sbnature.org; daily), which has an excellent collection of Chumash artifacts and a huge blue whale skeleton outside. A satellite, the **Sea Center**, is an interactive aquarium located down on historic **Stearns Wharf**, at the bottom of State Street.

Santa Barbara Harbor is the spot to enjoy fresh-off-the-boat seafood. Daily whale-watching excursions are available here between Christmas and late March, as well as year round trips to Santa Barbara Island, critical habitat for elephant seals in winter and California sea lions in spring, and a good birdwatching venue.

RED TILE WALKING TOUR

Explore downtown Santa Barbara using the self-guided Red Tile Walking Tour booklet, available at the **Santa Barbara Visitors** Center at Garden Street and Cabrillo Boulevard (tel: 805-965-3021; www.santabarbaraca.com; daily), the palm tree—lined seafront promenade. Two highlights include the handsome 1929 **Santa Barbara County Courthouse** (tel: 805-568-3070; www.santabarbaraca.com/businesses/santa-barbara-county-courthouse; daily), on East Anapamu, which has a lobby lined with mosaics and murals, grassy picnic areas, and one of the city's best views from its rooftop; a block away is **Santa Barbara Museum of Art** (tel: 805-963-4364; www.sbmuseart.org; Tue–Sun), a treat for art lovers. Among its large collection of world-class art are many French Impressionist paintings, including more Monets than any museum on the West Coast, as well as an antiquities collection to rival the Getty.

El Presidio de Santa Barbara State Historic Park (tel: 805-965-0093; www.sbthp.org; daily), on Canon Perdido

⊙ **Fact**

Los Padres National Forest (www.fs.usda.gov/lpnf) helps reintroduce California condors to the wild, manages the Black Mountain Wild Horse Territory, contains some of the best pictographs created by the Chumash Indians on rock outcroppings, and has numerous hiking and off-road vehicle trails.

Mission Santa Barbara.

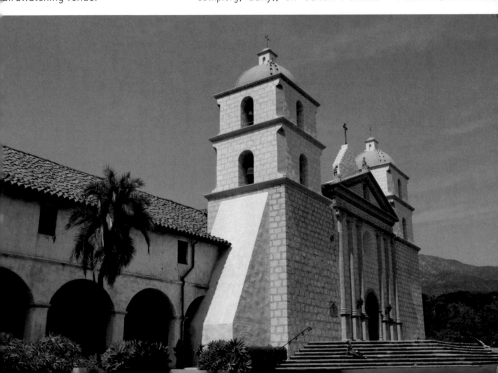

☉ Tip

The premier scenic drive in the Santa Barbara area heads over San Marcos Pass (State 154) to Los Olivos, for gorgeous views over the Santa Barbara Channel and the Santa Ynez Valley, the wine-growing region featured in the film *Sideways*. Continue west on State 246 through the Danish town of Solvang to Buellton to rejoin US 101. Loop back along the coast to Santa Barbara or continue north on 101.

Central Californian hillsides turn a verdant green after spring showers.

Street, housed the Spanish soldiers who protected Mission Santa Barbara. Tour the restored adobe chapel and other buildings, then have lunch in the charming 1920s shopping arcade of **El Paseo**, whose theater once featured a dancer named Rita Cansino, better known as Rita Hayworth.

SANTA BARBARA TO BIG SUR

After meandering through **Gaviota State Park** (tel: 805-968-1033; daily), Highways 1 and 101 turn inland and split. Continue on Highway 1 to sleepy **Lompoc**, home to **Mission La Purisima Concepcion** (tel: 805-733-3713; www.lapurisimamission.org; daily), California's 11th mission. North of town, the landscape is dominated by agribusiness, including irrigated fields of broccoli, cauliflower, and strawberries, and extensive fields of flowers, which in season offer an extraordinary display of magentas, pinks, golds, and purples.

This continues past **Guadalupe**, a quiet, old-fashioned town with an Amtrak station and one-story buildings dating to the turn of the 20th century. Eighteen miles (29km) north **Pismo State Beach**, once famous for its huge clams (still celebrated with a Clam Festival every October), has fabulous sandy shores stretching all around the bay and leads directly into San Luis Obispo, which is more or less the midway point between Los Angeles and San Francisco. Pismo is one of the few beaches where driving is allowed, so watch for dune buggies. Just before San Luis Obispo, keep an eye open for the extraordinary **Madonna Inn** (tel: 805-543-3000; www.madonnainn.com), whose 109 rooms are individually decorated in memorably kitsch fashion.

The attractive, low-key college town of **San Luis Obispo** ⑯ (SLO) also has an 18th-century mission (tel: 805-781-8220; daily), with a downtown community located around its plaza. There's a **Museum of Art** (tel: 805-543-8562; www.sloma.org; Tue–Sun, summer daily) and, across from the mission, the **History Center Museum** (http://historycenterslo.org; Wed–Mon).

MORRO BAY

Morro Bay is dominated by its 576ft (176-meter) -high volcanic rock, a nesting site for peregrine falcons, which divebomb their prey at astonishing speeds of 175mph (282kmh). You may catch glimpses of threatened snowy plovers if you hike and camp at popular **Montana de Oro State Park** (tel: 805-772-7434; www.slostateparks.com; camping reserations May–Sept), southwest of town. Morro Bay has a beautiful, sweeping, sandy beach and a restaurant-fringed harbor. Note: the harbor drive dead-ends in both directions, and parking can be difficult. Follow it to the end below Morro Rock, where you can watch sea lions and playful sea otters wrapping themselves in kelp. **The Museum of Natural History** (tel: 805-772-2694; daily) in **Morro Bay State Park** has exhibits on Central Coast wildlife and migratory Monarch butterflies. This short-lived beauty, with its amber and black wings, can be seen near Pacific Grove in winter.

Thirteen miles (21km) north, beyond the pretty town of **Cayucos**, is pastoral **Cambria**, set below the hills with its lovely Moonstone Beach. In between the two towns, State 46 winds east through the barren but beautiful hills of the Santa Lucia range, linking US 101 and **Paso Robles** (pronounced "paso ro-buls"). This is a charming, small, wine-producing region where most of the wineries offer free daily tastings. A map of local wineries is available from the Paso Robles Chamber Visitor Center (tel: 805-238-0506; www.pasorobleschamber.com), not far from **Paso Robles Pioneer Museum** (tel: 805-239-4556; www.pasoroblespioneermuseum.org; Thu–Sun pm).

HEARST CASTLE

Back on the coast, the hamlet of **San Simeon** sits below late newspaper and movie tycoon William Randolph Hearst's 250,000-acre (101,171-hectare) estate, best known for its owner's ravishingly beautiful home, **Hearst Castle** ⑰ (tel: 800-444-4445; www.hearstcastle.org; daily). Perched on what Hearst called "The Enchanted Hill," so high the house is often wreathed in fog, this was once the largest private residence in the US. Today, it rivals

Dune buggy on Pismo Beach's sand dunes.

⊘ **Tip**

Every Thursday night, part of San Luis Obispo's Higuera Street closes to traffic and transforms into a farmers' market and street fair with bands and entertainment.

Disneyland for California's most popular attraction.

Designed by architect Julia Morgan, the mansion began construction in 1919. Craftsmen labored for 28 years to create the twin-towered home, which Hearst then filled with carvings, furnishings, and works of art from European castles and cathedrals. (During his lifetime, Hearst accumulated one of the largest collections of private art in the world, with a value measured in the hundreds of millions of dollars.) All materials had to be brought up the coast by steamer, then hauled up that impossible hill. San Simeon's grounds were stocked with animals from all over the world, and Jean Harlow, Clark Gable, and other Hollywood royalty were invited to visit and stroll the beautiful gardens or enjoy the magnificent indoor and outdoor swimming pools.

Reservations are strongly recommended for one of the six daily tours leaving from the staging area below, some of which include the home movies of Hearst, whose lonely, lavish lifestyle

The stunning rocky coastline of Big Sur.

was the subject of Orson Welles's most celebrated movie, *Citizen Kane*. Tou[r] 1 is best for first-time visitors, as i[t] offers an overview of the castle an[d] main rooms. Although Hearst Castle i[s] extremely busy, especially during th[e] summer, the estate is efficiently run and timed entry means you can go awa[y] and have a picnic on the beach below i[f] the wait proves to be a long one.

Four miles (6km) north, Piedra Blancas is the birthplace each Janu[-]ary of thousands of elephant seals[.] Well into spring, from the walkwa[y] overlooking the beach, you can watc[h] the young pups learning to swim. Th[e] sheer number of these long-nose[d] creatures is amazing, and nowher[e] else on the coast can you see ther[e] this close.

BIG SUR

The 94-mile (151km) stretch of coast[-]line between San Simeon and the Mon[-]terey Peninsula is known as **Big Sur** ⑱ a legendary wilderness of holistic heal[-]ing retreats and remote homestead[s] inhabited by third-generation pioneer[s]

The area was barely accessible to traffic until 1937, and even now the sheer cliffs of the Santa Lucia Mountains hugged by the highway occasionally slide into the sea, leaving residents in complete isolation until the road is rebuilt. There are no roads inland between Cambria and Monterey, so check road conditions before proceeding. Fill your tank, preferably in Morro Bay, as prices leap in Cambria and gas stations beyond are few – and expensive – along this stretch.

The dark, thicketed mountains rise steeply to the right; the foamy sea to the left constantly changes shape and color. Only the two-lane road separates the two, which means the curling ribbon of road has its own distinct weather pattern. For this read: fog. Although the sun may be shining brightly on the other side of the mountain, and can often be seen slatted through the trees, Highway 1 can be distinctly chilly, and the fog comes on quickly, obliterating the world for unexpected moments. Infrequent guardrails, looking suspiciously flimsy, are small comfort in the face of the menacing rocks below.

Driving here is not for the faint-hearted, but for those with a sense of adventure and time on their side, this stretch of the California coastline is one of the most exhilarating routes in the US. Traveling nonstop with good weather, you could arrive in Carmel in about three hours, but the best way is to pause, at least for lunch or dinner. This is especially important for the person at the wheel, as the view is fabulous, but the road hazardous, and it can be frustrating (not to mention vertigo-inducing) if you don't take frequent stops. Luckily, scenic overlooks are numerous.

Coming from San Simeon, the hills begin gently enough, and the road is fairly easy to navigate. The first sight on the right is **Los Padres National Forest**, the southern tip of the coastal redwood belt, which contains several almost preternaturally beautiful state parks. **Julia Pfeiffer Burns State Park** and **Pfeiffer Big Sur State Park** have wonderful trails that lead up into the mountains or down toward the sea; Julia Pfeiffer

Hearst Castle.

Burns has a waterfall near McWay Cove, accessible via an easy hike.

BIG SUR COASTLINE AND ESALEN INSTITUTE

Big Sur Village ⑲ is just a stop in the road, really, with a few shops, a post office, and a handful of lodgings and eating places. If you're planning to stay overnight in summer or on a weekend, book well in advance. Accommodations range from campgrounds to luxury resorts and historic hostelries, such as Djeetjen's Big Sur Inn (www.deetjens. com), a charming family-run rustic inn built in the 1930s that is a good place to have a meal and mingle with interesting locals.

Until 1945, Big Sur was mainly populated by ranchers, loggers, and miners, but soon after began to attract writers. The **Henry Miller Memorial Library** (tel: 831-667-2574; www.henrymiller. org; daily), near spectacular **Nepenthe Restaurant** (www.nepenthebigsur.com), where everybody goes for drinks at sunset, preserves works by and about the world-famous author, who called the area "the face of the earth as the creator intended it to look."

In 1962, Michael Murphy and Richard Price moved to Murphy's cliffside family ranch at Big Sur, with others attracted by the human potential movement. Their idea was to create a residential retreat and center for alternative humanistic education, exploring and integrating ideas from the East and West, to help build a better world. Named **Esalen Institute** (www. esalen.org), after the Esselen tribe who once used the famous hot springs on the property, the stunning setting and intellectually challenging environment quickly attracted leading pioneers in spirituality, bodywork, psychology, and New Age thinking, from Fritz Perls, Ida Rolf, and Milton Trager to Allan Watts and Buckminster Fuller. Today, the nonprofit institute offers 500 residential workshops a year, lasting from a weekend to a week, including all meals from the organic gardens, (clothing-optional) hot springs access, and the chance to receive one of the world's best massages. The property is off

Paraglider along the coast on the Monterey Peninsula.

limits to non-workshop attendees, but occasionally, during the low season, its rustic lodgings are available for overnight stays. Check with the institute.

North of Big Sur is the area's crowning man-made achievement, **Bixby Bridge**. Spanning the steep walls of Bixby Canyon and often obscured by fog, the bridge was called an engineering marvel when it was constructed in 1932.

BIG SUR TO SAN FRANCISCO

Leaving the lush lands of Big Sur for the cities on the Monterey Peninsula can be a shock to the system. A way to ease this uncomfortable transition is to visit one last natural wonder on the way, the undramatic but still lovely **Point Lobos State Natural Reserve** (tel: 831-624-4909; daily). Miles of trails offer glimpses of deer, rabbits, sea lions, and sea otters. Robert Louis Stevenson is said to have been inspired to write *Treasure Island* while at Point Lobos. Several short footpaths traverse the rock-strewn headland, on which is one of two existing groves of ghostly Monterey Cypress trees.

CARMEL AND MONTEREY

Carmel ⓴, "Gateway to the Monterey Peninsula," once attracted famous artists and writers like poet Robinson Jeffers and photographer Edward Weston. It's a sign of the times that the cost of living here now makes pretty Carmel more of a place for selling creative works than making them. It's a classically beautiful little town, which has outlawed high-rises, neon signs, traffic lights, parking meters – anything possessing the foul taint of city life, including artificial house plants. Its residents include actors Clint Eastwood, who famously did a stint as the town's mayor, and Doris Day. Downtown is lined with upscale shops and galleries. **Mission San Carlos Borroméo del Río Carmelo**, otherwise known as **Carmel Mission** (tel: 831-624-1271; www.carmelmission. org; daily) and **Carmel Beach** are very appealing, and just to the north is **Pebble Beach**, home to the challenging golf course of the same name.

Motorcyclists are not barred from the peninsula's **17-Mile Drive**, which charges a hefty entrance fee to drive

Highway 1 runs almost the entire length of California. The Big Sur stretch is not for the faint-hearted.

Nepenthe restaurant overlooking Big Sur.

⊙ Tip

From the boardwalk behind the fog signal building at Pigeon Point Lighthouse, just south of San Francisco, keep an eye out for gray whales on their annual migration back to Alaska from Mexico, between January and April. The lighthouse grounds are open to the public.

around admiring its luxurious private homes. These look, in fact, much like any other affluent American neighborhood, and given the proximity to the exquisite Big Sur coast, this is a drive you can probably miss.

Cannery Row in **Monterey ㉑**, at the north end of the peninsula, basks in the glow of John Steinbeck's brilliant novel of the same name. Steinbeck's world withered with the mysterious disappearance of the sardines in the mid-1940s, and today his legacy is celebrated in nearby **Salinas**, at the **National Steinbeck Center** (tel: 831-796-3833; www.steinbeck.org; daily).

Cannery Row has become a bit of a tourist trap. A visit is redeemed, however, by a few hours spent at the excellent **Monterey Bay Aquarium** (tel: 831-648-4800; www.montereybayaquarium. org; daily), one of the best in the world, which offers innovative exhibits and interpretation on the marine life found in a Grand Canyon-sized trench just offshore. Wall-length tanks house sharks, regal salmon, and schools of tiny fish amid beds of kelp that writhe with the

simulated tides. Highlights include the Seahorses and Jellies exhibit. Try to time your visit to coincide with feeding time, when keepers in wet suits climb into the glass tanks and talk to spectators through underwater microphones. The sea otters are especially amusing.

Fisherman's Wharf is a delightful pier, lined with tourist shops, restaurants, and stands selling clam chowder in sourdough bread bowls. In the boat-filled harbor you'll see – and hear – resident seals. Inland from the pier, **Monterey State Historic Park** has 17 interesting museums and buildings from the town's days under Spanish, Mexican, and early American rule. Traffic on the stretch of coast north toward San Francisco can sometimes be horrendous. If so, you may wish to detour on State Highway 183 to **Castroville**, the "Artichoke Capital of the World," where the Giant Artichoke Restaurant serves the delicious deep-fried leaves.

SANTA CRUZ AND HALF MOON BAY

The communities in this heavily agricultural area of California have a

Vintage clothing store, Santa Cruz.

strong Mexican flavor, and all along Highway 1, you'll be surrounded by flat agricultural fields producing California's finest artichokes, cherries, and strawberries (all available fresh at roadside stands). The cute, colorful beach town of **Capitola** is a pleasant place for a stroll, its beach wall decorated with bright tiles. The university city of **Santa Cruz** ㉒ is famous for its century-old Beach Boardwalk, with a popular amusement park, thrilling roller coaster, and arcade games alongside the beach. Dine on yummy Dungeness crab in season in one of the restaurants on the pier, then drive along West Cliff Drive, lined with beautiful homes, to see surfers hitting the waves below the cliffs near the Santa Cruz Surfing Museum (www.santacruzsurfingmuseum.org).

Farther up the coast is the attractive wide beach at **Scott Creek**, north of **Davenport**. Tan, black, and white cows graze in fields high on the cliffs before Highway 1 swoops down to **Waddell Creek** and driftwood-lined beaches (such as Bean Hollow State Beach and Pescadero State Beach) all the way up to the Santa Cruz county line. Thin veils of fog sometimes obscure the view, but when it shifts (which it does every few minutes), drivers are rewarded by glimpses of **Pigeon Point Lighthouse** ㉓. At 115ft (35 meters), it is one of the tallest lighthouses in the country and has been in use since 1872.

Heading toward San Francisco, wide, flat fields lie between the highway and the coast. **Half Moon Bay** ㉔ is only half an hour's drive from the city and is famous not only for its pumpkins and nurseries but for the huge waves that pound its shores. Surfers from all around come to tackle the big ones – up to 40ft (12 meters) high – and the talk in the bars is of "mavericks" and "tubes." Sunday lunchtimes at Half Moon often include jazz or rock concerts.

With the city suburbs on the horizon, the coastline becomes rocky and untrafficked again. **Gray Whale Cove State Beach** or **Big Basin Park** are peaceful places for a final walk or picnic before hitting the big time – **San Francisco** (see page 344).

Bixby Bridge.

SAN FRANCISCO: CITY BY THE BAY

Fisherman's Wharf, Chinatown, the Golden Gate Bridge – this city wins hearts straightaway and effortlessly.

Each visitor takes away a different memory of San Francisco: the steep street that drops off toward the bay, the fog drifting through the Golden Gate Bridge, the dishes expertly blended to make the perfect meal, or the simple fun of a cable-car ride, admiring Victorian houses along the way.

Begin at **Union Square,** where a winged statue commemorates Admiral George Dewey's naval victory over the Spanish in 1898. **Chinatown Gate** appears just to the northeast. Chinatown is touristy, certainly, but the jostling crowds of Chinese residents on the sidewalk indicate that the area still caters to the Asian community. Tiny herb shops in mysterious alleys promise everything from rheumatism relief to the restoration of sexual prowess.

Chinatown ends where **North Beach** begins. While a few seedy clubs still promise lap dances,

Cable car trundles along Hyde Street.

critically acclaimed restaurants and posh nightclubs entice a different crowd altogether. But this traditional Italian neighborhood still attracts writers and artists, particularly legendary **City Lights** Booksellers and Publishers (www.citylights.com), co-founded by poet and publisher Lawrence Ferlinghetti in 1955, an unofficial meeting place for the Beat poets, including Jack Kerouac and Allen Ginsberg. At the time of this update, Ferlinghetti, almost 100 years old, is still active at the store.

To the east, **Telegraph Hill** rises above North Beach, offering spectacular views across San Francisco Bay. **Coit Tower** (tel: 415-249-0995; daily), with its momentous views and frescoes, crowns the hill and can be climbed. Follow Columbus Avenue to **Fisherman's Wharf** (www.fishermanswharf.org). Fishing boats put out before dawn; their catch determines the daily special at restaurants clustered around the wharf. A must for every visitor.

At the opposite end of the Embarcadero is another San Francisco landmark. Built in 1903, the **Ferry Building** survived the Great Fire and in its heyday was a hub for water transport between the bay communities. It has now been renovated to house the **Ferry Building Marketplace** (www.ferry buildingmarketplace.com), a foodie haven with a fantastic farmers' market and stalls selling artisan foods. From here you can ride the vintage electric streetcars of the F-line to **Fisherman's Wharf** or along Market Street to the **Castro district**.

A mile offshore from San Francisco is windswept **Alcatraz Island** (boat tickets – tel: 415-981-7625; www.alcatrazcruises.com; www.nps.gov/alca; daily), part of **Golden Gate National Recreation Area** (www.nps.gov/goga), the extensive Bay Area park system managed by the National Park Service. Once home to such hardened criminals as Al Capone and notorious Machine Gun Kelley, officials closed the prison in 1963, when repair costs grew too great. A tour of the prison is a fascinating and haunting experience; it also offers many surprises, including rare flora and fauna communities and historic buildings, as well as a deeper human past than you might expect, from Indian occupation to prison guard families. Bring a sweater for the breezy boat ride over.

A ride on the **Powell-Hyde cable car**, beginning two blocks inland from Hyde Street Pier, offers a tour of Russian Hill's high-rise apartments and mansions. The cable car passes near the curvy section of Lombard Street often seen in movies and continues to **Nob Hill**, dubbed the "hill of palaces" by Robert Louis Stevenson.

At the corner of Washington and Mason streets, **San Franciso Cable Car Museum** (tel: 415-474-1887; www.cablecarmuseum.org; daily) exhibits the city's transit history alongside the operating machinery that pulls the glamorous transportation through town.

The Financial District holds three impressive landmarks. **The Embarcadero Center; the Bank of America building** – so tall its roof sometimes disappears in the fog; and the distinctive **Transamerica Pyramid**, with 48 floors the tallest building in San Francisco.

"South of Market," or **SoMa**, is a focal point for art galleries, cafés, nightclubs, and local theaters. **San Francisco Museum of Modern Art** (tel: 415-357-4000; www.sfmoma.org; Thu–Tue) spearheads attractions that include Yerba Buena Gardens, Yerba Buena Center for the Arts, the Cartoon Art Museum, the California Historical Society research library and gallery, and independent bookstore Alexander Book Company. The **Asian Art Museum** (tel: 415-581-3500; www.asianart.org; Tue–Sun) is in the Civic Center district. It contains 10,000 artifacts dating back 3,500 years.

Mission Street heads south into the heart of the **Mission district**, San Francisco's melting pot of Latin American cultures. The thick adobe walls of **Mission Dolores**, built in 1776, protect the oldest building in San Francisco open to the public.

To the west lies the celebrated gay community of **The Castro**. Same-sex couples and rainbow flags fill the streets lined with table-hopping bars. It's a lively, fun, and light-hearted area, regardless of your gender.

Farther west is the **Haight-Ashbury district**. Haight Street was once so gaudy and bizarre that tour buses full of goggle-eyed tourists ran up and down it. Like most such radical departures from the social norm, the hippie experiment fell victim to time and fashion. The neighborhood retains its anti-establishment roots, but today piercing shops and tattoo parlors replace flower power. It's still a fun stretch, however, with great shopping and a wide range of inexpensive restaurants and cafés.

Golden Gate Park (tel: 415-831-2700; www.goldengatepark.com), 3 miles (5km) long and almost half a mile wide, consists of tree groves dotted with lakes, meadows, windmills, and dells. Despite 13 million visitors a year, it's surprisingly easy to find tranquility. In addition to peace, the Conservatory of Flowers offers sweet scents and botanical beauty, and the Music Concourse holds free Golden Gate Park Band performances at 1pm on Sundays.

California Academy of Sciences (tel: 415-379-8000; www.calacademy.org; daily) includes animal dioramas, 16,000 specimens of marine life at Steinhart Aquarium, and a laser light show at Morrison Planetarium. **The Japanese Tea Garden** (http://japaneseteagardensf.com) claims to be the birthplace of the fortune cookie.

The beautiful and neoclassical **Legion of Honor** (tel: 415-750-3600; http://legionofhonor.famsf.org; Tue–Sun) is unmissable. At the entrance is one of five bronze casts of Rodin's *The Thinker*.

Golden Gate Bridge extends beyond Golden Gate National Recreation Area. A promenade goes through Crissy Field, an airfield-turned-picnic area that belongs to the 1,480-acre (600-hectare) **Presidio**. A military post for over 200 years, it is now a shoreline park with beaches, woods, historical sites, a golf course, and 11 miles (18km) of hiking trails.

Street in the Castro district.

Drive-Thru Tree, Klamath.

SAN FRANCISCO TO OREGON

The Pacific Coast Highway, also known as Highway 1,
threads its way past golden beaches, hot-tub hideaways,
famed wineries, and the tallest living things on Earth.

's 363 miles (548km) north from San Francisco to the town of Crescent City, about half an hour's drive from the California-Oregon border. Beaches, wineries, and redwood forests are the attractions of this beautiful journey, with trees so massive you can even drive through a few of them.

PCH passes through windblown San Francisco ㉕ (see page 344), traversing Golden Gate Park and Golden Gate Bridge, two units of 75,000-acre (30,351-hectare) **Golden Gate National Recreation Area** (tel: 415-561-4700; www.nps.gov/goga; daily), the largest urban park in the world, preserving significant natural and cultural sites (including Alcatraz Island) in a setting that is hard to beat.

The pretty little harbor town of **Saualito** ㉖ is right off Highway 1/101, after Golden Gate Bridge and Marin Headlands. With its bustling marina, ricey waterside boutiques, and hillside mansions, it's a postcard-pretty place to stroll and enjoy seafood. Just north, Highway 1 (Shoreline Highway) heads west, twisting and turning to the coast.

South of the highway is **Green Gulch Farm Zen Center** (tel: 415-863-3136; www.sfzc.org/green-gulch), a popular retreat center that offers workshops, lectures, public meditation programs, and overnight accommodations on a gorgeous organic farm. Nearby are

Mount Tamalpais State Park (tel: 415-388-2070; www.parks.ca.gov; daily) and the giant redwoods of 300-acre (120-hectare) **Muir Woods National Monument** (tel: 415-388-2595; www.nps.gov/muwo; daily) – both with terrific hiking, sweeping views, and local history.

At rugged **Stinson Beach**, a popular beach destination for San Franciscans, the slow coast road heads north past **Bolinas Lagoon**, a rich wetland protected by Audubon, and on to spectacular **Point Reyes National Seashore** (tel: 415-464-5100; www.nps.gov/pore;

Map on page 348

⊙ Main attractions
Point Reyes National Seashore
Sonoma Valley
Napa Valley
Bodega Bay
Mendocino
Avenue of the Giants
Ferndale
Eureka
Redwood National Park

Wine tasting in Napa Valley.

San Francisco to Seattle

California

- Napa (12, 121) (116) Petaluma
- (29) Sonoma (12) (116)
- Santa Rosa
- Salt Point State Park
- Van Damme State Park
- **31** Avenue of the Giants – Humboldt Redwoods S.P. (101)
- Humboldt Bay National Wildlife Refuge
- Patrick's Point State Park (101)
- Redwood N.P.
- Jedediah Smith Redwoods State Park
- Gasquet (199)
- **California / Oregon**
- Harris Beach State Park
- Cape Blanco
- Bandon Marsh National Wildlife Refuge
- Oregon Dunes National Recreation Area **40** (101)
- Cape Perpetua
- **44** Yaquina Head Lighthouse
- Devil's Punchbowl ★
- Cape Meares Lighthouse
- Oswald West State Park (101)
- Lewis and Clark National Historical Park
- **Oregon / Washington**
- Ilwaco
- (105)
- (12)
- **53** Seattle (101)

- San Francisco **25**
- ◎ Sausalito **26**
- Point Reyes National Seashore (1)
- Inverness ●
- Bodega
- Bodega Bay **27**
- Jenner
- ★ Fort Ross State Historic Park
- Stewarts Point
- Gualala
- ★ Point Arena Lighthouse **28**
- Elk
- Albion
- ◎ Mendocino **29**
- Fort Bragg **30**
- ◎ Westport
- Leggett — Lost Coast
- Garberville
- Phillipsville — Cape Mendocino Lighthouse
- Scotia
- (211) Ferndale **32**
- Fortuna
- Eureka **33**
- Arcata
- McKinleyville (101)
- Trinidad **34**
- Orick
- Thomas H. Kuchel Visitor Center
- Klamath **35**
- Trees of Mystery
- Crescent City **36**
- Brookings-Harbor **37**
- Samuel H. Boardman State Scenic Corridor
- Gold Beach
- Humbug Mountain State Park
- Port Orford **38**
- Langlois
- Bandon **39**
- Coos Bay — Charleston
- North Bend — Shore Acres State Park
- Umpqua Lighthouse
- Reedsport
- Gardiner
- Florence
- Sea Lion Caves
- Yachats **41**
- Waldport **42**
- Newport **43**
- ★ Depoe Bay
- Lincoln City **45**
- Devil's Lake State Recreation Area
- ● Siuslaw National Forest
- Cloverdale (101)
- Tillamook **46**
- (6) Portland **47**
- Garibaldi
- Rockaway Beach
- Manzanita
- Cannon Beach **48**
- Seaside **49**
- Warrenton
- Astoria **50**
- Lewis and Clark National Wildlife Refuge
- Columbia
- (103) Long Beach
- Oysterville
- Willapa Bay — Cape Disappointment State Park & Lighthouse
- South Bend **51**
- Raymond
- Grayland
- Aberdeen **52**
- *Olympic Peninsula*

---

daily), the highlight of this scenic drive with its sweeping shoreline, marine life, cows grazing on lush grass, and historic **Point Reyes Lighthouse** (tel: 415-669-1534; visitor center and light house stairs: summer Thu–Mon, rest of the year Fri–Mon). Plan on stopping for a meal or spend the night in inviting **Inverness**, which has several inns and a good deli diner.

The delicious milk from those grazing cows is the secret to the spectacular farmstead and artisan cheeses now being made in Marin. Some of the best come from **Cowgirl Creamery** (tel: 415-663-9335; www.cowgirlcreamery.com; Wed–Sun), with creameries in Petaluma and Point Reyes Station where you can watch their award-winning cheeses being made, take a class, and buy cheese. Prince Charles and his wife Camilla, Duchess of Cornwall, visited in 2005, largely drawn by the excellent local foods in this region.

WINE COUNTRY

You can take the road east from Point Reyes Station (or Highway 101 north from Sausalito through Novato) to **Petaluma**, turning east on Highway 116. After the upscale communities crowded around the bay, the beautifully open, rolling hills and farmland of Marin County make for a very enjoyable drive to historic **Sonoma**, hub of the Sonoma Valley wine country.

With numerous distinguished wineries and tasting rooms spread throughout the 17-mile (6.9-hectare) valley, Sonoma feels less hectic than its famous neighbor, Napa. Highlights include the Gloria Ferrer Champagne Caves, Château St Jean, and Buena Vista Winery, California's oldest winery, dating from 1857. A guide to wine-tasting throughout the valley is available from Sonoma Valley Visitors Bureau in the Historic Plaza on First Street (tel: 707-996-1090; www.sonomavalley.com; daily).

On the east side of the mountains Highway 29 runs through America's most renowned wine region, **Napa Valley**. Some 400 wineries lie cheek by jowl in this beautiful rolling landscape, ranging from boutique winemakers to vast corporate operations. It can be a little overwhelming for first-time visitors, so stop by the Napa Valley Welcome Center (tel: 707-251-5895; www.visitnapavalley.com; daily) in downtown **Napa** for a guide to tastings and tours.

There are tasting rooms in Napa itself, an attractive riverside town with good restaurants, gourmet food shops, and galleries. Pretty **St Helena**, with its lovely old homes and upscale shopping, is a favorite base. At the northern end of the valley, **Calistoga** is most appealing of all, with its mineral baths, arcaded Victorian-era Main Street, and casual air. Note: Large, destructive wildfires have become more common in California, and in the summer of 2018, the Mendocino Complex Wildfire, north of Napa, one of 16 major wildfires burning up California, became the state's biggest wildfire in history, burning more than 290,000 acres.

BODEGA BAY, BIRDS AND BEACHES

Back on the coast, Highway 1 winds along beautiful Tomales Bay, passing oyster farms and rustic hamlets like Olema and historic Tomales, with its 1850s wooden buildings.

It's no coincidence that Alfred Hitchcock filmed his 1963 movie *The Birds* around **Bodega Bay** ㉗, where hundreds of bird species can be found. Brown pelicans are especially abundant. Just to the south and slightly inland, in the separate village of **Bodega**, you can see the schoolhouse and St Teresa's church that featured in the movie.

After **Sonoma Coast State Beach**, another really dramatic portion of the California coast begins, where Rivers End sits overlooking the mouth of the Russian River at **Jenner**. For miles, Highway 1 snakes around the canyon at ascending levels. The top of a subsequent canyon has been plugged with stone, making a bridge on which to site the road.

The road passes the timbered stockade of **Fort Ross State Historic Park** (tel: 707-847-3437; www.fortross.

Hot-air balloons over Napa Valley.

Napa and Sonoma valleys are great destinations for scenic roadtrips.

org; daily). For history buffs, it's worth exploring the cannon-studded fort, with its church and blockhouses – if only to wonder how 19th-century Russian otter hunters withstood the rugged winters in flimsy wooden buildings on one of the windiest parts of the coast. So well fortified were they that their Native American and Spanish neighbors left them alone. In 1842, after 30 years of relentless otter hunting (for furs), they sold out to rancher John Sutter and left.

At **Salt Point State Park** (www.parks.ca.gov), the trees march down to the water's edge as you drive through this lovely pine-scented stretch. Off the highway, other beaches abound – such as Stump Beach and Fisk Mill Cove. Much of the time, you'll find yourself a solitary visitor, as swimming is unsafe due to riptides and what the US Coast Guard calls "sleeper waves." **Stewarts Point** was once a "doghole" for schooners, so-called because of its anchorages, so tiny "only a dog could fit into them." After Pebble Beach, Stengel Beach, and 8 more miles

On the road to Mendocino.

(13km) of a winding two-lane road, a bridge across the Gualala River marks the end of Sonoma County.

MENDONOMA

Mendonoma, a name derived from the adjoining counties of Sonoma and Mendocino, identifies the coastal region between the Russian River at Jenner and the Navarro River, north of Point Arena. A heterogeneous mix of Russians, Germans, and Spaniards settled **Gualala** (pronounced "wah-lah-lah") in the 1800s, which by the middle of the last century had four sawmills and four bars. Wells Fargo and Western Union had offices in the Gualala Hotel, built by the town's founder in 1903, when a room with bath and ocean view cost $5. The writer Jack London stayed here a century ago, and things don't appear to have altered much. Since the last mill closed, tourism has filled the gap.

The town's name is a local Native American word that translates as "where the waters flow down," and you can paddle up the estuary of the Gualala River in a canoe or kayak,

looking for the osprey, heron, king-fisher, and river otter that make their homes here. Many local artists reside in and around the town, which has numerous galleries and shops. A full program of concerts and theatrical performances takes place at **Gualala Arts Center** (tel: 707-884-1138; www.gualalaarts.org; daily), which also hosts the Art in the Redwoods festival in August and the Sonoma Mendocino Coast Whale and Jazz Festival in April.

A wooden Old West structure with a tower marks a general merchandise store at **Anchor Bay**. After this, the coast-hugging, sometimes lonely road seems mostly deserted. Fifteen miles (24km) of winding two-lane highway allow ample time to contemplate that state law decreeing that slow-moving vehicles must use a turn-off if five or more vehicles back up behind them.

Beyond the cute town of Point Arena, one of the truly great coastal experiences is **Point Arena Lighthouse** ㉘ (tel: 707-882-2809; www.pointarenalighthouse.com; daily), the tip of which can be spotted at the beginning of the 2-mile (3km) diversion. A classically beautiful 111ft (34-meter) -high white tower with 145 steps, it replaced an earlier light-house damaged by the 1906 San Francisco earthquake. Its 2-ton (1,800kg) French-made Fresnel lens (floating on a tub of mercury) was itself replaced in the 1970s with an aircraft-type beacon. It is maintained by a nonprofit group of local citizens, and you can even spend the night in one of several attractive vacation rentals in former keeper's apartments and houses.

Miles of open pasture dotted with ram-shackle barns and grazing cows follow Point Arena. The road then dips, turns, climbs, and dives, winding through tiny **Elk** and **Albion**, pretty roadside com-munities on either side of the Navarro River, with sloping tracks down to the beach. Look down as the road crosses the Albion River Bridge for a lovely view of the river flowing out to meet the sea,

with big rock outcrops framing the riv-er's mouth just offshore. There's another pretty crossing at Little River as the high-way twists and turns around high cliffs before descending to a leafy stretch past **Van Damme State Park** (which contains a "pygmy forest" of pines and cypresses), offering occasional glimpses of the sea.

MENDOCINO

The lovely old town of **Mendocino** ㉙ was established by New England whal-ers and is one of the most admired places on the coast. It is a big hit with day-trippers, but if you choose to linger and stay the night, you'll be rewarded with great restaurants (some with health-conscious menus), numerous small bed-and-breakfast inns, as well as art galleries, jewelry and gift shops, and quaint cafés. The entire village is on the National Register of Historic Places. Among several Victorian homes exhib-iting period pieces are the 1854 **Ford House Museum and Visitor Center** (tel: 707-937-5397; www.mendoparks.org; Fri–Mon) and the 1861 **Kelley House** (tel: 707-937-5791; kelleyhousemuseum.org;

Statue in Mendocino.

Point Arena Lighthouse.

⊙ Tip

If you don't feel like driving the fairly arduous four to five-hour round trip to see the hidden attractions of California's Lost Coast, you can hire a guide in Ferndale to do it for you. Inquire locally for details.

Fri–Mon). **Mendocino Art Center** (tel: 707-937-5818; www.mendocinoartcenter. org; Wed–Sun), founded by Bill and Jennie Zaca in 1959, showcases work by local and national artists. Paths lead along the cliffs overlooking Mendocino Bay with lovely views. Note: parking in Mendocino is tight.

North of Caspar, delightful **Mendocino Coast Botanical Gardens** (tel: 707-964-4352; www.gardenbythesea.org; daily) is worth a stop, if only to walk through the aromatic pine forest to the sea, enjoying the interplay of light and shade. It's a good place for whale watching in season. Plants can be bought here, too. Nearby **Noyo Harbor** was once the biggest lumber port between Eureka and San Francisco. It's now a marina for sport fishing boats and the waterfront has plenty of restaurants. Goldie Hawn and Kurt Russell sailed out of the harbor at the end of the movie Overboard.

FORT BRAGG

An 1820 shipwreck led to the founding of **Fort Bragg** ㉚, when treasure seekers came to loot the wreckage and discovered the redwoods. A fort was built, and the Bureau of Indian Affairs established a reservation for the Pomo Indians. Lumber mills sprang up, along with a railroad to transport their product. When the 1906 earthquake devastated much of San Francisco, it was Fort Bragg's mills that provided the wood for rebuilding. The famous old **Skunk Train** (tel: 707-964-6371; www.skunktrain.com), which once carried lumber across the mountains to the sawmill at Willits, has been a tourist favorite for years. It still follows the same picturesque route along the Noyo River and through redwood groves.

What remains of the original fort, along with surviving Victorian buildings, can be seen one block east of Main Street (Highway 1), near the Skunk Train depot at Laurel and Franklin. Both the 1892 **Guest House Museum** (tel: 707-964-4251; www.fortbragghistory.org; May–Oct daily, Nov–Apr Thu–Sun), with displays on local history, and award-winning **North Coast Brewing Company** (tel: 707-964-2739; www.northcoastbrewing.com), a pioneer in the microbrewery movement,

Walking through wildflowers along the Lost Coast Trail.

founded in 1988, are on Main Street. Fort Bragg is an unpretentious working town that also blossoms with nurseries, one of which grows millions of trees for reforestation projects.

THE LOST COAST

Pretty hamlets and gorgeous views of crashing breakers and surf mark the winding coastal road beyond Fort Bragg. North of **Westport**, after 22 miles (35km) of dramatic, picturesque coastline, Highway 1 takes a final look at the sea before heading 25 miles (40km) inland. Here, it merges with US 101 at Leggett and – apart from a brief stretch near Eureka – disappears forever.

The relatively inaccessible (and unpaved) coastal road travels through primitive **Sinkyone Wilderness State Park** (www.parks.ca.gov; limited facilities) on the celebrated **Lost Coast**, an area of "black sand beaches and old-growth forests on a wall of windswept peaks," as one writer noted. Beyond the state park, in **King Range National Conservation Area** (www.blm.gov/visit/king-range), 35 miles (56km) of coastal trails and six campgrounds are managed by the Bureau of Land Management.

Once slated for an extension of Highway 1, the coast can be visited via a loop road picked up at the town of Weott, north of Leggett. The narrow side road crosses the Mattole River at Honeydew, heads through Petrolia, site of California's first but disappointingly unproductive oil strike, and follows the coast north to Ferndale, where it veers inland again to rejoin US 101.

AVENUE OF THE GIANTS

South again, Highway 1 climbs through coastal redwood forest and merges into US 101 at **Leggett**, where you'll find redwood figures carved with chainsaws (Big Foot is a favorite) and **Confusion Hill** (tel: 707-925-6456; www.confusionhill. com; daily). The latter is a classic Forties roadside attraction that kids and adults will enjoy, including a funicular ride up

the mountain, the world's tallest carved totem pole, a house made out of a redwood log, and a gravity house, where water runs uphill, a golf ball climbs a slope, and a chair prevents you from getting up without using your arms. Some of the effects are obviously optical illusions, but the owner says there are things he still hasn't figured out.

Containing several restaurants and motels, **Garberville** is a pleasant little place to break your journey before heading into redwood country proper. Farther north, at **Phillipsville**, the 31-mile (50km) **Avenue of the Giants** ③ offers an irresistible alternative to US 101, to which it runs parallel, allowing occasional on-off access. Some trees here are more than 300ft (91 meters) tall and 20ft (6 meters) in diameter. "From them comes silence," wrote John Steinbeck.

A handful of buildings are all that remain of two small towns that straddled the route until they were washed away by floods in 1964. Otherwise, the route through this stupendous 50,000-acre (20,250-hectare) redwood forest shows

The Drive-Thru Tree (Chandelier Tree) in Leggett.

Avenue of the Giants.

no signs of human habitation. A series of small groves is dedicated to various groups and individuals that have fought to preserve this magnificent enclave. They are places for contemplation. "We do not see nature with our eyes," wrote William Hazlitt, "but with our under-standings and our hearts." Many of the trees on the east side were planted in the 1980s, as reforestation projects. Near the town of **Myers Flat** is the **Shrine Drive-Thru Tree** (tel: 707-943-1975; www. famousredwoods.com/shrine), where you can drive through a huge redwood tree, a favorite with children and tourists (con-fusingly, there is another Drive-Thru Tree nearby – the Chandelier Tree in Leggett). Before Weott, **Humboldt Redwoods State Park Visitor Center** (tel: 707-946-2263; http://humboldtredwoods.org; daily) offers useful interpretive exhibits about coastal redwoods *(Sequoia sempervirens)*, which attract arborphiles from around the world.

REDWOOD TREES

Redwood has long been prized for its density and deep color, and despite slumps in the building industry and competition from more common trees such as cedar, it remains in demand. The logging industry, which grew up with the Gold Rush, made hardly a dent in the red-wood belt until the advent of chainsaws in the 1940s, paving the way for acres of redwoods to be clearcut in a single day. It takes 40 years to raise a stand of red-woods for pulp, press board, and other uses, and 500 years to develop the fine grain and blood-red tint that have made the wood so popular. Conservationists estimate that trees are logged at two and a half times the rate of regeneration.

The redwoods inspire not only passing tourists but also constitute the entire livelihood of the Humboldt community. Sculptors carve timbers into life-sized grizzly bears for sale at the roadside. Others, for a pretty hefty admission fee, show off the stout trunks growing in their backyards. Huge logging trucks carrying both raw timber and finished boards along the highway are a constant reminder that the trees in this area are an economic necessity as well as a natural wonder.

Fortuna Depot Museum (tel: 707-725-7645; www.sunnyfortuna.com/museum; June–Aug daily, Sept–May Thu–Sun) features local logging and railroad-ing history. Located on a back road between Fortuna and Eureka is minus-cule **Loleta**, celebrated for cheese and ice-cream production. Its factory, which featured in the 1982 movie *Hallow-een III: the Season of the Witch*, makes supermarket ice cream in loads of vari-eties for numerous companies.

FERNDALE'S VICTORIAN HISTORY

Ferndale ㉜, on the Eel River west of US 101 (reached by turning west off the highway, just north of Fortuna) has so many brightly painted Victorian stores and houses – many of which have been converted into enticing bed-and-breakfasts – the whole town has been designated a state historical landmark.

Walking through the majestic groves in Humboldt Redwoods State Park.

The elaborately turreted and gabled **Gingerbread Mansion Inn** (http://ginger bread-mansion.com) on Berding Street is outstanding, and the town's oldest building, the 18-room **Shaw House Inn** (www.shawhouse.com) is fashioned after Nathaniel Hawthorne's *House of the Seven Gables*. The year-round mild climate encourages enthusiastic gardening – don't be surprised if you see cypress topiaries shaped like giant gumdrops; it's that kind of town.

At the top of Main Street is the 110-year-old **Victorian Inn** (www.victorian villageinn.com). Also notable is **Ferndale Emporium** (www.ferndale-emporium.com), farther down the street, which serves genteel afternoon teas from Thursday to Saturday. You can learn more about the town's history in the **Ferndale Museum** (tel: 707-786-4466; www.fern dale-museum.org; Wed–Sat).

A top-hatted driver offers rides around town in a horse and carriage, while there's a genuine soda fountain on Main Street. Understandably, Ferndale attracts moviemakers, who use its setting for movie and TV dramas. The town is also the birthplace of the delightful Kinetic Sculpture Race, which sees its people-powered models competing in the annual three-day race from Arcata.

CAPE MENDOCINO LIGHTHOUSE AND EUREKA

The drive south along the Lost Coast from Ferndale follows the old stage-coach route known locally as Wildcat Road, it climbs high into the hills, then, after 30 miles (48km) of twists and turns, descends to cross the Bear River and arrive at the defunct community of Capetown. Off the deserted black sand beach is the immense Sugarloaf Rock and nearby Steamboat Rock, which resembles a big tanker stranded at sea.

Cape Mendocino is the westernmost point in California. **Cape Mendocino Lighthouse** was completed in 1868 only after a two-year struggle to bring materials in by sea and haul them up the steep cliff. Although it warned countless vessels of the treacherous waters, at least nine ships were wrecked off this rugged shore during its 83-year history. Decommissioned

Ferndale's Victorian architecture.

The Gingerbread Mansion Inn in Ferndale is named for the lavishly ornamented style of Victorian architecture.

The highly embellished Carson Mansion in Eureka was designed by San Francisco architects Samuel and Joseph Newsome.

Eureka is known for its sizeable number of Victorian buildings.

in 1951, the wind and sea would have claimed the lighthouse, too, but it was rescued and restored in 1999 and now stands in a park at the edge of Point Delgada (open Memorial Day–Labor Day, when guides are available).

Back on the main road, Highway 101 returns to the coast at Humboldt Bay, where it passes several of 10 units of **Humboldt Bay National Wildlife Refuge** (www.fws.gov/refuge/humboldt_bay; daily). As a key stop on the Pacific Flyway, it provides protected wetland habitat for tens of thousands of migratory water birds, including Aleutian cackling geese and shorebirds.

The biggest coastal city on the California coast north of San Francisco, **Eureka** ⑬ (pop. 27,000) and its **Old Town** on the waterfront often stands in for Fog City in movies. Early guests at the landmark **Eureka Inn** (www.eurekainn.com), a massive Tudor Revival mansion built in 1922, included Laurel and Hardy, Shirley Temple, John Barrymore, and Britain's Winston Churchill, who stopped in Eureka to visit an old friend who was editing the local

paper. After closing for six years, the inn underwent renovations and reopened in 2010 under new owners. The town's distinctive 1886 **Carson Mansion** – built by a lumber baron with a yen for gables, towers, and turrets – is generally regarded as the handsomest Victorian building in the state, if not in the entire West. It is now a private club.

At **Blue Ox Millworks** (tel: 707-444-3437; www.blueoxmill.com; Mon–Fri, Apr–Nov Sat), a working Victorian sawmill, visitors can watch craftsmen at work and see how much of the characteristic "gingerbread" ornamentation for such houses was crafted. The old Carnegie Library on F Street, with its wonderful balconies and redwood pillars, has been converted into the enjoyable Morris Graves Museum of Art (tel: 707-442-0278; www.humboldtarts.org; Wed–Sun). It is named for painter Morris Graves, a founder of the Northwest School of Art in the Pacific Northwest, who, prior to his death in 2001, donated a substantial portion of his personal art collection, including some of his own works and the use of his name, to help with the creation of the museum. Other attractions include **Clarke Historical Museum** (tel: 707-443-1947; www.clarkemuseum.org; Wed–Sat), with its collection of weapons, Native American crafts, and Victoriana, and across the bay, on a peninsula, **Humboldt Bay Maritime Museum** (tel: 707-444-9440; www.humboldtbaymaritimemuseum.com; mid-Mar–Nov Tue–Sat, Dec–mid-Mar Thu–Sat), with its lighthouse memorabilia.

Next door to Humboldt Bay Maritime Museum is the famous **Samoa Cookhouse** (www.samoacookhouse.net), which is the last remaining example of the 1890s lumber camp cookhouses, whose rules included eating as much as you could for a fixed price and helping yourself to anything within reach as long as one foot remained on the ground. Today, huge meals are served family style at long tables – and the same rules apply.

EUREKA TO OREGON

Arcata, just north of Eureka, has been called "the Galapagos of North America," because the number of bird species found here is greater than anywhere else in the state. The focus of all this birding activity is **Arcata Marsh and Wildlife Sanctuary** (tel: 707-826-2359; www.arcatamarshfriends.org; daily), a 307-acre (124-hectare) wetland that has been created by the city's innovative wastewater treatment plant on Arcata Bay (which produces more than half of California's oyster crop).

Among the birds thriving at the sanctuary, which is on the Pacific Flyway, are endangered Aleutian geese, once down to less than 1,000 in number, but rebounding with federal protection. Other notable birds found here are marbled godwits, white-tailed kites, and cinnamon teals. Birdwatchers from all over the country converge on the town for Godwit Days (www.godwitdays.org) every April, when field trips and workshops are offered. Arcata Chamber of Commerce on Heindon Road (www.arcatachamber.com) publishes a free bird list. On G Street, two blocks north of the Plaza, Humboldt State University's **Natural History Museum** (tel: 707-826-4479; www2.humboldt.edu/natmus; Tue–Sat) exhibits everything from butterflies to dinosaur tails.

Arcata was founded by a group of miners from the Trinity River region in 1849 and grew up around the 1857 **Jacoby Building** on Arcata Plaza, built of masonry during an era of timber construction by a merchant serving the goldmines upriver. Elegantly restored and refitted, it now houses stylish shops, cafes, and Abruzzi Ristorante, a rustic-chic Italian eatery. A self-guided walking tour booklet of old Victorian homes is available at the chamber.

McKinleyville, the fastest growing town in Humboldt County, is also the nearest one to the misnamed Eureka-Arcata airport. It claims to have the world's tallest single-tree totem pole (at the shopping center). Its 30-acre

(12-hectare) **Azalea State Natural Reserve** (tel: 707-488-2041; www.parks.ca.gov; daily), which blooms in spring, can be reached via a trail off North Bank Road (take the Central Avenue exit from US 101).

MOONSHINE BEACH AND WEDDING ROCK

After traveling in tandem for the last 100 miles (161km), Highway 1 splits from US 101 at **Moonshine Beach**, just north of the airport, and for 20 or so delightful miles (32km), it runs along the coast through the lovely clifftop village of **Trinidad** ㉞ (pop. 367), named by a Spanish explorer in 1775 and the site of a small museum (http://trinidadmuseum.org). Fill up here; this is the last gas station on this scenic stretch.

Farther north is **Patrick's Point State Park** (tel: 707-677-3570; www.parks.ca.gov; daily), where you can admire seals basking on the rocks off Rocky Point and explore tide pools at low tide. The park was named for an Indian scout who settled here in 1851. **Wedding Rock** is a popular site for

Café on Arcata Plaza, Arcata.

⊙ Tip

Contact the long-established Tributary Whitewater Tours (tel: 800-672-3846; www. whitewatertours.com) to experience whitewater rafting on the Smith River in Northern California. This can only be done between March and May and the difficulty level varies from III (moderate) to V (extremely difficult).

marriage ceremonies conducted to the sounds of crashing waves below. The rock got its name from the park's first caretaker, Vieggo Andersen, whose marriage to his housekeeper in 1933 began a popular custom. Scenes from Steven Spielberg's 1997 *The Lost World: Jurassic Park* were filmed in the parking lot. Nearer the highway is the site of an old Yurok Indian village, where you'll see an old canoe made of a tree trunk that was hollowed out by fire near a native plant garden. The state park has campsites, and for those who enjoy the luxury of glamping, a Mongolian *yurt* (a comfortable circular tent with a raised wooden-floor).

About 14 miles (22km) north of Patrick's Point, on the highway before Orick, stop at beachside **Thomas H. Kuchel Visitor Center** (tel: 707-465-7765; daily) for information on hiking and camping in **Redwood National Park** (tel: 707-465-7335; www.nps.gov/redw; daily) and three state parks – Prairie Creek Redwoods, Del Norte Coast Redwoods, and Jedediah Smith Redwoods – protecting 132,000 acres

(53,418 hectares) of redwoods between here and Crescent City.

The redwoods can reach heights of more than 360ft (110 meters) and are the tallest living things on Earth. Fossil records indicate that millions of years ago, when the climate was warmer and wetter, the trees were found throughout the northern hemisphere. Today, only isolated patches of redwoods remain, mainly in California and China.

Near **Orick**, once a major logging center, turn onto the signposted Newton B. Drury Scenic Parkway through **Prairie Creek Redwoods State Park** (tel: 707-488-2039), a long avenue of incredibly tall trees. If you are interested in hiking, stop for information at **Prairie Creek Visitor Center** (tel: 707-488-2039; www. parks.ca.gov; summer daily, off season Wed–Sun) and take one of several trails that leave from here. If you continue driving, you'll probably see the resident herd of Roosevelt elk, which has a tendency to graze beside the highway. These animals should be treated with respect because they can be unpredictable. A worthwhile sidetrip is to drive down the narrow, potholed Coastal Trail along **Golden Bluffs Beach** (a good place to picnic, explore tide pools, bird, and watch whales). The trail goes through dense woodland to **Fern Canyon**, a magical ravine bordered on either side by sheer, fern-carpeted cliffs.

CHAINSAW TREE SCULPTURES

Just before **Klamath** ㉟, US 101 parallels the broad **Klamath River**, formerly used by Yurok Indians and now a haven for salmon and steelhead fishermen. For a spectacular view of where the river meets the ocean, take the Requa Road on your left to an overlook 600ft (183 meters) above the water. (This side road dead-ends after a few miles.) Gold mines farther up the Klamath River were once served via Klamath from steamers that brought supplies up the coast from San Francisco. Today, the river is popular for jet boat tours from

Roosevelt elk stag on Gold Bluffs Beach.

Klamath to see such wildlife as elk and bears. Huge likenesses of legendary lumberjack Paul Bunyan and his blue ox, Babe, and chainsaw-sculpted trees herald the popular tourist spot **Trees of Mystery** (tel: 800-638-3389; www. treesofmystery.net; daily).

A trail leads past some unusual groupings: nine trees growing from one root structure to form the so-called **Cathedral Tree**; a dozen others growing from a single Sitka spruce trunk. Admission is charged to each trail, but the absorbing museum, with its large collection of Yurok Indian costumes and crafts, is free. The **Sky Trail** nearby is a 1,570ft- (480-meter) -long lift that offers treetop views of the redwoods.

US 101 continues through **Del Norte Coast Redwoods State Park** (tel: 707-465-7335; www.parks.ca.gov; daily), the smallest of the state parks. The highway hugs the coast around many attractive bays before beginning a lengthy climb, where traffic along the narrow road is controlled by solar-powered lights. Tall trees flank most of the final 10 miles (16km) into Crescent City, until the sea comes into view once again just before town.

REDWOOD PRESERVATION AND FUR TRAPPER HISTORY

Crescent City ㊱, named for the shape of the bay on which it sits, sprawls somewhat unattractively behind an interesting harbor, replete with restaurants, a seafood market, and the **Northcoast Marine Mammal Center** (tel: 707-465-6265; www.northcoastmmc. org), where distressed seals and sea lions are rehabilitated. West of the harbor, **Battery Point Lighthouse** (tel: 707-464-3089; http://lighthousefriends. com; summer daily, Oct–Apr Sat–Sun) can be visited at low tide. A museum contains photographs of shipwrecks off this treacherous coast.

When environmentalist John Muir visited Crescent City in 1896, he went out on a logging train to see "the work of ruin going on." Some of the redwoods, he observed, were up to 200ft (61 meters) high and 20ft (6 meters) in diameter, yet two men could chop them down in a single day. His experiences led him to fight for the redwoods' preservation.

Jedediah Smith Redwoods State Park (tel: 707-458-3018; www. parks.ca.gov; daily), the 10,000-acre (4,050-hectare) state park to the east, is named after Jedediah Smith, the fur trapper who first explored the region in the 1820s. It's a great place for hiking, camping, and picnicking, and fishing, swimming or white-water rafting in the spectacular and turbulent Smith River, California's only undammed river system. Stop at **Jedediah Smith Visitor Center** (May–Sept) in Hiouchi for information on visiting the state park. The US Forest Service office (tel: 707-457-3131) in **Gasquet** provides maps and information on Six Rivers National Forest and reserving a night in the remote fire-lookout cabin atop Bear Basin Butte. Whether you head north from Crescent City or Gasquet, in less than 25 miles (40km), you'll be in **Oregon**.

On the shore, Crescent City.

Fishing at the mouth of the Columbia River, near Astoria, Oregon.

OREGON TO WASHINGTON

The rugged 400-mile (644km) Oregon coast is famous for basaltic cliffs, historic lighthouses, and pullouts offering views of migrating gray whales all along its coastline and into Washington.

Trusty US 101 trundles up the Oregon coast into the state of Washington, offering some of the best coastal scenery in the United States. Rural and more rugged than California, this section of 101, which is signposted "PACIFIC COAST SCENIC HIGHWAY," brings you into dramatic proximity with cliffs, beaches, wildlife, and attractive state parks.

BROOKINGS-HARBOR TO WALDPORT

The southern part of the Oregon Coast – the **Siskiyou Coas**t – begins calmly enough, with a drive through farmland. Ships are beached on dry land – first, a huge one beside the aptly named Ship Ashore Motel (www.ship-ashore.com), then an old tugboat converted into a souvenir store just south of **Brookings-Harbor** ㉗. Brookings, located at the mouth of the Chetco River, is the larger of the two communities. The sports-fishing fleet is anchored here, and it also contains the local visitor information bureau (tel: 605-692-6125; www.brookingsharborchamber.com).

Brookings is a popular retirement spot, as it's in the "banana belt," with winter temperatures often reaching 65°F (18°C). The scientific explanation for this is that the town's southeast-to-northwest geographical layout combines with constant low-pressure thermal troughs that pull down the

highly compressed air following a storm system. One consequence is that the area is famous for its spring blooms. It produces most of the country's Easter lilies, and the city's 33-acre (13-hectare) **Azalea Park** (tel: 541-469-1103) attracts visitors every spring, especially on Memorial Day weekend, when there's an Azalea Festival.

Some of Oregon's most spectacular coastal scenery is protected in **Samuel H. Boardman State Scenic Corridor** (tel: 800-551-6949), just north of town. The state park runs for about 12

Main attractions

Boardman State Corridor
Coquille River Lighthouse
Coos Bay
Oregon Dunes
Sea Lion Caves
Yachats
Newport
Depoe Bay
Portland
Cannon Beach
Astoria

Map on page 348

Rounding up horses in Oregon.

miles (19km) past exposed cliffs, sparkling coves, and offshore rock formations such as Arch Rock and Natural Bridges. March brings daffodils, May the wild azaleas, and July the snow lilies, while every month of the year brings eager photographers.

WHALE WATCHING SITES

North of Brookings-Harbor, near **Harris Beach State Park** (tel: 800-551-6949), is one of 28 places on the Oregon coast to be designated a whale-watching site. The whale-watching station is manned by some of the 450 trained volunteers who take part in Oregon's Whale Watching Spoken Here program every winter, headquartered at Depoe Bay's excellent Whale Watching Center on the seawall.

Gray whales leave the Bering Sea to head south to their breeding grounds in the protected lagoons of Baja California from mid-December to January, then make the return journey to Alaska starting in March, as soon as the newborn calves are old enough to survive the dangerous journey. It is a grueling

10,000-mile (16,000km) round trip, at a speed of around 5mph (8kmh). The whales typically stay 5 miles (8km) offshore, and during peak migration pass by at a rate of 30 whales per hour. You are almost guaranteed a sighting, if you time your visit right – a real thrill.

KISSING ROCK

US 101 soon crosses the **Thomas Creek Bridge**, the state's highest at 345ft (105 meters), then a string of dune-backed beaches begins just before Pistol River. The best of these are around the rather eye-catching **Kissing Rock**, popular with windsurfers, between Meyers Creek and Gold Beach. The latter's name dates from the 1850s, when prospectors discovered that the sands around the mouth of the Rogue River were salted with gold dust.

Today, several companies offer excursions in powerful hydro jet boats up this wild and scenic river through a beautiful, pristine landscape teeming with wildlife; its upper reaches encompass dramatic canyons hundreds of feet deep. Sportfishing for salmon and

View of the coastline at Brookings-Harbor.

steelhead trout can be arranged, as well as ocean fishing, and horses can be rented for riding on the beach. At **Gold Beach**, a laid-back town large enough for a couple of good restaurants, make time to visit **Curry Historical Society Museum** (tel: 541-247-9396; www.curry history.com; Feb–Dec Tue–Sat). Highway 101 then crosses the graceful Patterson Memorial Bridge over the Rogue River to continue up the coast.

Seven miles (11km) north, at **Nesika Beach**, the highway parallels the shoreline. Low-lying, tree-covered hills flank the right-hand side and marsh-land sits between road and sea. Massive moss- and lichen-covered rocks stick out of the water, and around **Humbug Mountain** the scenery is particularly stunning. Towering mountains taper down to the road, which flanks a series of bays enlivened by crashing white surf.

WESTERNMOST CITY IN THE US

Keep an eye out on the right for the painted dinosaur outside the **Prehistoric Gardens** (www.prehistoricgardens.

com; daily) in the rainforest. Perched on scenic bluffs, **Port Orford** ㊳ is the westernmost city in the contiguous United States, and was a major lumber shipping port more than a century ago. Just offshore is a wooded island called **Battle Rock**. In 1851, the island's original party of settlers was besieged by local Native Americans who resented the newcomers' claim to the land. A month later, a larger white group arrived and took possession.

From here, there's a beautiful view of the coast back to Humbug Mountain. Take a lingering look at Port Orford's lovely bay, because it will be your last uninterrupted view of the ocean for nearly 100 miles (161km), although frequent "COASTAL ACCESS" signs dot the highway. Northeast of town, on Elk River Road, is the **Elk River Fish Hatchery** (tel: 541-332-7025), where salmon smelts are raised.

LIGHTHOUSES AND LAZY COUNTRYSIDE

From here, you can make a 6-mile (10km) side trip to **Cape Blanco State**

Stegosaurus exhibit at Prehistoric Gardens.

TEGOSAURUS
ounced: steg-o-SAWR-us
rally, 'roofed lizard'

the armored Dinosaurs, the plant
saurs lived during the upper Jurassic times
earers ago. He was 26 feet long, weighed
and had a brain the size of a walnut.

⊙ Tip

Stop in the small parking area provided on the west side of Riverside Drive in Oregon's Bandon Marsh National Wildlife Refuge (tel: 541-347-1470; www.fws.gov/refuge/bandon_marsh) to find the observation deck. This refuge is one of the best places to spot rare shorebirds, such as the Mongolian plover, as well as being an oasis for bald eagles and the California brown pelican.

Park (tel: 541-332-2973) and take tours of its historic **Hughes House** and **Lighthouse** (tours Apr–Oct Wed–Mon). The lighthouse sits on the cliffs, 245ft (75 meters) above the sea, and was the first in the state to be outfitted with a first-order Fresnel lens in 1870. It is operated by the Bureau of Land Management. Next comes **Langlois**, located in serene countryside filled with grazing cows and sheep. There are many lonely sheep ranches in the surrounding hills, and knitters will find a factory outlet selling wool among Langlois's small shops.

Miles of bright yellow gorse line the approach to **Bandon** ㊴, twice destroyed by fire in the last century; a brick chimney on the site of the old bakery stands as a memorial just off the highway. Artists' homes and studios and craft shops surround Bandon's **Old Town** area. **Bandon Historical Society Museum** (tel: 541-347-2164; www.bandonhistoricalmuseum.org; daily) includes an exhibit about cranberry cultivation, which has been taking place in nearby bogs for more than

a century – ever since the early settlers learned the technique from local Native Americans. The town celebrates with a Cranberry Festival every fall and you can tour cranberry farms by appointment. Near Bandon is charming **Coquille River Lighthouse** (tel 541-347-2209; tours mid-May–mid-Oct daily), accessed through **Bullards Beach State Park** (tel: 541-347-2209), a large family-oriented state park.

Coos Bay is a major lumber shipping port, with warehouses and stacked logs lining the road. Even its Mill Casino, run by the Coquille Tribe, is in a converted sawmill. Back in 1850, Captain Asa Simpson established a sawmill and shipyard here, which built about 50 vessels before the end of the century. On a smaller scale, you can tour the **Oregon Connection** factory (tel: 541-267-7804; www.oregonconnection.com), one of the oldest myrtlewood factories on the Oregon coast, where you can see logs fashioned into bowls, goblets, and other products.

A 24-mile (39km) drive east leads to **Golden and Silver Falls State Natural Area** (tel: 800-551-6949), a hidden gem in the coastal forests with 100ft (30-meter) waterfalls. On the coast, the fishing village of **Charleston** is a good place for fresh crab and seafood at Fisherman's Wharf. Continue south on the scenic **Cape Arago Beach Loop** for stunning sea views and vantage points for spotting seals, sea lions, and whales. Cape Arago is home to elephant seals, known for their deep diving skills – up to 4,000ft (1,200 meters). The loop encompasses three state parks, including **Shore Acres State Park** (tel: 541-888-3732; http://shoreacres.net), formerly the gardens of the spacious house belonging to lumber baron Louis J. Simpson, Asa's son.

OREGON DUNES

Across the magnificent McCullough Bridge spanning Hayes Inlet is Coos Bay's neighbor, **North Bend**. Stop in at **North Bend Welcome Center** (tel:

Coquille River Lighthouse.

541-756-4613) for visitor information and to find out more about the **Coos History Museum and Maritime Collections** (tel: 541-756-6320; www.cooshistory.org; Tue–Sun), an intriguing archive of local history.

Oregon Dunes National Recreation Area ㊵ begins at North Bend and protects a broad expanse of towering sand dunes up to 500ft (152 meters) high, which block access to the coast for 40 miles (64km). There are 11 different places offering beach access, at least one of which, **Spinreel** (watch for the highway sign) offers a chance to rent dune buggies (tel: 541-759-3313; www.ridetheoregondunes.com) and cavort in the sandy wilderness. The dunes are constantly sculpted into different shapes by wind and water and are a refuge for a rich variety of animals and plants, including red and yellow salmonberries, thimbleberries (similar to raspberries), wild strawberries and, in the fall, huckleberries. At the **Umpqua Dunes Trailhead** (watch for the highway sign), you can park the car and climb the dunes.

"Glamping enthusiasts (luxury campers) will be glad to learn that camping facilities here include spacious Mongolian *yurts*: structurally supported domed tents with plywood floors, lockable doors, comfortable beds, and light and heating. They are designed to withstand high winds and retain heat in winter. You'll find them throughout the Oregon State Park System, from rustic to deluxe (tel: 800-551-6949 for information and reservations). In summer, take a 5-mile (8km) side trip to visit **Umpqua Lighthouse State Park** (tel: 541-271-4631). The 1894 lighthouse is 65ft (19 meters) high and its lens has a distinctive red-and-white flash. It replaced the 1857 lighthouse that had been built here.

Lower **Umpqua Bay** is said to be the most fertile place for big soft-shell clams, some weighing around half a pound (220 grams). The delicious Dungeness crab is found in the Winchester Bay area, where the Umpqua River meets the ocean. Shops sell crabbing equipment and bait.

Oregon Dunes National Recreation Area.

SALMON HARBOR TO GARDINER

Drive past **Salmon Harbor** (unsurprisingly the largest salmon fishing port on the Oregon coast), and then cross the bridge into **Reedsport**, which is located at the midpoint of Oregon Dunes NRA.

Here you'll find **Umpqua Discovery Center** (tel: 541-271-4816; www.umpquadiscoverycenter.com; daily), an attractive hands-on education center that interprets the dunes and much else besides. Also in Reedsport is **Oregon Dunes NRA Visitor Center** (tel: 541-271-6000; Mon–Fri, summer Mon–Sat) on US 101, run by the US Forest Service, which publicizes preservation efforts, issues bird checklists (there are five different types of seagull alone), and can help you book campground sites. A mile or two to the east, on State Route 38, visitors can admire herds of Roosevelt elk at the pleasant **Dean Creek Elk Viewing Area**, which is also a haven for bald eagles, osprey, and blue herons.

Continuing north, Highway 101 passes through **Gardiner**, with an historic district of quaint buildings and a pioneer cemetery. The **Tsunami Art Gallery** (tel: 541-271-1597; Tue–Sun) in the old Gardiner General Store, contains the bronze sculpture studio of Mack Holman and features sculptures, pastels, porcelain, bronze, and oil paintings. It is aptly named, given the number of "Tsunami Hazard Zone" signs along the coast. Thankfully, the Pacific Northwest coast was not damaged by the Japanese Tsunami in 2011, but debris continues to wash ashore, and you may see storm debris collection sites along the coast. Glimpses of lakes and mountains appear through the pines along the pretty forest-lined road. There are numerous campgrounds, and the dunes continue all the way to Florence.

FLORENCE AND SEA LION CAVES

Florence has a picturesque harbor with some very old buildings as a backdrop. It's especially pretty when the rhododendrons display their vivid pink blossoms in late spring. In the Old Town **Siuslaw Pioneer Museum** (tel: 541-997-7884; www.siuslawpioneermuseum.com; May–Sept Labor Day daily, Feb–Apr Oct–Dec Tue–Sun) has old photographs and household items. When landslides block US 101 to the north (as happened for months early in 2000), it's the last chance to turn inland before Waldport. If traffic conditions have been bad, check with the Oregon Department of Transportation (tel: 888-275-6368; www.oregon.gov/odot), because even when the road is closed, it's sometimes open for an hour or two each day, usually early morning and early evening.

Eleven miles (18km) north of Florence is the 1894 **Heceta Head Lighthouse** (tel: 866-547-3696; http://hecetalighthouse.com; tours Mar–Oct daily) in Heceda Head State Park. Just before the lighthouse is **Sea Lion Caves** (tel: 541-547-3111; www.sealioncaves.com; daily), the world's largest sea cave, at the bottom of cliffs accessed by an elevator. Only a wire screen separates visitors from hundreds of

Florence's harbor.

Steller's sea lions, the closest you'll get to their underground lair. Harbor seals (which have spotted coats) and elephant seals are the most common pinnipeds on this coast; neither has external ears – as opposed to sea lions. The latter can also rotate their hind flippers and walk on land.

Cape Perpetua is the highest point (803ft/245 meters above sea level) on the Oregon coast. **Cape Perpetua Visitor Center** (tel: 541-547-3289; daily), run by the US Forest Service, is an excellent place to stop, enjoy a ranger-led program, and get maps and suggestions for hikes in Siuslaw National Forest. Its overlook has a terrific view – the highway looks like a thin sliver of silver ribbon threading along the coast. Note: You will need to purchase a $5 National Forest Day Pass for recreation in Northwest national forests, available at US Forest Service visitor centers and kiosks.

Cape Perpetua Visitor Center is 2 miles (3km) south of the curiously named **Yachats** ④, an attractive and laid-back resort town nestled between the mountains and the sea, has beach trails, richly populated tidepools, and good fishing. Once known for the multitude of smelts (a silvery sardine-like fish) that spawned here, the numbers have steadily declined in recent years and the community now has to import the fish from California for its annual Smelt Fry in July.

Waldport ④ sits at the mouth of the Alsea River, which arrives at the ocean from its origin in Siuslaw National Forest, and US 101 enters the town over the huge bay bridge. Waldport is mainly known for its fishing, crabbing, and clamming. It's also a good base for hiking.

WALDPORT TO SEASIDE

Look to the right while crossing Yaquina Bay into **Newport** ④: the section below the bridge is Newport's **Historic Bayfront**, where the attractions include old taverns, gift shops, a harbor filled with fishing boats, and a trio of commercial attractions, including **Undersea Gardens** (tel: 541-265-2206; www.marinersquare.com; daily), an aquarium where divers cavort behind glass. Across the bay, **South Beach** has the larger and well-known **Oregon Coast Aquarium** (tel: 541-867-3474; www.aquarium.org; daily), whose famous former resident, Keiko the orca, starred in the film *Free Willy*.

To reach the Bayfront, turn off the main street at the traffic light (opposite the Mazatlan Mexican restaurant in a gray, wooden building) and head down Hurburt Street. Farther on through town, several streets lead west to the seaport with its pedestrian promenade and historic murals. One block farther, Third Street leads to **Nye Beach**, at one time the Oregon Coast's major draw and still a worthy destination to visit **Newport Visual Arts Center** (tel: 541-265-2787; www.coastarts.org; Tue–Sun), with excellent art exhibits. The center also has a memorial to the famed composer Ernest Bloch, who spent the last decades of his life at his home at nearby Agate Beach.

Yachats covered bridge crosses the North Forks of Yachats River in Lincoln County, Oregon.

Heceta Head Lighthouse.

On US 101, opposite Newport Visitor Center (tel: 541-574-2679; http://visittheoregoncoast.com), the ornate **Burrows House**, a boarding house from the 1890s, is part of the **Oregon Coast History Center** (http://oregoncoasthistory.org), run by Lincoln County Historical Society to interpret central Oregon coastal history. Just outside town is the much-photographed **Yaquina Head Lighthouse ⓭**, built in 1873 and part of the BLM-run **Yaquina Head Outstanding Natural Area** (tel: 541-574-3100; www.blm.gov/0c5c; grounds, interpretive center and lighthouse tours daily).

About 5 miles (8km) north of Newport, don't miss the signs for **Devil's Punchbowl**, where a huge stone basin fills dramatically – and noisily – as the tide crashes in. Waves are higher in the Pacific than the Atlantic because the wind blows uninterruptedly over a larger distance. The study of waves – whose height is measured as the distance between the highest point (crest) and lowest point (trough) – is understandably one of great interest to coastal communities.

OREGON'S WHALE WATCHING CAPITAL

Cape Foulweather was named in 1778 by British navigator Captain James Cook. It was his first sighting of the American mainland after he had "discovered" Hawaii. The winds here, 500ft (152 meters) above the ocean, can reach 100mph (161kmh). The small gift shop sells the much-prized green glass bubbles that have drifted here from fishermen's nets all the way from Japan. Lincoln City launches its own floats every year at its Festival of Glass.

The awesome cliffs and headlands are basalt, formed by molten lava hitting the ocean eons ago and hardening instantly. Sometimes, this instant cooling creates oddly shaped rock structures known as pillow basalt, which can be seen offshore near Cape Foulweather and at **Depoe Bay**, a pretty resort that claims to be the world's smallest navigable harbor. Depoe Bay is Oregon's Whale Watching Capital, and the state-run **Whale Watching Center** (tel: 541-765-3304; Tue–Sun) on the seawall is a terrific

Hiking on Cascade Head.

place to learn about whales. A resident pod of gray whales spends the summer feeding in the kelp beds off Depoe Bay. Boats in the harbor offer whale-watching and fishing tours, and this is your best bet on the Oregon coast to get out on the water.

At high tide, seawater shoots skyward through two rock formations known locally as the **Spouting Horns**. Visitors get a close-up look at the wave action just by walking along the sea wall, which runs the full length of the town. When a storm is about to hit, everyone heads to a Depoe Bay restaurant for a full-frontal view, complete with sound effects.

LINCOLN CITY

Trawling for glass floats, collecting driftwood and studying tide pools are all popular pastimes along this stretch of low-key coast. Tide pools could be regarded as miniature ocean habitats, where some creatures wait in anticipation for the waves to wash in their lunch. Orange and pink starfish, urchins, and sea anemones can usually be seen among the tiny fish that dart about the shallows, while rocky residents such as long-tapered mussels and white barnacles cluster on the rocks.

Lincoln City ⑮ has 7 miles (11km) of beaches, including a half-mile-wide strand when the tide is out at Siletz Bay. It's home to a cluster of antique stores and second-hand bookstores, as well as Chinook Winds Casino (www.chinook windscasino.com) for night-time action and a factory outlet center for daytime shopping. The tiny D River links nearby **Devil's Lake** with the ocean, providing both freshwater and oceanside fun. North of town, **Cascade Head** is a good place to see falcons, hawks, bald eagles, and other raptors, which use their keen eyesight, outstanding hearing, and amazing speed to hunt and kill their prey, then eat it using large clawed feet and hooked bills.

PASTURED DAIRY FARMS

The highway passes through the wonderful, fresh-scented **Siuslaw National Forest** (www.fs.usda.gov/siuslaw), its highest peak, Mount Hebo, ascending to

Rooms at the Cannery Pier Hotel in Astoria have fabulous views of the Columbia River.

PORTLAND: CITY OF ROSES

A ride-for-free transit system, stunning scenery, and micro-breweries everywhere – no wonder Portland smells like roses.

Portland is a famously livable city. It has always prided itself on its bike-and-pedestrian friendliness and trees-and-parks image. In a city that boasts 247 parks and recreational sites, including 196 neighborhood parks, the largest is 6,000-acre (2,438-hectare) **Forest Park,** the fifth largest municipal park in the US.

Portland Regional Arts and Culture Council (tel: 503-823-5111; www.racc.org; Mon–Fri) promotes the arts in the city through education, public sculpture, and grants and is a good first stop for information about museums and art galleries. One popular public space for the arts is **Pioneer Courthouse Square** in Downtown, which hosts more than 300 events a year.

View over Portland and Mount Hood.

Its *Weather Machine*, an earth-shaped sphere by local artist Terence O'Donnell on a 25ft (8-meter) column, comes to life with a musical fanfare at noon each day.

Top art spots include **Portland Art Museum** (tel: 503-226-2811; http://portlandartmuseum.org; Tue–Sun) and Portland's quirkiest attraction, the Church of Elvis (www.24hourchurchofelvis.com; 24 hours), is a coin-operated shrine offering marriage counseling and more. Washington Park subway is within easy access of many major attractions, including **Oregon Zoo** (www.oregonzoo.org), the **World Forestry Center** (www.worldforestry.org), **Hoyt Arboretum** (www.hoytarboretum.org), and the **Children's Museum** (www.portlandcm.org). A streetcar system links Downtown Portland with the **Pearl District** (an area colonized by local artists) and the **Nob Hill** neighborhood, with its fine Victorian and Georgian mansions. In the historic **Skidmore District**, there's a large weekend open-air market with live entertainment. Portland also has more microbreweries and brewpubs than any other city in the nation.

Oregon history comes to life in **Oregon History Museum** (tel: 503-222-1741; www.ohs.org; daily) and in **Pittock Mansion** (tel: 503-823-3623; http://pittockmansion.org; Feb–Dec daily), the 1914 home of the founder of Portland's well-regarded daily newspaper, *The Oregonian*. Literary pursuits are popular in rainy Portland, and no visit here is complete without a trip to famous **Powell's Books** (www.powells.com), an independent bookstore in Downtown.

At the **Oregon Museum of Science and Industry** (tel: 503-797-4000; www.omsi.edu; Tue–Sun and Mon during school holidays), you can experience a simulated earthquake. East of Portland is the basaltic Columbia Plateau, formed by hardened lava from erupting Cascade volcanoes like Mount Hood and later carved by Ice Age flooding and the now-dammed Columbia River into a spectacular gorge. The breathtaking cliffs, waterfalls, wildlife, and historic sites preserved in **Columbia Gorge National Recreation Area** make a perfect day trip.

The city's most notable landmarks also include some treats for horticulture lovers: the **International Rose Test Garden** (tel: 503-227-7033; www.rosegardenstore.org) and the **Portland Japanese Garden** (tel: 503-223-1321; http://japanesegarden.com).

,000ft (914 meters). The highway skirts residential **Neskowin** and then heads inland, passing meadows of grazing cows (which outnumber people in this pastoral county) owned by the 180 working farms that provide the milk for the delectable Tillamook cheese. After **Cloverdale**, with its colorful rustic buildings, sturdy wooden barns and springtime daffodils catch the eye before the towns of Hebo and Beaver appear.

Tillamook Air Museum (tel: 503-842-130; www.tillamookair.com; daily), a couple of miles south of town, is housed in an enormous hangar containing World War II vintage planes and a welcome 1940s-style café. **Tillamook** ⑯ is justly famous for its huge, pristine **Tillamook Cheese Factory** (tel: 503-815-1300; www.tillamook.com/cheese-factory; daily), which offers free tours of its recently remodeled manufacturing facility. You can admire a life-size, painted plaster cow, beribboned with a computer chip that has replaced the old cowbell. A wall chart lists "udderly amazing" facts such as that 2,600 pints of blood pass through the udder to produce one pint of milk

and that a cow yields 10,000 gallons of milk in her lifetime. Help yourself to the free cheese samples, because it's a sure bet that you're bound to buy something in the tempting gift shop. Not to be outdone, the **Blue Heron French Cheese Company** (tel: 503-842-8281; www.blueheronoregon.com; daily) offers wine tastings with its cheese tastings. Needless to say, the Dairy Parade is a major event each June.

West of Tillamook, a detour along 20-mile (32km) **Three Capes Scenic Drive** takes you to the "Octopus Tree" – a Sitka spruce with multiple trunks – and **Cape Meares Lighthouse** (www.capemeareslighthouse.org), built in 1890 with a lens imported from Paris. An early lighthouse keeper wrote of the harrowing all-night horse-and-buggy trip required to reach a doctor in Tillamook, a trip that today takes about 16 minutes.

Two miles (3km) out to sea is **Tillamook Lighthouse**, situated on a solitary rock amid crashing waves that in 1934 roared into a maelstrom, climbing more than 100ft (30 meters) high to engulf the entire building. "Terrible Tilly" was how

Sport fishing boat in Garibaldi Harbor.

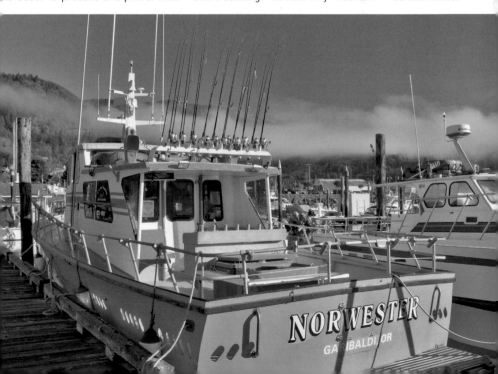

lighthouse keepers used to describe the building. Life on the rock was too hazardous to allow families to accompany staff to their jobs, who were rotated every three weeks and allowed 96 days' leave each year to recover. The lighthouse was decommissioned in 1980.

For a taste of big-city life, take a detour from Tillamook along State Route 6 east to the "City of Roses," otherwise known as **Portland** ❹ (see page 370). Past Tillamook, the highway hugs the 13-sq-mile (34-sq-km) shallow bay, which is rarely deeper than 6ft (2 meters). Estuaries such as this, where fresh water mingles with that of the ocean, are especially inviting to plant and marine life. Eelgrass provides shelter and nourishment to crabs as well as young salmon and other small fish; mudflats harbor gourmet treats for the stately great blue heron, which can often be seen prospecting for dinner.

GARIBALDI GHOSTS AND CANNON BEACH

Garibaldi is named for the 19th-century Italian liberator. Its down-home attractions include the battered Ghos Hole Tavern, the Lumberman's Memo rial Park, **Garibaldi Museum** (tel: 503-322-8411; http://garibaldimuseum.org Apr–Oct Thu–Mon, Mar and Nov Sat–Sun), and annual Crab Races, which presumably take place sideways.

At the cute, old-fashioned resort of **Rockaway Beach**, a red caboose beside the highway houses the tourist office (tel: 503-355-8108; Mon–Fri, albeit sporadically). Freight trains loaded with lumber can occasionally be seen running on the roadside track, which follows the course of the Nehalem River. Tiny **Wheeler** has antiques shops and a wildlife viewing area along the bay in the town center.

After the long climb from **Manzanita**, there are spectacular ocean views from an overlook where **Oswald West State Park** begins. Down to the trestle bridge over the canyon, Tillamook County ("the land of cheese, trees, and gentle breeze") comes to an end just before the tunnel.

Oregon's most iconic natural landmark can be found at **Cannon Beach** ❹,

A serene corner of the lovely Portland Japanese Gardens.

where 235ft (72-meter) -high **Haystack Rock** is home to nesting tufted puffins in spring and summer. Cannon Beach, named after a cannon washed ashore after an 1846 shipwreck, is an attractive artists' haven, with over a dozen visual arts studios and galleries. The vision of colorful stunt kites soaring overhead is matched only by the tranquil scene of families and friends gathered sround campfires on the beach as the silhouetted rock fades into the sunset.

Cannon Beach sponsors an annual Sandcastle Day in June and a dog show on the beach in October, with contests for best bark, Frisbee catch, and owner/dog lookalike. There's even a Stormy Weather Arts Festival (indoors) in November. The visitor center (tel: 503-436-2623; www.cannonbeach.org) can suggest plenty of things to do, but the big draw is strolling along the beach and investigating tide pools on this magnificent section of the Oregon coast.

HISTORIC SEASIDE

On the north side of town, Ecola State Park has beautiful views of the coastline and Haystack Rock. Eight miles (13km) north of Cannon Beach, US 101 descends into **Seaside** ㊾ (pop. 6,700), the largest resort town on the Oregon Coast. It is bisected by the Necanicum River, with its historic downtown area on the western side of Broadway. A wide sandy beach is flanked by a pedestrian promenade, where you'll find the **Aquarium** (tel: 503-738-7065; www.seasideaquarium.com; daily). Three blocks farther north is **Seaside Historical Society Museum** (tel: 503-738-7065; www.seasidemuseum.org; Mon–Sat).

It was at Seaside that members of the Lewis and Clark exploration party set up a camp to make salt by boiling seawater. After their epic journey west brought them to the mouth of the Columbia River and the Pacific in 1805, the expedition hunkered down for a cold, wet winter. They built **Fort Clatsop,** a 50-sq-ft (5-sq-meter) stockade with a parade ground and two rows of small cabins, southeast of what is now Warrenton and named it for the local Native Americans, who brought whale meat to trade (Clark cooked and ate some, describing it as "very palatable and tender").

The replica of the fort in **Lewis and Clark National Historical Park** (tel: 503-861-2471; www.nps.gov/lewi; daily), which protects Lewis and Clark sites on both the Oregon and Washington sides of the river, helps visitors imagine the challenging conditions. Its summer living history program features buckskin-clad rangers demonstrating daily life during the period. Another fort, located in nearby **Fort Stevens State Park,** was built to defend the mouth of the Columbia River during the Civil War.

ASTORIA TO ABERDEEN

Astoria ㉟ – 22 miles (35km) north of Seaside – was once known as "the salmon canning capital of the world," and in an 1872 book, Frances Fuller

Haystack Rock at Cannon Beach.

Cannon Beach.

Victor was able to write: "The immense numbers of all kinds of salmon, which ascend the Columbia annually, is something wonderful. They seem to be seeking quiet and safe places to deposit their spawn, and thousands of them never stop until they can reach the great falls of the Snake River, more than 600 miles (966km) from the sea." As late as 1915, fishermen were taking 21,000 tons of salmon from the river. But then came the giant dams. The protest by the Cayuse Tribe that it would abrogate their rights by eliminating most of the salmon sadly turned out to be true. Some salmon runs have declined 85 percent from what they once were, despite the production of 170 million fish each year by artificial hatcheries. Only here, at the mouth of the Columbia, can you experience the untamed river.

THE MIGHTY COLUMBIA

At its most powerful, the Columbia thrusts 150 billion gallons (682 billion litres) of water a day through the sandbars into the Pacific Ocean, a torrent that has capsized at least 2,000 boats in the two centuries since John Jacob Astor's Pacific Fur Company created the first American settlement on shore. In recent years, the Federal government has dredged a 40ft (12-meter) channel and placed long jetties at each side to narrow the channel, but despite constant dredging and other attempts to tame the river at its mouth, it remains one of the most dangerous sandbars in the world. The weather so consistently stirs up stormy seas that the US Coast Guard set up its National Motor Lifeboat School at the tip of Cape Disappointment, where waves sometimes reach 30ft (9 meters) in height. For all that, this is a spectacular place, and cruise boats regularly call at Astoria, depositing hundreds of passengers at the 17th Street Dock, used regularly by US Coast Guard cutters.

Columbia River Maritime Museum (tel: 503-325-2323; www.crmm.org; daily) is all about shipwrecks, lighthouses, fishing, navigation, and naval history. Much of Astoria's history is reflected in its handsome Victorian houses, which fall into particular styles: Italianate, whose overhanging eaves have

Crown Point overlooking Columbia River Gorge National Recreation Area.

decorative brackets and tall or paired windows and doors, or Queen Anne (multiple roof lines, towers and turrets, paneled doors, and stained glass). An interesting example of the latter is the **Captain George Flavel House** (tel: 503-325-2203; daily), dating from the 1880s, on Eighth Street.

It's a steep, winding drive past the historic homes up the hill to the newly restored **Astoria Column** (tel: 503-325-2963; http://astoriacolumn.org; daily), with its 164 winding steps. The Great Northern Railroad and Vincent Astor, great-grandson of Jacob Astor, were responsible for installing the 125ft (38-meter) -high tower in 1926. The views, of course, are stupendous, but once back on the ground you'll be glad to warm up in the hut as you buy a postcard.

WASHINGTON STATE'S DISCOVERY COAST

It took three weeks for the Lewis and Clark exploration party to cross the wide mouth of the Columbia River and set up another camp near today's **Chinook** on the Washington coast ("the Discovery Coast"). Motoring across the 4-mile (6km) -long bridge linking Oregon and Washington is one of the great thrills of driving this Pacific Coast route, even (or perhaps especially) in a fog. It climbs steeply above the water, as seagulls swoop overhead with keening cries and the wind reaches almost gale force.

US 101 continues past a bird-filled wildlife refuge to the attractive, unspoiled town of **Ilwaco,** with its murals and **Columbia Pacific Heritage Museum** (tel: 360-642-3446; www.columbiapacificheritagemuseum.org; Tue–Sun). The expedition stayed for three lonely months in this isolated area.

Ilwaco sits at the bottom of the Long Beach peninsula – 28 miles (45km) of sandy beach – which gets nicer the farther north you go. In the southwest corner, in **Cape Disappointment State Park** (tel: 360-642-3078), **Fort Canby** guarded the mouth of the Columbia for almost a century before it became part of the state park in 1957. Built in 1856, **Cape Disappointment Lighthouse** is the oldest operational lighthouse on the West Coast. So treacherous was

> **◉ Tip**
>
> Waikiki Beach is where the North Jetty meets the cape in Washington's Cape Disappointment State Park. This is an ideal place for storm watching as the waves crash into the cliffs, with Cape Disappointment lighthouse in the background. It's only a few miles from Ilwaco and great for photos.

A kayaking trip on Long Island Slough, Willapa National Wildlife Refuge.

Pacific fish and crabs find a ready market in Seattle and Portland.

Metal figures along the Wildlife-Heritage Sculpture Corridor in Raymond.

Cape Disappointment that another lighthouse had to be built in 1898 at nearby **North Head** (daily). There's a very interesting **Lewis and Clark Interpretive Center** (Apr–Oct daily; Nov–Mar Wed–Sun), where you can study biographies of members of the original party and entries from the actual journals they kept. This excellent park overlooks 28 miles (45km) of sandy beach that was voted top beach in Washington.

Nearby Long Beach is a perennially popular beach resort with weekenders from Seattle and Portland. It specializes in good, old-fashioned seaside fun and games and doesn't put on any airs or graces. Beaches on the peninsula are popular for clamming. **Nahcotta** and **Oysterville** at the northern end became prosperous from oyster gathering before the crop was overharvested, and some fine Victorian homes remain from those days. **Willapa Bay Interpretive Center** (Memorial Day–Labor Day Fri–Sun), in a replica of an oyster house in Nahcotta, explains the history. **Leadbetter Point State Park**, in Willapa Bay

separating the point from the Pacific, is also a wildlife refuge where waterfowl stop over on their way south.

SOUTH BEND AND RAYMOND

Back on "the mainland," US 101 crosses the Naselle River and a number of sloughs (inlets) before arriving at **South Bend** ⑤, which sits on a bay at the mouth of the Willapa River. Signs announcing oysters for sale in what calls itself the "oyster capital of the world" are a reminder that a century ago tons of these succulent bivalves were harvested by Native Americans, and now find a ready market in the gourmet restaurants of Seattle, Portland, and San Francisco. Also in search of the same is the black oystercatcher, a bird whose long red bill helps it open the shellfish once it has found them.

South Bend stages its annual Oyster Stampede every May. South Bend's neighbor, **Raymond,** is an unspoiled sort of place, with a library built in the style of a timbered English cottage, its art-glass panes depicting fairy-tale characters.

CRANBERRY BOGS AND LUMBER TOWNS

Architecturally, Raymond's pride and joy is the old courthouse, with its spiral staircase and stained-glass dome. "A gilded palace of reckless extravagance" was how the local paper described it when the courthouse first went up in 1910. Life-size metal silhouettes of sculptured animals and historical figures form the **Wildlife Heritage Sculpture Corridor**, which runs through the town along Highway 101. Four miles (6km) east of Raymond on State 6 is the (marked) grave of Willie Kiel, a 19-year-old who died of malaria just before the family wagon train left Missouri in 1855. Preserved in whisky in a lead casket by his doctor father, the body came along for the trip and was buried atop a grassy knoll, which is now crowned with towering cedars.

Access to beaches here is via State 105, which runs past the Shoalwater Indian Reservation and the cranberry bogs between North Cove and Grayland. Cranberries blossom in late June, and **Grayland** holds its annual cranberry festival in October, following the harvest.

Between Raymond and the lumber town of Aberdeen, US 105 bends and twists through a forest of mist-shrouded pines. Large tracts have been devastated by clearcutting, while others are covered in mono-cultural new plantings that give the forest a monotonous look. The road emerges just south of town, beside the century-old Weyerhaeuser sawmill, which closed as a result of the economic downturn. When the bridge over the broad Chehalis River is raised, vehicles must wait to continue their journey.

Like its Scottish namesake, **Aberdeen** ⑤ sits at the confluence of two rivers. It is known for **Grays Harbor**, the seaport that grew up after Robert Gray sailed in on the *Lady Washington*

in 1788 to help arrange fur trading between the Pacific Northwest and China. A replica of the 170-ton ship is used for educational trips, but is usually on show in the harbor, and more about the town's early days can be explored in **Aberdeen Museum of History** (tel: 360-533-1976; www.aberdeen-museum.org; Tue–Sun). By the time the first mill was built in 1852, the government was making treaties with Indian tribes in the region and Aberdeen was developing into a rowdy, honky-tonk shipping town.

ON TO SEATTLE

US 101 reaches the end of the journey that began all the way south in sunny San Diego with a flourish, by looping around the magnificent Olympic Peninsula (see page 168), ending up not far from Seattle. This is a real highlight of the trip, so try not to miss it. If you do decide to head straight for **Seattle** ⑤ (see page 172) from Aberdeen, you can take US 12 to **Olympia**, then hop on I-5N.

Diver with a sunflower sea star.

The General's Highway, Sequoia National Park.

USA ON THE ROAD

TRAVEL TIPS

TRANSPORTATION

GETTING THERE

Most travelers arriving in the United States do so by air. The routes in this book begin and end at major US cities with international airports: New York to Miami (Atlantic route); Boston to Seattle (Northern Route); Washington, DC to Los Angeles (Central Route); Atlanta to San Diego (Southern Route); Los Angeles to San Diego (Pacific Route). From here, connecting flights can be made all over the US to secondary cities and towns. It is also possible to arrive by ship. Transatlantic crossings include service between Southampton and New York on the Queen Mary 2; also, several "positioning voyages" (allowing cruise ships to switch from Mediterranean or Baltic to Caribbean service) are scheduled between European and Florida ports in the fall.

Important Note: Non-US residents from Visa Waiver countries such as the UK are required to submit information about themselves online to the Department of Homeland Security and be pre-approved for travel to the US at least three days before they travel.

Atlanta

Hartsfield-Jackson Atlanta International Airport (ATL; tel: 800-897-1910; www.atlanta-airport. com), located 10 miles (16km) from Atlanta, is one of the world's busiest airports by passenger traffic. The terminal has seven concourses with 209 domestic and international gates; international passengers arrive at Maynard H. Jackson International Terminal. There are over 300 food and beverage, retail, and high-end outlets, with more planned in the future.

Boston

Logan International Airport (BOS; tel: 800-235-6426; www.massport. com) handles more than 1,100 flights daily, with over 50 carriers serving the airport. It is the northern terminal of the world's busiest airline market: the Boston–New York–Washington, DC run. Delta Airlines, US Airways, and JetBlue run shuttles between these airports. Logan has four terminals (A, B, C, and E; for some reason, there is no D); all international arrivals are handled at terminal E. Note that domestic and international flights of the same airline do not necessarily use the same terminal. There is a free shuttle bus service between the terminals.

Los Angeles

Los Angeles International Airport (LAX; tel. 855-463-5252; www.flylax. co) is the city's main airport. It is the fifth-busiest airport in the world and serves most of the world's major airlines. LAX is 17 miles (27km) from downtown and a short drive to Santa Monica and other locations along the coast. Free shuttle buses connect its nine terminals. An information booth is located on the departure level of the Tom Bradley International Terminal, which offers a language translation link for non-English speakers. Other convenient airports serving the metro area with domestic flights include **Bob Hope Airport** (BUR) serving the San Fernando Valley; **John Wayne (Orange County) Airport** (SNA) is 35 miles (56km) south of Los Angeles in Santa Ana, convenient for Disneyland; and **Long Beach Municipal Airport** (LGB).

Miami

Miami International Airport (MIA; tel. 305-876-7000; www.iflymia.com) is the city's primary airport. It is sometimes also called Wilcox Field, and is one of the key airports serving the American South as well as other Central and Latin American destinations. Miami International is about a 30-minute drive from downtown, though traffic congestion at peak times can lengthen this considerably. Currently, there are eight concourses and 131 gates that serve almost all major domestic and international carriers. Information booths have Miami maps and can provide info about buses and shuttles to and from the airport via the train and Tri-Rail lines. Alternately, the **Fort Lauderdale Airport** in Broward County (FLL) can be used and is only 30 minutes north of Miami. Other airports are inconveniently distant, making Miami International or Fort Lauderdale the best choices for incoming travelers.

New York City

New York's two major airports, **John F. Kennedy International** (JFK; tel: 718-244-4444; www.jfkairport.com) and **LaGuardia** (LGA; tel: 718-533-3400; www.panynj.gov), are both in Queens, east of Manhattan on Long Island, respectively 15 and 8 miles (24km and 13km) from Midtown. Driving time to/from Kennedy is estimated at 90 minutes, but heavy traffic can often double this, so leave lots of time if you're catching a flight. LaGuardia is used only for shorter US domestic and some Canadian routes, and does not have any intercontinental flights.

San Diego

San Diego International Airport (SAN; tel: 619-400-2404; www.san. org), also called Lindbergh Field, is 3 miles (5km) northwest of, and about

⊘ Airlines

Air Canada: tel: 888-247-2262; www.aircanada.com
American Airlines: tel: 800-433-7300; www.aa.com
British Airways: tel: 800-247-9297; www.britishairways.com
Delta: tel: 800-241-4141; www.delta.com
Frontier Airlines: tel: 800-432-1359; www.flyfrontier.com
JetBlue: tel: 800-538-2583; www.jetblue.com
KLM: tel: 800-618-0104; www.klm.com
Lufthansa: tel: 800-645-3880; www.lufthansa.com
Norwegian Airlines: tel: 800-35-4159; www.norwegian.com
Southwest Airlines: tel: 800-435-9792; www.southwest.com
Spirit Airlines: tel: 801-401-2200; www.spirit.com
United Airlines: tel: 800-864-8331; www.united.com
Virgin America: tel: 877-359-8474; www.virginamerica.com

a 5-minute drive from, downtown San Diego. It is served by all the major domestic carriers and many international airlines. Free transportation between the airport's two terminals is provided on the Airport Loop Shuttle Bus system; color-coded parking shuttles also run between parking areas and the airport terminal. Over 350 Volunteer Airport Ambassadors in green polo shirts provide assistance to travelers around the airport and at the information booths in the baggage claim areas in Terminal 1 (tel: 619-400-2263) and Terminal 2 (tel: 619-400-2262) from 6am to 11pm daily.

Seattle

Seattle-Tacoma International Airport (SEA; tel: 800-544-1965; www.portseattle.org), known locally as Sea-Tac, is served by 35 domestic and international airlines. It is 14 miles (22km) south of Seattle city center, about a 25-minute drive depending on traffic. The airport has a central terminal and two satellite terminals for international flights, which are linked by a rail transit system. An airport information booth is located in the baggage claim area across from carousel 12 and is open daily from 6am until 2am.

Washington, DC

The city is served by three regional airports. **Ronald Reagan Washington National Airport**, or National, as it's often still called (DCA; www.flyreagan.com), is closest to the city, just 4 miles (6.4km) across the Potomac in Virginia. **Dulles Airport** (IAD; www.flydulles.com), the region's largest, is also in Virginia, 26 miles (42km) from DC. There is a convenient Super Shuttle service; Phase 2 of the Metro extension, from Reston to the airport, is due to open in 2020. **Baltimore-Washington International Airport** (or BWI; www.bwiairport.com) is 40 miles (64km) north, in the city of Baltimore in Maryland, about an hour by car. **Reagan National** offers mostly domestic service and also flights to and from some Canadian cities. Dulles and BWI are both international airports. Domestic flights through BWI are generally considerably less expensive than flying into Reagan National.

GETTING AROUND

The United States is so vast that, for most people, the only logical way to get around is by flying. Many flights connect through hub cities, served by major airlines. A number of regional airlines fly into smaller cities. A large road network offers a variety of driving options: rapid **interstate** and US **highways**, **scenic state routes**, and **slow county**, **forest**, and **Indian back roads.**

Federal and state highways are paved and kept free of snow by snow plows in winter. Rural backroads, which are maintained by towns, may be either paved or gravel and are also plowed, with the exception of some remote routes closed in winter. Even those gravel roads kept open all year can become impassibly muddy after heavy rains, making four-wheel drive a wise choice. Other transportation options include **trains**, operated nationally by Amtrak, and light rail within and between local cities. **Buses** operated by Greyhound crisscross the country, usually operating out of an easily accessible downtown depot with links to local transport.

By air

If, due to long distances, it is impractical to drive to the destinations listed here, an easy alternative is to fly. Airlines that serve the airports in the major hub cities include American, Delta, Southwest, and United.

You can also fly into cities along the routes, including Charleston, Savannah, and Tampa; Mobile, New Orleans, Houston, and Phoenix, San Francisco, and Portland; Buffalo, Chicago, Minneapolis/St Paul, Sioux Falls, Spokane. Smaller cities are often served by regional airlines.

Airport security

Since September 11, 2001, air travel in the US has changed drastically. Expect delays departing US airports due to recent Homeland Security anti-terrorism rules. These are apt to change, so check before flying. Leave gifts unwrapped, and take laptops out of bags for inspection by Transportation Security Administration (TSA) personnel. Consider wearing slip-on shoes as all footwear must be removed and scanned by x-ray machines.

Passengers are allowed one carry-on resealable 1-quart (1-liter) clear plastic bag, which can contain liquids, gels, or aerosols in containers of 3oz or less. The contents in the plastic bag must be sealed and may be subjected to x-ray inspection separate from the carry-on bag.

Allow plenty of time at the airport to clear security. Arrive at least one hour before departure for flights within the US; two hours for international flights. Expect searches and questions to be asked, and do not attempt to carry any sharp objects in your hand luggage. This includes scissors, nailclippers, penknives, and other seemingly innocuous items.

By train

Although passenger services were greatly curtailed in the latter part of the 20th century, it is still possible to travel the length and breadth of the continent by rail. **Amtrak** is the major rail passenger carrier in the US. Its network links many cities, but sadly bypasses many more. However, there are still some excellent trans-continental and coastal routes that glide through breathtaking scenery and often feature on-board entertainment, such as Native American storytellers and local historians. It's also possible to find Amtrak trains that allow you to take your car with you, such as the Auto Train between Lorton, Virginia, near Washington, DC, and Sanford, north of Orlando. You will also find an increasing number of light-rail options once you arrive in major cities.

Train passes

Passes for unlimited travel on Amtrak over a fixed period of time (15, 30, or 45 days) are available from a travel agent or online. The USA Rail Pass cannot be purchased onboard; proof of identity is required. For information about Amtrak's services, call 800-872-7245 or visit: www.amtrak.com.

By bus

The national bus line, Greyhound, as well as a number of smaller shuttle companies, provide an impressive network of ground travel throughout the country, offering daily service to major towns and cities. Routes and schedules are subject to change; it is a good idea to check all arrangements with local stations in advance.

Most cities also have municipal bus systems. As both Greyhound

---

⟳ Car rental companies

Contact details for major nationwide car rental agencies are listed below. Check the *Yellow Pages* for a full list of firms.
Alamo: tel: 844-354-6962; www.alamo.com
Avis: tel: 800-352-7900; www.avis.com
Budget: tel: 800-218-7992; www.budget.com
Dollar: tel: 800-800-4000; www.dollar.com
Enterprise: tel: 855-266-9289; www.enterprise.com
Hertz: tel: 800-654-3131; www.hertz.com
National: tel: 877-222-9058; www.nationalcar.com
Thrifty: tel: 800-847-4389; www.thrifty.com

---

and municipal stations are often situated in somewhat squalid areas, try to stay alert and do not wander too far, particularly after dark. Plan your journey for daylight arrival if possible. On the whole, the buses themselves are safe and reasonably comfortable; choosing a seat near to the driver may discourage unwanted attention.

For reservations and local bus station details, telephone 800-231-2222, or visit www.greyhound.com.

By car

The American love affair with the car is reflected in the excellent network of roads that has sprung up since World War II, creating access to the remotest areas. If you're in a hurry, the larger interstates are your best bet, with their fast, direct routes, 24-hour services, and year-round maintenance. But you will see more of the real America and its people if you drive at least some of the time on its folksy "blue highways." This book's routes offer a combination of both experiences.

Car rental agencies are located at all airports, in cities, and large towns; they are very hard to find in more remote areas of the US West. In most places you must be at least 21 years old (25 at some locations) to rent a car and you must have a valid driver's license and at least one major credit card. More agencies are accepting debit cards these days, but may hold back as much as $500 on the card to cover rental. Inquire at the time of reservation to avoid nasty surprises.

Be sure to check insurance provisions before signing anything. Cover is usually $15–25 per day. If you are a US citizen, you may already be covered by your own auto insurance or credit card company, however, so check with them first. **Loss Damage Waiver** (LDW) or **Collision Damage Waiver** (CDW) is essential. Without it, you'll be liable for any damage done to your vehicle, regardless of fault. You are advised to pay for supplementary liability insurance on top of standard third-party insurance. Be sure to walk around the rental car slowly, check it for existing damage, and make sure the agent notes any dents or dings before leaving the lot.

US rental car rates are excellent ($35/day average for a compact), if you return the car to the original location. One-way rentals are much more expensive: $100/day average. Good deals may be found in the US by checking online and booking through either a company or travel website.

Distances and driving times

The routes in this book are not designed to be driven straight through, so how long you take to drive them is entirely up to you: preferably, the slower the better. If you do decide to drive the whole route at once, allow two weeks for coastal routes and a month for cross-country routes so that you can spend two to three nights at major destinations and single nights in between. Where possible, the drives in this book are planned so that there are reasonable driving distances between towns and cities. Driving no more than 200 miles (320km)/day or four hours allows you to get the driving done in the morning, allowing you some of the afternoon to see the sights.

On cross-country routes across the West, you will inevitably have a few days of 500-mile (800km) pushes across empty highway to reach the next destination. Do a bit of planning and try to find a way of breaking up the journey to avoid burning out and having roads and towns blurring into one another.

Not counting stops, visits to attractions, side trips, traffic delays, and low-speed highways, the routes in this book could, theoretically, be driven Jack Kerouac-style straight through in the following time frames:
Atlantic Route: New York to Key West (1,761 miles/2,836km, allow 32 driving hours minimum)
Northern Route: Boston to Cape Flattery (4,095 miles/6,590km, allow 55 driving hours minimum)
Central Route: Washington, DC to Los Angeles (2,922 miles/4,702km, allow 42 driving hours minimum)
Southern Route: Atlanta to San Diego (2,572 miles/4,139km, allow 40 driving hours minimum)
Pacific Route: San Diego to Seattle (1,399 miles/2,251km, allow 30 driving hours minimum).

For detailed information on mileage between key cities along the route, see mileage charts at the back of the book.

Bikers in the Valley of Fire State Park, Nevada.

RV rentals

No special license is necessary to operate a motor home (or recreational vehicle – RV for short), but they aren't cheap. When you add up the cost of rental fees, insurance, gas, and campgrounds, you may find that renting a car and staying in motels or tent camping is less expensive. Keep in mind, too, that RVs are large and slow and may be difficult to handle on narrow mountain roads. If parking space is tight, driving an RV may be very inconvenient. Access to some roads may be limited. For additional information about RV rentals, call the **Recreational Vehicle Rental Association**, www.rvra.org; tel: 703-591-7130.

Open road survival skills

It is essential to inform yourself properly about the area you are traveling in, including weather and road conditions, and be prepared to change your plans at the first hint of potential danger, such as blizzards, heavy thunderstorms, and tornadoes.

Traveling in remote backcountry on foot is not recommended for solo travelers, but if you do, leave a note inside the car about your planned return time and don't hike off-trail or otherwise invite problems. It helps to know a few survival skills suitable for the terrain, including first aid, if you're traveling alone, especially in desert and mountain areas of the West.

It goes without saying that you should drive a reliable vehicle and carry plenty of supplies, including any medications, first aid kit, spare tire and a gallon jug of gas, large bottles of water (available at supermarkets), nutritious food, emergency flares, warm layers, and a cellphone.

Desert travelers: the single most important precaution you can take is to tell someone your destination, route, and expected time of arrival. Check tires carefully before long stretches of desert driving. Heat builds pressure, so have them at slightly below normal air pressure. The desert's arid climate makes carrying extra water – both for passengers and vehicles – essential. Carry 3-gallon water bottles in the car, and if hiking, drink at least one gallon per person per day; even on short day hikes, carry a 1-liter water bottle with you and drink often. Keep an eye on the gas gauge, and gas up whenever you have the opportunity. Remember, if you should have car trouble or become lost, do not strike out on foot. A car, visible from the air and presumably on a road, is easier to spot than a person, and it affords shelter from the weather. Wait to be found. Mountain drivers are advised to be equally vigilant. Winter storms in California's Sierra Nevada and Washington's Cascades occasionally close major roads, and at times chains are required on tires. Conditions often change fast, so check the weather forecast for road conditions before you depart.

AAA membership

Anyone spending a significant amount of time driving US highways is strongly advised to join the Automobile Association of America (AAA or Triple A); www.aaa.com. Benefits include battery and emergency breakdown service, free road maps, travel literature, and personalized trip planning. Premier level offers towing up to 200 miles (320km) from breakdown site – important if you are in the middle of nowhere – and lock-out, refueling, and jumpstart service. Insurance is also available through the association, which has a reciprocal arrangement with some of the automobile associations in other countries. For an eco-friendly alternative, try Better World Club (http://betterworldclub.com).

By motorcycle

For those with *Easy Rider* dreams, touring by motorcycle may be an inspiring option. Harley-Davidson and other major motorcycle vendors also offer rentals in some locations in the US. If you do decide to ride a motorcycle on any of the routes in this book, be conservative: you won't be able to cover as much ground as in a car in a day (probably no more than 250–300 miles/320–480km) to allow plenty of time for visiting attractions. And inevitably, you'll be riding on scenic highways and backroads off the Interstate, so factor that in, too. Vital clothing includes a helmet, stiff boots, and, in cool weather, leather chaps to cut down on road abrasion, should you take a spill. There are several organizations for enthusiasts of particular motorcycle makes, from Harley-Davidson to BMW. Several homegrown websites offer ideas on US motorcycle traveling.

By bicycle

Bicycle touring is gaining in popularity in the US. It's definitely the slow option of seeing the country, but that's not a bad thing in this age of rapid transit. Most cyclists average little more than 10–15mph (16–24kph), so your best bet is to cover a short scenic segment of any of the routes in this book, if you choose the bicycle option, and stick to areas with clustered attractions, scenery, and lodging/food services.

Hub cities

Atlanta

Public transportation
From the airport: Hartsfield-Jackson Atlanta International Airport is 10 miles (16km) from Downtown, farther to Midtown and Buckhead on the north side. Many hotels offer courtesy buses from the airport. Shared-ride shuttles provide service into the city: The ATL Airport Shuttle (tel: 404-641-0962; www. atlairportshuttle.com) serves downtown Atlanta, $16.50 one way. Taxis rates (minus tip) are fixed at $30 to Downtown, $32 to Midtown, and $38 to Buckhead. Public transportation from the airport to the city and within the metropolitan area is much cheaper and extremely safe, clean, and reliable.
Rapid Transportation/buses: Metropolitan Rapid Transit Authority (MARTA) is a rapid-rail and bus system comprising local bus service and north–south and east–west rail lines intersecting at the main Five Points Station in downtown Atlanta. Train stations are designated N, S, E, W, or P, denoting their compass points (P represents the current single station Proctor Creek line). The Hartsfield International Airport Station is designated Airport S7 and is the final stop on the South line. The trip to downtown Atlanta takes just 17 minutes. Trains operate daily 4.45am–1am. A one-way ticket costs $2.50. You can also buy a Breeze card and add value to it for your time in Atlanta. For more information, log on to www.itsmarta. com.
National buses: Greyhound operates from the depot at 232 Forsyth Street, tel: 404-584-1728.
National rail: Amtrak trains run from Peachtree Station, 1688 Peachtree Street NW, tel: 404-881-3060.

Private transportation
Atlanta – sprawling, suburban, and subject to extremes of weather – is not ideally suited for extensive walking tours.
Car rental: car rental companies may be found at the airport and/or downtown.
Taxis: Taxi companies are numerous. Hotels are always good places to find a taxi. Flat-rate fares within Downtown, Midtown, or Buckhead zones are $8, $2 each additional person. Outside the Business District, the following fares apply: first 1/8 mile, $2.50; each additional 1/8 mile, 25 cents; waiting, $21 an hour. Flat-rate fare from the airport to Downtown: $30, to Buckhead: $40. Fares are subject to 4 percent Georgia sales tax. Visit http://atlantacheckercab.com or call tel: 404-351-1111 for more information.
Bicycles: A public bicycle service launched in 2016, allowing rental of bicycles via online reservation or Social Bicycles mobile app (www. relaybikeshare.com). Visitors can rent at $3.30 for 30 minutes, and 15 cents per minute thereafter.

Boston

Public transportation
From the airport: Logan International Airport, just 3 miles (5km) from downtown Boston, is closer to town than any other major airport in the nation: this refers to distance, not to time. Traffic can back up at the tunnels under the harbor connecting the airport and city. Massachusetts Bay Transportation Authority's (MBTA) Blue Line from Airport Station is the fastest way to downtown (about 10 minutes) and many other places as well. Silver Line buses also serve downtown. Free shuttle buses run between all the airport terminals and the subway station. Cabs can be found outside each terminal. Fares to downtown should average about $20, including tip, providing there are no major traffic jams. Logan Express buses leave all terminals every 20 minutes for downtown and Back Bay hotels, and several major bus companies, including Boston Express Bus, Concord Coach Lines, Peter Pan, and C&J Bus Lines, serve many outlying suburbs and distant destinations.

Rapid transit: Boston's subway system (the "T") offers good value – just $2.25 per journey. A seven-day Link Pass, good for unlimited travel on subways, local buses, short-distance commuter rail, and inner harbor ferries costs $21.25; information at www.mbta.com.
City buses: The majority of the MBTA's 160-plus bus routes operate feeder services linking subway stations to neighborhoods not directly served by the rapid transit system. Some crosstown routes connect stations on different subway lines without going into downtown. Only a few MBTA buses actually enter downtown Boston, and most of these are express buses from outlying areas. The basic MBTA bus fare is $1.70.
Intercity buses: Several intercity bus companies serve Boston. The two largest, Greyhound (617-526-1808), and Peter Pan (800-343-9999), have frequent daily services from New York City and Albany, NY, as well as services from points within New England.
Commuter rail: The MBTA Commuter Rail extends from downtown Boston to as far as 60 miles (100km) away and serves such tourist destinations as Concord, Lowell, Salem, Ipswich, Gloucester, and Rockport. Trains to the north and northwest of Boston depart from North Station; trains to points south and west of the city leave from South Station. All south side commuter trains, except the Fairmount Line, also stop at the Back Bay Station. For information on trains from any of these stations, telephone 617-222-3200.
National rail: Amtrak Passenger trains arrive at South Station (Atlantic Avenue and Summer Street, 800-872-7245; TDD: 800-523-6590) from New York, Washington, DC, and Philadelphia with connections from all points in the nationwide Amtrak system. They also stop at Back Bay Station (145 Dartmouth Street).

Private transportation
Boston, it is justly claimed, is a walker's city – a good thing, for it is certainly not a driver's city. Early city planners laid streets along cow paths, Native American trails, and colonial wagon tracks, linked by crooked little alleys. However, in the middle of the 19th century,

impeccable grid systems were introduced in the Back Bay, South End, and, to a lesser degree, South Boston. If you attempt to drive, be aware that being stuck in a traffic jam, getting lost, and being unable to find a parking space is par for the course. Public parking facilities are found at Government Center, Post Office Square, the Public Garden, the Prudential Center, on Clarendon Street near the John Hancock Tower, and elsewhere. Private lots are scattered here and there.

Car rental: Most agencies have offices at the airport and/or downtown.

Taxis: Taxi stands are common at popular tourist sites. Companies to call include: Checker Taxi, tel: 617-536-7500; Red Cab, tel: 617-992-4404; Town Taxi Dispatch of New England, tel: 978-798-5972.

Bicycles: Boston's regional bikeshare system Blue Bikes (www.bluebikes.com) has more than 1,300 bikes at 140 dock stations. Single trips are $2.50, and the 24-hour membership fee is $10.

Los Angeles

Public transportation

From the airport: Public transportation is found on LAX's lower level, which is where arriving passengers claim baggage. At this level, there are stops for taxis, LAX shuttles, buses, courtesy trams, and vans in front of each airline terminal. Information boards about ground transport are located in all the baggage claim areas, and they are very easy to understand. Shuttles from the airport are reasonably priced; the fare varies depending on your destination. Among the companies operating 24 hours a day are FlyAway Bus Service, www.flylax.com/en/flyaway-bus; Prime Time Shuttle, www.primetimeshuttle.com; and The SuperShuttle, www.supershuttle.com. Hopping in a taxi at LAX should be avoided if at all possible. Los Angeles' cabs are very expensive – more so than most US cities – and are almost never found driving the streets looking for customers. Free shuttle service is provided to the Metro Green Line's Aviation Station (shuttle route G) for metro connection and to Parking Lot C (shuttle route C) for LAX City Bus

Center. Pick up is on the Lower/Arrival level under the LAX Shuttle sign. Check out the Metro Bus and Metro Rail routes and schedules on www.metro.net.

Metro: Los Angeles County Metropolitan Transportation Authority, known as **Metro**, serves an area of 1,433 sq miles (3,711 sq km). With 2,438 buses and six subway and rail lines. Metro Rail currently operates 105 miles (169km) of subway and light rail lines, with 93 stations stretching from North Hollywood south to Long Beach, and from the coast east to Pasadena, serving many key visitor destinations. The Metro Red Line subway serves Hollywood, Universal Studios, and several downtown locations. The Metro Blue Line runs from Downtown to Long Beach. The Metro Gold Line connects with the Red Line and a 2016 extension runs to Azusa. The Metro Green Line serves Los Angeles Airport. The Metro Orange Line serves the San Fernando Valley with Metroliner buses from Canoga Park to Chatsworth. The Purple Line subway runs from Union Station (downtown) to Koreatown along Wilshire Boulevard. The Silver Line bus serves South Bay via Downtown; The Expo Line runs to Santa Monica.

For information on **Metro Rail** and **Metro Bus**, tel: 323-466-3876 or use the trip planner on their website: www.metro.net. The base fare is $1.75 plus 50 cents for transfers. Bus drivers do not give change, so you must have the exact fare or a token. The **Metro Day Pass**, which allows unlimited bus and rail journeys, is good value at $7. You can buy them on the bus, or at vending machines in rail stations. Buses and rail lines operate from 4am to after midnight, though night services are less frequent.

The DASH **shuttle system** (tel: 213-808-2273; www.ladottransit.com) operates in Downtown during daytime hours, linking major businesses and the civic and entertainment centers. It costs 50 cents per ride and transfers are free. Separate DASH systems operate around Hollywood and other parts of the city, while Long Beach Transit (tel: 562-591-2301; www.lbtransit.com) is a similar service operating in Long Beach, with a free Passport Bus to local attractions.

Private transportation

The most efficient way to get around Los Angeles is to rent a car. Rental agencies may be found at the airport, your hotel, and in various locations around the city. Cars often can be delivered to you. Car rental companies all charge basically the same price.

Taxis: Taxis are fairly expensive. You will rarely find them cruising the streets, but they can be ordered or found at airports, train stations, bus terminals, and at major hotels.

Try LA Yellow Cab (tel: 424-222-2222) or Independent Cab (tel: 800-521-8294). LA Checker Cab Co (tel: 800-300-5007) also offers vans with wheelchair lifts. An average fare from LAX to downtown Los Angeles is a flat $46.50, plus tip.

Bicycles: Metro Bikeshare (www.bikeshare.metro.net), a public bikeshare scheme in downtown Los Angeles, with 1,100 bicycles at 65 stations, offers $1.75 single rides of 30 minutes and a $5 day pass.

Miami

Public transportation

From the airport: Miami International Airport is 7 miles (12km) from Downtown. SuperShuttle (tel: 305-871-2000) operates between the airport and major hotels. Metrorail's Orange Line connects Airport Station with downtown Miami and points south, and connects with the Green Line to points north. Several Metrobus routes also serve the Airport Station. Metrorail and Metrobusfare is $2.25. A taxi fare to Downtown costs a flat $21.70 minus tip to Downtown; $32 to South Beach, minus tip. **Rapid transit:** Metrorail is an elevated rapid transit system connecting Downtown with Dadeland and Hialeah. The free Metromover monorail system circles Downtown. Miami-Dade Transit runs both (tel: 305-891-3131; www.miamidade.gov). **City buses:** Miami-Dade Transit also runs the Metrobus fleet from stops indicated by distinctive blue and green signs.

Intercity buses: The main Greyhound terminal is at Miami Bus Station, 3801 NW 21ST #171 (tel: 305-871-1810).

Commuter rail: The Tri-Rail (tel: 800-874-7245; www.tri-rail.com)

service links Miami-Dade with Palm Beach, Broward, and the airport.

Trains: Amtrak trains run from the Miami Station at 8303 NW 37th Avenue (tel: 305-835-1223).

Private transportation

Miami is not a difficult city to negotiate by car, but try to avoid weekday rush-hour snarls. Parking in popular Miami Beach can be scarce, and restrictions are enforced by a fleet of efficient tow-trucks. Fortunately, Miami Beach is a delightful place to explore by foot. Most car rental companies have offices at Miami International airport or Downtown. Check the *Yellow Pages* for a full list of companies.

Ports: Florida has several major cruise ship ports, with Miami and Port Everglades leading with the most sailings. Others include Port Canaveral, Palm Beach, St Petersburg, Tampa, Port Manatee (in Tampa Bay), and Madeira Beach and Treasure Island (just north of St Pete Beach). PortMiami is the largest cruise port in the world. Seventeen cruise lines carry more than 4.3 million passengers a year into the port, which represents over two-thirds of all cruise passengers worldwide. The port is just a five-minute ride from Downtown and Miami Beach. Tel: 305-347-5515.

Taxis: Taxis are relatively plentiful in South Beach with fares under $5 per mile (1.6km). They can also be found at airports, train stations, bus terminals and the major hotels, or ordered by telephone. Call Yellow Cab Co (tel: 305-444-4444); Metro Taxi (tel: 305-888-8888); or Flamingo Taxi (tel: 305-759-8100).

Bicycles: Miami's public bike-share program, Citi Bike Miami (http://citibikemiami.com), has numerous rental options. A one hour ride is $4.50; a day pass is $24.

New York City

Public transportation

From the airport: AirTrain is a three-line airport rail system that connects JFK and Newark airports with subway and rail networks at Howard Beach (A train) and Sutphin Boulevard (E, J, and Z train) subways and at Jamaica Long Island

Railroad station for JFK, and at a special airport rail station in Newark. At each airport, AirTrain runs every few minutes and takes about 10 minutes from each terminal. Traveling between JFK and Midtown Manhattan by AirTrain and subway takes about one hour; traveling from Newark (by AirTrain and then Amtrak or NJ Transit train to Penn Station) can take only 30–45 minutes. For AirTrain information contact (JFK) tel: 877-535-2478; (Newark) tel: 888-397-4636 or visit www.panynj.gov/airtrain and choose one of the airports.

NYC Airporter (tel: 718-777-5111; www.nycairporter.com) express buses run between JFK and LaGuardia airports and Penn Station in Manhattan. Pick-up and drop-off points include: Port Authority Bus Terminal, Penn Station, and Grand Central Terminal, with a transfer service available to Midtown hotels (in such case you need to select Bryant Park as the drop-off location). Hotel pick-up is not available. Buses from JFK run 5am–11.30pm.

From LaGuardia, the SBS M60 bus to upper Manhattan subway stations operates 24/7, while bus Q-70 LTD runs to 74th St subway stop in Jackson Heights, Queens, from which various trains run to Penn Station, Manhattan.

Newark Liberty Airport Express (tel: 877-894-9155; www.newarkairportexpress.com) operates express buses daily between Newark airport and Midtown Manhattan, stopping at the Port Authority Bus Terminal, Grand Central, and Bryant Park (Fifth Avenue, at 42nd Street). Buses run 4am–1am.

There are several minibus services from all three airports to Manhattan. A big plus is that they take you door to door, direct to hotels or private addresses, but this can be slow, with many stops. SuperShuttle (tel: 800-258-3826; www.supershuttle.com) offers a frequent service. It can be booked online, at airport ground transportation centers, or from courtesy phones at the airports.

Rapid transit and buses: Subways and buses run 24 hours, less frequently after midnight, with the fare payable by token or (buses only) exact change, as well as by MetroCard pass (available at subway

ticket booths), which allows free transfers within two hours of use. Unlimited-ride passes for seven days or 30-day passes are also available, as is a day pass sold at newsstands, hotels, and electronic kiosks in some subway stations. For general bus and subway information and for other details about the MetroCard pass call: 718-330-1234; www.mta.info/metrocard/mcgtreng.htm has details. Greyhound buses run from the Port Authority bus terminal, 41st and 625 Eighth Avenue (tel: 212-971-6789).

Trains: National rail trains arrive and depart from Manhattan's two railroad terminals: Grand Central Terminal and Pennsylvania Station. City buses stop outside each terminal and each sits atop a subway station. Amtrak information, tel: 800-872-7245.

Private transportation

Car Rental: Driving around Manhattan is not much fun, but should the need arise, you'll find car rental companies at airports.

Taxis: All are metered, cruise the streets randomly, and must be hailed, although there are official taxi stands at places like Grand Central Station. Be sure to hail an official Yellow Cab, not an unlicensed "gypsy" cab. One fare covers all passengers up to four (five in a few of the larger cabs). After 8pm there is a 50¢ surcharge on all taxi rides. Telephone 212-302-8294 for lost property or to make a complaint.

Bicycles: Citi Bike (www.citibikenyc.com), the bike-sharing scheme, has operated in NYC since 2013. Single, 30-minute rides are $3; a 24-hour pass costs $12.

San Diego

Public transportation

From the airport: Various shuttle services operate from San Diego International Airport to downtown San Diego and are reasonably priced. Shuttle service companies include Advanced Shuttle (tel: 800-719-3499) and Sea Breeze Shuttle (tel: 619-297-7463). Metropolitan Transit System (MTS) bus route 992 travels from the airport to Downtown.

City buses and trolleys: City buses and the San Diego Trolley are run by San Diego Metropolitan Transit System (tel: 619-557-4555; www.sdmts.com). Fares start at $2.25 for

Washington DC's metro.

buses and $2.50 for trolleys, exact change required. Day passes cost $7 and include both bus and trolley routes. The **San Diego Trolley System** has three lines; the Blue Line travels from Downtown to the Mexican border at San Ysidro, the Orange Line travels Gillespie to Downtown, and the Green Line travels Santee to Old Town. Trolleys operate daily from 5am until midnight. Some bus services run later, but routes vary.

Trains: Amtrak (tel: 800-872-7245; www.amtrak.com) trains run from the Santa Fe Depot at 1050 Kettner Boulevard to Los Angeles with stops along the coast. **The Coaster** (tel: 760-966-6500; www.gonctd.com) is an express rail commuter service that runs between downtown San Diego and Oceanside.

Private transportation
Unlike Los Angeles, San Diego is a relatively easy city to explore, with or without a car. However, as in most big cities, journeys are best planned around the weekday early morning and late afternoon crush. Parking is generally easy to find and for the most part moderately priced. Most of the major car rental agencies have offices at the airport and in the downtown area.

Taxis: Try any of the following or check the *Yellow Pages* for a full list of companies – Orange Cab, tel:

619-223-5555, www.orangecabsandiego. net; San Diego Taxi Co., tel: 619-566-6666, www.sandiegotaxicompany.com; Yellow Cab, tel: 619-444-4444, www. driveu.com.

Traveling to Tijuana, Baja California, Mexico
About 300,000 people visit Tijuana, Mexico, over the border on the Baja California Peninsula every year. In the past, US citizens did not need a passport to travel to Tijuana for the day, but new Homeland Security border security rules now require that US citizens as well as non-citizens carry a valid passport (some US state-issued enhanced driver's licenses with embedded microchips are permitted but check first) and, if applicable, an alien registration card (green card), to reenter the country. Be sure you have these in hand before making the trip to avoid big headaches.

US car insurance is not valid in Mexico, so it's essential to obtain short-term car insurance at one of the many sales offices just north of the border if you plan on driving in Mexico. Crossing into Mexico is easy, with immigration officers at both sides usually just waving you along.

Because driving is not easy in Tijuana for those unfamiliar with the city (and the Spanish language), many drivers park in San Diego's San Ysidro, crossing into Tijuana via the

elevated pedestrian walkway. Avoid leaving your car in the parking places of merchants unless you want to have it towed away by police. There's an all-day secure lot off the "Last Exit US Parking" ramp – turn right at the stop sign to the Tijuana side. Cheap taxis and buses are available.

Return Crossing: Reentering the US is generally a much more tense experience than entering Mexico, as US Border Patrol officers scrutinize who is entering the country very carefully. Expect long lines, especially in busy vacation periods, and plan accordingly.

Finally, keep your wits about you while visiting Mexico to avoid getting caught up in any unrest or areas of high-crime activity. It's best to keep to well-traveled areas, and particularly avoid driving at night.

Bicycles: San Diego's bike-share system Discover Bike (www.disco verbikesandiego.com) has some 1,800 bikes and numerous dock stations located downtown and around Balboa Park. Single 30-minute rides are $5 and an 8-hour pass is $24.

Seattle

Public transportation
From the airport: The quickest connection between Sea-Tac and downtown Seattle is via Sound Transit's Link Light Rail (tel: 888-889-6368;

www.soundtransit.org), which runs from 5am to 1am, roughly every 15 minutes, and takes 40 minutes. One-way tickets are just $2.25–$3.25. Bus or van companies that link the airport with metropolitan Seattle or Bellevue include:
Airporter Shuttle (tel: 866-235-5247)
Shuttle Express (tel: 425-981-7000)
Capital Aeroporter (tel: 800-962-3579)
Quick Shuttle (tel: 800-665-2122)
Yellow Cab (tel: 206-622-6500) provides a taxi service to and from the airport. From the airport to downtown Seattle (or vice versa) costs a flat $40 minus tip.

National buses: The Greyhound terminal is located at 303 South Jackson Street, Seattle Amtrak (tel: 206-382-4127).

National trains: The Amtrak station is at Third Avenue and S. Jackson Street (tel: 800-872-7245).

Public transportation: Metro Transit (tel: 206-553-3000) operates commuter rail, buses, and water taxis.

Monorail: The Monorail (tel: 206-905-2620; www.seattlemonorail.com), which was built for the 1962 World's Fair, runs every 10 minutes between Seattle Center and Westlake Center. The ride is just under a mile (2km) and takes 90 seconds. It's clean and spacious with large windows.

Ferries: The Washington State Ferry system (tel: 800-843-3779; www.wsdot.wa.gov/ferries), the largest in the country, covers the Puget Sound area, linking Seattle (at Pier 52) with the Olympic Peninsula via Bremerton and Bainbridge Island. State ferries also depart from West Seattle to Vashon Island and Southworth, and from Edmonds, 7 miles (11km) north of Seattle, to Kingston on Kitsap Peninsula. They also go from Anacortes, 90 miles (145km) northwest of Seattle, through the San Juan Islands to Victoria, on Canada's Vancouver Island. Passengers to Canada need a passport. The Black Ball Ferry (tel: 360-457-4491; www.cohoferry.com) departs from Port Angeles on the Olympic Peninsula to Victoria, BC, on Vancouver Island, four times a day in summer and twice daily the rest of the year. Ferries carry cars.

Private transportation
When the weather is fine, Seattle is a pleasant city to walk in – it is hilly, but many of the sights may be toured comfortably on foot. Heavy traffic congestion and scarce, expensive parking make driving downtown a less attractive option. Many of the major car rental agencies have offices at Seattle-Tacoma Airport or in the downtown area. Consult the *Yellow Pages* phone book for a full listing of rental firms.

Bicycles: Seattle is currently trialing a new, private, for-profit bike-sharing program, with LimeBike (www.li.me) and Spin (www.spin.pm). Download the app to reserve; bikes can be left at your destination.

Washington, DC

Public transportation
From National: The Metro subway station is easily accessible from the airport terminal with quick service into DC (about $7). You can also take a taxi, available curbside when you pick up your bags, with fares that range from $10 to $30.

From Dulles: Take a Washington Flyer Taxi (tel: 703-572-8294) directly into the city, which will cost about $65. Metrobus service runs about every 30 minutes and costs $7. Buy your bus ticket at the kiosk on the airport Arrivals level. The Washington Flyer Silver Line Express leaves every 20 minutes from Arrivals Level door 4 and connects to the Metro for $5.

From BWI: A taxi from this airport to DC – the most distant, at 59 miles (95km) away – will cost an eye-watering average $127. A more sensible option is to take the free shuttle to the nearby Amtrak rail station (tel: 800-872-7245; www.amtrak.com) and ride the train to Union Station in DC for just $15–45 (the train leaves every 12 minutes from 5am to 1am). Alternatively, if you don't mind a long ride, take Metrobus B30 from BWI to Greenbelt Metro Station, and from there continue to Union Station, a combined journey of 67 minutes .

SuperShuttle: You can pick up one of these dependable blue minivans at any of the airports and share a ride into the city. Estimated cost from Dulles to DC is $25, from BWI to DC is $37, from National about $20. When you're ready to fly home, schedule a pickup to the airport by phoning 800-258-3826 (Blue Van).

International Limousine is one of the city's oldest limo services, available 24 hours. Tel: 202-388-6800 or visit www.internationallimo.com.

Metro: A $14.75 one-day Metrorail pass provides all-day subway travel after 9.30am. **City buses:** Metrobus (tel: 202-637-7000) operates a comprehensive but confusing network of routes covering the city and outlying areas. You need exact change to board. The Silver Line Express Bus Service between Dulles Airport and the Metrorail Wiehle-Reston East Station to pick up the rail to downtown DC is now open and costs $5; it runs every 30 minutes. For prices and schedules for both Metrorail and Metrobus see http://wmata.com.

National buses: Greyhound buses operate out of the Union Station at 50 Massachusetts Avenue NE (tel: 202-789-4318).

National rail: Amtrak runs from Union Station, 60 Massachusetts Avenue NE (tel: 800-872-7245).

Private transportation
Washington, DC is compact enough to make it one of the best cities in the country for exploring on foot.
Car rental: Another good way to get around – particularly if you are interested in some of the worthwhile day trips – is to rent a car. You can do this at the airport, your hotel, or any car rental agency.

Parking: A very few hotels in town offer free parking, but most charge a daily fee, which is in the $50/day range. Many hotels on the outskirts also charge, but generally in the $20/day range. Parking around DC is difficult on the street and expensive in parking lots.

Taxis: Long-distance taxi fares are steep; in the District, fees are $3.25 for the first eighth of a mile, with a $25/hour "wait fee," which kicks in whenever the cab is moving at less than 10 mph (16kph). For planned trips, reserve a taxi at least an hour in advance of departure. Two of the major taxicab companies are: Diamond Cab, tel: 202-387-6200 and Yellow Cab, tel: 202-544-1212; www.dcyellowcab.com.
Bicycles: Capital Bike Share (www.capitalbikeshare.com) operates a public bike system in Washington, DC, Arlington, Alexandria, and Montgomery County. You can choose between several membership options, including 24-hour and 3-day-passes.

A

Accommodations

Hotels and motels

Chain hotels and motels are reliable, convenient, and often reasonably priced, but tend to lack character. In general, prices range from $50 to $150 plus tax, depending on the location, the season, and additional amenities. Resorts and large hotels are often located on spacious properties outside the downtown area and cater to guests who want everything onsite, from pools, spas, health centers, and sporting facilities to restaurants and cafes, high-end shopping, ATM machines, business and meeting facilities, and in-room amenities such as fridges, microwaves, and coffeemakers. Their friendly, all-in anonymity may be just what you require when your nervous system needs to come down from the occasionally overwhelming sensory input of a long road trip.

Boutique inns and small historic hotels, on the other hand, are often located in converted historic buildings downtown. They offer B&B-like charm along with big-hotel sophistication and a surprising number of amenities, such as spas, fine dining, and in-room extras like Jacuzzi baths and robes. Their downtown location can make them a bit noisier than outlying hotels, and you'll usually pay more. But it's definitely worth it, if your budget allows, as these unique inns tend to be memorable and offer a quick way of getting to know more about the history and ambiance of a town – desirable if you're only in an area for one night.

Watch for hidden fees at luxury hotel chains. Most lodgings – even small ones – offer wireless internet in rooms, but beware of hefty access fees at major hotels. Phone connection charges may also be high. You can usually get free access to wireless internet in the lobby and use a pay phone there, if you don't have a cellphone. It is also common for resorts (and even some motels in resort areas) to tack on a daily fee to cover guests' use of facilities such as the swimming pool, spa facilities, and shuttle service. Be sure to ask when booking. Many hotels in larger cities will also charge a nightly parking fee, which can quickly push up a bill. Reservations made on the internet generally offer the best deal, but you can also call and ask specifically about special weekend or corporate rates and package deals. Motels, such as Best Western, offer a discount for AAA and AARP members. Book your room by credit card and secure a guaranteed late arrival, in case of any delays in your travel plans.

Hostels

A number of US cities and towns offer inexpensive hostels as a bare-bones budget option for travelers. Accommodations are typically dorm-style, but many also rent private rooms at a reasonable rate, making an expensive city stay viable for those on a strict budget. For more information, check www.hihostels.com or www.ymca.net.

Bed and breakfasts

B&Bs tend to be more personal than hotels. In some cases, you're a guest in a person's home, where the accommodations are fairly simple and may involve a lot of interaction with family and other guests; in others, the rooms are in separate (large) historic homes or inns decorated with antiques, quilts, art, and other period furnishings. Before booking, also ask whether the room has a private bathroom, telephone, television, and wireless internet access. Inquire about breakfast, too. Breakfast is included in the price but may be anything from a couple of muffins to a gourmet feast (expect the latter as a selling point at many high-end B&Bs in the US). For more information on B&Bs visit www.bbonline.com.

National parks

Lodgings inside popular parks such as Grand Canyon, Yosemite, and Yellowstone sell out a year in advance, so it's essential to book as soon as possible. Reservations are handled through the park's concessionaire, a company operating under license with the **National Park Service** (www.nps.gov) to manage accommodations, food service, gift shops, tours, and other services. Information is available on the park's website or by calling direct.

Campgrounds

Most state and national parks, US Forest Service areas, and some Bureau of Land Management sites have developed campgrounds. National Park Service campgrounds typically offer groomed tent and RV campsites with water, hookups, barbecue grate, picnic table, and a restroom with flush toilets; state parks usually also offer showers, electrical hookups, campstore, and other facilities.

Fees average $14–$25 per site, depending on whether it is a tent or RV site with hookups; sites in popular areas, such as the California coast, can cost double, are reservation only, and sell out fast. Primitive campgrounds in national parks and national forests are a good bet for those on a budget; they have designated campsites but only a pit toilet and often no water or other facilities. Such sites are less expensive (averaging $10–$15), and if you're lucky, they may even be free.

National forests also allow free "dispersed camping" away from trails and destinations. You must be entirely self-sufficient, as there are no facilities. Bring everything you need, including a gallon of water per person per day, nutritious food, and importantly, practice "leave no trace" camping.

If you plan on overnighting in national park backcountry or wilderness, you'll need to register with the park's backcountry office in person to receive a permit and a designated campsite. This may be free (although not necessarily): rangers use it to restrict backcountry numbers, safeguarding the resource and visitor experience of solitude. Most campgrounds are busy from mid-June to September (winter in Florida). You must make advance reservations for many popular camping regions, such as coastal state park campgrounds in California and Florida and the Northwest. Reservations for state park campgrounds and those under National Park Service or US Forest Service management may be made by logging onto www.reserveamerica.com or www.recreation.gov; tel: 877-444-6777; international: 518-885-3639. Reservations may be made up to six months in advance. Note: NPS campgrounds increasingly require reservations, but hold back a few first-come, first-served campsites. Plan on arriving very early in the day to get a spot.

Private RV campgrounds are typically very developed and more expensive and offer additional facilities such as coin laundries, pools, playgrounds, and restaurants. An extensive nationwide network of such sites is run by Kampgrounds of America (KOA); www.koa.com. Another good resource is *Go Camping America* (www.gocampingamerica.com).

Admission charges

Admission is usually charged at both private and public museums and attractions, although you will find quite a few free museums around the country. Special traveling exhibits at nationally known museums may charge as much as $25. Museums often offer free or reduced entrance fees certain days or evenings, often a Friday night. Most national parks and state parks charge an entrance fee valid for a week's stay. State parks are typically around $16. Entrance fees are currently charged at only 118 of 417 national parks, but charges at popular destination parks, such as Grand Canyon, have increased to an average $25–$30 per carload.

Consider buying **multi-site passes** for attractions in the larger cities, if available. Local visitor centers can assist you with planning, and many also offer discount coupons, with excellent deals on local attractions, hotels, and dining.

Anyone planning on visiting several national parks and other federally managed sites is strongly advised to buy an annual **America the Beautiful National Parks and Federal Recreational Lands Pass** ($80), which allows unlimited entry to over 2,000 federally managed public lands (NPS, BLM, USFS, and US Army Corps of Engineers) across the US as well as campground discounts. These interagency passes are available to anyone at park entrance gates or from the US Geological Survey (tel: 1-888-275-8747; https://store.usgs.gov/pass).

Age restrictions

Few age restrictions are imposed at attractions. Theme parks, such as Disney World, may state age, weight, and height restrictions for safety reasons. To enter premises serving alcohol, you must be 21 or over in most states.

B

Budgeting for your trip

Currently favorable exchange rates for the euro and pound against the dollar mean that the US remains a good destination for travelers, especially those on a road trip, where the main cost will be car rental, gas, lodging, and food, and you can search out bargains en route.

You can save considerably if you camp, stay in budget motels, eat in hometown cafés like the locals or bring your own food for picnics, and keep to a budget for visiting attractions. Allow $100–170 per day for good-quality lodgings for two people, although really memorable hotels and bed-and-breakfasts tend to run you closer to $200 per night (more in big cities). At the other end of the spectrum, you'll find an array of hostels and attractive campgrounds with full facilities for $16–35 per night; bare-bones motel lodgings can be found for about $60; and reliable chains are in the $80–100 range (look for AAA discounts and online deals at chains like Best Western and La Quinta). You can probably get away with $50 per day per person for basic meals if you stick to diners, food trucks, cafés, markets, and inexpensive restaurants and don't drink alcohol.

Meals in better restaurants cost a lot more, but if you're determined to visit that famous high-end establishment and don't have the cash, one insider trick is to eat lunch there: you'll find many of the items on the dinner menu at much lower prices and still get to say you've eaten at a hip eatery.

Budget roughly $3 per gallon for gas costs for your rental car (more in California); most economy vehicles get over 30 miles per gallon. Trams, light rail, buses, and other public transportation in cities like Tampa, Miami, Seattle, San Francisco, and Atlanta – even Los Angeles, Phoenix and Tucson – are just a few dollars per ride, allowing you to get around for much less.

C

Children

Two words of advice about traveling with children: first, be prepared and, second, don't expect to cover too much ground. Take everything you need, along with a general first-aid kit: Western towns may be small and remote with supplies limited. If you need baby formula, special foods, diapers, or medication, carry them with you along with those wonderful all-purpose traveler's aids: wet wipes and Ziploc bags. Games, books, and crayons help kids pass time in the car. Carrying snacks and drinks in a daypack will come in handy when kids (or adults) get hungry on the road. Give yourself plenty of time, as kids do not travel at the same pace as adults.

Be sure that wilderness areas and other backcountry places are suitable for children. Are there abandoned mine shafts, steep stairways, cliffs or other hazards? Is a lot of walking necessary? Are food, water, shelter, bathrooms, and other essentials available at the site? Avoid dehydration by having children drink plenty of water before and during outdoor activities. And particularly in summer, be sure they wear sunscreen with an SPF of at least 30, a broad-brim hat, sunglasses, sturdy sandals or hiking boots, and layered clothing. Don't push children beyond their limits. Rest often and allow for extra napping.

Climate

The US continent is vast, and the climate varies depending on region. Climatic norms continue to change, bringing unexpected weather extremes everywhere. Pack carefully, and be prepared.

Typically, it's temperate on the Pacific coast, semi-tropical in Florida and the Deep South, arctic in Alaska, semi-arid in the Great Plains west of the Mississippi River, and arid in the Desert Southwest.

Low winter temperatures in the Northwest are ameliorated occasionally in January and February by warm Chinook winds from the eastern slopes of the Rocky Mountains, but ice storms are common in the Columbia River Gorge, on the Washington-Oregon boundary, the only sea-level thoroughfare through the Cascade Mountains.

Hurricane season, which affects Florida and the Gulf Coast and runs from June 1 to November 30, annually produces some destructive tropical storms, hurricanes, storm surges, and torrential rain. Tornadoes, the bane of the Midwest, can strike suddenly and specifically in spring, and even late winter, if the right conditions arise.

Between early July and September in the Southwest, heavy "monsoon" rains arrive daily from the southwest following the summer change in the jetstream. They can be dangerous, creating flash-floods that sweep away everything in their path. The shift in jetstream in winter blows northwesterly winds onshore over mountain ranges that, along with frigid temperatures, typically bring heavy snows (depending on conditions

in the Pacific). Snowfall is often heavy in the Midwest, Great Lakes region, and the Northeast, paralyzing some of the country's busiest areas in winter.

When to visit

American schools typically break for the summer by June and begin the new school year by late August, earlier than in Europe. With long lazy summer days ahead and vacation days piling up, this is the traditional time for a family road trip. Consider this only if you don't mind soaring temperatures, hot and humid conditions near water, desiccatingly hot, dry, dusty conditions in the desert, and crowded freeways, hotels, campgrounds, and attractions across the US. Far better is to time your road trip to enjoy the singular glories of spring and fall across the magical US landscape (although do try to avoid spring break in March/April).

After Labor Day, the kids are back in school; roads, parks, and campgrounds are quieter; and weather conditions – usually warm days and cool nights – are perfect for outdoor activities. Winter has its own particular charm, but with frigid temperatures, heavy snows and winds, and road closures across the country, it's not the best time for a road trip.

Only the Southern, Atlantic, and Pacific routes are suitable for winter travel, and even then come prepared for bad weather that occasionally brings snow to low-desert areas like Tucson. Think twice before driving the Central, Northern, and Atlantic routes in this book in winter. If skiing is the main attraction, you'd do better to fly to a resort. Most winter travelers head for the Southern US, particularly Florida, where the sun shines 300 days of the year and winters are mild; the high season is January through April, rates plummet in summer. Many locals time their trips for the quieter, still-pleasant shoulder seasons of May and June and October to December.

What to wear

The US climate is varied and quite intense, often changing rapidly from one extreme to another. Your best bet is to bring layers of light-weight clothing, which can cover

exposed skin or be rolled up; a hat; polarized sunglasses; sturdy walking shoes or sandals; and a packable waterproof shell in summer. In winter, long underwear made of silk or breathable technical fabrics can be slipped under fleece or wool for warmth. Don't forget wool gloves, scarf, and hat, and possibly a lightweight packable down jacket in high-elevation areas and those in the northern US. A sunscreen with an SPF of 30 or above is a good idea at any time of year.

Crime and safety

If you are driving, never pick up anyone you don't know. Always be wary of who is around you. If you have trouble on the road, stay in the car and lock the doors, turn on your hazard lights and/or leave the hood up to increase your visibility and alert passing police. It's well worth carrying a sign requesting help. Do not accept a rental car that is obviously labeled as such. Company decals and special license plates may attract thieves on the lookout for tourist valuables.

Hitchhiking

Hitchhiking is illegal in many places and ill-advised everywhere. It is an inefficient and dangerous method of travel. Don't do it!

In the city

Most big cities have their share of crime. Common sense is your most effective weapon. Try to avoid walking alone at night – at the very least stick to livelier, more brightly lit thoroughfares and move about as if you know where you are going. Don't carry large sums of money or expensive video/camera equipment.

Keep an eye on your belongings. Never leave your car unlocked, or small children by themselves. Hotels usually warn that they do not guarantee the safety of belongings left in their rooms. If you have any valuables, you may want to lock them in the hotel safe. Many better hotels now have room safes with changeable codes.

Take particular care when using bank ATMs at night. If you are in doubt about which areas are safe, seek advice from hotel staff or police.

Customs regulations

You may bring in duty-free gifts worth up to $800 (American citizens) or $100 (foreign travelers). Visitors over 18 may bring in 200 cigarettes and 50 cigars or 4.4lbs (2kg) of tobacco. Those over 21 may bring in 34 fl oz (1 liters) of alcohol. Travelers with more than $10,000 in US or foreign currency, travelers' checks, or money orders must declare these upon entry. Among the prohibited goods are meat or meat products, illegal drugs, firearms, seeds, plants, and fruits. For a breakdown of customs allowances write to: United States Customs and Border Protection, 1300 Pennsylvania Avenue NW, Washington, DC 20229; tel. 877-227-5511; 703-526-4200 from abroad; www.cbp.gov.

D

Disabled travelers

The 1995 Americans with Disabilities Act (ADA) brought sweeping changes to facilities across America. Accommodations with five or more rooms must be useable by persons with disabilities. Older and smaller inns and lodges are often wheelchair-accessible.

For the sight-impaired, many hotels provide special alarm clocks, captioned TV services, and security measures. To comply with ADA hearing-impaired requirements, many hotels have begun

Gift shop on Route 66, Seligman, Arizona.

to follow special procedures; local agencies may provide TTY and interpretation services.

Check with the front desk when you make reservations to ascertain the degree to which the hotel complies with ADA guidelines. Ask specific questions regarding bathroom facilities, bed height, wheelchair space, and availability of services.

Many major attractions have wheelchairs for loan or rent; most national parks today also offer paved "barrier-free" or "accessible" trails. Some provide visitor guides and interpreters for hearing- and sight-impaired guests. The **Society for Accessible Travel and Hospitality** (tel: 212-447-7284; www.sath.org) publishes a quarterly magazine on travel for the disabled.

E

Electricity

Standard electricity in North America is 110–115 volts, 60 cycles AC. An adapter is necessary for most appliances from overseas, with the exception of Japan.

Embassies and consulates

Australia: 1601 Massachusetts Avenue NW, Washington, DC 20036 Tel: 202-797-3000; http://usa.embassy.gov.au
Canada: 501 Pennsylvania Avenue NW, Washington, DC 20001 Tel: 202-682-1740; http://international.gc.ca

⊘ Emergencies

Dial 911 (the operator will put you through to the police, ambulance, or fire services). The call is toll free anywhere in the US, including on cellphones. If you can't get through, **dial 0** for an operator. In national parks, it's best to **contact a ranger**. For free emergency roadside assistance in Mexico, contact the **Green Angels** at 078.

Great Britain: 3100 Massachusetts Avenue NW, Washington, DC 20008 Tel: 202-588-6500; https://www.gov.uk/world/organisations/british-embassy-washington
Ireland: 2234 Massachusetts Avenue NW, Washington, DC 20008 Tel: 202-462-3939; www.dfa.ie/irish-embassy/usa
Mexico: 1911 Pennsylvania Avenue NW, Washington, DC 20006 Tel: 202-728-1600; http://embamex.sre.gob.mx/eua
New Zealand: 37 Observatory Circle NW, Washington, DC 20008 Tel: 202-328-4800; www.mfat.govt.nz

Eating out

All-American

All-American (really German) mainstays like hot dogs and burgers and pretzels are associated with ballparks, corner stands, bars, and fast-food places throughout the country. In New York, look for Jewish deli favorites, such as lox, corned beef, pastrami, and sour pickles, and thin-crust Neapolitan pizza. In Chicago, Polish-style sausages and Italian deep-dish pizza are local favorites. In Philadelphia, Philly cheese steaks explode out of hoagie rolls, while in New Orleans, enormous muffaletta sandwiches, crammed with Italian sliced meats, olives, and dressing, are a specialty at Johnny's Po-Boys in the French Quarter, also home to the city's famous po'boy sandwiches, stuffed with everything from fried oysters to alligator sausage.

Barbecue

Slow-cooked barbecue leans heavily on pork in the South and East but, invariably, beef in the West. Each region has its own style and fan base. You'll find aged beef with a smoky tomato sauce in Texas

and "pulled" (shredded) pork in vinegar-based sauces in the South: Memphis, Tennessee, famous for its barbecue, offers both wet and dry versions.

Coastal America

Coastal America is a haven for fresh seafood – from lobster and clams in New England and grouper on the Gulf to snapper in California and Dungeness crab and salmon in the Pacific Northwest. Inland mountain lakes, rivers, and streams in the Rockies and the Cascades and the Mississippi Delta support rainbow trout, striped bass, catfish, and numerous other delicate freshwater fish.

The Pacific Coast's huge Asian population has led to a lighter fusion cuisine from California to Washington, combining traditional meat and fish with Chinese, Japanese, Vietnamese, and Thai flavors that linger in the mouth.

Southern food

Southern food, while playing up deep-fried chicken, boiled ham, collard greens, hush puppies, grits, pecan pie and sweet potato pie, and other "po' folks" foods, has a fusion all its own. The region's Latin, Afro-Caribbean, and French roots are major influences, with the latter's rich Continental-style cuisine as the main fine-dining option.

Rich meets spicy in New Orleans, with its complex gumbo stews and smothered Cajun dishes like crawfish étoufée, and in Florida, where "Floribbean" cuisine combines fresh fish, local citrus and other fruits, and West Indian spices.

Mexican and Southwestern

Mexican food is ubiquitous – sometimes authentic, but often involving quantities of meat and cheese in Tex-Mex concoctions that are a far cry from simple tortillas, tamales, and enchiladas. In Cowboy Country, blowout steak dinners are accompanied by the fixings – baked potatoes, sweetcorn, and coleslaw.

Out West, look for delicious, low-fat, grass-fed bison, venison, elk, and other game accompanied by wild greens, pinyon nuts, and wild berries, mainstays of Native American cuisine, which has a growing following.

Road food

Road food is a subject unto itself. Never pass up a slice of homemade pie made from local fruit in farm states like Arizona, Georgia, and Washington; backwoods barbecue, fried green tomatoes, and boiled peanuts in the South; and filled sweet Czech pastries called kolaches in Texas Hill Country. Lastly, when you're traveling hundreds of miles a day, the most important meal of the day is breakfast. Even the lowliest truck stop or diner can fuel you properly for your travels, with pancakes, waffles, and creative egg dishes for under $10. Reason enough to get up in the morning.

Etiquette

Visitors often associate the US with relaxed manners. While that may be true up to a point, particularly in dress and table manners, you should also be prepared for many Americans, particularly those who live in conservative areas of the Midwest and the South, to be surprisingly polite and formal, in speech, dress, and the intricate dance of social interaction.

Americans, as a rule, are positive, curious about others, generally accepting of differences, warm, effusive, and tactile. This being a nation of immigrants, care is generally taken in polite society not to give offence to any one group, and chauvinism and racism, though evident, are not tolerated in most social situations, so be careful about making off-color jokes or making assumptions about different regions of the country.

Visiting Indian reservations, which are sovereign lands within the US with their own laws and moral code, calls for unique sensitivity and cultural awareness. Make an effort to blend in, dress conservatively, behave modestly – particularly at Indian ceremonial dances, which are religious rituals, and never enter a home without being invited (nor refuse a meal if invited on a feast day, as that is considered rude). Many tribes rely on tourism for their income and have developed luxury resorts on their scenic lands to rival any in Las Vegas. In remote areas, you will usually be asked to pay a small fee to take photos of family members.

Health and medical care

Medical services are extremely expensive. Always arrange comprehensive travel insurance to cover treatment and emergencies. Check the small print – most policies exclude treatment for water, winter or mountain sports accidents unless excess cover has been included.

If you need medical assistance, consult the *Yellow Pages* for the physician or pharmacist nearest to you. The bigger hotels may have a resident doctor. In large cities, there is usually a physician referral service number listed.

If you need immediate attention, go directly to a hospital emergency room (ER); most are open 24 hours a day. You may be asked to produce proof of insurance cover before being treated. Walk-in medical clinics are much cheaper than hospital emergency rooms for minor ailments.

Avoid dehydration and overexposure to the sun. In the desert, or at high altitude, this can happen rapidly, even on cloudy days. A cover-up, high-factor sun lotion, hat, and one-liter water bottle are essential (try lightly salting your water to balance electrolytes and avoid hyponatremia). Avoid dehydrating alcohol, caffeine, and sugar, and pace yourself at high elevation. Allow yourself a day or two to acclimate.

Internet and websites

Many public libraries, copy centers, hotels, and airports offer high-speed or wireless internet access. Some (usually not libraries) charge a fee for access, either on their computer or your device. Surprisingly, lower-priced chain hotels are less likely to charge than expensive places. At all company-owned Starbucks coffeehouses Wi-Fi is free, as it is at many other coffeehouses and restaurants. At some airports, you must first purchase a Boingo Pass (www.boingo.com/mcr), before being able to log on. In big cities, public Wi-Fi hotspots are plentiful.

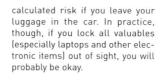

LGBTQ travelers

On the whole, urban areas in the US are safer places to visit for gay and lesbian travelers than rural destinations away from the cities. Keep a low profile in such areas, particularly in the conservative Bible Belt in the South, to avoid problems. Having said that, the lucrative LGBT market is one of the hottest targeted markets in the US, and most states now offer information on gay-friendly travel within their communities. Cities like New York, South Beach (Miami), Seattle, San Francisco, Los Angeles, Phoenix, and Tucson roll out the red carpet. Smaller arts and university cities, such as Santa Fe, Austin, and Flagstaff, also have surprisingly large gay communities.

Damron Company (www.damron. com) publishes guides aimed at gay travelers and lists gay-owned and gay-friendly accommodations nationwide.

Luggage storage

For security reasons, most airports and train stations in the US no longer operate luggage storage facilities for travelers, although some private companies do offer luggage lockers. Check with the individual location. Most hotels will allow you to check out and leave your luggage in a safe storage area. You will be taking a

Gay bar in San Francisco.

calculated risk if you leave your luggage in the car. In practice, though, if you lock all valuables (especially laptops and other electronic items) out of sight, you will probably be okay.

Lost property

If you lose property, your best bet is to immediately report it to management of the attraction or hotel where the loss occurred, then file a report in person at the local police station; some police stations allow you to file an electronic report via email. All airlines have lost luggage desks and will usually forward any delayed bags to your destination.

Maps

A detailed road map is essential for any road trip. They are widely available from state welcome and city visitor centers, large bookstores such as Barnes & Noble, outdoor stores, filling stations, supermarkets, and convenience stores. Cross-country travelers may find it useful to purchase a road-map book with maps of all 50 states, such as the one published by Rand McNally. The American Automobile Association (AAA) provides excellent maps free of charge to members (including the excellent Southwest Indian Country map). Maps of national and state parks, forests, and other public

lands are handed out at entrance stations. Extremely detailed topographical maps of states are available from the US Geological Survey (www.usgs.gov/pubprod). Topo maps are usually available in higher-end bookstores and shops that sell outdoor gear.

Media

Newspapers

Most communities across the US publish print and electronic editions of newspapers, and the opinions and endorsements of columnists and editorial boards continue to play an important role in American public life.

The **top 10 newspapers** by circulation in the US are: *USA Today*, the *Wall Street Journal*, the *New York Times*, the *Los Angeles Times*, the *San Jose Mercury News*, the *Washington Post*, the *New York Daily News*, the *New York Post*, the *Chicago Tribune, and* the *Chicago Sun-Times*. All are available online.

Television

Unlike many countries, the US does not have national broadcasting. Instead, three major TV networks – ABC, CBS, and NBC – are carried in local markets by affiliates who also produce local programming and news that can usually be watched for free. In addition to the Big Three, the conservative network Fox Broadcasting Corporation is gaining an increasing market share. Univision, a network of Spanish-language channels, is the fifth-largest TV channel.

Non-commercial broadcasting, a vital source of educational and news programming and high-quality documentaries and drama, is excellent. Look for local affiliate stations of Public Broadcasting System (PBS).

Among the most popular public interest channels on cable or satellite are CNN, ESPN, MSNBC, Discovery Channel, the Food Network, USA Network, TNT, TLC, BRAVO, Disney, National Geographic, and BBC America. Movie channels include HBO, Showtime, Stars, TMC, TCM, and pay-per-view movies through satellite providers such as DirecTV and Dish.

Radio

A good way to learn about American culture is to turn on the radio. Cities have a vast array of stations, from talk radio by right-wing host Rush Limbaugh to hip-hop, contemporary, and classic rock music. On long, lonely highways, country music and religion predominate along with Spanish-language shows and AM talk radio. You'll find more cultural programming at the lower and upper ends of the dial. National Public Radio (NPR), syndicated through local community radio stations, broadcasts the country's most listened-to public programs as well as opera, classical music, jazz, and often indigenous programming.

In the Southwest, Hopi Radio (KUYI FM at 88.1) and Navajo Radio (660 KTNN AM) broadcast locally in their native languages. Cajun Radio (1470 AM) in Lake Charles, Louisiana belts out zydeco and Cajun music throughout Cajun Country. You can tune in to Radio Sonora (96.9 FM) to enjoy lively polka-influenced Norteño music as you travel southern Arizona near the US-Mexico border.

A radio show dedicated to Route 66 is broadcast on St Louis station KMOX (1120 AM) every Saturday from 7pm to 1am. Information about local road conditions and attractions can often be tuned in at 95 AM. Truckers with CB equipment talk to each other on dedicated channels, usually Line 19 in most of the country (Line 17 on the West Coast). There is also a truckers' channel among the large lineup on satellite radio SiriusXM Radio, available in many rental cars. SiriusXM carries channels dedicated to just about every kind of music, including oldies' channels keyed to different decades.

Money

American dollars come in bills of $1, $5, $10, $20, $50, and $100, all the same size. The dollar is divided into 100 cents. Coins come in 1 cent (penny), 5 cents (nickel), 10 cents (dime), 25 cents (quarter), 50 cents (half-dollar), and $1 denominations (these last two are uncommon). Credit cards are accepted almost everywhere, although not all cards at all places. Most hotels, restaurants, and shops take the major ones such as American Express, MasterCard, and Visa; Diners Club less commonly. Along with out-of-state or overseas bank cards, they can also be used to withdraw money at ATMs.

Travelers' checks are widely accepted, although you may have to provide proof of identification when cashing them at banks (this is not required at most stores). Travelers' checks in US dollars are much more widely accepted than those in other currencies. The best rates of exchange for them are in banks. Take along your passport.

Tipping

Low-paid service personnel in the US rely on tips for a large part of their income. Going rates are: waiters and bartenders 15–20 percent; taxi drivers 15 percent; airport/hotel baggage handlers $1 per bag; chambermaids $2–5 per day, if staying multiple days; doormen $1 for helping unload a car or other services; more if you have a lot of luggage, and $4-5 if luggage is brought to your room. Hairdressers, manicurists, and massage therapists 15–20 percent.

N

National Park System

America currently has 417 units in its vast National Park System. The seed of the national parks came when Yosemite Valley was set aside as a small land grant by Abraham Lincoln in 1864. The first federally mandated national park was Yellowstone, which was set aside in 1872 to protect its unique scenery, followed rapidly by Yosemite, Mt Rainier, Glacier, and Mesa Verde national parks. Early parks were managed by the War Department, and soldiers were dispatched to patrol them. In 1916, the **National Park Service** was founded with the challenging mission to both protect parks and make them accessible for the public to enjoy.

Formally designated national parks are few in number, and the crown jewels of the system. They preserve large, relatively intact ecosystems and the natural and cultural history associated with them; many also have pristine areas managed as wilderness that allow no mechanized transport within them. **National historic sites** and historical parks are more numerous and found in cities as well as rural areas. They focus on telling America's unique history through diverse stories. **National recreation areas** are reservoirs next to dams managed by the US Army Corps of Engineers and operated by the Bureau of Reclamation.

National monuments are a special case: the US President may, without congressional approval, set aside areas of important scientific and archeological interest for preservation and research if they are in danger of being lost through destruction and overdevelopment.

Outdoor activities vary from park to park, but most offer excellent opportunities for hiking, fishing, wildlife watching, horseback riding, and scenic drives. All of the national parks listed in this book are open daily, year-round (except for Christmas and New Year's Day). For camping reservations for all of the national parks (except those that don't accept reservations) below, log on to www. recreation.gov or call 877-444-6777 (international: 518-885-3639). For general information, visit the park visitor center on arrival, telephone the numbers or log on to individual park websites, which are well laid out and full of information.

Atlantic route

Everglades National Park
Contact Tel: 305-242-7700 www.nps. gov/ever.

Permits and licenses Backcountry camping permits required.

General information Few parks conjure up more mystery or romance than the Everglades. This vast expanse of marshland, grasses, swamp, and cypress forest is the largest subtropical wilderness area in the US. Recently, federal wildlife managers in the Everglades, particularly Big Cypress Preserve, along with conservation programs at Naples Zoo and The Nature Conservancy, have been working together to bring back the endangered Florida panther to its native habitat; populations are growing – up to 230 in 2017 – but there's more to be done. Alligators are numerous, and drivers should be wary of reptiles crossing the road at all times. Note: June to November is the "wet season," and camping may be uncomfortable at this time.

Northern route

Badlands National Park
Contact Tel: 605-433-5361, www.nps.gov/badl.
Permits and licenses No.
Camping First-come, first-served.
General information Be prepared for sudden changes in weather – high winds and hail, rain or snowstorms. Hikers should carry and drink adequate water – 1 gallon (4 liters) per day per person.

Grand Teton National Park
Contact Tel: 307-739-3300, www.nps.gov/grte.
Permits and licenses Backcountry camping permits required.
Camping First-come, first-served.
General information Numerous park concessioners offer horseback rides at Colter Bay and Jackson Lake Lodge. The Teton Range offers many opportunities for climbers and mountaineers. Jenny Lake Ranger Station is the center for climbing information, routes, conditions, and so on. Contact Grand Teton Lodge Co. (tel: 307-543-2811; www.gtlc.com) for Jackson Lake cruises, float trips on the Snake River, boat rentals, and horseback riding.

Yellowstone National Park
Contact Tel: 307-344-7381, www.nps.gov/yell.
Permits and licenses Backcountry camping permits required.
Camping Half of the 2000 sites in Yellowstone's 12 campgrounds can be reserved in advance by contacting Yellowstone National Park Lodges, tel: 307-344-7311; www.yellowstonenationalparklodges.com/stay/camping. For same day reservations tel: 307-344-7901.
General information It is illegal to approach, feed, or take selfies with wildlife in the park. Bison appear placid and slow-moving but can charge quickly and suddenly if irritated; the same applies to bears. Stay back at least 100 yards (90 meters), for their safety and yours.

Glacier National Park
Contact Tel: 406-888-7800, www.nps.gov/glac.
Permits and licenses Backcountry camping permits recommended.
Camping Fish Creek and St Mary campgrounds can be reserved up to 6 months in advance; reservations through www.recreation.gov must be made 3 days in advance (Fish Creek tel: 406-888-7800, St Mary tel: 406-732-7708). Group sites at St. Mary's and Apgar may be reserved no more than 12 months in advance. Half the campsites at Many Glacier Campground are reservable; sites in the remaining 10 campgrounds are first-come, first-served, but get there early as they fill fast.
General information Never try to feed or approach wildlife; it is illegal and park authorities will prosecute. Sun Tours (tel: 406-732-9220; www.glaciersuntours.com) offers a variety of guided bus tours. Glacier Park Boat Co. (tel: 406-257-2426) offers cruises on McDonald, Many Glaciers, Two Medicine, and St Mary lakes.

Olympic National Park
Contact Tel: 360-565-3130 www.nps.gov/olym.
Permits and licenses Wilderness camping permits for designated campsites are required for all overnight stays in the backcountry. Reservations begin in early February and must be made at least two weeks ahead of your trip; quotas are in effect for popular areas (tel: 360-565-3100, charge). Reservation confirmations must be exchanged for actual permits at the Wilderness Information Center. Washington fishing license required when fishing in the Pacific Ocean from shore.
Camping First-come, first-served, except at Kalaloch Campground, where only 22 sites are first-come, first-served, and Sol Duc Hot Springs RV and Campground (information tel: 360-565-3131; reservations tel: 877-444-6777; www.recreation.gov; Mar–Oct)
General information Crossing snowfields may require special skills and equipment such as crampons. Hiking in high elevations can be extremely difficult, causing dizziness, nausea, and shortness of breath. Give yourself a few days to adjust. Obtain a tide table before hiking on the beach; incoming tides can trap hikers between headlands. Look for floating logs, too. An unexpected wave can send them hurtling toward the beach, crushing anything that gets in the way. The ocean is cold and currents are fierce; swim in the lakes instead of the ocean.

Central route

Shenandoah National Park
Contact Tel: 540-999-3500, www.nps.gov/shen.
Permits and licenses Visitors may obtain a five-day nonresident fishing license at Big Meadows or sporting goods stores. Camping in the backcountry requires a free permit, available online, at trailheads, and visitor centers.
Camping Most of the campsites in the park's four campgrounds are first-come, first-served and are very popular so get there early in the day to secure a site. Some 20 percent of sites may be reserved up to 180 days in advance through www.recreation.gov or by calling 1-877-444-6777.
General information Shenandoah is known for its historic architecture as well as its scenic beauty. It has 340 structures on the National Register of Historic Places, many built in the 1930s by the Roosevelt-era Civilian Conservation Corps (CCC). Shenandoah's 105-mile (169km) -long Skyline Drive, linking the Front Royal with the Waynesboro-Charlottesville area, is a major through-road for locals as well as visitors. The park strongly discourages biking, as there is no shoulder on the very winding road and drivers cannot always see bikers in time to maneuver away from them.

Grand Canyon National Park
Contact Tel: 928-638-7888, www.nps.gov/grca.
Seasons The South Rim is open year-round. The North Rim is open mid-May through mid-October.
Camping Sites can be reserved well in advance and are strongly recommended at year-round Mather Campground on the South Rim and seasonal North Rim Campground (tel: 1-877-444-6777; www.recreation.gov). Desert View Campground on the East Rim is first-come, first-served only; sites usually fill by noon. RV sites with hookups are only available at concessioner-operated Trailer Village, a year-round RV park on the South Rim (tel: 877-404-4611; for same day reservation, 928-638-3047; www.visitgrandcanyon.com/trailer-village-rv-park).
Permits and licenses Arizona fishing license. Inexpensive backcountry permits (for overnight hiking; not required for day hikes) must be requested from the

Backcountry Information Center at the South Rim on the 1st of the month four months ahead of your trip date. First, download and fill in a request form from the website, and either submit in person at the Backcountry Information Center at the South Rim; fax to 928-638-2125; or if necessary, mail to Grand Canyon National Park, Permits Office, 1824 S. Thompson Street, Suite 201, Flagstaff AZ, 86001. Note: phone and email requests are not accepted. Popular trails fill fast; submit as early as possible.

General information Most of the five million people who visit Grand Canyon each year view it from the more easily accessed South Rim; the higher, remote North Rim is 200 miles away and only open seasonally. Access to the canyon interior is by hiking, mule ride, or river. Shuttle buses travel around the South Rim leaving from the visitor center, hotels, campgrounds, and the airport at nearby Tusayan. The inner canyon is subject to extreme heat in summer. Hikers should carry adequate food and water, at least 1 gallon (4 liters) per person per day.

Southern route

Big Bend National Park
Contact Tel: 432-477-2251, www.nps.gov/bibe
Permits and licenses Backcountry camping permits required ($12).
Camping First-come, first-served in three front-country campgrounds; limited sites may be reserved at Rio Grande Village (Nov 15–April 15) and Chisos Basin (Nov 15–May 31). For reservations, tel: 877-444-6777, www.recreation.gov.
General information Big Bend is over 800,000 acres (323,000 hectares) in size and extremely rugged and remote; you will need at least two days to see most of the park on main roads. Hikers and four-wheel-drive explorers should allow a week. The sun is intense all year: wear a high SPF sunscreen, sunglasses, strong hiking boots or sandals, broad-brimmed hat, and clothing that can be rolled down for protection. Carry high-energy salty snacks and ample water in the car, and on every hike, no matter how short, take care to eat and sip water in equal measures to avoid electrolyte imbalances in the body (hyponatremia).

Allow 1 gallon (4 liters) per person per day. Don't overexert yourself: the nearest hospital is 100 miles (160km) away. This is wild country. Be alert for rattlesnakes, mountain lions, bears, and javelinas.

Pacific route

Redwood National and State Parks
Contact Tel: 707-465-7335, www.nps.gov/redw.
Permits and licenses California fishing license and free backcountry camping permits required (available from any visitor center). Due to difficult road access, visiting Tall Trees Grove also requires a permit.
Camping Four developed campgrounds run by California State Parks. Campsites may be reserved May through August (strongly suggested); first-come, first-served other times. For reservations, contact Reserve California (tel: 800-444-7275; www.reservecalifornia.com).
General information Access to Tall Trees Grove is limited; a summer shuttle bus transports visitors down the rugged 7-mile (11km) road to the trailhead. Otherwise, a limited number of free private-vehicle permits are distributed on a first-come, first-served basis. Backpackers must secure a free permit at any information center. Animal-proof food canisters are available to borrow free of charge at Thomas H. Kuchel Visitor Center. Swimming can be extremely dangerous. Ocean water is cold, currents are strong, and no lifeguards are on duty. National park entrance is free; state parks charge $35 overnight fee and $8 day use fee per carload.

O

Opening hours

Banks 8.30am–6pm, weekdays. Most close on Saturdays, or are open morning only.
Post Offices 8am–4 or 5.30pm, weekdays, Saturdays, usually mornings only, especially in small towns.
Shops 9am–5pm daily, later in tourist areas; shopping malls typically open 10am–9pm Mon–Sat, noon–5pm Sun.
All-hours services Most cities have 24-hour restaurants, convenience stores, and supermarkets.

Museums Usually open Tue–Sun, closed Mon.

Outdoor activities

The United States has a huge number of national, state, county, and city parks; lakeside recreation areas; and nature preserves. There is plenty of scope for walking, swimming, fishing, cycling, boating, and participant sports.

Water and wind

Coastal areas and parks on larger lakes are your best bet for water activities. **Deep-sea charters** offer fishing for grouper, sailfish, and tarpon in Florida and halibut, tuna, and salmon on the Pacific Northwest coasts. **Surfing** is big along wave-pounded beaches in southern California; swimming is popular on the Atlantic, Pacific, and Gulf coasts. **Parasailing** and **windsurfing** attract enthusiasts wherever there are prevailing strong winds. The Windsurfing Capital of the World is actually inland, though, at Hood River in Oregon's Columbia River Gorge. **Diving** and **snorkeling** are spectacular in Florida's Keys, where your companions are often dolphins. Limestone regions, such as Crystal River in central Florida, offer diving in crystal-clear spring-fed sinkholes frequented by manatees. Santa Rosa on the hot, dusty plains of eastern New Mexico is a unique find: its 80ft (25-meter) -deep, spring-fed Blue Hole is popular with desert divers.

Boating is virtually an art form in coastal regions, and along the US-Canada border regions of the Great Lakes in the Midwest and Finger Lakes of upstate New York. Boats are more than recreation on the calm Intracoastal Waterways and offshore islands of the Gulf Coast, New England, and Washington State: they are often residences and transportation. Above major dams, Western mountain rivers – such as the Colorado through the Grand Canyon and the Rio Grande in Big Bend National Park – have spectacular **whitewater** and **flatwater rafting**. Below the dams, flatwater sports are popular at Amistad Reservoir on the Rio Grande and Lake Powell on the Colorado, a good place to rent a houseboat or kayak.

Wherever there are bodies of water, people like to fish. Non-resident licenses are available at town offices and sporting goods shops. **Fishing** next to highways, along canal banks or in small boats, is common in the South, particularly in the Everglades and in the bayous of the Mississippi Delta where fishing for crawfish has deep cultural roots. Fishing in high mountain streams and lakes requires a little more effort, with fly fishermen often hiking (or, these days, riding all-terrain vehicles) to catch rainbow trout and salmon. Resorts offering log cabins near stocked lakes and streams are popular in mountain regions of the US as summer vacation spots.

Hiking

Hiking is popular in every region. Many of the best-known trails follow historic Indian and pioneer trails through mountains, valleys, and open deserts. National parks, and other federally managed lands, usually offer the greatest diversity of trails for hikers, from short paved accessible trails to scenic overlooks for disabled users to short day hikes for families and longer cross-country trails.

Walkers and **joggers** in cities will increasingly find designated urban trail networks linking the city and adjoining countryside in places such as Austin, Texas, and Flagstaff, Arizona.

Most challenging are **long-distance trails** like the Appalachian Trail in the East and the John Muir Trail in California's Sierra Nevada in the West. **Backcountry hiking** requires preparation, stamina, and time: many hikers split trails into segments hiked over years. Come well prepared and know your limits when you set out.

Desert cities

Cities such as Phoenix, Tucson, and Albuquerque, and Florida locations (Tampa and Fort Myers, for example), with their mild winter temperatures, are major destinations for **off-season outdoor activities** such as hiking, marathon training, bicycling, golf, tennis, and spring training for professional footballers and baseball players.

Mountains and "sky islands"

The Rockies, Cascades, Sierra Nevada, Appalachians, Smokies, and isolated young desert "sky island" ranges found in the Desert

Southwest and West offer an escape from 90–114°F (32–48°C) summer temperatures at lower elevations. These same mountainous locales are even busier when winter snows hit, attracting downhill and cross-country skiers and snowboarders to **ski resorts** as far south as Ski Apache in southern New Mexico's Sacramento Mountains. Most ski areas, though, are in the Rockies, Sierra Nevada, and northern New England.

The steady 58°F (14°C) temperature of subterranean limestone **cavern systems** such as Carlsbad Caverns in New Mexico makes them excellent for caving year round; Carlsbad offers wild-cave tours as well as main-cavern touring.

The western states

The western states – particularly Arizona, Colorado, New Mexico, and Utah, where the mile-high Colorado Plateau has been carved into sinuous canyons by the Colorado River and its tributaries – have the country's most enchanting combination of outdoor activities and tourism on the largest federally managed acreage in the Lower 48. Professional tour companies in gateway communities next to parks are usually the best way of experiencing **remote wilderness areas** where vehicles aren't allowed, particularly if it's your first time in an area. They take care of all the planning, permits, transportation, and meals, and some use low-impact horses and llamas to carry equipment so you don't have to, freeing you up to enjoy the experience.

Extreme sports, such as mountain climbing in Olympic National Park in Washington, are available through adventure companies. These are aimed at very experienced and fit outdoorspeople, familiar with the local environments, and should never be attempted by beginners. White-water rafting is very popular on the Colorado River and other rivers with designated wild and scenic sections; trips last a day to several weeks.

Bicycle tours of regions such as the Texas Hill Country, California's Wine Country, and New England in the fall are both cultural and challenging, often incorporating upscale amenities such as bed-and-breakfasts, wine tastings, gourmet meals, and guided tours with pedal time. In the city, you can usually

rent a bicycle (or rollerblades) to get around, often through bike share schemes. Some cities offer designated bicycle trails through historic communities, such as the Pinellas Trail between St Petersburg and Tarpon Springs on Florida's Gulf Coast and the Venice Boardwalk in southern California – the quintessential LA experience.

Photography

Even in this era of instant-view digital cameras, film is still widely available throughout the US. Business centers and discount chains often offer rapid development or conversion of digital to paper prints. The US is spectacularly photogenic. Some of the most rewarding photography is of cultural events, such as costume parades, Indian ceremonial dances, and wildlife.

If you plan on photographing in the desert, avoid the flat, washed-out light in the middle of the day and shoot in the early morning or evening instead; cloudy days will offer better contrast than bright sunny days.

Observe appropriate etiquette when photographing Indian people. Pueblos in New Mexico may ban photography, filming, and sketching of sacred ceremonial dances

---

☉ Public holidays

Holidays celebrated no matter on what day they fall in the year are:
January 1 New Year's Day
July 4 Independence Day
November 11 Veteran's Day
December 25 Christmas Day
Other holidays are:
Third Monday in January
Martin Luther King Jr Day
Third Monday in February
Presidents' Day
March/April
Good Friday, Easter Monday
Last Monday in May
Memorial Day
First Monday in September
Labor Day
Second Monday in October
Columbus Day
Fourth Thursday in November
Thanksgiving

and the pueblo; if permitted, you will likely have to pay for the privilege. Individuals may be willing to pose for you for a small fee. Always ask permission and get a photo release, if it's for commercial purposes, before taking a photo of anyone.

Postal services

Even the most remote towns are served by the US Postal Service. Stamps are sold at all post offices, plus at some convenience stores, filling stations, hotels, and transportation terminals, usually from vending machines.

Public toilets

Public toilets are rarely available in the US, unless you are visiting an attraction. Most businesses allow you to use their restrooms. At special outdoor events, you will often find temporary Port-a-Potties brought in to serve large crowds.

R

Religious services

Ninety percent of Americans believe in a form of God, and many attend religious or spiritual services regularly in their communities. Roman Catholic, Presbyterian, Baptist, and evangelical Christianity are the most visible religious expression across the US, but you'll also find Jewish synagogues (mostly in cities and suburbs); LDS (Mormon) meeting houses, tabernacles and temples; Muslim mosques; Quaker meeting houses; Japanese Buddhist zendos and Tibetan stupas; Penitente morada chapels in northern New Mexico; pagan Wicca ceremonies; evangelical tent revivals on Indian reservations; and other religious gathering places in the unlikeliest places, even remote national parks.

Visitors are welcome at most church services; however, whites attending Sunday services at black-majority gospel churches in the South should be prepared for a certain amount of suspicion as outsiders, particularly in light of the racially motivated shooting in a gospel church in Charleston in 2015.

S

Shopping

Shopping is a lot of fun in America. For lovers of kitsch, **Florida** and the **American West** won't disappoint, with their doctored postcards, fossil rocks, saltwater taffy, cactus jelly, snowglobes, and other Americana. **Cities** like New York, Los Angeles, San Francisco, and Houston are good places to buy contemporary art. Cowboy and pioneer art is easily found in towns adjoining **ranch country** in Arizona, New Mexico, Wyoming, and Colorado. In August, Indian Market in Santa Fe showcases Indian jewelry, pottery, carvings, sandpaintings, and other juried items, all for sale. Mexican souvenirs are best purchased in main **cities near the southern border** such as Tucson, Phoenix, San Antonio, and San Diego. Most American cities feature at least one large shopping mall, with chain stores, restaurants, cafés, and movie theaters.

Many are revitalizing their historic downtowns with unique shopping areas featuring boutique shops and hotels, local restaurants, quirky museums, and fun art galleries and weekly art walks. **Small towns** in rural locations and roadside stands are often the most interesting places to find unique souvenirs of the region, from preserved foods to handmade clothing and crafts.

Smoking

There are no federal bans on smoking, but increasingly, states and individual cities and towns in the US frown upon smoking in public and ban it in workplaces, on public transportation, in bars, hotels, restaurants, airports, and in and around public buildings and parks. Always check before lighting up.

Student travelers

The **International Student Identity Card** (ISIC) is recognized throughout the world. Major cities across the US, such as New York and Atlanta, accept the card and offer substantial discounts on everything from entertainment and restaurants to lodging and airport parking. The **International Youth Discount Card** (IYTC) offers travelers under 31

low-cost fares on buses, trains, flights, and hotels. The ISIC costs $20 a year and the IYDC costs $25 a year. The ISIC includes a comprehensive travel insurance policy and International SIM is a complete communication tool allowing international calls at low rates. For more information, log on to www.isic.org.

STA Travel (tel: 800-781-4040; www.statravel.com), headquartered in Zurich and London, also offers student discounts on airfares. Admission charges to attractions across the US are usually a couple of dollars less than full adult price for students, and children under 12 are often admitted free. Check at your destination.

T

Tax

Most cities impose a sales tax on goods and services. The amount varies (up to around 9 percent in some cities) and is in addition to the marked price. When looking at prices, beware of other taxes such as city lodger's taxes and car rental charges. These are especially hefty in tourist towns like Miami. If in doubt – ask.

Telephones

In this era of cellphones, you'll find fewer **public telephones** in hotel lobbies, restaurants, drugstores, garages, roadside kiosks, convenience stores, and other locations. The cost of making a local call from a payphone for three minutes is 50–75 cents, and charges for long distance or extra minutes can be astronomical. To make a long-distance call from a payphone, use either a **pre-paid calling card**, available in airports, post offices, and a few other outlets, or your credit card, which you can use at any phone: dial 800-CALLATT, key in your credit-card number, and wait to be connected. In many areas, local calls have now changed to a 10-digit calling system, using the area code. Watch out for in-room connection charges in upmarket hotels; it's cheaper to use the payphone in the lobby. Ditto: wireless and broadband internet connections in your room: many hotel lobbies and business

⊙ Time zones

The continental US spans four time zones. These are divided as follows:
Eastern (Greenwich Mean Time minus five hours)
Central (Greenwich Mean Time minus six hours)
Mountain (Greenwich Mean Time minus seven hours)
Pacific (Greenwich Mean Time minus eight hours)

centers offer free wireless but charge for it in guest rooms. Inquire ahead of time.

Toll-free calls

When in the US, make use of toll-free (no-charge) numbers. They start with 800, 844, 855, 866, 877, or 888. You need to dial 1 before these numbers.

Cheaper rates

Long-distance rates are cheaper after 5pm on weekdays and throughout weekends. Many wireless plans offer unlimited free cellphone minutes on weekends and between 9pm and 6am.

Useful numbers

Operator 0 (dial if you are having any problems with a line from any phone)
Local: 411
Long-distance: 1+area code +555-1212
Toll-free directory: 800-555-1212
Emergency: 911

Phone codes

With the proliferation of fax lines, modems, and cellphones, the US telephone system is seriously overloaded. To cope with these demands, the country has been forced to divide, then sub-divide, its existing telephone area codes, in some cases every six months. Although every effort has been made to keep the telephone prefixes listed here up to date, it's always a good idea to check with the operator if you're in any doubt about a number.

Tour operators and travel agents

The US has a huge variety of travel agents and tour operators to assist with both general and specialty travel packages. Even if you are planning on doing the driving yourself, you may want to hook up with a local tour operator to let someone else show you around for a few days. You can locate a US tour operator by checking listings on the websites of the **US Tour Operator Association** – USTOA (www.ustoa.com) and the **National Tour Association** (www.ntaonline.com) or contacting the visitor center at your destination for official listings.

Top tour operators serving all of the US include top-rated **Tauck Tours** (tel: 800-788-7885; www.tauck.com), a family-run Connecticut company that has been in business since 1924, and **Abercrombie and Kent** (tel: 888-611-4711; www.abercrombiekent.com), both of which specialize in small-group luxury tours. **The Smithsonian Institution** (tel: 855-330-1542; www.smithsonianjourneys.org) offers educational study tours to sites of archeological, historic, and scientific interest in the US, such as ancient Indian ruins in the Southwest, guided by authorities in the field. National park concessioners offer bus tours, mule rides, and other guided tours; park staff has listings of individual outfitters. Check individual parks for more information. **Gray Line** (tel: 303-539-8502, toll-free: 800-472-9546; www.grayline.com) runs guided bus tours in most large US cities.

Specialty tour operators offer guided trips tailored to your interests, from tours of ghost towns in Arizona to historic walking tours in cities like Santa Fe, Seattle, and Boston. Outfitters offer guided trips of the outdoors. You can enjoy hunting, fishing, river rafting, horseback riding, and skiing with outdoor outfitters in the Mountain West; rock climbing and bicycle and Jeep touring in the Southwest; wildlife watching in Florida; ballooning and wine tours in California; heritage tours on private ranches, Indian reservations, and archeological sites in the West; tours of Civil War battlefields and communities in the South; and tours aimed at those with special needs, health issues, disabilities, singles, women only, and the gay and lesbian community, among others.

Tourist information

Welcome centers are usually located at the state line. They are staffed by volunteers who can give you maps and general advice on your stay and have restrooms, snack machines, water, and often hot coffee. Most communities have visitor centers that offer information and trip planning. When visiting national parks, be sure to stop at the visitor center first. Rangers there can help you get the most out of your time in the park.

Visit www.usa.gov/visitors-driving for advice on driving in the US and www.fhwa.dot.gov/byways for information on America's designated **scenic byways** – a resource of great interest to road trippers meandering America's inspiring Blue Highways.

Route 66

National Historic Route 66 Federation
Tel: 909-336-6131
www.national66.org

State tourism offices

Alabama Tourism Department
Tel: 334-242-4169
www.alabama.travel
Arizona Office of Tourism
Tel: 602-364-3700
www.tourism.az.gov
Arkansas Department of Parks and Tourism
Tel: 501-682-7777
www.arkansas.com
California Tourism
Tel: 916-444-4429
www.visitcalifornia.com
Connecticut Commission on Culture and Tourism
Toll free: 888-288-4748
www.ctvisit.com
Visit Florida
Toll free: 888-735-2872
www.visitflorida.com
Georgia Department of Economic Development
Toll free: 800-847-4842
www.exploregeorgia.org
Idaho Division of Tourism Development
Toll free: 800-847-4843
www.visitidaho.org
Illinois Bureau of Tourism – Chicago Office
Toll free: 800-266-6328
www.enjoyillinois.com
Indiana Office of Tourism Development
Toll free: 800-677-9800
www.visitindiana.com
Louisiana Office of Tourism
www.louisianatravel.com
Maine Office of Tourism
Toll free: 888-624-6345
www.visitmaine.com

Maryland Office of Tourism Development
Toll free: 866-639-3526
www.visitmaryland.org
Massachusetts Office of Travel and Tourism
Toll-free: 800-227-MASS
www.massvacation.com
Explore Minnesota Tourism
Toll free: 888-VISITMN
www.exploreminnesota.com
Mississippi: Division of Tourist Development
Toll free: 866-733-6477
www.visitmississippi.org
Travel Montana
Toll free: 800-847-4868
www.visitmt.com
New Hampshire Department of Resources and Economic Development
Tel: 603-271-2665
www.visitnh.gov
New Jersey Division of Tourism and Travel Information
Toll free: 800-VISITNJ
www.visitnj.org
New Mexico Department of Tourism
Tel: 505-827-7400
www.newmexico.org
New York State Tourist Information
Toll free: 800-CALL-NYS
www.iloveny.com
North Carolina Division of Tourism
Toll free: 800-VISITNC
www.visitnc.com
Ohio Division of Travel and Tourism
Toll free: 800-BUCKEYE
www.discoverohio.com
Oklahoma Tourism and Recreation Department
Toll free: 800-652-6552
www.travelok.com
Oregon Tourism Commission
Toll free: 800-547-7842
www.traveloregon.com
Pennsylvania Tourism Office
Toll Free: 800-847-4872
www.visitpa.com
South Carolina Department of Tourism
Toll free: 803-734-0124
www.discoversouthcarolina.com
South Dakota Office of Tourism
Toll free: 800-732-5682
www.travelsouthdakota.com
State of Tennessee Department of Tourist Development
Toll free: 615-741-2159
www.tnvacation.com
Texas Tourism
Toll free: 800-452-9292 (TXDOT)
www.traveltex.com
Vermont Department of Tourism and Marketing

Daylight Saving Time

This begins each year at 2am on a Sunday in March, when clocks are advanced one hour ("spring forward"), and ends on the last Sunday in October ("fall back."). Arizona and Indiana do not observe Daylight Saving Time; however, confusingly for travelers, the huge Navajo reservation, spanning Arizona and New Mexico, does.

Toll free: 800-VERMONT
www.vermontvacation.com
Virginia Tourism Corporation
Toll free: 800-847-4882
www.virginia.org
Washington State Tourism Division
Toll free: 800-544-1800
www.experienceWA.com
Washington, DC
Tel: 202-789-7000
www.washington.org
Wisconsin Department of Tourism
Toll free: 800-432-8747
www.travelwisconsin.com
Wyoming Travel and Tourism
Tel: 307-777-7777
www.travelwyoming.com

V

Visas and entry

Immigration and visitation procedures can change rapidly depending on real and perceived threats to security. Check the relevant websites listed here for up-to-date information.

To enter the United States, foreign visitors need a passport and many also need a visa. You may be asked to provide evidence that you intend to leave the United States after your visit is over (usually in the form of a return or onward ticket).

You may not need a visa if you are a resident of one of 27 countries that participate in the Visa Waiver Program (VWP) and are planning to stay in the US for less than 90 days. You must, however, log onto the Electronic System for Travel Authorization's unmemorably named website, https://esta.us, at least 48 hours before traveling and provide personal information and travel details; either your application will be accepted (and will be

valid for multiple visits over two years) or you will be told to apply for a visa. If you don't have Internet access, you'll need to find someone who does.

Anyone wishing to stay longer than 90 days must apply for a visa in any case. This can be done by mail to the nearest US Embassy or Consulate. Visa extensions can be obtained in the US from the United States Immigration and Customs Enforcement (ICE). Online applications can be filled in and printed out at http://travel.state.gov.

Canadian and Mexican citizens traveling to the US by air or across the land border need a passport to enter the country.

The US Department of Homeland Security maintains a website at www.dhs.gov.

HIV: Travelers who are HIV-positive may enter the US under the Visa Waiver Program. For more information, visit https://help.cbp.gov.

W

Weights and measures

The US operates on the imperial system of weights and measures.

Women travelers

Driving is a wonderful, generally safe way for a woman to travel across the US. You are unlikely to have any trouble, and, from the safety of your vehicle, you will enjoy an unaccustomed, and possibly addictive, feeling of true adventure and freedom.

Although it's fun to meet new people on the road, if you are a lone female, be a little cautious to avoid unwarranted attention. Be conservative in dress and avoid engaging with anyone partying hard, especially groups of men in bars, where things can rapidly get out of control. Don't go home with strangers or pick up hitchhikers if you're a female traveling alone.

Plan on staying in slightly more expensive motels and public campgrounds, and get in the habit of keeping your car doors locked at all times. Avoid walking around at night in poorly lit areas, whether in the city or the country, and keep to public places. Try to let someone know your planned itinerary.

FURTHER READING

GENERAL

Basin and Range: In Suspect Terrain, Rising from the Plains, Annals of the Former World, and Assembling California by John McPhee. The definitive layman's account of the geology of the US and of the time the author spent with the people who study it.
The Great Deluge: Hurricane Katrina, New Orleans, and the Mississippi Gulf Coast by Douglas Brinkley. Historian Brinkley, a New Orleans resident and survivor of the hurricane, captures the experience and politics of the deadly storm.
Great Plains and **On the Rez** by Ian Frazier. The first is a thoughtful travelogue by the New Yorker writer on his 25,000-mile odyssey through the historic American heartland; the second is an account of contemporary life on the West's Indian reservations.
This House of Sky: Landscapes of a Western Mind by Ivan Doig. The lae western novelist's recollection of growing up in the vastness of 1940s and 1950s Montana.
Writing New York and Writing LA, Library of America. Two superb anthologies of fiction and nonfiction reveal the personalities of these huge, complex, and quintessentially American places.

FICTION

The Border Trilogy by Cormac McCarthy. McCarthy captures the feeling of Border Country, macho cowboys, and their love of horses.
Brokeback Mountain by Annie Proulx. This poignant short story of enduring love between two cowboys evokes the real American West of the 1960s with its spare prose, haunting characters, and authentic sense of place.
Death Comes to the Archbishop by Willa Cather. Based on the life of Santa Fe's 19th-century Archbishop Lamy who worked to "civilize" New Mexico's capital.
The Friends of Eddie Coyle by George Higgins. Set among Boston's criminal fraternity, this novel is celebrated for its dialogue and authenticity.
The Grapes of Wrath by John Steinbeck. This classic novel follows an Oklahoma family's experiences as migrant field workers in California during the Dust Bowl years of the Great Depression. It still resonates today.
Ernest Hemingway: Many of Hemingway's novels and short stories were written in the 10 years he lived in Key West, but To Have and Have Not is the only one set in the town

Send us your thoughts

We do our best to ensure the information in our books is as accurate and up-to-date as possible. The books are updated on a regular basis using local contacts, who painstakingly add, amend and correct as required. However, some details (such as telephone numbers and opening times) are liable to change, and we are ultimately reliant on our readers to put us in the picture.

We welcome your feedback, especially your experience of using the book "on the road". Maybe you came across a great bar or new attraction we missed.

We will acknowledge all contributions, and we'll offer an Insight Guide to the best letters received.

Please write to us at:
Insight Guides
PO Box 7910
London SE1 1WE

Or email us at:
hello@insightguides.com

(published in 1937). The Nick Adams Stories brings readers to a different Hemingway haunt, the woods and lakes of northern Michigan, where he spent boyhood summers.
Carl Hiassen: Miami Herald journalist Hiassen writes bestselling comic thrillers set in Florida, including Native Tongue (1992), which makes fun of theme parks.
Tony Hillerman: The late journalist's novels about Navajo policemen Sgt Joe Leaphorn and detective Jim Chee offer insights into the Navajo people and their vast reservation. His daughter, Ann Hillerman, is continuing the stories, focusing on Bernie Manuelito, wife of Jim Chee.
Lake Wobegon Days by Garrison Keillor. Charming stories about daily life in a mythical Minnesota burg based on the popular radio show Prairie Home Companion.
Lonesome Dove by Larry McMurtry. The classic evocation of life on a Texas cattle drive.

ON THE ROAD

Blue Highways: A Journey into America by William Least Heat Moon. This exploration of life along the blue-lined highways on the map by a Native writer is still essential road-trip reading.
The Lost Continent: Travels in Small Town America by Bill Bryson. Hysterical look at growing up in the Midwest by an expat American living in the UK.
On the Road by Jack Kerouac. A syncopated-jazz wild ride of a tale capturing the romance of the road and crazy, amped-up lifestyles of 1950s Beat poets.
Roadfood by Jane and Michael Stern. The ultimate guide to authentic American "eats" gives details on hundreds of diners, barbecue joints, homemade ice-cream stands, and other places that stand apart from the chains.
Route 66 Adventure Handbook: Expanded Third Edition by Drew Knowles. An exhaustive tome with lots of personal charm.
Route 66 Magazine quarterly from PO Box 1129, Port Richey FL 34673-1129, tel: 928-853-8148, www.route66magazine.com.
Travels with Charley: In Search of America by John Steinbeck. A classic road-trip book featuring the author's standard poodle companion and a vast continent.

CREDITS

PHOTO CREDITS

AL Gulf Coast CVB 250
Alabama Tourism 249, 251T, 251B
Alamy 22, 28, 32, 115, 116, 206, 241T, 257, 274B, 308, 363, 371, 376B
Alex Demyan /Apa Publications 254
Anon 192
Apa Publications 129T, 253T, 255T, 305T, 341T
Arizona Tourism 306T
Arkansas Tourist Board 193B, 193T, 195, 198
Atlanta Tourism 241B, 245
AWL Images 7MR, 10/11, 12/13, 14/15, 142, 200, 360
Beauvoir, Richard Flowers 256
Bellingrath Gardens 253B
Bigstock 55, 62, 63B, 65, 70B, 77, 87, 113, 143, 149T, 153, 166, 248B, 266T, 270B, 351B, 353B, 364, 367T, 374
Buffalo Bill Historical Center 154T
Busch Entertainment Corporation 90
Carol M. Highsmith/Library of Congress 129B, 227
Chris Gimmeson/Buffalo Bill Historical Center 155
Chris Hollo/Hollo Photographics, Inc. 196
Corbis 26, 27, 41
David Dunai/Apa Publications 7TR, 9B, 122, 123, 140, 141, 233, 234/235T, 235BL, 235TR, 235ML, 314, 315B, 316B, 317B, 317T, 318, 323, 324, 325, 327, 328, 329, 333, 334, 335, 336, 337, 340, 341B, 342, 343, 347, 349T, 349B, 350, 351T, 356T, 356B, 380, 388/389
Dreamstime 52/53T, 59, 66B, 86, 109B, 110B, 112, 118, 127B, 131, 134, 146, 154B, 156, 163, 165, 167, 169, 170, 179T, 197, 199, 203, 208, 209B, 246T, 248T, 292, 307, 367B
Fotolia 66T, 149B, 151B, 231T, 261, 339, 353T
Galveston Historical Society 269, 270T
Getty Images 1, 4, 30L, 50, 68, 242, 357

GPTMC 58B
Granger/REX/Shutterstock 16, 17B
iStock 6MR, 7BR, 7ML, 8, 9T, 18, 19, 40, 51B, 53B, 54, 57T, 57B, 58T, 60, 61, 64, 70T, 71, 74T, 74B, 75, 76B, 79, 81, 83T, 83B, 84, 85B, 91, 92, 94/95T, 94B, 95B, 95T, 96/97, 99T, 100/101T, 105T, 106, 107, 109T, 111, 114T, 125, 126, 130B, 132T, 132B, 133, 135T, 135B, 138, 145T, 150, 158, 159, 160, 161, 162, 171, 172/173T, 173ML, 183, 184T, 185B, 215, 220, 224T, 226T, 231B, 234B, 236/237, 238, 239T, 239B, 243, 255B, 258, 263, 264, 267, 268, 273, 275T, 275B, 276, 279, 281, 284, 287T, 287B, 315T, 316/317T, 321, 330/331, 338, 352, 354, 355B, 355T, 361, 362, 365, 368, 370, 372, 373T, 373B, 402
John McCarty 127T
Library of Congress 20, 24/25, 38
Louisiana Office of Tourism 260, 265
Macon GA CVB 247
Maid of the Mist 7BL, 121
Martyn Goddard 42/43, 63T, 69, 72T, 72B, 93, 108, 110T, 128, 152, 174/175, 177T, 185T, 229, 285, 346
Martyn Goddard/Apa Publications 358, 359, 378
Mary Evans Picture Library 23
Matt H. Wade 114B
Memphis Tourist Board 180
Metropolitan Museum of Art 211
Myrtle Beach SC Tourism 73
National Cowboy & Western Heritage Museum 204
National Park Service 266B
New Mexico Museum of Space History 286
New Mexico Tourism 277, 282B, 289T, 289B, 290T, 291, 293
New Orleans TB 259
NY Public Library 30R, 31L, 31R
Oklahoma Tourism 201
Oregon Tourism 369
Paul Karr/Apa Publications 130T

Photoshot 117, 240B, 366
Public domain 21
Robert Harding 119, 216, 230, 252
Ronald Grant Archive 29
Route 66 Magazine 34, 35, 36, 37, 39
Route 66 Museum 205B
Rudioso Valley Chamber of Commerce 288
San Antonio Tourism 280B
Savannah Tourism 78
Seneca Lake 120
Shutterstock 17T, 136, 147, 319, 322
South Carolina Tourism 76T
South Dakota Tourism 137, 139, 145B, 148T, 148B, 151T
Team Nowitz/Apa Publications 6BL, 6B, 6ML, 7TL, 44/45, 46/47, 51T, 52B, 53T, 80, 85T, 88, 89, 98, 99B, 100B, 101T, 101B, 102, 103, 105B, 176, 177B, 178/179T, 178B, 179B, 205T, 209T, 210, 212, 213, 214, 217, 218, 219, 221T, 221B, 222, 223, 224B, 225T, 225B, 226B, 232, 294, 295, 296, 297T, 297B, 298T, 298B, 299, 300, 301T, 301B, 302, 303T, 303B, 304, 305B, 306B, 309, 310, 311, 312/313, 332, 344, 345, 383, 387, 392, 394
Tennessee Tourism 181, 188T, 188B, 189, 190, 191, 194
Texas Tourism 207, 271T, 271B, 272, 274T, 280T, 283
The Coca-Cola Company 240/241T
The Georgia Trust for Historic Preservation 246B
The Kobal Collection 33
The National Archives UK 282T
Tim Thompson/Apa Publications 157, 172B, 173BL, 173TR, 376T
Virginia Tourist Board 67, 184B, 186, 187
Visit Baton Rouge 262
Washington State Tourism 164, 168, 375, 377
White Sands Missile Range 290B

COVER CREDITS

Front cover: Holiday Motel, Las Vegas Susanne Kremer/4Corners Images
Back cover: Grand Teton National Park iStock

Front flap: (from top) Grand Tetons, Wyoming iStock; Minneapolis Skyline iStock; Blue Ridge Parkway Bigstock; Ocean Drive, Miami iStock

Back flap: Death Valley iStock

INSIGHT GUIDE CREDITS

Distribution
UK, Ireland and Europe
Apa Publications (UK) Ltd;
sales@insightguides.com
United States and Canada
Ingram Publisher Services;
ips@ingramcontent.com
Australia and New Zealand
Woodslane; info@woodslane.com.au
Southeast Asia
Apa Publications (SN) Pte;
singaporeoffice@insightguides.com
Worldwide
Apa Publications (UK) Ltd;
sales@insightguides.com
Special Sales, Content Licensing and CoPublishing
Insight Guides can be purchased in bulk quantities at discounted prices. We can create special editions, personalised jackets and corporate imprints tailored to your needs. sales@insightguides.com
www.insightguides.biz

Printed in China by CTPS

All Rights Reserved
© 2019 Apa Digital (CH) AG and
Apa Publications (UK) Ltd

First Edition 2001
Fifth Edition 2019

Every effort has been made to provide accurate information in this publication, but changes are inevitable. The publisher cannot be responsible for any resulting loss, inconvenience or injury. We would appreciate it if readers would call our attention to any errors or outdated information. We also welcome your suggestions; please contact us at: hello@insightguides.com

www.insightguides.com

Editor: Sian Marsh
Managing Editor: Carine Tracanelli
Author: Donna Dailey, Mike Gerrard, Nicky Leach, Bill Scheller, Kristan Schiller and Fran Severn
Head of DTP and Pre-Press: Rebeka Davies
Updated by: Nicky Leach
Picture Editor: Tom Smyth
Cartography: original cartography Colourmap Scanning Ltd and Phoenix Mapping, updated by Carte

CONTRIBUTORS

This new edition of Insight Guides USA on the Road was commissioned by **Sian Marsh**.
This edition builds on earlier editions produced by **Donna Dailey, Mike Gerrard, Nicky Leach, Bill Scheller, Kristan Schiller,** and **Fran Severn.**
Many of the stunning photographs in this edition were taken by father-and-son team **Richard** and **Abraham Nowitz,** and **David Dunai.**

ABOUT INSIGHT GUIDES

Insight Guides have more than 45 years' experience of publishing high-quality, visual travel guides. We produce 400 full-colour titles, in both print and digital form, covering more than 200 destinations across the globe, in a variety of formats to meet your different needs.
Insight Guides are written by local authors, whose expertise is evident in the extensive historical and cultural background features. Each destination is carefully researched by regional experts to ensure our guides provide the very latest information. All the reviews in **Insight Guides** are independent; we strive to maintain an impartial view. Our reviews are carefully selected to guide you to the best places to eat, go out and shop, so you can be confident that when we say a place is special, we really mean it.

Legend

City maps
Freeway/Highway/Motorway
Divided Highway
Main Roads
Minor Roads
Pedestrian Roads
Steps
Footpath
Railway
Funicular Railway
Cable Car
Tunnel
City Wall
Important Building
Built Up Area
Other Land
Transport Hub
Park
Pedestrian Area
Bus Station
Tourist Information
Main Post Office
Cathedral/Church
Mosque
Synagogue
Statue/Monument
Beach
Airport

Regional maps
Freeway/Highway/Motorway (with junction)
Freeway/Highway/Motorway (under construction)
Divided Highway
Main Road
Secondary Road
Minor Road
Track
Footpath
International Boundary
State/Province Boundary
National Park/Reserve
Marine Park
Ferry Route
Marshland/Swamp
Glacier   Salt Lake
Airport/Airfield
Ancient Site
Border Control
Cable Car
Castle/Castle Ruins
Cave
Chateau/Stately Home
Church/Church Ruins
Crater
Lighthouse
Mountain Peak
Place of Interest
Viewpoint

INDEX

INSIGHT ⊙ GUIDES

OFF THE SHELF

Since 1970, INSIGHT GUIDES has provided a unique perspective on the world's best travel destinations by using specially commissioned photography and illuminating text written by local authors.

Whether you're planning a city break, a walking tour or the journey of a lifetime, our superb range of guidebooks and phrasebooks will inspire you to discover more about your chosen destination.

INSIGHT GUIDES

offer a unique combination of stunning photos, absorbing narrative and detailed maps, providing all the inspiration and information you need.

PHRASEBOOKS & DICTIONARIES

help users to feel at home, when away. Pocket-sized with a free app to download, they go where you do.

CITY GUIDES

pack hundreds of great photos into a smaller format with detailed practical information, so you can navigate the world's top cities with confidence.

EXPLORE GUIDES

feature easy-to-follow walks and itineraries in the world's most exciting destinations, with our choice of the best places to eat and drink along the way.

POCKET GUIDES

combine concise information on where to go and what to do in a handy compact format, ideal on the ground. Includes a full-colour, fold-out map.

EXPERIENCE GUIDES

feature offbeat perspectives and secret gems for experienced travellers, with a collection of over 100 ideas for a memorable stay in a city.

www.insightguides.com

Central Route — Washington, DC - Los Angeles (CA)

	Washington, DC	Memphis, TN	Joplin, MO	Amarillo, TX	Gallup, NM	Flagstaff, AZ	Los Angeles, CA
Washington, DC		940	1371	1850	2270	2452	2922
Memphis, TN	940		431	910	1330	1512	1982
Joplin, MO	1371	431		479	899	1081	1551
Amarillo, TX	1850	910	479		420	602	1072
Gallup, NM	2270	1330	899	420		182	652
Flagstaff, AZ	2452	1512	1081	602	182		470
Los Angeles, CA	2922	1982	1551	1072	652	470	

Atlantic Route
New York (NY) - Key West (FL)

Northern Route
Boston (MA) - Cape Flattery (WA)

Central Route
Washington, DC - Los Angeles (CA)

Southern Route
Atlanta (GA) - San Diego (CA)

Pacific Route
San Diego (CA) - Seattle (WA)

All distances shown are in miles.

Northern Route — Boston (MA) - Cape Flattery (WA)

	Boston, MA	Buffalo, NY	Chicago, IL	Pierre, SD	Cody, WY	Seattle, WA	Cape Flattery, WA
Boston, MA		872	1419	2309	2891	3961	4095
Buffalo, NY	872		547	1437	2019	3089	3223
Chicago, IL	1419	547		890	1472	2542	2676
Pierre, SD	2309	1437	890		582	1652	1786
Cody, WY	2891	2019	1472	582		1070	1204
Seattle, WA	3961	3089	2542	1652	1070		134
Cape Flattery, WA	4095	3223	2676	1786	1204	134	

Pacific Route — San Diego (CA) - Seattle (WA)

	San Diego, CA	Los Angeles, CA	San Francisco, CA	Eureka, CA	Crescent, OR	Newport, OR	Seattle, WA
San Diego, CA		124	504	785	867	1108	1399
Los Angeles, CA	124		380	661	743	984	1275
San Francisco, CA	504	380		281	363	604	895
Eureka, CA	785	661	281		82	323	614
Crescent, OR	867	743	363	82		241	532
Newport, OR	1108	984	604	323	241		291
Seattle, WA	1399	1275	895	614	532	291	

Atlantic Route — New York (NY) - Key West (FL)

	New York, NY	Baltimore, MD	Roanoke, VA	Savannah, GA	Orlando, FL	Miami, FL	Key West, FL
New York, NY		202	543	811	1170	1597	1761
Baltimore, MD	202		341	609	968	1395	1559
Roanoke, VA	543	341		268	627	1054	1218
Savannah, GA	811	609	268		359	786	960
Orlando, FL	1170	968	627	359		427	591
Miami, FL	1597	1395	1054	786	427		164
Key West, FL	1761	1559	1218	960	591	164	

Southern Route — Atlanta (GA) - San Diego (CA)

	Atlanta, GA	New Orleans, LA	Houston, TX	San Antonio, TX	Lordsburg, NM	Phoenix, AZ	San Diego, CA
Atlanta, GA		473	825	1070	1989	2213	2572
New Orleans, LA	473		352	597	1516	1740	2099
Houston, TX	825	352		245	1164	1388	1747
San Antonio, TX	1070	597	245		919	1143	1502
Lordsburg, NM	1989	1516	1164	919		224	583
Phoenix, AZ	2213	1740	1388	1143	224		359
San Diego, CA	2572	2099	1747	1502	583	359	

Interstate Route Marker

Even numbers indicate east-west routes: odd show north-south routes.

US Highway Marker

Four-way Stop Sign

Traffic from all four directions must stop. The first vehicle to reach the intersection should move first.

Yield Ahead

Reduce speed and allow vehicles crossing your path right-of-way.

No Entry

One-way road w traveling towar

Traffic Merges (from right)

Traffic flows merge from indicated direction.

2-Way Traffic

Traffic flows in both directions.

Traffic Lane Joins

Traffic enters carriageway with new lane.

Yield Ahead

A yield sign is ahead.

Divided Highwa

Divided highway to adjacent carria

Dead End

Not a through road, no access to other streets.

Crossing Traffic

Highway is crossed by road. Look to left and right for cars.

Stop sign ahead

Stop sign ahead, prepare to stop.

Slippery Surface

Road surface is slippery when wet. First half-hour of rain is most hazardous.

Animal Haz

Be prepared for crossing the ro

Construction Ahead

Distance given until construction begins. Watch for further signs.

Railroad Crossing Ahead

Slow and prepare to stop at crossing ahead.

Left Turn

All traffic must turn left.

Keep Right

Traffic is required to keep to the right of medians or obstructions.

Restricted L

The lane is rese certain purposes o Requirements ar usually shown o

One Way

One-way traffic in direction of arrow.

Camping

Direction to camping site.

Rest Area

Roadside park and rest area.

Hospital

Watch for pedestrians and emergency vehicles.

Tow Away Zo

No parking. Any vehicles removed.

School Zone

Follow speed limit displayed when lights above sign flash.

School

Children crossing road.

Lane Control

Travel in lane.

Lane Control

Clear the lane. If flashing, left turn is permitted.

Lane Cont

Don't use lane approachi